PLACE-NAMES OF SCOTLAND

PLACE-NAMES OF SCOTLAND

BY JAMES B. JOHNSTON, B.D., F.R.Hist.S.

WITH

ADDITIONAL NOTES ON THE AUTHOR

REPUBLISHED 1970 BY S.R. PUBLISHERS LTD.

First Published 1892
This reprint taken from the third edition, London, 1934

By kind permission of the heirs of the late J.B. Johnston

ISBN 0 85409 634 5

Reproduced and printed in Great Britain by
Lewis Reprints Limited, Port Talbot, Glamorgan

NOTES ON THE AUTHOR

THE Rev. James Brown Johnston (1861–1953) was inducted to Falkirk Free Church in 1888, where he remained as minister for 40 years, entering the United Free Church in the union of 1900.

The study of philology was one of the earliest of Mr. Johnston's leisure interests. He joined the staff of the Oxford '*New English Dictionary*' at Millhill in 1883, and had the distinction of being the last survivor of those who were engaged in that work when Sir J. A. H. Murray became the first editor. The first part was issued in 1884. Mr. Johnston was an honorary member of the staff from that year to 1915, and from 1926–27, which saw the completion of one of the greatest achievements of modern scholarship and research.

He was on the staff of the Scottish National Dictionary from 1931.

His work as a pioneer in the study and elucidation of place-names followed closely on that of the late Sir Herbert Maxwell and Mr. W. J. Liddall. His *Place-Names of Scotland* which has gone through three editions, and has for years been regarded as a standard work, found its germ in what he called "a very crude paper" read to a church society in 1887. The first edition. published in 1892, had a very favourable reception from the critics. The second, with some errors and doubtful derivations deleted and "the range of conjecture brought within much narrower bounds" followed 12 years later, and the third, of which this is a reprint, in 1934. Place-name study had made great strides in the intervening years, demanding drastic revision and making possible considerable additions to his original work.

Mr. Johnston was also the author of a booklet on *Place-Names of Stirlingshire*, *Place-Names of England and Wales*, *The Scottish Macs: their Derivation and Origin*, and *Place-Names of Berwickshire*. He also revised the names in several Scottish topographical works, and wrote articles on place-names, surnames and other subjects for Scottish journals, including *The Scotsman*.

PLACE-NAMES OF SCOTLAND

PLACE-NAMES OF SCOTLAND

By JAMES B. JOHNSTON, B.D., F.R.Hist.S.

Author of "Place Names of England and Wales,"
"Place Names of Stirlingshire," "The Scottish Macs."

LONDON

JOHN MURRAY, ALBEMARLE STREET, W.

1934

First Edition (*Douglas*) *1892*
Second Edition *1903*
Third Edition (*John Murray*) *1934*

CONTENTS

PREFACE

In a study like this perfection can never be attained, because of the ofttimes grave lack of evidence. But one would fain hope that this new issue makes a fair step nearer to perfection. The new issue is long overdue ; high costs of production have long been a barrier, and it is only made at all feasible now through a grant from the Carnegie Trustees and the willing co-operation of my publisher. The present work found its first germ in a very crude paper, read to a church society in Glasgow in 1887. The first edition was published in 1892, the second in 1903. Place-name study has made great strides since then. The revision demanded has been drastic, while the additions made are considerable. I hope that many students will now find some of their puzzles at last solved. I hope, too, that I have made the story of the Pict a little clearer. By far the most important work on our subject, issued during the last thirty years, has been Prof. W. J. Watson's *Celtic Place-Names of Scotland*, 1926. To it and to his other works my debt has been enormous, as the oft-recurring (W.) in the following pages will amply show. For all minute details as to Celtic phonetics and philology the student must still go to Prof. Watson. Along such paths I dare not try to follow him.

It may well be asked, Why, then, put out another book ? For one thing, of course, Prof. Watson deals only with Celtic names in his last book. But, besides, his omissions are serious. He has not a word to say about such ancient towns as Dunfermline and Stirling, not a word about a great ben like Wyvis or a great river like the Tweed, and its tributaries the Jed and Teviot. The visitor to the Trosachs will find nothing about Ben Ledi or Loch Lubnaig or Coilantogle, not even about Loch Katrine. And if this visitor goes on to Deeside, he will find no help about Aboyne or Invercauld or even about Balmoral and great Lochnagar. Prof. Watson also often omits important evidence, and, in several cases, the only Gaelic form he gives does not agree with that given by other competent Gaels.

That fine scholar Dr. Alex. M'Bain helped me a good deal directly with my second edition, and sent me his brochures up to the time of his all-too-early death. The late Kuno Meyer, then professor in Liverpool, helped me on several points by correspondence, and kindly sent me all his offprints up till the Great War. Dr. George Henderson, also sadly too soon taken, gave us a mine of scholarly wealth in his *Norse Influence on Celtic Scotland*. I have gleaned several helpful hints from Mr. W. C. Mackenzie's *Scottish Place Names*. Much useful information has been found in the veteran Sir Herbert Maxwell's last book on *The Place Names of Galloway*. The works of James M'Donald (Aberdeen), Rev. J. M'Neill (Islay) and E. Ellice (Glengarry) have been of very real service. But several of the books published of recent years on special districts have been found of little use. Mr. Hugh Marwick's work on the names of Orkney, however, is most scholarly; and the work of the late Dr. Jakob Jakobsen on both the names and the words of Shetland needs no praise of mine.

Sir J. A. H. Murray was to me a lifelong friend, so busy that he could only occasionally give me direct help. But the great Oxford Dictionary (*N.E.D.*) has been constantly consulted with much profit. I have gathered what I could from the published volumes of the English Place Name Society. They do not help much for Scotland; and it is little short of a calamity that the editors have never yet found anyone able and willing to be responsible for the Celtic names in England.

The Scots Register of the Great Seal (R.M.S.) has proved itself a rich quarry; and I have diligently gathered for myself hints and pronunciations, from Scalloway to Galloway, for a full half-century. A good many of the Gaelic forms here given could not be reproduced now, because, alas, Gaelic speakers in Scotland are dying out so fast. I also owe a very great deal to stray communications from all sorts of people, to whom I am truly grateful, though it is impossible to make individual acknowledgement of them here. I have done my best, but doubtless mistakes must have crept in time and again. I must, therefore, crave the student's forbearance with me in such a big and 'fikey' task, which has had all to be tackled single-handed. At any rate, I have tried hard to include all the relevant evidence, so far as the stern exigencies of space would allow, and to give most of the place-names likely to be sought after by ordinary enquirers. The expert no doubt will continue to fend for himself.

JAMES B. JOHNSTON.

EDINBURGH,
July 1934.

INTRODUCTION

EVERY science has its byways as well as its highways. It is along an interesting byway that this book invites the student to walk. The study of place-names may be said to stand to History and Ethnology in somewhat the same relation as the study of fossils stands to Geology. Each group of fossils represents, with more or less strictness, a distinct age of geologic time ; so, roughly speaking, does each group of place-names represent a period of historic or prehistoric time. Almost all the place-names worth studying are fossils ; no man now living was present at their birth. Sometimes the geologist who wishes to map out his territory finds his task the simplest possible ; *e.g.*, for hundreds of monotonous miles over the steppes of Russia he finds the same strata, the same soft Permian sandstones, lying horizontal and unaltered as on the day when first they hardened on the old sea-bottom. At other times, though he may have only fifty, or even twenty, square miles to map out, the geologist finds his task one of extreme difficulty and complexity. Half a dozen different systems crop up in that little space, and igneous rocks rise here and there among the aqueous, crumpling, distorting, and altering all things around ; such a region is the Isle of Arran, or the English counties along the Welsh border. Again, the eager fossil-hunter is sometimes delighted in splitting open a nodule, or in cleaving the thin laminæ of the shale, to discover an exquisitely symmetrical ammonite, or a yet more delicate fern, in shape as perfect as the day it died. But, just as often, the only specimens he can find are fragments crushed and broken, which require the trained eye of the expert to tell what once they were.

Now, if the devotee of such a physical science as geology will but lay aside his hammer and his pocket-microscope for a little while, he will find somewhat similar problems to study when he grapples with (Scottish) place-names. Sometimes his task will be fairly easy, if he have learnt the rudiments of the craft; *e.g.*, in Angus he will find himself in an almost purely Gaelic region, with a slight Pictish or British admixture. In sound and shape these names are mostly as they were ever since history began. But in other districts, more especially in those where English has long been spoken, the old names have often come down to us in much-corrupted and truncated forms, sometimes in a ludicrously-altered form, which it requires the greatest skill and patience to decipher—if, indeed, the name can now be deciphered at all.

The subject which is here to be treated, the Place-Names of Scotland, is one which has only recently been grappled with as a whole; and there is a good deal yet to be done. Too many of those who have tried their 'prentice hands at the task proceeded in the most reckless fashion, giving way to unscientific guess-work which, like the obstructive undergrowths in the virgin forest, had to be cleared away before one could begin to make a road at all. But much pioneering has already been done, and done well. Sir Herbert Maxwell and Mr. W. J. Liddall (1885) were first on the Scottish scene.[1] And now, thanks to the labours of Joyce (in Ireland) and Mackinnon and M'Bain, and Professor Watson and a few others, it should be impossible that, *e.g.*, *Poma Dei* should ever again be put forward as the etymology of that place which Glasgow railwaymen know so well—POLMADIE.[2]

Our treatment of the subject will be historic, and will proceed in the order of time. The first chapter will refer to all we know of the aborigines of Britain—call them Iberians, Silurians, or what you please—and then will rapidly discuss the largest and most complicated portion of our task—the Celtic names. Purely English or Anglo-Saxon, Scandinavian, and Norman names will each receive a chapter; and with the Norman we will treat the Roman names, a group too insignificant to call

[1] Capt. Thomas, R.N., was hard at work among the Norse Gaelic names of the Hebrides over thirty years before them. *Cf.* his *Place Names of Islay*, 1882.

[2] The printing of a name in capitals means that its origin is treated of in the Alphabetical List.

for separate handling. The modern names will be dealt with last of all; and as ecclesiastical names form so large and important a group, they will receive a chapter to themselves. Such study should be no mere dilettante trifling. The historian, the philologist, the antiquarian, the anthropologist will, each and all, find for themselves side-lights both helpful and interesting; and the great *Oxford English Dictionary* (N.E.D.) will sometimes be supplemented by earlier instances of words than any which its columns now record.

What further seems needful to be said in introduction, by way of rule, caution, or useful hint, we shall throw into a series of numbered paragraphs:

(1) It will be found in Scotland,[1] as in any other country, that the oldest place-names, the names which, like the hard granite, best resist weathering, are those of large rivers, mountains, promontories and islands. The names of rivers and islands especially are, as a rule, root-words, archaic, and so, often difficult to explain. In a very few cases we cannot explain them at all, we know so little of the ancient language to which they probably belong. The names of man's dwellings change pretty often; but the name of a big ben or a steady-flowing river has hardly ever been known to change.

(2) Every place-name means something, or at least once meant something. Only in the degenerate nineteenth century had men begun to coin silly, meaningless names. Only within late years could a Dickens or a Thackeray have had the chance of satirizing his neighbour for calling No. 153 in a dingy back street, full 20 feet above the level of the sea, *Mount Pleasant*, or for christening an ugly brick house, in full sight of a gas-work, *Belle Vue*.

(3) It may be taken as a general rule that every name was once fairly appropriate. Therefore try, if possible, to study names, as every honest student studies his quotations, *in situ*, on the spot. But one must not always expect to find the name appropriate to-day. The cause or circumstance which gave rise to the name may have utterly passed away. What was 'Kingsbarns' once need not be so now. Or the physical aspect of the site may have become entirely altered; *e.g.*, CAMLACHIE,

[1] *Cf.* Skene, *Celtic Scotland*, vol. i, bk. i, chap. iv, a once valuable chapter, though Skene is now out of date.

now a wilderness of stone and lime in the East End of Glasgow, probably means, 'the crook or bend of the swamp'; the swamp itself can be seen no more.

(4) Though every name has a real meaning, *never prophesy unless you know.* It is quite likely that a name does not mean what it says, or seems to say; and a name which looks like English pure and simple may possibly not be English at all. There is a constant tendency to assimilate the spelling of a word of unknown meaning to the spelling of a word which is known, a 'kent' word, as we Scots call it. The enquirer must always be on the outlook for this; many a true Celtic name has been thus disguised. Abundant illustration of this will be found further on. Meantime, take one illustration. There is a spot in the parish of New Abbey which at present goes by the sadly vulgar and English-looking name of SHAMBELLY. On examination this turns out to be pure Gaelic, *sean baile* (shan bally), which has the very innocent meaning of 'old house' or 'hamlet.'[1]

(5) It is thus of the highest consequence, wherever possible, to secure not only an old but the very oldest extant form or spelling of a name. For, though a name may be spelt so-and-so to-day, it by no means follows that it was always spelt thus. And frequently it is only when one sees the old form that an idea of the name's true meaning can be reached. This also will find copious illustration as we proceed. For the present, take just one instructive instance from the writer's own experience. YESTER, the name of a parish at the foot of the Lammermuirs, was long a puzzle. The writer communicated with the courteous Professor of Celtic in Edinburgh University, giving a somewhat foolish conjecture, which need not be repeated. The conjecture Professor Mackinnon repudiated, but said he could throw no light upon the name. Then his *confrère* at Oxford, Professor Rhys, was applied to, with the suggestion that Yester might be the same name as the hill Yes Tor in Dartmoor, and was asked for the latter's meaning. We then learnt that *Yes* is a Cornish superlative, and *Yes Tor* means 'highest hill'; but Professor Rhys would not venture to identify it with Yester, and declared himself puzzled. But one day we discovered that the oldest mention calls the place

[1] *Cf.* too KINGEDWARD, MONTROSE, etc.

Yestre, and the meaning appeared with a flash. For *ystre* is just the ordinary Welsh word for 'a house.' Thus were we supplied with a plain warning against rash guesses, and at the same time found a clear footstep of the Brython among the Lammermuirs. The joy of the palæontologist when he cracks open a limestone nodule and finds therein a magnificent *Productus*, every curve and line of the shell perfect, is hardly greater than the satisfaction of the historical philologist when he first discovers that a puzzling and prosaic name like CARSTAIRS originally was 'Casteltarres' (*sic c.* 1170), *Terras* being a familiar Scotch surname to this day. Even yet all will not be well unless the student also knows that the oldest usage of the word 'castle' in English was as a translation of the Vulgate's *castellum*, where *castellum* means always, not a fortress but a village. Thus Carstairs, if dressed in Saxon garb, would be Tarreston, in Norman garb, Tarresville. It may be taken as a rough rule, with many exceptions, that if we can find a name on record before the year 1200, we have a good chance of correctly surmising its meaning; whereas, if no record of it be found till after 1500, that record may be of small scientific value. In the sixteenth and seventeenth centuries all spelling either of names or words ceased to be under law, and was, generally speaking, regulated by mere caprice.

(6) If it be highly desirable to ascertain the old spelling of a name, it is almost equally desirable that we should know its local, native pronunciation. Celtic scholars are so thoroughly agreed as to the need for this, if Celtic names are to be rightly interpreted, that we hardly need to emphasize the rule—wherever you can get a native Gael to pronounce a name listen carefully to him. Such a proceeding will save one many a time from writing or talking nonsense. But the rule holds good, to a less extent, about all Scottish place-names, and about Celtic names even when the pronouncer himself no longer speaks Gaelic. The writer did not need to go far from his own Falkirk door to find very pertinent examples of this. If the reader will consult the List of this book he will find that, in the case of at least three of these local names, the present native pronunciation comes much nearer the true etymology than the present spelling. The names are the Celtic DENOVAN (pron. dunni′ven), and the English FALKIRK (fawkírk) and SHIELDHILL

(sheelhill). The liquids *l*, *m*, *n*, *r* always need special watching; and, when the whole truth is known, it will be seen that the Celt makes far sadder havoc with his *h*'s than the Cockney (see p. 17). He who would further this interesting and valuable study must himself first make some study of the Laws of Phonetics. To him indeed, in any difficult case, they are *sine qua non*. He must learn that any letter *cannot* become any other, as too many seem to think. *E.g.*, an esteemed correspondent, now dead, assured the present writer that MUSSELBURGH must be 'mouth-Esk-burgh'! And what is worse, he believed so till the day of his death!

(7) A hybrid is to be postulated with caution. Hybrid names do occur, but very occasionally, *e.g.*, the Celtic and English GARMOUTH or ARNPRIOR, the Celtic and Norse ARDALANISH or JURA, and the Norse and Celtic BLAVEN or FORSINARD. Nor must it be supposed that the names in any given district ought all to belong to one language—all Gaelic in the Highlands and all English in the Lowlands. This is far from being the case; though it is true that some districts are nearly unmixed in this respect, *e.g.*, Orkney and Shetland names are practically all Norse; the mainland of Argyle names nearly all Celtic, pure Gaelic too, with no Brythonic or Welsh admixture; whilst in Berwickshire there is scarcely a name left which is not English.

When all these seven caveats have been surely learnt and gripped, then, and only then, is the amateur investigator fit to advance with safety.

CHAPTER I

CELTIC NAMES

It is impossible to speak with accuracy on the point, but Celtic names in Scotland must outnumber all the rest by perhaps ten to one. Their importance may be measured well by the one fact that, up to so late a date as the death of Malcolm II in 1056, all the mainland of Scotland, except the shires between Edinburgh and Berwick, was purely Celtic. Wide and difficult though the Celtic problem still is, answers can be found far more surely than was at all possible a few years ago. Here, as in every other field, the last half-century has seen science advancing with swift, sure foot. Fifty years ago the subject of Celtic place-names spread out like a vast morass with a little solid footing round the edges alone—a morass, with no thoroughfares and no beacons, and with many a Will o' the Wisp dancing deceitfully about, to lead the luckless follower to confusion. Some solid footing there has always been; *e.g.*, nobody who knew Gaelic at all would ever be at a loss to say that *Achnacloich* meant 'field of the stone.' But whenever any name a little less simple than this was met with, or when men began to argue, Was this stone a Druid relic, or a mere boundary mark? Is *auchter* a true Gaelic, or a Pictish, or a Brythonic (Welsh) form?—then at once arose a bewildering Babel of tongues. But now the morass has been largely drained, and everywhere good footpaths run.

During the early part of last century all was wildest conjecture as to Britain's aborigines, and most of what had then been written was pure nonsense. Almost everybody was satisfied that our aborigines were Aryans [1] and Celts, and that in Scotland the eldest race was most likely the Picts. Learned

[1] The name *Aryan* was not actually applied to the great Indo-European family of languages till about 1846.

Pinkerton laboured hard with the names of the Pictish kings (many probably spurious), to prove the Picts Gothic, while industrious Dr. Jamieson plied a lusty cudgel in favour of a Teutonic origin. *Mais nous avons changé tout cela.* That new science called Anthropology, born *c.* 1862, but now in a vigorous youth, has supplanted the shifty, precarious methods of mere root guessing. Those who say they know now tell us, that what survives longest of a race is its type of skull and face, next longest its place-names; whilst that which most readily changes is its language. Anthropology has proved beyond question that the primeval inhabitants of our isles, down to the very close of the Stone Age, were those non-Aryan cave-dwellers of dark complexion, black hair, long skull, and short, feeble build, whose remains are found in the long barrows, a people typically represented by the tribe *Silures*, whom Pliny describes as dwelling on to-day's Welsh border. Their marks may still be recognized by the skilled observer almost all over Scotland from Galloway northwards, and very specially in such a Hebridean isle as Barra. Curious to relate, if we want to find the one living race which is a tolerably pure representative of these 'Iberians'[1] of old, both in build and speech, we must journey to the shores of the Bay of Biscay and see the Basques, the folk whose uncouth speech, 'tis said, the Devil gave up learning in despair. The Basque tongue is but a poor specimen at the best, and has left no literary remains earlier than the sixteenth century.

Naturally these old 'Iberians' would give a name to every prominent physical feature in the land; but what these names were we can hardly in any instance tell. Their tongue is dead, drowned by the many later comers in almost utter forgottenness. Written monuments of any kind the British 'Iberian' has none. However, Professor Mackinnon thought a pre-Celtic element may still be dimly recognized in the modern Gael's vocabulary; and there are a very few Scottish place-names which may with some confidence be identified with Basque roots, *e.g.*, Orr, Urr, river-names, almost certainly the same as the Basque *ur*, 'water.' I have traced over a score of old names in Southern France which can almost

[1] So called from *Iberia*, an ancient name of Spain, though it is only a scholar's guess to say that Britain's aborigines came from Spain.

certainly be derived from Basque.[1] It is very different with Scotland. Almost the only name except Urr which can with any confidence be equated with a Basque root is the River FARRAR. Other at least possible pre-Celtic names are the Cheviots, Islay, Mar, and the rivers Eden, Gadie, Nairn, Naver, Nethy, Teith, Tilt and Ullie. Professor Rhys has done his best to discover for us some more of our aboriginal, or 'Ivernian' names, as he prefers to call them. His method (*Rhind Lectures*, 1890, No. 3) is, if he can find Scottish names not readily explainable from Gaelic, which resemble the names of some princesses, heroes, or divinities mentioned in the earliest Welsh and Irish legends, then he conjectures that these Scottish place-names must be pre-Celtic, because all three countries have them in common. Such a method is precarious, and perhaps never reaches demonstration. See ATHOLE, BANFF, CLYDE, DUNFERMLINE,[2] EARN, ELGIN.

So, after the dim aborigines, came the Celts. Till about forty years ago it was considered a settled commonplace that the Aryans' cradle was somewhere in Western Asia, to the north of Persia. Here again all is changed. Max Müller was one of the last to remain by the old flag. And now the supplanting suggestion (perhaps first made by our own Dr. Latham), that the Aryan home must have been among the wide, swampy plains of Central Germany, is being largely supplanted too. No doubt there were early Aryans in Germany; but our latest authority, the erudite Dr. Schütte, holds that the Indo-European races 'have had a firm footing in Europe time out of memory,' and that the Celts, at any rate, cannot have been born in Germany, but in Gaul or France. Their cradle, he argues, must have been near the sea.[3] With this agrees our first mention of the Celts, in Herodotus II, 33 and 49, *c.* 440 B.C. The Father of History's knowledge is very vague. All he knows is, they dwelt in the far West, near the setting of the sun (? Portugal), and near the Pyrenees, which he calls 'a city'!

[1] No reference can be given to anything in print. One gets little encouragement to publish on such recondite themes.

[2] Here at least impossible, though there is a late form Dunferlyne, thought to come from Farlan, one of the first colonisers of Ireland.

[3] Gudmund Schütte, *Our Forefathers*, I (1929), pp. 6, 114, etc. *Cf.* Cæsar, *Bell. Gall.*, vi, 24.

These Celts must have early supplanted the aboriginal Basques over most of Gaul. How early, who shall say? It is, at any rate, now fairly agreed, that Celtic culture, of which our archæologists now possess ample and often very beautiful remains, shows almost no trace of going back to the Bronze Age.[1] It almost wholly belongs to the Iron Age or later, *i.e.* we have no grounds for dating the Celts before 1200 B.C. It is also agreed that the divergence in the Gaulish or Celtic tongue, between the Goidelic or Gaelic and the Brythonic or Welsh type, did not show itself for a long time. Zeuss, in his great *Grammatica Celtica*, 1853, thought it began only a few centuries B.C. Our data are sadly scanty, but they are fairly decided, and, if carefully pieced together, lead to fairly definite conclusions.

Some think the great Celtic migrations did not begin till *c.* 500 B.C. This must surely be too late. When Pytheas made his famous voyage from Marseilles to our shores, *c.* 330 B.C., he found Celts in possession of Britain away as far north as the Orkneys. At any rate, these isles then had a Celtic name. When he sailed on to Shetland the Celts probably had not reached so far, for its name, to him, was Thule, a pre-Celtic name. These same Celts must have also early spread to the farthest south of Scotland, as is shown by the name LOCH RYAN. For Celts to have been settled in Orkney by 330 B.C. seems to demand a departure from Gaul earlier than 500 B.C. And it must have been at a date before divergence in the language had apparently begun. Our recorded names before the incoming of the Picts—of whom anon—are painfully few. But it is the poet Lucan, *c.* A.D. 60, who first names the Caledonii. The elder Pliny gives us the Hebudes or HEBRIDES and Dumna, the Long Island. Tacitus, son-in-law of the Roman general Agricola, who invaded Scotland, *c.* A.D. 80, gives us the Clyde and the Tay, also Bodotria, the FORTH, and Mons Granpius, the GRAMPIANS. Then, from Ptolemy, the famous astronomer and geographer of Alexandria, *c.* A.D. 150, we have a more substantial quota, say about twenty names still existing, though some of them a good deal canvassed. We may venture

[1] Archæology now inclines to agree with what is here said about Celts and Picts. See Prof. Gordon Childe's Munro Lectures in *Scotsman*, 23 Feb. and 1 March, 1934.

on River Boyne, Carron (Ross-shire), River Clyde, River Dee (2), Loch Etive, River Farrar, Glen Devon, Hebrides, Loch Long (LEVEN), Mull, River Naver, River Nith, Ochils, Loch Ryan, Skye, CARN SMEART, River Spey, River Tay, River Tyne. Of course these are not nearly all the Scots names in Ptolemy. They, including some sixteen or eighteen names of tribes, will be found elaborately discussed by Dr. Watson.

But he who carefully studies Ptolemy's still existing names, along with the few earlier ones which have been preserved, will hardly dispute that these names represent a Celtic tongue still undifferentiated; Goidelic and Brythonic elements are still almost inextricably mixed. *E.g.*, both the poet Lucian and the historian Tacitus call the Caledonians 'Britanni.' Even so late as the history of Herodian, bk. iii, *c.* A.D. 238, we find only 'the regions of the Bretannoi'; and, though he describes their painted bodies, he never mentions Picts. The latest edition of the *Encyclopædia Britannica*, 1929, is disappointingly perfunctory about Celtic origins, and worst of all about the Picts. But it thinks that the Goidels or Gaels probably passed over to Ireland direct from Gaul, it may be from the mouth of the Loire, in the fourth century B.C. By this time, in Gaul, differentiation was fairly complete. For in Ireland and its speech we find no trace of Brython.

When these Gaels arrived in Ireland they found plenty of the dark, long-skulled aborigines, survivals, it seems, of Upper Palæolithic types. Irish tradition is clear and strong that they were there—these Fir-bolg or 'men with the bag,' these Cruithne [1] or 'painted men,' the 'Creenies' of Galloway tradition, called by the Welsh Prydyn and by the Latins Picti. It is by no means certain that these were the same as the Gaulish tribes called by Cæsar Pictones and Pictavi (seen now in the name Poitou), but it is at least possible. Archæology is now helping us to make things a little clearer. Celtic civilization, as we have heard, can hardly precede the Iron Age—1200 B.C. on; and far the most of it comes in late in that Age. We are confidently told that Celtic expansion must have taken place in the La Tène (northern end of Lake Neuchâtel, Switzerland) period, 500 to 1 B.C., during which culture reached 'a high

[1] The root is probably *cruth*, 'form, figure.' Like many another race the Cruithne soon lost their own tongue, of which no trace remains.

artistic level.' It is agreed that Celtic art first developed in Gaul, South-Western England and probably Eastern Scotland, and did not cross over to Ireland till about A.D. 400.[1] The earliest Celtic art in stone was 'Pictish,' and quite distinct from the later Irish or Columban art.

But now we must go back a bit. It is fully agreed that there was a second Celtic migration from Gaul to England, of tribes of a decidedly Brythonic or Welsh complexion, including the Belgæ. These would cross by the Straits of Dover, or farther down the Channel, and apparently did not arrive in Britain till say 250 B.C. or even later. This Brythonic invasion must have speedily spread all over England and Wales, and supplanted the earlier pure British or Celtic tribes, at least in speech. For to-day it is very hard to find any clearly Gaelic place-names south of the Tyne or Lune, and the few there may be in Wales were given by invaders from Ireland, probably long after the Birth of Christ. These Brythons, in the persons of the tribe Brigantes, also spread up into Scotland as far north as Antonine's Wall 'twixt Forth and Clyde. Of course, all the old kingdom of Cumbria and Strathclyde, from Ribble to Clyde, was Brythonic, and though it fell *c.* 950, still, in twelfth-century charters, we find mention of 'Strathclwyd Wealas' or 'Walenses,' *i.e.*, Welsh, 'foreigners.' In Berwick, Roxburgh, Peebles and the Lothians we still find many names for which the Welsh dictionary gives most help. Dr. Watson has surveyed this field fairly well, but by no means exhaustively.[2]

Now we seem ready properly to tackle the much-vexed question of the Picts. They are not so named until the days of the obscure panegyrist Eumenius, who mentions them as at war with the emperor Constantius Chlorus, *c.* A.D. 296, the time he wrote. But his words imply that they had been there long before, fighting with the Britons. Gildas, our earliest English

[1] See Dr. J. Galbraith in *Scotsman*, 14 Dec., 1933.

[2] The following Lowland names omitted are almost certainly Brython—Carrifran Gans, Cluden, Cochrane, Cummertrees, Dunipace, Fruid, Giffen, Giffnock, Glendinning, Jed, Kirtle, Knockdolian, Plenderleith, Restalrig, Tantallon, Tartravon, Tema, Teviot, Throsk, Torweaving, Tur, Tweed, Tyne, Wanlock, Yester. These others have a fair claim to be the same—Cadzow, Caruber, Cothil and Cuthill, Enterkin, Errol, Erskine, Gorgie, Govan, Pinvinnie. See the List, s.v., for further details.

writer, *c.* 550, does not contradict this when he makes them come from the north, across the sea, *i.e.*, at the Irish Channel. It can scarcely be disputed that these Picts were the Cruithne or aboriginal Irish Fir-bolg, who must have remained fairly pure in race, though they entirely lost their native speech, and adopted Irish Gaelic. Some time in the third century they must have invaded Galloway in fierce fashion, and very soon must have completely subdued the earlier pure British. They must have gone conquering right up to the North of Scotland, as is proved by the PENTLAND Frith and by several names in Orkney and Shetland[1] (see Norse Names, p. 31). But they must have speedily allowed themselves to adopt the British speech of the race they conquered, just as happened with the Normans and English. For when the Irish-speaking St. Columba visited the king of the Picts at Inverness, *c.* 560, he required an interpreter, even though the two tongues cannot have been very widely different.

Thus the much-talked-of Pictish tongue, as we find it in many Scots names, can have been none other than the early, undifferentiated British speech, of which we get traces away all over the Highlands, as far to the north-west as APPLECROSS and as far north as Pitfure, Pitgrudy and Pittentrail in Sutherland. This is a little upsetting; and yet the tongue the Picts brought with them out of Ireland must have been pure Gaelic. In Galloway, where they first landed, they themselves almost totally swamped the British speech. For traces to-day, in Galloway and its near neighbour Carrick, of anything Brythonic are hard to find, and probably the Strathclyde Britons never settled in any numbers there. Dr. Watson, p. 180, gives just three Welsh names in Galloway—Drumwalt, LESWALT and TROSTRIE; and in sooth these three are only half Welsh. He also refers to KIRKGUNZEON, probably named by a stray Welsh devotee, and to Loch RYAN, an original British name. In Carrick the only Brython name seems the curious KNOCKDOLIAN; but in Galloway there are a few more, *e.g.*, Kevan and Kevands, W. *cefn*, a ridge, L. Hempton, on Pont's map,

[1] *Cf.* too the poet Claudian (I, 288 Loeb.), A.D. 398: 'Incaluit Pictorum sanguine Thule,' 'impervia Thule,' as he calls it. The name of Gonwais, King of Orkney, in Layamon, p. 207 Dent, looks Pictish, O.W. *gwas*, 'a servant.'

Dyrhympen, which must mean ‘ boundary ’ or ‘ limit stream,’ W. *dwr rhimpyn*, MINNIGAFF and PLASCOW. Bede tells us that Galloway was inhabited by the Niduari, a tribe of Picts. If this be correct, as it most likely is, their speech must simply have been Gaelic. We have now sought to outline the whole early situation, and would respectfully submit that no other scheme will fit the known facts.

And now we must hark back again to Ireland. It was long thought that Scotland owed almost everything to Ireland in Celtic art and learning. But archæology's latest verdict is, that Celtic art, with all its marvellous and intricate beauty of design, passed from Great Britain to Ireland. Pictish art in stone, in Scotland, is said to be distinct from the Irish, and undoubtedly older in origin. But Ireland was not long in repaying its debt, first by the invasion of the sword, and then, a score or two of years later, by the more gracious invasion of the Gospel, headed by Columba, *c.* 563.

In the year 498 the true Scots,[1] the men of Ulster, came over in their wicker boats, conquered all Argyle and the Isles, south of Ardnamurchan, founded the kingdom of Dalriad Scots, and imposed their speech there too. Even as the Jute and Angle, whose prows were fast turning towards England at this same time, imposed their speech on all England and have left very few British names in any thoroughly English shire, so those Scoto-Irish, in course of time, imposed their tongue on all Scottish Celts, and largely, though not so universally, stamped their impress on the nomenclature too. Many hold that the difference between the speech of Pict and Scot must have been very small indeed. This, however, is certain, that Pictish, however close to Erse, was one of the *p* group of Celtic tongues, while Irish and Scottish Gaelic are of course members of the *c* or *q* group—a division or grouping for which we are indebted to those great philologists, Windisch and

[1] ‘ Scots ’ never meant anything but Ulstermen till the tenth century. Perhaps the earliest instance of our present use is in the *O.E. Chron.*, ann. 924. The arrival of the Scots under Reuda or Riada—hence Dalriada—mentioned by Bede, *Eccl. Hist.*, I, i, may have been as early as the second or third century. Scottia is used in contrast with Hibernia as early as Eddi's *Life of Wilfrid*, *c.* 709. *Cf.* Watson, *Celtic Pl. Names*, pp. 213–15 ; also Claudian II, 210 Loeb, A.D. 398, Quae Saxona frenat vel Scottum legio.

Whitley Stokes. Thus Pictish, in this respect, must have stood nearer Welsh, Breton, and Cornish than to Erse or Manx; and the substitution of the Pictish *p* for the Erse *c* offers a possible solution of some puzzles. See PANBRIDE, SPEY, etc.

Distinctly and typically British or Pictish are the many names in -four or -fuir 'pasture,' like Delfour, Trinafour, etc., and we have a typical ending in the common *-ais*, a locative or suffix of place, seen in Alves, Dallas, Geddes, etc.

A run through Joyce's *Irish Names and Places* will soon convince any Scotsman that his names and the Irishman's are largely alike; *e.g.*, all the Bals- or Ballys-, all the Carricks-, so common in those parts of Scotland nearest Ireland, as Carrickaboys, Carrickcow, Carrickglassen, etc., and all the Kils- and Knocks-, of which there are scores in either land. Yet, some common Scottish prefixes do seem rather British. In the *Postal Guide* list for Wales and for Ireland there is not a single Fetter-, Fodder-, Petti- or Pit-, except Pettigo, Donegal. However, this branch of our subject can never be thoroughly expiscated, owing to almost total lack of material. Scottish education practically began, and almost wholly spread, through the Donegalman Columba and his far-travelling monks, of whom the earliest were all Irish-bred; and down to the middle of the sixteenth century all Gaelic put into writing in Scotland was practically identical with Erse. The Book of the Dean of Lismore, which dates so late as 1512–40, is the first known MS. of any consequence in Scottish Gaelic. At any rate, to the surprise and sorrow of Henry of Huntingdon (chap. 12, 13), *c.* 1130, the Pictish tongue was quite extinct.

Even by the days of Kenneth M'Alpine, first king of the Scots, *c.* 850, the Welsh or Brythons of Scotland had been overrun and largely eclipsed by Gaels. Their chief tribes among us had been the Brigantes and the Damnonii, up from York, who once spread from Tweeddale away north, as far probably as to the Tay. In Tweeddale Gaelic forms are still quite scanty. The typical Gaelic *auchen-*, *bal-*, *craigen-*, and *mach-*, are here few and far between.[1] But, wherever we meet the letter *p*, there probably the Brython pitched his camp. That letter seldom occurs in true Gaelic; it is chiefly found in a few imported words like *pibroch*, from *piobair*, our English 'piper.'

[1] *Cf.* Professor Veitch, *History of the Scottish Border*, 1878, chap. i.

At a very early stage *p* vanished from true Gaelic; witness that word which must be one of the oldest in every tongue, *athair*, the L. *pater*, Eng. *father*; also *orc*, a pig or sea-pig, *i.e.*, whale, the L. *porcus*, found in ORKNEY, which is the earliest Scottish name on record. Strabo (bk. ii), who preserves for us the narrative of the great voyager Pytheas, *c.* 330 B.C., gives it in the form *'Ορκὰς*; even then the *p* was gone. A modern Gael, even when he sees *p* printed before him, will often read it *b*—*iompachadh* ('conversion') he will pronounce imbacha, etc. But, curiously enough, in some quarters the reverse process is found, where Brythonic influence is hardly possible, *e.g.*, on the west coast the Norse *bol* not seldom becomes *pol*, see p. 42; BONSKIED, Pitlochry, is pronounced by some natives Pownskütch; and *a.* 1300 we find 'Palgoueny' as the spelling of BALGONIE.

As *p* is not found in pure Gaelic, most of the *pens* will be Brythonic, the Gaelic being *ceann*, locative *cinn* (Ken- or Kin-). North of Stirling we find only PENDRICH, just beyond the Forth, and PENNAN, near Fraserburgh; *pen* in the former case is a contraction for *pitten-*, and the latter's origin is unknown.[1] A common prefix, not found in pure Gaelic or Irish, is *pit* or *pet*, with their genitives, *pitte-*, *petti-*, first met with in the Pictish Gaelic entries of the *Book of Deer*; *e.g.*, 'pette meic Garnait,' homestead of Garnait's son, etc. Gaels call PITLOCHRY *Bailechlochre*, and this is the general rule, the G. *baile*, 'house, hamlet,' being the equivalent of the Pictish *pit-*. Then some names in *tra-* and all in *tre-* are Brythonic; for this is the W. and Cornish *tra*, *tre*, *tref*, also Ir. *treb*, 'house, home.' It also occurs as an ending, as in NIDDRIE, RATTRAY, etc., *cf.*, THRIEVE.

A fierce battle was once waged over the question, 'Is the common prefix *aber-*, "at the mouth" or "confluence of," a purely Brythonic form or no?' This *aber* is O. Welsh *aper*, Corn. and Breton *aber*, glossed *gurges*; and analysed by Whitley Stokes *at-bor*.[2] In old Gaelic it also means 'a marsh', with which we may compare the modern G. *eabar*, 'mud, mire,

[1] But note also RESCOBIE, the old Rosolpin. Besides there is a farm called Penick near Nairn. This will be one of several names where the Pen- or Penny- means 'penny land.'

[2] Giraldus Cambrensis in his *Itinerary*, *a.* 1200, says: '*Aber*, lingua Britannica, dicitur locus omnis ubi fluvius in fluvium cadit.'

marshy land.' A little islet called Aber stands at the mouth of the River Endrick, Loch Lomond. Welshmen are eager to assert that '*aber-* is Welsh, pure and simple, the Gael always uses *inver-*.' The *ber* or *ver* is the same root in both, and may be cognate with the Eng. *bear*, L. *ferre*, Gk. *φέρειν*. The oldest extant spelling is *abbor* or *aebber* (see ABERCORN and ABERDOUR); but in old charters we often find the British *p* for *b* (see ABERARGIE, ABERDEEN, etc.). Possibly we have an example as early as Ptolemy. His *Ἀβραουάννου ποταμοῦ ἐκβολάι* may be for *aber aimhne* or Avon, 'mouth of the river' Luce, Wigtonshire; though Dr. Watson says, No. The *a* in *aber-* was thought to be *ath*, pron. *āh*, a ford; for *aber-* is sometimes found in a name where there is no river-junction or mouth, but where there is or was a ford, *e.g.*, ABERNETHY, near Perth, and ARBIRLOT, the old Aberelloch. Scholars say the first syllable really is O. Celt. *ad* 'to' or *od* 'out,' but that may imply a ford. The first syllable in Inver is *inn*, *ind*, 'over.' Down the River Nethy from Abernethy we find Invernethy, where Nethy and Earn actually meet. This much is certain about *aber-* and *inver-*, that in Wales there are scores of *abers-*, but of *invers-* not a solitary one. But in Scotland we find *Aber* all over from Aberlady to Aberchirder and Aberchalder. On the west coast and north of Inverness, however, it barely exists. ABERSCROSS, Sutherland, is no case in point. There are only two in Argyle,[1] land of the Dalriad Scots; none in Selkirk, Peebles, Lanark, Stirling, Dumbarton,[2] Renfrew, Ayr; none in Galloway; and none in Cornwall. Then, in Aberdeen, Kincardine, Forfar, Perth, and Fife, there are said to be seventy-eight *invers-* and only twenty-four *abers-*. In Forfar the *aber* gets hardened into *ar*, as in ARBROATH, the famous Aberbrothock, and ARBUTHNOT, at first spelt Abirbuthenoth; just as *fothir*, later *fetter*, becomes in this region hardened into *for*. Thus we have FETTERANGUS and FETTERNEAR in Aberdeen, but FORDOUN and FORTEVIOT,

[1] Both in Islay, *viz.*, KINNABER and Badabery, which probably means, 'thicket by the little confluence.' But there are said to be 63 invers.

[2] Except the afore-mentioned islet of Aber. There are 13 in Perthshire, 11 in Inverness, 10 in Aberdeen. See Erskine Beveridge, *Abers and Invers*, 1923.

the old Fothuirtabaicht, farther south. To complete the discussion of *aber-*, it may be remarked that, on the whole west coast, the solitary instance (unless we count LOCHABER, as Stokes does) is one which would not easily be guessed under its cheating mask, *viz.*, APPLECROSS in West Ross, which is a modification of Abercrosan or ' Apurcrossan,' the Crossan being a river there. We may safely say that *aber* belonged to the old British or Pictish speech. But it does occur, rarely, in Donegal.

To sum up, then—in the study of the Celtic names the aid of the Welsh or Cornish dictionary will occasionally be required for the district south of the Grampians, particularly Tweeddale ; but the largest number of our place-names are to be interpreted from the dictionary, and by the laws, especially the pronouncing laws, of Scottish Gaelic.

By far the best-known form of Gaelic is Irish ; and Scottish Gaelic is as much a variety of Irish as Broad Scots is of Anglic or Old English—being nearer Connaught Irish than any other. Perhaps the most distinctive note of the Scottish tongue is, that the primary accent is always on the first syllable. In some grammatic peculiarities Scottish Gaelic is more like Manx than Irish, which means, in other words, that Gaelic and Manx have ceased to develop at a further or later stage of disintegration than Irish ; and to this day a Manxman—the few hundred Celts of them now left—can understand a Gael better than a man from Erin's isle.

The assistance in our study to be gained from names in Ireland is immense, assistance splendidly systematized and clarified for us by Dr. Joyce in his two handy volumes. The aid from Ireland is all the more precious to the scientific student, because we possess copious remains of early Irish literature, annals, historic poems, and the like, which give us the early forms of many of the Irish names. Abbot Tighernac, *c.* 1080, and the *Annals of Ulster*, *c.* 1300 and later, have quite a number of Scottish names too ; and sometimes we get forms as old as the fifth or sixth century A.D.[1] From these early,

[1] Our Alphabetical List will be found to take note of nearly 50 still-existing Celtic names of which we have record before the year 900. There may be one or two more still to be identified in Adamnan. In addition, the List contains fully 100 names of all kinds recorded before 1100 ; and probably this total can only be very slightly increased.

uncorrupted forms scholars can usually tell with certainty the meanings of the names. Irish names are as a rule easier to interpret, because they have never, to the same extent, been so mangled and corrupted as in Scotland, either by Dane or Englishman. Again, the Scottish student is not nearly so fortunate as his Irish neighbour, because early literature is with us sadly wanting. Not that early Scotsmen could not handle a pen, and handle it well; but their writings have not been allowed to survive. For this we have to thank the kindly attentions of our invaders; not so much the armies of England's two Edwards,[1] though they did their share, but rather the rough hands of pagan Vikings from Norroway, who hated anything which seemed to smell of the mass, and flung hundreds of precious Scottish MSS. to the sea or to the flames. These same rude pirates have made early Celtic MSS. very scarce all over Britain. This country contains only about six MSS. which date before A.D. 1000; but the Celtic clergy fled from their native cells to the Continent, bearing their books with them; and the libraries of Central and South-West Europe have now rich store of early Celtic MSS.; but their subjects make them to be seldom of much service for place-names. Nor do the many later bundles of Scottish Gaelic MSS. in the Edinburgh National Library and elsewhere yield us much fruit either. Of annals or topographic works they are said to contain hardly any, though there are rare exceptions, like the Islay charter of 1408, so luckily rescued from a peat-hag in Antrim.[2]

Of two other precious survivals every student of Scottish history has at least heard:

(1) *The Book of Deer* in Aberdeenshire, discovered by Mr. Bradshaw in Cambridge University Library in 1860. This manuscript contains the gospel of John, and parts of the three other gospels, in Latin; and then, what is important for us, in the blank spaces of the MS.—parchment was costly in those days—there are written in Pictish Gaelic, grants of land and privileges to the church of Deer, containing several place-

[1] *Cf. Calendar of Documents relating to Scotland*, 1881, vol. i, pref. pp. vi *sq.*, where the gross neglect of our own public record-keepers in early days is much commented on, and Edward I vindicated.

[2] See Prof. Mackinnon in *Inverness Gaelic Society's Proceedings*, xvi, pp. 287 foll.

names. The original MS. is written in a hand which may be of the ninth century, whilst none of the later entries come beyond the reign of David I, *c.* 1150.

(2) *The Pictish Chronicle* of the monks of Brechin, a brief work writ in Latin, but clearly a translation from Gaelic, containing a good many examples of place-names, which will all or nearly all be found embodied in our List. It breaks off at the year 966, and its date cannot be much later, although the only known MS. must belong to the fourteenth century. Besides, we have many instructive name-forms in Abbot *Adamnan's* (d. 704) well-known life of his great predecessor, Columba. One MS. dates from A.D. 710. Then, from the days of King Duncan (1094) onwards, we have the copious Abbey Chartularies, whose stores of names of hill and dale, town and hamlet, have largely been made available by the zeal of the Bannatyne Club. Specially have we to thank the huge industry of Cosmo Innes and Brichan in the *Origines Parochiales*, which, alas! cover only half of Scotland (see p. 327). The famous *Inquisitio de Terris Ecclesiæ Glasguensis*, made in 1116 by Prince David, afterwards David I, and now printed in the Chartulary of Glasgow, is the oldest authentic example of such documents now preserved in Scotland. The only earlier ones are certain Coldingham Priory Charters, now preserved at Durham, which go back some twenty-two years earlier. They may be conveniently studied in the noble collection, so carefully edited, of *The National Manuscripts of Scotland*. The Chartularies of Glasgow, Paisley, St. Andrews, Holyrood, and Melrose are perhaps those most deserving of note. But when, as is often the case, the chartularies have been written by scribes wholly ignorant of Gaelic, their phonetic attempts at the spelling of a place-name often sadly disfigure the real word (see AUCHTERMUCHTY, etc.). A famous scribe's error with permanent results is to be found in the name of the cradle of Scottish Christianity, IONA, whose original spelling certainly was *Ioua*. Like so many of the names in Adamnan, it is probably an adjectival formation, we are not sure from what. Equally notable is HEBRIDES, at first Hebudes.

As an example of what we may find in a charter, and of how little after all place-names change, even in 780 years, take the following list, being all the names mentioned in the charter (in the *Paisley Chartulary*) granted by King Malcolm IV to Walter, Stewart or Seneschal of Scotland, in 1158: 'Francis (*i.e.*, Normans) et Anglis, Scotis et Galovidiensibus . . . . . de terris de Reinfrew, Paisleth, Pullock, Tulloch, Kerkert (*i.e.*, CATHCART), Le Drip, Egilsham, Lochynoc, et Inerwick, Inchenan, Hastenden (*i.e.*, HASSENDEAN), Legerwood, et Birchensyde, ... Roxburgh, ... St. Andrae, Glasgow, Kelcow, Melross.' Among others, there are the following noteworthy personal names: 'Colvill, Sumervilla, et Macus'; the latter has not yet the appended *-wiel* to make him Maxwell.

The Celt gave names to all Scotland, so we must be prepared to find thousands of Celtic names to study; but, unfortunately for those who wish to make sure of the true pronunciation of a puzzling name, Gaelic is now spoken over much less than half its old area. It has been retreating up the glens ever since the days of foreign, Saxon Queen Margaret, and is destined to retreat farther still, till finally, at no distant future—*eheu fugaces !*—it may give up the ghost altogether, even as Cornish has already done.[1] Take the region north of a line drawn from Forres to Campbeltown, and there, roughly speaking, is the area in which Gaelic is still a living speech. But Gaelic lived on in most parts of Scotland much longer than is commonly thought. We have the evidence of George Buchanan that it was spoken in Galloway down to the days of Queen Mary; and it lingered in Glenapp (south of Ballantrae) a full century later. Little wonder then that Galloway, though now English in speech, is crammed with Celtic names, some of which like KILLINTRINGAN must be quite late. But, south of the above-mentioned line, we cannot be so sure about the real pronunciation and, consequently, the real meaning of many of the names. And, *nota bene*, it will not always do to trust local pronunciations and interpretations, even when given by a true Gael, *e.g.*, Loch MAREE, so commonly and wrongly thought to be 'Mary's Loch.'

The Gael, even the scholarly Gael, is apt to exaggerate the

[1] In 1931 the census showed 7,069 speaking Gaelic only, 137,149 Gaelic and English. On Gaelic being spoken in Fife as late as about 1680, see the old *Statist. Acct. Scotld.*, IX (1793), 478. Already by 1220 English names like Raperslaw and Fithelers flat had appeared even in Strathearn, but they were very rare then.

importance of his present-day pronunciations. A typical instance is COULTER, in Lanark and in Aberdeen, a name often mentioned in charters from 1170 on, always spelt Cul-, never Col- ; and always pronounced with *u* long, so that it certainly seems G. *cùl tir* 'back land.' But Gaels adduce two little-known names, with no history, Inchcoulter, Kiltearn and Sgorr a' Choltair, Glenglass, the former being in G. *innis a'choltair* 'meadow of the coulter' or 'ploughshare,' said to be an early loan from L. *culter*, where, be it noted, the *u* is short. And Gaels think this should counterbalance the above strong evidence. One must leave the student to judge. At any rate, Gaelic pronunciations are by no means so stable and reliable as is often asserted. The writer has found two different pronunciations of a name in one farm-yard. This is specially true of names not Gaelic in origin, but of genuine Gaelic names also. The writer once stayed a month at Duallin, Lawers. All Loch Tay natives then spoke Gaelic, yet none could tell for certain whether the name was Du-ăllin or Du-āllen. This is important in connexion with such a common name as ALLAN and also ALNESS. To connect with L. *pălus* a marsh, as Dr. Watson has suggested, will not do here, for Duallin is 'a dark meadow,' lying on a steep slope.

Gaelic names have undoubtedly changed fairly often. See BALCONY, COLONSAY, FINHAVEN, and many more. Dr. Watson, in his *Pl. Names Ross and Crom.*, notes at least thirty-three cases where the Gaelic has changed or is misleading ; and with some names, like CALLANDER and Ben VORLICH, there has been serious confusion. Take one name more, not in the thirty-three, yet in a purely Gaelic region, Ardmair, north of Ullapool. Old Gaels in Ullapool to-day all say Ardmair, though some think it should be Ardmara. Dr. Watson says, it is *Ard mheàra* 'finger promontory,' exactly the site. But how came the change ? One must add, that the 'oldest inhabitant' is apt to be extremely ignorant and misleading in his ideas of Celtic etymology. This can be illustrated from the old *Statistical Account* (end of eighteenth century) passim.

No sure progress can be made until at least something is learnt of the difficult laws of Gaelic inflection and pronunciation, difficulties which Scottish Gaelic shares with all the other Celtic tongues. The inflections are sometimes a little difficult, because they largely take place within the word, *e.g.*, nom. *cu*, 'a dog'; gen., the very different-looking *coin*, 'of a dog,' *corp*, 'a body,' *cuirp*, 'of a body,' etc. Then it is the rule—and this is of great moment for our study—that whenever certain consonants come between two vowels they aspirate or add an *h*; these aspirating (and the tyro may well call them also exasperating) letters are *b*, *c*, *d*, *f*, *g*, *m*, *s*, *t*; *e.g.*, Adam in Gaelic is *Adhamh*, and Adamnan, more correctly Adhamnan, is the diminutive, 'little Adam,' 'Adie.' For the extraordinary results produced on the name Adamnan by these aspirations see p. 68. Whenever these said consonants are preceded by certain other consonants they also aspirate, *e.g.*, always after *an* 'the,' *beinn* 'ben,' etc. But this does not apply to non-Gaelic words. *E.g.*, *bail fuar* becomes *bail'uar*, but *bail feur* ('pasture') keeps to *f*, hence BALFOUR.

The laws of pronunciation are yet more difficult. Many will re-echo the wish that Gaelic, like Manx, had been written phonetically, according to sound, and not according to what Prof. Mackinnon calls 'the strict and highly artificial rules of the schools.'[1] As things now stand, there is probably no language in the world in which the eye gives less help to the tongue. Of course, there is method in the seeming madness; but, to an untrained eye, the spelling gives almost no clue to the sound, and is often altogether misleading. Thus, an ordinary Englishman consulting a Gaelic dictionary will find himself altogether at sea, and M'Bain in his later days openly revolted against some scholastic spellings. The north-country Gael prefers an *ia* sound where the Gael south of the Grampians adheres to the true long *e* or *eu*, *e.g.*, *bial* and *beul*, *fiar* and *feur*, etc. Local differences in pronunciation are almost endless; and Gaelic scholars to-day lament the slovenly fashion of speech predominant all over the land.

But it is the 'aspiration' which causes the chief troubles. When *h* gets next to any letter in the middle or end of a word it

[1] The vowel sounds in Gaelic are so varied that they can only be learned by considerable experience. They also differ a good deal in different localities, and in different centuries (*cf.* KYLE, MULL, etc.). Gaelic diphthongs tend to become a single vowel: *bealach* becomes Balloch, *beinn* Ben, *ceann* Ken, etc. But to sound *ea* in *bealach* as a dissyllable with very short *e*, as Scott did in Bealach-nam-Bo, is by no means misleading.

has always a tendency to eclipse its neighbour, and to make both it and the *h* silent altogether.[1] Thus, many of those strange *mh*'s and *dh*'s, with which Gaelic is so thickly peppered, have no sound at all; *Amhalghaidh*, which looks such a monstrous mouthful, subsides into Awlay, so well known to us in the name Macaulay. Hence, too, such pronunciations as Stracathro for STRATHCATHRO, or, say, Gael for Gadhel—here *dh* is called evanescent. Only, in scores of cases, as early spellings show, the letters mute to-day were sounded long ago, and indeed were not aspirated at all, see *e.g.*, DUNBEATH or DOUGLAS, in *Nennius*, Dubglas, etc. The usual sound of *mh* is *v* nasal as in *mhòr*, 'big,' hence SKERRYVORE, and of *bh* a thin *v* as in *dà bharr*, 'two heights,' or DAVARR. Sometimes it is nearer *w*, as in Craigwhinnie, the G. *creag mhuine*, 'crag of the thicket'; sometimes the *v*-sound goes all the way to *b*, though not in good Gaelic, as STRATHBUNGO = 'Mungo's vale'; and then often, as we have seen above, the aspirate and its neighbour have no sound at all. Yet more puzzling is it when the original consonant falls away altogether, leaving only the *h*, or else leaving no trace. In modern G. *th* never has any sound; nor has initial *fh*, hence such puzzling names as KILLIN and KILLINTAG, from *fhionn* and St. *Findoc*. But it is to be noted, that Old Gaelic was not always the same as that of to-day, and letters did not always aspirate as they do now. Examples will be found in our List *passim*. Some have forgotten this.

As to Brythonic or Welsh words, it will be helpful to remember that *au* final very nearly sounds ay, *aw* sounds ow, *dd* makes a soft th and when final may almost disappear, *f* sounds v, the Gaelic *mh*, it is *ff* which sounds f, *ll* sounds a soft thl and *w* sounds u. The aspirations are somewhat similar to those in Gaelic.

Another matter of crucial importance is the accent. In Gaelic, which here differs from Irish, the accent tends to fall on the first syllable. Thus, in many names, the second or unstressed syllable is corrupted by indistinct pronunciation, and often falls away altogether; *e.g.*, *achadh*, 'field,' has in hundreds of names become *ach* or *auch*. Seldom has the final

[1] Of course, this often happens even in English, especially with *g*; in Eng. *h* almost always silences *g*, as in high, naughty, straight, etc. This does not apply to Lowland Scots.

syllable survived in a name ; though we have, *e.g.*, Achanancarn and Achanamoine in Benderloch (plural forms), and Auchamore, Dunoon. Here is another interesting example. In a charter of Malcolm the Maiden, *c.* 1160, we read of a place in the Don Valley, 'Brecachath quod interpretatur campus distinctus coloribus'; and there is still a Breakachy, or 'speckled field,' near Beauly and in Caithness. Similarly, *tulach*, 'a hill, mound,' usually appears in names as Tully- or Tillie-, as in TULLYMET and TILLIECHEWAN, though we have the whole word in TULLOCH, and the second syllable intact in MORTLACH. It may be called a firm rule in Gaelic phonology, in compound names, which Gaelic place-names usually are, that the accent falls on the qualifying word or attributive. Attention to the accent in the native pronunciation will thus save many an incorrect guess at a name's meaning; thus Knóckan would mean 'little hill' (dimin. of *cnoc*), but Knockárd, 'high hill,' *àrd* being here the qualifying word; thus, too, TYRIE, name of a farm near Kirkcaldy, might from its look mean 'king's house' (*tigh righe*), but when we know it is accented Týrie, it can only be the locative of G. *tìr*, *tìre*, 'land, a bit of land.' However, even this rule has a few exceptions. *E.g.*, natives of Central Perthshire do certainly speak of Kénmore, just as natives of Galloway speak of Kénmure; and though we do say Kinlóch, we do also say currently Kínloch-Rannoch. Hence we may justify the meaning assigned to MOCHRUM, MOFFAT, POLMONT, etc.

English speakers often put 'The' before a name, as 'The Methil,' 'The Lochies' (see p. 55); but in the forms of Gaelic place-names used by English speakers the article is almost never prefixed, except in the form *t'*. The nominative of the article, *an*, is then rarely met with in English use (on Gaelic lips it is common enough); but the genitive *an* masc., *na* fem., in plur. *nan*, before labials *nam*, is very often met with; *e.g.*, Bal*na*bruaich, 'village on the bank,' Coir*nan*uriskin, 'ravine of the goblins,' Bealach-*nam*-bo, 'pass of the cattle.' The *an* or *na* of the article is very liable to abrasion or corruption; *e.g.*, it may become simple *a* as in Dal*a*rossie, or simple *n* as in Kil*n*inver, or may even slip down into *i*, as in Culli*i*cudden (*cf.*, Welsh *y* in Bettws-y-Coed, 'house in the wood'). It is also worth remembering that, except in feminine polysyllables, the gen. plur. of a noun is always the same as the nom. singular. With masculine nouns beginning with a vowel the article is *an t'*, or *t'*, as in TOB, 'the bay.' The same is true of nouns beginning with *s*, here the *t* eclipses the *s* ; as in the names COLINTRAIVE and KINTAIL, which are in G. *caol an t'snaimh*, and *cinn t'saile*.

The mediæ *b*, *d*, *g* approach in sound much nearer to our English tenues *p*, *t*, *c*, and are often found interchanging in names, *cf.*, ARNGASK, DUTHIL, etc. Final *dh* sometimes sounds like *k* or *ch*, but is often mute. The letter *d* seems often to insert itself, as in DRUMMOND, G. *dromainn*, and in LOMOND, old G. *Lomne*. The letter *l* always seems ready to run away from a name ; see, *e.g.*, BOGIE, COCKBURNSPATH, or COWDENKNOWES, in which last both the *w*'s represent an original *l*. The *s* of the English plural in many cases affixes itself to Gaelic names, as in LEUCHARS or WEMYSS. In names like CROMLIX and TORBREX the final *c* has amalgamated with this *s* and become *x*. In olden days Gaels were not so careful about genders as now. Well-attested cases like BALNAGOWAN are too common to be all set down to careless scribes. There is similar though not so plentiful evidence as to old Welsh. If Henry Bradley had known this and one or two other things he would probably have sometimes modified the truculence of his criticisms on place-name work. The ending *-ie* is very freely found, usually spelt scholastically *-aidh*, representing the old Gaelic locative, 'at the place of,' as in BRODIE, CAMLACHIE, etc. In our river-names *-ie* is specially common—Feshie, Lossie, Trommie, Urie, etc., and perhaps points to the same ending as is seen in Ptolemy's Libn-ios, Nov-ios, Tob-ios, etc.

Of Scottish place-names those sprung from Celtic lips show by far the most sympathy with nature. The Celt's warm, emotional heart loved to seek out the poetry and colour in the world around, and many of his place-names show that 'stern nature was his daily companion and friend.' Indeed, *the majority of Celtic names give either the simplest possible description of the site named, or describe some prominent feature, or else the colouring or appearance of it as it strikes the eye.* Thus the traveller up Strathtay, when he passes striking CRAIGIEBARNS, will see in a moment the appositeness of the true name, 'crag at the pass or gap.' A large number of Gaelic names mean simply, 'house on the bank,' 'village by the straits,' 'field of stones,' or the like. The first two are represented in Gaelic by those Cockney terrors TIGH-NA-BRUAICH and BALL-A-CHULISH; whilst that mouth-filling name MACHRAHANISH, Kintyre, just means 'plain' or 'links of a man Sanas,' plus the Norse *nish*, *i.e.*, ness. Thus we may almost venture to lay it down as a general rule that *the simpler the meaning conjectured, the more likely is it to be correct.* From what has been said the reader will not be surprised to find that the words for 'water,' 'river,' 'stream,' occur very often in names—*dobhar* or *dôr* (see ABERDOUR, etc.); *abhuinn* or *ân*[1] or AVON; *abh*, found in AWE, and very likely in AVOCH, the *bh* here being quiescent; also *uisg*, *uisge*, so familiar in the shape and sound of that 'strong water,' commonly called 'whisky'; this word we see in COR-UISK, and in a little hill in Gartly parish called Wisheach, 'the watery' or 'wet' hill. ESK is a cognate, and in England the same root rings the changes on almost all the vowels, as in Ax, Ex,[2] Isis, Ock (in Ockbrook, Derby), Usk, and Ux (in Uxbridge); whilst Ox-, in Oxford, is perhaps a brother of the same family. A softer form of this word may perhaps be seen in OUSE, a river-name found not only in England, but on this side the Border too; see OXNAM.

Whether the last rule be accepted or not, there is no question that personal acquaintance with a spot is highly desirable before we make any attempt to solve its name. One sight of a place may prevent ludicrous mistakes, and may also suggest with a flash the real meaning. It was personal inspection which brought that happy inspiration which translated COLINTRAIVE, on the quiet Kyles of Bute, as *caol an t'snaimh* (pron. traive, for *t* eclipses *s*, and *n* changes to its kindred liquid *r*), 'narrows with the swimming-place,' where the cattle for market swam over. ARDENTRYVE, opposite to Oban, has a similar origin.

Where Gaelic names now survive in an English-speaking region, and to some extent in Gaelic-speaking regions too (few

[1] The final -an in a good many Celtic names like ABRIACHAN, etc., is purely terminational.

[2] *E.g.*, Simeon of Durham speaks of Exeter as, 'Brittanice Cairuisc, Latine Civitas Aquarum.'

Gaels can spell their own tongue), the place-names are apt to get so corrupted by generations of illiterate speakers that one requires to know, not only the look of a place and the true pronunciation of its name, but also something of the laws of phonetics, something of the lines on which these corruptions or alterations usually run. Phonetics is a science with real laws, and these must be mastered.[1] We already know how apt *b* and *p* are to interchange, so too are *d* and *t*; *e.g.*, take Dulnan for *tuilnean*, or take *alld* or *allt*, a very remarkable word, for it means both 'river,' 'glen,' and 'heights on either side a glen,' thus being apparently akin to the L. *altus*, high; Diack contests this. It occurs again and again in Gaelic names, in the guises of All-, Alt-, Auld-, Ault- (see List). As showing the length to which the Gael can go in flinging away his alphabet, we may cite BEALLACHANTUIE, on the Atlantic side of Kintyre, meaning 'pass of the seat,' G. *suidhe*; but the name is now pronounced Bállochantée, which means that all that is now left of the six letters *suidhe* is the final long *e*!

The commonest names are those giving a bare, brief description of the site named; next in frequency are those which give the general appearance of the place as it strikes the eye—rough (*garbh*) or smooth (*mìn.* also 'level, gentle-looking'), straight (*deas*) or crooked (*cam*), black or dark (*dubh*), speckled or spotted (*breac*), long (*fada*) or short (*gearr*), little (*beag*) or big (*mòr*); such names as GARVALT, 'rough glen,' MINGARRY, 'smooth enclosure,' MORVEN, 'big ben,' are legion. Almost all of Nature's common colours figure largely in the sympathetic nomenclature of the nature-loving Gael. Specially common are *dubh*, 'black,' which everyone knows in the guise of Duff, but often also sounded *du*, as in DOUGLAS, DHU HEARTACH, ROSSDHU; and *fionn*, 'white, light-coloured, clear to the view,' as in CARFIN, FINDON. Names denoting red or reddish are also plentiful. Here we have two words, *dearg*, 'red,' also 'the colour of newly-ploughed land,' as in Ben Dearg; when the *d* is aspirated it sounds almost like *j*, as in Barrjarg, 'red height,' near Closeburn. The other word is *ruadh*, familiar to us all in the name of Rob Roy, 'red Robert,' with his ruddy tartan

[1] For Norse-Gaelic phonetics the serious student will find Watson's table invaluable. *Pl. Names Ross and Crom.*, Introd., pp. lvii *sq.* *E.g.*, Norse *ei* usually equates with Gaelic *ao*, Norse *t* with Gaelic *d*, and so on.

plaid ; but also pronounced rew, and something very like roch, as in TANNIEROACH, 'reddish meadow.' The *dh* is preserved in the spelling of the name RUTHVEN, though the name itself is now often pronounced Rivven, and the whole name is a little doubtful. Green, chief colour in Nature's paint-box, is *gorm*. Everyone knows CAIRNGORM, and every lover of Scottish song has heard of 'Tullochgorum,' *i.e.*, 'green hillock.' Then there is *glas*, 'grey, pale, wan,' as in Glass Maol, 'the grey, bare hill,' so frowningly conspicuous on the road between Braemar and Glenshee, GLASSARY, and possibly too in the name of the great Western Metropolis. On that much-controverted subject, the etymology of GLASGOW, see the List. Common and expressive is such a name as Tonrigaoith, 'back to the wind.' Already in a charter of William the Lyon we find a Tunregaid near Morebattle : in Arran it has been turned into Thundergay.

Few objects are more striking in a landscape than a clump or forest of trees ; thus we are prepared to find tree-names bulking largely in Gaelic topography. Common as any, perhaps, is *beath* (bay), the birch, one of the few natural or indigenous trees of Scotland. This we find pure and simple in Beath and Beith, where the *th* retains its sound ; often the *th* is mute, as in AULT-BEA, Ross-shire, and TOMBEA, Pass of Leni. The word *dair*, gen. *dara*, an oak, its derivative *darach*, an oakwood, and its cognate *doire*, a grove, have also many representatives. We have the simple Darroch at Falkirk, etc., and we have a Scottish as well as an Irish Derry, near Braemar. Then there are DAR-VEL, AUCHTERDERRAN, and DALJARROCH, near Girvan, etc. The Gaelic for an elm is *leamhan* (louan), which appears in many a dress. One of these is the common name LEVEN. The Vale of Leven was once called Levenax or LENNOX, whilst the old form of Loch LOMOND was Lomne, which may also be *leamhan* ; and its sea-neighbour Loch LONG is probably the *Loch Lemannonius* of Ptolemy. He, by the way, wrote *c.* A.D. 150, but is thought to have taken his names from an old Tyrian atlas at Alexandria, and so the forms he gives may be a good deal older than this date. Humbler plants have also contributed their quota, like the sedge, *siosg*, as in DERNA-CISSOCK, Wigtown, and the rush, *luachair*, as in LEUCHARS.

If trees and plants give feature to a landscape, animals have their own prominence too. And the Celt was very fond of raising a monument to his dumb cattle by means of a place-name; *e.g.*, the Gaelic for a cow is *bo*, = L. *bos*; this we find in the name which Scott has made all the world know by the *Lady of the Lake*, Béalach-nam-bo, *i.e.*, 'pass of the cattle,' *bealach* better known to most of us in the shape of BALLOCH; then there is BOCHASTLE, and BOYNE, near Banff, which seems to be G. *bo-fhionn*, 'white cow.' *Madadh*, the wild dog or sometimes the wolf, is commemorated in LOCHMADDY. A wolf is mentioned in a Court of Barony case at Taymouth in 1622; and it seems to have lingered on till the end of that century: *cf.*, Culmaddie or 'wolf's neuk,' in Sutherland. The ordinary dog is *cu*, gen. *coin*, as in Loch Con. The unsavoury pig, *muc*, has left many a sign of his former abundance, as in AUCHTERMUCHTY, DRUMMUCKLOCH, and MUCKHART, all of which imply the site of a swinefield or pen. Even the shy otter, *doran*, gives name to Ben Doran; and so forth.

Not only did the Gael give the names of animals to many spots associated with them, he was also constantly seeing in some landmark a resemblance to some part of an animal. Most common of all do we find *druim*, = L. *dorsum*, the back, especially a long back like that of a horse, hence a long hill-ridge. Sir H. Maxwell gives about 200 instances in Galloway alone, and we find them everywhere—DRUMCLOG, DRUMLANRIG, DRUMSHEUGH, DROMORE, etc. DRUMMOND and DRYMEN are just the G. *dromainn* with the same meaning. Then there is *crubha*, 'a haunch or shoulder,' hence the shoulder of a hill, as in DUNCRUB, but not, as was once thought, in CRIEFF. *Sròn*, 'the nose,' equivalent of the Norse *ness*, and the English Naze, is found in a good many names of headlands, where it is always spelt *stron*, but the *t* is like the *t* in *strath*, a mere Sassenach intrusion to enable the Lowlander to pronounce the word. Examples are STRONE itself, Stronbuy, and that little cape on Loch Katrine, so unpronounceable to English lips, STRONACHLACHAR, 'cape of the mason.'[1] Besides, there is the widely scattered *ceann*, 'a head,' and so, a promontory, usually found as ken-, or in its old locative form of *cinn* or kin- (see KINALDIE); instances stand everywhere.

The Gael has been a more modest man than his English

[1] On CAMERON, see the List.

supplanter. John Bull dearly loves to perpetuate his own or his own kith's name, be it in a town, a castle, an hospital, or even by surreptitious carving on his bench at school. There are scores of towns and villages in England, and Scotland too, called by the names of Saxon men (*cf.*, p. 50 and foll.). The Celt adopted this fashion much more rarely. But a good many of the heroes of Ossian and other early legends are commemorated in this way, *e.g.*, CORRIEVRECKAN, off Jura, is 'the cauldron' or 'whirlpool of Brecan,' grandson of the famous Niall of the nine hostages. COWAL is called after Coill, the 'old king Cole,' of the well-known rhyme; LORN, after Loarn, first king of Scots in Dalriada or Argyle. In Angus we have INSHEWAN, 'meadow of Eogan or Ewan.' The seven sons of that legendary eponymous personage, *Cruithne* or *Cruidne*, reputed father of the Cruithnig or Pictish race, are always cropping up. According to the *Pictish Chronicle*, the seven were Fib, Fidach, Floclaw, Ce, Fortrenn, Got, Circinn. Fortrenn was the old name of Strathearn and its vicinity; for the others see ATHOLE, CAITHNESS, FIDDICH, FIFE, MEARNS, etc. The old man's own name we find in Cruithneachan, Lochaber. It should be said, however, that some scholars vehemently object to our deriving any names from this Cruithne, or his sons. They consider them pure myths, *noms pour servir*, deliberate inventions to conceal ignorance. How that hill in Badenoch, 'Craig Righ Harailt,' came to be called after the Norse king Harold nobody seems to know; perhaps from his passing through on his ill-fated expedition to Athole. Certainly Celtic names of the type of BALMACLELLAN, 'M'Lellan's village,' and BALMAGHIE, in Galloway, are quite rare. Near Lesmahagow is the curious name, Auchtigammell, 'field of the house of Gemmell'; the common Norse *gammel*, 'old,' or in its Scots form, so common as a surname among us, Auld. The Celt did little[1] in the way of handing down his own or his folk's name; but, having always been a pious man, there was nothing he liked better than to call a church or a well after some favourite saint who once upon a time may have sojourned there. This, however, demands separate treatment (see chap. v).

It is often said that several place-names preserve the memory

[1] But *cf.* DUNDONALD, DUNROBIN, DUNVEGAN, etc.

of the ancient Druidic or Pagan sun and fire worship. This is conceivable, *cf.* Ben Ledi, though it is absolutely certain that no Bal- in Scotland, nor yet Tulliebeltane, represents or preserves the name of Baal, the Phœnician sun-god ; and one is surprised to find this unscholarly superstition so often repeated. Even though Greenock be the G. *grian-aig*, 'sun-bay,' that will just mean 'sunny bay' ; and Ardentinny, 'height of the fire,' on the west shore of Loch Long, refers to the old signal fire for the ferryman, whilst Auchendinny does not mean 'field of the fire' at all.

The inquisitive amateur, somewhat dismayed by the many difficulties in the study of Celtic names now detailed, will yet, we hope, begin to take heart again. He ought to be further reassured when he hears that acquaintance with about a dozen Gaelic words will enable any one to interpret a big bunch of the Gaelic names in Scotland. As fitting close to the section, let us enumerate these :

(1) *Aber*, already discussed.

(2) *Achadh*, 'a field,' also already discussed in part. From *achadh*, with its unaccented second syllable, comes the common prefix *ach*, as in Achnacarry, or Achray. As a prefix the form is as commonly *auch-*, as in Auchinleys, Auchmithie, etc. ; and *ach-* and *auch-* often interchange, as in Ach- or Auch-nasheen, Ach- or Auch-engane, etc.

(3) *Auchter*, in Gaelic *uachdar*, Welsh *uchder*, O.Ir. *ochter* ; but even the oldest charters spell it *auchter* or *ochter*, or *octre* ; *au* and *o* are here found freely interchanging as in Auchtertyre or Ochtertyre, Auchterneed, in 1619 Ochterneid, etc. This *uachdar* is literally 'the summit or upper part,' hence 'a high field.' In Achtercairn, Ross-shire, the first part is really the hard West Coast pronunciation of *achadh,—ach'd-a'chàirn* (1638 Auchitcairne).

(4) *Bail, baile*, 'a hamlet,' or simply 'a house.' We all know the multitudinous Irish *Ballys* ; and *ball-* or *balla-* is a common prefix in the Isle of Man. But it is as common in Scotland—Balnabruaich, Ballinluig, and so on. In the Lowlands of Aberdeen alone there are said to be no less than fifty instances. Occasionally the *b* has become *p*, as in Balgonie, *a.* 1300, Palgoveny.

(5) *Barr*, a height or hill, as in Barr, Barlinnie, etc. ; in

Lochaber, once a swampy region, *barr* means a road, because these roads could only be made along the high ground. The aspiration of the *b* appears in CRAIGIEVAR, and in the name of 'young LOCHINVAR' (G. *lochan a' bharra*). But BARRA and perhaps DUNBAR refer to an Irish St. Barr.

(6) *Blàr*, 'a plain,' as in Blair, BLAIRGOWRIE, etc.

(7) *Còil*, or *cùil*, 'a corner, a nook,' as in COLFIN, COLLACE, CULROSS, etc. There is apt, here, to be confusion with *cùl*, *cùil*, 'the back,' and *coille*, 'a wood' (see the List *passim*). COLL itself probably means a 'hazel.'

(8) *Dail*, 'a field or meadow,' W. *dol*; the prefix *dal-* is always Gaelic, and has this meaning, as in DALAROSSIE, DALNASPIDAL; but the suffix *-dale* is always either Norse (see p. 38) or English, in Scotland usually the former, and means 'valley.'

(9) *Gart* or *Gàrradh* (a late loan-word from English), 'an enclosure, garden,' akin to the Mid. Eng. *garth*, and the ordinary Eng. *yard*, usually found as Gart-, as in GARTCOSH, GARTNAVEL (= APPLEGARTH); sometimes as Garry-, as in GARRYNAHINE, 'Garden on the river,' in Lewis. But GARRABOST, another Lewis name, we should probably interpret the man 'Geirra's place.' Just as in the case of *dal* or *dale*, the prefix *gart-* is Gaelic, but the suffix *-garth* must be English or Norse.

(10) *Inver* or *Inbhir*, already referred to (p. 11). Unlike *aber*, and contrary to Isaac Taylor's idea, *inver* is found, practically all over Scotland, save in those northern isles where the Norseman has clean swept the board; but it is much commoner north than south of the old Roman Wall. The simple INVER occurs again and again—on the Dornoch Firth, as name of a little village, formerly Inverlochslin, and near Crathie, and where Bran joins Tay; also in Loch Inver, so well known to the Sutherland salmon-fisher. *Inver* always tends to slide into *inner*, as both old charters and modern pronunciations amply testify, *e.g.*, Inver- or INNER-ARITY, Inner- or INVER-KIP, etc. *Inver* does not exist in Brythonic Wales; it is rare in Ireland; and we can hardly call it Pictish.

(11) *Magh*, 'a plain,' probably akin to *mag*, 'the palm of the hand,' as in MACHRAHANISH; but the final guttural usually vanishes. Thus we get such curious-looking names as CAMBUS

o' MAY, which just means 'crook of the plain'; and MAGGIKNOCKATER, q.v.; whilst *magh*, in its locative, appears twice in Inverness as MOY, and more than once in Stirling as Mye. MEARNS, the old name for Kincardine, in its only existing early form, Moerne, strongly points to an original Moy Erne, 'plain of Eire,' see EARN.

(12) The Pictish *pet*, *pit*, gen. *pette*, found in names as Pit-, Pitte-, Petti- (see p. 10); also, in 1211, we find the form Put-mullin ('land of the mill'). After the common fashion of such words—*cf.*, the Eng. *ham* and *ton*—*pit*[1] (G. *cuid*, W. *peth*, O.W. *pett*, 'a thing') first means 'an enclosed bit of land,' then a farm, then the cottages round the farm, and so, a village. The word seems still to linger in Assynt as *put* or *poot*, applied to a small patch of cultivated land among the rocks. In Gaelic, *i.e.*, the tongue of the Dalriad Scots, which afterwards overspread the whole land, *pit* is commonly rendered by *baile*; it is doubtful if it is ever rendered by *both*, 'a hut' (see PITGAVENY). The region of *pit-* is the east centre of Scotland from the Firth of Forth to Tarbat Ness. It occurs as far north as Golspie—Pitfure and Pitgrudy; also at Pittentrail, Rogart, and *a.* 1350 a 'Petcarsky.' But there seem to be none at all in the west, so we may call this Pictish.

(13) *Tulach*, 'a hillock or hill': the unstressed second syllable usually drops into *y* or *ĭ*; but we have the full word in TULLOCH, near Dingwall, already so spelt in 1158. *Tulach* occurs both as prefix and suffix, as in TILLYFOUR, TULLYMET, GRANDTULLY, KIRKINTILLOCH. It has somewhat more disguised itself in MORTLACH, and yet more in MURTHLY, both of which represent the G. *mòr t(h)ulach*, 'big hill.'

To these, the amateur can, of course, at once add all those Gaelic words entering into place-names which have already become part of ordinary English speech. Such a word is *ben*, as a suffix, usually aspirated into *-ven*, as in MORVEN, SUILVEN, rarely thus as a prefix, *e.g.*, VENLAW and VENUE. Then there are *brae*, G. *braigh*, the upper part of anything, hence BRAEMAR, the Braes of Balquhidder, etc., but also quite common in Lowland names, as in Cobble Brae (Falkirk), Whale Brae (Newhaven); *cairn*; *corrie*, G. *coire*, lit. 'a cauldron or kettle';

[1] Often identified with late L. *petia*, *pecia*, 'a fragment,' then 'a bit of land,' Eng. *piece*, see *N.E.D.*, s.v.

craig or *crag*, and its diminutive *craigan* ; *glen* ; *inch*, G. *innis*, ' an island or links ' ; *knock*, G. *cnoc*, ' a hill ' ; *kyle*, *kyles*, G. *caol*, *caolas*, ' narrow place, straits ' ; *loch*, and its diminutive *lochan* ; and *strath*. Most of these words have only been used by Southron tongues for a century, or a little more or less ; though *crag* is found in the *Cursor Mundi*, before 1300, and in Barbour's *Bruce*, whose date is *c.* 1375 ; *loch*, in Barbour too, still sounded new and strange to Dr. Johnson, although already in Domesday Book, *c.* 1086, we find Hoiloch, now Hoylake, Cheshire. Barbour also tells us of Ben Cruachan: ' Crechanben hecht (was called) that montane.' Sibbald, in his well-known *History of Fife* (ed. 1710), cumbrously refers to Ben Lomond as ' Lomundian mountain.' Bishop Pococke has ' Benevis ' in 1760 ; but the earliest quotation for *ben* which one has found is for the year 1771, when in Denholm's *Tour Through Scotland* (1804, p. 49) we read : ' Prompt thee Ben Lomond's fearful height to climb.' *N.E.D.*'s earliest instance is for 1788 ; and the earliest example in that great dictionary for the use of the word *cairn* as a landmark is from John Wesley in 1770. *Corrie* is unrecorded till 1795, and was first popularized by Sir Walter Scott. *Strath* is not used in English till 1639.

Note.—It may be useful to say that the invaluable maps of Timothy Pont, compiled *c.* 1610, and so often cited in our List, were first published in Blaeu's great Atlas, *Theatrum Orbis Terrarum*, Amsterdam, 1654.

CHAPTER II

NORSE NAMES

WHEN we come to deal with the Norse names[1] in Scotland,—perhaps to say Scandinavian names would be more correct,—we find ourselves amongst a group most interesting, and far more numerous than the outsider would think. The story of the Norseman's deeds in Scotland has been skimmed over but lightly by most historians, and therefore it may be useful to set at least the bones of that history before the reader. Dr. Skene held there is proof of Frisians, *i.e.*, men from the mouth of the Weser, in Dumfriesshire even before the year A.D. 400; then Dr. Jakob Jakobsen thought he had found, in Shetland place-names, proof of Norse settlement there in pre-Viking days, *a.* 700. He bases on words like *bolstað-r* 'homestead,' *heim-r* ditto, and *vin* 'pasture,' found in Shetland but never in Iceland, which was settled before 900. He thought the Shetland dialect proved settlement from South-Western Norway—Vest Agder and Rogaland, while the place-names suggest colonization by peasants from Möre in the West. However that may be, we have certain evidence that, before the eighth century passed away, bold Vikings from Denmark and Norway had already begun to beach their galleys on our long-suffering coasts. In 793 we find their rude feet on holy Lindisfarne, close to the modern Scottish border; and in 794 they swooped down among the Hebrides, being forced away from their homes because their own barren rocks could not sustain the growing population. This search for resting-place and sustenance drove some as far away as the Volga; it urged others over the cold seas, to Iceland and Greenland, and some rested not till they had coasted

[1] Their importance and greater difficulty incline us to put this chapter before the English names, of which some are earlier in historic time.

down to where mighty New York now spreads and grows. The uprise in the next century of ambitious Harold of the Fair Hair (Haarfagr), who at length made himself absolute king of Norway, drove out many more of his most active opposers, who, from 826 on, found in the many rocky bays and friths of Western Scotland the quarters most suited for their plundering forays. King Harold followed after them, conquered all the isles away as far south as Man (A.D. 875), and made his brother Sigurd their first Jarl. Even before this the Orkneys had been a station of call for the Vikings; while by the tenth century Norse rule had spread over all the Hebrides, Caithness, and all but the south-west of Sutherland. It has little affected Scottish topography south of the River Oykel, except in Argyll; though latterly it included the west of Inverness, and all Arran, even reaching as far as Dumbarton.

In Orkney and Shetland the Viking completely superseded the Pictish Celt, who, so far as place-names are concerned, has—strange to tell—left very few traces behind, a result almost unique in history. One exception, it is just half a one, is the name ORKNEY itself; another partial instance is the Moulhead of Deerness, Orkney, the *Múli* of the Saga, which is the G. *maol*, 'brow of a rock, cape.'[1] It must be remembered that here the Norseman had 600 years and more in which to do his obliterating work. Yet the memory of the Pict, who reached north before A.D. 400, does survive in such names as the PENTLAND Frith, Pettawater and Pettidale (Delting), Pettasmog (Burrafrith), Pettister, Unst, etc., where the Pent- or Pett- must mean 'Pict.' But, says Brögger, these are names given by the Norse in memory of the defunct Picts. He thinks the few surviving Celtic names are late, and were given by Celtic servants of the Norseman. The *Nordreyar*, 'northern isles,' so called in contrast with the *Sudreyar*, 'southern isles' or Hebrides, did not escape from his dominion till 1469, when

[1] A few other names used to be plausibly pressed as Gaelic, like CORRIGALL Burn and Deasbreck (Dea's *brekka*, O.N. for 'slope'). These must now be given up. But a small residuum is still conceded, *e.g.*, Nockan, G. *cnocan*, 'little hill,' off North Ronaldsay and Knucker Hill (*cf.* W. *cnwc*, 'hillock'), Westray, also Diamonds, Deerness, which its site shows is, Ir. *di-muinn*, 'two tops.' There are two or three more probable. See H. Marwick, *Celtic Pl. Names in Scotland*, Socy. Antiq., 1922–3.

James III of Scotland married Margaret, daughter of Christian I of Denmark, and received these northern isles as her dowry. But the Hebrides only remained an appanage to the Norwegian crown for a scant three years after King Haco's fleet was shattered, after the brave battle of Largs in 1263.

In these parts of Northern and Western Scotland, Scandinavian names are found in more or less abundance.[1] They also form quite a notable colony in Dumfriesshire, especially between the Rivers Esk and Nith ; but the distinctive *gill*, *beck*, and *rig* spread a good deal farther than that—away into Kirkcudbright, and up Moffat Water, and not a few have even flowed over into Peebles ; though on all Tweedside there is not a single representative of the characteristic Norse suffixes *beck*, *force*, *thorpe*, *thwaite*, and *wald*. The Dumfries colony of names, like the Scandinavian names in the Isle of Man, bear a more Danish cast than the others, and it is now a generally-admitted fact that this special group of names is due to a Norse irruption from England *via* Carlisle, and not to any landing of fair-haired pirates direct from the sea. The native Gaels called the Norsemen 'the fair strangers,' and the Danes 'the dark strangers' or *gaill*. The most hurried comparison will show how like the Dumfries Scandinavian[2] names are to the kindred names across the Border in Cumberland—*fell* and *beck*, *bie* and *thwaite*, are alike common to both.

In other parts of Scotland, especially those at some distance from the sea, Norse footprints are few and far between, though a few, like SNAEGOW near Dunkeld, are clear enough. Even on the east coast itself, south of Dingwall, undoubted Norse names are very rare ; because the snug *viks* or bays are so very few. But INNERWICK, south of Dunbar, seems one exception, and there are a few south of the Moray Frith, like ENZIE, RATHVEN, Scar Nose (Cullen), etc. Note also EDZELL, Angus, MEIGLE, Perth, and CRAILING, Roxburgh. Mr. W. J. Liddall[3] has drawn attention to a series of interesting names connected, he thinks, with the doings of one of these pirate Northmen called

[1] Though we can remember none in Dumbarton and there seem none in Moray, Nairn or Lochaber.

[2] The latest verdict is, that the place-names of Cumberland are, on the whole, much more Norse than Danish.

[3] See *Scottish Geograph. Mag.* for July 1885.

Buthar, corrupted into Butter, the man after whom, he thinks, Buttermere is named. He, it is said, has also given his name to Butterstone or Butterstown, near Dunkeld, and his path from thence to the sea is marked by an old road over the Ochills, still called the Butter Road, and past a Kinross-shire farm called Butterwell, on to Largo Bay; and the surname Butter still occurs. However, Mr. Stewart of Moneydie held Butterstown to be from G. *bothar*, ' a road or lane,' its name having once been Bailebothar. There is another ' Buter mere ' away down in Wilts, mentioned in a charter of King Athelstan, 931, and there are several spots in Galloway called Butter Hole ; all probably refer to the bittern and its haunts, the Scotch name for that bird being *butter*, the Mid. Eng. *bitourc*, Old Fr. *butor*. It may be noted, *en passant*, that here we have several instances of names which seem to say ' butter,' and yet have nothing to do with that useful commodity.

It is usually said that Icelandic is the nearest modern representative of the tongue which these Viking-invaders spake; it would be more correct to say it was Icelandic itself.[1] Before 1300 all the lands peopled by the Northmen—Norway, Sweden, Denmark, Iceland, the Faroes, Orkney, Shetland, and the Hebrides—used much the same speech, and so did the Norse or Danish settlers in England, Ireland, and the mainland of Scotland. And this northern tongue, the language of the old Eddas and Sagas, differed as little from modern Icelandic as Shakspere's English from Browning's. The Arctic isle has preserved the mother-tongue with little change. Thus in studying the Scandinavian place-names of Scotland it is chiefly the Icelandic dictionary on which we must rely ; though the amateur must again be warned that unless he have some little knowledge of Norse speech, knowing to seek the origin of a name in *wh-* under *hv*, knowing when to expect the *r* of the genitive (see Aros, Brora, etc.), and the like, he will find himself unable, even with his dictionary, to explain many unquestionably Norse forms. Modern Swedish and Danish are to Icelandic as Italian and Spanish to Latin. They did not begin palpably to diverge from the parent stem till the thirteenth century. Yet scholars are fairly agreed that in the

[1] In our List will be found both ' O.N.,' *i.e.*, Old Norse, and ' Icel.,' but these mean almost the same thing.

Scottish names which we are now dealing with, all of which probably existed before 1300, there are some which have a decidedly Danish cast, whilst the majority are rather Norse. The Norsemen seem to have loved mountainous regions like their own stern, craggy fatherland; hence it is chiefly Norse forms which we find in the names among the uplands of Southern Scotland and North-West England, and chiefly Danish forms on the flat and fertile stretches of Dumfries, a district so like the Dane's own land, where hills are a rarity as great as trees in Caithness.

It is also well understood that the old Norse speech was near of kin to our own Old English, which came from the flat coast-region immediately south-west of modern Denmark; and the Norsemen themselves emphatically recognized this near kinship. The best living representative of Old English is Lowland or Broad Scots, that most expressive of tongues, so rich in vivid adjectives, whose rapid decay is almost as much to be regretted as that of Gaelic. Broad Scots is the survival of Anglian or Northern English, giving to us still, in its pronunciations, the same sounds as fell from the lips of the old warriors of Bernicia and Deira. And Broad Scots, both in vocabulary and pronunciation, approximates, in scores of cases, far more closely to Danish and Icelandic than modern English does.[1] In consequence of this, when we have no external evidence to guide us, it is sometimes impossible to say whether a given name is of Anglo-Saxon or of Norse birth.

In quite another direction there are proofs that the West Highland Gaels borrowed a few words from the Northmen, who settled so plentifully upon their bays and lochs, without leave asked. There is the Icel. *gjá* or 'goe,' a chasm, which the Gael has made into *Geodha*. In Colonsay there is a *Rudha Gheadha* or 'red cleft,' where the old Norse *a* is still preserved. The word *firth* or *frith*, the Icel. *fjörðr*, and N. *fjord*, is, of itself, sufficient proof that the Norse galleys sailed round every angle of our coasts, north and south, east and west. There are firths everywhere from Pentland to Solway, and from Dornoch to Clyde. The Gael has copiously adopted this word *fjord*, but in his mouth the *f* gets aspirated, and, therefore,

[1] See Worsaæ, *The Danes and Norwegians in England, Scotland, and Ireland*; and J. Veitch, *History of Scot. Border*, pp. 31–6.

soon disappears. Thus on the west coast we have few 'friths,' but plenty of names ending in *-ord*, *-ort*, *-ard*, *-art*; the usual pronunciation in modern Gaelic is *arst*. Such is the origin of KNOYDART, 'Cnud's' or 'Canute's fjord,' ENARD, MOYDART, SNIZORT. The *f* remains in MELFORT, but Broadford is modern. And if the Gael borrowed from the Norsemen, we are told there are traces in modern Norse of *vice versa* borrowing from the Gael.

The student is well served with early forms of our Scandinavian place-names. For all the Norse region, except Dumfries, Orkney, and Shetland, the *Origines Parochiales* liberally supply us with old name-forms, and the Dunrobin charters cited there often take us back to *c.* 1220. For Orkney itself we have the curious early rental-books of the Bishops of Orkney, which have all been printed, the oldest dating from 1497. For the northern counties we also have Torfæus' *History of Norway*, 1696, based on the Sagas; but here, far above all else in value, is the famous *Orkneyinga Saga*, so well edited for English readers by Dr. Joseph Anderson. Its date seems *c.* 1225, but it embodies songs from several earlier skalds. The oldest existing Norse manuscript dates from about 1100. Of course the Norse names have not altered nearly so much as have Celtic names in a now English region, and thus early forms are not so often of crucial importance; but the names NORTH and SOUTH RONALDSAY (q.v.) are pertinent examples to the contrary.

No one in Scotland now speaks a Scandinavian tongue, but it seems to have lingered on in far sequestered Foula, away to the west of the Shetlands, till *c.* 1775; and the local speech of Shetland and Orkney is still full of Scandinavian words.[1] This is little to be wondered at, seeing that, for centuries, Norwegian kings were wont not seldom there to live, and even there to die. And though the speech be gone, the physiognomist can still pick out the Norse face, with the blue eyes and fair hair, almost all over Scotland. One usage borrowed from a Norse source has had large influence in Scottish place-names, *viz.*, the measuring of land by rental, the unit being the *ounce-land*—Old G. *unga*, Mod. G. *unnsa*, L. *uncia*, as in UNGANAB in North Uist, the land for which the abbot (*ab*) was paid an

[1] A Shetland deed has lately been found written in Norse, of so late a date as 1597. Mr. Goudie speaks of one of as late a date as 1627.

ounce of silver as rental. ‘Ounceland’ rarely is met with; but the smaller amounts are quite common. In an ounce of silver there were held to be 18 or 20 dwts., and ‘penny’[1] lands (O.E. *penig*, *pening*, Icel. *penning-r*, Dan. *penge*) abound, *e.g.*, PENNYGHAEL, Pennymuir, etc.; so do all the lesser sums down to the farthing or *feorling*—there is a place of this name in Skye—and even to the half-farthing. Names like Shillingland and Twomerkland and Threemerkland, which may also be found in our directories, have, of course, a similar origin. Only, *merk* and *pound* indicate Saxon rather than Norse influence. There is a Merkland at Dunscore, and a Poundland at Parton. In the Orkney early rentals we read of a ‘cowsworth’ of land, which was $= \frac{1}{3}, \frac{1}{4}$, or $\frac{1}{6}$ of a mark of land. In the same rentals (*c.* 1500) we find a ‘Cowbuster’ or ‘cow-place’ in Firth, and a Noltland or ‘cattle-land’ in Westray.

Though the Danes visited Ireland too, and were there in power all along the east coast for at least a century, having Dublin for a time as their chief seat, there are now barely thirty names of Danish origin in all Ireland. This is rather remarkable when we find their print so plain and oft in Scotland. The leading place-names in several Scottish counties are all Norse—in Shetland, LERWICK and SCALLOWAY; in Orkney, KIRKWALL and STROMNESS; in Caithness, WICK and THURSO; in Sutherland, GOLSPIE, HELMSDALE, and TONGUE; in Ross, DINGWALL and TAIN; in Bute, ROTHESAY and BRODICK. It has been already stated that in Orkney and Shetland Norse names have a nearly complete monopoly; in the Outer Hebrides, where now every man speaks Gaelic, the Norse monopoly is wellnigh as complete. Captain Thomas, R.N., who very carefully investigated the subject some eighty years ago, reports that in Lewis Norse names outnumber the Gaelic ones by four to one, and that in all Harris there are only two pre-Norse or Celtic names. In Skye the Valuation Roll gives about 60 per cent. of Norse names, 40 per cent. Gaelic. In Islay they are about one to two, in Kintyre one to four. Tiny Fetlar alone has about 200 Norse names! No place-name of any consequence in the whole Long Island is of Celtic origin, unless we call that queer name BENBECULA an exception. The marks of the

[1] But Monypenny, formerly Hattis of Erth (Airth), 1450 RMS. was called after Wm. Monypenny, miles.

Viking grow rarer in the isles south of Ardnamurchan, for here he dwelt about a century less. Jura has very few,[1] Islay has a good many—Conisby, Laxay, Nerby, Oversay, Scaraboll, etc.; Captain Thomas says, here Norse names are to Gaelic as three to one.[2] But, though both JURA and ISLAY are words with a Norse look, and commonly reputed of Norse origin, they are not so (q.v.). Islay's real spelling is Ile, and it may be pre-Celtic; but *Ile* has been 'improved' by some would-be clever moderns into *Islay*, which literally means 'island-island.'

Norse and Saxon names sometimes give us a little glimpse of mythology, sometimes of natural, and yet more frequently of family, history. The Teuton was much fonder of leaving the stamp of his name behind him than the Celt. The Saxon was even prouder of his own name than the Northman; and Norse names of the common Saxon type of DOLPHINTON and SYMINGTON are rare. HELMSDALE may be called after some Viking of the name of Hjalmund; 'Hjalmundal' is the form we find in the *Orkneyinga Saga*; OCCUMSTER may be called after some man; GAIRSAY surely is. And from Scottish place-names we can pick out some of the gods and men oft sung in the grand Old Norse epics. Take, *e.g.*, Thor, the thunder-god, not to be found in THURSO, but in TORBOLL, while we have a Woden Law hard by Jedburgh. Woden's or Odin's name may enter into several other place-names. But Ran, the giant goddess, queen of the sea, can hardly have her name preserved in Loch RANZA, Arran; in 1433 the name is Ransay, while the genitive of *Rán* would give Ranaray. Hero-names are seen in HAROLDSWICK, Shetland; CARLOWAY or 'Carl's bay,' Lewis; and SUNART or 'Sweyn's fjord,' Morven. Then there are those two Orkney isles, North and South Ronaldsay, which everyone would naturally think must both be called after the same man, Ronald, Rognvald, or Reginald—these names are all one. But it is not so. SOUTH RONALDSAY was formerly *Rögnvalsey* or 'Rognvald's isle'; but NORTH RONALDSAY was originally *Rinansey*, in which name we, following Prof. Munch of Christiania, may safely recognize the much-commemorated St. Ringan or Ninian of Whithorn. It is

[1] We have Lussa = *lax-á*, Asdale = *ask-dal*, Sannaig = *sand-vik*, and, besides, Bladda, one of the small Isles.

[2] See Brøgger, *Ancient Emigrants* (1929), pp. 58–60.

popular corruption and ignorance which have assimilated the two. Wherever we find *hov-* in Orkney and Shetland, as in Hovland, Fetlar, that implies the site of an old heathen 'holy' place. We have been giving only northern examples of places called after gods or men; but they occur, more sparsely, in the south also, *e.g.*, THURSTON, Dunbar, Pierceby or PERCEBIE, 'Percy's town,' and Sibbaldbie, 1561 Sibbulbic, in Dumfriesshire.

Unlike Celtic, Norse yields us few prefixes for the making-up of our place-names. They are chiefly two:—(1) *Fors*, the Icelandic for 'water-fall,' familiar to every tourist in the English lakes as *force*, Stockgill Force, and all the rest. FORSE, pure and simple, is the name of a Caithness hamlet. As prefix we find it in FORSINARD and FORSINAIN in East Sutherland. (2) *Toft*, Icelandic and Danish for 'an enclosed field near a house,' as in TOFTCOMBS, near Biggar; but it is commoner as a suffix, as in Ecclestoft (Berwicksh.), Aschantoft, and Thurdistoft (Thurso). But, if the prefixes be few, Norse has yielded us suffixes in abundance. To *garth* (Icel. *garð-r*—there are 115 gaards and 11 gardies in Shet.)—and to *dale* (Icel., etc., *dal*) we have already referred (p. 27); examples of the latter are easily found, as in BERRIEDALE and HELMSDALE; occasionally it is suffixed to some Celtic word, as in Esk- and Nithsdale. Sometimes the Gael has forgotten the meaning of *dale*, and so has added his own prefix *strath-*; hence that tautology 'Strathhalladale.' An interesting set of names is connected with the suffix *-shiel*, *-shiels*, *-shield*, *-shields*; all of these forms appear. This, like the Scottish *shieling* or *shealing*, 'a hut or bothy,' comes from the Icel. *skjól*, a 'shelter.' The O.N. *skali* is still used in Norway for a temporary or shepherd's hut. The *shel-* in 'shelter' is in root the same, being connected with the O.E. *scild*, Icel. *skjöld-r*, a shield. A *shiel* is, therefore, 'any place which gives shelter,' and so, 'a house'; it is still the common name on Tweedside for a fisher's hut; as a suffix, it is seen in GALASHIELS, POLLOKSHIELDS, etc. The word is seen too in SHIELDHILL, in 1745 Shielhill, and so often pronounced still. *Shiels* enters into many names of Lowland farms—Biggar Shiels, Legholm Shiels, etc. Another very common suffix is *-fell*, Icel. *fjall*, N. *fjeld*, 'a mountain or hill,' as in the Dovrefjeld of the Romsdal. In the Outer Hebrides, through Gaelic influence, this aspirates into *-bhal* or *-val*, as in Bens HALLIVAL, HASKEVAL, and Oreval in Rum, and Iseval in S. Uist; though this ending, in the case of the smaller eminences, is more probably from Icel. *hváll*, 'a small hill.' Fells are very common in Northern England, but almost equally so in Southern Scotland, *e.g.*, Coulter Fell, Goat Fell, Hart Fell, etc; whilst in Galloway we have CRIFFEL and Ben SCREEL or 'scree-fell.' Noteworthy also are: *-holm*, the Dan. and O.E. *holm*, 'a small island in a river, an islet,' Icel. *holm-r*, 'an island, also a meadow near river or sea.' Those in the far north, like HOLM itself, one of the Orkneys, and like GLOUPHOLM, are, without doubt, Norse; while those in the south, like BRANXHOLM and MIDHOLM, are probably English in their origin, and they are perpetually interchanging with the purely English *ham* (see YETHOLM and HODDOM): *-hope* is not the O.E. *hopa*, 'hope,' but the Icel. *hóp*, 'a haven of refuge,' as in the two ST. MARGARET'S HOPES; the Lowland *-hope*, as in SOONHOPE, Peebles, is the same word (see HOBKIRK). Soonhope means 'pen, shelter-place, for swine'; there are both a Chapelhope and a Kirkhope near St. Mary's Loch, and a DUDHOPE as far north as Dundee: *-thwaite*, Icel. *þveit*, (*lit.* 'a piece cut off,' from *þvíta*, to cut, hence 'a small piece of land,') is common enough in England, but rare north of the Border, MURRAYTHWAITE, Ecclefechan, being one of the very few Scotch examples, though we can add Raggiewhat and Crawthwaite east of Lockerbie, also Suchayt, old form of SOUTHWICK. The original form of the name of the MOORFOOT Hills was 'Morthwaite.' With this we may compare Nether Murthat, Kirkpatrick Juxta.[1].

Beck and *gill* are pure Scandinavian, and common to both Northern England and Southern[2] Scotland. The former, Icel. *bekk-r*, Dan. *baek*, Sw. *bäck*, 'a brook,' is seen in Bodsbeck and WATERBECK; but it is rarer in Scotland than *gill*, Icel. *gil*, 'a ravine or gully.' Quite a cluster of gills are found far inland, to the west of the sources of the Tweed—Duncan, Ram, Snow, Wind Gills, etc.: *-rigg*, Icel. *hrygg-r*, Dan. *ryg*, Sw. *rygg*,

[1] The personal name Garthwaite is common about Ecclefechan. Where is the place?

[2] There was a 'Ravengille' about 1230 near Kinnethmont, *Lindores Chartul.*

also O.E. *hrycg*, 'a ridge of land,' literally the back, the equivalent of the common G. *drum-* (p. 24), is a frequent suffix, chiefly in the south, as ROUGHRIGG, TODRIG, etc. But these 'riggs' are seldom of pure Norse descent; BONNYRIGG and DRUMLANRIG, for example, cannot be. *-land* 'clearing' is not so common as in Norway, and may also be English: but fifty-five have been counted in Shetland. *-voe*, Icel. *vö-r*, 'a little bay or inlet,' is common in the far north, as in AITHSVOE and CULLIVOE, Shetland: *-goe*, Icel. *gjá*, already referred to (p. 34), is of similar meaning; literally it is 'a cleft or gap,' as in GIRNIGO and Whaligoe in Caithness.

A very large group of words end in *ey*, *ay*, *a*, the O.N. and Icel. *ey*, Dan. *oe*, cognate with O.E. *íg*, an island. The ending is found all over the north and west, as in PAPA WESTRAY, a double instance, RAASAY, ULVA, and that very curious name COLONSAY (q.v.). Almost in no case has the original *-ey* been retained. PLADDA, off Arran, is the old Flada or 'flat isle,' another instance of the Celt's very shifty use of the letter *p*. The name remains uncorrupted in Fladay, off Barra. An almost equally important group are the *wicks*, O.N. and Icel. *vík*, a (little) bay; hence *vik-ing* or 'bayman.' *Wick* we have still in English in the expression 'the wicks' or corners of the mouth. LERWICK and BRODICK, or 'broad bay,' are certainly Norse; but this suffix is, in the south, apt to be confused with the O.E. *wíc*, a dwelling, village, as in BERWICK and HEDDERWICK. Another Old Norse word for a bay or cove is *vág-r*; but the *r* of the nominative generally falls away, and we get *-way*, as in SCALLOWAY, STORNOWAY, etc. In other cases the *r* in *vág-r* changes into its brother liquid *l*, as in Osmundwall, PIEROWALL, and especially KIRKWALL. This last town first appears in the *Orkneyinga Saga*, under the spelling *Kirkiuvag*; before 1400 it has become *Kirkvaw*, and already by 1497 it is *Kirkwall*, and Kirkwall, to many a one's puzzlement and misleading, it is to this day. In Harris and Benbecula *vágr* appears as *-vagh*, as in FLODAVAGH and Uskevagh. Of like meaning is the suffix *-vat* (Icel. *vatn*, N. *vand*, 'water, a lake'), as in Loch LANGAVAT, Lewis, etc.

The Norsemen have not only named many of our inlets with their own names of firth and voe and goe, they have named many of our 'outlets' too. Every 'ness' is Norse,—Icel. *nes*,

Dan. *naes*, a nose ; hence a cape or 'Naze,' a transfer of meaning parallel to that of the G. *sron* (p. 24) ; *cf.* too Ben NUIS in Arran. But though names like STROMNESS and DEERNESS are pure Norse, it does not follow that names like BUCHAN Ness and BUDDON Ness are all Norse too ; what Buddon actually does mean no one seems sure. *Ness* often becomes in Gaelic mouths *nish*—for the Gael, in this common case of a palatalized *s* before the slender vowels *e* and *i*, always aspirates his *s* (*cf.* ARDALANISH, MACHRAHANISH, etc.). 'Head' for 'headland' is usually applied to a bold, steep cliff overhanging the sea, as in FITFUL HEAD or the Heads of Ayr. Almost the only purely English instance which occurs early seems ST. ABB'S HEAD. The early cases, like FITFUL and SUMBURGH Heads, are purely Norse. BURG-HEAD is Norse too, but it has not been found in any early record. However, in 1116 *Inquis. Pr. David* we have a Brumeseheyd. The Viking has largely fixed the nomenclature of our stormy northern and western shores. All the 'stacks,' O.N. *stak*—these wild-looking lonely juts or columns of rock, in Caithness, are Norse ; so are all the 'skerries,' N. and Dan. *skjaer*, 'a cliff or rock,' of which there are numerous examples around the wild Pentland Firth —SCARFSKERRY, SULESKERRY, etc. ; and such names as SUMBURGH ROOST are from the N. *röst*, 'a whirlpool.'

Two remarkable suffixes remain, and demand special attention. The first is *-by* or *-bie*, which probably indicates the foot of the Dane rather than the Norwegian. This is the north. O.E. *by*, Mid. Eng. *bi*, Dan. and Sw. *by*, all derived from the *Icel. boe-r*, O.N. *by-r*, and all meaning 'a dwelling, a hamlet or town.' The root is the same as that of the good old Scottish word *big*, to build, but not the same as that of 'bury' or 'borough' (O.E. *burh*). The suffix *-by* is frequent in the north of England, and almost as frequent in South-West Scotland —CANONBIE, LOCKERBIE, MIDDLEBIE, PERCEBIE, SORBIE, etc. There are nine examples in the Dumfries district, three in Ayr (Crosby, Magby, and Sterby), and only four in the south-east, Newby, Peebles, etc. There is one near Glasgow, BUSBY, and just one north of the Forth, HUMBIE, near Aberdour, Fife. In the extreme north *by* reappears in the misleading guise of *-bay*, as in CANISBAY and DUNCANSBAY ; and there are half a dozen in Shetland, MELBY, etc. But perhaps the most remarkable group of suffixes in the whole study of Scottish names is that evolved out of one compound O.N. word *bolstaðr*, a dwelling-place, which has been chopped and changed into almost every conceivable shape. It occurs alone, as a place-name, again and again, and in many shapes, as in Bosta, Lewis, Boust, Coll, and Busta, Shetland. Perhaps nearest to the original are the forms *-bolsy*, found in 'Scarrabolsy,' mentioned in Islay in 1562, now Scarabus, and *-bustar*, *-buster*, and *-bister*, as in 'Skelebustar,' 'Swanbuster,' in Orphir, mentioned in the early Orkney rental books, *c.* 1500, Cowbuster (Firth, Orkney), and Libister, old form of LYBSTER. This last shows us the first vowel dropped out, as is also seen in BIL-BSTER and SCRA-BSTER (1201 Skara-bolstad). As common as any is the form *-bost*, as in Colbost, GARRABOST, Shawbost, all in Long Island; there are thirteen names in *-bost* in Lewis alone. In Islay poor *bolstaðr* is squeezed down into *-bus*, as in Eorabus, 'beach-house,' Persebus, 'priest's farm,' etc. There are twenty-five such names in the island, including one with *p* for *b*, Keppus. Then *-bol* often occurs alone, and, indeed, *bol* is itself the O.N. for a dwelling, thus we have BORROBOL and ERIBOL in Sutherland; and then that shifty liquid *l* drops away, and so we get EMBO and SKIBO, near Dornoch. In Islay, Coll, Tyree, and Mull the *b* may become *p*, and so for *bol* we get *pol* or *poll*, as in CROSSAPOL, GRISAPOLL. In Caithness it is the second or *staðr* half which has been chiefly used, *staðr* being the Norse equivalent of the O.E. *stede* or 'stead,' a place, as in 'homestead.' But in Caithness the *-sters*—OCCUMSTER, THRUMSTER, etc., and especially those in Orkney and Shetland, also come from N. *sætor* 'summer pasture,' seen unabridged in DALSETTER, INGSETTER, etc. Instead of *-ster* we usually find, in the Long Island, *-stra*, as in SCARRI-STRA, or even *-sta*, as in TOLSTA. Further, metamorphosis could hardly go.[1]

An interesting little group is formed by the three names, DINGWALL, TINGWALL (Shetland), and TINWALD (Dumfries), which are all shapes of the same word, *þingavöllr*, 'meeting-place of the Thing, diet, or local parliament.' In Norse *th* is sounded *t*, hence the latter two forms; and everyone who

[1] In all matters regarding West Coast names this chapter is largely indebted to Prof. Mackinnon's valuable series of articles on the *Place-Names of Argyle*, in the *Scotsman*, 1887–8.

knows Grimm's law, knows how naturally *th* becomes *d*, hence Dingwall, or, as it first occurs *c.* 1250, Dinkeual. The Icel. *þing* and the Dan. and Sw. *ting* mean, properly, a court or assembly, but in our own O.E. the *thing* is originally the cause or matter which the Thing met to discuss. The second syllable of Dingwall, etc., is the O.N. *völl-r* or *vold*, Sw. *falla*, O.E. *fald*, Dan. and Mod. Eng. *fold*, an enclosure, or what is enclosed, hence 'an assembly.'

Several Scottish counties have a Norse element in their names, *e.g.*, CAITHNESS, a name never used by any Gael. He always speaks of *Gallaibh*, 'land of the Galls' or 'strangers,' these, of course, being the marauding Northmen; *-aibh* is the old locative case-ending. The name Caithness is the O.N. *Catanes*, 'ness' or 'projecting land of the tribe Cat.' Cat is the name actually given to the district by the Irish Nennius. This tribe are said to have taken their name from one of the sons of the legendary Cruithne (see p. 25). The next neighbour of Caithness, SUTHERLAND, which, curiously enough, contains nearly the whole of the extreme north of Scotland, is the O.N. *Sudrland*, so named because it lay to the south of the Norse settlements in Orkney and Caithness; just as the Hebrides were termed *Sudreyar*, 'Southern isles,' as contrasted with the more northerly Orkneys and Shetlands. We meet this name again in the title of the Bishop of *Sodor* and Man. Already in a Latin document of 1300 we find the name as *Sutherlandia*. The ending of the name ORKNEY, at least, is Norse (see List). SHETLAND or Zetland is the O.N. *Hjaltland* or *Hetland*, which Dr. Vigfusson in his Icelandic dictionary makes no attempt to explain. Some think it was because the islands, or the chief island, look like the hilt—Icel. *hjalt*—of a sword.

One or two noteworthy scraps in conclusion: be it noted that the PENTLAND Frith has nothing to do with the word *pent*, which would be singularly inappropriate as applied to this swift-running sea-channel, which is no true frith at all. Pentland frith is the O.N. word *Petland*, the Norse for 'Picts' land,' which conveys to us some useful information as to the migrations of the Picts. Cape WRATH, standing in its stormy solitude at the far north-west corner of Scotland, has doubtless been thought to bear a very appropriate name. So it does;

but what it means is, not rage and fury, but ' corner, turning point,' or ' shelter,' Icel. *hvarf* and Sw. *hwarf*, the same word as our Eng. *wharf*. And that far northern isle in Shetland, YELL, seems to bear a very startling name. But Yell is the O.N. *Jali*, Icel. *gelld* or *gall*, which means nothing more than ' barren,' as may be seen in the Scots phrase ' a yell coo,' *i.e.*, a cow which gives no milk. This last is also the root of that ugly name JAWCRAIG, near Slamannan, spelt in a 1745 map, Jallcraig. The present form is one among many examples of ' popular etymology,' or, as likely, of popular carelessness. As curious a corruption as any is the name applied to the remains of an old turf-built fort in Islay—DUN NOSEBRIDGE ; which Capt. Thomas says must really be meant for O.N. *hnaus borg*, ' turf fort ' !

CHAPTER III

ENGLISH NAMES

To the student who has fairly tackled the Celtic, or even the Norse, names of Scotland, the purely English names are mere child's play. Considering that English is now the vernacular of thirty-two out of every thirty-three persons in the land, the number of our English or Anglo-Saxon place-names is surprisingly small. We are not aware, however, if the proportion of English to Celtic and to Norse names in Scotland has ever been exactly ascertained or even estimated. The calculation would be rather a difficult one, but full of interest. English has for some time been the language of all the most populous districts; but over a very wide area in the Highlands English influence had scarcely any existence before the Rebellion in 1745; and very few place-names of any interest to us have originated since that date. The place-names of yesterday are of small account.

Both the contemporary historian Ammianus Marcellinus and the rather later poet Claudian prove, that as early as A.D. 360, Saxons had invaded the Roman province of Britain.[1] How soon they entered Scotland we are hardly able to tell; but we have already alluded to the possible presence of Frisians in Dumfriesshire before 400. Octa and Ebissa, leaders of the Frisians, were probably established in Lothian *c.* A.D. 500; and, at any rate, by 547 Angles and Frisians, *i.e.*, men from the swamps and plains around the mouths of the Weser, Rhine, and Scheldt, had spread from Tees to Forth, soon after Ida, 'the Flamebearer,' set up the kingdom of Northumbria. Permanent Angle settlement, however, was probably later.

[1] 'Domito quod Saxone Tethys mitior aut fracto secura Britannia Picto.' Claudian I, 168 Loeb, A.D. 398. 'Maduerunt Saxone fuso Orcades,' *ibid.*, 288.

A district on the south of the Frith of Forth was early known as the 'Frisian shore'; and the name of the frith itself in Nennius is *Mare Freisicum* or 'Frisian Sea.' The true modern representatives of these Frisians are, of course, the Dutch or Low Germans of Holland and Hanover. Lothian was for at least 400 years (*c.* 560–960, and perhaps a good deal later) an integral part of England, forming the northern half of the Northumbrian kingdom of Bernicia. But it can hardly have been so purely English as Freeman represented it, in these early days. This is specially true of the western portion of Scottish Northumbria, as figured in his map, *Norm. Conquest*, vol. i. The student should consult the appendix to that volume, p. 582, 3rd edition. For long, too, all South-Eastern Scotland was an integral part of the See of Durham.

Though the Angle and the Frisian were thus early on the ground, very few English names can be *proved* to have been in use in Scotland before the days of Malcolm Canmore, *c.* 1070; therefore is it that we have made this Chapter III when strictly it should have been Chapter II. Among the very few exceptions are TYNINGHAME and WHITTINGHAM. The eighth-century *Historia Sancti Cuthberti* mentions the hybrid JEDBURGH (Gedwearde), also YETHOLM, then Gatha'n, and one or two unimportant places in its vicinity. To this it may be added that Simeon of Durham (*c* 1060–1130), when writing of the year 756, mentions Niwanbyrig, which must be NEWBURGH in Fife; and Eddi and the venerable Bede (both *c.* 720) mention 'Coludesburg,' in Bede's Latin *Coludi Urbs*, the modern COLDINGHAM. Of course, probably many more English names than these actually existed as early; but our extant information is very scanty. It is tantalizing that the many English chroniclers who write of events before the Norman Conquest, though not seldom referring to Scotland, almost never mention the name of any place in it, Simeon alone excepted.

Freeman informs us that exiles were welcomed from England as early as the days of Macbeth, who, 'as every schoolboy knows,' was slain at Lumphanan in 1057. So far as Scotland, apart from Lothian, is concerned, the chief inflow of English blood came not till Macbeth's equally famous successor, Malcolm Canmore, had been seated for fully ten years upon his throne.

By that time the Norman Conquest was a sad reality to Saxon and to Angle ; whilst King Malcolm at that time made a cruel invasion of Northumberland and Durham on his own account, and carried back thousands of English-speaking slaves. To quote our Durham chronicler, 'Scotland was thus crammed with slaves and maidservants of the Anglic race, so that even to this day there is, I do not say, not one little village, but not even one little mansion-house, where these are not to be found.' [1] At the same time Malcolm gladly welcomed the exiled Saxon royal family to his palace at Dunfermline. Nor was he long in espousing the devout Saxon princess, Margaret, who has left her trace in North and South QUEENSFERRY, hard by Dunfermline. From the marriage of Malcolm with Margaret (1070), and from the incoming of the English exiles about the same time, we may safely date the decay, not only of the old Celtic Church, but also of the Celtic speech. Through his much intercourse with England Malcolm was, from his youth, a bilinguist, and spoke English 'perfectly,' to use Turgot's adverb. Henceforth Gaelic was a courtly language no more. But just after the Norman Conquest many of our English town and village names must have sprung up. By the aid of the old charters, of which we have a rich abundance after 1100, we can see many of these names coming in and taking shape before our very eyes. And to the student of history the process is quite as interesting as the embryologist finds it to watch the steady growth of the ascidian or the tadpole under the microscope. Here, too, is evolution.

The English ending denoting 'town,' 'village,' is *ton* or *ham*. We might, for illustration, select almost any Scottish name ending thus. Let us take SYMINGTON, which occurs twice, in Lanark and in Ayr. Both take their name from the same man, Simon Lockhart, a local knight, about whom we read a good deal in the records of the middle part of the twelfth century, and whose surname is still preserved in Milton Lockhart, Carluke. In 1160, in one of the oldest charters of Paisley Abbey, we read, 'Inter terram Simonis Loccardi & Prestwick,' which shows us Knight Simon already in Ayrshire, and prepares us for the entry in 1293, 'Symondstona in Kyl.' Again, *c.* 1189, we find 'Villa Symonis Lockard' in Lanarkshire, which,

[1] Simeon of Durham, ann. 1070.

before 1300, has become 'Symondstone'; in either case the further advance to 'Symington' is easy. Take one other very similar case, Covington, near Lanark. About 1120 we find among the followers of David Prince of Cumbria a certain Colban. About 1190 we find mention of a 'Villa Colbani,' *villa*, by the way, being just the Latin form of the Norman-French *ville*, literally, a country house, then a town. In 1212 we find 'Colbaynistun'; in 1434 this has become 'Cowantoun,' showing one way how the name *Cowan* has arisen; but *c.* 1480 it has slipped into its modern shape of 'Covingtoun'; for *toun* is still the good Scottish way of pronouncing *town* or *ton*.

As might be expected, genuine English names are to be found all over the Lowlands; but as all the hills and streams had, long ere his coming, received Celtic names, the Angle has named for us very few of these; though sometimes he managed to add an adjective, as in the Black and White Adder. Perforce he adopted the names he found, though seldom had he much inkling of their meaning. English names for Scottish natural features are rare. As for hills, neither Moorfoots nor Pentlands are true cases in point, and a name like Norman's Law or North Berwick Law cannot be called a very serious exception; as for rivers, if few even of England's rivers bear English names, there seem almost none of any consequence in Scotland, not even Gala. There are several *hows* (O.E. *holg*, *holh*) or hollows or valleys, as 'the How o' the Mearns,' and famous Habbie's How at Carlops.

The region [1] for true English names is that which lies between Edinburgh and Berwick, whose original population were the Celtic Otadeni. But 1400 years of Anglian settlement have largely obliterated the traces of the old Celt here, especially as regards the name of the towns or villages. Almost the only notable exception is Dunbar, mentioned as early as the days of Eddi (*c.* 720), certainly a Celtic name, and perhaps commemorating St. Bar or Finnbarr, bishop of Cork. Considering the usual paucity of our early material, it is right pleasant for the student to find quite a store of Berwickshire names in the afore-mentioned eleventh-century Coldingham charters. All the leading present-day names are to be found there, and had

[1] Readers of Armstrong's sumptuous *History of Liddesdale*, etc., will see that English farm and manor names are very plentiful here too.

probably existed already for 300 or 400 years more. The village and farm names are pure English. Only a few rivers like the ADDER are Celtic.

In the Highlands, English names, unless they be quite modern, are very rare. Wherever an English or partly English name occurs, the Gael is sure to have a name of his own, *e.g.*, he calls Taymouth BALLOCH, and so forth. And the Gael deals precisely so with Norse names also; he speaks not of *Tain*, but of *Baile Dhuthaic*, 'the town of St. Duthac.' Sometimes an English name is just a translation of an older Gaelic one, as in the town now erroneously spelt and called by outsiders FALKIRK, but which is really Fahkirk (1298, Faukirke), and so pronounced by the natives to this day. This is Simeon of Durham's Egglesbreth, and the modern Highland drover's *An Eaglais bhreac*, 'the spotted church,' referring to its mottled stone.

Place-names of English origin are a faithful reflection of the typical Englishman—stolid, unemotional, full of blunt common sense. They almost all spell plain 'John Bull his mark,' 'John Bull his house.' Anglo-Saxon names are, as a rule, abrupt, matter-of-fact, devoid of aught poetic, having of music none. How different, *e.g.*, are the two Fat Lips, or 'Brummagem,' or Wolverhampton, from 'Be-a-la-nam-bo,' or COILANTOGLE! And even Balla-chu-lish has something pathetically Celtic about it, if pronounced by understanding lips. For pure expressiveness, however, few names can beat the name (it cannot be very ancient) given to a conspicuous, monument-capped hill near Linlithgow, and also found near Bamborough, 'Glower-o'erem' or Glowrórum. To translate *glower* into 'English' would be to make the name feeble indeed. A little to the south, near Drumshoreland, is found the feebler name 'Lookabootye.' Some other expressive names in good broad Scots, found in the *County Directory*, are Reekitlane, Dustyriggs, Gathercauld, Ducksdub, Gowksknowe and Deil-ma-care (a fishing station on the Tay). Breed-sorrow, Largs, has that name as early as 1610—'Breed-sorrow alias Kempisland.' The Scots-looking Dinna Muck must be the G. *dùn-na-muic*, 'sow's hill.'[1] The Englishman but rarely shows in his names the Celt's inner sympathy with nature either in her sterner or in her softer

[1] Just as Innernighty, Ballinluig, seems to have the innocent meaning, 'confluence at the gullet or narrow opening,' *G. inbhir an eitìghich.*

moods. And the modern Socialist will not be too well pleased to find that most of our O.E. town names give strong expression to the idea of individual rights, and the sanctity of private property. Many of them are the very embodiment of the adage, ' Every Englishman's house is his castle ' ; so many of the commonest O.E. place-endings imply ' enclosure, fencing-off.' This is the root-idea in *burgh*, *ham*, *seat*, *ton*, and *worth*.

And the English thane, as well as the Norman baron, regularly called the little village, which grew up under the shadow and shelter of his castle walls, after his own noble self. The burghs, tons, and hams are all English. *Burgh*, or more fully *borough*, is the O.E. *burg*, *burh*, gen. *byrig*, dat. *buri*, *biri*, hence its other form ' Bury ' or *-bury*, common in England but not in Scotland, though on the Ayrshire coast stands TURNBERRY (1286 Turnebyry). The root of *burgh* is probably the Old Ger. *bergan*, to shelter, seen already in Pliny's Burgundiones ; and its earliest meaning, given in a Kentish glossary *c.* A.D. 820, is *arx*, ' citadel, castle ' ; then it comes to mean, ' a fortified town ' ; but the idea of ' civic community ' or ' town ' arises very early also. In names the word occurs chiefly as a suffix, *-burgh*, but occasionally as a prefix, as in Borrowstoun-ness or BO'NESS. BURGHEAD is Norse. But we find it in the heart of the name in that very interesting name, HALYBURTON. The Old Norse form *borg* (used by Charles Kingsley in his *Hereward*) also occurs, on the west coast of Lewis, as Borgh, as readers of the *Princess of Thule* know.

The O.E. *tun(e* or *ton(e* never originally meant a large town ; and we still have the common Scots phrase, ' the farm toun,' which means a collection of houses very different in size from Leeds or Bradford. In O.E. the word occurs both with and without the final *e* ; thus JOHNSTONE means not ' John's stone,' but ' John's town.' *Ton* seems also to have implied a village belonging to a certain class, as FULLERTON or ' fowler's town,' HALKERSTON or ' settlement of the hawkers,' *i.e.*, falconers. Genuine cases of Scottish names in *-burgh*, called after some man, are hard to discover ; but COLDINGHAM was originally Coludesburg or ' Colud's town,' and ROXBURGH may be another case in point. The peculiar case of EDINBURGH is fully dealt with in the List, where it is shown that the name of Scotia's capital is of British origin—O.W. *din eiddyn*, or

Dunedin, 'fort on the hill-slope,' *i.e.*, what was the backbone of Edinburgh, its High Street, from the Castle to Holyrood. The name was merely remodelled, though it certainly was remodelled, in honour of King Edwin of Northumbria. With these exceptions, all other Scottish *-burghs* are comparatively modern, except perhaps three or four—CUNNINGSBURGH and SUMBURGH, in Shetland, which are Norse; ROXBURGH, which we find away back as early as 1127; and thirdly, and most curious of all, NEWBURGH in Fife, which, as we saw a few pages back, is the oldest extant English name in Scotland. Of recent *burghs* we may mention COLINSBURGH, built in 1682; MARYBURGH, near Dingwall, *c.* 1690; and HELENSBURGH, which only dates from 1776. But if *burghs* called after Saxon thanes or knights are rare, *tons* are found in a rich plenty, *e.g.*, DOLPHINTON, DUDDINGSTON, EDDLESTON or 'Edulf's ton,' STEVENSTON, etc. Wherever this suffix *-ton* is spelt *-town*, the name is sure to be modern, of which we see examples in the two CAMPBELTOWNS, Hutchesontown, PULTNEYTOWN, SINCLAIRTOWN, etc. Moreover, the amateur must always walk warily in dealing with English-looking *tons* in the north, aye, and in the south too, for *ton* is not seldom a corruption of the G. *dùn*, a hill or fort, *e.g.*, EDDERTON, near Tain, is *eadar dùn*, 'between the hillocks'; and away in the south, near the Tweed, stands EARLSTON, a simple name enough, one would think; but Earlston is just the result of careless tongues. In 1144 the name was Ercheldon, the 'Ercildunc' famed as the birthplace of Thomas the Rymer.

Ham, O.E. *hám*, is just our winsome English word 'home,' the original *a* being preserved in the Sc. *hame*. A typical example is COLDINGHAM or WHITTINGHAM, though *hams*, called after Saxon men, are much rarer north than south of the Tweed. Instances not connected with any man's name are BIRGHAM in Berwick and KIRKPATRICK-DURHAM, near Dumfries. *Ham* often gets clipped down, for *h* easily vanishes in an Englishman's mouth, and in a Scotsman's too, if only he were aware of it. Almost no Scotsman, *e.g.*, will pronounce the *h* in such a sentence as 'John told me that *h*e said,' etc. Thus *ham* becomes *am*, as in BIRNAM, and EDNAM, 'home on the River Eden,' or yet more disguised, as in MIDDLEM, or EDROM, 'home on the River Adder.' There is one lonely but very interesting *ham* away up near Forse in Caithness, 'Notingham,' which is so spelt in the *Bk. of Scone* in 1272.

It is generally said that *-ing-* in O.E. place-names implies 'descendants of'; *e.g.*, SYMINGTON was thought to be the *ton* or village of Sym's sons. But in most cases of *-ing-* occurring in a Scottish place-name, so far as we have been able to trace, the *-ing-* is a later corruption, generally of *an*, *in*, or *on*. See ABINGTON, COVINGTON, DUDDINGSTON, LAMINGTON, LEDINGHAM, NEWINGTON, UDDINGSTON, etc.[1] The only certain exceptions are COLDINGHAM and TYNINGHAME; perhaps also FOTHRINGHAM and WHITTINGHAME. There is a Hillington near Innerwick (*a.* 1246 *Paisley Chart.*).

As with names Norse so with names English, of English prefixes there are but few (*burgh* has been already referred to), but English suffixes are almost innumerable, the most of them requiring little or no elucidation. There is, *e.g.*, the little cluster signifying some kind of height or eminence—*hill* itself, as in Maryhill, Townhill; *knowe*, the softened Scottish form of *knoll*, O.E. *cnoll* (just as How is the Scottish form of the O.E. *holg*, and Pow the Scottish form of the G. *poll*, a stream or pool); this we find in BROOMIEKNOWE, COWDENKNOWES, etc.; *law*, the Scottish form of the O.E. *hláew*, a hill, a mound, a barrow, as in (1215–21 Rapereslaue, *Inchaffray Chart.*) GREENLAW, HARLAW, LARGO LAW, and also in the LAMMERLAWS, the well-known cliffs at Burntisland, and in MINTLAW. The English form *low*, as in Ludlow and Taplow, plentiful though it be south of the Border, seems to occur only in FERRIELOW. To this group of suffixes *mount* can hardly be added, for Scottish *-mounts* or *-monts* almost all represent the G. *monadh*, a mountain or moor, as in ESSLEMONT, GLASMONT, etc.

In many cases it would be more correct to say that a given suffix or word is Scots rather than English; which just means that the word, or often simply the form, though once used in northern literary English, is now preserved only in Lowland Scots. Neither *knowe*, *e.g.*, nor *law* is to be found at all in Annandale's most reliable *Concise English Dictionary*; another

[1] Not only are such English names as Barking and Woking real patronymics, denoting the abode of a family or clan, but in England undoubted patronymic names, like Birmingham, Gillingham, etc., are very common.

instance is that very interesting word *kirk* or 'church,' fully dealt with in our List. It may be added that a charter dating *a.* 1124, which mentions 'Selechirche' or SELKIRK, is earlier than any document quoted by Dr. Murray for the soft or *ch* form of the O.E. *cyrc*, our modern *church*. Only, names ending in -cherche are quite common in Domesday, and in these cases the Norman scribes may have meant the *ch* to be sounded hard. An interesting instance is *-gate*, which in place-names like CROSSGATES, Trongate, WINDYGATES, always has its Scottish meaning of 'way,' 'road.' 'I gae'd a weary gate yestreen, A gate I fear I'll dearly rue.' In Scots, unlike both O.E. and Mod. Eng., it never means a door or entrance; but the well-known Border pronunciation 'yet,' which is the English not the Scottish *gate*, is to be found in YETHOLM, that Roxburgh hamlet at the 'gate' between Scotland and England. Similar is *-water*, still on the Scottish borders pronounced like the O.E. *waeter*, which means not only the brook or burn itself, but also the valley through which it flows, as in Galawater, Jedwater, Rulewater: 'Not Yarrow braes nor Ettrick shaws can match the lads o' Galawater.' A curious and deceiving suffix is *-battle*. MOREBATTLE, near Kelso, looks very like some bloodthirsty borderer's cry. But when we find the name on record in 1170 as Merebotle, we see that the true meaning is the 'dwelling (O.E. *botl*) by the mere' or lake. By 1575 it had become Morbottle; it is only within the present century that the *o*, through ignorance, has become permanently changed to *a*; and the same is true of fair NEWBATTLE Abbey, near Dalkeith. The Northumbrians still retain the *o*, as in Harbottle; and there is a Newbottle near Durham. O.E. *botl* is also found disguised in BOLTON, which, *c.* 1200, was spelt Botel- or Bothel-tune.

So far as sound goes, the ending *-haven* might indicate either an English (O.E. *haefen*) or a Norse (Icel. *höfn*, Dan. *havn*) name; but, as a matter of fact, most of the 'havens' are demonstrably English, and late in origin; *e.g.*, both BUCKHAVEN and NEWHAVEN, on the Frith of Forth, date only from the sixteenth century. And some 'havens' do not mean a haven at all; such a one is that tautological-looking name belonging to an Islay village, spelt PORTNAHAVEN, but pronounced portnahávn, which at once shows that this is really the G. *port na h'aibhne*, 'harbour on the river.'

In looking for truly English names two of our preliminary cautions must always be kept well in view: (1) Many names may be partly English and partly something else; *e.g.*, that name dear to every Scottish heart, BANNOCKBURN. 'Burn' is good Scottish or O.E., but 'bannock' can hardly have anything to do with flour or pease-meal scones; it is just the Celtic *ban oc*, 'white' or 'gleaming brook.' BARRHEAD has nothing to do with toll-bars or any other bars, the 'head' simply repeating what has already been said in the G. *barr* (a head or height). Another well-known name is GLASSFORD, near Hamilton, a name which pictures to the mind's eye some shallow spot in a river of glassy smoothness. 'Ford,' indeed, is English, but it is not original; and the 'glass' is just the common G. *glais* or *glas*, grey or dark, as in DUNGLASS, GLASMONT, and many more; or else it is the Old G. *glas*, a river, as in DOUGLAS.

All the examples given for our first caveat would serve well for the second, *viz.*: (2) An English-looking name may not be English at all. Look well before you leap. We shall only point out one or two more conspicuous instances of the need of this. There are several glens with deceptively English-like names, *e.g.*, mighty Glen LYON, which is of quite doubtful origin. A little to the south is Glen ALMOND; both the Scottish rivers called Almond were formerly spelt Awmon, showing that here we have simply one of the many guises of G. *amhuinn*, a river. Glen Howl, in the Stewartry of Kirkcudbright, has no connexion with cries or roars; it is but the G. *gleann a' ghabhail*, 'glen of the fork,' where two streams join. And again, in the Highlands, as in Ireland, we meet with many a Letter-. But they were all there long before the days of the Post Office. The first syllable in LETTERFEARN or LETTERFINLAY is just the G. *leitir* (*leth-tir*), 'land on the slope of a glen.' We have it simply in Letters near Beith.

There is some manuscript reason for thinking that English scribes were rather fond of prefixing an *h* to Scottish place-names beginning with a vowel, especially those in Aber- and Inver-, which are never so spelt now.[1] But there is no doubt

[1] See, *e.g.*, Jos. Stevenson's interesting collection of *Documents Illustrative of the History of Scotland*, vol. i, for 1289–92, and the itineraries and accounts of expenditure of Englishmen quoted there.

that the Celt, both in Scotland and in Ireland, often prefixed such an aspirate himself. See the old spellings of ERCHLESS, ERSKINE, IONA, etc. The Celtic definite article, as we have seen, is very rare at the beginning of Celtic names on English lips. The English article is common enough ; but, for euphony's sake, it seems only to be used with words accented on the first syllable, as The Lochies (Burntisland) or The Redding (Polmont).

Many types of names very common in England seem wholly wanting in Scotland. In England 'Great' abounds as an appellation—Great Malvern, and the like ; but in Scotland there are none. The same remark holds true about 'Little,' with the exception of 'Little Franco,' Dalkeith, 'Little Dunkeld,' and 'The Little Ferry,' near Dornoch. Again, 'Market' and 'Stoke' (*i.e.*, place) are very common Anglican prefixes and suffixes, as in Market Drayton, and Bishopstoke, and many more ; but in Scotland they are never used at all. See, however, OLDHAMSTOCKS.

CHAPTER IV

ROMAN, NORMAN, AND PURELY MODERN NAMES

In strict propriety the Roman names should have been dealt with before either the English or the Norse ones; but they form a group so small and so unimportant, that little harm can be done by treating them along with those names which stand last in historic sequence, the little handful from the Norman-French, which is, of course, one of Latin's many daughters. The Roman left a deep mark on Southern Britain, and his memory is preserved in many a name there. But even though Rome's legions, from the days of Agricola onwards for more than 300 years, may have marched many a league and thrown up many a camp in North Britain, they never could make much dint upon the hardy savage of Caledonia in his bogs and woods; and traces of Roman influence north of the Roman Wall 'twixt Forth and Clyde are but trifling. England is covered with *-casters*, *-cesters*, and *-chesters*, often denoting the site of a camp or fort of the invaders, L. *castrum* or *castra*; but, surprising to relate, there are hardly any such compound names in Scotland, save Kerchester, near Kelso, a tautology, Bonchester Bridge, near Hawick, and one or two obscure spots in Berwickshire, like Habchester and Whitchester. Close to Hawick is a place called the Chesters; and any large map of the Border district will show a good many names like Chester Knowes (Chirnside), Chester Hill and Rig (Traquair), Chester Lees (Tweedsmuir); and at most of these spots there are remains of circular or oval hill forts. It is quite certain that the Romans were in Berwick and Peeblesshire; yet it is all but certain that these names are not of Roman origin. Veitch thought that these Peeblesshire 'Chesters' were the last retreats of the Cymri or Brythons of Forth and Clyde, the forts where they made their final but unsuccessful stand against Pict, and Scot, and Angle. That curious-looking compound near Gatehouse, Castramont,[1] cannot be from *castra*. In early charters of Kelso Abbey we find names like 'Cauchester lawe,' 'Stamkilchestre,' etc. Of any real Roman names there seems no trace.

Many a broad acre of Scotland's best land was gifted into Norman hands; and Florence of Worcester, writing of the year 1052, informs us that, even at that early date, several Norman nobles betook themselves to Scotland, fleeing from the wrath of the English King to the court of Macbeth. But Dr. Skene (*Celtic Scotl.*, i, 430) held that the Normans, who are just our old friends the Norsemen back again with an infusion of new blood and a new tongue, had no perceptible influence on Scottish affairs till the reign of David I (1124–53), a date too late to allow of much result in the way of place-names. And the later frequent intercourse between the courts of France and Scotland had practically no influence on our topography. Even as the Gael's common name for his village was *bal* or *baile*, and as the Saxon's regular name for the hamlet round his thane's castle was *ham* or *ton*, so the Norman's regular name for the castle-village was *ville*, from the L. *villa*, a country-house or farm. *Ville*, in Scotland, has seldom survived uncorrupted, though we have both a MELVILLE and a MOUNT MELVILLE in Fife. Now, in Fife charters of the days of Alexander II (1214–49), we find notice of a Norman knight called 'Philippus de Malavilla'; and so Melville has the strange meaning of 'the bad (? unhealthy) town.' A 'Galfred de Melville' is found in the Lothians in 1153. He would come from one of the four Mallevilles in Normandy. The writer does not know of any other *villes* in Scotland; for, of course, such a vile compound as JEMIMAVILLE is not a case in point.[2] But we have still among us such common surnames as Colvill (*sic* 1158), and Somerville (*c.* 1124, Sumerville); and probably it was the influence of this Norman *-ville* which has changed St. Boisil's name into ST. BOSWELL'S.

[1] In 1610 Castraman, *Pont* Karstromen, which Sir Herbert Maxwell says is *cars traman* or *droman*, 'carse of the elder-trees.'

[2] The place called Coshieville at the mouth of Glen Lyon is an attempt to render the G. *cois a' mhill*, 'the foot of the hill.' So Belleville (*sic* 1788), Kincraig, is G. *bail-a'-bhile*, 'village at the brae-top.'

A Norman noble, De Belassize, has given his name to one of the railway stations on the Waverley route, BELSES. One of the most famous Norman families in Scotland was the Lindsays, whose name we see in Lindsaylands, near Biggar. In an appendix to the *Lives of the Lindsays* (vol. i) we find a curious list of no less than eighty-eight spellings of this name, which have all actually been found in some old charter or letter, varying from the ten letters of *Lyndyssaye* to the five of *Lynse*, which last, if the final *e* be sounded, gives the exact modern pronunciation. BEDRULE, near Jedburgh, does not come from the W. *bedw*, 'a birch,' as Professor Veitch supposed. In 1280 its name was Rulebethok, and Bethoc was wife of the Norman Radulph, the earliest-known lord of the manor here (*c.* 1150). The name Bedrule is still locally pronounced bethorule, or was so quite recently, as Sir J. A. H. Murray informed the writer; though, of course, his old schoolmaster at Denholm, near by, was wont to teach that such a pronunciation was ignorant and vulgar! Bethoc, however, is hardly a Norman name; we find it again, *a.* 1300, in the *Registrum Aberdonense*, in a 'Kynbethok'; and RULE is the name of a river. Traces of the Norman knights are also to be seen in BARRASSIE and TURNBERRY, Ayrshire.

On a beautiful spot at the head of what is now the BEAULY Frith the monks *Vallis umbrosæ* founded a priory (*c.* 1220), which we, in 1230, find styled *Prioratus de Bello Loco*. The French spelling *Beau lieu*, 'beautiful spot,' also occurs; and in 1497 we meet with 'Beulie,' the present pronunciation. There are a Bewlie Mains and a Bewlie Hill near Belses; and Beaulieu is also the name of a village in Hants, formerly seat of a Cistercian monastery; which name is also pronounced *bewly*. Well did the old monks know how to choose the fairest sites. Bowprey, Aberdour, Fife, was in 1320 Beaupre, 'fine meadow'; and BELMONT, 'fine hill,' is a common name for modern residences; but we also find it attached to hills, not only in the Sidlaws, but even away up in Unst. Perhaps, however, the naming has been quite recent. MONTROSE is very French-looking, but we already know that it was once G. *moine rois*, 'moss' or 'bog on the promontory.' BURDIEHOUSE, near Edinburgh, is, according to common tradition, a corruption of 'Bordeaux-house.' Grant, in *Old and New Edinburgh*, thinks it was probably so called as the residence of some of the exiled French silk-weavers, the same exiled Huguenots who settled so largely in Spitalfields, London. They also founded the now swamped village of Picardy, between Edinburgh and Leith, whose name is still preserved by 'Picardy Place.'

Cape, a headland, is the Fr. *cap*, 'head or cape'; thus we have few 'capes' in Scotland, and those few, such as Cape Wrath, of quite modern application.

A few recent names still call for a passing word. And, be it remarked, even though a name has sprung up within the last couple of centuries, its origin is by no means invariably easy to trace; *e.g.*, it took the writer over fifteen years to trace the exact origin of ALEXANDRIA in the Vale of Leven, although the place is only a little more than a century old. After some trouble he also found why a little railway station near Holytown has been dubbed with the Honduras name of OMOA. He presumes it must have been some Bible lover (?) who christened JOPPA, near Edinburgh, about 150 years ago, and who planted both a Jordan and a Canaan Lane on the south side of that city. There is also a JORDANHILL, west of Glasgow, and a PADANARAM near Forfar. The place marked Succoth on the Ordnance Survey of the parish of Glass does not belong to this category. It is the G. *socach*, 'place full of projecting points or snouts' (*soc*).

Some recent names are, of course, very easily solved; as, for instance, the three well-known forts planted along the Caledonian valley to overawe the Highlanders at different periods from 1655 to 1748, and called after scions of the reigning house, FORT WILLIAM, FORT AUGUSTUS, and FORT GEORGE. Battles have pretty frequently been commended to the memory of posterity by a place-name; *e.g.*, we have a farm on the south shore of the Dornoch Frith called BALACLAVA, its former name having been Balnuig ('farm town on the bay'). PORTOBELLO, near Edinburgh, like Portobello near Wolverhampton, takes its name from a seaport on the Isthmus of Darien, where Admiral Vernon won a great victory for Britain in 1739. The name means 'beautiful harbour'; but, as most people know, the Edinburgh watering-place is not specially beautiful, and it certainly has no harbour. BEESWING is the curious name of a little village on the high road between Dumfries and

Dalbeattie. It is a famous race-horse which has been immortalized in the present village.

The suburbs of the large cities have, of course, modern, and often purely fancy, names ; such are Golden Acre, near Edinburgh, MAGDALEN GREEN, Dundee, and MOUNT FLORIDA and MOUNT VERNON, on the outskirts of Glasgow. The latter name occurs in the *Glasgow Directory* of 1787. Nearly all the place-names north of Inverness, which are neither Gaelic nor Norse, are quite recent ; *e.g.*, THE MOUND and THE POLES, near Dornoch, BETTYHILL, near Tongue, and The Fendom, Tain. But WARDLAW, Beauly, goes back to at least 1210, Davidston, Cromarty, is 1449 Dauiston, and both Bennetsfield and Castleton, Avoch, go back at least to 1456.

CHAPTER V

ECCLESIASTICAL NAMES

FROM the earliest times a distinguishing and far from unpraiseworthy feature of the Scot has been his warm attachment to the Church. The Norseman, drinking to Thor and Wodin, dreaming of Asgard and Valhalla, and, long after his nominal conversion to Christ, a pagan at heart, has left little mark on the ecclesiastical nomenclature of Scotland; the Angle, whose conversion, thanks largely to Iona missionaries, was more real, has left a considerable impress here. But the warm-hearted, pious, and somewhat superstitious Celt has left far more. His personal names, too, have often a churchly flavour; *e.g.*, Macnab, 'abbot's son,' Mackellar, 'the superior's son,' MacBrair, 'the friar's son,' Gilchrist, 'servant of Christ,' Gillespie, 'servant of the bishop,' etc. Carmichael, which looks like a place-name, is in Gaelic *mac gille Micheil*, 'son of the servant of St. Michael.'

Till 1469 Orkney and Shetland had the Bishop of Trondhjem as their ecclesiastical superior; but, for all that, the Norse churchly names may be dismissed in a few sentences. All northern 'kirks' have received their name from Norse lips, as HALKIRK, KIRKWALL, and KIRKABY; but these are not many. Near Kirkwall, seat of the Bishop of Orkney, stands QUANTERNESS, and *quanter-* is the Icel. *kantari*, which enters as an element into a good many Icelandic words; it is an adaptation of the Canter- in holy Canterbury (O.E. *Cantwaraburh*), being used in Icel. for 'bishop.' Then we have the oft-recurring PAPA, and its derivatives PAPILL and PAPLAY, as local names in Orkney and Shetland. *Papa* is a Latin name for 'a bishop,' in use as early as Tertullian; the Norsemen at first gave the name to any Christian, but soon it came to be applied only to 'a priest.' We have already explained North RONALDSAY as = 'St. Ringan's' or 'Ninian's isle.' He reappears in St. Ninian's Isle in the south of Shetland. We do not remember any other Orcadian or Zetland isle bearing the name of a saint.[1] But Celtic missionaries did work there. Adamnan tells of a visit to the Orkneys by Cormac, a disciple of Columba, *c.* 580. A curiously corrupted name, half Celtic, half Danish, is CLOSEBURN, in Dumfriesshire. It has nothing in the world to do with either a close or a burn. Before 1200 the name appears as Kylosbern, but already in 1278 it has donned its present guise. The early form shows that here we have another of the many Celtic *kils*; only this was the 'cell' or 'church' of a Norse saint; for Osborne is the N. *Asen-björn*, 'the bear of the Asen' or 'gods.' The same name is equally disguised in Orbiston near Bothwell, which was 'Osbernston' in 1399. An interesting specimen is Cannamesurdy, name of a well on the beach at Rousay, Orkney. This is almost certainly 'water-pot, can (O.N. *canna*) of my dear Servandus,' a companion of St. Boniface, named in the *Aberdeen Brevy.* Boniface himself is commemorated in Papa Westray. On the -me- or *ma*, see p. 67.

Over the true English church-names we must linger a little longer. Seeing that English-speaking monks were at one time owners of a large proportion of Scotland, it is not strange that we should find a good many English ecclesiastical place-names. We have both a MONKTON and a NUNTON, the one near Troon, the other away beside Lochmaddy, but both pronounced almost alike, *i.e.*, the local inhabitants usually talk of 'the Munton.' 'Abbey' and 'Abbot' occur again and again in places—ABBEY CRAIG, Abbey Hill, ABBOTSFORD, ABBOTSGRANGE, ABBOTSHALL, as well as ABBEY ST. BATHAN'S. The 'bishop' has left his name too, as in BISHOPBRIGGS and BISHOPTON: even the humble priest (O.E. *preost*) has come in for his share of mention. There are at least fifteen Prestons in England, and several in Scotland, besides PRESTONKIRK, PRESTONPANS, and PRESTWICK.

Probably all the many 'kirks' south of Caithness are of English origin. 'Kirk' is the O.E. *cyrc*; but in Scotland, as well as in England, the hard *c* often became soft *ch*; and perhaps it may be useful here to inform the benighted Southron

[1] Except DAMSEY, for which see p. 68.

that ordinary Scottish people do *not* now, as a rule, speak about their 'kirk.' *Kirk* occurs both as prefix, suffix, and alone, as in KIRKMAIDEN or Maidenkirk, Wigtown, KIRKBUDDO, KIRKCOLM, CHANNELKIRK, FALKIRK, LAURENCEKIRK, and Kirk o' Shotts. There are many Kirktons in Scotland, corresponding to the Kirtons of England, just as the Scotch KIRKABY (O.N. *kirkia-bi*) corresponds to the English Kirby, in West Kirby, Kirby Stephen, etc. The old, full name of Golspie was 'Golspiekirktoun,' and there is a farm called Kirkton there still. KIRKCALDY is not English at all. Popular etymology long explained the name as 'church of the Culdees.' But in the St. Andrews charters, *c*. 1150, the name is 'Kircaladinit,' which is most likely Gaelic for 'fort by the harbour of refuge.'

All place-names in the form of St. ——'s are also, of course, to a certain extent, English; but only a few are called after really English saints. Take the first two examples which would occur alphabetically—ABBEY ST. BATHAN'S, Berwick, and ST. ANDREWS; Bathan, or rather Baothen, was a Scot, *i.e.*, an Irish Celt, and was the man who succeeded Columba in the abbacy of Iona, A.D. 597. St. Andrew, Scotland's present patron saint, is of course the apostle of that name, whose bones, as a dubious tradition declares, were brought to the east of Fife by St. Regulus. But the church built by this last saint (? A.D. 400) was called by his own name, till rechristened in the middle of the ninth century as 'St. Andrews,' by King Kenneth Macalpine. For long, whenever this ancient bishop's see is referred to in any document it is in its Latin form, *e.g.*, in 1158, 'St. Andrae'; but as early at least as 1434 we find 'Sanctandrowis.' The old Celtic name of the place was Kilrymont, or, as Abbot Tighernac has it, *Cindrighmonaigh*, 'the church,' or 'the head, the promontory of the king's mount.'

Among real English or Anglian saints who have given their names to places in Scotland are the Abbess Æbba, sister of Oswald of Northumbria, commemorated in ST. ABB'S HEAD, and St. Boisil, contemporary of Æbba, and Prior of Melrose while the great Cuthbert was being educated there, whose name is preserved in the well-known railway junction, ST. BOSWELL'S; however, the old name of the parish here, until the seventeenth century, was Lessuden. Then, of course, there is St. Cudberct, better known as St. Cuthbert, great pastor and bishop, missionary too all over Northumbria, most lovable of all the Saxon saints. By far the most populous parish in Scotland, 'St. Cuthbert's,' Midlothian, embracing a large portion of Edinburgh, is called after him. His name appears in a slightly altered spelling in KIRKCUDBRIGHT, whose present pronunciation, Kircóobry, must have been in vogue as early as *c.* 1450, when it is recorded as 'Kirkubrigh.' The Scot has slurred his name down to 'Cuddie,' while the Gael has made the saint's name into Cudachan, as in Killiemacuddican, 'church of my own little Cuthbert,' in Kirkcolm. CLACHNACUDDAN is quite another word. Near Kirkcudbright is a curiously misleading name, Kirklaugh, Pont's Caerclach, 'fort on the rock.' The name of Canmore's saintly Saxon queen is still preserved in 'St. Margaret's,' King's Park, Edinburgh, and in the two ST. MARGARET'S HOPES, or ship-refuges, at Queensferry, and at South Ronaldsay.[1]

The Celtic ecclesiastical names form, perhaps, the most puzzling and complex portion of our subject, a portion which it needs much care and skill to unravel. One can hardly say that the whole subject has been set in clear daylight yet, notwithstanding all that members of the Scottish Society of Antiquaries have done.[2] Many of the old Celtic saints, male and female, are to us very dim and hazy, almost lost in the clouds of legend and the mists of antiquity ; and their identity is often very difficult to establish, specially when, in many cases, two or more bear the same name.

Though, as we know, the Celt never showed great anxiety to hand down the name of his own humble self attached to some village or glen, he never wearied of thus commemorating his favourite or patron saints. The majority of the saints brought before us in Scottish place-names were either friends and contemporaries of St. Columba, or belong to the century immediately thereafter, the seventh. After 700 the Celtic Church began to wax rich and slothful, and its priests were embalmed in grateful memory no more. Foreign saints are

[1] Some think the latter place was called after Margaret, the Maid of Norway, who died not far from here on her voyage to Scotland.

[2] Dr. G. A. F. Knight has given us a most laborious conspectus in *Archæological Light in the Early Christianizing of Scotland*, 2 vols., 1933.

rarely met with. KILMARTIN (Lochgilphead), called after good St. Martin of Tours, the preceptor of St. Ninian, is an easily understood exception. Why the French St. Maurus should appear in KILMAURS is not quite so plain. A local St. Paldoc, not Palladius, Rome's missionary to Scotland, has probably received recognition in ABERFELDY, as well as in Paldy's Fair and Paldy's Well at Fordoun, and in Kilpallet, South Haddington. First in the Scottish calendar, and, presumably, first bringer of Christianity to Scotland, was St. Ninian of Whithorn, born *c.* A.D. 360, whose name also appears as Ringan and Rinan, and in St. Innian's Well, Lanark. He is commemorated in over fifty churches or chapels, from Ultima Thule to the Mull of Galloway; and there are several more in England, while MAIDENKIRK, near the above Mull, is probably the kirk of St. Medana, a friend of Ninian.

If Ninian, first of Scottish saints and missionaries, has received over fifty commemorations, it is no marvel that Columba of Iona (521–97), greatest of them all, has had at least fifty-five Scottish places called after him, either places of worship, or spots or wells sacred to him; and there are forty-one others in his native Ireland. The saint's name is seldom or never now found as Columba, 'dove,' its Latin shape, but rather in its Celtic form, *Colum*; *e.g.*, on the west coast there are six isles called Eilean Coluim or 'Colm's isle,' in Loch Erisort, Loch Arkeg, the Minch, etc. Then there is Iona itself, often called alternatively Icolmkill, 'island of Colum-cille' or 'Colm of the churches.' For, if men called John Henry Newman 'father of many souls,' other men might well call earnest, much-travelling Columba, 'father of many churches.' Sometimes his name is clipped down into *Comb*, as in Eilean Comb, Tongue; or even into *Com*, as in GILCOMSTON, Aberdeen, 'the place of the gillie' or 'servant of Columba,' and Clumlie, Dunrossness, has been claimed as simply a corruption of Columcille.

With the exception of two about to be mentioned, the saint most frequently honoured, next to Columba and Ninian, has been Donan, the former's contemporary and friend, and, to their honour be it said, the only martyr who died by pagan hands in Scotland. Even his death at Eigg, by order of the Pictish queen, is said to have been rather for political reasons.

Donan's name lies sprinkled all over the map of Scotland from the north of Sutherland to the south of Arran and to Wigtown. 'St. Bride the Calm,' Brigida or Bridget of Kildare (*c.* 450–523) is also widely commemorated, from Kirkmabreck in Galloway to Papa and Stronsay in Orkney, and from Borve in Lewis to Dunottar. This is but natural, if she was indeed, as she is claimed to be, 'the greatest woman of the Celtic Church.' These things being so, it is somewhat strange that the great Kentigern or Mungo, bringer of the glad tidings to Glasgow and Strathclyde, should have received such very scanty remembrance. No place-name seems to embody 'Kentigern'; there is, of course, STRATHBUNGO. There are too a BALMUNGO, and Mungowells, near Ormiston; quite likely they have nothing to do with the saint. But there is also the modern parish of St. Mungo, formerly part of Hoddam, Dumfriesshire, a place said to have been visited by St. Mungo on his return from Wales, and to have been his headquarters for some time.

Bishop Reeves, the valued editor of *Adamnan*, has drawn attention to the marked contrast between names of the parishes on the east and on the west of Scotland. On the east the names are chiefly secular, even though chiefly Celtic, and probably date from remote pagan times. But on the west the parochial names, in a large number of cases, are found to combine with the prefix Kil- (G. *ceall*, locative *cill*, 'a monk's cell, then a church, also a grave'; see KILARROW) the name of some venerated Scoto-Irish saint. Undoubted instances of this on the east coast are rare. We have, near Beauly, KILMORACK, 'church of St. Moroc,' and KILTARLITY from St. Talargain, and KILRENNY (Anstruther), probably from St. Irenæus, but not many more. There are many other names in Kil-, as KILDRUMMY (Aberdeen), KILLEN (Avoch), KILMENY (Fife), and Kilmore (Loth); but in these the kil- may be G. *coil*, a wood; and their second halves do not stand for any saint. KILCONQUHAR (Elie) and KILSPINDIE (Errol) are two very curious names, which can hardly commemorate any saint either (q.v.). Dr. Reeves' contrast is true not only of the parish names, but the names generally; *e.g.*, take the case of St. Columba. All along the east coast we find but one INCHCOLM, while there are six instances of an Eilean Coluim

(' Colm's isle ') on the west. Yet the monasteries of Deer (Aberdeen) and St. Serf (Kinross) are, to say no more, sufficient proof that Columban missionaries did not neglect the east.

Students of the *Origines Parochiales* know that there were many more ' Kils - ' among the names of the ancient parishes than among the modern ones. And, just as we still have churches called ' Christchurch ' or ' Trinity Church,' so do we find that the old name of the parish of Strathy in Skye, and the old name of the parish now Muir of Ord, was KILCHRIST, the variants Kirkchrist and Cristiskirk also occurring. The first Norse church in Orkney, built *a.* 1064, was known as ' Christ's Kirk in Birsay,' such a name being given by the Norse only to a cathedral church. There was also at least one Kil Iosa, ' church of Jesus,' and near Beauly is KILTEARN, 1269 Keltyern, G. *ceall Tighearna*, ' church of the Lord ' ; whilst on Blaeu's map of North Uist we find a KILTRINIDAD, now called *Teampul-na-Trianaide*, ' church of the Trinity.'

Many of these ancient Celtic saints have had their names so twisted and distorted by centuries of tongues, ignorant alike of spelling and hagiology, that now the personages themselves are hardly recognizable. It needs clever eyes to see St. Comgan in KILCHOAN, and yet cleverer to recognize Talargain in KILTARLITY, or Begha in KILBUCHO. St. Begha, disciple of St. Aidan and Abbess Hilda, is the well-known English St. Bees. One of the obscurest cases is Kilchousland, Kintyre (G. *cill Chuisilein*), said to be ' Church of St. Constantine,' a Cornish prince, whose conversion is dated A.D. 588, said to have been martyred here. But the corruption is strange, and little light is yielded by the charter-spellings Kil-, Quhit- lauisland. Recognition is made all the more difficult from the warm-hearted Celt's frequent habit of prefixing to the saint's name *mo* or *ma*, ' my own,' which signifies endearment, and of affixing an *-oc*, *-og*, or *-aig* (*cf.*, G. *òg*, ' young '), which is a kind of pet diminutive. Thus KILMARONOCK, near Alexandria, like Kilmaronog, on Loch Etive, means ' church of my dear little Ronan.' But KILMARNOCK is really Kilmaernanog, from St. Ernan, of the seventh century. This unaccented *ma* explains the true and still largely-preserved pronunciation of that pretty Renfrewshire village, KILMA(L)COLM, pronounced Kilmăcóm, ' church of my own Columba' ; and Robert of Gloucester in 1297 writes of our Scottish monarch as 'Kyng Macolom.'[1]

The two names which, above all the rest, have gone through the most extraordinary vicissitudes, almost rivalling the fate of the Norse *bolstaðr* (p. 42), are Adamnan and Maolrubha. Adamnan, a man of royal Irish blood, and Abbot of Iona (679–704), is far famed as Columba's biographer. His name means 'little Adam,' and in Lowland Scots it would be 'Adie.' The unaccented initial A easily goes ; and we find that, through aspiration, the two aspirable consonants here, *d* and *m*, in many cases go too. Thus all that is left of 'Adamnan' is sometimes no more than *eon*, as in ARDEONAIG, pronounced arjónaig, on Loch Tay, 'height of little Adamnan.' In Orkney all that is left is *dam*, as in DAMSEY, the old Daminsey, 'Adamnan's isle.' The saint's name appears as *veon* (v = dh) in KILMAVEONAIG (Blair-Athole), and as *ennan* in KIRKENNAN (Galloway) ; whilst in the north-east his name is pronounced Theunan or Teunan. Till lately this last was the name of the parish of Forglen, Banffshire.

Maolrubha is a saint from the Irish Bangor, who seems to have been almost as great a missionary as Columba himself. In 671 he came over to Kintyre, travelled slowly north, and founded the monastery of Applecross in West Ross ; and in that district his name is still preserved in Loch MAREE, which, contrary to popular tradition, does not mean, 'Mary's Loch.' The Modern Gaelic for Mary is *Maire*, but the older form, and that which is always applied to the Virgin Mother, is *Moire* ; thus we have in Scotland, as in Ireland, several Kilmorys ; hence, too, TOBERMORY, 'Mary's well.' But the name of St. Maolrubha has had to endure far more than this. In the older forms of the place-names his name is sometimes preserved with tolerable plainness, *e.g.*, the old name of Ashig in Strath (Skye) was *Askimilruby* ; and in 1500 the name of KILARROW (Islay) was Kilmolrow, in 1548 Kilmarrow, whilst to-day the *m* has, through aspiration, clean vanished away. A common modern form of the old saint's name is Marui, as in Innis Marui, Loch Shin and Aiscag Marui, or 'Maolrubha's ferry,' near Kyleakin,

[1] However, in *O.E. Chron.* (Worcester), ann. 1075, we find 'Kynge Malcholom,' which implies the G. *maol Choluim*, 'servant,' lit. 'shaveling of Columba' ; *ibid.* (Laud), ann. 1079, we have 'Melcolm.'

whilst yet another form is seen in Cill Mharu, Muckairn. There is no proof that Maolrubha, or Sagart ruadh, as he is also called —'ruddy priest'—ever visited AMULREE (Dunkeld), nor is it likely that it derives its name from him. But Sammareve's Fair, held in Keith and Forres, helps to keep alive his name.[1]

Maolrubha must be carefully distinguished from St. Moluag of Lismore, patron saint of Argyle and friend of Columba, who died in 592. His name is to be found unaltered in Kilmoluag (Tiree, Mull, and Skye), and almost so in Kilmolowok (Raasay). The change is more violent in Knockmiláuk, 'Moluag's hill,' near Whithorn. KILMALLOW (Lismore) has sometimes been thought to come from Maolrubha; but the form *Kilmaluog* shows that this cannot be. The parishes of Raasay and Kilmuir, in Skye, both once bore this same name, Kilmaluog; and Kilmalew was the old name of the parish of Inveraray, whilst we have Clochmaloo near Rhynie. Moluag's original name was Leu or Lua, perhap L. *lupus*, a wolf; in Gaelic it is Lugaidh. The final syllable has been dropped, and the endearing *mo* and the pet suffix *-oc* have been added, hence the forms Moluoc, Moluag, or Molua; the curious spellings Malogue, Mulvay, and Molingus also occur. Somewhat similar in composition is the name of St. Modoc, or Cadoc of Llancarvan, a saint of the Welsh calendar—a rare thing to find in Scotland. His name we see in KILMADÓCK, Doune. On the other hand, we have a few pseudo-saints, like St. Brycedale, long the residence of worthy Patrick Swan of Kirkcaldy. There never was such a being; the name is really St. Bryce's dale, Bryce being a corruption, less common than Bride, of that worthy woman St. Brigid, whose name is so dear to Irish tongues as Bridget. A worse fraud is ST. FORT, near Dundee, a silly modern corruption of Sandford, the old name of the estate there. Hard by is 'St. Michael's,' as the Ordnance Survey calls it, which really commemorates one Michael Irvine, who kept a public-house there early in the eighteenth century!

In Scotland by far the commonest prefix to denote 'church' or 'chapel' is *kil*. But the Brythonic and Pictish *llan*, *lhan*, or *lan* is also found. This word means (1) a fertile, level spot, (2) an enclosure, (3) a church, with which three meanings the student may find it interesting to compare the similar mean-

[1] See Rev. A. Scott on St. Maolrubha in *Scott. Hist. Rev.*, April 1909.

ings of the L. *templum*, itself also often adopted into Gaelic as *teampull*, a church or holy cell. Scottish *lans* are rare; the chief is LHANBRYDE, Elgin, 'St. Bridget's church.' In Wales *llan-* superabounds. Professor Veitch, in his *History of the Scottish Border*, says there are 97 there; but there are actually 221 given in the Postal Guide alone.

Besides *kil* and *lan*, the Scotch Celt also occasionally adapted for himself the Latin (or Greek) *ecclesia*, a church; thus we have ECCLES, near Coldstream, as well as three others south of the Tweed; thus, too, comes ECCLEFECHAN, 'church of St. Fechan,' that saint's name having the pretty meaning of 'little raven'; also ECCLESMACHAN (Linlithgow) and ECCLESIAMAGIRDLE (South-Eastern Perthshire), which queer-sounding appellation means 'church of my own Griselda' or 'Grizel'; but LESMAHAGOW probably does not belong here. In a charter of 1147 we find St. Ninian's, Stirling, called 'the church of Egglis,' which approximates to the G. *eaglais*, a church; itself, of course, like the W. *eglwys*, an adaptation of *ecclesia*, while in 1207 it is 'the Kirketoun.' M'Dowell (*Hist. Dumfries*, p. 37) mentions an estate of Eccles, Penpont, which he says was called after an Elsi or Eklis, a knight-templar of the reign of David I. Many wells (G. *tiobar*) have also been dedicated to saints, as at TOBERMORY and many another Tober- or Tibber-. The word is a little disguised in TIPPERLINN, and still more in such Galloway names as CHIPPERDINGAN, sacred to St. Ninian, and Chipperdandy, which is really *tiobar t' Antoin*, 'well of St. Anthony.'

That same modesty which kept back the Celt from giving his own name to his hamlet or farm led him, when he became a devout Christian, to dwell much in seclusion. Hence, it was once thought, the very name Culdee or *Cuilteach*, 'man of the recess' or 'nook.' But our best authorities say the name is *Cele De*, 'fellow of God,' *i.e.*, an anchorite. There is no trace of the name till after the days of Adamnan and Bede, *i.e.*, till after the partial Romanizing of the Celtic Church. But the zeal for solitude can hardly be traced to the influence of Rome. The Roman missionaries sought busy, wealthy Canterbury or York; but the men of Iona, like the hermits of Egypt and Syria long before, chose rather some dwelling-place like wild Tiree, as did Baothen, or wilder North Rona, as did Ronan. Their retreats or cells or caves were wont to be called *deserta*, adapted into Gaelic as *diseart*, where it also means a place for the reception of pilgrims. Hence we have DYSART, in Fife, still called by George Buchanan Diserta, and Dysart, near Montrose; and hence, *e.g.*, the old name of the parish of Glenorchy, Dysart or Clachandysert. These Diserts or Dyserts are still more common in Erin's isle.

One more interesting point, and then we must leave the student to his own devices. The lonely isle, Scotland's most westerly, commonly called ST. KILDA, bears a name which has caused much puzzlement. It is first mentioned in a charter of King Robert II, 1373, by the name of Heryte, whilst Fordoun, the well-known historian of the same age, calls it Irte. Then, in Mercator's earliest map, 1564, and in one map published by Ortelius in 1573, we first light upon the track of the present name; it is there St. Kylder, plainly a seaman's carelessly ascertained form. In J. Lesley, 1579, Nicolay and Speed, it is S. Kilder. But, by 1698, in Martin's well-known *Voyage to St. Kilda*, it has assumed its present form. There is no proof that such a personage as St. Kilda ever existed; though no doubt 'St. Kilda,' like every other lone Hebridean islet, was once the dwelling-place of some saint; and there once were chapels there to both Columba and Brendan. The inhabitants for a time had quite lost the *r* sound, and always made it *l*; so that the original Hyrte became on their lips Childa; and there is a *tiobar Childa* on the island to-day. This is no well dedicated to a saint, but probably means, as Martin already hints, 'well of the western land,' from G. *iar*, the West. The old Hirte or Hirta is thus a similar name to that of the well-known West Coast Lighthouse, DHU HEARTACH or Hirteach. *Irt* or *iort* in old Gaelic means 'death.' Possibly the old Celts imagined this isle of the far west to be the gate to paradise. Others derive the Kilda from O.N. *Kelda*, 'a spring, a well,' as in Salkeld and Threlkeld in the North of England.

ALPHABETICAL LIST OF ALL THE IMPORTANT PLACE-NAMES OF SCOTLAND

WITH

EXPLANATIONS OF THEIR ORIGIN

ABBREVIATIONS

Dan., Danish.
Dom., Domesday Book, *c.* 1087.
Fr., French.
G., Gaelic.
Icel., Icelandic.
Jam., Jamieson's Scott. Dicty.
L., Latin and Loch.
(M.), Dr. M'Bain.
(Mack.) W. C. Mackenzie.
M.E., Mid. English (1100-1500).
N., Norse.
N.E.D., *New* or *Oxford English Dicty.*
O.E., Old English or Anglo-Saxon.
O.G., Old Gaelic.
O.N., Old Norse, the Sagas.
Sc., Lowland Scots.
Sw., Swedish.
W., Welsh.
(W.), Prof. W. J. Watson, sometimes W.
a., ante, 'before.'
accus., accusative case.
adj., adjective.
ann., anno, 'in the year.'
c., circa, 'about.'
cf., compare.
cny., century.
corrup., corruption.
dimin., diminutive.
esp., especially.
fr., from.
gen., genitive case.
loc., locative case.
Onom., Searle's *Onomasticon Anglo-Saxonicum.*
orig., originally.
O. Stat. Acct., old *Statistical Account of Scotland.*
perh., perhaps.
phonet., phonetically.
prob., probably.
pron., pronounced.
R.M.S., Register of Great Seal.
syll., syllable.
termin., terminational.
var., variant.

4–7, or the like, means, found from fourteenth to seventeenth centuries.

A'AN Ben (L. Katrine). 1810, Ben An. ? invented by Sir W. Scott. But Aan is also var. of R. AVON, Banff.

ABBEY ST. BATHAN'S (Chirnside). 1250 Ecc[a]. ('church') sci. boythani, *i.e.*, *Baothen* of Tiree, Columba's successor at Iona, 597. The old church of Bothans (G. *bothan*, 'little hut') Yester, has nothing to do with a saint.

ABBOTRULE (Roxburgh). *a.* 1153 Rule Herevei; 1220 Ecclesia de Rule Abbatis ('of the abbot'), 1275 Abotrowl. See R. RULE and, as to Herevei, HALLRULE. The lands in Rulewater of Jedburgh Abbey.

ABBOTSFORD. The Abbot of Melrose Abbey.

ABBOTSGRANGE and -HAUGH (Grangemouth). Lands of Newbattle Abbey. Grange, med. L. *granagium* (*granum*, 'grain'), now often 'a farm,' orig. place where an abbey's rates and tithes were paid. See HAUGH.

ABBOTSHALL (Kirkcaldy). 1539 Abbotishall. He of Dunfermline.

ABB'S HEAD, ST. (Berwick). 1461 Sanct Abbis Heid. *Æbba*, sister of K. Oswald of Northumbria, was first abbess of Coldingham, close by, *c.* 650. Earlier, *Lib. Eliensis*, it was Coldeburcheshead, see COLDINGHAM. 'Head,' like O.E. *heafod*, O.N. *hofuð*, G. *ceann* and Fr. *cap*, means both 'the head' and 'a cape.'

ABDEN (Kinghorn). *c.* 1280 Abbethayne, also Abthen, -thania, lands of (Dunfermline) Abbey. G. *abdhaine*, 'abbacy, abbotric,' fr. *abaid*, 'abbot.' *Cf. a.* 1200 *Chart. Arbroath*, Ecclesia Sanctæ Mariæ de veteri Munros (Montrose) . . . quæ Scotice (*i.e.*, in Gaelic) Abthen vocatur ; and *Excheq. R.* 'Abden of Kettins,' Angus.

ABDIE (Newburgh). 1248, Ebedyn. Prob. as above, referring to Lindores close by. Or else loc. of G. *abaid*, 'beside the abbey' ; the *n* will then be, as often, a scribe's flourish. Abdy, Rotherham, *sic* 1379, will be Fr. *abadie*, 'abbey lands.'

ABERARDER (Strathnairn, Deeside, L. Laggan). Str. A. 1456 Aberardor, Lag. A, *c.* 1645 Abirairdour. Aber see p. 10. O.G. *aber àird dobhair*, 'confluence of the high water or stream.' *Cf.* Auchterarder.

ABERARGIE (Perth). *c.* 970 *Pict. Chron.*, Apurfeirt (*t* for *c*). G. *feargach* 'fierce,' *fearg* 'anger' ; *f* lost by aspiration. So, 'confluence of the fierce river.'

ABERCAIRNEY (Crieff). 1218 Abercarnich, 1221–3 -charni. O.G. *abar carnach* (in loc.), 'rocky marsh.' No confluence here. *Cf.* CAIRNIE and LOCHABER.

ABERCHALDER (L. Oich). 1238 Abbircaledouer ; also Aberchalladour. Prob. Brit., same root as in CALLANDER and CALLATER. The ending is O.G. *dobhar*, 'stream.' *Cf.* R. CALDER.

ABERCHIRDER (Banffsh.). Pron. -hírder. *c.* 1212 Aberkerdouer, 1291 Abirkerdor, *c.* 1370 -kyrdore. O.G. *aber chiar dobhair*, 'confluence of the dark or brown stream.'

ABERCORN (Bo'ness). *c.* 720, *Bede*, Aebbercurnig, *a.* 1130 : *Hen. Hunt.* Ebercurn and *Sim. Durham* Eoriercorn, *c.* 1300 *Trivet* Abourcorn. Prob. Brit. or W. *aber corniog*, 'horned confluence.' (W.)

ABERCROMBIE (or St. Monan's, Fife). *a.* 1165 Abercrumbi, 1250 Abircrumbyn, 1270 Abbercrumby, 1461 Abircumby. 'Crooked marsh,' O.G. *crumb*, G. *crom* 'crooked,' here in loc. *Cf.* ABERCAIRNEY.

ABERDALGIE (Perth). 1150 Abirdalgyn, 1348 Aberdalgy. 'Confluence among the thorns,' G. *dealg*, here in loc. *Cf.* ABDIE.

ABERDEEN. *a.* 1100 *Bk. Deer*, Abberdeon, 1114 Aberdon, 1136 Villa de Veteri Abbirdon, *c.* 1137 Aberden, 1153 *Snorro* Apardion, 1178 Aberdoen, *c.* 1225 *Orkn. Sag.* Apardjón. Mod. G. Obairdheathain. 'At the month of DEE' or 'DON.'

ABERDOUR (Fife, Gamrie). Fif. A. 1126 Abirdaur ; also Aberdovar. Ab. A. *Bk. Deer*, Abbordoboir. See R. DOUR.

ABERFELDY. G. Obair Pheallaidh. Prob. not fr. *Palladius*, Rome's missionary to Scotland, 5th cny., but fr. *Paldoc* or *Paldy*, disciple of St. Ninian, who went to Fordoun, *cf.* PALDY'S WELL. W. derives fr. Peallaidh, a river name, used in Lewis for a water-sprite or demon. *Cf.* Castail Pheallaidh, Den of Moness, and Eas Pheallaidh, Glen Lyon.

ABERFOYLE (S. Perthsh.). 1481 Abirfull. G. *aber phuill* (gen. of *poll*), 'confluence of the streams.' *Cf.* Ballinfoyle, Ireland.

ABERGELDIE (Braemar). 1451 -gheldy, *Pont* Galdy, 1611 Abiryeldie. G. Geallaidh; *cf. geal* 'clear, fair.' M. derives fr. Pict. *geld* 'a well,' same as N. *kelda*, in Salkeld, etc. *Cf.* PITYOULISH.

ABERLADY (N. Berwick). *Life Kentigern* Aberlessic, *c.* 1221 -lauedy, 1275 -lefdi, 1328 Abirleuedy, 1507 Aberlathye, 1528 -ladye. W.'s 'mouth of stench,' G. *lobh* 'to rot,' will not do. As Mack. hints, the forms, *c.* 1221 on, come fr. *lady* (see *N.E.D.* s.v.), *i.e.*, Our Lady, The Virgin. Though abnormal this seems certain. Aber- is here 'marsh.'

ABERLEMNO (Forfar). 1250 Aberlevinach, -lemenach, *c.* 1320 Abberlennoche, 1533 Abirlemno. 'Confluence of the elm-stream,' G. *leamhan* 'elm,' adj. *leamhanach*. *Cf.* LENNOX.

ABERLOUR (Banffsh.). 1226 -lower, 1275 -logher. 'Loud confluence,' G. *labhar*. (W.)

ABERMILK (Annandale). 1116 -melc. Now St. Mungo. See R. MILK.

ABERNETHY (Perth, Grantown). Per. A. *c.* 970 *Pict. Chron.* Abur-Apurnethige. *c.* 1097 *Flor. Worc.* Abernithici, *a.* 1107 -nethyn, *a.* 1130 *Sim. Durham* -nithi, Ir. *Nennius* Apuirnige. Inv. A. 1461 Abirnethi. G. Ob.air Neithich, see NETHY and NITH, with which M. connects. Per. A. is the 'ford,' Invernethy is at the confluence with R. Earn. Early forms suggest G. *an eitighich*, 'at the narrow opening,' lit. 'gullet.'

ABERNYTE (Inchture). *Sic* 1415. 1338 -nuyt, *a.* 1517 -nyde. Perh. fr. G. *naid, -de* 'a lamprey.'

ABERSCROSS (Sutherld). G. Àbarscaig. 1512 Abirsskor, 1518 Aberscors. W. suggests, N. *á-búr-skiki* 'river-bower-strip,' *cf.* OVERSCAIG and SHIBBERSCROSS. But the last syll. is quite doubtful.

ABERTARFF (Lochaber). 1231 -terch, *c.* 1240 -terth, 1282 Abirtarf, *c.* 1400 *Bk. Clanranald* Obuirthairbh, gen. of G. *tarbh*, 'a bull.' *Cf. c.* 1130 Abercarf (*c* for *t*) where Tarth joins Lyne, Peeblessh., and TARFF.

ABERUCHIL (*e* here mute) and ABERUTHVEN (Perthsh.). *c.* 1198 Aberrotauin, -ruadeuien, 1200 Abirruotheven. See RUCHIL and RUTHVEN.

ABINGTON (S. Lanark). 1459 Albintoune. 'Village of *Albin*,' in O.E. *Ealhwine*.[1] Abingdon, Berks, and Abington, Cambs, are not the same.

ABÓYNE (Deeside). *Sic*. 1643, but *c*. 1260 Obyne, 1282 -eyn, 1639 Oboyne. Forms apt to be confused with OYNE. A- or O- is O.G. *abh* 'water, river,' *cf*. AWE, and -boyne is G. *bo fhionn* 'white cow.'

ABRÍACHAN (L. Ness). 1239 Abirhacyn, 1334 Aberbreachy and Abriach. G. Ob'ritheachan. M. is doubtful. Perh. 'confluence of the beggars,' G. *dhìtheach*. The -an is termin.

ACHALEVEN (Argyle). G. *achadh a' leamhain*, 'field of the elm.' *Cf*. LEVEN and *a*. 1500 *Reg. Aberdon*. Auchlevyn. Ir. names write Agh- for Ach-.

ACHANAULT (Contin). 'Field of the streams,' G. *allt*, *uillt*.

ACHÁRACLE (Strontian). A mod. spelling. The proper name is Āharkle, N. *á Thorkill*, 'river of Torquil' (Thor's kettle'), *i.e.*, R. Shiel.

ACHÁRN (Kenmore). G. *ath chàirn* 'ford at the cairn.'

ACHAW (L. Creran). G. *achadh an chath* 'field of the battle.'

ACHBRECK (Ballindalloch). 'Field spotted or speckled,' G. *breac*.

ACHENGEOCH (Cadder). 'Field of the goose,' G. *an geòidh*.

ĀCHILTY L. (Strathpeffer). 1479 Auchquhilye, 1528 Hechely. G. Achillidh. Also Achalties, Stirlingsh., and Torachilty, Ross-sh., (G. *torr*, 'hill'). Pict. or Brit. *achil*, 'a height,' W. *uchel* 'high,' *cf*. OCHIL and Gaul. *uxello*, also Achil, Mayo. But ACHILTIBUIE (Ullapool) is G. *achadh a'ghille buidhe*, 'field of the yellow-haired lad.' In all cases the *ty* or *t* is late and euphonic.

ACHLÚACHRACH (Ft. William). 'Rushy field,' G. *luachrach*, fr. *luachair*, 'rushes.'

ACHNABA (Ledaig). G. for 'field of the cows,' *bò* 'a cow,' pl. *bà*.

ACHNACARRY (Ft. William). 1505 Auchnacarre. 'Field of the weir,' G. *cairidh*.

ACHNACLOICH (Oban[2] and Rosskeen). 'Field of the stone or boulder,' G. *clach*, *cloch*. *Cf*. Auchincloch, Kilsyth.

ACHNASHELLACH (W. Ross-sh.). 1543 Auchnashellicht, 1584 -nasellache; 'field of willows,' G. *seileach*. *Cf*. Glaickshellach, Rosskeen, *glac* 'a valley.'

ACHNASTANK (Ben Rinnes). *Sic* 1474, *a*. 1500 Auchynstink. 'Field of the pool or ditch,' G. *an staing*.

[1] One must also note Roger de *Albini* or Aubigny, a Norman baron, who came over in 1066.

[2] The Campbells of Achnacloich transferred the name in its Eng. shape to their new estate at Tarbert, L. Fyne—Stonefield.

ACHÓSNICH (Strontian). 'Field of sighing,' G. *osnaich*, in pl. 'blasts of wind.'

ACHOYNANIE (Keith). *Sic* 1703, but 1545 Auchquhennany, 1667 Achynannie. Here G. *achadh* has its rarer sound achoo, achoy. So, 'field in the marsh,' *eanach*, here in loc.

ACHRAY L. (Trossachs). *Sic* 1791, but 1800 *Leyden* Loch-a-chravy, and *O. Stat. Acct*—the writer was a Gael—says, it is *achadh-a' chràbhadh*, 'field of devotion.'

ACKERGILL (Wick). 1547 Akirgill; also Acrigill. O.N. *akr*, O.E. *æcer*, *acer*, cognate with L. *ager*, lit. 'open country, untilled land'; later *acre* meant what was tilled. Gill is O.N. *gil* 'ravine,' see p. 39.

ADD R. (Crinan). W. thinks it doubtful if this is Ptolemy's R. *Longos* or is G. *fhada* 'long,' *fh.* lost by aspiration. But *cf.* Drum-ad, Ireland, and Cloined, S. Arran, 'long slope,' G. *claoin*.

ADDER Black and White (Berwicksh.). *a.* 800 *Hist. St. Cuthbt.*, Edre, *c.* 1098 Blacedre and Ederham, *a.* 1130 *Sim. Durham* fluvius Edre. The pron. is Whít-adder. Perh. 'dividing' river, G. *eadaradh* 'a division,' fr. *eadar* 'between.' Prob. not O.E. *édre* 'vein, fountain,' Eng. river names are very rare.

ADDIEWELL (W. Calder). Seems modern. *Addie* is for *Adam*. For absence of 's *cf.* MOTHERWELL.

ADEN HO. (Mintlaw). *a.* 1150 *Bk. Deer* Aldin Alenn. Prob. G. *alldan aluinn*, 'bonnie little burn.'

ADVIE (Cromdale). Prob. G. *fhada* (*fh* lost by aspiration), *faide* 'long,' with -vie termin. Or else = IDVIES.

AFFRIC L. and Glen (Inverness-sh.). 1538–9 *R.M.S.* Foresti de Auffrik. M. suggests G. *ath bhraich*, 'ford of the boar,' and *ath-breac*, 'somewhat speckled.' It may conceal the name of a Celtic water-nymph.

AFTON WATER (New Cumnock). Prob. G. *abh donn*, 'brown stream.'

AIKENHATT (Finhaven). Prob. same as AIKENHEAD (Cathcart, etc.). 1260 Akinhede, 'oaken head,' 'height covered with oaks,' Sc. *aik*.

AIKET HILL (Urr). 1550 Aikhead. As above, fr. O.E. *ac*, O.N. *eik*, Sc. *aik*, 'an oak.' *Cf.* Akatover and -nether, N. Ayrsh.

AILORT L. (Skye). 'Snow-shower *fjord*,' O.N. *él* 'snow-shower,' also 'a hot fight.' See p. 34.

AILSA CRAIG (Frith of Clyde). *Bk. Leinster* Aldasain, 1404 Ailsay, 1596 Elza. In G. Creag Ealasaid (W.). Prob. N. 'Isle of *Æla*' or '*Ailsi*,' short form of O.E. *Ælfsige*. See p. 40.

AINORT L. (E. Skye) = ENARD.

AIR POINT (Mainland, Orkn.), AIRY, Birsay. N. *eyri*, 'gravelly point or spit.'

AIRD DHAIL (S.W. of Butt of Lewis). G. *àird dhail*, 'height, cape of the meadow.' *Cf.* The Aird of Sleet.

AIRDS MOSS (E. Ayrsh.). Might be fr. a man, but prob., like AIRDS (Appin), G. *àird*, 'height, hill.' For adding Eng. plur. *cf.* WEMYSS.

AÍRDRIE (Lanark, Crail). *Cf.* 1570 Airdrie, Cromarty. Prob. G. *àird airigh*, 'high hill-pasture,' the N. *saeter* or summer hill-farm. Lan. A. might be the 577 battle of Arderyth, in *Brit. Triads*. If so, Celt. *ard tref*, 'high dwelling'; *cf.* NIDDRIE.

AIRLIE (Forfar). 1219 Eroline; later Eroli, Herolin. Must be same as ERROL. Prob. Pict. or Brit. W. *ar ole*, 'on the ravine,' or *aroll*, 'cleft, rift,' would suit Airlie, but hardly Errol.

AIRTH (Larbert). 1128 Hereth, *c.* 1214 Harth, 1296 Erth. G. *airidh*, here, 'a level green among hills.'

AIRTH-, AITHRIE (Stirling). *c.* 1142 Atherai, *a.* 1200 Athran, 1317 Athray, 1488 Athra. Doubtful. Perh. 'at the cows' place,' a loc. fr. O.G. *aithre*, 'ox, cow.'

AITHSVOE (Lerwick). O.N. *eið vö-r*, 'isthmus inlet.' Also AITHSTING (W. Shetld.), *old* Eidsting; see TINGWALL.

AKIN or Kyle Akin (Broadford). 'Straits of *Haco* or *Hakon*,' K. of Norway. He is said to have sailed through, returning from defeat at Largs, 1263. The name recurs at Ukinster, Sheſld. See KYLE.

ALBANY, old name of Scotland. *a.* 1160 *Gest. Steph.* Scotia quae et Albania dicitur, *c.* 1175 *Fantosme* Albanie, Aubanie. Same as Albion, Pliny Senr's name for Britain. Root Celt. *alb*, 'white' or *alp*, 'high.' Albainn is the regular G. name for Scotland, but till *c.* 1100 it was the name of Pictavia or the Kingdom of Scone.

ALCAIG (Dingwall). 1430 Alcok, 1611 -caik. N. *alka-vík*, 'auk's bay'; *aig* is regular Norse G. for 'bay.'

ALD-, OLDCAMBUS (E. Berwicksh.). 1098 Aldcambus, 1212 Aldchābos, Aldecambus. G. *allt camuis*', 'burn,' or perh. 'cliff, at the bay.'

ALDCLUNE (Blair Athol). G. *alld*, *allt cluain*, 'glen of the meadow.'

ALDER, AULER Ben (Laggan). Pron. Yallar. *Pont* Aildir. Perh. G. *alld dobhar*, 'rock stream,' the burn here.

ALDIE (Buchan and name of Water of Tain). G. *alld*, 'burn,' here in loc. *Cf.* Balaldie, Fearn, 'farm at the burn.'

ALDIVALLOCH (Cabrach), ALDNAVALLOCH (L. Lomond). G. *alld*, *allt a' bhealaich*, 'stream in the pass.' *Cf.* BALLOCH.

ALDOÚRIE (L. Ness). G. *allt dobhraidh*, loc. of *dobhar* or rather *dobhrag*, name of the burn here. Both halves mean 'stream.'

ALE R. (Ancrum). *c.* 1116 Alne. Prob. G. *àluinn, àilne,* 'exceeding fair, lovely.' Alnmouth, Northumbd, is also pron. Alemouth. *Cf.* ANCRUM. But ALE Water, trib. of R. Eye, is prob. G. *àl, àil,* 'a rock,' fr. the great Kip Rock which stands where it joins the Eye.

ALEXANDRIA (Dumbarton). Called, *c.* 1760, after Alexander Smollett, M.P., of Bonhill.

ALFORD (Aberdeensh.). *c.* 1200 Afford, 1654 Afurd, and so still pron. Prob. G. *ath òrd* (var. of *àrd*), 'high ford.' For *th* become *f, cf.* RAFFORD.

ALINE L. (W. Argyll). G. *àluinn, ailne,* 'very fair, lovely.'

ALLADALE (Kincardine, Ross.). 'Ali's dale.'

ALLAN R. (Stirling). 1187 Strathalun, 1373 Alon, 1508 Inneralloun. G. and Ir. *àluinn, àlainn,* 'bonnie.' The 1st *a* has become short in such Ir. names as Moy- and Kenallen, Down, as it has on the Eng. lips which have pron. this Allan for 7 c'nies. ALLEN (Fearn) 1357 Estir Alane, 1529 Alen is prob. G. *àilean,* 'a green plain.' The length of the *ai* is very fluctuating ; *e.g.*, L. Tay Gaels say, both Duăllin and Duāllin (Lawers). It is a meadow on a steep slope, so cannot be equated with L. *palus,* 'a marsh' (W.). *Cf.* KENTALLEN and SALEN ; also the W. and Corn. Alun. ALLAN Water, Melrose, is also Elwand ; see ELVAN.

ALLANTON (Chirnside, Galston, etc.). 'Village of *Allan.*' Chirn. A. was so named by a Stewart of Allanton, Galston.

ALLERMUIR (Pentlands). *Old* Alamore. Prob. G. *àl mòr,* 'big rock.'

ALLIGIN, ALEGIN Ben (Torridon). Perh. fr. G. *àilleag,* 'jewel, pretty woman.' W. is doubtful, for the G. is *àiliginn. Cf.* ELGIN.

ALLOA. *Sic* 1707, but 1357 Alwey ; also Alloway. Prob. = ALVA, ALVIE.

ALLOWAY (Ayr). 1236 Auil-, 1302–4 Aule-, *c.* 1340 Auylway. W. connects with above. Might be G. *àl a' mhaigh,* 'rock in the plain.'

ALLT GRANDA or GRAD (Kiltearn). G. for 'ugly burn.'

ALMANACK Hill (Inch). G. *allt manach,* 'monks' glen.'

ALMOND R. (Perth, Edinburgh). Ed. A. *c.* 1128 Avin, 1178 Amonth (see CRAMOND) ; also Awmon. Per. A. *Ulst. Ann.* 686 Aman (so still in G.), *Cron. Elegiac.*, Amon, Aven, Awyne, 1461 Almond, 1640 Amond. G. *amhainn, -uinn,* 'river' ; so = AVON. For suffixing of *d, cf.* DRUMMOND.

ALNESS (Invergordon). 1226 Alenes, very near the G. pron. now. It is not Alanáis (W.) but Àlnais, very rarely Àleinais. Prob. G. *àilean,* 'green plain,' with common Pict. loc. *-ais.*

ALTASS (Bonar Br.). G. *allt giuthais*, 'stream of the pinewood.'

ALTNABREAC (Caithness). 'Stream of the trout,' G. *breac, bric.*

ALTNAHARRA (Farr). 1834 Aultnaherve. 'Stream,' *na h-eirbhe*, 'with the stone and turf fence,' O.Ir. *airbe*, lit. 'ribs.'

ALTON (Beith). G. *alltan*, 'little burn.'

ALTRIVE Burn (Yarrow). (? *Reg. Neubotle* p. 27 Will. de Auetrive). 1587 Eltryve. Prob. G. *allt t'snaimh*, 'stream with the swimming-place.' *Cf.* ARDENTRYVE.

ALTVENGAN Burn (Aberfoyle). 'Burn with overhanging boughs,' G. *mheangan.*

ALTYRE (Elgin). (*Bk. Deer* Altere). 1492 Altre, 1573 Alter. G. *allt tìr*, 'river-land.'

ALVA (Alloa). *c.* 1180 Alueth, 1301 Alwthe. G. *ailbheach*, 'rocky place,' *ailbhe*, 'rock, flint.' So ALVAH (Banff). *a.* 1300 Alueth, and ALVIE (Aviemore), *c.* 1350 Alveth, -way, *c.* 1400 -vecht.

ALVES (Elgin). Also 'rocky place,' G. *ailbhe*, 'rock,' with common Pict. loc. *-ais*, 'at the.'

ALWHAT Hill (E. Ayrsh.). G. *àl chàtt*, 'rock of the wild cat.' *Cf.* Macherwhat near by, *machair*, 'plain, links.'

ALYTH (Angus). Pron. áylith. *Sic* 1327, but *a.* 1249 Alicht, 1296 -yght, 1651 Ellit. G. *ail-, eileach*, 'mound, bank,' lit. 'rocky place.' *Cf.* ELLIOT.

AMISFIELD (Dumfries and Haddington). Dum. A. pron. Emsyfield, *a.* 1175 Hempisfield, 1298 Amesfelde. Prob. fr. *Hemmi* (in *Onom.*), mixed up with *Ames* or *Amyas* de Charteris, early lord of manor here. The Had. name is a transferred one.

AMPLE Glen (L. Earn). 1471 Amble. Given me *c.* 1900 as G. *gleann amaill.* But W. says, Ambuill, fr. L. *amphora*, 'a large jar,' hence, 'a vatlike pool.'

AMULREE (Aberfeldy). G. Amalruighe. Perh. not, as commonly said, 'Ford,' G. *ath*, 'of St. *Maolrubha*,' the famous st., b. Derry, 642, but 'ford at the shieling' or 'outstretched arm of the hill.' Site and G. would admit either. But *cf.* MAREE.

ANCRUM (Jedburgh). *Sic* 1522, but *c.* 1116 Alnecrumba, *c.* 1150 -cromb, 1147–50 Alvecromber (scribe's error), 1275 Ankrom. 'Crook, bend of R. Alne or ALE,' O.G. *crumbadh*, G. *cromadh*, 'a bending,' fr. *crom* crooked. *Cf.* Abercrombie.

AN-, INDAÍL L. (Islay). 1703 Loch -Dale. 'Duckdale,' fr. O.N. *önd*, gen. *andar*, 'a duck.' So also Lochindaal, Sleat, *sic* 1772.

ANDREW'S, St. (Fife, Elgin, Orkney). Fif. A. *a.* 1130 *Sim. Durham* ann. 1074 and *Eadmer* Ecclesia Sancti Andreae, *c.* 1144 apud Sanctum Andream, 1158 St Andrae, 1434 Sanctandrowis. Prob. K. Kenneth M'Alpin, *c.* 850, first named St. Regulus' church here, St. Andrew's. Still in G. Baile Reuil, 'Rule's town.' Its old name was KILRIMONT. Scotland's patron st. also gives name to Lhanbryd church, Elgin. But *a.* 800 the Sc. patron saint was St. Peter.

ANGUS or Forfar. *a.* 1150 *Bk. Deer* Engus, *c.* 1175 Anegus, *a.* 1200 Enegus. Said to be fr. Anegus, Oengus (Corn.) or Hungus, son of Fergus and K. of Picts, 729.

ANNAN R. and town (Dumfries). *Sic* 1300, but *c.* 1150 *chart.* and *c.* 1180 *Bened. Peterb.* Anant, coin *a.* 1249 'Thomas on An.' Prob. back-formation fr. next. But Celt. roots, *an* 'swift' or *han*, 'separated, parted,' seem possible.

ANNANDALE. *c.* 1124 Estrahanent (W. *ystrad*, 'strath, valley'), *a.* 1152 Stratanant, *c.* 1295 Anandresdale, 1297 Vallis Anandi, 1487 Annander-. The -dres-, *c.* 1295, is a double gen., *r* is O.N. and *es* early Eng. 'Dale of *Önand-r*,' an O.N. name, found, 1198, at Gt. Yarmouth as *Anund*, 1292 *Anant*, and in *Landnamabok* as *Onund*, *c.* 874.

ANNAT (Inverness, Perth, Appin, etc.) and ANNAIT (Dunvegan). G *anait*, 'a parent church.' There are *Tobar na h' annait* or Well of Annat, at Strath, Skye and Calligray, Harris, Balnahanait, Glen Lyon, and ANNOTHILL, Airdrie; and *cf.* KILDALTON. But F. Macleod, *Iona*, p. 171, speaks of 'that mysterious Anait whose Scythian name survives in the Gaelic West, and nothing else.'

ANNICK Water (Irvine). ? G. *eanach*, 'a marsh.'

ANNIÉ (Callander). 1791 Aney. G. *ath an fheidh* (all aspirates mute), 'ford of the deer.' ANNIEGATHEL (Glen Queich) may be G. *ath an Gadhail*, 'ford of the Gael,' a late comer.

ANSTRUTHER. *c.* 1205 Anestrothir, 1231 An-, 1270 Aynestrother, 1362 -oythir. Looks like G. *an sruthair*, 'the stream'; in 1225 we find a Kynstruther, 'at the head (*cinn*) of the stream.' Local pron. is An-, Ainster. But prob. the name means 'marshy meadow.' Ane-, Ayne- reminds of ENZIE, N. *engi*, 'meadow,' and *stro-*, *struther* is common in O.Sc. and North. Eng. for 'a marsh'; *cf.* O.E. *stród*, 'marsh' and *strood*, s.v. in *N.E.D.*; also *c.* 1190 Estrother, now Strother, Boldon, RAVENSTRUTHER and WESTRUTHER. *Pont* has Struhers in N. Ayrsh.

ANWOTH (Kirkcudbt.). *c.* 1200 Anewith, *c.* 1280 Avinvethe, 1575 Anuecht. Doubtful; 1st syll. is AVON 'river.' Mack. thinks the 2nd, Brit. *weth*, 'hill-face.' *Cf.* MIGVIE.

AONACH, Mhòr and Beag (near Ben Nevis). G. for 'big and little height, heath, desert place.' *Cf.* TEANINICH.

AONAIN Pt. (Mull, Lismore, Iona). 'Harbour of St. Adamnan.' See p. 68.

APPER, Beag and Mhor (Tobermory). 'Little and big mudbank,' G. *eabar*, *abar*, 'mud, marsh.'

APPIN (Argyll, also burn, N.W. Dumfries). G. Apuinn. *Old* Apthania, -thane, 'Abbeylands' of Lismore. See ABDEN.

APPLEBIE (Wigtown). As in Westmorld., 1131 Aplebi, usually thought fr. O.N. *æpli*, *apli*, O.E. *æpple* ,'apple,' and O.N. or O.E. *bý*, *bí*, 'hamlet.' To derive fr. a man *Hiálp*, a saga name, accords more with analogy. *Cf.* 5 Appletons in England.

APPLECROSS (W. Ross-sh.). *c.* 1080 *Tighernac* ann. 673 Aporcrosan, ann. 737 Apuorcrossan, 1510 Appillcroce, 1515 Abilcros. O.G. *apor Crossain*, ('little cross'), 'mouth of the Crossan.' But this stream name is now forgotten, and natives now speak of A' Chomaraich, 'the sanctuary'; *cf.* Balwhomrie, *sic* 1517, Leslie, and Inverquhomery, Longside. See too *aber* p. 10, and *Pl. N. Eng.* s.v. Appledore. Also *cf.* the Sc. appleringie fr. L. abrotonum.

APPLEGARTH (Lockerbie). *c.* 1190 Apilgarth, 1578 Aplegirth, 'apple orchard,' O.N. *garð-r*, O.E. *geard*, *a.* 1300 *garth*, 'yard, court, enclosure.'

AQUHADLIE (Aberdeensh.). Perh. G. *achadh a' chadail*, 'field of sleep,' here in loc.

AQUHORTIES (Inverurie). 1390 Athquhorthy, *a.* 1500 Auchquhorty, 1538 Authquhorties; *cf.* an old Achorthi, Barony of Troup. 'Field,' G. *achadh*, or 'ford,' *ath*, 'full of circular hollows,' G. *choirteach*, fr. *coire*, 'a cauldron.' The -y is the loc. The Eng. plur. -es is late.

ARAY R. (Inveraray). O.N. *eyri*, 'gravelly bank.' *Cf.* AYR.

ARBÍRLOT (Arbroath). *c.* 1210 Abereloth, 1250 -elloch, -ellot. 'Ford on R. ELLIOT.' See *aber* p. 10, and *cf.* ARBROATH.

ARBOLL (Fearn). *Sic* 1507, but 1463 Arkboll. Now G. *earbil*, 'point, extremity of land' (the Tarbat peninsula). *Cf.* Urbal, common in N. Ireland and Darnarbil, Kirkcudbt. But orig. N. *ork-bol*, 'ark place,' or fr. *orkn*, 'a seal,' as in Orbost, Skye (W.).

ARBROATH. 1178 Aberbrothoc, *c.* 1190 -bruthoc, *a.* 1300 Abbirbroth, 1456 Arbrothat, 1456 Arbroth, 1546 Abirbrothoke. 'At the mouth of R. Brothock,' G. *brothach*, 'filthy, muddy.' *Cf.* Curbrottack, Pitlurg, and PARBROATH. See *aber* p. 10.

ARBUCKLE (Airdrie). *Old* Ironbuckle, *cf.* IRONGRAY; 1546 Arbucle. As surname 1506 Arnbuckle, *c.* 1560 Arbuchell. G. *àrd an buchaille*, 'height of the shepherd.'

ARBUTHNOTT (Fordoun). *Sic* 1482 but 1202 Aberbuthenot(h, 1206 -bothenoth. G. *abar baothanaich*, 'marsh of the silly fellow.'

ARCHIESTON (Moray). Founded 1760. *Archie* is short for *Archibald*; *cf.* 1361 *Paisley Chart.* Archiston Renfrew.

ARD L. (Aberfoyle). G. *àrd*, 'high.'

ARDALANISH (S.W. Mull). G. *àird gheal* (*gh* lost by aspiration), 'white cape' + N. *næs*, 'ness.' So a tautology. *Cf.* MACHRAHANISH.

ARDALLIE (Mintland). G. *àird àille*, 'very lovely height.'

ARDARGIE (Perth). G. *àird fheargach*, here in loc., 'fierce-looking height.' *Cf.* ABERARGIE.

ARDBEG (Rothesay). G. *àird beag*, 'little height' or 'cape.'

ARDCHALZIE (Breadalbane). G. *àrd choille*, 'height of the wood,' G. *coille*, Ir. *caill*; *z* is the Sc. *y*.

ARDCHATTAN (L. Etive). 1296 Ercattan. G. *àird Chattain*, 'height of abbot Cattan,' friend of Columba. Also called Balmhaodan, fr. St. Modan.

ARDCHULLERIE (L. Lubnaig). 'Height of the quarry,' G. *a' choileire*.

ARDCLACH (Nairn). 1545 -clauch. 'High rock,' G. *clach*.

ARDEER (Stevenston). G. *àird iar*, 'west cape.'

ARDELISTER (Islay). Hybrid. G. *àird*, 'height' and N. *hellis setr*, 'cave seat or residence.'

ARDELVE (Lochalsh). G. *àird ailbhe*, 'height of the rock.'

ARDENCONNEL (Row). *Sic* 1351 but 1429 Ardinconvale. 'Height of *Convall*.' See KIRKCONNEL.

ARDENTINNY (L. Long). 'Height of the fire,' G. *teine*, as signal for the ferryman. *Cf.* Achateny, N.W. Argyll, and Craigentinny, Edinburgh.

ARDENTRYVE (Oban). 'Point of the swimming-place,' G. *an t' snaimh*. Cattle used to be swum over here. The *t* eclipses *s* and *n* changes to its kindred liquid *r*. *Cf.* COLINTRAIVE.

ARDEONAIG (L. Tay). Pron. Arjónaig. 1494 Ardewnan, 1723 -ownaig. 'Height of little St. *Adamnan*,' see p. 68; *-aig* is a G. dimin.

ARDEONAN (on R. Tay). As above. *Eonan* is contraction of *Adamnan*. *Cf.* Balvoulin Eonan, 'mill-village of Eonan,' Glenlyon.

ARDERSIÉR (Nairn). The old name of Cromarty was similar. 1227 Ardrosser, 1257 -erosseir, 1570 Ardorsier, 1661 -nasier. G. *àrd ros ear*, 'high east point.' But now in G. *àrd an saoir*, 'point of the carpenter.'

ARDFERN (Lorn). 'Height of the alders,' G. *fearn(a*.

ARDFIN (Jura). 'White cape.' G. *fionn*, 'white, clear.'

ARDGAY (Bonar Br.). 1642 Ardgye; so now pron. 'Windy height,' G. *gaoith*, 'wind.' *Cf.* MILNGAVIE.

ARDGOIL (L. Goil, q.v.). Name suggested by J. A. Stewart, Glasgow, for the Cameron Corbett estate gifted to Glasgow in 1905.

ARDIMERSAY (Islay). Hybrid. G. *àird*, 'height' and N. *emmers-ay*, 'isle of the ember-goose' a kind of Northern diver, O.N. *himbrin*.

ARDINCAPLE (Gareloch). 1305 Airddengappil, *c.* 1390 Ardincapel, 1405 Ardenagappil. 'Height of the mare,' G. *capull*. *Cf.* PORTINCAPLE.

ARDKINGLAS (Inverary). 1560 Ardkyn(d)glas. 'Height of the grey dog,' G. *choin ghlais, cu*, gen. *con, choin*, 'a dog.'

ARDLÁMONT (L. Fyne). 1550 -lawmonth. 'Height of *Lamont*,' N. *lagamað-r*, pl. *lögmenn*, 'law man.' A *Lauman* at Kilmun, 1240. *Cf.* Kerrylamont, Bute.

ARDLAIR (Perthsh.), ARDLER (Coupar Angus). Pe. A. 1391 Ardelare, 1538 Ardlayr, For. A. 1384 Ardillar. G. *àrd a' làir*, 'height of the (? threshing) floor.' But *cf. c.* 1253 *Reg. Dunferm.* Ardlather quae nunc vocatur Milnetun, perh. fr. G. *làthair*, 'the company.'

ARDLUI (L. Lomond). The true G. pron. cannot now be got. Prob. G. *àrd laoigh*, 'height of the calf.' *Cf.* Ardluie, Cabrach and Glen Luie, Glen Garry, which is G. *gleann laoigh*.

ARDMADDY (L. Etive). 'Height of the dog or wolf,' G. *madadh*.

ARDMARNOCK (Tighnabruaich). 1403 -mernak. 'Height of my little Ernan.' See KILMARNOCK.

ARDMILLAN (Girvan). 'Height of the mill,' G. *muillean*.

ARDMORE (Islay etc.). G. *àrd mòr*, 'big height' or 'cape.'

ARDMUCKNISH (Ledaig). 1772 -muchnaye. True name of the L. Nell there. Hybrid. G. *àrd muic*, 'sow's height,' and N. *næs*, 'ness, cape.' *Cf.* ARDTORNISH.

ARDNADAM (Kilmun). Looks like 'height of Adam'; but Gillies was sure it is G. *àird nan damh*, 'height of the oxen.' *Cf.* CRAIGDAM.

ARDNAHUATH (Bute, Islay). Pron. Arnanoe. Bu. A. 1440 -nahow. G. *àird na h-ùghadh*, 'height of the burial mound,' N. *haug-r*.

ARDNAMURCHAN (N.W. Argyll). *Sic a.* 1500 *Bk. Clanranald, a.* 700 *Adamn.* Art Muirchol, Artdaib M., 1292 Ardenmurich; but 1309 -namurchin, 1325 -murcon, 'of the sea-hound' or 'otter,' *muirchu*. The name has changed. Reeves and M. held -chol O. Celt. for 'hazel.' W. thinks -muirchol will mean 'sea sins,' piracy. McKinnon said, Gillies' *àird na murduchain*, 'cape of the mermaid,' is phonet. impossible.

ARDOCH (Perthsh., etc.). G. *àrdach*, 'high place.'

ARDOW (Mull). G. *àrd dubh*, 'dark height.'

ARDRISHAIG (L. Fyne). 'Height of the briers,' *driseag*, dimin. of *dris*, 'brier, thorn.'

ARDROSS (Invergordon). G. for 'high moor.' All central Ross used to be called Ardross. *Cf.* ARDERSIER.

ARDROSSAN. *Sic* 1375. G. for 'height of the little cape,' *rosan*.

ARDTAL(A)NAIG (L. Tay). Perh. G. for 'height of the castle (*talla*) of Eonan.' *Cf.* ARDEONAIG near by and p. 68.

ARDTELIGAN (Ardrishaig). *Tighern.* Delgon, *Ulst. Ann.* 574, Telocho. Prob. 'height of thorns or briers,' G. *dealgan.* Gillies said, it is Ardtilligain = *àrd Uilleagain*, which he cannot explain.

ARDTORNISH (Sound of Mull). 1390 -thoranis, 1461 -tornys. Hybrid. G. *àird*, 'cape,' and N. *Thorinæs*, 'of Thori's ness.' *Cf.* ARDALANISH.

ARDTUN (Mull). G. *àird tunna*, 'height, cape of the waves,' *tonn*, or better, 'like a tun or cask,' G. and O.N. *tunna*. *Cf.* An Tunna, Glen Sannox.

ARDVASAR, -VARSAR (S.E. Skye) 'Fatal headland,' G. *bàs'ar* or *bàsmhor*, 'fatal, deadly.'

ARDVERIKIE (L. Laggan). 'Height for the standard,' G. *mheirge*.

ARDVORLICH (L. Lomond and L. Earn). In both cases near a Ben VOIRLICH, q.v. 1543 *Chart. Colquhoun* Ardiiurlik, *Pont* -vouyrlig.

ARDWELL (Stoneykirk). Prob. G. *àrd ghaill* 'height of the stranger' or 'foreigner,' as in Corn-wall. *Cf.* the local proverb, 'The Kirkmaiden folk were aye Fenians.' But J. Macdonald makes A., Strathbogie, G. *àrd bhail*, 'high dwelling.'

ARGYLE, -GYLL, *c.* 970 *Pict. Chron.* Arregaithel, *c.* 1150 Ergaithel, 1240 Erregaithle, 1289 Er-, 1292 Argail, *c.* 1425 *Wyntoun* Argyle, 1643–1700 *Dunoon Presby. Recds.* always Argyll. G. Earghaidheal, Araghàideal, Ir. Airer Gaedhil. G. *earr a' Ghaideal*, 'imit, boundary of the Gaels.' The adj. Argathelane is found, 1650. *Cf.* Anniegathel, Glen Queich, 'ford of the Gaels.' Earlier it was, *Albanic Duan* Oirir Alban, 'coast lands of Alban'; also Mergo Scottorum.

ARISAIG (W. Inverness), 1250 Arasech, *a.* 1292 -iseg, 1309 -yssayk. Prob. = AROS + *aig*, Norse G. for 'bay,' N. *vík*.

ARKAIG ((Ft. William). *c.* 1310 Logharkech, 1372 -arkage, 1516 -arcag. Prob. O.G. *arc*, 'black' with ending as above. With *c.* 1310 Logh, *cf.* the Ir. lough.

ARKLET (L. Katrine). Skene thought Loirgeclat (*i.e.* loch Irgeclat), battle in *Tighern.* ann. 711, is L. Arklet. ? G. *àr cleit*, 'battlefield of the snow-flakes.' W. says it is, *Air-claid* 'difficulty slope.' *Cf. Pont* Lin arklat, Glencairn. M. puts with ARKAIG.

ARLARY (Kinross). 1450 Ard-, Arlory. Old charter Magh-erderrly Doubtful. Perh. contains G. *làrach* 'ruin, house, farm.'

ARMADALE (Bathgate, Skye, Farr). Sk. A. 1703 Armidill, 1723 -odel. The root *arm* may be either 'arm of the sea' or 'land.' It may be fr. a man *Eorm*. *Cf.* Armathwaite, Cumberland.

ARNAGE (Ellon). 1488 Mekle Arnage (? this place). *Arn* is Sc. for 'alder.' The -age is uncertain; perh. as in BROOMAGE, so 'arn-tree meadow.' *Cf.* Wellnage, Duns, 'meadow with the wells,' O.E. *wellan*.

ARN- ARINAGOUR (Coll). G. *airidh nan gobhar* 'shieling of the goats.' *Cf.* next and ARDGOUR, also Airntully, Murthly.

ARNAHEAN (Argyll, several). G. *àrd na nighean*, 'height of the maiden'; or fr. *airidh*, 'shieling.'

ARNBURN (Luss), ARNS (Cumbernauld). Sc. *arn*, 'alder-tree.'

ARNCROACH (Elie). 'Height of the stack-like hill,' G. *na cruaiche*. *Cf.* Croach, Inch and Kelton, and CRUACHAN.

ARNGASK (Kinross). *c.* 1147 Arringrosk, 1250 Ardgrosc, 1389 Aryngosyk, 1548 Arnegosc. G. *àrd an croisg*, 'height of the crossing or pass.' *Cf.* Ardingrask, -grosk, Inverness. GASK is not the same.

ARNHALL (S. Kincard., Huntly). 'Hall, manor, among the arns.'

ARNISDALE (Lochalsh). 'Dale of *Arni*,' prob. some Viking.

ARNISORT (Skye). As above and -ort = N. *fjord*, 'firth, sea-loch.' See p. 34. *Cf.* SNIZORT. But ARNISH (Lewis and Raasay) is 'eagle's ness,' N. *örn*, 'an eagle.'

ARNISTON (Gorebridge). 1354 Arnaldistoun. '*Arnald's* village.'

ARNOT (L. Leven), ARNOTHILL (Falkirk). Lev. A. 1429 Arnut. (1541 'Arnothil,' Liddesdale.) Usually thought fr. Eng. *ernut* (*sic* 1551) or *earth-nut* or pig-nut: *cf.* Arbury or Erbury, *old* Erdsbery, Erthbery. Knockharnot, Leswalt, is 'barley knoll,' G. *ornacht*; while 1296 *Ragman R.* we have David Arnot, which makes things doubtful. Arnot might be for *Arnold*; *cf.* Arnodestorp, now Arnoldstoft, Yorks.

ARNPRIOR (Kippen). G. *àrd an*, 'height of' the *prior* of Inchmahome. To the W. is ARNGIBON, fr. G. *gibean*, 'a hunch on the back.'

ARNSHEEN (Ayr). 'Height of the foxgloves,' G. *sion*, or fr. *sìan*, *sìne*, 'of the storm of rain or snow.' Cf. AUCHNASHEEN.

AROS (several, Hebrides). 1410 'dun Aros in Mulle.' The Dan. Aarhus, N. *ár oss*, 'river's mouth,' *á*, gen. *aar*, 'river.' In G. *àros* is now 'house, mansion.' Gillies says, Jura A. is G., not N. *Cf.* Inveraros, Raasay.

ARPAFEELIE (Cromarty). So to-day in G. M. says, fr. G. *àrd na fhaolinn*, 'height of the sea-gull.' Curious corrup.! W. calls it 'obscure.'

ARRAN. 1154 *Four Masters sic*, but 1251 Araane, *c*. 1294 Aran, 1326 Arram. W. *aran*, 'peaked hill,' is very appropriate. But in mod. G. Arainn, with -inn old loc., 'at Ara.' Dr. Cameron, Brodick, said, G. *àra*, *àran*, 'a kidney,' exactly Arran's shape. *Cf*. Aran Isles, W. Ireland. W. denies they are the same.

ARROCHAR (L. Long). *Sic c*. 1350; also Arachor, -thor, G. and Ir. corrup. of L. *aratrum*, 'plough,' 'a carrucate,' used as a land-measure of 104 or 160 acres. We also find, *Cartul. Levenax*, passim, *c*. 1248 Letharathor, -archore, 'a half carrucate.'

ARTAFAILLIE (Munlochy). 1526 Ardirfalie, *c*. 1590 -thirfairthlie, 1599 Ardafailie. Perh. = ARPAFEELIE. W. says, prob. G. *àrd tir fàillidh* (gen. of *fàlach*), 'high land of the place of sods,' a rather abnormal name.

ARTFIELD Fell (Old Luce). *Pont* Artfell, a triple tautology, G. *àrd*, 'height.' O.N. *fiall*, 'hill,' Dan. *fjeld*, 'hill, mountain.'

ARTHURLEE (Barrhead). 1439 -lie, 'Arthur's meadow,' O.E. *léah*, 'pasture.'

ARTHUR'S OON (once at Carron, Stlg., and in Tweeddale). Car. A. *sic* 1727. 1293 *Reg. Neubot*, Furnum Arthuri. 'Arthur's Oven,' O.E. *ofen*; popularly but wrongly connected with K. Arthur's battles. It may be the 'Stan hus' in STENHOUSEMUIR. The first reference is in 1146 *Hermann* (Migne *Patrolog*. CLVI, 983), Furnum illius famosi regis Arturi, placed in Devon and *re* 1113. *Cf*. BESSIE YON.

ARTHUR'S SEAT (Edinburgh). 1508 Kennedy *Flyting* Arthurissete; *cf*. Girald. Camb. *Itin*. Kaer (for *cader*) Arthur, id est, cathedra Arthuri. Named fr. the famous 6th c'ny. king, in *Nennius* Arthur, *Dom*. Yorks and Lincs, Artor, prob. Rom. name, as in Juvenal *Sat*. 3. 29 Artorius, which may be fr. O. Celt. *arth*, 'a bear.'

ARTNEY GLEN (Comrie). 1573 -artnay, 1580 -arknay, -artharnay. In G. usually Artair = Arthur. But it is prob. 'pebble-place,' loc. of G. *airtein*, *artan*, 'a pebble'; and sometimes one hears gleann Artain.

ASCAIG, L. (Sutherld.), ASCOG (Bute), Port ASKAIG (Islay). Bu. A. 1503 Ascok, Is. A. 1703 Escock. Prob. 'bay,' Norse G. *aig*, *N. vík*, 'of the small boat,' N. *ask-r*. Perh. fr. O.N. *ask-r*, O.E. *æsce*, 'an ash tree.' G. Henderson, doubtfully, connects with Strathasgag, Lochalsh, which is N. *á-skiki*, 'river strip.'

ASCRIB Isls. (N.W. Skye). Perh. O.N. *áss kryppa*, gen. *-pu*, 'ridge with the hump or hunch.'

ASHA-, ESHANESS (Shetland). Prob. N. *esja*, 'a kind of clay, soapstone.'

ASHKIRK (Hawick). *a*. 1244 Aschirche, 1505 Askirk, O.E. *æsce*, 'ash-tree.'

ASHIESTEEL (Yarrow). 'Place of ash-trees,' O.E. *steall, stæl,* 'a place,' then 'a stable stall.' *Cf.* STEELE.

ASLOON (Alford). 1654 Asloun. Perh. G. *ath sleamhuinn,* 'smooth ford'; *cf.* Craigslouan, New Luce. But ASWANLEY, Glass, may be G. *eas bhan slèibh,* 'white waterfall on the hill.' *Cf.* too ASLOSS (N. Ayrsh.) 1493 Auchinloss, become in 1561 Assinloss, G. *achadh an lios,* 'field with the enclosure or garden.'

ASSARY (Caithness). *Flatey Bk.* Asgrims ærgin (-in, N. art.), 'Asgrim's shieling.' Norse G. *ærg,* G. *airigh.*

ASS of the GILL (ravine on R. Cree). Ass here is prob. for Sc. *hawse, halse,* O.N. and O.E. *háls,* 'neck, throat, defile,' while Gill is N. *gil,* 'ravine, gully.'

ÁSSYNT (S.W. Sutherld.). 1343 Asseynkt, -synkte, 1455 -send, 1502 -sent, 1595 -syn. Difficult. The *a* is short, which rules out many guesses. Perh. N. *asynt,* 'visible, seen fr. afar,' referring to its many peaks seen fr. the Minch. But, 1632, 'the chapel of Assind in Brakadaill,' Skye, is N. *áss endi,* 'ridge end.'

ATHELSTANEFORD (Haddington). Local pron. Elshinfurd. c. 1150 Alstanefurde, *c.* 1200 Alstanesfurth, 1250 Elstan-, 1461 Athilstanfurd. Said to be where *Athelstane,* general of Eadbert of Northumbria, was defeated by the Pict. K. Angus, *c.* 750. In Flodoard of Rheims, *c.* 960, King Athelstan of that time is Rex Alstanus.

ATHOLE, -OL (N. Perthsh.). *c.* 970 *Pict. Chron.* Athochlach (prob. for -clath), *Tighern.* ann. 739, Athfoithle, *c.* 1140 *saga* Atjoklis, *a.* 1200 Adtheodle, *c.* 1250 *Matt. Paris* Athole. In G. Athall. G. *ath Fhotla* or *Fodla* (in Pict. Chron. *Floclaid*), 'ford of Fodla,' one of the 7 sons of the legendary Cruithne. *Cf. a.* 1300 *Reg. Aberdon.,* Badfothel. Some hold, Fodla was wife of an early Welsh prince; and Fodia was an old poetic name for Ireland. K. Meyer posited *ath Fhòdla,* 'new Ireland.' But *ath* is lit. 'again, a second time,' which would yield a very abnormal Celt. name. Coire Fodla, Athole, certainly supports 'ford of Fodla.'

ATTACHOIRRIN (Islay). G. *atta chaoruinn,* 'house of the rowan tree.'

ATTADALE (2, W. Ross-sh.). Prob. fr. N. *at,* 'a fight.'

ATTOW BEN (Central Ross). G. *fhada,* 'long,' *fh* lost by aspiration. Final *a* here takes, as often, the sound *aw.* *Cf.* Callow, Cowal, for G. *cala,* 'a bay.'

AUCHELCHANZIE (Crieff). Brit. *uchel Chanice,* 'height of Kenneth,' W. *uchel,* 'high,' and O.Ir. *Canice,* G. *Coinneach,* Kenneth. *Cf.* Chonzie, Ochils, and Tibberchindy, Aberdeensh., 1523 Toberchenze, 'well of Kenneth.'

AUCHEN Cas. (Moffat). G. *achan,* 'banks.'

AUCHENAIRN (Glasgow). Prob. = AUCHENCAIRN, *c* lost by aspiration.

AUCHENBOWIE (Stirling). 1329 Auchinbothy, 1483 -bowy. G. *achadh an botha*, here in loc., 'field with the house.'

AUCHENCAIRN (S. Kirkcudbt.). 1305 Aghencarne. G. *achadh an càirn*, nom. *càrn*, 'field with the cairn or barrow.'

AUCHENCLOICH (Kilmarnock), AUCHENCLOY (Stoneykirk). 'Field with the boulder stone,' G. *cloiche*, nom. *clach*, *cloch*.

AUCHENCROW, -CRAW (Ayton). *Sic* 1510, but 1202–81 Aldengrave; also -krawe, *c*. 1230 Hauchincrew, 1298 Aldencraw. AUCHENCRUIVE (Ayr and Dumbarton). Du. A. 1208 Hackencrow. Ay. A. now pron. Edincraw. Anglian influence has mingled Eng. or Lowl. Sc. *haugh* with G. *achadh*, 'field.' However, the name orig. is G. *alld an craoibhe*, 'glen or burn with the trees.' *Cf*. BUNCHREW.

AUCHENDINNY (Penicuik). 1335 Aghendini. AUCHINDINNY (Gartly). 'Field of refuge,' G. *dion*, *-a*, or 'of the flowers, daisies,' *dithein*, here in loc. But *cf*. ARDENTINNY.

AUCHENFEDDRICK, -RIG (Glencairn). 'Field of Patrick,' G. *Padruig*.

AUCHENGANE (Falkirk). 1458 Duae ('two') Auchingavennis, *Pont* Achingein. 'Field of the yearling cattle, stirks,' G. *nan gamhna*, sing. *gamhainn*.

AUCHENGRAY (Carnwath, Dalry, Ayrsh. and Kirkcudbt.). Dal. A. *Pont* Achingray, 1610 -grie, and now -gree. 'Field of the herd,' G. *greagh*, *greighe*. *Cf*. Drumgray, Airdrie, and IRONGRAY.

AUCHENHEATH (Lanark). Prob. 'field of birch,' G. *an bheith*, nom. *beath*, *beith*, *b* lost by aspiration.

AUCHENMALG Bay (Wigtown). *Pont* -inmalg. G. *mealg*, 'milt of a fish.' The name might refer to the manuring of the field.

AUCHINBLAE (Fordoun). 1506 -inblay. Prob. 'field of the flowers or blooms.' Auchin- and -en often interchange, both representing the art. *an* or *na*, 'of the.'

AUCHINCREOCH (Kinross). 'March, boundary field,' G. *crioch*. *Cf*. CRIECH.

AUCHINCRUVE (Ayr, Kirkcudbt.). See AUCHENCROW. But -cruive may also be fr. G. *cruibha*, 'paw, hoof,' from the field's shape. *Cf*. Dalcruive, Methven.

AUCHINDACHY (Keith). Here pron. Auchínachie, hence the fairly common surname, 'Field of the meeting' or 'the fastness,' G. *dàil*, *dàlach*, or simply, 'in the plain,' *dail*, *dalach*. DALLACHY, Aberdour, is also called Daichy.

AUCHINDOIR (Alford). 'Field of the grove,' G. *doire*, or 'of the chase or diligent search,' *toir*.

AUCHINGILL (Wick). Pron. Oukin-. 1410 Ochyn-. 'Hawk's gill' or 'gap.' O.N. *hauka gil.* Name also found in Iceland. Gill may mean 'ravine' or 'little bay.'

AUCHINHOVE (Grange, Moray). 1574 -hovis; *cf.* 1430 Auchinhufe, Kilburnie. 'Field of the cave,' G. *na h 'uamha.* *Cf.* Glenhove, -huve, Cumbernauld, with several caves, and CULTENHOVE.

AUCHINLECK (Ayrsh., Newton Stewart, etc.). Ay. A. *a.* 1239 Auchinlec, 'field of the flat- or tomb-stone.' Same as Affleck, Lesmahagow and Monikie, 1296 Aghelek. Also name of an old estate in Kyle.

AUCHINLEYS (Ayr, Perth). 'Field of the glimmering light' or 'torch,' G. *leus.*

AUCHINLOCHAN (Tighnabruaich). G. 'field of the little loch.'

AUCHINTORLIE (Bowling). *Sic* 1541. 'Field of Sorlie' or Somerled, G. *t'Somhairle*, *t* has eclipsed *s.*

AUCHINVALLEY (Kilsyth). 'Field of the village,' G. *an bhaile*—'township field.'

AUCHLECKS (Blair Atholl), 'Field of the flat stone' or 'tomb,' G. *leac.*

AUCHMACHAR (Deer). *c.* 1150 *Bk. Deer* Achad Madchor. 'Field of St. Machorius,' see MACHAR.

AUCHMACOY (Ellon). 'Field of Mackay,' G. *mac Aoidh.* But in Argyle Mackay is Macàidh.

AUCHMEDDEN (Aberdour, Abdn.). 'Middle field,' G. *miadhon,* 'the middle.' *Cf.* Middlefield, Falkirk, and PITMEDDEN.

AUCHMITHIE (Arbroath). 1434 Achmuthy. 'Field of the herd,' G. *muthaidh.*

AUCHMULL (Aberdeen). 'Bare field,' G. *maol,* 'bald, bare.'

AUCHNAGATT (Old Deer). 'Field of the wild cat,' G. *cat.* *Cf.* Carnagat, Ulster.

AUCHNARROW (Moray). 'Field of corn,' G. *arbh.* *Cf.* YARROW.

AUCHNASHEEN (Ross-sh.). 1548- schene. 'Field of the foxgloves,' G. *sion,* or 'of the stormy weather,' *sìan, sìne.* *Cf.* Auchensheen, Dalbeattie.

AUCHTARSIN (L. Rannoch). 'Oblique field,' G. *tarsuinn.* *Cf.* Ben TARSUINN and Pennytersan, Kilmacolm.

AUCHTERARDER (Perthsh.). *c.* 1200 Eohterardeuar, Vchterardouere, 1295 Eutrearde, Outreart, 1330 Huchtirardor, 1597 Ochterardour. G. *uachdar àrd dobhair,* 'upland of the high stream,' W. *uchdar* (fr. *uch,* 'above'), 'top, summit.' The 1295 forms are Eng. bad shots! *Cf.* ABERARDER. AUCHTERAIVE (Ft. Augustus) may be Pict., *uchdar tref,* 'upland of the house', *cf.* THRIEVE.

AUCHTERDERRAN (Kirkcaldy). 'Upland with the thickets or groves,' G. *doirean.*

AUCHTERGAVEN (Perth). 1296 Ostergavene (Eng. scribe's spelling), Ogtergeven, *a.* 1300 Huctirgauen, 1336 Aughtregauen. 'Upland of the sticks,' G. *gamhainn.* *Cf.* AUCHENGANE.

AUCHTERHOUSE (Dundee). *c.* 1235 Hutyrhuse, 1245 Hwuchtyruus, *c.* 1375 Ouchtirhouse; -house, here pron. hoos, is G. *fhuathais,* 'field of the spectre or bogle.' Cf. AULDHOUSE and WYVIS.

AUCHTERLESS (Turriff). *a.* 1300 Ochthrelyss, *c.* 1280 Uchterless, 1364 Othyrles. 'Highland with the enclosure,' G. *lios.*

AUCHTERMUCHTY (Fife). 1204–14 Vchtermukethin, 1250 Hucdirmukedi, *c.* 1290 Hichermakedi, 1293 Utermokerdy, 1294 Utremukerty. Prob. 'height, rising of the swine-herd,' G. *mucair,* with -ty or -dy termin. as in CROMARTY. Forms 1293–94 give the Eng. pron. to this day!

A(U)CHTERNEED (Strathpeffer). 1447 Wethirnyde, 1499 Ouctirnede, 1619 Ochterneid. Perh. 'upland with the nests,' G. *neade, nid.* W. doubtfully connects this *uachdar nìad* with W. *nant,* 'a valley.' With form 1447, *cf.* Ballywater, 'upper town,' Wexford.

AUCHTERSTRUTHER (Largo). *c.* 1150 Ochter-. Perh. 'upland like a cart-saddle,' G. *srathair.* But *cf.* ANSTRUTHER.

AUCHTERTOOL (Kirkcaldy). 1174 Ochtertule, *a.* 1200 Octretul, *c.* 1240 Huctartule, 1289 Houthyrtullech. This last must be G. *uachdar tulaich,* 'top of the hill.' Yet W. may be right in connecting with a man *Tuathal* or Toole.

AUCHTOGORM (Moray). G. *ochdamh gorm,* 'green eighth' of a davoch. *Cf.* OCTAVULLIN and DAVA.

AUCHTOSE (Lesmahagow). 'Field above,' G. *tuas.*

AUCHTRIEVANE (Kirkmabreck). G. *uachdarach* (here in loc.) *bhàn,* 'white upland.'

AUCHTYFARDLE (Lesmachagow). 1662 Auchterfardel. G. *uachdar fardail,* 'upland of the detention or delay.'

AUGUSTUS, Ft. (L. Ness). Founded 1716, and so called, 1730, by Genl. Wade, after Wm. *Augustus,* Duke of Cumberland. Its G. name is Kilchumein, 'church of St. *Cumin,*' abbot of Iona, 7th cny.

AULASARY (N. Uist). '*Olaf's* shieling,' G. *airigh.*

AULDBAR (Forfar). 1250 Aldbar. G. *alld barra,* 'burn by the height.'

AULDEARN (Nairn). 1238 Aldheren, *c.* 1340 Aldyrne. G. *alld Eireann,* 'stream, den of the EARN.' *Cf. Reg. St. Andr.* ann. 954, Ulurn.

AULDGIRTH (Dumfries). 'Old garden,' N. *garth.* *Cf.* next and APPLEGARTH, 1578 Aplegirth.

AULDHAME (N. Berwick). 1094 Aldeham. O.E. *ald hám*, 'old house.'

AULDHOUSE (Pollokshaws). 1265 Terra de Auldhus, -house. Now a burn crossed by Bogles' Bridge. Early corrup. of G. *alld fhuathais*, 'burn of the spectre or bogle.' *Cf.* AUCHTERHOUSE.

AULISTON Pt. (Sound of Mull). Natives say, G. *rudha nan amhlaistean*, 'point of the difficulties or troubles,' var. of *amhluadh*, 'trouble.' It may be N. *Olafstein*, 'Olaf's rock.' *Cf.* AULASARY.

AULTBEA (Poolewe). Pron. -bay. G. *allt beath*, 'glen with birches.'

AULTNAPADDOCK (Glass). 'Glen or burn of spectres or clowns,' G. *bodach*, influenced by Eng. *paddock*, 'a toad.' But perh. 'burn of the thirsty,' G. *padhach*.

AULTYORN (Moray). G. *allt eorna*, 'barley burn.'

AVEN, Water, Kincardine, R., Lanark, L. and Ben, Banff. See AVON.

AVERNISH (Lochalsh). 'Oats ness,' O.N. *hafre*, Da *havre*, M.E. *haver*, 'oats.' *Cf.* ARDALANISH.

AVICH (Lorn). *Sic* 1589, but 1297 Awath (*t* scribe's error for *c*). Doubtful. ? N. *á vík*, 'river bay'; *cf.* Avik, Lewis. Perh. G. *amhach*, *-aich*, 'neck of land.'

AVIEMORE (Kingussie). 1654 Avimoir. Not really G. *abh mòr*, 'big river,' the Spey, but now in G. *agaidh mhòr*, prob. 'big hill-face.' Blargie, Badenoch, 1603 Blairovey, shows a like change; and the same ending is seen in Dalmigavie, Strathearn, G. *dail Mhigeaghaidh*.

AVOCH (Cromarty). *c.* 1333 Auauch, 1481 Avauch, 1493 Alvach, 1580 Awach. Now pron. Auch. O.G. *abh-ach*, 'river place.'

AVON, R. (Linlithgow and Banff), and L. (Ben Macdhui). The L. is pron. A'an, the Linl. R. is prob. *O.E. Chron.*, ann. 710 Haefe, *c.* 1128 Avin. Ba. A. *Sim. Durham*, ann. 756 Ovania, *c.* 1190 Strathouen. G. *abhuinn*, 'river,' W. *afon*. For Antona, Tacitus, *Ann.*, xii. 31, now Avon, trib. of R. Severn, read Aufona. Same root is seen in Segu-*ana*, the Seine, Guadi-*ana*, Spain. Dan-*ube* and Punj-*aub* ('five rivers'). Evan, Tweeddale, is also the same, so is Oun-dle, N'hants; see also AVEN. Five Avons in England.

AWE, L. and R. (Argyll). Former in G. *ou* or ow, latter, G. *atha* or āh. *a.* 700, *Adamn.*, Aba, 1292 Lochaue, 1304 Lochaua, 1322 Louchaby, 1361 Lochawa, 1580 fluvius et lacus Avus, 1682 Owe. The L. is prob. O.G. *abh*, W. *aw*, 'water'; *cf.* Eu, Normandy, *c.* 1110 Owe. The R. is prob. same root as G. *ath*, 'ford, shallow part of a river.'

AWELLS (Polmont). Prob. O.E. *æwiell*, 'river spring.' *Cf.* the Eng. Awell and 3 Ewells; also *a.* 1328 *R.M.S.* Awelochis, Carrick.

AYR, town and county take name from the R. *a.* 1177 Ar, 1197, Are, *c.* 1230 Air, *c.* 1400 Aare. O.N. *eyri*, 'tongue of land, gravelly bank.'

AYTON (Berwick and Abernethy, Perth). Be. A. 1098 Eitun, 1250 Aytun. Town on R. EYE. *Cf.* the Aytons, Yorks, *Dom.* Atun, *c.* 1160 Etona, prob. fr. O.E. *éa*, M.E. *oe*, 'running stream.'

BABERTON (Colinton, Gogar). Co. B. 1335 Kilbaberton. Difficult. Kil- in 1335 may be Dan. *Kilde*, 'a well,' and Baber- may be for *Badburh*, a woman, seen in Babraham, Cambs.

BACK (Lewis, burn S. of Hawick). G. *bac*, 'a bank,' same root as O.E. *bœc*, O.N. *bak*, 'back,' O. Icel. *bakki*, 'a ridge,' Dan. *bakke*, Sw. *backe*, 'a hill, hillock.'

BACKIES (Golspie and Glenbuchat, Aberdn.). As above, with dimin. and Eng. pl. -es. *Cf.* The Lochies, Burntisland.

BADANTOIG (Glengarry). 1512 -intawag, 1785 Battenteog. G. *badan t'seobhaig*, 'thicket of the hawk.'

BADDINSGILL (Peebles). 1410–11 Baldwynesgille. 'Gill, narrow dale of *Baldwin*'; *cf.* baldric and baudric. 'Baldwinus the Fleming' occurs in a local deed, *c.* 1150.

BADENLONGART (Badenoch). G. *bad an longairt*, 'thicket of the camp or shieling.' *Cf.* LUNCARTY.

BADENOCH (S. Inverness). 1229 -nach, 1290 -naghe, *c.* 1300 -nau, Baunagd, 1372 Baydenach, 1522 Badzenoch. Early forms suggest G. *badanach*, 'bushy place,' but later ones and the mod. pron. báh-janach, make it G. *bàidheanach*, 'marshy land,' fr. *bàdh*, 'to drown' (M.). *Cf.* LOCHABER, which is *Adamn.* Stagnum Aporicum.

BADENSCOTH (Auchterless). Looks like G. *badan sgothu*, 'little thicket like a boat.' But W. derives fr. obs. G. *scoth*, 'flowers.'

BADICAUL (Lochalsh), BADCALL (Applecross, Rosskeen). G. *bada call*, 'hazel clump or thicket.'

BAD-NA-CARBAD (Assynt). G., 'spot (thicket) of the bier, where the mourners halted for refreshment.' *Cf.* UISKENTUIE.

BADYCHARK (Leochel). G. *bad a' choirce*, 'grove among the oaks,' G. *coirc*.

BAILLIESTON (Glasgow). Quite modern.

BAINSFORD (Falkirk). *Sic* 1785, 1797, 'Briansford commonly called Bainsford.' This connexion with Sir Briande Jay, slain here in the bog in the battle of Falkirk, 1298, seems quite fanciful. The Pest Burn once flowed through here, and the name's origin may have been as in next.

BAINSHOLE (Insch). From a man *Bain*.

BALACLAVA (Johnstone, Portmahomack). Jo. B., a village founded 1856, two years after the famous Charge. Po. B.'s old name was Balnuig, 'village on the bay.'

BALADO (Kinross). G. *bail*, *-e*, 'village, farm, house'; *cf.* Sc. use of toun. The root is common in Ir. and Manx but not in W. names. The -ado is G. *fhada*, 'long'; *cf.* ADVIE and Ben ATTOW. Wester, Middle and Easter B. all lie along the same straight road.

BALAGIECH (S. Renfrew). Prob. G. *bail an gheoidh*, 'village of the goose.'

BALBEGGIE (Perth, Dysart). 'Little village,' G. *beag*, here in loc.

BALBIRNIE (Markinch). *Sic* 1517 but *c.* 1170 -berny, *a.* 1266 Balebranin. 'Village of *Brendain* or *Brandon*.' See KILBINNIE.

BALBLAIR (3 in Ross-sh.). 'Village in the plain,' G. *blàr*.

BALCAITHLY (Denino, Fife). 'Village, farm of the seeds or chaff,' G. *càithlich*. But *cf.* PITKEATHLY.

BALCANQUEL, -QUHAL (Strathmiglo). Pron. Bakánkal or Bawcónkill, 1294 Balmaccancolle, 1414 Balmacancoll, 1490 Balcancole. Seems abnormal. Prob. 'village at the prow or tapering extremity,' G. *ceann -caol*, here in nom., though one expects gen.; *ma* should be *na* or *an*, 'of the.' But *ma* makes one think of the pet name of some st. None likely seems known.

BALCARRES (Colinsburgh). Seems 'village at the rocky place,' G. *carrais*, *-ais* being common Pict. ending.

BALCARY Pt. (Kirkcudbt.). Prob. 'village at the mound or bank,' G. *cairidh*.

BALCASKIE (Anstruther). 1296 -caski. Seems 'village of the stopping or checking,' G. *casgaidh*.

BALCOMIE (Crail). 1253 -colmy. Prob. 'village of St. *Colman*,' prob. a 7th cny. Northumbrian.

BALCONY (Kiltearn). 1297 -conie, keny, 1333 -kenny, 'village of *Coinneach* or *Kenneth*,' perh. a friend of Columba. Some say the G. now is Bailcòmhnuidh, 'the residence.' W. is sure it is Bailcnidh, G. *bailc*, 'strong,' with extension as in DELNY.

BALCRISTIE (Newburn, Fife). *a.* 1100 Ballecristin, *c.* 1150 Belacristin. Prob. 'village of the Christian,' O.E. *Cristen*.

BALDERNOCK (Milngavie). *c.* 1200 Buthirnok, 1238 -ernokis, 1745 Badernock. O.G. *buth*, G. *both*, 'house,' then *bail*, 'village,' *airneag*, 'among the sloes.' *Cf.* BALQUHIDDER, and Incharnock, Moray, 'links (G. *innis*) with the sloes.'

BALDOVIE (Broughty Ferry). 'Poor hamlet,' G. *doimh*, here in loc.

BALDRAGON (Broughty Ferry). Pron. -draygon. 'Hamlet among the thorns,' G. *draighionn*.

BALELIE (Denino, Fife). 'Other farm,' G. *eile*, contrasted with BALCAITHLY.

BALERNO (Edinburgh). 1289 -nauch. 'Barley farm,' G. *eòrnach*.

BALFÓUR (Markinch, 2 in Angus, Kirkwall). Ma. B. 1187 Balfor, 1219 -fur, 1304 -fure. The -four is Pict., cognate with W. *pawr*, Bret. *peur*, 'pasture land.' *Cf.* Delfour, 1569 Dallefour, Kincraig, Inchfuir, E. Ross, and TRINAFOUR.

BALFRON (Stirlingsh.). *a.* 1300 Bafrone, 1303 Buthbrene, 1503 Buthrane. G. *bail*, 'hamlet,' or O.G. *buth*, G. *both*, 'house' (*cf.* BALDERNOCK) and prob. *fraon*, 'place of shelter among hills.' But commonly said to be 'house of mourning,' *bhròin*.

BALFUNNING (Drymen). *a.* 1300 Buchmonyn. 'Hamlet' or 'house' (*cf.* above) of the heaths or hills, G. *monadhean*, with *m* aspirated to *f* as in W., not in G. For the -ing *cf.* Ardinning, Strathblane, G. *àrd dunain*.

BALGARNIE (once in Perth and Inverness). 1285 Ballygernauch, 1306 -garnach, 1365 Balghigernache. G. *baile gearnach*, 'discontented village.'

BALGEDIE (Kinross). 'Village with the bit of arable land,' G. *geadaig*, here in loc.

BALGONIE (Markinch, Aberdeen). Ma. B. 1163 -gone, Ab. B. prob. *a.* 1300 Palgoveny, 1487 Balgowny, 'Village of the smith,' G. *gobhann*. But BALGONE (E. Lothian), 1337 -negon, is G. *bail an gcon*, 'Hounds' farm.' The -ie is sign of the loc.

BALGOWAN (Perth, etc.) = BALGONIE.

BALHARVIE (Kinross). 'Village of the bull,' G. *tharbh*, here in loc. But Achinhervie, Kilmaurs, will be fr. *airbhe, eirbhe*, 'a well.'

BALINTORE (Fearn, Kirkhill, Abriachan). G. *bail an todhair*, 'bleaching village,' where flax was cultivated. *Cf.* the Ir. Ballitore and Tintore.

BALISHARE (Lochmaddy). N. *bals eyri*, 'gravelly spit or point with the beacon,' N. *bál*. *Cf.* Alisary, L. Aylort.

BALLACHULISH (N. Argyll). Pron. -hóolish, 1552 -echeles. 'Village on the straits,' G. *chaolais*, fr. *caol*, 'narrow.' *Cf.* EDDRACHILIS.

BALLANTRAE (S. Ayr). 'Village on the shore,' G. *traigh*. *Cf.* Ballintrae, Antrim.

BÁLLATER (Deeside). Prob. G. *bealaidh tìr*, 'broom land.'

BALLÉNDRICK (Br. of Earn). 1779 -enrick, 1827 Ballendra. G. *bail anrach*, 'stormy village.' For intrusive *d cf.* ENDRICK. It may be c. 1260 *chart.* Ballindurich. If so, G. *bail an duraidh*, 'hamlet by the water.' *Cf.* DURIE.

BALLIKINRAÍN (Killearn). *Sic* 1680, but 1441 Ballekyrrain, *Pont* -achendrain, -ekendrain. G. *bealach*, 'pass' or *bail*, 'hamlet,' *a' chinn rainn*, 'at the head of the division.'

BALLINDÁLLOCH (Moray, Balfron). Mo. B. *c.* 1300 and Ba. *c.* 1238 Balinodalach, 1508 -indaulach, 'Village in the field,' G. *dail*, gen. *dalach*.

BALLINDEAN (Fife, Inchture). Fi. B. 1459 -dain. BELLENDEAN (10 mls. W. of Hawick). Pron. -teén. These are the origin of the surnames Bellenden, *sic* 1486, and Ballantine, -tyne. In 1531 Archdeacon Bellenden is called Ballentyne, *a.* 1615 Adam Ballendene, Falkirk. Often confused with (PT.) BANNATYNE. W. thinks, G. *bail an deadhain*, 'the Dean's stead.' But Ballindean, Inchture, is just beside B. Hill, so prob. *bail an duìn*, 'village by the hill,' which phonet. would more easily give -den and -tyne. The official *dean* is not found in Eng. till *c.* 1330 *dene*, and G. *deadhan* must be later. The local DEAN clearly influenced the endings.

BALLINDORE (Muckairn). 'Village of the stranger,' G. *Dearaidh*, now Dewar, surname of St. Maelrubha.

BALLINGALL (Kinross, 2 Fife). 1294 -negal, 1590 Bamgall, 'Village of the stranger or Lowlander,' G. *gall*. *Cf.* Baligal, Melvich.

BALLINGRY (Lochgelly). Pron. Bíngry. *a.* 1400 -yngry. Perh. 'farm of the flock,' G. *greigh, -e*.

BALLINLUIG (Pitlochry). 'Village in the hollow,' G. *lag, luig*.

BALLINTUIM (Blairgowrie). 'Village on the knoll,' G. *tom, tuim*. Tuam, Ireld., is fr. Ir. *túaimm*, 'a grave.'

BALLOAN, -LONE (4, Ross-sh.). 1479 -lone, 'Village in the damp meadow,' G. *lòn, lòin*.

BALLOCH (L. Lomond, etc.). L. B. *c.* 1213 rí Bealaigh, 1238 Bellach, *c.* 1370 le Balach. Also *c.* 1190 near Abernethy, Perth, Belach, and 1570, Taymouth, Balloch. G. *bealach*, W. *bwlch*, 'a gap, a pass.'

BALLOCHMYLE (Mauchline). 'Bare pass,' G. *maol*. *Cf.* Craigmyle, Glassel.

BALLYGRANT (Islay) = GRANTSHOUSE, G. *baile*. But McKinnon thought the true name, *bail a' ghrànda*, 'village by the ugly ford' (*ath*).

BALLYGRINDLE (Lismore). 'Farm with a good foundation' or 'frugal, economical,' G. *grunndhail*.

BALLYMENACH (Arran). 'Middle farm,' G. *meadhonach*.

BALLYNAN STINBHAICH (Blair Athole). 'Farm with the cowsheds awry,' G. *nan staoin bàthaich*.

BALLYNAVIN (Perthsh.). 'Village on the River,' G. *abhuinn, aibhne*.

BALLYOUKAN (Pitlochry), 'Village with the graves,' G. *uaghaichean*, pl. of *uagh*.

BALMACARRA (Lochalsh). 1548 Ballimacroy, 1554 -amaccara, 1574 -emakcarrane. There has been confusion. W. thinks, 'village of Mac Carra,' the sons of Carra or Ara.

BALMACLELLAN (New Galloway). *Sic* 1505, 'Village of John Maclellan,' whose charter dates 1466. *Cf.* 1183 *Chart. Dunferml.* Balmacglenin, 'of M'Lennan.'

BALMAGHÍE (Cas. Douglas). *Cf.* 1420 Balmeceth, -magye, Fife, 'Village of M'Ghie,' var. of Mackie.

BALMAHÁ (L. Lomond). *Pont.* -macha, 'Village of St. *Maha* or *Mahew*,' companion of St. Patrick. St. Maha's Well is near by.

BALMANNO (Abernethy, Perth). 1312 -managhe, 1488 -mannoch. Prob. 'farm abounding in kids,' G. *meannach.* For the -o *cf.* BALERNO and CRAIGO.

BALMASHANNER (Forfar). *a.* 1400 -moschenore, 1439 -maschener. Prob. 'village of my dear bard or elder,' G. *ma seanair.* *Cf.* p. 67.

BALMERINO (N. Fife). Pron. Bamérnie. *c.* 1200 Balmerinach, 1227 -morinach, 1629 -merinoch. Might be 'wanton, drunken village,' G. *mearanach.* But prob. fr. St. *Merinach* who accompanied St. Regulus to St. Andrew's. St. Merino's Croft, Barry, belonged to the Abbey here.

BALMÓRAL (Deeside). 1451 Bouchmorale. Looks like O.G. *buth,* G. *both* (*cf.* BALDERNOCK) or *bail,* 'village' and *mòral,* 'majestic.' In G. to-day it is Baile mhòireir, 'laird's dwelling.' (W.) But M. said, Moral is Pict. for 'big clearing,' W. *ial,* 'open space.'

BALMUCHIE (Fearn). 1529 -mochi. 'At the farm of the swine,' G. *muc,* here in loc., Corn. *moch,* W. *mochyn,* 'a pig.' The form -mochi seems Pict.

BALMUNGO (St. Andrew's). 'House of (St.) *Mungo,*' pet name of St. Kentigern.

BALNAB (2 Galloway, Islay). 'Village of the abbot,' G. *ab, aba.* The Gall. ones are Whithorn and Saulseat Priories. *Cf.* Lochanabb, Kildonan.

BALNABRUAICH (E. Ross, etc.). G. for 'village on the bank.' *Cf.* TIGHNABRUAICH.

BALNAGOWAN (Invergordon, Appin). In B. 1375 -negoun, 1475 -nagovin, 1490 -gown. 'Smith's village' = BALGONIE. Here, as sometimes in G. place-names, we have a wrong gender, for *na* is fem., *an* masc., for 'the.' However BALNAGOWN, Urray, is 1476 Ballingovnie.

BALNAKILL (Kintyre). 'Village of the church,' G. *ceall, cill.*

BALQUHATSTON (Slamannan). *Pont* Banhatstain, Hybrid. G. *bail an chat,* 'farm of the wild cat' (*cf.* BANKNOCK), and Sc. *stane,* Eng. *stone.*

BALQUHIDDER (Perthsh.). *Sic* 1536, but 1266 Buffudire. *c.* 1268 Buchfydir, *c.* 1272 Butfuder, 1304 Boffodyr. Prob. 'fodder farm.' G. *fuidir*, fr. Eng. *fodder*. *Cf.* BALDERNOCK, BUCHANAN, and Balquhidderock, Stirling, 1471 Buquadrok, fr. G. *fhodarach*, 'abounding in fodder or straw.' G. *bail* and *both*, *buth*, often interchange.

BALRUDDERY (Forfar). 1513 -rudree, 1546 -dry. 'Place of the rider or knight,' G. *ridere* loaned fr. O.E. *rídere*. *Cf.* Kilruddery, Bray.

BALRYMONTH Hill, E. and W. (St. Andrew's). 1141 Balri-, Barrimund. 'Village on the royal hill,' see KILRIMONT.

BALSHÁGR(A)Y (Partick). 1515 -shagre. Perh. 'village, farm of the withered flock,' G. *seaca graighe*. *Cf.* AUCHENGRAY.

BALSUSNEY (Kirkcaldy). Pron. -sísney. *c.* 1560 -sussnie. Prob. 'village of the Englishman,' G. *Sassunach*. *Cf.* Carsawsen, Cornwall, but also BLAIRCESSNOCK.

BALTA Sound (Shetland). *Sagas* Balt(a)ey, 'belt isle,' O.N. *balti*, Dan. *baelt*, and *ey*, *ay*, *a*, 'island.' Some derive fr. *Balti*, a man found in Shetland in 13th cny.

BALTHANGIE (Aberdeensh.). 'House of thanks,' G. *tang*, *thaing*, here in loc.

BALTHAYOCK (Kinfauns). 'House of the guest or visitor, an inn,' G. *tathach*, *thathaich*, 'visitor.' Cf. Tayock, Montrose.

BALVENIE (Dufftown). *c.* 1200 -begno. Doubtful. Perh. fr. *Baine*, daughter of the K. of Alban, *Four Masters*, p. 10.

BALWEARIE (Kirkcaldy). 1247 and always, *Reg. Dunferml.* -weri. Also near by, 1386 *R. M. S.* Balgeuery. W. says, fr. G. *geamhraidh*, 'winter,' good wintering place. But as likely fr. G. *iarach* (here in loc.), 'western.' *Cf.* Blaw and Castle Weary, Galloway.

BAMFLAT (Biggar). *Old* Bowflat, 'plain for cattle,' see BOWLAND. Bam may be for *bean*; like change is seen in Bamboro'.[1] Northbld and BALLINGALL become Bamgall. *Flat* sb. occurs as early as *c.* 1200 *Coldstrm. chart.* Kaldstre' flat.

BÁNAVIE (Ft. William). 1461 Banvy. G. Banabhidh. M. said, 'place of pigs,' Ir. *banbh*, 'sucking pig.' *Cf.* Banavie burn, Blair Atholl, G. Bainbhigh, and L. Vanaire, near L. Shin. Not 'Vicus Bannavem,' *c.* 450 Patrick's *Confessions*.

BANCHORY DEVENICK and TERNAN (Deeside). *a.* 1300 Banchery defnyk, 1361 -chory deveny; *a.* 1300 Bancheritarny, 1481 -quhori-terne; also 1164 Benchorin. G. *beannachar*, 'place of peaks,' *beannach*, 'peaked, pinnacled'; same as Bangor, Wales (*c.* 1120 Banchor) and Ireland, Ir. *bennchor*, 'row of points,

[1] It is 709 *Eddi*—Bebbanburg.

circle of peaks,' W. *bangor*, 'an upper row of rods, a coping, battlement.' Its L. adj. is in *Ulst. Ann.* 671 Maelrubha Benchorensis. *Cf.* Beannacher, 1603 Benchar, Kingussie, and L. Beannachar, Ross-sh. 1479 Benquharene, 1508 Kinloch Banquhar, 1571 Beancharan ; also 1471 *Excheq. R.* Tulibanquhara, Perthsh. The -y in Banchory is the old loc. VENNACHAR is the same. Devenick is fr. St. *Devinicus*, prob. contemporary of Columba, who worked in Caithness, perh. seen also in Landewednack, The Lizard. St. *Ternan*, *a.* 500, was a Pict. convert of Ninian, then abbot of Bangor, Co. Down.

BANFF. *a.* 1150 *Bk Deer*, Banb, *c.* 1136 Banef, 1290 Bamphe, 1291 Banffe. *Banba* in Ir. Nennius, was a W. or Ir. queen, said to have come fr. Scotland. *Banbha* is also an early poetic name for Ireland. K. Meyer, with no strong evidence, favoured this derivation. Quite possibly, Ir. *banb*, 'a sucking pig,' so perh. a relic of totemism ; *cf.* Bannow, Wexford, and Bamff, Perthsh.

BANGÓUR (W. Lothian). 1335 Bengouer. G. *beinn gobhar*, 'hill of goats.'

BANKNOCK (Dennyloanhd). 1510 Ballinknok. G. *bail an cnoc*, *cnuic*, 'village on the knoll.' Near by is the similar BANKIER, 1510 Ballinkeyre, 'village by the fort,' G. *cathair*, W. *caer*. It is near the Roman Wall.

BÁNNACHRA (Balloch). 1489 -achar. Prob. = BANCHORY and VENNACHAR.

BANNOCKBURN (Stirling). *Sic* 1314 but 1215 Vtred (*i.e.*, Auchter), Banoc, 1494 Bannokysborne. Prob. Brit. *ban oc*, 'white) shining stream,' as in Ock, see *Pl. N. Eng.* s.v. A Welsh Life of St. Cadoc speaks of Mons Bannauc (O.W. for W. *bannog*, 'peaked, horned' hill), which may have been in this region ; and W. connects the burn with this. The grounds seem slender. It is abnormal to derive, as many have, fr. O.E., *bannuc*, 'a bannock,' as in Ach ta bannock, Urray. There seems no analogy for such an early Eng. stream name.

BANTASKIN (Falkirk). *Sic* 1774, but 1450 Pettintostale, 1451 -toskale, 1497 Pettentoskane, 1617 Pantaskin, 1745 Pen-. A name much confused. Prob. orig. Pict. G. *pett an t'soisgeil*, 'croft of the gospel,' ? once a glebe to a priest. *Cf.* near Brechin *c.* 1470 Pettintoscall, 1461 Pantoscal, 1463 -oscane, and Godscroft. But *pett an tosgail* or *tostail* means 'croft of arrogance,' a strange name. For *pett an* become Pan-, Pen-, *cf.* PENDRIECH.

BANTÓN (Denny). *Pont* Bantoin. W. thinks, G. *bail an toìne*, 'farm on the rump or bluntly rounded ridge.' *Cf.* BANKNOCK.

BARCÁLDINE Cas. (N. Argyll). G. *barr calltuinn*, 'height of the hazels.' *Cf.* CALTON.

BAR-, BARNDANNOCH (Glencairn). 1593 Bardannoch, *Pont* Barnedannoche. 'Height of the fastness,' G. *daighneaich*.

BARDOWIE (Baldernock). 'Black, dark height,' G. *dubh*, here in loc.

BARDRISHACH (Argyll). 'Height covered with brambles,' G. *driseach*, fr. *dris*, 'bramble, brier.' *Cf.* Portdrishaig, Tighnabruaich.

BAREMMAN (Rosneath). 'Height of *Adamnan*,' see p. 68.

BARGEDDIE (Coatbridge). 'Height with the little croft,' G. *geadaig*.

BARGRENNAN (Newt. Stewart). 'Height of the summer house or sunny spot,' G. *grianain*. *Cf.* Arngrennan, Tungland.

BARJARG (Closeburn). 'Red height,' G. *dhearg*.

BARLINNIE (Glasgow). 'Height with the pool,' G. *linne*.

BARMEKIN of ECHT (S.E. Aberdeen). B. is the outer rampart or barbican of a castle, also a turret, found *c.* 1340 *barmeken*. *N.E.D.* says, perh. fr. O.N. *barm -r*, 'brim, border, wing of a castle,' but cannot explain -kin, perh. a dimin. See ECHT.

BARNAICH (N. Ayrsh. and Alva). G. *bàirneach*, 'a limpet,' name of a house clinging to the hillside.

BARNBOGLE (Dalmeny). Perh. *c.* 1177 *Lennox Chart.* Berenbouell, *c.* 1320 Prenbowgal, 1481 Berenbougale. Orig. Brit. *pren*, 'tree,' then G. *barr an*, 'height of the,' *buaigheail*, 'cowstall.' But BARNBAUCHLE, Galloway, will be fr. *buachaille*, 'of the shepherd.'

BARNÉGO (Dunipace). Perh. *c.* 1177 *Lennox Chart.* Brenego, 1503 Byrnago, 1510 Bar-, *Pont* Barnegy. 'Height of the stallion,' G. *an aigich*. For -o *cf.* BALERNO, etc.

BARNEYWATER (Kirkcudbt.). G. *bearna uachdar*, 'upper pass or cleft.' *Cf.* AUCHTERNEED.

BARNHILL. Several, may all be plain Eng. But BARNHILLIE, Kirkcudbt., *old* Barnkylie, is G. *barr na coille*, 'height with the wood.'

BARNSHOT (Colinton). *Old*, 'the barnshot.' *Shot* is O.E. *sceata*, 'angle, nook, bit of land,' as in Aldershot, etc.

BARNTON (Edinburgh). *c.* 1400 Berntoun, 1493 Barnetoun, 'farm with the barn,' lit. 'barley-house,' O.E. *bere-ern*, M.E. *beren*.

BARNYARD (Irongray). G. *bearn àird*, 'high gap or pass,' Ir. *bearna*, 'gap, notch.' *Cf.* CRAIGIEBARNS and RAWYARDS.

BARR (S. Ayr, etc.). G. for 'top, height.' BARONE, Bute, adds *sròn*, 'point.'

BARRÁSSIE (Troon). M.E. *barras, -es*, O.Fr. *barras*, fr. *barre*, 'a bar.' 'Tilt-yard, knightly lists.'

BARRA(Y) (Out. Hebrides). *a.* 1100 *Gael. MS.* Barru, *sagas* Barey, 1292 Barrich, 1373 Barre, -ech. In 1549 the parish is Kilbarr. 'Isle,' O.N. *ay, ey,* 'of St. Barr.' See DUNBAR.

BARRHEAD and -HILL. Tautologies made by ignorant English.

BARROCK (Thurso). Dimin. of G. *barr,* 'a height.'

BARROGILL Cas. (Caithness). O.N. *baru gil,* 'wave, billow cleft or gully.'

BARRSHAW (Paisley). Hybrid. 'Height with the wood,' O.E. *scaga.*

BARSKIMMING (Mauchline). 1639 -kinning. Said to be 'height of *Simeon,*' Manx *Shimmin,* 1511–15 *Symyn. Cf.* the surname Miskimming = Mac Shimmin.

BARTHOL (Old Meldrum). 'Height over the hollow,' G. *toll, thuill,* 'a hole, hollow, crevice.'

BARVAS (Lewis). 1536 -was. Perh. N. *bára oss,* 'wan, pale river-mouth.'

BASS ROCK (N. Berwick). *a.* 1300 Bass. Also The BASS (Inverurie). Prob. G. *bathais,* 'forehead, front,' fr. the curious shape of the rock. *Cf.* BASQUHARNIE, Cairnie, 'rocky forehead,' fr. G. *càirneach,* here in loc.

BATHGATE. *c.* 1160 Bathchet, *c.* 1200 Betchet, 1250 Bathket, 1316 -getum. Brit. *bath* or *both chet,* 'house in the wood, O.W. *chet,* W. *coed. Cf.* Chetwode, Bucks, etc. For the *g cf.* Geth, earliest form of KEITH; also *cf.* PENCAITLAND.

BATTOCK Mt. (Kincardine). G. *monadh biataich,* 'hill of the raven.' But *cf.* BEATTOCK.

BAVELAW (Currie). *c.* 1240 Baueley. First syll. prob. some man's name, ? *Beowa,* one in *Onom.*; *-law* is Sc. for 'hill,' and *-ley* is *lea* or meadow.

BAYBLE (Lewis). Corrup. of N. *papa-bol,* 'priest's dwelling.' *Cf.* PAPLAY.

BEALACH COLLUSCARD (Kilmuir, Skye). Tautology, G. *bealach,* 'pass' or BALLOCH, and N. *koll-r skarð,* 'top of the pass.'

BEALACH NAM BO (Aberfoyle). G., 'pass for the cattle.' *Cf.* BALLOCH.

BEALLACHANTUIÉ (Kintyre and Applecross). Pron. -antée. 'Pass of the seat,' G. *an t'suidhe. Cf.* MEALLANTSUIDHE.

BEAM, The (farm, Bonnybridge). Prob. O.E. *béam,* 'a tree.' *Cf.* the hornbeam.

BEANCROSS (Falkirk). *Pont* Beanscorse, and now pron. Beancorse, prob. for *carse,* as it is on the CARSE of Stirling, where beans are largely grown. *Cf.* brod for board, etc.

Bearsden (Glasgow). Modern; though Scotland had bears 900 years ago. O.E. *denu*, 'den,' is akin to Eng. *dean*, Sc. *den*, 'a valley.'

Beath (Dunfermline), **Beith** (Ayr). Du. B. *c.* 1140 Beeth, Beith. Ay. B. *Taliessin* Beit, 1178 Beth. G. *beath*, *beith*, 'a birch.' Final *th* is preserved in this early name, but is lost in Aultbea.

Beattock (Moffat). G. *biod-ach*, 'sharp top place.' But Jam. says, *battock* is a piece of land between two burns, as this is.

Beauly (Inverness-sh.). In G. a 'Mhanachain, 'the Priory.' 1230 Prioratus de Bello Loco, *a.* 1300 Beaulieu, 1497 Beulie and so now pron. L. *bellus locus*, Fr. *beau lieu*, 'lovely spot.' *Cf.* Beaulieu, Hants, pron. Bewly. Monasteries in both, that in our B. founded by the monks Vallis umbrosæ, *c.* 1220. Bewlie, Belses, is the same. Beaufort Cas., *a.* 1200 Beufort, is near Beauly, 'fine castle.'

Bedrule (Jedburgh). 1275 Badrowll, 1280 Rulebethok, 1310 Bethocrulle, *a.* 1600 Bethrowll. Still at times pron. Bethorule. 'Lands on R. Rule of *Bethoc*,' wife of Randolph, first lord of manor here, *c.* 1150. *Cf. a.* 1300 *Reg. Aberdon.* Kynbethok.

Beeslack (Penicuik). 'Bee hollow,' O.N. *slakki*, 'a small, shallow valley, a dip in the ground.' *Cf.* Catslack.

Beeswing (Dumfries). Fr. a picture of *Beeswing*, famous race-horse a cny. ago, sign of a public house round which the village grew.

Begbie (Stenton, Kirkcudbt.). St. B. 1458 and Ki. B. 1537 Bagby. *c.* 1584 Baigbie, surname, E. Lothian. Prob. 'dwelling of *Bæga*, *Beagu* or *Begu*,' all 3 occur. On analogy of Crosby, 'village of the ring,' O.E. *béag*, 3 *beg*, O.N. *baug-r* is also possible; -bie is O.E. *bý*, Dan. *bæ*, by, 'dwelling, hamlet.'

Belhaven (Dunbar). 1379 -havyn. Perh. fr. Fr. *bel*, 'fine,' found in Eng. *c.* 1314. But *bell-haven* seems likely too.

Belhelvie (New Machar). 1292 Balheluy, 1293 -helwy, 1450 -helfy. Perh. G. *bail chailbhe*, 'village by the headland'; *calbh* is lit. 'a bald pate.' W. says, fr. a man *Sealbach*, as in Selvieland, Renfrew. This seems doubtful.

Belivat (Nairn). Said to be G. *buail fhiodaid*, 'fold in the thicket.'

Bellahouston (Glasgow). 1578 Ballahaustane, 1598 -owstane. G. *bail a 'cheusadain*, 'village with the crucifix.' *Cf.* Crosby. The present form is popular etymology.

Bellanoch (Crinan). Perh. G. *beul-atha nan each*, 'ford of the horses,' or *baillean-ach*, 'place full of bosses.'

Bellie (Fochabers). Perh. G. *baile*, 'village, farm.' *Cf.* Billie, Coldingham, *c.* 1400 Bilie, and 1386 Billymire.

BELL ROCK (Arbroath). From the warning bell formerly hung on the Inchcape reef.

BELLYBOUCHT Hill (Thornhill). G. *baile bochd*, 'house of the poor man.' *Cf. Reg. Neubot.*, Balnebueth, Bellyboucht, near R. Esk, Midlothn.

BELMONT (Sidlaws and Unst). Fr. *bel mont*, 'fine hill.'

BELSES (Hawick). *Pont* Belshies, and so still pron. 1541 Belsis, fr. *de Bel Assize*, a Norm. knight. Belasis, Durham, is 1300–1400 Belasise, Bellassys, Belas.

BEMERSIDE (Melrose). 'Seat, abode of the trumpeter,' O.E. *beamere, bemera*, fr. *beme*, 'a trumpet.' *Cf.* Bemerton, Salisbury; also MUIRAVONSIDE.

BENARTY Hill (Kinross). *c.* 1420 *Wyntoun* Bennarty. *Chart. St. Andr.* Cabennartye. First part = *Cæsar* Cebenna, Fr. Cevennes, W. *cefn*, 'a ridge'; second part perh. = ARTHUR. *Cf.* ARTNEY.

BENBECULA (Out. Hebrides). 1449 Beanbeacla, 1495 Bendbagle, 1549 Benvalgha, Buchagla, *c.* 1660 Benbicula; also 1535 Beandmoyll, 1542 Beanweall, prob. fr. G. *mhaoil*, 'bare height.' In G. *beinn a' bhaodla*, perh. for *na faodhail, faoghail*, or *fhaodla*, 'hill of the fords.' But how comes its present form in Eng. or in G.?

BENDERLOCH (Oban). 1304 Menderaloch, 1723 Benedera. Usually thought 'hill between (G. *eadar*) lochs' Etive and Creran; *cf.* EDDRACHILIS. Diack says, Meudarloch, 'black district.' Perh. it is *Ulst. Ann.* 735 Etarlinddu, 'between the dark lochs.'

BENDOCHY (Coupar Angus). *c.* 1130 Bendacthin, 1183 -chin, 1232 Bennacthin, 1275 Bendaghthyn. Said to be G. *beannachta*, 'the blessed'; final *n* scribal flourish. *Cf.* PT. BANNATYNE.

BENDOURAN or DOIREANN (Tyndrum). G., 'mount of storms.'

BENHÁR (N. Lanark.). 'Near hill,' G. *ghar*.

BENHOLM (Kincardine). 1262 Bennum, *c.* 1280 Benam. Doubtful through its North. site. If in England Bennum would be a loc., 'at Benna's.' There is such a man in *Onom.*, and the type of name was common early in Yorks.

BENJOCK (Stobo). 'Hill of the drink,' G. *dheoch*; *cf.* Barrjarg, fr. *dhearg*. This, with Benhar and Benrig, Roxb., seem the only Lowland bens.

BENNACARRAIGAN (S. Arran). G., 'hill of the cliffs.' *Cf.* CARRICK.

BENNACHÍE (Insch.). *c.* 1170 Benychie, *c.* 1356 Benechkey, 1359 -chye. 'Hill of the pap,' G. *a 'chithe*. *Cf.* The Paps of Jura.

BEN NAN AIGHEAN (L. Etive). 'Ben of the hinds,' G. *agh*.

BENNOCHY (Kirkcaldy). 1585 -ochquhy, will be similar to Tigh Beannachadh, Lewis, G. for 'house of blessing.'

BENTPATH (Langholm). 'Path through *bent, bennet* or reedy grass.'

BENVIE (Dundee). *Sic* 1479, but *a.* 1300 Banvy. Prob. = BANAVIE.

BEN Y GLOW (Blair Atholl). 'Veiled, hooded, cloud-capped ben,' G. *glo*, 'a veil.' *Cf.* 1231 Lochglo, Cleish.

BEREGONIUM (Ledaig). *Sic* 1527 *Boece*. He says, 'castle of K. Fergus over against the Western Isles.' G. *Buchanan* Bergon. ? G. *barr a' goine*, 'height of the hurt or wound.'

BERNERA (Out. Hebrides and Lorn). Lo. B. *Sagas* Bjarnarey, 1580 Bernera, '*Bjorn's, i.e.*, bear's isle,' N. *a, ay, ey*.

BERRIEDALE (Caithness). *Sagas* Berudal, 1340 Beridale, and prob. *Orkn. Saga* Beruvik (Jos. Anderson). The first part is doubtful. Like Birgidale, S. Bute, this may be = BORRODALE.

BERVIE (Kincardine, river and town). *Sic* 1199; *c.* 1212 Bervyn, 1290 Haberberui. M. held, fr. root *borv*, 'bubbling spring,' as in Bourbon. *Cf.* O.G. *bir, bior*, 'water, a well,' W. *berwi*, 'to bubble.'

BERWICK and NORTH B. 1097 Berwick, *a.* 1150 Berwich, -ewic, Berrewyk, 1187 Suth Berwyc, *c.* 1225 *Orkn. Sag.* Beruvik, 1250 Northberwyk. *Cf. a.* 715 Bereueg, Kent, 1060 Uppwude cum Ravelega berewico suo. O.E. *berewíc*, 'a demesne farm,' fr. O.E. *bere*, 'barley, bere,' and *wíc*, 'dwelling, village,' and so = the Eng. Barton. *Cf.* Berwick, Sussex, *Dom.* Berewice.

BESSIE YON (Glasserton). 'Bessie's Oven,' O.E. *ofen*, Yorks. *yoon*. *Cf.* Sc. *yin*, 'one,' and ARTHUR'S O'ON.

BETTYHILL (Farr). Market knoll called after Elizabeth, M'chioness of Stafford, *c.* 1820. But BETTYFIELD, Smailholm, is *old* Bedesfeld, 'Beda's field.'

BIDEAN NAM BIAN (Glencoe). G., 'hedge, fence of the skins or hides.'

BIEL (Drem). = Beal, Northumbld., 1228 Beyl, 1248 Behulle, which Mawer thinks 'bee hill.' As likely, 'by the hill,' O.E. *be, bi*, 'by.' See *Pl. N. Eng.* s.v.

BIELD, The (Tweedsmuir). Sc. *bield*, found so *c.* 1450, is 'a shelter, a refuge.' Root doubtful.

BIGGAR (Lanarksh.). *c.* 1170 Bigir, 1229 Bygris, 1524 Begart. Prob. N. *bygg garð-r*, 'barley field.' *Cf.* Biggart, Beith, Biggarts, Moffat, and APPLEGARTH.

BILBSTER (Caithness). *Old* Bilbuster. Seems 'sword place,' O.Sw. and O.E. *bil*, 'sword, bill,' and N. *bolstað-r*, see p. 42.

BINDLE (Portmahomack). N. *bind-dal*, 'sheaf dale.' Found also in Norway (W.).

BINNEND (Burntisland). Binn is for ben, G. *beinn*, as in BINNS (Abercorn), 1335 Bynnes, *i.e.*, 'hills.'

BINNY (Uphall). 1250 Binin (*n* scribe's flourish). Loc. of above.

BIRGHAM (Coldstream). Pron. Bírjam. *c.* 1098 Brycgham, *a.* 1166 *Ben. Peterb.* Birgham, *c.* 1180 Brigeam, prob. 1250 Capella Brigham Letham. 'Village, house (O.E. *hám*) at the bridge,' O.E. *bricg*; here *r*, as often, has been transposed.

BIRKET's Hill (Urr). O.E., Sc. and Dan. *birk*, 'birch.' The -et may be 'head' as in AIKET. *Cf.* too Burchetts, Surrey, 1292 atte Byrchette; *-ette* being common suffix for 'group of.'

BIRKISCO (Skye). N. *birk-skóg-r*, 'birch wood or shaw.' *Cf.* Burscough, Lancs.

BIRNAM (Dunkeld). 1508 -nane. 'Hero's, warrior's home,' O.E. *biorn, beorn*, M.E. *berne, birn* and *hám*. *Cf.* BIRGHAM.

BIRNESS (Ellon). Formerly also Bishop's Brynnes. 1392 Brenes, Byrnes. Prob. Pict. G. *brionn-ais*, 'pretty place.' See *-ais*, p. 9.

BIRNIE (Elgin). *c.* 1190 Brenin, *a.* 1200 Brennach, 1384 Brynnay. Not 'Brendan's field.' Prob. G. *braonach*, 'moist, oozy place,' here in loc.; or, as above, 'pretty place.'

BIRNIEKNOWE (Cumnock). Prob. fr. St. *Brendan*, as in KILBIRNIE. Sc. *knowe*, O.E. *cnoll*, N. *knoll* is 'a knoll, a hillock.'

BIRRENSWARK (Ecclefechan). 1542 Burniswarke, 1608 -work. '*Bruna's* work,' O.E. *weorc*, often, as in 'outwork,' a fortification. Identified by G. Neilson with *O.E. Chron.* 937 Brunanburh, *a.* 1130 *Sim. Durh.* Brunnanwere, *c.* 1150 *Gaimer* Bruneswerc.

BIRSAY (Orkney). *c.* 1050 and *Orkn. Sag.* Birgisherad, O.N. for 'hunting land,' *hérað*, 'a district, a valley.' Here the jarls of Orkney lived. *Cf.* HARRAY.

BIRSE (Aboyne). 1170 Brass. Prob. G. *bras*, 'rash, impetuous' as of a torrent (Burn of Birse), with commonly transposed *r*.

BIRTHWOOD (Biggar). Prob. O.N. *byrði*, 'a board.' So, 'wood from which planks were got.' It may be fr. Eng. *barth*, 'shelter,' root unknown.

BISHOPBRIGGS (Glasgow). 1665 Bishop Bridge, 1666 Bishop brigs, he of Glasgow. *Cf.* BIRGHAM.

BISHOPTON (Paisley). Also referring to Glasgow, and dating *a.* 1332.

BIXTER (Walls). 1628 Bigseter. O.N. *bygg set-r*, 'barley farm,' or fr. a man *Bygg*. *Cf.* INGSETTER.

BLACKBARONY (Eddleston). 1507 Haltoun alias Blakbarony.

BLACKBURN (several). Liddesdale *c.* 1160 Blachaburne = DOUGLAS.

Black Isle (Cromarty). 1794 Ardmeanach ('mid high land') or the Black Isle.

Blackness (Linlithgow). *c.* 1200 Blackenis, 1508 Blaknes, *i.e.*, 'cape.'

Blacksboat (Craigellachie). 'Boat' enters into many names of ferries hereabouts. Boat of Forbes, Garten, Inch, etc.

Blackshiels (Edinburgh). On Sc. *shiels*, 'group of huts or houses,' see Galashiels.

Blackwaterfoot (Arran). Natives to-day say only Dubh Abhuinn, 'dark stream.'

Bladnoch (Wigtown). 1456 -enoch, 1563 Blaidnoo, *Pont* Bluidnoo. Difficult. Perh. G. *bloideanach*, 'place full of little splinters.'

Blaiket (Wigtown), also Blacket Ho. (Middlebie). *c.* 1280 Blaket. Prob. as in Aiket, 'black head' or 'height.' *Cf. c.* 1260 Ecclesia Sce. Brigide de blacket.

Blair (several). N. Ayr 1220 Blar. G. *blàr*, 'plain, field, battle-field.' Blairadam, Kinross, was called after its proprietor.

Blaircessnock (Perthsh.). Prob. 'marshy plain,' G. *seasganach*.

Blairgowrie. 'Plain of the goat,' G. *gobhar, goibhre*.

Blairhoyle (Pt. of Menteith). *c.* 1600 -guhoille. 'Plain with the wood,' G. *c(h)oille*.

Blairingone (Alloa). 1390 Blayrygon. G. *blàr an gobhainn*, 'field of the smith,' Smithfield.

Blairlick Hill (Cabrach). 'Plain of the flat stone,' G. *leac, lic*.

Blair Logie (Stirling). 1508 Blair de Logy. G. *lag, luig*, 'a hollow,' here in loc.

Blairmore (L. Long). 1248 Blar mor. G. for 'big plain.' The village was named fr. the farm near it. Blairbeg, G. *beag*, 'little,' is close by.

Blairnroar (Glen Artney). *Ulst. Ann.* 878 Civitas Nrurim. Perh. G. *blàr an ruire*, 'plain of the knight or champion.'

Blairvaddick (Gareloch). *c.* 1240 Blarvotych, *c.* 1350 Fynvoych que scotice dicitur Blarvotych et similiter Drumfynvoch, 1545 Blairwaddych. Orig. fr. G. *bothach*, 'full of cottages,' but now prob. fr. G. *b(h)adach*, 'full of bushes,' G. *bad*, 'bunch, thicket.'

Blalowan (Cupar Fife). G. *bail a' leamhan*, 'house among elms.'

Blanefield (Dumbarton). Named after Strathblane.

Blantyre (Bothwell and Findochty). Bo. B. Blantthyre, 1290 -tire, 1319 Blauntyr. Pict. or W. *blaentir*, 'projecting land, foreland.'

Blarnavaid (Drymen). *c.* 1350 Blarefode, -nefode. 'Plain with the peat or turf,' G. *an fhoìd.* Now rather, *an bhaid,* 'of the thicket.'

Blaven (Skye). G. Blàbheinn. Hybrid; 'blue ben,' N. *blá,* 'blue.'

Blawrainy (Kirkcudbt.). G. *blàr raithneach,* here in loc., 'ferny plain.'

Blebo (Cupar). *Sic* 1570. Prob. 1144 Bladebolg, 1567 Blebow. Prob. O.G. *blàda, blàtha bolg,* 'meal sack' place. *Cf.* Bogie.

Blingery (Wick). Prob. N. *bliong airigh,* 'lythe shieling.' *Cf.* Assary.

Blinkbonny (several). Prob. = Belle Vue, but Craigbonny, Galloway, is fr. G. *banbh,* 'a young pig.'

Blocháirn (Baldernock). 1504 Blacharne, 1665 Blairquhairen. G. *blàr a' chàirn,* 'plain with the cairn.' The *o* may have come fr. O.G. *blot,* 'cave, den.'

Blythebridge (Dolphinton). Near to Blyth Hill. Root unknown. *N.E.D.* has no quotations *re* a place, s.v. *blithe.* Blyth, S. Yorks, is 1097 Blida; R. Blythe, Notts, is *Dom* Blide, and 944 *chart.*, N'hants, has a stream Blithe.

Blythswood (Glasgow, Renfrew). *c.* 1560 Blythiswod. Prob. fr. a man *Blythe.*

Boarhills (St. Andrew's). *c.* 1120 Alexander I gave Cursus Apri, 'boar's chase,' to the see of St. Andrew's; interesting proof of the boar's existence here. Yet the present spelling is said to come fr. an 18th cny. dominie. Before it was always Byre- or Byir-hills; *cf.* Byrecleugh. *c.* 1420 *Wyntoun* calls it Barys Rayk.

Boat of Forbes (on R. Don), of Inch (Kingussie), etc. Names of old ferries, see Forbes, Inch, etc. Boat of Garten (Grantown) is fr. G. *gairtean, goirtean,* 'field of corn, croft,' fr. *gart,* 'standing corn.'

Boath (Forres, Alness). For. B. may *a.* 1100 Bothguanan, see Pitgaveny. Al. B. 1583 Bothmore, 'big house.' Later syllables are at times dropped, leaving G. *both,* 'house' (same as Sc. bothy), alone. *Cf.* Inver.

Bochastle (Callander). *Sic* 1791. W. says, in 1452 Mochastir, 1579 Moucastell. G. *both chaisteail,* 'house by the castle or fort.' But in 1478, Bochossil, ? *both chosdail,* 'dear, costly house.'

Boddam (4 in Aberdeensh., Stirlingsh. and S. Shetland). 1523 'le Boddoms,' Alford. Sc. for 'valley' or 'bottom,' O.E. *botm,* North. Eng. *bodome,* in 1513 Gav. Douglas *boddum.* *Cf.* a 'Bothams,' E. Lothian, and Buddon.

Bogie (R. and strath, Aberdeensh.). G. *srath Bhalgaidh.* 1187 Strabolgin, 1335 -bolgy, 1594 Strathbolgie. Perh. same root as the legendary Ir. Firbolg, ' bag-men,' fr. Ir. *bolg,* ' bag, sack.' *a.* 1093 Bolgin is prob. Bogie, Abbotshall. *Cf.* Cairnbulg, Aberdeensh. W. identifies Bogie with Balgie, Glenlyon, etc., and says it means ' bubbly stream.'

Boglily (Fife). G. *bog lilidh,* ' marsh with the lilies.' This is really half Eng.

Bognamoon (Aberdeensh.). Prob. G. *bog na moine,* ' bog with the peats.' *Cf.* Balnamoin, Angus, now pron. Bonnymoon !

Bogriffie (Aberdeensh.). ' Brown, heather-coloured bog,' G. *riabhach,* here loc.

Bogroy (Inverness). ' Red,' G. *ruadh,* ' bog ' or clayey ground.

Bogue Fell (Kirkcudbt.). G. *bog,* ' soft, moist.' *Fell,* see p. 38.

Bohally (L. Rannoch). Perh. G. *both chaile,* ' house of the vulgar hussy.' But *cf.* Cally.

Boh*á*rm (Banff). *c.* 1220 Boharme, 1306 Botharm, 1325 Bocharme, Bucharm. Also 1488 ' Bocquharne,' Brechin, and 1534 Bogquharne, now Bucharn, Gartly. Prob. G. *both chàirn,* ' house by the cairn ' ; perh. ' house of arms,' G. *airm.* The liquids *m* and *n* easily interchange.

Boh*ú*ntin (Glenroy). 1568 Bohintene-villie (G. *bhaile,* ' village '). G. *both chunndainn,* ' house at the confluence.'

Boisdale L. and parish (Out. Hebrides). G. Baoghasdail. *c.* 1400 Boysdale, 1427 Baegastallis, 1549 Baghastill. N. *bugis-dal-r,* ' slight bay dale ' (M.). The gen. of N. *bui,* pron. boy, ' a goblin,' would be *bua.*

Bold (Peeblessh.). *Old* Boild, O.E. and M.E. *bold,* ' a dwelling,' akin to O.N. *ból.* *Cf.* Bolton.

Bol*é*skine (Foyers). 1226 Buleske(n. 1451 Bulleskyn. Prob. G. *bual esguin,* ' place of fen.' *Cf. a.* 1207 Boghesken, Ayr. W. prefers, *both fhleasgain,* ' booth of withies,' *cf.* Auchleskine, Balquhidder. But it is nearly certain that would not have been pron. Bulesken so early as 1226.

Bolin (Glengarry). G. *both lion,* ' booth for flax.'

Bolshan (Angus). *Old* Ballishane. G. *baile sean,* ' old village.'

Bolton (E. Lothian). *c.* 1200 Bot(h)el-, Bowel-, Boeltun, 1250 Boultun, 1297 Boltone. O.E. *botl-tún,* ' dwelling enclosure, village,' influenced by O.N. *ból,* ' dwelling ' ; 9 Boltons in England. *Cf.* Morebattle.

Bonally (Colinton). G. *both na h'àile,* ' house on the rock or cliff.'

Bonar Br. (Sutherld.). 1275 Bunnach, still pron. nearly so, only with *ā* for *u,* 1566 Bonach, 1686 Boanarness. Doubtful ; though

W. says, G. *am bonnàth*, 'the bottom ford.' Bonar is a mod. corrup., influenced by the Eng. surname.

BONCHESTER Br. (Hawick) and Hill (Abbotrule). Early history unknown. Perh. G. *bon*, 'foot,' and O.E. *cæster*, L. *castra*, 'a camp.' *Cf.* Bonjedward near by.

BO'NESS or BORROWSTOUNNESS, *sic* 1649, 1783 Boness; *cf.* 1745 Borroustoun, Kirkintilloch, and 1538 ibid. Reay. Fine example of contraction. The orig. village is a mile fr. ness and sea. *Borrowstoun* is common for a Sc. municipal burgh, O.E. *burh*, 'fort, shelter-place.' *Ormin*, c. 1200, has *burrghess tun*, and *burrowstoun* is a common Sc. word fr. Henryson to Scott.

BONHILL (Alexandria). 1225 Buchlul, *c.* 1270 Buthelulle, 1273 Bohtlul, 1278 Bullul, *c.* 1320 Buchnwl. Good example of corrup. Now pron. Bonill. Prob. O.G. *buth an uillt*, 'house by the stream,' *allt*.

BONKLE (Lanark). 1290 Bonkil. G. *bun*, *bonn coill*, 'foot of the wood'; *cf.* BUNKLE. *Cf.* 'The Foot of the Wood' in Falkirk.

BONNINGTON. Peebles B. *c.* 1380 Bonnestoun, Leith B. *old* Bonnytoun, Lanark B. 1776 Boniton, Maryton B. *c.* 1600 Bonitone [*Dom.* Kent Bonintone, and *a.* 1296 Bonigtone]. Some may be fr. Sc. *bonnie*, *c.* 1300 *bonie*, prob. not. Some may be O.E. *Bonan tun*, 'village of Bona.' Prob. is O.E. *Bondan tún*, 'village of Bonda,' or 'Bond,' *i.e.*, the householder or husbandman. There are 8 Bondingtons in *R.M.S.*, vol. I, 1306–1424, and we have 1371 Bondyngtona, Ratho, 1372 Bonyngtona. On *-ing* see p. 52. *Cf.* BONNY-TOUN.

BONNYBRIDGE and WATER (Falkirk). *Pont* Bony. Perh. G. *buinne*, 'rapid stream' (Mack.), W. *buan*, 'swift.' River names are rarely Eng.

BONNYRIGG (Dalkeith) will be 'bonnie ridge.' But BONNYTOUN (Linlithgow) is 1451 Bonyntone, *a.* 1500 Bondington, and so = BONNINGTON.

BONSKIED (Pitlochry). Pron. Baunsküd, rarely Pownskütch. G. *bun*, *bonn sgaoid*, 'low place with blackthorns'; so the late Rev. R. Barbour; *cf.* Baunskeha, Kilkenny, Ir. *sceach*, 'hawthorn.' Perh. fr. G. *sgòd*, *sgòid*, 'a corner.'

BO-, BUCHQUHAPLE (Thornhill, Perthsh.). 1508 Buchquhoppil. O.G. *buth*, G. *both chaibeail*, 'house of the chapel,' one of 6 belonging to Inchmahome.

BORDLANDS (Peebles), BOR(E)LAND (several). *c.* 1199 Borland, Kincardine on Forth, *Pont* Boirland over and nether, Cunningham. 1444 le bordland, central Perth. 'Board land,' O.E., Sw. and Dan. *bord*, 'board, table,' O.N. *borð*, plank, table, maintenance at table, 'board.' So, land held on the rental of a food-supply. *c.* 1250 *Bracton* Quod quis habet ad mensam suam et proprie, sicut sunt Bordlandes, Anglice. *Cf.* BORLUM.

Borgue (Kirkcudbt., Caithness). Ki. B. *c.* 1150 Worgis, 1260 Borg. O.N. and Dan. *borg*, O.E. *burg*, *burh*, 'a fort, shelter place, burgh.' The dimin. Borgan is in Minigaff.

Borlum (Ft. Augustus, Urquhart). Corrup. of Borland (McKinnon).

Bornish (S. Uist). N. *borg-nes*, 'fort cape,' see Borgue. *Nish* is the common W. coast form of O.N. *nes*, Dan. *næs*, ness, lit. 'nose.'

Boroughmuirhead (Edinburgh). 1575 the burrowmure of Edinr. See Borgue and Bo'ness. The -muir is O.E. and Dan. *mór*, 'moor.'

Borreraig (Dunvegan). N. *borgar-aig*, 'castle bay,' Norse G. *aig*, N. *vík*, 'bay.' *Cf.* Boreray, N. Uist.

Borrobol (Sutherld.). N. *borg-bol*, 'fort place.'

Borrodale (Ardnamurchan). 1332 Borubal, *cf.* above. 'Fort dale.' *Cf.* Birgidale, Bute, Borradale, Inverness and Borrowdale, Cumberld., 1210-12 Borcherdale.

Borthwick (Gorebridge, Roxburgh). Go. B. 1430 Borthuic, Ro. B. *a.* 1185 Bordewich. 'Fort place or village,' O.E. *wíc*. See Borgue, and *cf.* Borwick, Carnforth. So = Castleton.

Borva, -ve (Lewis). Corrup. of N. *borg*, 'fort.' See Borgue.

Boswells, St. (Melrose). From *Boisil*, prior of Melrose, *c.* 650, preceptor of St. Cuthbert; -well comes through influence of Norm. *ville*, *vil*, 'town.' But *a.* 1600 the parish was Lessuden or Lessedwyn.

Botarie (Nairn). 1226 Butharrie, but 1662 Pittarie. *Cf.* Pitgaveny. O.G. *buth*, G. *bòt airidh*, 'hut on the hill-pasture.'

Bothkennar (Falkirk). *c.* 1250 Buth-, 1291 Bothkenner, 1304 Boghkener. O.G. *buth*, G. *both ceannaire*, 'house of the driver or ploughman.'

Bothwell. *a.* 1242 Botheuill, *a.* 1300 Bothvile, -wile, *c.* 1340 -euyle. M.E. *bothe wiel* or *weel*, O.E. *wœl*, 'booth, hut by the eddy or fish pool,' referred to in an old charter. *Cf.* Maxwell.

Botríphnie (Keith). 1226 Buttruthin, 1275 -ruthie. Seems O.G. *buth*, G. *bòt ruaidh*, 'red house.' The -phn- seems to point to *aibhne*, gen. of *abhuinn*, so, 'house on the red river.' *Cf.* Ruthven.

Botúrich (Dumbarton). 1498 Duæ le Boturchis. G. *bòt Mhurich*, 'house of Murdoch.'

Bourd, Ben y (Ben Macdhui). G. *beinn a' bhuird*, 'mountain of the board,' G. *bord*, or Table Mountain.

Bourtie (Aberdeen). *c.* 1182 Boverdyn, *c.* 1200 Bourdyn. Perh. G. *bothar*, 'lane, road,' and *-dyn* or *-tie* termin. *Cf.* Cromarty.

BOURTRIEBUSH (Aberdeen). Sc. for 'elder bush,' M.E. *burtre*; further origin unknown.

BOUST (Coll). N. *bolstað-r*, 'place'; see p. 42. *Cf.* Colbost, Skeabost, etc.

BOWDEN (Melrose, Torphichen). Me. B. 1124 Bothendene, *c.* 1150 Boul-, *c.* 1250 Bowelden (*cf.* forms under BOLTON and BONHILL). Prob. G. *both an duin*, W. *din*, 'house on the hill'; so not = the Eng. Bowdens. If it had been an O.E. name—'St. Bathan's or Bothan's dune'—the *th* would have remained.

BOWER (Wick). *c.* 1230 Bouer, 1605 Boar. O.N. *búr*, Dan. *buur*, O.E. *búr*, 'house,' and then 'bower'; *cf.* byre.

BOWFIDDLE Rock (Cullen). 1728. 'The rocks near Portknockie called Scarr noss (see NOSS) or Bowfiddle.' So called from the rock's shape.

BOWHILL (Selkirk, Colvend). Sir H. Maxwell thinks, G. *buachaill*, 'cowherd,' name often in Ir. for standing stones. As likely fr. Sc. *bow*, M.E. *bu*, O.N. *bú*, 'farm, farm stock, cattle.'

BOWLAND (Galashiels). Prob. as above, 'cattle land.' It may be for BOKELAND.

BOWLING (Dumbarton). Perh. for BOWLAND. But *cf.* Bowling Bank, Wrexham and Bowling, Bradford, *Dom.* Bolline, 1303 Bollyng, prob. a patronymic, 'place of the sons of *Bolla*,' 5 in *Onom.* *Cf.* BUTT of LEWIS.

BOWMORE (Islay). G. *both mòr*, 'big house.'

BOW of FIFE. *Sic* 1770. Perh. fr. its shape, fr. O.E. *boga*, Dan. *bue*, 'a bow.' But perh. fr. O.N. *bú*, 'house, village'; *cf.* The Bu, Bow or Butt of Orphir, Orkney, 1503 Bu.

BOWPRIE (Aberdour, Fife). 1320 Beaupre, Fr. for 'fine meadow.' *Cf.* BEAULY.

BOYNAG, BYNACH Burn (Crathie). Perh. G. *bonnag*, *bannag*, 'a jump, a spring.'

BOYNDIE (Banff). Pron. Bŷnedy. *c.* 1170 *chart.* Inverbondin, 1552 Boynd. Perh. same as Ir. R. Boyne; in old Ir. MS. is Inber-in-Bhoinde at the Boyne's mouth. Perh. Ptolemy's Buvinda, see next. Letter *d* often adds itself.

BOYNE (Portsoy). Pron. Byne. 1368 Boyen, 1426 Boigne, 1491 Boyne, 1521 Bone. O. Celt. *buvind*, 'white cow,' see above, G. *bo fhionn*. *Cf.* ABOYNE.

BOYSACK (Angus). *Old* Balecisæ. G. *both*, *bail easaige*, 'house, village of the squirrel.' *Both* and *bail* often interchange.

BRABSTER (Deerness), BRABSTERMIRE (Caithness). De. B. 1492 Brabustare, 1538 Brabastermyre. O.N. *breiðr bolstaðr*, 'broad place'; and *myrr*, 'moor, bog.'

BRACADALE (Skye). 1498 Bracadoll, 1459 Vrakdill. N. *brekka dal*, 'dale, glen with the steep slope,' confused with G. *bhreac*, 'spotted, speckled.' *Cf.* Brackness, Stromness, *old* Brekness.

BRACARA (Arisaig). G. *breac cara*, 'speckled, mottled haunch' (of the hill).

BRACKLINN Falls (Callander). G. *breac linne*, W. *llyn*, 'speckled, foamy pool.' Brackland, 'mottled land,' G. *lann*, is close by.

BRACHO (Beith), BRACO (Dunblane, Cruden). *a* pron. as *ay*. Prob. G. *bracach*, 'greyish place'; *cf.* CRAIGO. But Breagho, Fermanagh is Ir. *breagh mhagh*, 'wolf field.'

BRAE (Lerwick). *Old* Brai-ai. O.N. *breið eið*, 'broad neck or isthmus.'

BRAEHEAD (Lanark, etc.). O.N. *brá*, O.E. *bráew*, *bréaw*, lit. 'eyelid,' 'a steep bank.'

BRAEMAR (W. Aberdeensh.). 1560 the Bray of Marre. *Pont* Brae of MAR, 1682 Brea-marr. In North. names, rather G. *bràigh*, 'upper part,' not Sc. *brae*, a different root. The BRAES, Skye, is G. an Bràigh.

BRAID (Edinburgh). 1165 Brade. G. and Ir. *bràghaid*, *-ad*, 'neck, gully,' really gen. of *bràigh*, 'upper part.' The gully is S. of Blackford Hill. *Cf.* R. Braid, Antrim, and BREADALBANE.

BRAIDWOOD (Lanark). *Braid*, Sc. for 'broad.' *Cf.* 1179–80 *Pipe R.* Yorks, Bradewude.

BRAIGO (Islay). N. *brá-gjá*, 'brae inlet or goe.' *Cf.* BRAEHEAD.

BRAN, Falls of (Dunkeld). *a.* 1200 Strathbranen (? -uen), 1488 -bravne, 1499 -braun. G. Breamhainn, fr. *breaman*, 'the tail or backside of a sheep.' But R. Bran, Contin, is O.G. and Ir. *bran*, 'a raven.'

BRANDER, Pass of (L. Awe). W. says, G. *brannradh*, 'a trap, an obstruction.' But perh., like Glen BRANTER, Cowal, G. *branndair*, 'a gridiron.' BRANDERBURGH, Lossiemouth, seems mod.

BRANXHOLM (Hawick). *a.* 1400 Brancheshelm, 1478 Brankishame. 'Holm' or 'home of *Brance*.' O.E. and Dan. *holm* is 'a small island,' then, 'rich land by a riverside.' *Cf.* Branscombe, Axminster, *Dom.* Branchescome and BRANXTON, Coldstream. 1251 Brankiston.

BRAWL (Strathy). *c.* 1375 Brathwell. Prob. O.N. *breið völl-r*, 'broad field.' (W.)

BREADALBANE (Perthsh.). *c.* 1600 Bredalban. G. *bràighad Albainn*, 'upper part (*cf.* BRAID) of Alban.' Prob. *c.* 970 *Pict. Chron.* Brunalban, 'east slope of Drum-alban,' great dividing ridge of Scotland, with Bruneire (G. *iar*, 'west'), the 'west slope.' *Brun* is O.G. for 'bank, slope, brae,' W. *brynn*, 'a hill'; *cf.* BRUAN. Alban did not include Argyll.

BREAKACHY (Beauly, Kincraig, Caithness). *c.* 1170 *chart*, etc., Don Valley, 'Brecachath quod interpretatur campus distinctus coloribus.' G. *breac achadh*, 'mottled field'; one of the rare cases where the 2nd syll. of *achadh* survives in a place-name. *Cf.* GARIOCH.

BREAKISH (Broadford). G. *breac innis*, 'speckled meadow,' confused fr. O.N. *brekka*, 'hill-side, slope,' as in BRACADALE.

BRECHAM Wood (Longformacus). Here withes were cut for draught-horse collars, in Sc. *brecham*, M.E. *berhom*, perh. fr. O.E. *beorgan*, 'to protect,' and *hame*, *hem*, 'iron guard of the collar.'

BRECHIN (Angus). Pron. Bréehin. *Sic a.* 1150, but *Pict. Chron.* ann. 966 Magna civitas Brechne (gen.), *a.* 1150 *Bk. Deer* Brecini (gen.), 1248 Brekin, 1435 -quin. Perh. fr. a man *Brechan*, *Brychan*. See Skene *Celt. Scotl.* (1887) ii. 36, and *cf.* Brecknock, Wales, 1094 Brecheniauc.

BREICH (Holytown), BROICH (Crieff). G. *brèoch*, 'brim, bank.'

BRERACHAN, Glen (Pitlochry). G. Briathrachan, *c.* 1392 Glenbrerith. Doubtful. Root perh. G. *briathrach*, 'wordy,' fr. the babbling sound (W.). The *-an* is suffix of place.

BRESSAY (Lerwick). Doubtful. May be fr. a man *Bresti*, or fr. O.N. *brest-r*, 'crack, burst,' or *brjóst*, Sw. *bröst*, so 'isle like a breast'; *-ay* is N. for 'island.'

BRIDGENESS (Bo'ness). Pron. Brigness. 1670 Brignies. O.N. *bryggja næs*, 'landing-stage cape.' O.N. for 'bridge' is *brú*. *Cf.* The Briggs, Rattray Head, and Filey Brigs, Yorks.

BRIDGE of ALLAN, EARN (*Pont* Brig of Ern), etc. The first reference to a bridge in Scotland seems to that of Berwick in 1199.

BRIMS, BRINS NESS (Thurso). 1559 Brymmis. O.N. and O.E. *brim*, 'surf or the sea'; *s* is gen.

BRITTLE L. (S. Skye). Pron. braé-tel. Not Eng. *brittle*, a rather late word, but O.N. *breið-r dal-r*, 'broad dale.' *Cf.* BRODICK.

BROADFORD (Skye). Mod., not Norse. BROADLAND, Cairnie, is for BORDLAND.

BRODICK (Arran). *c.* 1306 Brathwik, 1391 Breth-, 1450 Brade-1595 Brydik. O.N. *breið-r vík*, 'broad bay,' Eng. *broad*, 3–4 *brade*. *Cf.* Breibister, Shetland.

BRODIE (Nairn). *Sic* 1311; 1380 Brothie. Loc. of G. *brothach*, 'at the muddy place'; *cf.* ARBROATH. Its other name, DYKE, might be Eng. transl. of G. *brothag*, 'little ditch.' *Cf.* 1250 *Reg. Dunferm.* Ecc[a] de Dulbrodoch, Elgin.

BROGAR (Stennis). Prob. O.N. *breið-r garð-r*, 'broad enclosure.' *Cf.* BRODICK and GARTH.

BROOM L. (W. Ross, Pitlochry). Ro. B. 1227 Braon, 1310 Bren, 1499 Brene, 1573 Brune, 1580 Brian, 1586 Brume, 1682 Broom or Brian. G. *braon*, 'drizzling rain, dew.'

BROOMAGE (Larbert). 1452 Bremis, 1488 Bruminche. 'Broom mead,' O.E. *brom*, 'broom, gorse,' and *inch*, as in Perth Inches, taken fr. G. *innis* 'island, meadow.' Suffix -age is always difficult, often mod.; see *Pl. N. Eng.*, p. 46. *Cf. Inquis. Pr. David* Brumeseheyd.

BROOMIEKNOWE (Lasswade) and BROOMIELAW (Glasgow). 'Broom clad knoll or hill,' O.E. *hláew*, 'hill.' 1325 Bromilaw; *cf.* 1293 *Inq. p.m.* Surrey, Bromyknoll. *N.E.D.* has no quots. for *broomy* before 1647.

BRORA (Golspie). 1499 Strabroray, 1595 Browra. 'Bridge river,' O.N. *brú*, Dan. and Sw. *bro*, gen. *broer*, 'bridge' and *á* 'river.' Here once was the only important bridge in Sutherld. *Cf.* BROOSTER, Walls, 'bridge place'; see p. 42.

BROUGH (Thurso), B. NESS (S. Ronaldsay), BROUGH of BIRSAY, an islet in Orkney. Th. B. 1506 Brucht. By common transposing of *r*, fr. O.N. and Dan. *borg*, O.E. *burg*, 'castle, fort, broch.' *Cf.* BORGUE, BURGHEAD and Brough, Westmorld., *Dom.* Burg.

BROUGHTON (Edinburgh, Biggar). Ed. B. 1128 Broctuna, *c.* 1200 Brouhtune; then Bruchton, still the vulgar pron. Bi. B. *c.* 1200 Brouhtune. Usually thought fr. O.E. *bróc*, 'a brook,' perh. fr. *broc*, 'a badger'; and O.E. *tún*, 'village.' *Cf.* Broughtons, Yorks, *Dom.* Broctun.

BROUGHTY Ferry (Dundee). 1541 Bruchty Craig, 1595 Brochty. G. *bruach*, 'bank, slope,' with -ty termin.; or loc. of *bruachdach*, 'at the magnificent place.'

BROWNDEAN Law (Oxnam). (Not *Barbour* The Boroundoun.) Perh. *c.* 1290 *Melrose Chart.* Sir Wm. de Barondoun. 1436 Broundean. Doubtful. Perh. O.G. *bruan, duin*, 'slope of the hill.' *Law* is Sc. for 'hill' too.

BROXBURN (Bathgate), BROXMOUTH (Dunbar). 1094 Broccesmuthe. 'Burn' and 'mouth of the badger,' O.E., G. and Ir. *broc*. *Cf.* Brockly, Kinross and Broxbourne, Herts.

BRUAN (Wick). O.G. for 'bank.' See BREADALBANE.

BRUAR, Falls of (Blair Atholl). Jas. Macdonald derived Cairn-a-Bruar, Cabrach fr. O.G. *brothaire*, 'cauldron,' root *bruith*, 'to boil'; *cf.* R. Brue, Somerset. W. makes it O. Celt. Brivara, 'bridge stream'; but *cf.* BRIDGE.

BRUCKLAY (New Deer). *c.* 1220 Brachlie, 1654 Bruclaw. Orig. fr. G. *brach*, 'a bear,' later fr. *broc*, 'a badger,' *broclach* or *-luidh*, 'badger's den, a cavern.' The endings -lie 'meadow' and -law, 'hill' are later, and they often interchange.

BRUICHLADDICH (W. Argyll). G. *bruach chladaich*, 'bank on the shore or stony beach.'

BRUNTON (Cupar). Said to be for Bryantoun, fr. some Norman. But B., Northumbd., is *c.* 1250 Burneton.

BRYDEKIRK (Annan) = KILBRIDE and LHANBRYDE, 'church of St. *Brigida*' or *Bridget*, friend of St. Patrick.

BUACHAILL (Staffa) and BUACHAILL EITE (L. Etive). G. for 'shepherd of Etive,' fr. *bò-ghille*, 'cowherd.'

BUCCLEUCH (St. Mary's L.) *a.* 1600 Bockcleugh, Buckcleuch. 'Buck's glen,' O.E. *buc*, O.N. *bukk-r*, 'male of the goat or fallow deer,' and Sc. *cleugh*, Eng. *clough*, earlier *clou*, *clog*, 'cleft, ravine, gorge.' *Cf.* Doe- and Wolf-cleuch near by and Catcleuch, Bonnybridge, perh. 1253 *Cart. Levenax* Cattisclothe; 1315–21 Catteclouche; also *c.* 1200 *Coldstream Chart.* Heseliclov and *c.* 1200 Hamestalesclogh, Lancs. But the orig. name was Balcleuch, G. *bail cluiche*, 'house of the sports' or 'funeral solemnities.' Possibly the name is found too in *c.* 1200 *Coldstm. Chart.* 21 Selbukleche.

BUCHAN (N. Aberdeen and Minigaff). Ab. B. *c.* 1150 *Bk. Deer* Buchan, *Pict. Chron.* Buchain, 1249 Bochan, *c.* 1295 Bouwan. Mi. B., 1456 Buchane. Prob. O. Celt. *Cf.* G. *baogh*, 'a calf,' W. *bwch*, 'a cow,' with -an termin.

BUCHANAN (L. Lomond). *c.* 1240 Buchquhanane, 1296 Boughcanian, 1562 Bowhanan, O.G. *buth*, G. *both*, *chanain*, 'house of the canon.' *Cf.* BOTHKENNAR.

BUCHANTY (R. Almond). 1428 -ondy, 1633 -indye. Perh. O.G. *buth chainntaig*, 'house of the peevish young woman.' W. connects with BUCHAN.

BUCHARN, see BOHARM.

BUCHLÝVIE (Aberfoyle), Easter and Wester B. (Aberdour, Fife). Fife B. *old* Boclavies. Prob. O.G. *buch*, G. *both sleìbhe*, 'house on the moor or hill,' *sliabh* (here *s* is silenced). *Cf.* 1517 *Inquis. Fife*, Wester Bucklevie.

BUCKET (trib. of R. Don). 1654 Buchet. Perh., like R. BUCKIE, Balquhidder, fr. G. *boc*, *buic*, W. *bwch*, 'a buck.'

BUCKHAVEN (Leven). Founded *c.* 1555. Doubtful. Prob. fr. O.E. *buc*, 'a buck.'

BUCKIE (Banff). 1362 Buky, 1580 Bukkie; BUCKIES (Glen Queich). Prob. G. *bucaidh*, 'a pimple, a knob.'

BUDDON Ness (Barry) may go with Bodden Pt. (Montrose). Old forms needed. *Cf.* BODDAM, also Eng. *boud*, 'a weevil.'

BUITTLE (Cas. Douglas). Pron. Bittle. 1304 Botle, 1572 Butill. O.E. *botl*, O.N. *bol* for *boðl*, in Eng. *c.* 1200 *buttle*, 'a dwelling.' *Cf.* NEWBATTLE and Bootle, Liverpool.

BULLERS of BUCHAN (Peterhead). A rocky recess where the sea boils like a cauldron. Sw. *buller*, 'noise, roar,' Dan. *bulder*, 'tumbling noise,' Gav. Douglas, 1513, uses 'bullyer.'

BULLIONFIELD (Dundee). 1509 Bulyeoun. Prob. not fr. *bullion*, not found in Eng. till 1463, but fr. G. *builgean*, 'blister, pimple, bubble, bell.'

BUNACHTON (Inverness). O.G. *buth*, G. *both Neachdain*, 'Nectan's booth.' *Cf.* CAMBUSNETHAN.

BUNAVEN (Islay). G. *bun aibhne*, 'foot, mouth of the river,' *abhuinn*.

BUNAVOULIN (Morven). 'At the foot of the mill.' G. *m(h)uilinn*.

BUN-, BONAWE (Argyll). 'Bottom, foot,' G. *bun*, *bonn*, 'of the R. AWE.'

BUNCHREW (Inverness). 'At the foot of the trees,' G. *c(h)raobh*.

BUNESSAN (Mull). 'At the foot of the little waterfall,' G. *easan*. *Cf.* Moressan, Aberfoyle.

BUNKLE (Chirnside). *c.* 1130 Bonekil = BONKLE.

BUNZION (Kingskettle). Pron. Bunion. Prob. G. *bun-fheann*, 'the tail.'

BURDIEHOUSE (Edinburgh and Beith). Said to be 'Bordeaux[1] house,' fr. some unrecorded Fr. settlers, ? weavers, or Q. Mary's French attendants.

BURGHEAD (Moray). Here *g* is hard. Site of a *borg*, see BORGUE, built by the Norse *c.* 880. They called the cape Torfnæs.

BURGIE (Moray). *c.* 1240 Burgyn (*n* scribe's flourish). Loc. of O.G. *burg* (loaned fr. N.), 'at the village or fort.'

BURN of CAMBUS. O.E. *burna*, O.N. *brunn-r*, 'burn, brook,' lit. 'a spring or fountain.' *Cf. c.* 1160 *Melrose Chart.* ad burnam de fauhope. See CAMBUS.

BURNESS (N. of Orkney). Prob. N. *byrr naes*, 'fair wind point.' But *cf.* BURWICK.

BURNHERVIE (Inverurie). Perh. G. *beur an h'eirbhe*, 'point, pinnacle of the boundary or wall.' But W. makes it a hybrid.

BURNMOUTH (Berwick). 1171 *Newminster Chart.* Burnemuth. But prob. 1098 *Durham Chart.* Cramesmuthe. A creek here was till lately called Cramsmoo.

BURNSWARK. See BIRRENSWARK.

BURNTISLAND (Fife). 1538–1710 Bruntisland, 1543 Brunteland. Said to be because of fishers' huts *burnt* or, in Sc., *brunt*, on an islet E. of the present harbour. Named *a.* 1500 Wester Kingorne. BRUNTSFIELD Links, Edinburgh, is 1681 Brandsfield.

BURRA (Shetland). 1299 Borgarfiord, O.N. for 'castle frith or bay,' *borg*, 'a fort.'

BURRELTON (Coupar Angus). Prob. a man '*Burrell's* town.'

BUR(S)WICK (S. of Orkney). *c.* 1225 *Orkn. Sag.*, Bardvik. Prob. O.N. *barð vík*, 'edge, brim of the bay.'

[1] In Strabo *Bourdigala*, plainly fr. Basq. *berdogala*, 'the herb sea-purslane.' It reappears in the monastery of Bordgal or Bordeaux, West Meath.

Busby (Glasgow). *c.* 1300 Busbie, 1787 Bushby. 'Bush town,' O.N. *busk-r,* Dan. *busk,* Sc. *buss,* 'a bush,' and O.E. and Dan. *bý,* 'place, village.'

Busta (Shetland). Pron. Bista. Corrup. of N. *bolstað-r,* 'place.' *Cf.* Bosta, Lewis, and Boust.

Bute. *c.* 1093 *Norse chron.* Bot, 1204 Bote, 1292 Boot. In G. Boite. Some say, O.G. *bot,* O.N. *búð,* Dan. and Sw. *bod,* 'hut, bothy,' ? of St. Brendan. M. thought, 'Victory isle,' fr. Pict. G. *buaidh.* W. favours O. Ir. *bòt,* 'fire, beacon fire.'

Butt of Lewis. (1716 Bowling Head). *N.E.D.* says, fr. *butt,* 'to jut out,' fr. *buter.* The only quot. given for *butt,* 'cape,' is 1598 Florio's *Ital. Dict.* '*Capo* or but of any lands end.' More likely fr. Dan. *but,* 'short, blunt, stumpy.' *Butt* = buttock occurs *c.* 1450.

Buttergask and -stone (Dunkeld). 1200 Buthyr-, Buthurgasc, 1296 Bother-, 1461 Buttergask. Prob. O.G. *bothar gasc,* 'causeway hollow,' see Gask. From Ir. *bòthar* come 4 Batterstowns. *Cf.* too p. 33, Butterdean, E. Berwicksh., which is 'wooded glen of the bittern,' and Burghill, Brechin, 1574 Buthirgille, 'valley, ravine, with the road,' G. *bothar.* But Butterflats, S. of Stirling, is *c.* 1610 Battelflats.

Buxburn (Old Machar). 'Buck's burn.' *Cf.* Buccleuch.

Byrecleugh (Lammermuirs). 'Cowhouse glen,' O.E. and Sc. *byre,* 'cowhouse, shed,' lit. 'dwelling,' same root as Bower. See Buccleuch. Byres (E. Lothian) is 1294 Byrys.

Byth (Turriff). The *y* pron. as in by. Doubtful. ? G. *bàith,* 'a lure, a decoy.' But *cf. bythwind* spelling, 1647, of the plant withwind, fr. O.N. *vithja, vith,* 'withy, willow, osier.' Pont's map has a Pow-byth, N. Ayrsh., *pow,* 'a sluggish burn.'

Cabrach (Jura), and Buck of (Rhynie). 1374 Cabrauche. G. *cabrach,* 'a thicket'; it also means 'a deer.'

Cadboll (Fearn). 1281 Kattepoll, 1478 Catbollis, 1529 Cathabul. Prob. not 'place,' N. *bol,* 'of the Cat or Cataibh,' see Caithness, but 'place of wild-cats,' which abounded in the rocks here. O.N. *kött-r,* gen. *kattar,* Dan. *kat.* *Cf.* Catmore, Berks., *Dom.* Catmere, 'wild-cat lake.'

Cadder (Glasgow). 1170 Chaders, 1186 Cader, = Calder and Cawdor.

Cad(d)on Water (Selkirk). Cadonlee (Clovenfords). *c.* 1175 *Fantosme* Keledenelee, 1296 Kalndene. Perh. W. *caled din,* 'hard fort' or 'hill'; perh. 'lea, meadow of the springs.' *Keledene* seems Anglian gen. of O.N. *kelda,* 'well, spring.' *Cf.* Cadden Cas., Kinneff.

CADELAW and -MUIR and CADEMUIR WHAUM, WHYM (Peebles). *Old* Cadmore. Prob. fr. W. *cad*, G. *cath*, 'a battle.' On *law* see p. 52, on *muir*, MUIRAVON. *Whaum* is O.N. *hvamm-r*, 'grassy slope, vale.'

CADESLEA (Earlston). *c.* 1150 Cadysleya. Prob. 'Cade's lea,' O.E. *léah*, 'fallow land, pasture.' *Cada*, *Cade* and *Cado* are all on record.

CADZOW (Hamilton). *c.* 1150 Cadihou, -yhow, *c.* 1360 Cadyow. Doubtful. Looks like W. *cad y ?*, 'battle of the ?' Perh. it is W. *cad du*, 'dark battle,' and Sc. *how*, O.E. *holh*, *holg*, 'a hollow.'

CAERDON (Tweeddale). W. *caer din*, 'fort on the hill.' The Brit. form *caer* prevails over the G. *cathair* in this region.

CAERKETTON (Pentlands). 1317 *Reg. Neubot.* Karynketil (1539 Carketill, surname). Not 'fort of *Catel*,' a well-known Celt. name (W.), for the 1317 *yn* is plainly the art., but 'fort of the retreat or refuge,' as in Balnakettle, Fettercairn; see KETTLE.

CAILLEACH Head (L. Broom). G. *sròn na caillich*, 'point of the nun' or 'old wife.'

CAIPLIE Coves (Crail). *c.* 1420 *Wyntoun* Caplawchy. Loc. of G. *capallach*, 'at the horse-place,' G. *capull*, L. *caballus*, 'a horse.' *Cf.* CAPLICH, 3 in E. Ross.

CAIRNAQUHEEN (Balmoral). G. *càrn na chuimhne*, 'cairn of memory or recollection.' It was a great rendezvous.

CAIRNBAWN (Crinan and W. Sutherld.). 'White cairn' or 'heap,' G. *bàn*. *Cf.* the Ir. colleen bawn.

CAIRNBEDDIE (Perth). 'Cairn of *Beth*' or Macbeth. O.G. *mac bead*, *bethad*, 'son of life,' here in loc. Traditionally Macbeth's fort was placed near here.

CAIRNESS (Lonmay). 'At the cairn,' Pict. loc. *-ais*, as in ALVES, etc.

CAIRNFECHEL (Aberdeensh.). 'Cairn of the tooth,' G. *fiacaill*. *Cf.* Beul na Fiaclaich, Kiltearn, 'mouth of the tooth-place.'

CAIRNGORM (Braemar). G., 'Green or bluish cairn.'

CAIRNGRASSIE (Stonehaven). 'Cairn of the blessing,' G. *gràs*, *gràise*, 'grace, divine blessing.'

CAIRNIE, -EY (Huntly). G. *càirneach*, 'rocky place,' here in loc.

CAIRNNORRIE (Methlie). 'At the East cairn,' G. *noir*, here in loc.

CAIRNRYÀN (Wigtown). See RYAN. Till a century ago, when the name was changed by the Post Office, it was Macharyskeeg, G. *machar a' sgitheig*, 'links with the hawthorn.'

CAIRNTABLE (Muirkirk). *c.* 1315 Kaerntabel. Prob. 'cairn of the sling,' G. *tabhail*. But *cf.* next.

CAIRN TOUL (Braemar). 'Cairn, hill like a barn,' G. *t'sabhail*. The hill near by is called 'Barn.' *Cf.* TOMINTOUL.

CAITHNESS. *c.* 970 *Pict. Chron.* Kathenessia, *c.* 1150 *Bk. Deer* Catness, and Ir. *Nennius* Cat., *a.* 1130 *Sim. Durh.* ann. 934 Cathenes, *c.* 1150 Cataneis, *c.* 1155 Chatenois (Fr.), 1196 *Hoveden* Cathania id est Catenes, *c.* 1225 *Orkn. Sag.* Ness. 'Ness or nose of the *Cataibh*, or 'cat-men'; why so called we know not; *cf.* the Cattegat. In G. Gallaibh, 'strangers' (Norse) land.' Possible also is derivation fr. O.N. *kati*, gen. *kata*, 'a kind of small ship.' *Cf.* CATACOL.

CAITLOCH (Glencairn). 1559 Cadhelaucht, 1624 Cadzelauch, 1587 Catloch. Prob. G. for 'place full of colewort,' *càdhal*. See -ach.

CAKEMUIR (Borthwick). Prob. 'moor at the opening or entrance.' W. *ceg*.

CALAVA Bay (Sutherld.). Tautology. O.N. *kjala-r vag-r*, 'keel bay,' *cf.* Calabost, Lewis; see p. 42.

CALDALE (Kirkwall). Perh. fr. O.N. *kol*, 'coal,' from the abundance of peat. Or fr. O.N. *kald-r*, Sw. *kall*, 'cold.'

CALDER, many instances. Thurso C. is *c.* 1225 *Orkn. Sag.* Kalfadal, O.N. for 'calf's glen.' But Midl. C. is 1250 Kaldor, and other South. cases are 1293 Caldovere, 1294 -der, and *Chart. Paisley* Kaledour. O.G. *call dobhar*, 'hazel stream.' *Cf.* Creag Challdarais, Shieldaig, 'rock of the gloomy hazel wood,' G. *call* and *dubhras*, 'dark wood.' Some Calders may be fr. O.N. *kald-r*, 'cool.' *Cf.* CADDER, CALLANDER, CAWDOR and SCOTSCALDER.

CALDERCRUIX (Bathgate). 1561 -cruikis. '*Crooks*, windings, of the CALDER.'

CALDWELL (Renfrew). *Cf.* Coldwells, Cruden.

CALEDONIAN Canal (Inverness-sh.). *Caledonia* occurs first in *c.* 60 Lucan's *Pharsalia*; root prob. W. *caled*, 'hard.' *Cf.* DUNKELD.

CALF (Eday, Orkney), CALF of MULL (Tobermory), CALVA (islet, W. of Sutherld.). Ed. C. *Norse chrons.* Kalfey. To. C. in *ditto*, Mylarkalfr; G. an Calbh. O.N. *kálf-r*, 'a calf,' hence, a small island near a large one + N. *ay*, *ey*, 'island.' *Cf.* the Calf of Man.

CALIFORNIA (Polmont). Fancy name.

CALLAD-, CALLATER L. (Braemar). Same root as in ABER-CHALDER, CALDER and CALLANDER.

CALLANDER (Falkirk and Perthsh.). Fa. C. 1164 Calentare, 1296 -tyr, *c.* 1350 Callanter. The district here and to E. was called *c.* 1145 *Ailred* Calatria and in Ir. annals Calathros, Ir. for 'hard wood'; this can hardly be the same name. Pe. C. 1451 Calyn et Calendrate, 1457 -drade, 1509 Calen et Calendrath, -treth, 1580 *Buchanan* Caolrathad. M. derives Falk. C. and also

CALDER fr. root *cal*, 'sound, call.' *Cf. a.* 1173 *Paisley Chart.* Kalenter, ? Ayrsh., also 1504 Kalentaremore and -beg, then belonging to Earl of Montrose, in Perthsh. The ending -ter, -tyr, -tare, -der may be G. *tìr*, 'land.' Perth C. must be a different word.[1] Its true G. pron. is very uncertain; lately given to me as Calltraid. The ending may be G. *triath*, gen. *triaith, treith.* So, 'hazel.' G. *call*, 'of the chieftain.' The 2 Callanders were assimilated because they once had the same lords, The Livingstones, earls of Linlithgow.

CALLERNISH (W. of Lewis). Like Kjalarnes, Iceland, 'keel cape.' *Cf.* CALAVA.

CALLERT (Ballachulish). Pron. Cáw-yert. Perh. G. *call àird*, 'hazel height.'

CALLY, Br. of (Blairgowrie). *a.* 1214 Kalathin. Prob. old loc. of G. *caladh*, 'a ferry.' But Corriehallie, Urray, is G. *coire shallaidh*, 'fat corrie,' rich in grass.

CÁLROSSIE (Fearn). Perh. O.G. loc. of *call ros*, 'hazel wood.' But 1476 Glossery, G. *glas airidh*, 'green shieling.'

CALTON (Glasgow and Edinburgh). Ed. C. *c.* 1600 Caldton. G. *caltuinn, calldainn*, 'hazel, hazel copse.'

CALVINE (Blair Atholl). O.G. *caill mhìn*, 'smooth wood.' *Cf.* Cavin, Resolis, which W. thinks is for G. *caol mhìn*, 'smooth pass,' and Dalveen Pass.

CAMBO (Crail). 1288 Camboc, 1327 -ou. O.G. *camb ou*, 'crooked stream,' same root as in L. AWE. The -oc, 1288, also means 'stream.' Cambo, Northumbld., 1253 Cambhou, 1298 Camou, is fr. *how.*

CAMBUS (Alloa). *Cf. Adamn.* Ait-Chambus, Ardnamurchan. G. and Ir. *camus*, 'bay, creek.' For the *b cf.* CAMERON, CROMARTY, CUMBERNAULD. Also *cf.* ALDCAMBUS and 1471 *R.M.S.* Mure -Camboss.

CAMBUSBARRON (Stirling). 1215 -barroun, *c.* 1270 -run. 'Crook, bend at the little height,' G. *barran.* CAMBUSDRENNY, G. *draighneach*, 'thorns' (here in loc.) refers to the same crook of Forth.

CAMBUSCURRY Bay (Tain). *Sic* 1487. 'Bay at the wet plain,' G. *currach*, here in loc. *Cf.* CURRIE.

CAMBUSKENNETH (Stirling). *Sic* 1147, but *c.* 1142 -kinel, 1296 -shenel. Seems orig. G. *camus sgeanail*, 'clean, tidy crook or bend'; but now, 'Bend of Kenneth,' Ir. *Canice*, Adamn. *Cainnachus*, friend of Columba and patron of Kilkenny.

[1] See full evidence in the author's *Place Names Stirlingsh.*, 2nd edit., pref., p. viii.

CAMBUSLANG (Glasgow). 1296 Cameslank, *a.* 1300 Cambuslank, 1319 Cameslong, 1344 Camyslang. ‘Creek, bend of the boat or ship,’ G. *long*, confused with O.E. and Sc. *lang*, ‘long.’

CAMBUSMORE (Dornoch). G. *camus mòr*, ‘big bay,’ *i.e.* L. Fleet.

CAMBUSNETHAN (Wishaw). *a.* 1153 Kambusnaythan, 1159 Cambusneithan. ‘Bend of *Nechtan*,’ in Bede *Naiton*, perh. he K. of the Picts *c.* 700. *Cf.* NENTHORN.

CAMBUS O’ MAY (Aberdeensh.). ‘Crook in the plain,’ G. *a’ maigh*. *Cf.* May, Mochrum, and ROTHIEMAY.

CAMELON (Falkirk and Balmaghie). Gueith Camlann, ‘battle of Camelon,’ 977 *Hist. Briton.* must have been in England. Fa. C. was orig. CARMUIRS. 1526 *Boece* called it in error Camelodunum, 1535 *Stewart* Camelidone, 1536 *Bellenden* Camelon, 1777 *Nimmo* New Camelon. Boece’s confusion arose because a Rom. fort was here. Ba. C. is G. *cam linne*, ‘crooked pool.’ *Cf.* Camling, Carsphairn.

CAMERON (Leven, Stirling, S. Edinburgh). Le. C. 1199 Cambrun, *c.* 1306 -bron. St. C. *a.* 1200 Cambroun, *c.* 1280 Cameron. Ed. C. *c.* 1210 Camberoun. *a.* 1236 Camerun. [1467 Gilla Camsroin; 1594 clan chamron.] Often said to be G. *cam sròn* (*s* here mute), ‘crooked nose or point.’ But Whit. Stokes rightly makes it ‘crooked hill,’ G. *brun*. *Cf.* BREADALBANE.

CAMLÁCHIE (Glasgow). From the accent, prob. G. *camadh làthaich* (here in loc.). ‘At the crook or bend of the swampy place or mire.’ A zigzag burn used to flow here.

CAMPBELTOWN (Kintyre and Ft. George). Ki. C. named *c.* 1598 from the Earl of Argyll, head of Clan Campbell. Ft. G. C. named, 1623, after John D. Campbell of Calder. Campbell occurs in 1243 *Close R.* as ‘Galfridus de bello campo,’ in Nor. Fr. as Beauchamp or ‘Fairfield,’ As early as *c.* 960 *Flodoard* we find Campellis as name of an abbey, ? S. of Laon, while *c.* 1190 *Bened. Peterb.* we have Torencus de Chambel. The earliest Sc. mention of the name is a ‘Gillespic Cambel,’ 1263, G. *cam beul*, ‘crooked mouth’ or *cambel*, ‘wry-mouthed.’ *Cf.* CAMERON.

CAMPERDOWN (Dundee and Resolis). Called after the place of Adml. Duncan’s victory over the Dutch in N. Holland in 1797.

CAMPFIELD (Banchory, Falkirk). The former prob., the latter certainly, a battle-field, in 1298. True also of Camptown, Jedburgh.

CAMPSIE (Glasgow, Glenalmond, Cargill), and CAMPSIE FELLS. Gl. C. *c.* 1200 Camsy, 1208 Kamsi, *c.* 1210 Campsy (through fancied connexion with *camp*). G. *cam sìth*, ‘crooked hill or hill-range.’ Fell is O.N. *fiall*, Dan. *fjeld*, ‘mountain, hill.’ Also near Londonderry.

CAMSTRADDAN (L. Lomond). 1427 Caumstradan. G. for 'crooked lanes,' *sraddan*, pl. of *sraid*.

CAMUSESKAN (Cardross). 1351 Camiseskane, 1367 Camceskane. G. *camus seasgain*, 'inlet on the moorland.'

CAMUSNAGAUL (Ft. William). G. for 'creek or bend of the stranger,' *gall*.

CAMUSTANE (Monikie). *Old* Cambstowne. Must be fr. G. *camus*, 'inlet.' The Dan. chief *Camus* is mythical.

CAMUSTEEL (Applecross). W. thinks of G. *teile*, 'a lime tree.' But the pron. -till or -tchill does not suit. *Cf.* INVERTIEL.

CANISBAY (John o' Groats). *c.* 1240 Cananesbi, 1274 Cranesby, 1455 Cannasby. Crane in O.N. is *trani*, Dan. *trane*, so form 1274 is prob. a mistake. *Pont* gives Conansbay, which Dr. Jos. Anderson thought pointed to an early Celt. chief, *Conan*. But most prob. it is 'canon's place.' *Canon* is found in Eng. *c.* 1205. *Bay* is O.N. *bœ-r*, *bý-r*, Dan. and O.E. *bý*, *bí*, 'village, dwelling.' *Cf.* CANONBIE and DUNCANSBAY.

CANISP Ben (Assynt). ? N. *kenna ups*, 'well-known house-roof,' fr. its shape.

CANNA (Arisaig). 1549 Kannay. Prob. 'island like a can or pot,' O.N. and Sw. *kanna*, O.E. *canne*, 'a can,' and *-ay*, *-ey*, N. for 'island.' But M. says fr. O.G. *cana*, 'a porpoise.' *Cf.* Canna Mill, Wooler.

CANNERTON (Campsie). Prob. G. *ceann airtean*, 'head, height covered with little flints or pebbles.'

CANNICH R. (trib. of R. Glass). Perh. 1538–9 *R.M.S.* Inverchanais; and CANNY R. (Kincardine). Perh. fr. G. *cannach*, 'sweet willow, myrtle.'

CANONBIE (Dumfriessh.). 1290 Canne-, Canenby = CANISBAY. An Austin priory founded here in 1165.

CANTY BAY (N. Berwick). O.G. *canta*, 'a lake, a puddle.'

CAPPLEGILL (Moffat). N. *kapilla-gil*, 'chapel glen,' see AUCHINGILL. Shows how far inland Norse influence went.

CAPUTH (Dunkeld). Pron. Kaypŭt, and prob. G. *ceapach*, 'full of heights like shoe-lasts,' as in Edinkyp. L. Earn. So Rev. J. McLean. *Cf.* Caputhall, Bathgate, and Cappuck, Jedburgh. But W. says it is, 1275 Cathbathac, -bethac, fr. G. *beitheach*, 'birchwood.'

CARBERY (Inveresk). *c.* 1143 Crefbarrin, *c.* 1160 -arri, 1450 Carbarrin, 1543 Carberry. G. *craobh barran*, 'tree-hedge' (W.). No connexion with *Cairbre*, K. in Antrim *a.* 200. But he may be seen in Dunharberry, Girthon.

CARBETH (Killearn). Prob. G. *cathair beath*, 'fort among the birches.' But *cf.* CAIRNBEDDIE.

CARBOST (Skye). 'Copse dwelling,' N. *kjárr-bost*, short form of *bolstað-r*, see p. 42. *Cf.* SHEABOST.

CARBROOK (Plean). 1497 -brok. No 'brook' here, so prob. G. *cathair broc* or *bruic*, 'fort of the brocks or badgers.' Three in England.

CARDENDEN (Dunfermline). W. says, prob. Brit. or Pict., *cf.* W. *cardden*, 'a brake, a thicket,' and KINCARDINE + O.E. *denu*, 'den, dean or dell.' *Cf. c.* 1310 Cardynside, Lindores.

CARDONALD (Paisley). 'Fort,' G. *cathair*, W. *caer*, 'of *Donald*.'

CARDORCAN (Newton Stewart). *Old* Garrowdorkan. This is G. *ceathramhadh*, 'a land quarter,' fr. *ceithir*, 'four'; *cf.* Kerrow, Kingussie. The last part is *darcan*, 'a coot, a teal, also an acorn.' So prob. 'acorn quarter.'

CARDOWAN (Wishaw). Prob. G. *carr dubhain*, 'rock like a hooked claw.' *Cf.* PARDOVAN.

CARDRÓNA (Peebles). *Sic* 1534, but *c.* 1430 -dronow, 1530 -ono. Perh. G. *cathair drothanach*, 'breezy fort.'

CÁRDROSS (Helensburgh). 1208–33 Cardinros, Cadinros, 1275 Cardrois, 1401 -rose. W. *cerrdin ros*, 'rowan tree promontory.'

CARDWELL (Delting, Shetld.). Prob. '*Korti's* field,' O.N. *völl-r*, as in Cartworth, S. Yorks, 1274 Carte-, 1486 Corteworth. *Cf.* CARTER and SCATWELL.

CARESTON (Brechin). *Old* Keraldiston, 1529 Caraldstoun, 1643 Carralstoun. 'Dwelling of *Kerald*,' judge or 'dempster' of Angus, 1227.

CARFIN (Holytown). G. *carr fionn*, 'white, glistening rock.'

CARFRAEMILL (Lauder). 1458 Carffra. 'Fort at the border or edge,' G. *fraighe*.

CARGILL (Stanley). *c.* 1180 Kergill, 1296 Carghill. Pict. G. *ker*, 'fort,' or *carr*, 'rock,' 'of the pledge or wager' or 'of love,' G. *geall*, gen. *gill*.

CARINISH (Lochmaddy). 1389 Karynche. 'Ness of *Kari*,' a man; or fr. N. *kjárr*, 'copse.' *Cf.* CARBOST and Carness, Kirkwall.

CA(E)RLANRIG (Hawick). W. *caer*, 'fort,' and see DRUMLANRIG.

CA(E)RLAVEROCK (Dumfries). *Sic* 1299, in 1275 Carlauerok. Perh. a hybrid, 'fort of the lark,' Sc. *laverock*, O.E. *láwerce*, *-ferce*. As likely fr. G. *leamhreach*, 'an elm-wood.'

CARLETON (Galloway 3, Colmonell). *a.* 1300 *chart.* Karlaton (so it is said), which is = the Eng. Carleton, O.E. *ceorla tún*, 'churls', serfs' dwelling,' often in *Dom.* as Ceorlatona, Cerlatune, etc. But for most of the Gall. places *Whithorn Priory Rentals* has Cairiltoun, 'dwelling of the *Cairils*,' who are said to have come fr. Antrim to Carrick, 1095. Hence the name McKerlie. *Cf.* Minnie, (G. *moine*, 'a moss') Carlie, on Carleton Fell.

CARLONAN LINN (Inverary). G. *càrr lonain*, 'rock of the prattling' and *linne*, 'a pool.'

CARLOPS (W. Linton). *c.* 1425 *Wyntoun* Karlyn-, Kerlinlippis, 'Carline's, old woman's, leap,' Nor. M.E. and O.N. *kerling*, 'old woman,' fem. of *karl*, 'churl,' in Sc. *carl*; and *loup* Sc. for 'leap,' O.N. *hlaup*. Carlops Burn is an old name, the village only founded in 1784. *Cf.* Loch Carlinwark which gave its first name to Cas. Douglas, and *Pont* Karling-craige, N. Ayrsh.

CARLOWAY (Lewis). 1716 Carlvay. 'Karl's bay,' O.N. *vág-r*. *Cf.* STORNOWAY.

CARLOWRIE (Kirkliston). 1336 -louri. Prob. G. *càrr labharaidh*, 'rock of the echo,' lit. 'of speaking.' *Cf.* Craiglowrie, Girthon. W. prefers deriving fr. a man *Lowrie* or Laurie.

CARLUKE (Lanark). 1304 Carlug, *c.* 1320 Carneluke, 1567 Carlouk. G. *càrr na luig*, 'rock by the hollow.' Its old name was Eglismalescok, 'church of ? *Malisius*.' A man so called is found in Strathblane, 1398, and in Finnich Malise. But no such st. is known. W. says, *cf.* St. Loesuc, Brittany. Also *cf.* Kilmalisaig, N. Knapdale.

CARMUIRS (Falkirk). 1458 Duae Carmuris, 1632 Wester and Easter Carrmure. Prob. like DALMUIR, 'big,' G. *mòr*, 'fort,' not fr. *moor*. *Cf.* CAMELON.

CARMUNNOCK (Glasgow). *c.* 1177 Cormannoc, 1359 Curmanok. G. *coire manaich*, 'glen, corrie of the monk.'

CARMYLE (Glasgow), CARMYLIE (Arbroath). Gl. C. 1223 Kermill, -myl, 1510 Cermyle. G. *càrr maol* (-lie is loc.), 'bare, rounded rock'; *cf.* MULL in sagas Myl. Or *cathair mill* (nom. *meall*), 'fort on the hill.'

CARNBEE (Anstruther). *c.* 1450 Carnbe, 1457 Carnbene. Perh. G. *càrr an bein*, 'rock of the hide, wild beast's skin.'

CARNBO (Kinross). *Sic c.* 1210, *c.* 1370 Carnibo. 'Rock of the cattle,' G. *bo*.

CARNÉGIE (Carmyle). *a.* 1300 -egey, *c.* 1350 -innegi. G. *cathair an eige*, 'fort at the gap or nick.'

CARNETHY (Pentlands). Prob., as the site shows, W. *carneddi* (*dd* = *th*), 'cairns' or 'cairnlike hills.' (Rhys). *Cf.* 1116 *Inquis. Pr. David* Carnethyn, and Carneddan Hengwm, Barmouth.

CARNOCH, -OCK (Airth, Dunfermline, Ross-sh., etc.). St. Ninian's C. 1185 *Jocelyn* Kernach. Du. C. 1215 Carnock, 1250 Kernoch; Ai. C. 1449 Crannok, 1468 Kernok. G. *càrnach*, 'rocky place, quarry.' G. *crannag* is 'a pulpit.'

CARNOUSTIE (Angus). G. *cathair, càrr* or *carn na fheusta* (*fh* here mute), 'fort, rock or cairn of the feast.' But *c.* 1575 Carnusie, ? *carn guithais*, 'cairn of the firtree.'

CARN SMEART (Strathcarron) preserves Ptolemy's tribe *Smertae* (W.).

CARNTYNE (Glasgow). ? *c.* 1200 Prenteineth. Seems Brit. for 'tree among the green plots.' W. *tyno*. The earlier W. *pren* has become the later G. *crann*, 'tree'; then, by common transposing of *r*, the more familiar *càrn*. W. says, the ending is a G. *teineadh*, 'fire.'

CARNWATH (Lanark). *c.* 1165 Charnewid, 1174 Karnewic (*c* for *t*), 1108 Carnewith. W. *carn gwydd* (*dd* = *th*), 'cairn, mound in the shrubs or woods.' *Cf.* O.N. *við-r*, O.Dan. *wede*, 'a wood.'

CAROY (Skye). G. *càrr ruadh*, 'red rock.' *Cf.* Rob Roy.

CARPOW (Abernethy, Perth). Prob. *Pict. Chron.* Ceirfull, W. *caer pwll*, 'fort at the pool.' *Cf.* POWBURN.

CARRADALE (Kintyre, Skye). In Kint. there is a R. Carra. River names are rarely N., but this may be *kjarr-á*, 'copse river.' *Cf.* GLENRISDELL.

CARRBRIDGE (Aviemore). G. *Drochaid charra*, 'bridge of the rock-ledge.'

CARRICK (Ayrsh., Lochgoilhead). Ay. C. *Taliessin* Carrawg, *c.* 1140 Karric, 1286 Carryke. G. and Ir. *carraig*, 'a sea cliff or rock,' very common in compounds in Galloway and Ireland, Carrick-cow, etc. *Cf.* Carrickdubh, Whiting Bay.

CÁRRIDEN (Bo'ness). *a.* 1000 *Capitul.* of *Gildas* Cair Eden, prob. *Brit. Triads* Caer Eiddyn, *c.* 1140 Karreden. O.W. *caer eiddyn*, 'fort on the slope or hillside.' *Cf.* G. *aodann*, 'front, face,' and Dunedin or EDINBURGH.

CARRINGTON (Midlothn.). 1296 Keryngton. Prob. 'village of the descendants of *Ker* or *Carr*.' See -ing, p. 52.

CARRON (Falkirk, Elgin, W. Ross-sh., etc.). Fa. C. prob. *O.E. Chron.* 710 Caere, *Ir. Nennius* Carun, 1208 Caroun. Ro. C. prob. seen in *c.* 150 *Ptolemy's* tribes, Carnones and Cerones, in that region. Prob. G. *car abhuinn* (pron. ŏwn), 'bending, winding river,' G. *car*, 'a turn.' The Ir. Carrons are said to be corrup. of Ir. and G. *càrn*, 'cairn, rock.' W. holds to a Pict. Carsona, 'rough river.' The ending -on is seen in the Fr. Marne, L. Matrona, Garonne, L. Garumna, etc. *Cf.* CONON.

CARRONFLATS and -SHORE (Falkirk). 1552 Carrounflat. The latter built *c.* 1750. The tide comes up the river to here.

CARR ROCKS (Crail, Berwick-on-Tweed). Tautology. G. *càrr*, W. *caer*, Bret. *ker*, *cear*, also North. O.E. *carr*, 'a rock.'

CARRIFRAN GANS (hill, N.E. of Moffat). W. *caer y fran*, 'fort of the crow,' and *gans*, in Jam. as Roxb. Sc. for 'jaws without teeth'; root seen in obs. vb. *gane*, and in Sc. *gant*, Eng. *yawn*.

CAR(R)UBER (Linlithgow; farm, Fife). Li. C. 1296 Caribre, 1454 -ibris. Brit. *caer aber*, 'fort by the marsh.'

CARRUTHERS (Ecclefechan) and -STONE (Lockerbie). 1334 Carrothres, *c.* 1350 Caer Ruther, he being some old Celt. *Cf.* Karruderes, ? Berwicksh., Raine's *N. Durham* app. 39. G. Henderson suggests, 'fort of *Rydderch*,' King Roderc in *Adamn.*

CARSCURDO (Ladybank). Prob. *carse* (here adopted as G.) *cordach*, 'corded-looking CARSE,' G. *còrd, cùird,* 'a cord.'

CARSEBRECK (Auchterarder). 'Speckled, mottled CARSE,' G. *breac.*

CARSE of FORTH, GOWRIE, etc. *N.E.D.*'s earliest quot. is *c.* 1375 *Barbour* Kerss. But *c.* 1143 *chart.*, 'apud Streuelyn,' we find: 'Una salina in Carsach' (-ach suff. of place), *i.e.*, Carse of Forth, and *c.* 1200 *chart.* lie Carse de Gowrie, 1296 *Oath of fealty* to Edw. I, Johan Strivelyn de Cars. In Sc. still called *kerss*, as in KERSE. It means 'low, alluvial land along a river.' Root doubtful; *cf.* W. *cors,* 'pool, marsh, fenland,' in O.N. *carr*, Dan. *kaer*; *cf.* too O.N. *kjarr*, 'copse wood,' common in M.E. as *carr.* *Cf.* Kersie, 1195 Carsyn (*n* scribe's flourish), S. Alloa, Hungry Kerse, Br. of Allan, and Muckersie, Forteviot, 1263 Muckyrsy, G. *mùc,* 'a sow.'

CARSHOGLE (Hill, Thornhill). 1375 Corschogyll. 'CARSE for rye,' G. *sheagail.* *Cf.* Branshogle, Killearn, 1680 Blarinshogle, 'plain with rye.'

CARSKÉY (Kintyre). 1545 Karschaych, 1549 *Munro* Carraig Sceath, 1618 Carskeay. G. *cathair sgèith,* 'fort with the spur or wing,' or fr. *sgitheach,* 'hawthorn.' For Carraig see CARRICK.

CARSPHAIRN (N. Kirkcudbt.). 'CARSE with the alders,' G. *fearna.*

CARSTAIRS (Lanark). 1170 Casteltarres, *c.* 1250 Castrotharis, 1301 Castrum de Tarres, 1500 Carstaris, 1540 Castalstaris. O.E. *castel Tarres,* 'castle of Tarres,' Terras is still a Sc. surname. Also see CASTLEBAY; and *cf.* 1376 Tarrisholme, Liddesdale.

CART, R. (Renfrew.). Forms see CATHCART. The White and Black Cart join to form R. Cart. G. *caraid,* 'a pair.' The Water of Kilmarnock is called CARTH, for it too is made up of two streams; *cf.* Cartmel, Lancs. M. prefers to connect with W. *scarth,* 'scouring.'

CARTER Fell (Cheviots). *Sic a.* 1540. Prob. an O.N. nickname, *kört-r,* 'short horn,' *cf.* Ger. *kurz.* Sc. *cærter* is very near in sound to *kört-r.* Fell is O.N. *fjall, fell,* 'hill, mountain.'

CARWHINELOW, R. (S. Dumfries). Prob. W. *caer Gwendolew,* 'fort of G.,' leader in the battle of Ardderyd, 573.

CASHEL DHU (Sutherld.). G. and Ir. *caiseal,* L. *castellum,* 'circular stone fort,' common name in Ireland. G. *dubh* is 'black.'

CASKIEBEN (Aberdeen). 1261 Caskyben. Prob. G. *gasc a' bheinn,* 'nook, hollow between the hills.' *Cf. a.* 1300 Kaskybarran, Fife, G. *barran,* 'a hill top,' Caskardy, G. *àirde,* 'by the height,' and GASK. G. *casg* is 'a stopping, a stop.'

CASSILIS (Maybole). 1385 Casselys = CASHEL, with Eng. plur.

CASTLEBAY (Barra). Here stood the castle of the McNeills. In dealing with names in *castle*, remember, O.E. *castel* was orig. = L. *castellum*, the Vulgate N.T. transl. of Gr. *κώμη*, 'village' or 'ton.' Only through the Normans did it come to mean 'fortress.' *Cf.* Freeman *Nor. Conq.*, II, app. S.

CASTLE CAMPBELL (Dollar). Prob. *Pict. Chron.* ann. 877 Ach Cochlam, and formerly Castell Gloume, prob. G. *goch leum*, 'mad leap.' Name changed, 1489, after its owner, first earl of Argyll.

CASTLECARY (Falkirk). *Sic* 1450, but *c.* 1200 *Lennox Chart.* Castelcarris. Prob. tautology, fr. W. *caer*, 'fort.' Roman fort here. Castle Cary, Somerset, is fr. the surname Carey.

CASTLE CAVAN (Perthsh.). O.G. *cabhan*, 'a field,' in Ir. 'a hollow place.' Common in Ir. names, but not cognate with *cabin.*

CASTLE DOUGLAS (Kirkcudbt.). Sir Wm. *Douglas*, great builder here, changed the name fr. Carlinwark, in 1792. *Cf.* Castle Kennedy, Stranraer.

CASTLE GYLEN (Kerrera). N. *geil, gil*, 'a narrow glen,' with suffixed N. art. *-en*, 'the.'

CASTLE HEATHER (Inverness-sh.). Corrup. of Cas. Leather, older, Lathir, Leffare, G. *leathair*, 'a side.' *Cf.* Leathair nan Manach, Beauly, 'hillside of the monks.'

CASTLEMILK (Dumfries, Glasgow). Du. C. 1170 Casthelmile, 1189 Kastelmilc. Gl. C. 1387 Castel mylke. See CASTLEBAY and MILK.

CASTLE STALKER (Appin). On Island Stalker, *sic* 1501, G. *eilean an stalcaire*, 'falconer's isle.' *Stalker* is fr. O.E. *staelcan*, Dan. *stalke*, 'to go warily, stalk.' Said to have been built for James IV's hunting expeditions.

CASTLE SWEN (Knapdale). Old *Ir. MS.* Dun Suibhne, 'fort of Sweeny.' He was abbot of Iona, 766. But Dr. McLauchlan said, fr. *Sweyn*, a chief who d. 1034.

CASTLE TIRRIM or TIORAM (Moydart). G. *tioram*, 'dry, barren.'

CASTLETON, -TOWN (several). Roxbh. C. 1220 Caseltoun, 1260 Castleton. Eight in England. *Cf.* pp. 50, 51.

CASTRAMONT (Girthon). See p. 57.

CAT, Hill of (Angus). O.G. *cat*, G. *cath*, 'a battle.'

CATACOL (L. Ranza). 1433 Catagill, 1452 Cathaydill. Prob. 'Ravine,' O.N. *gil*, 'of the wild cats,' O.N. *kött-r*, gen. pl. *katta*. *Cf.* AUCHINGILL, and AUCHNAGATT, where too *g* is for *c*.

CATERLINE (Bervie). *Old* Katerlyn, Pictish. W. *Cader*, G. *cathair*, 'fort,' and W. *llyn*, G. *linne*, 'pool.' *Cf.* Catterden, Cumbld., 1201 Katerlen.

CATHCART (Glasgow). 1158 Kerkert (W. *caer*, 'fort'), *c.* 1170 Kat-Ketkert, *c.* 1375 Catkert. 'Battle (see CAT) on R. CART.'

CAT(H)KIN BRAES (Glasgow). G. *cat(h cinn*, dat of *ceann*, 'at the battle height.' See BRAE.

CATHLAW (Torphichen). Hybrid. G. *cath*, 'battle,' and O.E. *hláew*, Sc. *law*, 'a hill.'

CATRAIL or Picts' Work Ditch (said to run fr. Peel Fell to Mossilee near where Tweed joins Gala). Sir J. A. H. Murray said, an invented name for an invented rampart. First described in Gordon's *Itinerar. Septentrion*, 1726; improved on by the imagination of Chalmers, *Caledonia*, 1807. But some say it is *a.* 1304 *chart.*, 'the fosse of the Galwegians.'

CÁTRINE (Mauchline). O.G. *cat roinne*, 'battle point or headland.'

CATSLACK (Yarrow). 1473 Cattislak, 1487 Catslak, 'Little shallow valley of the wild cat.' *Cf.* CATACOL, BEESLACK and Knockslack, Wamphray.

CAULDCOTS (Arbroath). 1335 Caldecotes (1296 *Ragman's R.* Geoffrey de Caldecote). 'Cold cots or cottages.' *Cf.* Calcots, Elgin.

CAULRIG (Inverness). Prob. Sc. for 'cold rigg or ridge.'

CAUSEWAYBANK (Chirnside), -END (Manuel), -HEAD (Stirling). At Stirl. C. stood the Spittal, to which a causeway ran fr. Stirling Bridge, *c.* 1220 La chausee, *Stlg. Burgh Sasines*, Lang Calsay. From Eng. *causey*, M.E. *caucé*, O.Nor. Fr. *caucie*, late L. *calceata*, 'beaten, trodden way,' fr. *calx*, 'the heel.' *Cf.* 1202 *Reg. Dunferm.* A capite de la chaucee.

CAVAY (Orkney). Not 'cheese isle,' but prob. *Kalf-ey*. See CALF, CALVA.

CAVERS, CAVERTON (Hawick). 1291 Kauirs, 1298 Cauers; 1533 Cavertone. Perh. fr. a man. *Onom.* has only a *Caber*; *cf.* Caversham, Reading. But early O.E. *ceber-*, *caebrtun* is a 'forecourt,' and later O.E. *cafortun*, 'a mansion.'

CAWDOR (Nairn). Pron. Kāhdor. *c.* 1280 Kaledor, 1501 Caldor, = CALDER.

CEANNACROE (Inverness-sh.). G., 'peak, head of the hill.' G. *ceann* in names is usually Ken-. Croe is G. and Ir. *croagh*, *cruach*, 'stacklike hill.' *Cf.* Croaghpatrick, etc.

CEANN A' MHAIM (Inverness-sh.). 'Head, point of the rounded hill.' G. *màm*, *màim*, cognate with L. *mamma*, 'the breast.'

CELLARDYKE (Anstruther). 1600, 'the Silverdyk,' Sc. Sillerdyke. *Dyke* is O.E. *díc*, our *ditch*. *Cf.* Sillerford, Strathbogie.

CERES (Cupar). 1199 Syreis, 1517 Siras, Pict. G. *siar-ais*, 'western place.' *Cf.* Alves, etc.

CESNOCK, R. (Mauchline). 1625 Cesnok. Prob. G. *seasgan -ach*, 'marsh, moor place.' But CESSFORD Burn, Morebattle, 1596 Cesfurde, must be fr. Eng. *cess*, 'a peat-bog.' *N.E.D.*'s earliest quot. is 1636.

CHALLOCH (Girvan, etc.). G. *teallach*, 'a hearth, a forge.' Initial *t* in G. is often *ch*. *Cf.* CHIPPERDINGAN.

CHALMAN I. (Iona). Prob. for *Colman*, name of some 60 Irish saints.

CHAMPFLEURY (Linlithgow). Fr. *champ fleuri*, 'flowery field.' Thought to be a reminiscence of Q. Marie of Lorraine, but it seems quite modern. *Cf.* 1631 *R.M.S.* Blakfuird alias Champunyie, Edinburgh and *a*. 1328, 'Mountflory in schira de Scoone,' Fife.

CHANNELKIRK (Lauder). *a*. 1200 *Lib. de Ortu Cuthbt*, Childeschirche, then said to have been built in honour of St. Cuthbert, who was there as a child, O.E. *cild*, esp. a child of gentle birth. Then 1160–1300 *Dryburgh Chart.* Childenechirche, -inchirch ; *-ene-* either irregular gen. pl. of *cild* or the rare adj. *childene*, 'pertaining to children' ; 1535 Chyndylkirk, 1620 Chingel-, 1634 Cheinil-, 1834 (given as the local pron.) Ginglekirk. It is a curious corrup., but the liquids *n* and *l* easily interchange. *Channel* in mod. Sc. is 'gravel.'

CHANONRY (Fortrose). 1503 'The Canonry of Ross,' 1570. Channonrie, 'The jurisdiction,' O.E. *ríce*, 'of the canon,' the cathedral precincts : *cf.* CANONBIE. Fortrose in G. is *A'chanonach*, 'the canonry.'

CHAPEL (several, Fife, etc.). Common too in England. Chapel, late L. *cappella*, fr. *cappa* 'cape, cope,' is so spelt in Eng. *c*. 1275.

CHAPELERNE (Carmichael). 'Chapel-house,' O.E. *erne*. *Cf.* Blackerne, Kirkcudbt. and WHITHORN.

CHARTERSHALL (Bannockburn). *Pont* Chartreushall. So, prob., not fr. the family of *Charteris* (*i* mute), but fr. a *charterhouse* or house for Carthusians, fr. the Chartreuse near Grenoble.

CHESTERS, The (Hawick, Bolton, E. Lothian), CHESTER Knowes (Chirnside), CHESTER Lees (Tweedsmuir), and CHESTER Rig and Hill (Traquair). L. *castra*, 'camp,' *castrum*, 'fort' : *cf.* Chester and the many -chesters in England. Remains of hill-forts are found at nearly all the above. The Romans certainly were in Peeblessh. ; but it is doubtful whether these be Roman or British. Veitch thought they marked the final, unsuccessful stand of the Cymri or Britons against their many invaders.

CHEVIOT Hills. 1181 *Pipe R.*, Chiuiet, 1239 Chyviot, *c*. 1250 Montes chiueti, *a*. 1300 Mons chiuioth. A puzzle, prob. pre-Celt. The only possible and very abnormal suggestion is Fr. *chevet*, 'a pillow,' and so, pillow-like hill ; *cf.* Chevet, Barnsley, *Dom.* Cevet.

CHICKEN Hd. (Stornoway). Eng. transl. of its G. name *rudha na circe.* But *circe* is a Gael's mistake for *kirke*, it being prob. a spot where a church was built.

CHIPPERDINGAN Well (Wigtown). G. *tiobar Dingan*, 'well of St. Ninian,' see p. 65, and *cf.* CHALLOCH, TIPPERLINN, and Auchtercheper, Moray, 'upland with the well.'

CHIRNSIDE (Duns). Local pron. Chirsit. *Sic* 1250, but *c.* 1098 Cirnside, 'Hillside like a churn,' O.E. *cyrin*, M.E. *chyrne*, Sc. *kirn.*

CHISHOLM (Roxburgh). 1254 Cheseholme. 'The Chisholm,' G. *an Siosalach*, a branch fr. the Norm. Sysilts or Cecils, early settled in Roxburgh. But the place-name means 'waterside meadow good for producing cheese.' *Cf.* Chiswick, *Pl.N.Eng.* and the many Eng. Butterleys. See HOLM.

CHONZIE Ben (S. Perth). Pron. Hony (z = old Sc. y). Prob. O.G. loc. of *Choinneach*, 'Kenneth,' and not fr. G. *chon.* gen. of *cu*, 'a dog'; though L. Con is near; *cf.* Carchonzie Woods, Callander.

CHRYSTON (Glasgow). 1721 Chrystoun. 'Christ's village.' *Cf.* Christon, Exeter and Christskirk, old name of Strath, Skye.

CIR MHÒR (Arran). G. 'the great comb or crest.'

CLACHAIG (Dunoon, Arran). Loc. of G. *clachag*, Ir. *clochag*, 'a stony place,' fr. *clach*, *cloch*, 'a stone.'

CLACHAN (about 20), also CLACHAN of ABERFOYLE, etc. G. for 'village,' often also 'church.' Root as above.

CLACHAN EASY (Wigtown). 'Village of Jesus,' G. *Iosa. Cf.* CHRYSTON.

CLACHDIAN (Ben Macdhui). 'Stone of shelter,' G. *dìon.*

CLACHNACUDDAN (stone at a street corner, Inverness). G. for 'stone for the tubs,' *nan cudainn. Cf.* CULLICUDDEN.

CLACHNAHARRY (Inverness). G. for 'stone of watching,' *na fhaire*, which it actually was: but W. says, 'stone of repentance,' *na h'aithrige.* Clachcharra, Onich, is prob. fr. G. *cara*, 'a haunch'; while Knockenharrie, Kirkcolm, is 'little watch hill,' *cnocan fhaire.*

CLACKMANNAN. *Sic* 1221, but *c.* 1133 Clacmanan, 1147 -anant, *c.* 1148 -anet; also *c.* 1143 Clamance, prob. an error. 'Stone of *Manu*,' gen. *-nan*, prob. same as the Manannan Maclir of Ir. legend, who gave name to I. of Man. This huge stone in the middle of the village is prob. glacial. The district, in G. Manann, in W. Manan, stretched fr. here over the Forth through Stirling to SLAMANNAN Moor and E. to R. Avon.

CLADICH (Inverary). G., 'at the shore,' *cladach. Cf.* BRUAN.

CLAIDVILLE (Islay). McKinnon said, N. for 'well-clad *fjall* or hill,' O.N. *klæða*, pa. pple, *klædd*, 'to clothe.'

CLAIGINN (common Sc. and Ir. hill-name). G. *claigionn*, Ir. *claigeann*, 'a skull,' hence 'a dry, round hill.'

CLA(I)RDON Hill (Thurso). G. *clàr dun*, 'smooth, bare hill.'

CLAIRINCH (L. Lomond). *c.* 1225 Clarines. G. *clàr innis*, 'island like a table or plate.' *Cf.* above.

CLARKSTON (Airdrie and Busby). *Cf.* CLERKINGTON.

CLASHBREAC (Morvern). 1496 -brake. G. *clais breac*, 'spotted, speckled hollow, ditch or trench.' Clash- is common in Galloway and Ir. names. *Cf.* Clashmore, Assynt, and CLASHBENNIE, Gowrie, *a.* 1215 Glesbanin.

CLASHMACH Hill (Huntly). 'Hollow of the battlefield,' one of the meanings of G. *magh*, 'a plain.' Tradition tells of 3 battles here.

CLASHNEACH, Nick of (Minigaff). Tautology. G. *clais 'n 'eich*, 'trench, furrow of the horse.'

CLATT (Aberdeen). 1137 Clat = CLETT.

CLATTO (Kingskettle). 1541 Clatty-dene. Sc. *clatty*, 'dirty,' fr. *clat*, 'a clot, a clod of dirt.'

CLAUCHLANDS (Lamlash). *Old* Clachelane, -ellane, Cleuchtlanis. Dr. Cameron thought fr. G. *clach*, 'rock' and *lann*, 'enclosure'; -elane reminds of G. *eilean*, 'island,' only there the 1st syll. is long.

CLAVAGE (Dunning). *c.* 1240 Clatheueys. Perh. Pict. for 'sword-place,' G. *claidheamh-ais*. *Cf.* ALVES.

CLAVERHOUSE (Dundee). 1594 The Barns of C. O.E. *clafre*, *clæfre*, 4–7 *claver*, 'clover.' *Cf.* Claver-don, -ing, and -ley, England.

CLAY of ALLAN (Fearn). G. *Criadhach ailean mhòr*, 'big, clayey plain,' phonetics as in CRIANLARICH. Of course *criadhach* may mean 'clayey place,' but there seems no evidence of its use thus, nor of *clay* in this sense in Eng. See ALLAN.

CLAYSLAPS (once a village, now a street, in Glasgow). 1635 Clay-sclope, 1714 -slap. From *slap* sb², 'opening, gap,' at times confused with *slope*.

CLEGHORN (Lanark, Cairnie). La. C. *sic* 1483, but 1230 Clegerne. Ca. C. *old* Clegern. O.E. *cláeg erne*, 'clay house,' Dan. *kleg*, 'clay.' *Cf.* DREGHORN and WHITHORN.

CLEISH (Kinross). 1231 Kles, *c.* 1280 Cleth. G. and Ir. *clais*, 'a ditch, a furrow.' Near by is CLASHLOCHIE, G. *locha*, 'ducks' ditch.'

CLELLAND (Motherwell). Prob. 'clay land,' O.E. *clæg*, M.E. *cley*, *clei*, 'clay.'

CLEPINGTON (Dundee). Perh. '*Clephane's* village,' *cf.* Clephantown, Nairn. Clephane is a corrup. of Clapham.

CLERKINGTON (E. and once in Mid. Lothian). Mi. C. *c.* 1141 Clercketune, 1173 Clerkynton. 'Village of the cleric or clerk.' *Cf.* Clerkenwell, London, 1185 Fons clericorum.

CLETT, The (Thurso). 1329 Klaet, S. Ronaldsay. O.N. *klett-r*, G. *cleit*, 'a rocky pillar, a cliff.' *Cf.* CLATT.

CLIBRECK Ben (Sutherld.). 1269 Clybry. G. *cliath breac*, 'spotted side or slope.' W. thinks it may be, N. *klif-brakka*, 'cliff slope.'

CLICKIMIN (Lerwick). O.N. *klakk-minni*, 'rock mouth.' *Cf.* Cleckhimin, Lauderdale and Airmyn, *Pl.N.Eng.*

CLIFTON (Morebattle). *a.* 800 *Hist. St. Cuthb.*, Cliftun. O.E. for 'cliff-dwelling.'

CLINTMAINS (St. Boswell's). Sw. and Dan. *clint*, 'brow of a hill, promontory.' *Cf.* Clent Hills, Staffs., and Clint, Yorks. But Clinty, Antrim, is Ir. *cluainte*, 'meadows.' *Mains* is common in Sc. for 'farm steading' or 'mansion house,' the *main* or chief building. *N.E.D.* says, short for *demesne* or *domain*, but gives no evidence.

CLIPPENS (Kilbarchan). G. *clibein*, 'a small excrescence,' with Eng. pl.

CLOCH, The (Gourock). *a.* 1600 *chart. Jas. VI* Clochstane. G. *cloch*, *clach*, 'rock, stone.'

CLOCHAN (Fochabers). Dimin. of above. In Ir. it means a beehive-shaped stone house.

CLOCHNABEN, -BANE (hill, Kincardine). G. *cloch na beinne*, 'rock on the ben.' But also called White Stone Hill as if fr. *bàn*, 'white.'[1]

CLOCHODERICK (Kilbarchan). *c.* 1202 Cloghrodric, 1456 -rodryge. 'Rock of *Roderick*.'

CLOCKSBRIGGS (Forfar). Explanation needed. The 1st syll. may be G. *cloch*, 'a rock.'

CLOLA (Mintlaw). Doubtful, ? 'cleft law' or 'hill.' O.N. *klof*, 'a cleaving,' *klofi*, 'a cleft.' But *cf.* CLOVA and CLOVULLIN.

CLONE (Galloway 3). 1456 Clune, 1557 Cloyne; *c.* 1230 Clon, Ross-sh. now CLYNE. Prob. G. *claon*, 'a slope.'

CLOSEBURN (Dumfries). *Sic* 1278, but *a.* 1200 Kylosbern, 1683 Closburn. G. *cill Osbern*, 'cell, church of St. Osborne,' N. Asenbjörn, 'bear of the gods.'

CLOUSTA (Shetland). Perh. O.N. *klof-sta*, 'cleft, cleaving place,' see p. 42.

CLOVA (Angus, Aberdeen). *a.* 1300 Cloueth, 1328 Cloveth. Perh. fr. G. *cloidh*, 'a paddock' or *clòth*, 'a victory,' with *-ach* suff. of place. *Cf.* next.

[1] *Cf.* too Clochmabanestane, 1398 in Bain's *Cal. Doct. Sc.*, a trysting place, fr. *Mabon*, a Celt. hero, see LOCHMABEN.

CLOVULLIN (Ardgour). G. *cladh a' mhuilinn,* 'mound of the mill.'

CLOY Glen (Arran). From the McLoys or Fullertons, who got lands here fr. Robert the Bruce. McLoy is *mac Loui* or 'son of Louis.'

CLUDEN, R. (Dumfries). *Sic* 1449. *Taliessin,* Glut vein. Perh. W. *clwyd,* 'warm,' with *-en* suff. for 'stream.' *Cf.* AVON and R. Clwyd, Wales.

CLUGSTON (Wigtown) (1230–40 *Chart. Lindores,* Klogestoun). Prob. 'dwelling' of some man. One *Clofige* in *Onom.*

CLUNAIG (Skipness). 1511 Clynage. Dimin. of G. *cluan,* 'a meadow' or *claon,* 'a slope.' *Cf.* next and CLONE.

CLUNAS (Nairn). As above, with *-ais* Pict. suff. of place. *Cf.* ALVES.

CLUNIE, -Y (several). Blairgowrie C. *Pict. Chron.* ad Cluanan, *c.* 1164 Kluen, 1291 Clony. Laggan C. *c.* 1603 Cloonye. As above. The -ie is loc. *Cf.* Clun, Salop, and CLUNITER, Innellan, G. *claon oitir,* 'slope at the reef.'

CLUTAG (Kirkinner). Refers to land valuation of 'pennylands,' G. *clitag* being the 8th of a farthing.

CLYDE, R. *c.* 90 *Tacitus* Clota, *c.* 150 *Ptolemy* Klōta, *a.* 700 *Adamn.* Cloithe, *c.* 720 *Bede* Alcluith, *Nennius* Cluth, *a.* 1100 *scholiast* Ail-Cluada, *c.* 1145 *Geoffr. Mon.* Alclud (G. *àl, àil Clud,* 'rock on the Clyde, *i.e.,* Dumbarton), *a.* 1249 Clud ; *cf.* 1116 *Inquis Pr. Dav.* Canclut, prob. = Clydehead. See also STRATHCLYDE. Rhys thought *Clota* might be a pre-Celt. river goddess, and says the name is not the same as R. Clwyd, Wales, which means 'warm,' W. *clyd.* However, *Dom.'s* form of this river, 'Cloith, Cloit' is practically the same as *Adamn.'s* for Clyde. R. Clwyd is *c.* 1200 *Girald. Cambr.* Cloid, 1250 Cloyd ; *Pict. Chron.* ad Cluiam is prob. this too. *Cf.* Joyce *Ir. Names,* 2nd series, pp. 371–2. Wh. Stokes says, root is as in L. *clu-,* 'wash.'

CLYDESDALE. 1250 *Matthew Paris,* Cludesdale.

CLYNDER (Gareloch). *Old* Clyndairg. G. *claon dearg,* 'red slope.'

CLYNE (Golspie and E. Ross). Go. C. *c.* 1240 Clun, Ro. C. 1231 Clon, 1264 Clyne, 1375 Clyn. G. *claon,* 'a slope.'

CLYNELISH (Sutherld). G. *claon lios,* 'slope with the garden.'

CLYTH (Lybster). 1377 Westerclithe. G. *cliath, cliathach,* 'the slope of a hill.'

CNOC AINGIL (many). G. fr. 'knoll, hill of angels.' Usually Knock.

COALSNAUGHTON (Tillicoultry). 1620 -nauchtant, 1629 Cussnachtane. Seems, G. *caolas Nechtain,* 'narrow pass of Nechtan'; see CAMBUSNETHAN.

COALTON (Dysart). A colliery village.

COATBRIDGE (bridge not made till *c.* 1800) and near it COATDYKE and COATS. Corn. *coat*, O.W. *chet*, W. *coed*, 'a wood.' The Eng. Coathams and 3 Coats are prob. all fr. M.E. *cote*, 'cot, cottage.'

COBBLER, The (Arrochar). *Sic* 1800. G. *an Greusaich chrom*, 'the crooked shoemaker.' The ben looks like a cobbler at his work.

COBBINSHAW (Carmdath). Prob. '*Colban's* hill.' Sc. *shaw*, O.E. *scaga*, strictly 'a wood,' often used for 'a hill.' COBBIE ROW'S CAS, Weir, Orkney, is corrup. of 'Kolbein Hruga's Castle,' mentioned *c.* 1150; *hruga* is 'a heap.' *Cf.* COVINGTON and COPINSHAY.

COCH- COCKNO (Duntocher). 1594 Cochno, 1699 Cockneugh; *chart.* Cochynnach, -inach, G. *cuachanach*, 'place of little cups,' fr. *cuach*, 'a cup' (W.).

COCHRANE (old barony, Paisley). *Sic* 1384. W. *coch rhen*, 'red brook.'

COCKAIRNIE (Aberdour), E. and W. COCKAIRNEY (Kinross). Ab. C. *a.* 1169 Kincarnathar, 1178 Kincarnyne. The earlier form is for Kincarn Nether, and there are still Nether and Upp. Cockairnie. G. *cinn càirn*, 'at the head of the cairn or heap.' Also *cf.* COCKENZIE. Ki. C. 1304 Cultcairn is G. *cuilt charnaigh*, 'rocky nook' (W.).

COCKBURNSPATH (Berwicksh.). *c.* 1128 Colbrandespade, 1461 Coburnispeth, 1503 Cowburns pecht, 1508 Cokburnis-, 1529 Cokbrandispeth. 'Path of *Colbrand*,' a fairly common O.E. name. Transposed *r* is common and liquid *l* easily drops. But COCKBURN, Duns, 1166 Koke-, 1381 Cokburn, is fr. *cock*.

COCKENZIE (Prestonpans). Local pron. Cockénnie. 1590 Cowkany. Prob. = Culkenzie, Rosskeen, G. *cùil Coinnich*, 'Kenneth's nook.' *Cf.* next and COWDEN.

COCKLARACHY (Drumblade). 1423 Culclerochy, 1557 Coclarachquhy. G. *cul cleirich* (here in loc.), 'hill back of the cleric or priest.' For the Cock- *cf.* above.

COCKLEROY, -RUE (hill, Linlithgow). Prob. G. *cochull ruadh*, 'red cap or hood'; *ruadh* would yield both -roy and -rue.

COCK of ARRAN. *Sic* Pont. G. An Coileach, 'the cock.' *Cf.* Cocklaw, Walston, 1461 Coklaw.

COCKPEN (Dalkeith). 1250 Kok-, *a.* 1300 Cockpen. W. *coch pen*, 'red head' or 'hill.'

COIGACH (Ullapool). 1502 Cogeach (and so now pron.), 1530 Coidgeach. Really G. *còigeach*, 'a fifth.' Natives say, *còig-ach*, 'five fields,' fr. 5 places there with names in Ach-.

COIGNAFEARN (Inverness). G. *còig na fearn*, 'fifth part with the alders.' There are 5 farms at the head of Strathdearn—Cuignasith, etc.

COILANTOGLE (Trossachs). G. *cùl an teocheil* or *tiochail*, corrup. of *t'saoghail*, 'at the back of the world,' name also of a place in ? Mull. Or fr. *t'ocheil*, 'at the back of the height'; see OCHIL.

COILTON (Ayr). From King *Cole*. See KYLE.

COIRECHATACHAN (Skye). G. *coire*, see next, and prob. based on G. *cat*, 'the wild cat' (W.).

COIR NAN URUISGIN (Ben Venue). G. for 'cave of the goblins'; it was thought haunted. *Coire* is 'cauldron, circular hollow, dell, cave.'

COLABOLL (Lairg). Norse for '*Kol's* place.' See *bol*, p. 42.

COLDBACKIE (Tongue), COLDBACKS (Shetland). See BACK, 'hill ridge.' Backie is a dimin.

COLDINGHAM (Berwick). *Sic c.* 1098, but *c.* 709 *Eddi*, Coludesburg, *c.* 720 *Bede* Coludi Urbs, *a.* 800 *Hist. St. Cuthb.* Colodesbyrig, *c.* 1100 Coldingaham and Coldingamscire; *a.* 1500 often spelt with G. At first 'fort of *Colud*,' now 'home, village of his descendants,' see p. 52. The part of Berwicksh. near the priory was early called Coldinghamshire.

COLDSTREAM (Berwicksh.). *a.* 1178 Kaldestrem, *c.* 1207 *Gervase* Caldestream, 1290 Coldstreme, referring to R. Tweed.

COLFIN (Portpatrick). Col- in names may be either G. *còil*, *cùil*, 'a nook, a corner,' or *coill (e*, 'a wood.' G. *fionn* is 'white, clear.'

COLINSBURGH (Fife). Founded by *Colin* Lindsay, 3rd earl of Balcarres, 1682.

COLINTON (Edinburgh). 1296 Colgyntone, 1538 Colintoun. 'Village of *Colgan*,' an Ir. name.

COLINTRAIVE (Kyles of Bute). G. *caol an t'snaimh*, 'strait, kyle, at the swimming place,' where cattle were swum over; *cf.* ARDENTRYVE. The liquids *n* and *r* often interchange.

COLL (island, and in Lewis). Perh. *Adamn.* Colosus (so W.). 1449 Coll, *c.* 1590 Collow. G., Ir. and W. *coll*, 'a hazel'; *cf.* COLONSAY. But N. *koll-r* is 'hill-top, summit.'

COLLACE (Perth). 1250 Kulas, 1403 Cullace. Prob. G. *cùl eas*, 'nook at the waterfall.' A rocky burn tumbles down here.

COLLESSIE (Newburgh). 1253 Cullessy. Prob. G. *cùl easaige*, 'nook of the squirrel or pheasant.'

COLLI(E)STON (Ellon, Arbroath). *Collie* is a common Sc. surname, and also Sc. for 'sheep-dog.' It is prob. N. *Kolfi*, *Kolli*, as in Collister, now an Aberdeen surname, fr. Kolvister, Yell.

COLLIN (Kirkcudbt). G. *cuileann*, 'holly.' *Cf.* COWIE.

COLMONELL (Girvan). 1179 Kirke colmanele, *c.* 1240 Colmanel. St. *Colmonella*, d. 611, in *Adamn.* Columbanus, is G. *Colum an Eala*, 'C. of the Eala,' a stream in King's Co. *Cf.* KILCALMONELL.

COLONSAY (Hebrides). 1335 Golwonche, 1376 Colowsay, 1463 Colonsay, 1549 -vansay. Doubtful. Some connect with COLL; many say, '*Colum's*, Columba's isle,' N. *ay*, or Norse G. *aoi*, 'isthmus,' for this island and Oronsay once joined. W. fancies N. *Kolbeins-ey*, 'Colvin's isle.'

COLPACH, -PY (Aberdeen). O.G. *colpa*, 'cow, heifer,' *colpach*, 'pasture for cows.' *Cf.* 1461 Colpley, Renfrew. *Colpa* was a son of the legendary Milesius; hence Colp, on R. Boyne.

COLQUHOUN, Mains and Chapel of (Old Kilpatrick). *Sic* c. 1246, but 1308 Kelquon, *a.* 1328 Culchen, 1373 Culquhone, also Colquhan. Local pron. Cuchúin. First syll. see COLFIN; the 2nd is G. *cumhann*, 'narrow.'

COLTNESS (Newmains). Early history unknown. Prob. not fr. Eng. *colt* as in COLTBRIDGE, Edinburgh, but G. *coillte an eas*, 'woods by the waterfall.'

COLVEND (Dalbeattie). 1513 Culevane, 1560 Colven, 1610 Culwen, *Pont* Cov-, Cawenn. Prob. 'at the back of the hill,' G. *cùl a' bheinn*. See COLFIN.

COLZIUM (Kilsyth). Now pron. Coal-zium. *Pont* Colyam. Looks like G. *coil leum*, 'wood of the leap,' yet prob. = Coylum, Aviemore, G. *cuing leum*, 'gorge leap,' *cf.* Knockchoilum, Stratherrick. The Laird's Loup is near Colzium.

COMAR (Ben Lomond). G. *comar*, 'confluence, meeting of two waters.' *Cf.* COMRIE and CUMBERNAULD. COMERS, Aberdeen, is the same.

COMISTON (Edinburgh). 1335 Colmanston. Five *Colmans* in *Onom.* But COMPSTONE, Kirkcudbt., 1331 Combistoun, 1504 Cumyston, will be fr. a man *Comb*, prob. for *Columba*.

COMRIE (Crieff, Contin), CUMRIE (Cairnie). Cr. C. *c.* 1268 Comry, Co. C. 1479 Cumre. G. *comar*, 'confluence,' in loc. *Cf.* COMAR.

CON, L. (L. Katrine). G. *cu, coin*, 'a dog.' For CONA see GLENCOE and next.

CONAGLEN (Ft. William). G. *con-gleann*, 'double glen' (M.). This is the L. prefix *con-*, in G. usually *comh-*, 'together.' *Cf.* Cona Mheall ('hill') Durness.

CONCHRA (Strachur, Lochalsh), CÓNOCHRA (Drymen). Lo. C. 1554 Concry, 1558 Conachry, Dr. C. *Pont* Connochra. G. *con-cra*, 'collection of folds,' G. *crà, crò*, 'fold, weir.' *Cf.* Contullich, Alness.

CONDORRAT (Cumbernauld). 1553 *RMS.* Cundurat. G. *con, comh-dobhar-ait*, 'joint-river-place.' *Cf.* CONAGLEN and CONWHISK, also Le Dorat, Hte Vienne, France.

CONGLASS (Tomintoul). G. *con ghlais*, 'dog stream' (W.).

CONISBY (Islay). Prob. fr. O.N. *kóng-r*, 'king'; *cf.* Coniston, Cumbld., and CUNNINGSBURGH. On *-by*, 'village,' see p. 41.

CONNEL Ferry (Oban). Not fr. *Conall*, K. of Dalriada, *c.* 560, or some other Celt. hero, but G. *coingheall*, 'a whirlpool,' referring to the falls on L. Etive. W. says, Achachonleich, Lochalsh, has the same root.

CONNING- CUNNINGSBURGH (Lerwick). [1251 *Chart. Lindores* Cunigburch.] Fr. O.N. *konung-r*, Dan. *kon(g)e*, 'a king.' *Cf.* Coningsby, Boston, CONISBY, Kingstown, Queensborough, etc.; also Cummister, Yell, 1639 Cunnyngsitter (N. *sæter*, 'summer farm').

CONON, -AN, R. (Ross-sh.). ? 1309 Strathconon, 1479 Strquhonane. Prob. not fr. *Conan* the Ossianic hero, but fr. G. *cu*, *coin*, 'a dog'—'dog-river,' *-on* being a regular river ending, see CARRON. So W.

CONRICK (Glencairn, Badenoch). Gl. C. 1506 Conrauche, 1580 -rach. Perh. G. *comar-ach*, 'confluence place.' W. says, *còmhrag*, 'a meeting.'

CONTIN (Strathpeffer). G. Cunndainn. 1226 Conten, 1510 -tan. Not G. *cointin*, 'a dispute, debatable land,' but prob. means 'confluence'; *cf.* BOHUNTIN and Contuinn, S. of Cavan.

CONWAY (Beauly). *c.* 1215 Coneway, 1291 Convathe, *a.* 1330 -veth. G. Confhadaich, 'noisy, stormy,' fr. *confhadh*, 'a storm' (M.). But W., p. 220, seems to favour G. *coinmheadh*, 'free quartering, billeting'; *cf.* Laurencekirk. Conva and Convoy, Ireland, are fr. Ir. and G. *con mhagh*, 'hound's plain.'

CONWHISK (Dumfries). G. *con uisg*, 'joint streams.' *Cf.* CONDORRAT.

COODHAM (Kilmarnock). *Old* Cowdams. A mod. refinement, *c.* 1850, and prob. orig. a cows' drinking-place.

COOKNEY (Stonehaven). Doubtful; *cf. a.* 1400 Quikenne, near Hawick. Perh. O.G. loc. of *caochan*, 'at the rivulet.'

COOMLEES (Tweeddale). W. *cwm*, 'a hollow,' and Eng. *lee*, *lea*, 'a meadow.' *Cf.* Coomb Hill, Tweedsmuir, Eng. *coomb*, O.E. *cumb*, 'a bowl, a valley,' root *cimban*, 'to join.'

COPINSHAY (Orkney). *c.* 1260 Kolbensey, N. for '*Kolbein's* or Colvin's isle.' *Cf.* COBBINSHAW.

COPPERCLEUCH (Selkirk). *Older* Capper-, Sc. var. of *copper*. Jam. says, in Mearns it means 'a spider'; so perh. 'spider glen.' See BUCCLEUCH.

CORBY (Roxburgh). Like Corby, Grantham, *Dom.* Corbi, and C., Kettering, *Dom.* Carbi, 'Dwelling of *Cor* or *Carr*,' one in *Onom.* But CORBIEHALL, Carstairs, and CORBIE DEN, Cults, are fr. Sc. *corbie*, N. and Sw. *korp*, L. *corvus*, 'raven, crow.'

COREHOUSE (Lanark). 1362 la Corrokys. G. *coireach*, 'place full of circular hollows or corries,' with Eng. pl. -ys. Curious corruption.

CORNCOCKLE Muir (Dumfries). Named fr. the common *cockle* flower, *Lychnis githago*. CORNTON (Br. of Allan), 1202–10 Cornetune, is the oldest *tun* or -ton in Stirling.

CORNSILLOCH (Dalserf). 1379 Carynsalach. G. *càrn seileach*, 'cairn, mound of willows.'

CORPACH (Ft. William, Jura). G. for 'corpse-place,' where corpses used to be kept overnight, when travelling to a burial isle.

CORRA LINN (Lanark). *Corra* prob. means 'round,' *cf.* G. *corran*, 'reaping hook.' Some prefer G. *coradh*, 'a weir,' with W. *llyn* or G. *linne*, 'a pool.' *Cf.* Corra Pool, Kirkcudbt.

CORRAN (L. Linnhe). G. 'a reaping hook,' Ir. *carran*, as in Carran Tual. *Cf.* Zancle, now Messina, Sicily. Some prefer the dimin. *corran*, 'a little excess or outgrowth, a beak, a snout.' Both suit the site.

CORRIE (Arran, Dumfries). Ar. C. 1807 Currie. G. *coire*, 'a cauldron, then a circular glen.' CORRIÉACHAN (L. Lomond) is fr. *Eachan*, 'Hector.'

CORRIEFECKLACH (Minigaff). 'Glen of the polecat,' G. *feòcullach*, or *fiaclach*, 'toothed, jagged' (W.).

CORRIEGALL (Harray). 1572 Corigilles, and CORRIGILL, CORRIEGILLS (Brodick), 1558 Corriglis, 1590 Corrigills. O.N. *karri-gil*, 'cock-ptarmigan valley.' *Cf.* CATACOL.

CORRIEMULZIE (Braemar and Oykell Br.). Brae. C. G. *coire mùllidh*, which natives take to be, 'corrie fit for driving a mill,' G. *muileann*. Seven mills once near Oykell Br.

CORRIEVAIRACK, -YARRICK (Boleskin). G. *coire eirich*, 'rising corrie or glen.' M. thought perh. connected with *earrach*, 'spring.'

CORRIEVRECKAN (Jura). *a.* 700 *Adamn.* Vortex, Charybdis Brecain, *c.* 1380 *Fordoun* Corbrekane. G. *coire Bhrecain*, 'cauldron,' here, 'whirlpool, of Brecan,' grandson of the famous Niall, *c.* 450.

CORSEWALL Pt. (Stranraer). 1430 Corswel. 'The cross well,' here dedicated to St. Columba. For transposed *r cf.* BEANCROSS, CORSBIE, Earlston, and CORSAPOOL, Islay. *Well* in Sc. is *wall*.

CORSOCK (Kirkcudbt.). 1527 Karsok. W. and Corn. *cors*, 'bog, fen,' with dimin. *-oc*, *-og*. *Cf.* CARSE and Corscleugh, Yarrow.

CORSTÓRPHINE (Edinburgh). Local pron. Carstérfin. *c.* 1130 Crostorfin, -phin, *c.* 1140 Crorstorfin, 1508 Corstorphyne. Accent shows, not G. *crois torra fionn*, 'cross of the clear hill,' though Torphin Hill is opposite, near Juniper Green. It is 'Cross of *Thorfinn*.' The famous Earl of the Orkneys, 1014–64, seems to have had no connexion here, but the name was common. *Cf. c.* 1130 *Dunkeld chart.* Incheturfin, and Macbet Mac Torfin in a *c.* 1143 charter of David I.

CÓRTACHIE (Kirriemuir). 1257 Cortachyn, *c.* 1320 Carcathie. G. *cor tathaiche*, 'turn of resort,' frequented turning. But *c.* 1320 is G. *cathair catha*, 'fort of the battle.'

CORUISK (Skye). G. *coire uisge*, 'glen of the stream.' *Cf.* Hill of Corskie, Gartly.

COSHLETTER (Skye). G. *cois leitir*, 'foot of the hill-slope.'

COTHAL (Kinaldie). Doubtful. Perh. = CUTHILL. *Cf.* 1329 *Arbroath Chart.* Couthal.

COULBEG and -MORE (Sutherld.). G. *cùl beag* and *mòr*, 'little' and 'big corner or nook.'

C(O)ULÍSS (Nigg). 1296 Culisse, 1351 Culuys, 1550 Culles. G. *cùl lios*, 'at the back of the garden.'

COULL (Aboyne). *a.* 1300 Coul, 1454 Colle. G. *cùil*, 'nook, corner.'

COULMONY Ho. (Nairn). G. *cùl moine*, 'at the back of the moor or moss.'

C(O)ULTER (Biggar, L. near Stirling, Aberdeen). Bi. C. *c.* 1210 Cultyr, 1229 Cultir. St. C. 1457 Cultir. Ab. C. *c.* 1170, Kultre, Culter. G. *cùl tir*, W. *tre*, 'back land.' *Cf.* TILLICOULTRY. Inchcoulter, Kiltearn, is in G. *innis a'choltair*, see p. 16. 1153 contin. of *Sim. Durh.* Holmcultran is now Holm Cultram, Cumberld.

C(O)ULTER ALLERS (Biggar). See above. Allers is *alders*, O.E. *alor*, *aler*, O.N. *ölr*. *Cf.* Allerbeck, Ecclefechan, and Ellerlie, Dumfries.

COULTERSAY (Islay). Hybrid. G. *cùl*, 'the back' and *Thors-ey*, 'Thor's isle,' see p. 40.

COUNTESSWELLS (Aberdeen). *Sic* 1613. Origin unknown.

C(O)UPAR FIFE and ANGUS. Fi. C. 1183 Cupre, 1294 Coper. An. C. *c.* 1169 Cubert, *c.* 1190 Cupre, 1296 Coupre in Anegos; also 1150–53 *Reg. Dunferm.* Cupermaccultin, now Couttie. Long a puzzle. Mack.'s G. *comh-pairt*, 'partnership, common land, common,' seems quite possible.

COURANCE (Lockerbie). Information needed.

COUSLAND (Dalkeith and Linlithgow). Da. C. *sic c.* 1150. 'Cows' land,' O.E. *cú*, O.N. *kú*, Sc. *coo*, 'a cow.' *Cf.* Cousley Wood, Sussex.

COVE (several). O.E. *cófa*, 'chamber, cave,' O.N. *kofi*, Sw. *kofwa*, 'a hut.'

COVINGTON (Lanark). *c.* 1190 Villa Colbani, *c.* 1212 Colbaynistun, 1434 Cowantoun, *c.* 1480 Covingtoun. '*Colban's* or *Cowan's* village.' He was a follower of David, Prince of Cumbria, *c.* 1120. *Cf.* COBBINSHAW and Covington, St. Neot's. See -ing, p. 52.

COWAL (S. Argyll). 1361 Congall, 1461 *Lib. Pluscard.* Touvale (T error for C). K. *Comhgall,* Coill or Cole was king of the Dalriad Scots, 6th cny.

COWCADDENS (Glasgow). Native pron. Kú-káddens. 1510 Kowcawdennis, 1521 -kadens, 1531 -caldenis. G. *cuil calldainn* or *-tuinn,* 'nook of hazels.' For the Cow- *cf.* COCKENZIE, COWDEN and CULROSS, now pron. Kū-ros. The change was the easier because C. used to be a loan by which cows went to pasture.

COWDENBEATH (Dunfermline). See next and BEATH.

COWDENKNOWES (Earlston). 1460 Coldoun, 1604 Couldenknowes, 1827 Coldingknowes. Hybrid. G. *cùl duin,* 'at the back of the hill,' and Sc. *knowe,* 'hillock.' *Cf.* Cowdenhill, Bonnybridge, also a tautology.

COWIE (St. Ninian's, Kincardine, Huntly). St. N. C. 1147 Collyne, later Collin, Collie. Hu. C. *c.* 1340 Collie, Kin. C. 1375 Colly. G. *coille,* 'a wood'; the *n* a scribe's flourish; *cf.* how and hollow. W. prefers to say, extension of G. *coll,* 'a hazel.'

COWLAIRS (Glasgow). 'Cow lairs' or 'pastures,' O.E. *leger,* 'couch, bed.'

COXITHILL (St. Ninian's). 1328 Kokschote, 1584 Cockshothill. 'Plot of ground for cocks.' For -shot, O.E. *sceat,* see Bagshot, *Pl. N. Eng.*

COYLET (L. Eck). G. *cuing leathad,* 'narrow hill-slope.' Cf. COLZIUM and CROMLET.

COYLTON (Ayr). Old Cuil-, Quiltoun. Perh. G. *caol dùn,* 'narrow hill.' See KYLE and *cf.* EDDERTON.

CRACKAIG, -GAIG (Jura). G. *creag,* 'crag, rock,' with *-aig* loc., 'among the crags.'

CRAGABUS (Port Ellen). N. *kraka-bus,* 'crows' place.' See *bolstað-r,* p. 42.

CRAGGANMORE (Craigellachie). G. *creagan mòr,* lit. 'big, little rock.'

CRAGGIE or CREAGACH (Ben, Mull, Loch, 2 in Sutherld.). G. *creagach,* 'rocky place,' with -ie its loc.

CRAICHIE (Angus, Parton). Par. C. 1535 Crauchy. G. *cruachach,* 'hilly place,' here in loc. *Cf.* CRUACHAN.

CRAIG(A)NURE (Mull). 'Rock of the yew,' G. *iubhar.*

CRAIGCROOK (Edinburgh). 1335 Cragcrok. Prob. Brit., in G. *creag cruaich,* 'stack-like crag,' W. *crug,* 'a heap, a stack.'

CRAIGDAM (Old Meldrum). 'Rock of the ox,' G. *daimh,* O.G. *dam.*

CRAIGDUCKIE (Kinross). Prob. 'crag of the bugle-horn,' G. *dùdaiche.*

CRAIGELLACHIE (Aberlour). *c.* 1680 Craig Ilachie. Often said to be G. *creag eagalach*, 'rock of warning,' lit. 'causing fear,' war-cry of Clan Grant. *Cf.* 'Stand fast, Craigellachie.' But *g* in *eagalach* is hard and M. thinks, fr. *eileachaidh*, prob. 'stony, rocky,' *ail*, *ailech*, *eilech*, 'a rock.' W. compares with Glen Elchaig, Kintail, which also, and ELCHO too, means 'rocky.' Jas. M'Donald was wrong in saying Eallachie Burn, Cabrach is G. *allt lochan*, 'stream of the pools.'

CRAIGENPUTTOCH (Nithsdale). Said to be 'rock of the kite,' same root as L. *buteo.* The Dicty. only gives *putag*, 'a small ridge of land.'

CRAIGENVEOCH (Old Luce). 'Rock of the raven,' *bhfhiaich*, pron. veeagh.

CRAIGFOODIE (Cupar). 'Rock with the turf,' G. *fòide.*

CRAIGIE (several). Per. C. 1266 Cragyn. G. *creag*, in loc., 'at the crag.'

CRAIGIEBARNS (Dunkeld). As site shows, 'crag at the gap or pass,' G. *'a beirn*, nom. *bearna.* *Cf.* above and Carbarns, Wishaw.

CRAIGIEBUCKLER (Aberdeen). Fancy name given to his estate by James Blaikie in 1815. Its old name was Burnieboozle.

CRAIGIEBURN (Falkirk, Perth). Pe. C. 1466 Cragyburn. Hybrid. See CRAIGIE.

CRAIGIEVAR (Alford). G. *creag a' bharra*, 'rock with the point or head.'

CRAIGLOCKHART (Edinburgh). 1278 *Newbottle Chart.* Crag quam Stephanus Locard miles tenuit (one of the Lockharts of Lee, here *c.* 1250). This shows W., p. 495, wrong. 1528 Craglokhart. The man's name is prob. the N. or O.E. *Loker* or *Locær* ; *t* readily suffixes itself. *Cf.* Symington. But Bar- and Drumlockhart, Wigtownsh., are prob. fr. G. *lùchairt*, 'encampment, castle,' root as in LUNCARTY.

CRAIGLUSCAR (Dunfermline). 1561 -cer. Perh. 'crag of the sudden noise,' G. *lasgar.* *Cf.* *c.* 1150 *Reg. Dunferm.* Duæ villæ Luscer, -char.

CRAIGMILLAR (Edinburgh). *Sic* 1212 but *c.* 1130 Cragmilor ; also Craigmoilard. 'Rock of the bare height,' G. *maol àrd.*

CRAIGMORE (Rothesay, Aberfoyle). 'Big crag,' G. *mòr.*

CRAIGNEUK (Motherwell, New Abbey). Perh. not fr. *neuk*, 'nook,' but 'crag of the death,' G. *an èig*, nom. *eug.*

CRAIGNISH (Lochgilphd., Ayrsh.). Lo. C. 1434 Cragginche, 1609 Creginis. 'Rock with the inch or meadow,' G. and Ir. *innis.*

CRAIGO (Montrose). 1359 Craggow. G. *creagach*, 'rocky place.' *Cf.* ABERLEMNO, etc.

CRAIGROTHIE (Cupar). Prob. 'crag with the fort,' G. *rath*, here in loc. *Cf.* ROTHIEMAY, etc.

CRAIGROWNIE (Rosneath). Prob. 'crag with the rowans,' Dan. *rön, rönne -træ*, Sw. *rönn*, 'the rowan or mountain ash.' But it may be loc. fr. *rudhan*, 'little point'; *cf.* Row.

CRAIGROSTAN (Ben Lomond). *Sic* 1793, but 1272 Cragtrostane. 'Rock of St. *Drostan*' pupil of Columba. *Cf.* Allt Rostan near by, G. *allt*, 'a burn.' The late spelling -royston comes fr. connecting with Rob Roy.

CRAIGVAD (Aberfoyle). G. *creag fhada*, 'long rock.'

CRAIL (E. Fife). *c.* 1150 Cherel, *a.* 1153 Caraile, *c.* 1160 -ele, 1195–1639 Carrail. Prob. G. *cathair àille*, 'fort on the cliff,' as in CRAMOND. But the Carr Rocks are close to the east, G. *càrr*, 'a rock'; and Tomcrail and Pitkerril, Perthsh., are prob. fr. the Ir. family Cairill or O'Carroll.

CRAILING (Jedburgh). *c.* 1147 Creling, Craaling. Prob. N. *krá lyng*, 'nook of the ling or heather.'

CRAMOND (Edinburgh). 1178 Caramonth, *c.* 1200 Karramunt, 1292 Cramunde, 1293 Karamunde. 'Fort,' W. *caer*, 'on R. ALMOND.' *Cf.* CRAIL. But CRAMALT Craig, Tweeddale, is G. for 'bent, bowed cliff.'

CRAMONERY (Minigaff). Seems, 'mountain-grass place,' G. *mòin-fheoir*, here in loc.

CRANSHAWS (Duns), CRANSTOUN (Dalkeith). 1250 Craneshawes, *c.* 1160 Craneston. O.E. *cran*, 'a crane,' used also as nick-name. See SHAW.

CRARAE (L. Fyne). 1412 Charree. G. *crà reidh*, 'smooth land' (Gillies).

CRASK, The (Sutherld.), CRASK of AIGUS (Strathglass). G. *crasg*, 'a cross, crossing, pass.' Aigus prob. means 'abyss,' which suits the site. *Cf.* ARNGASK and Loch-a-Chraisg, Eddrachilis.

CRATHES (Kincardine) = next, with *-ais* suff. of place.

CRATHIE (Braemar). G. *creathach*, 'brushwood,' here in loc.

CRAVIE (Banff). G. *craobhach*, 'wooded place,' here in loc. fr. *craobh*, 'a tree.' *Cf.* Corncravie, Stoneykirk, and Corriecravie, S. Arran.

CRAWFORD (Lanark). *c.* 1150 Crauford, *a.* 1300 Croweford. O.E. *cráwe*, Sc. *craw*, 'a crow.'

CRAWFORD JOHN (Lanark). 1275 Craufurd johnne, *c.* 1300 Craw-fordeione. See above. The *John* was stepson of Baldwin, sheriff of Lanark. As a place-name it is almost unique.

CRAWICK (Sanquhar). Prob. W. *caer Rywc*, 'fort of Rywc,' prob. he in *Taliesin*.

CRAY (Blairgowrie) = Ir. *crathaidhe*, 'a quaking bog' (W.).

CREAGORRY, -GARRY (Lochmaddy). M. hesitates. G. *creaga* is said to be 'a cluster of houses' and *gaire, goire* is 'shouting, laughter.'

CREE, R. (Kirkcudbt.). 1301 Crethe, 1363 Creth, *c.* 1375 Cre. G. *crioch, criche*, 'the boundary' between E. and W. Galloway. *Cf.* next.

CREICH (N. Fife, Bonar Br.). Fi. C. 1250 Creyh, 1298 Creegh. Bo. C. *c.* 1240 Crech, 1275 Creych. = CREE. *Cf.* Coil-a-creich, Ballater.

CREITYHALL (Buchanan). 1723 Creitchael. Corrup. of G. *croit an choille*, O.G. *chaill*, 'croft in the wood.' *Cf.* CREITENDAM, Drymen, fr. G. *damh*, 'an ox'; *cf.* CRAIGDAM.

CRÉRAN, R. and L. (N. Argyll). *Old* Creveren for a G. *Craibhrionn* fr. *craobh*, 'a tree.'

CRETANREE (Banff). G. *croit an fhrìthe*, 'croft in the wood.'

CREWE (Edinburgh). Borrowed fr. Crewe, Cheshire. O.W. *creu*, W. *crewyn*, 'a pen, sty, hovel.'

CRÍANLARICH (W. Perth). 1603 Creinlarach. Perh. G. *crion làrach*, 'little farm or ruin.' W. prefers G. *crithionn*, 'aspen tree.' The name is abnormal.[1]

CRICHTON (Gorebridge). *c.* 1145 Crechtune, 1250 Krektun, 1367 Creigchton (*ch* guttural as still in Sc.). 'Village on the border,' G. *crioch*. Thus an early hybrid. *Cf.* CREE and CREICH.

CRIEFF. *a.* 1178 Creffe, 1218 Crefe. Must be as in MONCRIEFF, so O.G. loc. of G. *craobh*, 'among the trees.' *Cf.* Ballincrieff, Aberlady and Dumcrieff, Moffat.

CRIEFFVECHTER (Crieff). Local pron. Currievechter. Looks like loc. of G. *currach uachdar*, 'higher wet place'; *cf.* Currocks near by.

CRIFFEL (Kirkcudbt.). *a.* 1330 Crefel. 'Split fell or hill,' fr. O.N. *kryfja*, 'to split,' and *fell*, Dan. *fjäld, fjeld*.

CRIMOND (Buchan). 1250 Creymund, *a.* 1300 Crechmond, *c.* 1550 Crichmound. G. *crioch monadh*, 'boundary hill.' W. connects with G. *creachann*, 'bare, wind-swept hill-top.'

CRINAN (W. Argyll). Doubtful. W., p. 23, seems to connect with the tribe *Cerones*. Gillies says, root, G. *crion*, 'small, withered.'

CROCKETFORD (Kirkcudbt.). G. *crochaid*, 'hanging.' *Cf.* 1452 Crockatshot, 'hanging place,' Renfrew (see COXITHILL) and Craigcrocket, Carsphairn.

[1] What of *cridhean*, 'a gallant'? Did anyone ever hear a Perthshire man say Crion-?

CROE Glen (Argyll). G. *crò*, 'a circle,' from the encircling hills.

CROFTÁMIE (Drymer). G. *croit Sheamais* (*sh* mute), 'croft of Jamie,' *cf.* Arntamie, Kippen, and Croit Sheocaidh ('Jockie'), L. Lomond.

CROFTHEAD (Bathgate). O.E. *croft*, 'a field'; Veitch said, in Sc. properly 'enclosed, cropped land.' Croft-an-righ, Holyrood, is 'king's field.'

CROICK (Bonar Br.). W. thinks, prob. loc. of G. *cròc*, 'an antler,' hence, 'a branching or side glen.'

CROMAR (Aberdeen). G. *cro*, 'circle, enclosure.' See MAR.

CROMARTY. 1257 Crumbathyn, 1264 -bauchtyn, 1296 Crombathie, 1398 -ardy, *c.* 1425 -baghty, 1565 -arte. O.G. *crumb*, G. *crom*, 'crooked,' with *-ach* and *-tan* suffixes. In O.Ir. *bath* is 'sea.' The -ardy, -arty is due to influence of *àrd*, *àirde*, 'height.' To-day, as in 1794, the G. is *crom bàdh*, 'crooked bay.'

CROMBIE (Banffsh., S.W. Fife). Loc. of G. *crombach*, 'at the crooked place.'

CROMDALE (Grantown). 1224 Cromdol, 1237 Crumbdol, Pict. forms. O.G. *crumb*, G. *crom*, 'crooked,' and G. *dail*, W. *dol*, 'meadow.'

CROMLET (Nigg, Rosskeen) [*c.* 1570 *Reg. Neubotl.* Crumlat]. G. *crom leathad*, 'crooked slope.' *Cf.* PAISLEY.

CROMLIX (Dunblane, Inverness). G. *crom leac*, 'crooked stone,' with Eng. pl. x = cs.

CRONBERRY (Muirkirk). Prob. a tautological hybrid, like BARRHEAD. G. *cronag*, 'a circular fort,' fr. G. *cruinn*, W. *crwn*, 'round,' and O.E. *byrig*, 'fortified place, burgh.' *Cf.* TURNBERRY.

CROOK (several). O.N. *krók-r*, Sw. *krok*, 'a hook, a crook.' *Cf.* CROOKSTON.

CROOK of DEVON (Kinross). See R. DEVON and *cf.* Cambusdoon, Ayr.

CROOKSTON (Paisley, Stow). Pa. C. *c.* 1160 Crocstoun, 1262 Cruikston [1304 a 'Crokedeston' in Lanark]. Given by Robert de Croc or CROOK to his daughter on marrying a Stewart, *c.* 1160. *Cf.* Krukster, Shetland; see p. 42.

CROSBY (Troon). *Sic a.* 1214, but 1230 Crosseby, 1367 Corsbi. 'Cross village,' 4 in England. *Cf.* Corsbie, Earlston. See -by, p. 41.

CROSS (Orkney, Lewis). N. *kross*, G. *crois*, Fr. *croix*, L. *crux*, 'a cross.'

CROSSAIG (Kintyre). As above and Norse G. *aig*, N. *vík*, 'a bay.'

CROSSAPOOL (Mull), L. CROSSPUILL (Durness). Mu. C. 1542 Crosopollie. Here the ending will be *pol* or *bol*, 'place,' as in ULLAPOOL; see *bolstað-r*, p. 42. But in Du. C. it is G. *poll*, *puill*, 'pool.'

CROSSBASKET (E. Kilbride). 1426 Corsbasket, 1445 -at. Doubtful. W.'s suggestion of St. *Pascent* does not look very likely; nor does origin fr. Eng. *basket*, *sic a.* 1300. Perh. 'Cross at the exit of the wood,' O.W. *pâs cet* (W. *coed*); *cf.* BATHGATE.

CROSSBOST (Stornoway). Really the same as CROSSAPOOL.

CROSSFORD (Lanark, Dunfermline). La. C. 1498 Corsefoord; *cf.* CORSAPOOL.

CROSSMICHAEL (Cas. Douglas). *c.* 1370 Corsmychell, 1607 Crocemichael. 'Cross of St. Michael.'

CROSSMYLOOF (Glasgow). The tradition that Q. Mary, at the battle of Langside, 1568, cried, 'By cross i' my loof' (palm, hand), is popular etymology. It is, as Rev. Geo. Calder says, G. *crois Maoldhuibh* (*dh* lost by aspiration), 'cross of Malduff,' whose name recurs in Kilmalduff, old name of Inverary.

CROSSRAGUEL Abbey (Maybole). *Sic* 1306. Pron. Crossráygel. *a.* 1200 Cosragmol, 1225–65 Cros-, Corsragmol, 1372 Crosragmere, *c.* 1560 Corsragvell. G. *crois rathaig mhaoil*, 'cross at the bare, untowered fort'; *cf.* KILRAVOCK and RAIGMORE. The L. name, Monasterium Crucis Regalis, shows what the monks thought it was.

CROWLIN (W. Ross). G. *Cròlaig* or *-lainn*, which W. hesitates over.

CROWNPOINT (Glasgow). Country house built there by Wm. Alexander, and called after the frontier fort on L. Champlain, just (1775) captured from the French.

CROY (Kilsyth, Ft. George, Gartness). Ki. C. *sic* 1369, Ft. G. C. *sic* 1473, Ga. C. *sic* 1745. G. *cruaidh*, 'hard, firm ground, a hillside.' Three in Ireland.

CRUACHAN Ben (Argyll). *c.* 1375 *Barbour* Crechanben. G. *cruachan*, 'the haunch, also a conical hill,' *cruach*, 'a stack.' Cruachan Eile, now Cruach Phadrig, Connaught, is mentioned in *Nennius*.

CRUACH LUSSA (Knapdale). See above. Lussa is, 'of plants,' G. *lus*, *lusa*. *Cf.* Ardlussa, Jura.

CRUDEN (Aberdeensh.). 1163 Invercrwdan, 1501 Croudane. 1163 is prob. 'confluence of the kingfisher,' G. *crùidein*. See INVER.

CRUITHNEACHAN (Lochaber). 'Picts' places,' fr. G. *Cruithnig*, said to be people who painted the forms (*crotha*) of beasts, birds, etc., over their bodies; hence Picti or Picts. But Rhys thought *Pict* non-Aryan, and W., p. 68, is non-committal. *Cf.* p. 6.

CUCHULLIN Hills, *sic* 1772, better CUILLINS (Skye). G. Cuilionn. 1702 Quillins. *Cuilinn* or *Coolin* is G. *cu Chulainn*, 'hound of Culann,' a hero in *Ossian*, 'noble son of Sualtain.' But Collin Hill, Buittle, is G. *cuilionn*, 'holly.'

CUFF Hill (Beith). Prob. corrup. of G. *cuibhioll*, 'a wheel.'

CUICH, R. (Kinross). G. *cuach*, 'a drinking cup, a quaich.'

CUIL (Appin). G. *cùil*, 'corner, retired nook.'

CUILFAIL (L. Melfort) is 'nook with the hedge,' *fàil*.

CULBEN (Banff), CULBIN (Kiltearn). Ba. C. *c.* 1270 Coul-, Culbin, -byne, pron. Kóo-ben. G. *cùl beinne*, 'at the back of the hill.'

CULBOKIE (Dingwall). 1456 -oky. G. *cùil bocain*, 'nook of the bogie or goblin'; here in loc.

CULCRIEFF (Crieff). Local pron. Culchree. 'At the back (G. *cùl*) of the trees.' See CRIEFF.

CULDUTHIL (Inverness). 'North back,' G. *tuathail*. *Cf.* DULNAN.

CULLEN (Banff, Gamrie). *c.* 1190 Inverculan, 1290 Colane, 1517 Culane. Prob. not Celnius Fl. in *Ptolemy*. G. *cùilan*, 'little nook.'

CULLENDOCH (Girthon). 13– Culyndavach, 1456 -dach. G. *cuilionn dabhach*, 'holly vat'; *cf.* Cullendeugh, New Abbey, 1527 Culindaich. But CULLENOCH, Balmaghie, is *cuilionnach*, 'place of hollies.'

CULLICUDDEN (Resolis). 1227 Culicuden, 1551 Cullicuddin. 'Nook, creek,' G. *a'chudainn*, 'of the cuddies,' small fish once common here. But 'Drumnecudyne,' once near here, is fr. *cudainn*, 'a tub, a large dish.'

CULLIPOOL (Oban). Prob. as in next and ULLAPOOL. 'Colla's dwelling.' See *bol*, p. 42.

CULLIVOE (Shetland). *Sagas* Kollavag. Either fr. N. *koll-r*, 'a hill' (Jakobsen) or a man *Kolla*, and O.N. *vag-r*, 'bay' or Icel. *vogr*, 'little bay.'

CULLODEN (Inverness). 1238 -odyn. G. *cùl lodain*, 'at the back of the little pool.' In mod. G. Cùlodair, perh. 'at the back of the ridge or sandbank,' G. *oitir*.

CULNAGREEN (Perthsh.). G. *cùl na grèine*, 'at the back of the sun.'

CULNAHA (Nigg). G. *cùl na h'atha*, 'at the back of the kiln or kiln-like hill.' *Cf.* 1346 *Paisley Chart.* Joh. de Kulnahath, clericus Glasguensis, and CULNAKNOCK, Uig.

CULRAIN (Bonar Br.). Looks like G. *cùil rathan*, 'nook with the ferns.' W. says, imported fr. Coleraine, Ulster. Its old name was Carbisdale.

CULROSS (Dunfermline). Pron. Kú-ross. *c.* 1110 Culenross, 1295 Culneross; also Kyllenros. G. *cuileann ros*, 'holly wood.'

CULSALMOND (Insch.). 1195 Culsamiel, 1198 -samuelle, both in foreign, papal writs, 1446 –salmond. Perh. 'Nook,' G. *cùil*, not 'of Samuel,' but 'of *Salmond*,' though this surname does not seem to occur in Sc. till 1479; perh. fr. G. *sèaman*, 'little stout man.'

CULTENHOVE (Bannockburn). 1358 Qwytilhoue (for Quyllti-), 1369 Cultnehoue, 1391 -tynhuf. Prob. G. *cùiltean na h'uamha*, 'nooks with the caves.' *Cf.* Glenhove, -huve, Cumbernauld.

CULTERCULLEN (Ellon). Prob. a recent combination. See COULTER and CULLEN.

CULTOQUHEY (Crieff). Perh. G. *coillte a' Che*, 'woods of Ce,' see p. 25.

CULTS (Aberdeen, 2 in Galloway). Ab. C. 1450 Qhylt. Ga. C. 1426 Qwyltis, 1456 Cuyltis. G. *coillte*, 'woods,' with Eng. pl. *s*.

CULZEAN (Maybole). Pron. Kull-éen. 1636 Cullen. G. *cùil ean*, 'nook of the birds.'

CUMBERNAULD (Castlecary). Pron. Cummer-náud. *a.* 1300 Cumbrenald, 1417 Cumyrnald, 1427 Combernald. O.G. *cumber*, G. *comar an allt* or *uillt*, 'meeting, confluence of the streams'; not same root as Cumberland, fr. the *Cymri*. *Cf. c.* 1280 *Reg. Neubotl.* Combrecolyston, E. Lothian, and Combermere, Chesh., 1135 Cumbermere. We may have *p* pro *b*, as in Donaghcumper, Kildare and in Quimper or Kemper, Brittany, the same root.

CUMBRAES (Firth of Clyde). 1264 Cumberays, *c.* 1270 Kumbrey, *Sagas* Kumrey-ar, 1515 Litill Comeray. 'Isles,' N. *ay*, *ey*, 'of the *Cymri*' or Welsh.

CUMINESTOWN (Turriff). 'Town of the *Cumines*' of Auchry, branch of the great Comyn family, now in Sc. *Cumming*. Robt. de Comines (Nord, France) came over in 1066—'Rodbertus cognomento Cumin,' *Sim. Durham*. *Cf. Dom.* Salop, Comintone.

CUMLOD(D)EN (Inverary, Minigaff). Mi. C. 1475 Camlodane. G. *cam lodan*, 'crooked little pool.' *Cf.* CULLODEN.

CUMMERTREES (Annan). 1223 Cumbetres, *a.* 1245 Cumbertres, 1553 Cummirtreis. O.G. *cumber*, G. *comar dreas*, W. *cymmer drysi*, 'confluence among thorns or brambles.'

CUMNOCK, OLD and NEW (Ayrsh.). *Sic a.* 1300 but 1297 Comnocke, 1298 -enok, 1461 Cunnok. Dimin. of O.G. *cuman*, 'a shrine'; *cf.* St. Bride's Bank near here, and GIFFNOCK, etc.

CUNNINGHAM (Ayrsh.). 1153 Cunegan, 1180 Cuninham, 1181 Chunigham, *Brev. Aberd.* Coninghame, ? fr. G. *cuinneag*, 'a milk pail.' The -ham is the 'improvement' of a Saxon scribe.

CÚNNOQUHIE (Cupar). Pron. Kínnowhy. 1480 Cunyochy. Perh. G. *cùinneach*, *-iche*, 'place abounding in coins,' fr. some find of coins there. *Cf.* 1561 Pitconquhy, Dunfermline.

CURLEY WEE (hill, Minigaff). G. *car, cuir le gaoith*, 'bend, turn in the wind.' *Cf.* THUNDERGAY.

CURRIE (Midlothian). *Sic c.* 1230. Loc. of G. *currach*, 'wet plain, marsh,' *cf.* The Curragh, Kildare; or, W. *cyri*, G. *coire*, 'a circular glen, a corrie'; *cf.* Currie Rig, Carsphairn, and 1365 *R.M.S.* Walter de Corry, Edinburgh, called, 1368, de Curry. *N.E.D.* for 1795 has 'Corries or Curries.'

CURROCHTRIE (Kirkmaiden). 1492 le duæ Currochtyis, 1550 Corrouchtrie. Doubtful; prob. G. *currach uachdar* (here in loc.), 'upper wet plain.' *Cf.* CRIEFFVECHTER.

CURSETTER (Firth and N. Ronaldsay). *Sic* 1574. O.N. *ky-r sœter*, 'kye, cow pasture.' *Cf.* Rossiter, Aberdeensh.; fr. O.N. *hross*, 'a horse.'

CUSHNIE Glen (Alford). *a.* 1300 Cuscheny, 1395 Causchini; also Cussenin. Prob. G. *cuisneach*, here in loc., 'frosty, freezing place.'

CUTHILL (Prestonpans, W. Calder). Prob. W. *cuddigl*, 'a retreat, private place,' fr. *cuddio*, 'to hide'; *cf.* KETTLE. But for CUTHEILL BHEAG ('little') and MHOR ('big'), Urray and L. Broom, W. suggests N. *kúa-fjall* or *kvi-fjall*, 'cow' or 'fold fell or hill.' *Cf. c.* 1500 Cuthilgarth, Sanday.

CYDERHALL (Dornoch). *c.* 1160 Siwardhoch, 1230 Sywardhoth, *Pont* Siddera. Interesting corrup. fr. Earl '*Sigurd's how*' or '*haugh*,' O.N. *haug-r*, 'grave-mound.' He was buried here, 1014.

CYRUS, St. (Montrose). Pron. St. Seerus. From St. *Cyricus*, *Ciricius* or *Cyr*, of Tarsus. *Cf.* EGLISGIRIG.

DAER Water (Elvanfoot). *c.* 1170 *Reg. Neubotl.* Deiher, so not = Aber-dare, Wales (W.). Prob. G. *deifir*, 'haste, speed.' It is a 'rapid, frolicsome' stream.

DAILLY (Girvan, Urr). Gi. D. 1625 Daylie. G. *dealge*, 'thorns.'

DAIRSIE (Cupar). 1234 Dervesyn (*n* scribe's flourish), 1639 Dersey. Perh. O.G. *dair bheus* (here in loc.), 'oak of fornication'; *cf.* W. *derw*, 'oak.'

DALAROSSIE (Moy). 1208 Dulergus, *c.* 1230 -gusy. G. *dail*, W. *dol*, *Fhearghuis*, 'field of Fergus,' prob. the companion of St. Drostan, 6th cny.; *cf.* L. Fergus, Kirkinner, and Kilfarassy, Waterford, Ir. *cill Fhearghusa*.

DALAVICH (Lorn). 'Field,' G. *dail*, 'on R. AVICH.'

DALBEALLIE (Aberlour). G. for 'field at the rim or margin,' *bile*.

DALBEATTIE (Kirkcudbt.). 1469 -baty, *Pont* -bety. 'Field of the birch trees,' G. *beath*, here in loc. *Cf. Ulst. Ann.* 679 Dunbaitte and Dalbeathie on Tay.

DALCHREICHART (Glen Morison). Often pron. Dul-, *cf.* W. *dol,* 'meadow,' G. *dail chreaich àrd,* 'high-up field of the foray' or 'division of the spoil,' *creach.* In same glen, Duldreggan, fr. G. *droigheann,* 'a thorn.'

DALCROSS (Croy, Invnss.). Corrup. of Dealganross or Dalginross, name in Athole and Strathearn. G. for 'spit of the promontory,' *ros.*

DALDERSE (Falkirk). *Pont* -darse. G. *dearsach,* 'bright, shining' field.

DALE (Halkirk). *c.* 1255 *Orkn. Sag.* Dal. Norse for 'dale, valley.'

DALGARDIE (Perthsh.) = DALNACARDOCH, but here in loc.

DALGARNOCK (Closeburn). 'Field with the noisy burn,' G. *gairneag.*

DALGETTY, -GATY (Aberdour, Fife). 1178 Dalgathyn. 'Field of the wind,' G. *gaoith,* here in loc., 'windy field.'

DALGLEISH (Ettrick). 1383 -glas. May be 'field of activity,' *gleòis.* To derive fr. *glais,* 'green' (W.) is phonet. less likely.

DALGUISE (Dunkeld). 'Field of firs,' G. *giuthais. Cf.* KINGUSSIE.

DALHOUSIE (Cockpen). *c.* 1235 Dalwussy, 1298 -wlsy, -wulsy, 1461 -wosy. Perh. 'field of slander,' G. *thuaileas,* here in loc. *Cf.* Balhousie, Perth, *c.* 1275 -ulsi. But Dalchoisne, Rannoch, is 'field in the corner or angle,' G. *a' h'oisinn.*

DALIBORG, -BURGH (Lochmaddy). 'Field of the fort' or BORGUE.

DALJARROCH (Girvan). G. *dail dharach,* 'field of oaks.' *Cf.* Barrjarg, G. *dhearg,* 'red height.'

DALKEITH. 1140 -kied, *c.* 1145 -keth, also Dolchet. Brit. for 'field in the wood,' W. *dol,* G. *dail,* 'field,' and O.W. *cet, chet,* W. *coed,* 'a wood.' Balkeith, Tain, 1548 Ballecuth, is now in G. *baile na coille,* 'village by the wood.' *Cf.* KEITH.

DALLACHY (Fochabers, Aberdour, Fife). In Fife pron. Daichy. G. *dail,* gen. *dalach,* and here in loc. 'at the field.'

DALLAS (Forres, Edderton). Fo. D. 1306 Dolays. Ed. D. 1560 Doles. Pict. *dol-ais,* 'place on the plain,' W. *dol,* 'meadow,' and *cf.* ALVES, etc.

DALMAHOY (Ratho). 1272 -mohoy, 1295 -mehoy. 'Field of my dear Hugh,' G. *mo h'Aoidh.* On *-ma -mo* see p. 67. W.'s derivation fr. St. *Tua* is phonet. very difficult.

DALMALLY (Argyll). Also once called DYSART. G. *dail mhàilidh,* perh. for G. *màile, màille,* 'a helmet, coat of mail.' W. takes it, like KILMALLIE, fr. an uncertain saint. *Cf.* Knight, *Early Christ. Scotl.* II, 188.

DALMELLINGTON (S. Ayr). Pron. Damelinton. 1275 Dalmellingtoun, 1302–04 -meledone. Hybrid. Perh. G. *dail meallan,* 'field among a cluster of knolls or hills'; but *cf.* DUNFERMLINE; and *-ton,* Eng. for 'village.'

DALMENY (Queensferry). *c.* 1180 Dumanie, 1250 Dunmanyn. G. *dubh, du* is 'black' and *moine,* 'a moss.' But D. is prob. G. *dùn mainne,* 'hill of delay or procrastination.'

DALMUIR (Dumbarton). *c.* 1200 -more, 1680 -muire. G. for 'big field,' but G. *mòr* confused with Eng. *moor,* Sc. *muir,* O.N. *mór.*

DALMULLIN (Ayr). *a.* 1214 Dalmulin super Are. 'Field of the mill,' G. *muileann, -inn.*

DALNACARDOCH (N. Perthsh.). 'Field of the smithy,' G. *ceàrdach,* fr. *ceàrd,* 'a smith.' *Cf.* DALGARDIE.

DALNAGLÀR (Glen Shee). 'Field of the loud noise, clang of arms,' G. *gleadhar.*

DALNAMEIN (N. Perthsh.). 'Field of the mine,' G. *mèin,* 'ore, a mine.'

DALNASPIDAL (N. Perthsh.). 'Field of the spittal or inn,' G. *spideal,* Eng. *hospital.* There was a hospice here. *Cf.* The Spittals in Glen Cluny, Glenmuick and Glenshee.

DALNAVAIRD (Angus, Kincardine). 'Meadow of the bard or rhymer,' G. *an bhaird,* gen. of *bard.* But DALNAVERT, Aviemore, *sic* 1338, is 'field of graves,' G. *feart,* O.Ir. *fert.*

DALQUHARRAN Cas. (Dailly). Perh. 'field of the scurvy grass,' G. *c(h)arran* ; *ch* becomes *quh* or *wh* in Sc. *Cf.* SANQUHAR.

DALREOCH (Rosskeen, Cabrach, Dumbarton). 'Grey, brindled,' G. *riabhach,* 'field.'

DALRY (several). Edinburgh D. *sic* 1336, Cas. Douglas D. 1497 Dalrye. 'Meadow of the king,' G. *righ, -ghe.* *Cf.* Dalree, Tyndrum, and PORTREE.

DALRYMPLE (Ayr). *a.* 1300 -rimpill, 1467 -rumpill. As its site shows, 'field on the curving stream,' G. *chruim puill,* nom. *crom poll.*

DALSERF (Hamilton). Formerly Mecheyn (1116) or Machan ; *cf.* METHVEN and ECCLESMACHAN. 'Field of St. *Serf,*' prior of Loch Leven, 5th cny.

DALSETTER (Lerwick). N. *dal saeter,* 'valley of the summer, hill or dairy farm' ; orig. same as *setr,* 'dwelling.' *Cf.* INGSETTER.

DALSWINTON (Dumfries). 1292 -suyntone, also *c.* 1295 Bale -swyntoun, a tautology fr. G. *baile,* 'village.' See SWINTON.

DALTON (Ecclefechan, Ayr). Ec. D. *c.* 1280 *Bagamund* Paradelton [*c.* 1200 *Lib. Melros* Dalton, ? in England]. Either 'dale town,' or perh. G. *dall dùn,* 'dark hill.' *Cf.* DUBTON and EDDERTON.

DALWHINNIE (S. Inverness). G. *dail chuinnidh,* 'champion's dale' (W.). But Sir H. Maxwell takes Craigwhinnie, Girthon and Kirkmaiden, fr. *mhuine,* 'a thicket.'

Dalziel (Motherwell). *a.* 1200 Dalyell, -iel, 1352 Daleel. Now pron. Dalzéll. Prob. not 'field of the sungleam,' G. *ial*, but 'white field,' fr. *g(h)eal*. *Cf.* Dalgheal, Alness, G. *dail ghil* and pron. in Eng. Dalyil, 'at the white field.'

Damph or Daimh (L. Broom). G. *damh*, 'an ox.'

Damsey (Kirkwall). *c.* 1225 *Ork. Sag.*, Daminsey, Demisey. Corrup. of '*Adamnan's* isle,' N. *ay*, *ey*. See p. 68.

Dand-, Dundaleith (Rothes). G. *dùn da leathad*, 'hill with two slopes.'

Darnagie (New Luce). G. *dobhar na gaoithe*, 'stream of the winds.'

Darnaway (Forres). 1226 Terneway, 1453 Tarnewa, 1498 Darnway. Difficult. May go back to O. Celt. *taranu -magos*, W. *taran*, G. *torunn*, 'thunder,' and G. *magh*, 'a plain.' But Diack suggests, G. *taranmhaich*, 'plain across.'

Darnconner (Auchinleck). Doubtful. Perh. O.G. *dobhar na conair*, 'stream with the path' (W.). But perh. fr. a man *Connor*. Connor, Antrim, is glossed in old Ir. MSS. *doire na con*, 'thicket of wild dogs.' *Cf.* Gartconner, Kirkintilloch.

Darngavel (N. Lanark). 1304 Derngable. G. *dobhar an gabhail*, 'stream with the fork.'

Darnick (Melrose). *a.* 1150 Dernewick. O.E. *derne wíc*, 'out of the way, dark, dreary dwelling or village.' *Cf.* Darnrig, Slamannan.

Darvel (Galston). *Pont* Darnevaill. Doubtful, but perh. G. *dobhar an bhaile*, 'oakwood by the hamlet.'

Daughtie Mill (Kirkcaldy). Pron. Dáwty ? G. *deagh tigh*, 'excellent house.'

Dava (Grantown), fuller Davoch, Bk. Deer *dabach*, a land measure, 4 plough gates, G. *dabach*, 'a tub, a corn measure.' *Cf.* Davochbeg and -fin, Dornoch.

Davárr Isl. (Campbeltown). G. and Ir. *dá bharr*, 'two heights'; *cf.* Inishdavar, Ireland. But the name was once Sancte Barre, *cf.* Barra.

Daven, -an L. (Ballater). Not Ptolemy's Devana. In G. Dabhain. Doubtful.

Davidson's Mains (Edinburgh). Called fr. the Davidsons of Muirhouse, the family of the late Abp. of Canterbury, long there. Also called Muttonhole.

Daviot (Old Meldrum, Inverness). O.M.D. 1136 Dauyot, *a.* 1300 Daviot; also Davyoth. In. D. prob. *c.* 1210 Deveth. Perh. = Dava. But M. says, perh. the same as the S. Wales *Dyfed*, the tribe Demetae, Pict. *dem-*, 'sure, strong,' G. *deimhin*.

Dawick (Stobo). *c.* 1200 Dauwic. O.E. *dá wic*, 'doe's abode.' *Daw* for jackdaw is not found till *c.* 1450.

DAWSTANE Burn and Rigg (Liddesdale). Skene thought, *c.* 720 *Bede* Degsastan, 'Degsa's stone' (O.E. *stán*, Sc. *stane*), scene of K. Aidan's defeat, 603. This is doubtful. It is *a.* 1150 *Gaimar* Dexestane.

DEAN (Edinburgh, etc.). Ed. D. *c.* 1145 Dene. O.E. *denu*, M.E. *dene*, *dane*, 'valley, glen, usually deep and wooded.' Cognate with *den*. But DEANSTOUN, Doune, is presumably fr. the Dean of Dunblane Cathedral.

DEARG Ben (Ross-sh.). G. *beinn dhearg*, 'red ben.'

DEARN, R. (Carrbridge). Can it be fr. G. *dèarn*, 'the palm of the hand'?

DECHMONT (Cambuslang, Uphall). G. *deagh monadh*, 'fine hill.' *Cf.* ESSLEMONT.

DEE, R. (Aberdeen, Kirkcudbt.). G. Dèabhadh. *Ptolemy* Dēoua; for other forms see ABERDEEN, they intermingle with DON. Connected with river-worship, common among early Celts; *cf.* L. *diva*, 'goddess' and the river-nymph *Devona*, or *Divona*. L. name of Cahors, France.

DEER, OLD and NEW (Aberdeen). *a.* 1150 *Bk. Deer* Dear, *c.* 1320 Der. So called, says Bk. Deer, fr. the tears (Ir. *dear*, *deor*, G. *deùr*) shed here at the parting of St. Columba with his friend Drostan, who founded the abbey here. Scholars prefer to derive fr. G. *doire*, 'a forest,' such as once was there. *Cf.* DURRISDEER.

DEERNESS (Kirkwall). 1492 Deirnes. Prob. not *deer-ness*, but N. *dyr-nes*, fr. the *door*like recess in the headland here.

DEGENISH (Lorn). 'Ness of the dairy-maid,' N. *deigja*, which also means 'a damp, a wetness.' *Cf.* ARDALANISH.

DELNY (Invergordon). *Sic* 1463, but 1356 Dalgeny, 1398 Delgeny, 1381 -gny. G. *dealganach*, 'place full of prickles or thorns' (here in loc.), fr. *dealg*, 'a thorn, a bodkin.'

DELÓRAIN (Ettrich). 1456 Dallorjane. Not fr. St. *Oran*, but G. *dail odharain*, 'field of the cow-parsnip.'

DELTING (Shetland). *a.* 1500 Dalating, 1597 Daleting. N. *dal þing*, 'valley of the thing or meeting.' *Cf.* TINGWALL.

DENBURN, DENHEAD, etc. *Den* is O.E. *denn*, 'wild beasts' lair.' In Sc. it usually means 'a wooded glen,' so = DEAN and dingle. DENHOLM, Hawick, is 1296 Denum, 1304 Denhom. *Cf.* BRANXHOLM.

DEN-, DUNINO (St. Andrew's). Pron. -ínno. 1250 Duneynach, 1517 Dinnino, G. *dùn aonaich*, 'hill on the heath or moor.'

DENNIS Hd. (N. Ronaldsay). 1653 Dunnas Ness. O.N. *dyn-nes*, 'ness of din,' fr. the noise of the surf.

DENNISTOUN (now in Glasgow). Orig. in Renfrewsh.—perh. still earlier in Lennox, as Hugh, lord of Denniestoun, is said to witness a Luss charter temp. Alex. III—1298 Danielestoun, and spelt Danyelston up to 1400. The family was early in the Glasgow district called after them, first feued in 1836.

DENNY (Falkirk). *Sic* 1691, but 1510 Litill Dany. Seems DEAN and O.E., *eg.*, 'wet land.' *Cf.* 1509 Forgundynye, FORGANDENNY; also Danny, Sussex, 1343 Danye, and Denny Bottom, Tunbridge Wells. DENNYLOANHEAD, Denny, see LOANHEAD.

DÉNOVAN (Denny). *Sic* 1691, an Eng. refinement, but 1462 Denovane, 1510 Dunnovane, and still pron. Dunníven. G. *dùn aibhne*, 'fort by the river.' *Cf.* Craigniven, Stirling and *a.* 1272 Donouen, 1475 Dunnown, Cromarty.

DERNACISSOCK (Kirkcowan). G. *dobhar na siosg*, 'stream with the sedge.'

DERRY (L. Earn, Braemar). G. and Ir. *daire, doire*, 'an oak, oakwood.' *Cf.* 1630 *Gordon*, Diri -moir, -chat, and -meanigh (G. *meadhonach*, 'middle'). But L. DERRY, Tongue, is G. *loch an dithreibh*, 'loch in the desert or moor.'

DERVAIG (Tobermory). O.N. *djarf-r*, Dan. *diœrv*, 'terrible, dreadful,' orig. 'bold, daring,' and Norse G. *aig.*, N. *vík*, 'a bay.'

DERYNGTON (Lammermuirs). *c.* 1250 Diveringdounes, 'shaking, quaking hill,' fr. obs. vb. *diver.* The -ton, as often, was orig. -don, 'hill.'

DESKFORD (Cullen). Pron. Déskurd. 1406 -furde, 1493 Desfurde. Pict. G. *du esc*, 'dark stream,' and O.E. *ford*, 'a ford.' *Cf.* next.

DESKIE Burn (Elgin). As above, but in loc. Similar is DUSK WATER, Beith, but it is G. *dubh uisg*, 'dark water.' Then, DESKRY Burn, Tarland is prob. same as 1568 *R.M.S.* Glendescherochie, now Glendessary, L. Arkaig. This seems fr. G. *deasghair*, 'on the right hand,' though the G. now is said to be Deiseiridh.

DEVANNOC, INCH (L. Lomond). *Sic* 1776 but 1804 Tavanach. Prob. G. *tigh da mhanach*, 'house of the two monks.' A hermit once dwelt here.

DEVERON, R. (Banff). 1273 Douern, *a.* 1300 Duffhern; later Duvern, and same as Ptolemy's Ir. Dabrona. Looks like G. *dobharan*, 'little stream'; *cf.* Devoran, Cornwall, and Wendover, Bucks, O.E. *chart.* Wændofron. But 'Duffhern' must be fr. G. *dubh earn*, 'dark R. EARN.' *Cf.* FINDHORN and Lindifferon, Monimail; also an Dobhran, Edderton and Dufferin, Ireland.

DEVON, R. (Kinross). *c.* 1210 Glendovan, 1271 -dofona. G. *dubh abhainn*, 'black, dark river'; on the ending *cf.* CARRON. The district seems to have been the land of the Mæatæ, outlier of the great tribe *Damnonii*, inhabiters and namers of the Eng. Devon, W. Dyvnaint. Rhys thought all these names identical.

DEWAR (Heriot). Prob. W. *du ar*, 'dark ploughed land,' rather than G. *dubh àrd*, 'dark height.'

DHU HEARTACH (rock off Colonsay). G. *An dubh hiortach*, 'the dark, deadly one.' *Cf.* Hirta Dhu, old name of St. Kilda, see p. 71.

DHUSKER (L. Eriboll). G. *dubh*, 'black, dark,' and *sgeir*, N. *skjaer*, *sker*, 'rock' or 'skerry.'

DIBIDALE (Kincardine, Ross). 1623 Debadaill. O.N. *djúp-r dal-r*, 'deep dale.' Several Glen Dibidils in the Hebrides.

DILLOT, The (Menteith). G. *diollaid*, 'a saddle, a saddle-shaped ridge.' *Cf.* DIOLLAID a' Mhill Bhric ('of the speckled hill'), L. Broom.

DINGWALL (Ross). 1227 -well, *c.* 1250 Dinkeual, 1263 Dignewall, 1463 Dingvale. O.N. *þinga-völl-r*, 'meeting of the thing' or local council, = TINGWALL and TINWALD. Gaels call it Inverpefferon, 1256 *Papal bull* Inverferan.

DINLABYRE (Liddesdale). Perh. W. *din lla byr*, 'fort of the short hand,' commemorating some forgotten deed.

DINNET (Aberdeen). Perh. G. *dìon-aìte*, 'place of refuge, sanctuary.'

DINWOODIE (Lockerbie). 1296 Dinwithie, Dunwythye, 1482 Donwethy, 1503 Dunwedy, 1578 Dumwiddie. W. *din gwydd* (*dd* = *th*), 'hill with the shrubs.'

DIPPIN (S. Arran). 1807 'The Dipping Rocks,' 300 ft. of perpendicular basalt. Older it is Dupennylandis or 'twopenny lands.' See p. 36.

DIPPLE Burn (Beith). [1336 Duppoll near Ayr.] W. *du pwll* or G. *dubh poll*, 'dark stream.'

DIRLET (Caithness). Prob. *dirl clet*, 'stack-like rock with the hole dirled or drilled in it.' There is a CLETT here.

DIRLETON (N. Berwick, Kirkinner). N. B. D. 1270 Dirlton, 1288 Driltone, 1298 Drillintone. 'Village of *Dirl*' or 'the *Dirlings*.' *Onom.* has no *Dirl*, but has the patronymics *Derl- Dirling*.

DIRRIEMORE (L. Broom). G. *dìridh mòr*, 'the big climb,' often called by Southerners 'Dreary moor.'

DISTINKHORN Hill (Galston). Prob. O.E. *disc-þegn erne*, 'dish-thane's or steward's house.' *Cf.* Distington, Cumbld, and CLEGHORN.

DOCHART, L. and R. (W. Perth). *c.* 1200 Glendochard, 1238 -chir, 1428 Dochirde. Prob. G. *daboch àrd*, 'high ploughed land.' See DAVA and *cf.* Dawachnahard, Coigeach.

DOCHFOUR (Inverness-sh.). Pict., 'land for pasture,' see DAVA and BALFOUR and *cf.* PITFOUR.

DOCHGARROCH (Inverness). 'Rough, ploughed field.' The -och will be suff. of place attached to G. *garbh*, 'rough.' *Cf.* GARROCH Hd.

DOCHLAGGIE (Strathspey). 'Ploughed land in the hollow.' G. *lag*, here in loc.

DODD, common name of rounded hills in S. Scotland. *Cf.* Sc. *doddy*, *doddit*, 'without horns, bald.' *Cf.* Dodridge, Ford.

DOE, R. (2 in Inverness). G. Dobha, prob. fr. *dobh*, 'boisterous, swelling, raging.' *Cf.* R. Dove, Derby, and R. Dovey, Wales.

DOLLAR (Alloa), DOLLAR Law (Peebles). *Pict. Chron.* Dolair, 1461 Doler, 1639 Dolour; also 1544 Dolorbeg (G. *beag*, 'little'). W. *dol*, 'meadow, dale,' and *ar*, 'ploughed land' or perh. O.G. *ar*, *air*; or -ar may be a mere suff. (W.). Dollar Law is of itself proof enough against the legend that Dollar is Fr. *douleur*, L. *dolor*, 'grief,' as overlooked by Castle Gloom or Cas. Campbell.

DOLLERIE (Crieff). 1454 Dullory. G. *doilleir*, here in loc., 'at the dark (place).'

DOLPHINTON (Peeblessh., Tranent). Pe. D. 1253 Dolfinston, 'Dolfine's town.' He was brother of the first earl of Dunbar, *c.* 1240. *Cf.* Dolphinholme, Lancs., called after Dolfin of Cumbria, *c.* 1080.

DON, R. *Sic c.* 1170; other forms see ABERDEEN. Not G. *donn*, 'brown,' but G. Dian, Dèan, older Deon; so connected with Ptolemy's Dēouāna, prob. same as L. *Diana* and as Divona, mentioned by Ausonius the Gaul, 'Divona, Celtarum lingua, fons addite divis' (L. *divus*, 'divine'; hence, 'a god,' 'a goddess'). Thus Don like DEE points to the Celts' river-worship. *Cf.* DOON.

DONIBRISTLE (Aberdour, Fife). *a.* 1169 Donibrysell, 1178 -ybrisle. G. *dùn* (here in loc.) *brisg-gheal*, 'at the clear, bright hill.' But W. prefers to derive fr. O.Ir. *breasal*, 'a warrior,' *cf.* Bally- and Clonbrassil, Ireland.

DOON, R. and L. (Ayr). 1197 Inter Don et Ar, *c.* 1300 Logh Done. Prob. = DON.

DORBACK (Edinkillie). 'Place abounding in tadpoles,' G. *doirb* (M.). *Cf.* LOCHANDORB; *-ach* is suffix of place.

DORES (L. Ness). 1263 Durris, *c.* 1350 -rys. G. Durais. Contested. Might be Pict. G. *dur-ais*, 'water-place,' See p. 9. M. says, root *dur*, 'strong,' and prob. meaning 'stronghold,' though it may be G. *dorus*, 'the door,' the same root. W. says, *dubh ros*, 'black wood.' *Cf.* DURRIS.

DORLINN (between Morven and Oronsay, Kintyre and Davaar, and Mull and CALF). G. *doirlinn*, 'bit of land or isthmus temporarily submerged by the tide.'

DORNIE (Lochalsh). DORNOCH (Sutherld.). *a.* 1145 Durnach, 1199 Durnah, 1456 Dornouch. G. *dornach, -ag,* 'pebble place,' a pebble being a stone easily held in the fist, *dorn, dùirn*; *cf.* Durnovaria, lit. 'fist-plays,' Rom. name of Dorchester. DORNOCK, Annan, and Durno, Pitcaple, *a.* 1182 Durnack, are the same. *Cf.* Drum- and EDINDURNO.

DÓRRATUR (Falkirk). Prob. G. *doithir oitir,* 'dark, ill-featured promontory or ridge.' There is such here at a bend of R. Carron. *Cf.* CLUNITER.

DOUGLAS (S. Lanark, and 2 burns, L. Lomond). La. D. *c.* 1150 Duuelglas, Duue-, Duglas, *c.* 1220 Dufgles, 1298 Douglas. L.L.D. *Nennius* Dubglas, 1272 Douglas. O.G. *dub glas,* 'black, dark stream.' *Cf.* Douglas, I. of Man, and Dowlais, Glam.

DOUGLASTOWN (Maybole, Forfar). From the great Scottish family of that name.

DOUGRIE (W. Arran). [1540 *R.M.S.* Dugerre ? where.] *Old* Dowgare, Dougarre. G. *dubh garaidh,* 'dark den or thicket.' *Cf.* Dugary. E. Ross.

DOUNBY (Stromness). 'Dwelling on the hill,' Sw. and O.E. *dún,* and see -by p. 41. So = HILTON.

DOUNE (Callander). G. *dùn,* 'a hill.' DOUNIE, Ardgay, is the loc.

DOUR, R. (Fife). Forms, see ABERDOUR. O.G. *dobhar, dobboir,* O.W. *dubr,* W. *dwfr,* Corn. *dour,* 'water, stream.' *Cf. Adamn.* Dobor Artbranani.

DOVECRAIGS (Bo'ness). G. *dubh creag,* 'dark rock.'

DÓWALLY (Dunkeld). Pron. dú-ally. 1505 Dowalye. G. *dubh àille,* 'dark, black cliff.' *Cf. a.* 1300 *Reg. Dunferm,* p. 223 Douely, prob. near Kincardine O'Neil.

DOWHILL (Kinross). Pron. dú- (c)hill. G. *dubh choill,* 'dark wood.'

DOWNFIELD (Dundee). G. *dùn,* 'a hill,' as in Co. Down.

DOWNIES (Kincardine, Beith). Loc. of G. *dùn,* 'hill,' with Eng. pl. *Cf.* 1254 Dunny, now Downie, a thanage at Monikie.

DRAINIE (Lossiemouth). G. and Ir. *draighionn* or *-neach,* here in loc., 'among thorns.' *Cf.* Drain, Drains, Ireland.

DRANIEMANNER (Minigaff). G. *mainnir,* 'sheep pen, cattle-fold, among thorns'; see above.

DREGHORN (Irvine, Colinton). Ir. D. *c.* 1240 Dregern, 1275 -arne, *Pont* -gorne. O.E. *drýge* (2 *dreie*) *erne,* 'dry house.' *Cf.* CLEGHORN.

DREM (Haddington). *Sic a.* 1150. G. *druim,* 'the back, then a hill ridge.' *Cf.* Dreim, Urray, and DRUM.

DRENG (St. Magnus Bay, Shetld.). O.N. *drang-r,* 'pointed cliff.'

DRIMNIN (Morven). G. *druinnein*, dimin. of *dronn*, 'the back, a ridge.' *Cf.* Drimna and Drimmin, Ir. *druimin*, Ireland.

DRIP, The (Stirling, on R. Forth), and DRIPPS (Renfrew). St. 1295 Trips, *a.* 1300 Passagium de drippes. Re. D. 1158 Le Drip. Sc. *dreep*, 'a jump or drop down,' same as Eng. *drip*, O.E. *dryppan*, O.N. *drjúpa*, 'to drip, drop.' *Cf.* Bawdrip, Bridgewater.

DROCHIL (Peebless-sh.). *a.* 1200 Drochyl, 1296 Droghkil. G. *droch choill*, 'bad, calamitous wood.' *Cf.* DOWHILL.

DROMA, L. (Ross). Gen. of G. *druim*, 'back, hill ridge.' It stands where the backbone of Scotland, Drumalban, crosses the valley at the head of L. Broom. *Cf.* Drom, Dromagh, Ireland. DROMAN, Eddrachilis, is a dimin.

DRO-, DRUMMORE (Kirkmaiden). 1486 Drummore. G. *druim mòr*, 'great ridge.'

DRON (Br. of Earn). *Sic c.* 1190. G. *dronn*, 'the rump, the back, a hill-ridge.'

DRÓNGAN (Coylton). DRONNAN (Min i gaff), DRUNGANS (3 in Galloway). G. *dronnan*, 'little rump,' or, double dimin., *dronnagan*, 'little ridge.' W. prefers Ir. *drong*, 'troop, tribe,' and so, 'meeting-place,' as in 3 Ir. Drungs and Drungan, Leitrim.

DRONLEY (Dundee). Perh. hybrid, 'meadow, lea on the ridge,' see above. Perh. 'meadow of the drones or male bees,' 1508 Dunbar, *dron*. *Cf.* Dronfield, Sheffield.

DRUM (many). G. *druim*, L. *dorsum*, 'the back, then, hill-ridge like a back.' Sir H. Maxwell gives about 200 names in Drum- in Galloway alone. We have it in Drum Alban, the great dividing ridge of Scotland, found in an Ir. prophecy *a.* 400. Drum, dum and dun 'hill' constantly interchange in Sc. names.

DRUMBLADE (Huntly). 1403 -blathe, *a.* 1500 -blate. Either fr. G. *bladh*, *blatha*, 'smooth,' or *blàth*, 'a flower, a bloom.'

DRUMCHAPEL (Dumbarton). Prob. 'mare's back,' G. *c(h)apull*, 'a mare.'

DRUMCLOG (Strathaven). Either fr. G. *clog*, 'a bell,' or W. *clog*, 'rock, crag' (W.).

DRUMDOLLO (Forgue). 'Hill-ridge with the field,' G. *dail*, *dolach* (W.).

DRUMÉLDRIE (Largo). 'Hill-ridge of the miller,' G. *mèildear*, here in loc.

DRUM(M)ELZIER (Broughton). Pron. -mélyer, *c.* 1200 Dunmedlr, *c.* 1305 Dumelliare, 1326 Drummeiller, 1492 -melzare. Either as above or fr. G. *meilleir*, 'blubber-lipped fellow.' *Cf.* Drumalzier, Denny, pron. -míler.

DRUMFAD (Helensburgh), -FADA (hill, Banavie). Hc. D. 1342–62 -fade, but already *f* lost by aspiration in 1272 Drummade. G. *druim fhada*, 'long hill-ridge.'

DRUMGLOW or DUN- (Cleish). 1231 Dunglo. 'Hill of the veil,' G. *glo*, 'veiled hill,' as in BEN Y GLOW.

DRUMLANRIG (Thornhill). 1375 -langryg, 1663 -lanerk. As it stands a hybrid tautology. But the latter part may be as in LANARK. *Cf.* Carlenrig, N. of Langholm.

DRUMLEMBLE (Campbeltn.). In G. *druim leamhan*, 'hill ridge of the elms.' But Gillies thinks the ending, N. *lamba-fjall*, 'lamb hill.'

DRUMLITHIE (Fordoun). 'Grey,' G. *liath*, here in loc., 'hill-ridge.'

DRUMMOND (Kiltearn, Crieff, Whithorn). Cr. D. 1296 Droman [1296 *Ragman's R.* Gilbt. de Dromund del County de Dunbretan is DRYMEN]. Already in 1297 Joh. Dromand, the *d* has suffixed itself, as often. G. *dromainn*, 'a ridge,' fr. *druim*, 'the back.' Ireland has several Drummonds and Drummins too.

DRUMMÚCKLOCH (Anwoth, Inch). An. D. 1426 -muchloch. G. *muclach*, 'piggery,' *muc*, 'a pig.' *Cf.* Drimnamuclach, Argyll.

DRUMNADROCHIT (L. Ness). From G. *drochaid*, 'a bridge.' *Cf.* DRUMDROCHAT, Minigaff and KINDROCHIT. Droch Head, Kirkcolm, is just G. *drochaid*.

DRUMOAK (Peterculter). *Sic* 1407, but 1157 Dulmayok, *c.* 1250 Dumuech, and till lately pron. Dalmáik. 'Field,' G. *dail*, W. *dol*, 'of St. *Mayota*,' Ir. Virgin, friend of St. Bridget, 5th cny. St. Maik's well is still here.

DRUMOCHTER (Dalnaspidal). 'Upper hill-ridge, summit,' see AUCHTERARDER.

DRUMPÉLLIER (Coatbridge). 1174 Dumpeleter in Cludsdale, 1203 Dunpeleder, 1232 -peldre. Orig. British. W. *din peledyr*, pl. of *paladr*, 'fort of the spears.' *Cf.* Dunpelder or TRAPRAIN LAW.

DRUMSHEUGH (Edinburgh). Often mistaken. It is a contraction of 1699 Meldrumshaugh; see HESTERHEUGH. Often confused with the old forest of Drumselch, *sic* 1507, near Edinburgh, fr. G. *seilich*, 'a willow.'

DRUMSHORELAND (Ratho). G. *druim soir*, 'east hill ridge,' + *land*, or else G. *lann*, 'land.' *Cf.* PENCAITLAND.

DRUMSMITTAL (Knockbain). G. *druima smiotail*. Prob. 'vapoury, misty,' G. *smùideil*, 'ridge.' W. prefers G. *spital*, 'hostelry.'

DRUMSUY (Coylton). *Old*, -soy, -soyis, -souie; now pron. -swée. The name has varied between 'ridge of the warrior,' G. *saoi*, *cf.* PORTSOY, and 'ridge with the seat,' *suidhe*.

DRUMTOCHTY (Fordoun). Perh. 'obstructing, lit. choking, hill-ridge.' G. *tachdach* here in loc., fr. *tachd*, 'to stop up, choke.'

DRUMVUICH (Perthsh.). 'Ridge of the buck,' G. *boc, bhuic.*

DRUMWHINDLE (Aberdeensh.). Perh. 'hill-ridge like a head-dress,' G. *binndeal, bhinndeil.*

DRUNKIE (Trossachs, Glencoe). Tr. D. 1567 Dronge, 'Loch of the little ridge or knoll,' G. *dronnag, -aige.* But *cf.* DRONGAN.

DRYBURGH (Melrose). *Sic c.* 1150, but *c.* 1160 Drieburh, *c.* 1211 Dryburg, -borch, 1544 -brough. 'Dry,' O.E. *dryge, drie,* 'fort,' see BROUGH. *Cf.* Dryhope, Yarrow, and Drylaw, 1299 Drilaw.

DRYDEN (Roslin, Ashkirk). 1329 *Sc. Excheq. R.* Driden, 'Dry vale,' see DEAN.

DRYFESDALE (Lockerbie). Pron. Drysdale, 1116 Drivesdale. R. Dryfe is prob. fr. N. *drífa*, 'to drive, like spray'; *drífa*, 'snow, sleet.'

DRYMEN (S. of L. Lomond). Pron. Drímmen. 1238 Drumyn; also Drummane. See DRUMMOND.

DRYNACHAN Ho. (Nairn). *c.* 1170 *chart.* Trenechinen quod Latine sonat lignum recte extensum; 1497 Drynahine. A dimin. of G. *draighneach*, 'thicket, place abounding in thorns.' *Cf.* next.

DRYNIE (Dingwall, Killearnan). Di. D. 1479 Drynee. G. *droigheann*, 'thorns,' here in loc. *Cf.* DRYNOCH, Bracadale.

DUBFORD (Banff). Sc. *dub*, found fr. *c.* 1500, 'a pool, a puddle.' *Cf.* Dubbieside, Leven.

DUBTON (Montrose). Prob. O.G. *dub*, G. *dubh dùn*, 'dark hill.' *Cf.* EARLSTON, EDDERTON.

DUCAT, R. (Laurencekirk). Perh. Brit. *dub chat* (W. *coed*), 'dark wood.'

DUCHRAY (Aberfoyle), DUCHRAYS (Dumfries), DEUCHRIES (Glen Tanar). G. *dubh chraobh*, 'dark, black trees'; with Eng. pl. *s.* But Ducharry, Ullapool, W. suggests, is *dubh chàthraigh*, 'black, broken, moorland.'

DUDDINGSTON (Edinburgh). *c.* 1150 *chart.* Dodinus de Dodinestun, 1295 Dodingstone. *Doding* is a patronymic fr. *Doda* or *Dodda*. *Cf. c.* 1147 Dodinus de Berwic. Six Doddingstons and a Duddingston in England. Doddington, March, is *Dom.* Dodinton.

DUDHOPE (Dundee). 1430 Dudup (so pron. still), *c.* 1500 -ap. 'Hope, shut-in valley of *Dudda* or *Dudde*.' See p. 39.

DUFFTOWN (Banffsh.). From the clan *Duff*. We have Gillemichel Macduf, afterwards Earl of Fife, *c.* 1140.

DUFFUS (Elgin). 1274 Duffhus, 1512 -fous. Perh. G. *dubh uisg*, 'dark water.' W. takes *-us* as the common *-ais*, see p. 9. Phonetic. this seems unlikely. It may be *Orkn. Saga* Dúfeyrar, where the ending is O.N. *eyri*, 'spit of land.'

Duich, L. (Glenelg). G. Dubhthaich. Prob. fr. St. *Duthac*, d. Armagh, *c*. 1062. *Cf*. Bailedhuich, G. name of Tain. But Duich, Islay, is G. *dubh fhaich*, 'dark field.'

Dúirinish (Skye, Lochalsh). Sk. D. 1567 Durynthas. Lo. D. 1548 Durris, 1554 Durness, 1607 Dowrnes, Durinische. Prob. as Mackinnon thought = Durness or 'deer ness.' *Cf*. Craig-durnish, L. Etive, 1613 -durinche.

Dull (Aberfeldy). *Sic* 1380, but 1206 Dul. Pict., W. *dôl*, G. *dail*, 'a plain, a meadow.' *Cf*. Doilweme mentioned in Ir. *Life of St. Cuthbt*. as near by. *c*. 1170 *chart*. re Don Valley, says, 'Rivulus . . . Doeli quod sonat carbo ('coal') Latine, propter ejus nigridinem'; *cf*. G. *dúlach*, 'misty gloom.'

Dúllatur (Castlecary). *Pont* Dulettyr, G. *dubh leitir*, 'dark hill slope.'

Dulnan, R. (Badenoch). *Pont* Tulnen. G. *tuilnean*, *tuil* 'a flood,' often a very appropriate name.

Dulsie, Br. (Nairn). G. Dulasaidh, for *dul-fasadh*, 'haugh stance' (W.).

Dumbarton. *a*. 1300–1445 Dunbretane, 1498 -bertane, *c*. 1600 Dumbarten, 1639 -briton. G. *dùn Breatuin*, 'fort or hill of the (Strathclyde) Britons.' Its old name was Alcluith, see Clyde. Dum- and Dun- constantly interchange.

Dumbuck (Old Kilpatrick). 'Hill of the buck or he-goat,' G. *boc*, *buic*.

Dumcrieff (Moffat). 'Hill among the trees.' See Crieff.

Dumfries. Perh. *Nennius* Caer Pheres (error for Phrees), *c*. 1183 Dunfres, 1395 Drumfreiss, 1465 Dumfrise. Skene thought, 'fort of the Frisians,' here *a*. 400. They called themselves *Frésa*, *Frésen*. But prob. fr. W. *prys*, G. *phreas*, 'copse, shrubs' = Shrewsbury, O.E. Scrobbesbyrig. *Cf*. the name Monfries, G. *monadh phreais* or Shrubhill.

Dumgree (Kirkpatrick Juxta). 'Hill of the herd,' G. *greighe*.

Dun (Montrose). *Sic* 1250. G. and Ir. *dùn*, 'a hill,' then 'fort on a hill,' W. *din*, cognate with the ending -dunum, so common in Cæsar, Camalodunum, Lugdunum, etc. *Cf*. too the Eng. *downs* and *dune*. As early as *a*. 800 *Hist. St. Cuthbt*. we find Duna, now Dunion, a hill near Jedburgh.

Dunad (Crinan). *Chron. Iona*. ann. 683 Duin-Att. W. thinks not G. *dùn fhada*, 'long hill'; but *cf*. Attow.

Dun Alastair (Pitlochry). G., '*Alexander's* hill.'

Dunan (many). G., 'a little hill.'

Dunaskin (S. Ayrsh.). 'Hill by the fen,' G. *esguin*, *easgin*.

DUNAVERTY (S. Kintyre). *Chron. Iona*, ann. 712 Aberte, 1252 Dunaverdin, *c.* 1375 *Barbour* Donaverdyne, which seems, G. *dùn a' bhardainn*, 'hill of the warning or summons.' *Cf.* TULLIBARDINE. But W. derives fr. a man *Abhartach.*

DUNBAR (Haddington and Kirkbean). Ha. D. *c.* 709 *Eddi* Dynbaer, *Pict. Chron.* Dunbarre, *Sim. Durham* ann. 1072 Dunbar. Prob. 'fort on the height,' G. *barr.* But possibly fr. St. *Barr* or Finbarr, bp. of Cork, *c.* 360, to whom Dornoch church is dedicated.

DUNBARNEY (Br. of Earn). *c.* 1128 Drumbernin, *a.* 1214 Dunbernyn, 'Hill with the gap,' G. *bearna. Cf.* CRAIGIEBARNS and DUMBARTON.

DUNBEATH (S. Caithness). *Sic* 1450, *Ulst. Ann.* 680, Duinbaitte. 'Hill with the birches,' G. *beath.*

DUNBLANE (S. Perthsh.). *c.* 1200 Dumblann, -blein, Dunblain, *c.* 1272 Dumblin ; also Dubblain. 'Hill of *Blann*' (gen. *Blainn*), head of a monastery here, *c.* 600, prob. an Irish-trained Briton.

DUNBOG, DINBUG (Cupar). ? in *Chron. Iona*, ann. 598 Duinbolg, *c.* 1190 Dunbulcc, 1250 -bulg, 1517 -bug. 'Massive, bellying hill,' fr. G. *bolg, builg,* 'the belly.' *Cf.* Drumbulg, Tarland.

DUNCANSBAY (N. Caithness). *c.* 1225 *Orkn. Sag.* Dungalsbaer, 1553 -gasbe, 1682 Dungisby. 'Village of Donald,' O.G. *Donnghal*, G. *Dònull.* The *Orkn. Sag.* tells of a 10th cny. Celtic chief, Dungad or Dungal, who prob. named this place. For *-bay* or *by,* 'dwelling,' see p. 41. *Cf.* CANISBAY.

DUNCOW (Dumfries). 'Hill of the gow or smith,' G. *gobha*, or fr. O.G. *coll*, 'a hazel.' *Cf. poll* or *pow.*

DUN-, DRUMCRUB (Strathearn). *Pict. Chron.* ann. 965 Dorsum Crup. 'Hill with the haunch or shoulder,' G. *crubha*, W. *crwb*, 'a hump.'

DUNDAFF (Fintry, Lanark). Fi. D. *sic* 1237 ; 1480 Dundafmore. Prob. G. *dùn daimh,* 'hill of the stag' or 'ox.'

DUNDAGU (Mull). G. *dùn da gaoith,* 'hill of the two winds,' *i.e.*, where the wind seems to blow two ways.

DUNDAS CAS (Winchburgh). *Sic* 1296. G. *dùn deas,* 'south hill.'

DUNDEE. *a.* 1177 Donde, *a.* 1182 Dunde, *c.* 1200 *Lib. de Scon* Dundo, -de, -dho. [*Cf. Ulst. Ann.* 691 Dundeauae dibsi.] Prob. G. *dùn Dè* (gen. of *Dia*), 'hill of God.' W. says, the G. is *dùn dèagh*, 'excellent hill.' This is a very rare pron. It is usually Dundé ; and there is no evidence that, as W. says, the -deagh refers to a man *Daig.*

DUNDONALD (Troon). *Sic* 1461 but *Acta Sanct.* -devenel ; and DUNDONNELL (Ullapool) 1548 Auchnadonill. [1183 Dundouenald, Angus.] 'Hill of Donald,' G. *Dònull* or *Domhnull.*

DUNDRENNAN (Rerwick). *c.* 1160 -drainan, 1290 -draynane, 1461 -dranan. 'Hill with the thicket,' G. *draighnean*. *Cf.* DRYNACHAN.

DUNDURN (L. Earn). Prob. *Chron. Iona*, ann. 683 Duin Duirn, 'hill of the fist,' like a fist, G. *dorn, duirn*.

DUNEATON Water (Abington). 'Hill of the junipers,' G. *aitean*. *Cf.* TOMATIN.

DUNECHT (Aberdeen). Modern. See ECHT.

DUNFALLANDY (Logierait). *c.* 1200 -folenthi, -foluntyn. 'Hill of the sea-gulls,' G. *faoileann*; with ending as in CROMARTY. *Cf.* Creag na Fhaolinn, Durness.

DUNFERMLINE. *Sic* 1251, but *a.* 1092 *Turgot* Dumfermelyn, 1124 -ferlin, *c.* 1134 Dunfermelitanus, *c.* 1142 -mlin, 1160 -melin, -ermling, *c.* 1375 -ferlyne. Two names seem to have intermingled. The short form -ferlin is fr. *Farlan* (*cf.* M'Farlane and Parlane) said to be, with Nemed, first colonizer of Ireland. The longer form may either be for 'fort on the hillock,' G. *meallain*, or G. *dùn fiar Melain*, 'crooked hill of Melin,' a man seen also in LECKMELM; *cf.* STIRLING.

DUNFION (Lamlash, L. Lomond). G. for 'clear hill.'

DUNGLASS (Cockburnspath). 'Grey, wan,' G. *glas*, 'hill.'

DUNGLOW. See DRUMGLOW.

DUNIPACE (Denny). *Sic* 1195, but 1183 -past, *c.* 1190 Dunypais, 1580 *Buchanan* Vulgo appellatur Duni pacis ('hills of peace'). Locally thought, G. *dùn na bais*, 'hill of death,' but, as the site suggests, prob. W. *din y pás*, 'hill, hills of the pass or exit.'

DUNIQUOICH (Inverary). 'Hill like a drinking cup,' G. and Ir. *cuach*, *-aiche*. *Cf.* R. Quaich, Kenmore.

DUNIRA (St. Fillans). 'Western hill,' G. *iar*, 'west.'

DUNJUMPIN (Colvend). 'Fort on the hillock,' G. *tiompain* (*ti* sounded *chi*). *Cf.* Dinchimpon, Buittle. G. *tiompan* also means 'cymbals,' perh. with reference to some religious rites. *Cf.* *a.* 1395 Tympane and *c.* 1240 *Reg. Neubot.* Tympaneochau.

DUNKELD (Perthsh.). *Sic a.* 1150, but *Pict. Chron.* Duncalden, Ulst. *Ann.* 865 Duincaillen, *Bk. Deer* Dunicallenn, *c.* 1141 Duncheldin, *c.* 1420 *Wyntoun* Dwnkaldyne. Fr. same root as the tribe *Caledonii* (Tacitus), which Rhys derived fr. a man '*Caledo*,' name found on a Colchester tablet. *Cf.* 'the wood of *Celidon*' (Nennius), 'of *Caledon*' (Geoffr. Monm.). The root seems Celt. *caled*, 'hard.'

DUNKIRK (Kells). 'Hill of grouse,' G. *cearc, circe*.

DUNLAPPIE (Fern, Angus), DUNLOP (Stewarton). Fe. D. 1172 Dunlopyn. St. D. *sic* 1489 but *c.* 1523 -loppie, earlier Dounlap. G. *dùn làpach* or *làpanach*, with loc., -ie., 'muddy, miry hill.'

DUNMORE (several). G. *dùn mòr*, 'big hill.' The Airth name was borrowed fr. Perthsh. There is no hill there.

DUN-, DUMMYAT, DEMYAT (Ochils). 'Hill of the *Mœatae*' (Mæ- pron. Mai-) or *Miati* (Adamnan), outliers of the tribe Damnonii; *cf.* R. DEVON near by. *c.* 230 *Dion Cassius* lxxvi 12, 'The Mæatae dwell close by the Wall (of Antonine).' Rhys derived *Miati* fr. W. *meiddio*, 'to dare.' *Cf.* Myothill, Denny.

DUNNET (N. Caithness). *c.* 1230 Donotf, 1275 Dunost, 1455 Dunneth. Seems a hybrid, G. *dùn*, 'a hill' and O.N. *hofuð*, 'head, headland'; *cf.* AIKET for Aikhead.

DUNNICHEN (Forfar). *Tighernac* Duin Nechtain, *a.* 1220 Dunnachtyn. 'Fort of *Nechtan*,' K. of the Picts, d. 481. *Cf.* Dunachton, Alvie, 1381 Dionachtan.

DUNNIKÍER (Kirkcaldy). *c.* 1250 Duniker. G. *dùn* (here in loc.) *ciar*, 'dark brown hill.' Perh. 'hill of the fort,' as in BANKIER.

DUNNING (Perth). 1200 Dunine, later -yn. G. *dùnan*, 'little hill or fort.' *Cf.* several DUNAN.

DUN NOSEBRIDGE (Bridgend, Islay). An old fort. Curious corrup. of O.N. *hnaus borg*, 'turf fort,' with G. *dùn* tautologic.

DUN(N)OTTAR (Stonehaven). *Ulst. Ann.* 681 Duin foither, *Sim. Durham* ann. 934 Dunfoeder, *c.* 1270 -notyr, 1461 -otir. Perh. G. *dùn oitire*, 'castle on the reef or low promontory,' which it is, mod. G. having lost the *f* by aspiration; *cf.* 1373 Dalnotire, Dumbtn., and OTTER Ferry. But W. prefers O.G. *fother*, 'a slope.'

DUNOLLY (Oban). *Ulst. Ann.* 685 Duin Ollaigh, *Tighernac* ann. 714 Dunollaig, 1322 -ollach. Prob. 'castle of a man *Ollach*.'

DUNOON. *Sic* 1472, but *c.* 1240 Dunnon, 1270 -hoven, *c.* 1300 -hon, 1476 -novane, 1478 Dunnune. 'Castle on the water,' G. *obhainn*, pron. in S. Argyll o'an; *cf.* AVON, DENOVAN, and PORTNAHAVEN. G. *omhan, odhan*, 'foam,' seems possible here too. Dunoon and Dunowen are common in Ireland.

DUNPHAIL (Forres). *c.* 1250 *Matt. Paris* Dunfel. 'Hill with the hedge,' G. *fàl, fàil*.

DUNRAGIT (Glenluce). Prob. *c.* 800 *Martyrol. Oengus* Dun-rechet. Perh. 'hill of keen sorrow,' G. *reachd*. W., p. 156, derives fr. the district *Rheged*.

DUNRINGIL Cas. (Skye). Hybrid. G. *dùn*, 'fort' and N. *hringa-gil*, 'ring gill,' cleft of circular shape.

DUNROBIN Cas. (Golspie). 1401 -robyn, 1512 Drumrabyn; also Drum Raffn. In 1222 *Raffn*, 'The Raven,' was Lögmadr, 'law-man' or crown representative here. Name remodelled prob. in honour of *Robin* or *Robert*, Earl of Sutherland, *c.* 1400. But good scholars make it G. *druim rabhain*, 'hill-ridge with the long grass.' *Cf.* Allt bad a rabhain, Dunrobin Glen and Raffin, Assynt. Drum and Dun constantly interchange in names.

DUNROD (Kirkcudbt.). *Sic* 1160; also Dunroden. Either fr. G. *roid*, 'sweet gale, bog myrtle,' or fr. *ròd*, 'a road.'

DUNROSSNESS (S. Shetland). *Sic* 1510. *Sagas* Dynröst, -raust, 'din, noise,' O.N. *dyn-r*, 'of the whirlpool,' *röst*, *i.e.*, SUMBURGH ROOST; 1524 Dunrostnes. See NESS.

DUNS (Berwicksh.). *Sic* 1296. G. *dùn*, 'a hill,' with Eng. pl. No proof that it is contracted fr. *Dunstan*.

DUNSAPPIE (Edinburgh). Prob. the Celt's name of Arthur's Seat, *dùn seàpach*, here in loc, 'hill with the long tail,' as it exactly looks fr. the south. Evidence for connecting with Torsoppie (W.) is weak. G. *sop* means properly 'a wisp, a loose bundle of straw,' very unlikely here.

DUNSCAITH, -SKAIGH Cas. (Skye). 1505 -skahay. Prob. G. *dùn sgathe*, 'fort of dread or fear.' W. says, 'fort of *Sgàthach*.' *Cf.* the now vanished Dunskaith, Nigg, 1461 Dunschath, -scacht.

DUNSCORE (Dumfries). *a.* 1300 Dunescor, 1465 -scoir. 'Hill of the sharp rock,' G. *sgòr*.

DUNSHELT, -SHALT (Auchtermuchty). Prob. 'fort of the hunt,' G. *sealg*, *seilg*. *Cf.* Auchensalt, Stirling.

DUNSINANE (Dunkeld). *c.* 970 *Pict. Chron.* Dunsinoen and prob. *Tighernac*, ann. 596, Arsendoim, -oin. Prob. 'hill with the dugs or breasts,' G. *sine*, *sineachan*. Derivation fr. *sithean*, 'of the fairies,' is impossible.

DUN SKUDABORG (Skye). 'Projecting Castle,' N. *skúti*, Dan. *skydi*, 'to project.' On *borg* see BORGUE, and *cf.* DUNRINGIL.

DUNSTAFFNAGE (Oban). 1322 Ardstofniche, *a.* 1328 -scodinche (*sc* for *st*), *c.* 1375 Dunstaffynch, 1595 -stafage. The true pron. seems now lost, though natives say it is G. *dùn sta innis* (*sta* for *da*), 'fort by the two islands,' which is dubious. Prob. it is Dun-staff (O.N. *stafr*, 'a staff') -ness. Ard- of course is 'height.' Rudha Stathish, Kintyre, is prob. the same name, with G. *rudha* = N. *ness* and -ish a tautologic *nish* or *ness*. *Cf.* ARDTORNISH and BROOMAGE.

DUNSYRE (Dolphinton). 1180 -syer, *a.* 1300 -sier. 'West,' G. *siar*, 'hill.'

DUNTOCHAR (Dumbarton). 1225 Drumthoker, 1265 -toucher, 1273 -tocher. 'Fort' or 'ridge of the causeway,' Ir. *tócher*, not in mod. G. *Cf.* Cantochar, Ireland.

DUNTREATH (Kilsyth). 1497 -treth. 'Fort of the chief,' G. *triath*, *-eith*.

DUNTULM (Uig). 1498, -tullen. 'Fort on the meadow by the sea,' G. *tuiln*, borrowed fr. O.N. *holm-r*. See HOLM and TALISKER.

DUNURE (Ayr). 1371 Donouure, 1385 -hower. 'Hill of the yews,' G. *iubhar*.

DUNVALANREE (Ledaig). *Sic c.* 1770 *Pennant*. G. *dùn a' bhail an righe*, 'hill of the king's house.' But W. says it really is *dùn Bhalaire*, fr. the well-known Balar of the evil eye, a Firbolg chief.

DUNVEGAN (Skye). 1498 -begane, 1517 -veggane, 1553 -nevegane. Prob. 'fort of *Began* or *Bekan*,' an O.N. name on record. But *cf.* G. *b(h)eagan, -ain*, 'a few, a small number.'

DUPPLIN Cas. (Perth). *Pict. Chron.* Duplyn, 1639 Dublin, which is the same name, O.G. *dub linn*, G. *dubh linne*, 'black pool.' *P* and *b* readily interchange.

DURA DEN (Cupar). G. *dobharach*, 'watery place,' fr. *dobhar*, 'stream.' *Cf.* DOUR and Durie, and see DEN.

DURHAM (Kirkpatrick-Durham and name of hill there). *c.* 1280 *Bagamund* Kirkpatrick Dureant, which is only perh. = Durham. That is thought the name of an early proprietor, as in the case of Kirkpatrick Fleming; *cf.* Sir Wm. Durham at Monifieth, 1322. As to the Eng. Durham, its oldest and its common form till after 1200 is Dunelm, 'hill of the elm' or 'fort made of elm,' O.E. *ealm*, loaned by the Celts. *Dunholm*, fr. which it is often derived,[1] is ruled out, because there is no trace of *holm* in the north till long after Durham's founding, 995; and its present form does not occur till 1231.

DURIE (Leven). Same as DURA, with -ie loc. *Cf.* Dourie, Mochrum.

DURNESS (W. Sutherld.). *c.* 1230 Dyrnes, *c.* 1542 Ardurness, *Camden* Duirness. 'Deer cape,' O.N. *dýr*, Dan. *dyr*, 'a beast, a deer.' *Cf.* DUIRINISH.

DUROR (Appin). (1343 Durdoman, *i.e.*, 'deep water.') 1501 Durroure, which suggests O.G. *dur* or *dobhar odhar*, 'grey stream.' The G. to-day is Dúr-or, ? fr. the rare *dur*, 'uncultivatable land.' W. says, 'hard water' or 'fort water.' *Cf.* ORR.

DURRIS (Banchory). 1266 *Sc. Exch. R.* -res. = DORES; *cf.* Durrus, S. of Ireland.

DURRISDEER (Thornhill). 1275 Durisdeir, 1303 Doresdore, 1306 Dorresdere. G. *dorus doire*, 'door, entrance of the forest.' There was one here. *Cf.* Deerhass near by, and Dunindeer, Insch, 1536 Doundore.

DUSK Water (Beith). See DESKIE.

DUTCHMAN'S CAP (isle off W. of Mull). So called fr. its shape.

[1] The name is fully discussed by the writer in *Anglia*, March 1930, p. 91 sq. The serious deficiencies of Dr Mawer's art. in his *Pl. Names of Northumberland and Durham* are there detailed.

DUTHIL (Carrbridge). *c.* 1230 Dothol, 1336 Dotheleie. G. *tuathail*, 'north,' north side (of Creag-an-fhithich). M. approves this local derivation. *Cf.* Polhullie, Strathdon.

DYCE (Aberdeen). G. *deis*, loc. of *deas*, 'to the south.'

DYE, R. (Kincardine and Berwicksh.). Perh. Celt for 'goddess'—river worship—as in Dwyfor and -bach, Criccieth, which Anwyl thought, 'great and little goddess.'

DYSTER's Brae and Rig (Stoneykirk and Balmaclellan). The -ster is the common, usually fem., suffix, *cf.* spinster, webster, etc.; 1098 Dyesterhale, Berwicksh. *N.E.D.*'s earliest quot. for *dyester* is 1350.

DYKE (Forres). *Sic* 1311, but *c.* 1190 Dich, 1238 Dike, 1263 Dych. Its Celtic name is BRODIE. O.E. *díc* is, in its soft form, 'ditch,' in its hard, North form, 'dyke.' Wherever *dyke* or *dykes* occurs, as in Battledykes, Forfar, Cleaven Dyke on R. Isla, Raedykes on R. Ythan, it usually marks an old camp.

DYKEBAR (Paisley). *Barre*, 'barrier,' is found in Eng. by *c.* 1220.

DYSART (Fife, Montrose). Fi. D. *c.* 1210 Disard, 1250 -hard, *c.* 1530 *Buchanan* Deserta. G. *diseart*, L. *desertum*, 'desert place, then hermit's cell, house for pilgrims, church.' The earliest monkish 'desert' was Le Desert de St. Bruno, *a.* 1100, at La Grande Chartreuse. *Cf.* Clachandysert or Dysart (*sic* 1446), old name of Glenorchy parish. Cladh ('graveyard') an Disert and Port an Disert, Iona; also 1156 *Pipe R.* Derby, Desertelaw, and *a.* 1200 Disserth, now Dyserth, Flint.

EAGER-, EGGERNESS (Sorby). *c.* 1185 Egernesse, 1456 Egyrnes. O.N. *œgir*, 'the ocean' or 'a sea-god.' Eng. *eagre*, 'tidal wave,' is a late word.

EAGLESFIELD (Ecclefechan). Said to be called fr. a Mrs. Smith's Christian name.

EAGLESHAM (Paisley). 1158 Egilsham, 1309 Eglishame. Not fr. *eagle*, which is Fr. *aigle*, nor fr. G. *eaglais*, 'church,' but fr. a man *Egil* or *Egli*, still a Swiss name. This is the only *hám* or 'home' in this district. *Cf.* EGILSHAY.

EARLSFERRY (Elie). *c.* 1296 Erlsferie, 1492 the Erlys fery. Prob. fr. the Macduffs, earls or thanes of Fife fr. 12th cny. The ferry was over to N. Berwick.

EARLSTON (Melrose). Local pron. Yirsiltoon. *c.* 1144 Ercheldon, *c.* 1180 Ercildune, *a.* 1320 Essedoune, 1370 Hersildoune, 1541 Ersiltoune. Perh. G. *àird choill*, 'high wood,' still there, to which Anglian immigrants added O.E. *dún*, 'hill.' As likely fr. the common *Earcil* or *Earcytel*; *cf.* *c.* 1215 Arkilleshow, S. Lancs. For *dun* become *ton* *cf.* DUBTON, EDDERTON, etc.

EARN, R. and L. (Perthsh.). *Pict. Chron.* Sraithherni, *a.* 1100 *Proph. St. Berchan* Eirenn, *c.* 1190 Erne, *c.* 1195 Eryn, *a.* 1300 Eran, Strathere, 1615 Lockerrane; also *old* Sraith hirend. In G. Eire, gen. Eireann. Perh. fr. *Eire,* Ir. queen in the Ir. Nennius who is said to be fr. Scotland. *Eire,* acc. *Ērinn* was also an old name of Ireland; orig. a local goddess; Gk. Iernē, *Juvenal* Iuuerna, corrup. into Hibernia; so Rhys. Eren was also the old name of R. FINDHORN. *Cf.* AULDEARN, BANFF and DEVERON.

EARNOCK (Hamilton). Prob. G. *earnach,* 'place of sloes,' *earnag.*

EASDALE (Oban). G. Henderson thinks that this, in G. Eisdeal, is prob. N. *hest-r fjall,* 'horse fell or hill.' It might be 'East,' O.N. *aust-r,* 'dale.'

EASSIE (Meigle). 1250 Essy. Loc. of G. *eas,* 'at the waterfall.' *Cf.* ESSY.

EAST NEUK O' FIFE. Sc. *neuk,* taken into G. and Ir. as *nuìc,* is Eng. *nook,* first found *a.* 1300 as *noke,* of doubtful origin.

EATHIE (Cromarty). G. Àthaigh, loc. of *àth,* 'ford, fordable river.' M. thought the root *it* 'going.' *Cf.* ETHIE.

ECCLEFECHAN (S. Dumfries). 1303 Eglesfeghan, 1570 Hecklefeugham. G. *eaglais Fiachan,* 'church of St. Fechan' or the Little Raven, Abbot of Fother, W. Meath, in Kentigern's time. *Cf.* ST. VIGEANS.

ECCLES (Coldstream, Penpont). Co. E. 1297 Hecles. L. *ecclesia,* G. *eaglais,* 'church'; St. Mary's Cistercian nunnery founded here, 1155. *Cf.* 1147 Egglis, now St. Ninian's, Stirling. Three in England.

ECCLESIAMAGIRDLE (S.E. Perth). Pron. Exmagirdle (*sic* 1476), *a.* 1214 Eglesmagril, 1568 -magirll, 1618 -magirdill. 'Church of my dear *Grill,*' in dimin. *Grillan,* devoted missionary to Picts and Scots, *c.* 620 (W.). See *ma,* p. 67. The liquid *l* in Eccles has dropped, then Ecces- easily becomes Ex-.

ECCLESMACHAN (Uphall). *c.* 1250 Eglismanin, -mauchin, 1296 Egglesmauhy, 1404 Eglismauquhy. Prob. 'church of St. *Machan,*' disciple of St. Cadoc, *c.* 570. *Cf.* ECCLES.

ECHT (Aberdeen). *Sic a.* 1300. Perh. G. *eachd,* 'an exploit.' Duneight, Lisburn, is Ir. Dun Eachdach, 'Eochy's hill' or 'fort.'

ECK, L. (Dunoon). G. Aic. 1595 *Mercator* Heke. Perh. O.Celt. for 'water,' *cf.* Esk, Exe (L. *Isca*), etc. But Gillies connects with G. *each,* 'a horse,' and compares R. Eachaig near by.

ECKFORD (Jedburgh). *c.* 1200 Eckeforde, 1220 Hecford. 'Ford of *Ecca,*' a common O.E. name. *Cf.* Ecton, Northants, *Dom.* Echentone.

EDAY (Orkney). *Sagas* Eidey, *c.* 1260 Eidoe. O.N. *eið-ay,* 'isthmus isle,' which it is.

EDDERTON (Tain). G. Eadardan. 1275 Ederthayn, 1461 Edirtonne, v.r. Ederconne, 1532 Eddirtane, 1565 -thane. Corrup. of G. *eadar dùn*, ' between forts,' perh. influenced by its nearness to Tain. *Cf.* EARLSTON.

EDDLESTON (Peebles). *c.* 1200 Edoluestone, 1296 Edalstone, *c.* 1305 Edwylstone. ' *Edulf's* village ' ; *a.* 1189 lands granted here to a Saxon Edulf or Edulphus. The Celt. name had been Pentejacob. *Cf.* 1289 Edilisheude, *c.* 1335 Eddlesheued, ' Edulf's head.'

EDDRACHILIS (W. Sutherld.). Pron. -híllis. 1509 Eddiraquhelis. G. *eadar a' chaoilais*, ' between the straits,' G. *caol*, ' a KYLE, a narrow sound.' *Cf.* Eddergoll (' between the forks,' G. *gobhal*), Breadalbane and Eddraven (' between the bens '), Assynt ; also BALLACHULISH.

EDEN, R. (Fife, Roxburgh). Fi. E. *c.* 1260 Edyn, and perh. Ptolemy's Tina. Origin obscure. Roxb. E. is prob. a back-formation fr. Æden-ham or EDNAM. The forms of R. Eden, Cumberld., are quite different.

EDENAMPLE (L. Earn). G. *aodann ambuill*, ' face of the vat or cauldron ' (W.). *Cf.* AMPLE.

EDGERSTONE (Jedburgh). 1455 Eggerhope Castell ; also Adgurstone. Prob. ' *Eadgar's* town.' O.N. *Ægir* was a sea-god.

EDINBANE (Portree). G. *eadann ban*, ' white slope or hill-face.' *Cf.* Edinglassie, Strathdon, 1219 Adynglas, *c.* 1440 Edinglasse, fr. G. *glas*, ' gray,' and here in loc.

EDINBARNET (Duntocher). 1381 Edyn-, *a.* 1400 Edenbernan, G. *eadann bearna*, ' slope at the gap or pass.'

EDINBURGH. *a.* 700 *Gododin* (Welsh bard), Eydden, Eidden, *Taliessin* Dineiddyn, *Black Bk. Caermarthen* Mynyd (' mount ') Eidden, *Ulst. Ann.* 638 Etin, *Nennius* and *Geoffr. Monm.* Mons Agned, *c.* 970 *Pict. Chron.* oppidum (= *dun*, ' fort ') Eden, *a.* 1100 *Tighernac* Dunedene que Anglica lingua dicitur Edineburg. It is perverse to dispute that the name is Celt., W. *din*, G. *dùn*, ' fort,' and O.W. *eiddyn*, G. *eadann*, ' hill-slope,' that fr. the Castle down to Holyrood ; O.E. *burh*, O.N. *borg* (as in *c.* 1225 *Orkn. Sag.* Eidiniaborg), *Eng. burgh* being = G. *dùn*. But without doubt the name of K. *Edwin* of Northumbria, 613–33, influenced some of the oldest spellings we have—*c.* 1128 *Holyrood chart.* Ecclesia Sancte Crucis Edwinesburgensis, and *Sim. Durham*, d. 1130, Edwinesburch. Charters of K. David have *c.* 1126 Edenburge, *c.* 1130 Edensburc, while a Welsh MS. *c.* 1300 has Dinas (' castle ') Etwin. As late as 1680 we find Edenburgh. Another name in K. David's charters, 1140–50, is Castellum puellarum, ' castle of the maidens,' *c.* 1155 *Brut* Le Castel des Pucèles, 1163 *Cambuskenn. chart.* Oppidum puellarum, *c.* 1205 *Layamon*, ' Ane newe burh vppen Agnetes munte (edit.

1275, hulle) . . . Maidene[1] Castel icleoped.' There is also a Dunedin in Roxburgh, *Dryburgh Chart.* p. 83. *Cf.* BORGUE.

EDINDURNO (Huntly). 'Hill-slope with the pebbles,' see DORNOCH, and *cf.* Drumdurno, *old* -dornach, Aberdeensh.

EDINGIGHT (Banff). Prob. G. *eadann gaoith,* 'hillside exposed to the wind,' more prob. than W.'s *gaoth,* 'a marsh.' *Cf.* 1522 Edingeyth, near Glasgow.

EDINGTON (Chirnside). *Sic* 1166, but *c.* 1098 Haedentun. *Cf.* HADDINGTON, prob. the same name. *Edwin* is less likely.

EDINKILLY (Dunphaill). 'Hill-face with the wood,' G. *choille.*

EDNAM (Kelso). *c.* 1105 Aednaham, 1116 Edyngahum, *c.* 1120 Ednaham, 1316 Ednam. Prob. 'home, village of *Ædan* or *Aidan,*' name of a St. and a Sc. king. *Cf.* EDEN, Edenham, Bourne and EDROM.

EDRADYNATE (Logierait). G. *eadar diòn-àite,* 'between the refuges.' *Cf.* EDDRACHILIS and DINNET.

EDROM (Duns). *c.* 1098 Ederham, *i.e.,* 'home, village on R. ADDER.' *Cf.* EDNAM and WHITSOME. EDRINGTON on the Whiteadder, 1098 Hædrintun, shows the -ing as meaning 'river-dweller.' See *Pl. N. Eng.,* p. 56.

EDWARDSLEY (Jedburgh). 1147–50 Edwardisley. 'Lea, meadow of *Edward.*' It is too early for the royal Edwards.

EDZELL (Brechin). Local pron. Åydel. 1250 Adel, 1267 -all. Prob. O.N. *áa,* O.E. *ea,* M.E. *œ,* 'river, running water,' and N. *dal,* 'dale,' rare type of name for this region. *Cf.* Edale, Derbysh., *Dom.* Aidele.

EGILSHAY (Orkney). *Orkn. Sag.* Egilsey. 1529 *Jo. Ben,* Egilshay, quasi ecclesia insularum. Prob. not fr. G. *eaglais,* 'church,' but fr. a man *Egil, e.g.,* the son of Skallagrim in the well-known saga. *Cf.* EAGLESHAM.

EGLINTON (Irvine). 1205 Eglunstone. Fr. some Saxon settler, ? *Ægelwine,* in *Onom.* as var. of the common *Æthelwine.* *Cf.* Eglingham, Alnwick, *c.* 800 Ecgwulfincham, Eglin Lane, New Luce, and Eglin Hole, Yorks.

EGLISGIRIG, -GREIG (now St. Cyrus). 1243 Ecclesgreig. W. says, 'church of St. *Cyricus*' or Cyrus, martyr in Antioch; hence our name Greig.

EGLISMONICHTY (Monifieth). *c.* 970 *Pict. Chron.* Eglis Monichti, 1211 -menythok, 1245 -meneyttok, 1482 -monichto. W. thinks, 'church of *Mo-Nechtan* or *-toc*'; see DUNNICHEN and *ma, mo,* p. 67, also MONIKIE.

EIGG (Hebrides). *Adamn.* Egea, *Ulst. Ann.* 725 Ego (a gen.), 1292 Egge, old *Celt. MS.* Eig, in O.Ir. 'a fountain.' But this is Ir. and G. *eag, eige,* 'the nick or hack,' which runs through the island.

[1] But, from its site, Maiden Castle, Dorchester, must be W. *maith din,* 'large, ample fort.'

EILDON Hills (Melrose). *c.* 1120 Aeldona, *Sim. Durh.* Eldunum, 1143 Eldune. Prob. hybrid, G. *àill*, 'rock, cliff,' and O.E. *dún*, 'hill.' *Cf.* EARLSTON.

EILEAN DONAN (W. Ross). *c.* 1425 Elandonan, 1503 Alanedonane, 'Island of St. *Donan*,' martyr, d. in Eigg, 617. G. *eilean*, 'island,' is seen in Adamn.'s Elena, now unknown.

EILEAN, ELANMUNDE (Glencoe). 'Isle of *Munnu*,' Columba's friend. *Cf.* KILMUN.

EILEAN NA BEARACHD (Eddrachilis). G., 'island of the precipice,' or 'of judgement.'

EILEAN A' NAOIMH (The Minch). G., 'isle of the saint.'

EILLER, HELYER HOLM (Orkney). O.N. *hell-r holm-r*, 'cavern isle.' *Cf.* Jam. s.v. *helyer* and HOLM.

EISHORT, L. (Skye). O.N. *eiðs-fjord*, 'isthmus bay.' On *-ort* suffix see KNOYDART.

ELCHIES (Craigellachie), *sic* 1226. ELCHO (Perth), *c.* 1230 Elchok, 1281 Elyoch. Prob. G. *ailcheach*, 'rocky place' (W.). The *s* is the Eng. pl.

ELDERSLIE (Renfrew). 1398 -sly, 1499 Ellirsly. 'Alder lea' or 'meadow,' O.E. *ellærn*; *cf.* COULTER ALLERS. The Sc. for the elder is bourtree.

ELGIN. *Sic* 1140; on old corporation seal Helgyn. W. says, in G. Eilginn, an old loc., but competent Gaels say, Ailigin and in N.W. Perth Elgnidh; *cf.* Alligin, Achnasheen, in G. Ailigin. Often held pre-Celtic. *Elg*, gen. *Elgga*, is found in mythic Ir. history, and is also poetic name for Ireland. K. Meyer thought Elgin a dimin.—a very rare type in Sc.; though there is still a Little Ireland in Elgin.

ELGOLL (Broadford). G. Fala-, Falghol, which is perh. *fàl a' ghoill*, 'enclosure, fold of the stranger or Lowlander,' G. *gall*.

ELIE (Fife). 1491 Port and havin of the Elye, *c.* 1600 The Alie. W. thinks, prob. G. *eilaidh*, 'at the grave.' Many think it = Ely, England, *Bede*, Elge, O.E. *el-ige*, 'isle of eels.' The present harbour was once an island.

ELLIOT (Arbroath). *Old* Elloch, Eloth; see ARBIRLOT. Prob. G. *eileach*, 'a dam, mound, bank,' so not the same as the Border name Elliot. *Cf.* ALYTH, Elliothead, Br. of Earn, *c.* 1720 Elithhead, and ELLIOCK, Sanquhar.

ELLON (Aberdeen). *c.* 1150 *Bk. Deer* Helian, Eilan, 1265 Elon. Perh. G. *eilean*, 'an island.' The tide comes up here.

ELLSRIDGEHILL, ELSRICKLE (Biggar). 1293 Elgirig [? *c.* 1470 Henry, *Wallace*, ii, 266, Elrisle]. Perh. G. *àil Girig*, 'rock of Ciric' or 'Greig'; see EGLISGIRIG. Col. Lumsden suggested, O.N. *elds hrygg-r*, 'ridge of the fire or beacon,' *eld-r*.

ELPHIN (Lochinver). G. *ailbhinn*, 'rock peak,' so not = Elphin, Ireland.

ELPHINSTONE (Airth). *c.* 1320 Elfyngston, 1593 Elphingstoun. *Elpin*, *-phin* for *Alpin*, *Albin*, was the name of one of the Pict. kings. But PT. ELPHINSTONE (Inverurie) was named, over 100 years ago, after Sir Robt. E. It is the end of a canal.

ELRIG, ELRICK, ELDRICK (several), ELRICK MORE ('big'), Dalguise. Inverness Elrick, 1576 Allerik, Galloway E.'s, 1466 Elrik, 1507 Heilrig beg ('little') and mor, 1538 Alrig. M. said, loc. of G. *eileareag*, 'a cul de sac bounded by fallen trees'; but W. spells that *iolairig*, and says, No, it is G. *eileirg*, in *Bk. Deer* ind elerc. metathesis fr. O.Ir. *erelc*, 'an ambush.'

ELSICK (Pt. Lethen). *Sic* 1654. Prob. not = Elswick, Newcastle, pron. Elsick. Prob. loc. of G. *aillseach*, 'place of fairies.'

ELVAN Water and Foot (Beattock). *c.* 1170, and same date and district, Brothyr-alewyn. Prob. W. *al-gwen*, 'very white, bright.' *Cf.* R. Alwen, N. Wales, *c.* 1170 Elwan, Alewyn, and ELWAND, *c.* 1160 Alewent, Aloent, other name of Allan Water.

EMBO (Dornoch). *c.* 1230 Ethenboll, 1610 Eyndboll. Forms difficult. Perh. fr. N. *Eyvind*, as in next, 'Eyvind's stead or place.' But now in G. Eiripol = ERIBOLL, N. *eora-ból*, 'beach town or place,' just its site. See -bol, p. 42.

ENARD, EYNARD Bay (W. Sutherld.). 1632 Eynort. Prob. '*Eyvind's fjord*' or 'bay'; see p. 34, and *cf.* AINORT and EYNORT.

ENDRICK, R. (Dumbartonsh.). 1238 Anneric, -rech. But Strathendry, Leslie, is *a.* 1169 -enry. Perh. G. *anrach*, 'stormy'; on the *d* see p. 20. Perh. *an* (for *abhainn*) *éiridh*, 'river of the rising, spatey river.' W. compares Endrick, Glen Urquhart, which he says is G. *eunaraig*, 'a snipe.' The Dicty. spells this *eun-ghurag*, and 'snipe' is not a likely name for a river. *Cf.* BALLENDRICK.

ENHALLOW (Orkney). *c.* 1225 *Orkn. Sag.* Eyin Helga, O.N. for 'holy isle.' *Hallow* is fr. O.E. *halgian*, 'to hallow,' *hálga*, 'a saint,' O.N. *heilag-r*.

ENOCH (Durrisdeer), ENOCH DHU (Pitlochry). G. *eanach dubh*, 'dark, black marsh.' But ST. ENOCH'S, Glasgow, is fr. Thennach or Thenew, *c.* 500, mother of Kentigern or Mungo—1429 St. Thenew's Gate, 1509 St. Tennoch.

ENTERKIN Burn (N. Dumfries). Difficult. Perh. same as 1303 Michael de Enderkelyn, Midlothn. Prob. British, W. *entyrch celyn*, 'summit with the holly trees.'

ENZIE (Buckie). Pron. Íngee. 1295 Lannoy (*L* the Fr. article), 1490 Anze, 1497 Aynye, 1654 *Gordon's Survey* Ainia (Ainyee).

Prob., like ENSAY (Hebrides), fr. N. *engi*, *-ge*, 'a meadow.' But W. prefers G. *eanga*, 'a nook, a corner.' *Cf.* Pittenzie, Crieff.

EOCHAR (Lochmaddy). G. *iochdar*, 'low place, bottom.' *Cf.* YOKER.

EOROPIE (Lewis). Wrongly spelt Europa. N. *eyrar-bœ* (*by*, *bi*), 'beach place or village.' *Cf.* ERIBOLL and 1562 Eurobolsey, Islay.

EPORT (Lochmaddy). *Sic* 1705. Prob. N. *a*, *ey*, 'island' and *fjorð-r*, 'frith,' influenced by G. or Eng. *port*. *Cf.* KNOYDART.

ERCHLESS (Beauly). *Sic* 1403, but *c.* 1220 Herkele, 1258 Er-Herchelys, 1539 Hereichlis. M. says, G. *air ghlais*, 'on the stream.' But the G. rather is *airidh ghlais*, 'shieling on the stream.' Old forms suggest *chaolais*, 'kyle, pass'; *cf.* EDDRACHILIS.

ERIBOLL (N. Sutherld.). 1499 Erribull, Ereboll, 1530 Ireboll. N. *eyri-ból*, 'place on the tongue of land or gravelly bank,' loaned in G. as *earbil*. *Cf.* ARBOLL, AYR, EMBO and Eirebal, Lismore.

ERICHT, R. and L. (N. Perthsh. and Blairgowrie). As the *e* is short, M. suggested G. *eireachdas*, 'handsomeness.' But Coire Eirigh, L. Katrine, is fr. *èiridh*, 'ascent, rising slope,' and W. derives Ericht and Glen Erichdie, Struan, fr. *eireachda*, 'an assembly.'

ERICKSTANEBRAE (Moffat). *c.* 1375 *Barbour* Arikstane. '*Eric's* stone or rock.' The form *Aric* is in *Dom.*

ERISKA(Y) (L. Creran, S. Uist). Cr. E. 1558 Yriskay, Ui. E. 1549 Eriskeray. Not fr. *Eric*, but G. *ùruisg*, 'a goblin, a diviner,' and N. *ay*, *ey*, 'island.'

ERISORT, L. (Lewis). '*Eric's fjord*' or bay; see p. 34. *Cf.* Ericsolt, which G. Henderson says is '*Eric's holt*' or heath.

ERNANITY (Crossmichael). 1565 -nannidy. G. *earrann annaid* (here in loc.), 'land belonging to the church,' while ERNESPIE close by, 1565 -esbe, will be 'land of the bishop,' G. *easbuig*. *Cf.* ANNAT.

ERN-, IRONGATH Hill (Bo'ness). 1337 Arnegayth, 1488 Ardyngaith. G. *àird an gaoith*, 'height of the wind, windy hill.'

ÉRROGIE (Ft. Augustus). Doubtful. ? G. *àird raoig* (here in loc.), 'height of rushing.' But *cf.* ROGIE.

ERROL (Carse of Gowrie). *c.* 1190 Erolyn, *a.* 1199 Erolę. Perh. Pict., W. *ar ole*, 'on the dingle.' *Cf.* AIRLIE.

ÉRSKINE (Renfrew). 1225 Erskin, 1227 Yr-, 1262 Ire-, *a.* 1300 Harskin, Irschen. Mack.'s suggestion, W. *ir ysgyn*, 'green ascent,' suits the site well. *Cf.* FARSKIN.

ESBIE (Hoddam). *c.* 1124 Ascherbie. 'Hamlet at the ashtree.' See -by, p. 41.

ESCART (Skipness). 1511 Escarde, N. *ask-r* (O.E. *æsce*) *fjord*, 'ash-tree bay'; see p. 34. *Cf.* ESKADALE.

ESK, R. (Midlothn., Berwick, Forfar). Mi. E. *a.* 800 Escemuthe, *a.* 1145 Esche, Be. E. *a.* 1130 *Sim. Durh.* Esca, *c.* 1200 Northesk, Fo. E. *c.* 1260 Glenesch, 1369 North and Suthesk. Celt. for 'water,' cognate with G. *uisge*, Axe, Ex, Usk, and R. Esk, Cumberld., also O.Ir. *esc*, 'marsh, fen.' *Cf.* INVERESKANDY.

ESKADALE (Beauly). 1508 Escadell, 1538 Eschadillis, 1568 Aeskedaell. 'Ash-tree dale.' See ESCART.

ESSACHOSEN (Inverary). G. *easer-chasain*, 'a thoroughfare.'

ESSLEMONT (Ellon). *a.* 1600 Essilmontht. Prob. G. *eoisle monadh*, 'incantation, spell hill.' W. prefers *iosal*, 'low,' but notes, Gaels allow prefix of nouns of 2 syllables, almost never adjs. *Cf.* TULLYNESSLE.

ESSY (Strathbogie, Angus, Moray). 1187 Esseg in Strabolgin, 1227 Essy. G. *eas* in loc., 'at the waterfall.'

ETHIE (Arbroath). *c.* 1212 Athyn, 1483 Athe, -y. G. *àth*, in loc., 'at the ford.' Ethie Beaton near by is fr. O.G. *beitin*, 'withered grass.'

ETIVE, L. (Argyll). Old *Ir. MS.* Loch-n-Eite. Perh. G. *èite*, *èiteag*, 'white pebble,' fr. the streaks of quartz with which its rocks abound. W. says, *Eite* is 'foul, dreadful one,' goddess of the loch. Gillies pleads for O.G. *étibh*, 'cattle,' which would suit BUACHAILL ETIVE.

ETTRICK (Selkirk). *c.* 1235 Ethric, Etryk, Hetterich, Etreyich, 1776 Atric. Doubtful. ETTERIDGE, Badenoch, 1603 Ettras, is G. Eadrais, *i.e.*, *eadar dhà eas*, 'between two waterfalls'; and Ettrick may contain *eadar*, or *eadaradh*, 'a division'; or W. *atre*, 'playful' (Mack.).

EUNAICH Ben (Dalmally). G. *eunach*, 'hunting,' fr. *eun*, 'a bird.'

EVANTON (Dingwall). Named, *c.* 1800, after *Evan* Fraser of Balcony.

EVIE (Orkney). *Orkn. Sag.* Efju; also Efja, N. for 'backwater, eddy.'

EWE, L. and R. (W. Ross). G. Eu. Prob. G. *eugh*, *eubh*, 'an echo, a cry'; *cf.* Aird na h'eugh opposite Letterewe. Wh. Stokes said, the same as Eo, Ioua, oldest forms of IONA. W. prefers Ir. *eo*, 'yew tree.'

EWES, EWESDALE (Langholm). 1179 Ewichedale, *c.* 1280 Ewycedale (in both cases *c* scribe's error for *t*), 1296 le Vale de Ewithe, *c.* 1300 Ewytesdale. 'Newt's, eft's dale,' O.E. *efete*, M. E. *evete*, *ewte*. The *n* in *newt* comes fr. the Eng. article *an*.

EYEMOUTH AND -WATER (Berwicksh.), EY R. (Braemar). Be. E. 1098 Ei, *c.* 1130 Eiford, 1250 Aymouthe, 1595 Hay-. *Ei* is prob.

O.E. for 'stream.' See Ayton. But L. Eye, Tain, is G. *loch na h'uidhe*, 'loch of the isthmus,' as in next.

Eye Peninsula (Stornoway). 1506 Fy, 1552 Y. Norse G. *y*, *iu*, *aoi*, 'isthmus, island, peninsula.' *Cf.* above and Iona.

Eynard, L., and Eynort, L. (W. Skye). See Enard.

Fad, L. (Bute, Colonsay). G. *fada*, 'long.' *Cf.* Inchfad, L. Lomond.

Fairgirth (Dalbeattie). From O.E. *fæger*, O.N. *fag-r*, Dan. *feir*, 'fair, pleasant,' or fr. O.N. *faer*, 'sheep,' and *garth*, 'enclosure, garden.' *Cf.* Applegarth.

Fair Isle. *Orkn. Sag.* Friðarey. O.N. for 'isle of peace.' But 1529 *Jo. Ben*, 'Faray, quasi clara ('fair, clear') insula,' *c.* 1600 Fear Yll. Fair I., like the Faroes, is prob. fr. O.N. *faer*, 'sheep.'

Fairburn (Urray). 1476 Ferburny, 1527 Fairburneglis, 1538 Farbrawne, 1542 Ferburn. G. *far brasin*, 'over the wet place,' changed into a 'kent' Eng. name.

Fairlie (Largs). 'Fair lea or meadow,' O.E. *léah*.

Fala (Stow). 1250 Faulawe, 1508 Faulohill. O.E. *fah hlæw*, 'pale, dun hill.' *Cf.* next and *c.* 1160 *Melrose Chart.* Fauhope.

Falkirk. *Sim. Durh.* ann. 1065 Egglesbreth, 1166 Ecclesia de Eiglesbrec, que varia capella dicitur, 1253 Varie Capelle, 1298 *Cotton* Faukirke quae a quibusdam vocatur la Chapelle de Fayerie, 1298 *Norm. writs* La vaire, veyre Chapelle, *a.* 1300 *MS. Digby* Locus qui Anglice vocatur ye fowe chapel, 1381 Fallkirk, 1382 Fawkirc, *c.* 1600 the Fawkirk, still the local pron. Prob. the only place in Britain with a name in 4 tongues. Orig. and still, G. *eaglais breac* or W. *eglwys brith*, 'speckled church,' *i.e.*, of mottled stone, of which Fah-, Fawkirk and La vaire Chapelle are translations ; Sc. *faw*, *fauch*, O.E. *fah*, 'dun, pale red.' *Cf.* Fallside and Faside, Newton Mearns, 1338 Fausyd. The name reappears in Vowchurch, Hereford, 1291 Fowchurche, not till 1538 Vouchurch.

Falkland (Fife). *Sic a.* 1150, but *c.* 1128 Falleland, 1160 Falecklen, *c.* 1440 Facland. Perh. fr. O.E. *fealca*, 'a falcon,' so, 'land for hawking.' *Cf.* Falkedin, S. Devon, Faulkbourne, Essex and Fawkham, O.E. Fealcaham, Kent.

Falloch Glen (L. Lomond). G. *falach*, 'a hiding, a veil.'

Fallside (Bothwell, Inveresk). In. F. *c.* 1150 Fageside, *c.* 1189 Faussyde, now often Fawside. 'Speckled hillside.' See Falkirk and Muiravonside.

Falmouth (Cullen). So on Ordn. Surv. map. But it is 'Whale's mouth,' locally pron. fal's mou. O.N. *hval-r*, Dan. *hval*, 'a whale.'

FANDOWIE (Strathbraan). *c.* 1200 Fandufuith. Prob. O.G. loc. of *fan dubh*, 'dark, black slope.'

FANNYSIDE, L. (Slamannan). Prob. fr. G. *feannag*, 'ridge of land,' then 'lazy-bed.' *Cf.* FALLSIDE, Port-na-Feannaige, S. Arran, and Feinag More, Eddrachilis. FANNYCAPPLE, Kirkinner, is G. *fàn na geapull*, 'slope of the horses' (W.).

FARG, R. (Kinross). *c.* 970 *Pict. Chron.* Apur-feirt. See ABERARGIE.

FARNELL (Brechin). 1219 Ferneval, 1410 Fernwell. G. *fearna bhail*, 'alder village.' But 1098 Farndun, Berwicksh., will be O.E. for 'fern hill.'

FARNESS (Cromarty, Wigtown). Cr. F. *a.* 1272 Fernenes, 1578 Farnes. W. says, G. *fearn-ais*, 'place of alders,' see p. 9. It may be O.N. *far næs*, 'ness, cape by the passage for ships'; *far* also means 'a ship.' *Cf.* FARR.

FAR OUT, FARRID Head (N. Sutherld.). *Pont* Row na farrif, G. *rudha na fàraidh*, 'cape of the ladder' or fr. *faraidh*, 'freight.' Now G. an Fharaird, which W. says is 'projecting cape.' This seems doubtful.

FARR (N. Sutherld.). *c.* 1230 Far, which in O.N. is 'passage for ships, ship'; *cf.* FARNESS. Ships sail up the river here. But M. connects L. Farr, Insh, with G. *far*, 'below,' so 'lower place.'

FARRER, R. and Glen (N. Inverness-sh.). Prob. *c.* 150 Ptolemy *Ouarar*, his name for Beauly Frith. M. connects with L. *varius* and W. with W. *araf*, 'slow.' But prob. this is one of our rare pre-Celt. names. *Cf.* R. Var, S.E. France, in Strabo *Ouaros*, which is Basq. *uar*, 'thick, muddy water.' Glen Strathfarrar is sometimes heard.

FARSKIN (Cullen). 1366 Farskane, 1560 Farskyne, 1581 Froscan. Seems G. *far sgaineadh*, 'over the cleft.' *Cf.* FAIRBURN.

FASKALLY (Pitlochry). 1611 -chailyie. Perh. G. *faisg àille*, 'near rock.'

FASLANE (Garelochhead). *Sic* 1351, but 1373 Fosselane. 'Abode, station,' G. *fas*, O.Ir. *foss*, 'on the enclosed land,' G. *lann*, *lainne*.

FASNACLOICH (Appin). G. *fasadh na cloiche*, 'protuberance of the stone or rock.'

FASQUE Cas. (Laurencekirk). 1471 Fasky; so pron. still. Prob. G. *fasgadh*, 'a shelter.' *Cf.* Straufasket, pron. -fasky, Kells.

FASSIEFERN (Banavie). 1553 Faschefarne. G. *fàsach a' fearna*, 'forest of alders.'

FAST Cas. (Coldingham). *Sic* 1461, but 1404 Fascastell. O.E. *fest*, O.N. *fast-r*, Dan. *fast*, 'firm, solid.' *Cf.* 1216 *Newminster Chart.* Le Swire de Fastside.

FAUGHLIN Burn (Kilsyth). Prob. like FAUCHLANDS, S. of Falkirk, fr. Sc. *fauch*, *faugh*, found fr. 1513 meaning 'fallow.'

FAULDHOUSE (Whitburn). O.E. *fald*, 'a fold, a pen'; *cf.* GUSHETFAULDS. Names in Fauld- are common in Galloway, where this will be G. *fàl*, 'pen, fold, circle.'

FE(A)RINTOSH (Dingwall). 1499 Ferintosky. G. *fearainn toìseaich*, 'land of the thane' (of Cawdor) or 'land-officer.' *Cf.* Ferrindonald, Kiltearn, fr. Donald, ancestor of the Munros.

FEARN (Tain, Brechin). Ta. F. 1529 Ferne. The name was transferred with the monastery, fr. Fearn, Edderton, *c.* 1245, and called then Nova Farina, 1349 Noue Farine. G. *fearna*, 'an alder.' *Cf.* COULTER ALLERS.

FEDDERAT (Brucklay). *c.* 1205 Fedreth, 1265 Feddereth. *Feder* or *foder* is Pict. G. and hardened form of O.G. *fother*, contracted *for*, of doubtful meaning, perh. 'field' or 'wood.' W. prefers to derive fr. *fo-thir*, 'lower place.' The -at or -eth is termin. *Cf.* FETTERANGUS, FODDERTY, FORDOUN, FORGAN.

FENDER Br. (Blair Atholl). G. *fionn dobhar*, 'fair, clear stream.'

FENDOCH (Amulree). 1543 Fin-. Pron. fiánnach. So G. *fionn-ach*, 'fair, clear place.'

FENTONBARNS (Haddington). 1291 Fenton, 'Village in the fen or bog.' O.E. and O.N. *fen*.

FENWICK (Kilmarnock). As above, and O.E. *wíc*, 'dwelling.' Common in N. England.

FEORLIN(G) (Skye), N. and S. FEORLINE (Arran). Ar. F. *old* Furlangis, Forling. G. *feòirlinn*, 'a farthing,' a land-measure. See p. 36.

FERNAN (Fortingall). *Black Bk. Taymouth* Stronferna, G. for 'point of the alders'; -an is a dimin.

FERNIEGAIR (Hamilton). 'Ferny gair,' O.N. *geire*, Eng. for 'a strip of tender grass.' See *N.E.D.* s.v. *Cf.* GREENGAIRS.

FERRIELOW (Colinton). Perh. 'ferry hill,' O.E. *hlœw*, Sc. *law*; *cf.* the Eng. Houndslow, Marlow, etc. Possibly G. *feurach* here in loc., 'at the grassy place,' and Eng. *low*.

FERRYHILL (Aberdeen). 1451 Fferihill.

FERRYTONFIELD (Forfar). 1359 Feryntoun. Hybrid, G. *fearainn*, 'enclosed land, farm,' and -ton.

FESHIE R. (Kingussie). *c.* 1230 Ceffy (error for Fessy). Perh. pre-Celt. M. said Pict., and compared R. Gwesyn, Brecon, fr. W. *gwes*, 'that which moves or goes.' W. suggests G. *feith*, 'a bog,' which does not look likely.

FETLAR (Shetland). *Sagas* Fætilar. N. *fetill*, pl. *fetlar*, 'a belt, a strap.' But Jakobsen refuses this.

FETTERANGUS (Mintlaw). Fetter- is a hardening of Pict. G. *fothir*, which Ir. glosses and dicts. suggest may mean 'field or forest'; but W. holds it means 'a terraced slope,' which suits some cases, hardly all.[1] And if, as he says, the root is *fo*, 'under,' we should hardly have forms in fether-, fetter- so early as the 12th and 13th c'nies. *Cf.* FEDDERAT and FORGAN, and see ANGUS.

FETTERCAIRN (Laurencekirk). *c.* 970 *Pict. Chron.* Fotherkern, *c.* 1250 Ffetyrkern, *chart.* Dav. II, Fettercardin, Fetherkern. Pict. G. *fothir ceàrn*, 'field or wood in the corner.' For Dav. II's -cardin see KINCARDINE.

FETTERESSO (Stonehaven). *Pict. Chron.* Fodresach, 1251 Fethiresach, *c.* 1270 Ffetyressach. See above. 'Place abounding in waterfalls,' G. *easach*, fr. *eas*, 'waterfall.'

FETTERNEAR (Chapel of Garioch). 1163 Fethirneir. See above. 'Place to the west,' G. *an iar* or *'niar*.

FETTYKIL (Leslie). *c.* 1200 Futhcul, *c.* 1320 Ffythkyle. Perh. G. *fuidh cùil*, 'under the back part'; or fr. *cùil*, 'nook, corner.'

FEUGH R. (Kincardine). Perh. cognate with G. *fuachd*, 'cold, chilliness.'

FIDDICH Glen (Mortlach). *Fidach* was one of the sons of the legendary Cruithne. But W. connects with O.W. *guid*, 'a wood.'

FIDRA (N. Berwick). Pron. Fíthera. 1509 Fetheray. '*Fethere's* isle,' N. *ay*, *ey*. *Cf.* the many Featherstones; see *Pl. N. Eng.* s.v.

FIFE. *Bk. Deer* Fib, *c.* 1153 *Snorro* Fifi, 1165 Fif. *Fib* was one of the 7 sons of Cruithne, legendary father of the Picts.

FIGGATE Burn (Portobello). 1486 Fegot. 'Cattle-watercourse'; see *N.E.D.* s.v. *fee* sb.[1] and *gote*. But Sc. *gate* is 'road.'

FILLAN'S, ST. (L. Earn). 1317 Strathfulane. *Fillan* succeeded St. Mund as abbot on the Holy Loch; d. 777.

FINCASTLE (Pitlochry). In G., says *Old Statist. Acct.*, *fonn chaistil*, 'land with the fort or castle.'

FINDHORN R. and town (Forres). 1153 Eren, 1595 Fyndorn; also Fynderan, -erne. On part of its course still called Findearn; *cf.* AULDEARN, 1238 Aldheren. G. *fionn earn*, 'EARN with white, clear banks.' On the *d cf.* next and p. 20; and on -erne become -horn *cf.* WHITHORN.

FINDLATER Cas. (Portsoy). 1266 Finletter, 1455 Finlatir, 1511 Findelatir. G. *fionn leitir*, 'white, clear hillside.' On *d*, in pron. here usually mute, see above.

FINDLAY Seat (Rothes). [*c.* 980 Finlay, mormaer of Moray.] Prob. G. *fionn laigh*, 'clear calf' or hill like a calf. *Cf.* Calf of Man.

[1] The facts are fully set forth in Watson's *Celtic Pl. Names Scotd.*, pp. 509–12. There are several Fodderletters, 1428 and 1502 *R.M.S.* Fothirlettir, where 'slope slope' seems unlikely.

Fíndochty (Cullen). 1440 Fyndectifeilde, 1492 -dachy feilde, 1521 -dachtie. G. *fionn dabhach, -och,* 'clear, fair davoch'; see Dava. The -ty will be termin.

Findon (E. Ross, Gamrie, Pt. Lethan). E.R.Fi. 1456 Fyndoun. G. *fionn dùn,* 'clear, white hill.' Three in England, perh. not the same.

Finfan (Garmouth). G. *fionn fàn,* 'white, clear meadow.'

Fingland (Peebles, etc.), Finglen (Lorn). *a.* 1100 *Tighernach* Findgland, which is O.Ir., G. *fionn gleann,* 'white, clear glen.'

Finlagan L. (Pt. Askaig). *Sic* 1427. St. *Findlugan* or *Finlagan,* dimin. of *Finnlugh,* 'fair one of Luga,' god of the sun, was an Irish contemporary of St. Columba.

Finhaven, -avon (Oathlaw). 1370 Futhynevynt, 1379 Fothenevyn, are fr. G. *fodha, fotha,* 'under,' but *c.* 1445 Fynewin, 1453 Finevyn, fr. G. *fionn abhuinn,* 'clear, white river,' which it is. *Cf.* Denovan, Methven, Portnahaven, and 1272 *Cart. Levenax* Fynobhyn.

Fínlarig Cas. (Killin). G. *fionn lairig,* 'clear, sloping hill.'

Fínnart (L. Long). *a.* 1350 Fynnard. G. *fionn àrd,* 'clear height.'

Finnieston (Glasgow). Named, 1768, fr. Rev. John *Finnie,* tutor of the proprietor, Matt. Orr.

Fins-, Phinstown (Kirkwall). *Phin* is a Sc. surname. Here the reference prob. is to the *Finns* of the sagas.

Fintray (Kintore), Fintry (Denny, Cumbraes). Ki. F. *a.* 1182 Fintreth, 1203 -trith, *a.* 1300 Fyntre. De. F. *a.* 1225 Fyntryf, 1238 -trie. Celt. for 'white, fine house,' W. *tref, tre*; though perh. -treth may mean 'shore, beach of river or sea,' as in Pentraeth, Menai Br., and Pentreth, Cornwall.

Finzean (Aboyne). *c.* 1150 Feyhan. Doubtful.

Firth (Orkney). *Orkn. Sag.* Fiörd. Mod. N. *fjord,* 'a frith, a bay.'

Fishwick (farm, Hutton, Berwicksh.). *c.* 1098 Fiscwic, O.E. for 'fish house.'

Fiteach Ben (Islay). The *t* is radical, so cannot be G. *fitheach,* 'a raven.' But *cf.* Glen Fiddich, perh. fr. a man *Fidach.*

Fitfull Hd. (S. Shetland). *Saga* Fitfugla hofdi. O.N. *fitfugl,* 'a web-footed bird,' fr. *fet,* 'a step' and *fugl,* 'fowl.' Here sea-birds love to alight. Hofdi is for O.N. *hofuð,* Dan. *hoved,* 'headland.'

Five Mile House, from Dundee.

Flanders Moss (Buchlyvie). *Sic* 1707. Many Flemings settled early in Scotland, *e.g., c.* 1350 *Cart. Levenax,* Dominus Willelmus Flandrensis de Barruchane.

FLANNAN Is. (Minch). Perh. by a monk's corrup., 1231 *bull* Insulae Alne. From St. *Flannan,* famous Ir. hermit, d. 680.

FLASHADER (Skye). O.N. *flat-r set-r,* 'flat sheiling or summer pasture or sæter.'

FLEET R. (Sutherld., Kirkcudbt.). O.E. *fléot,* O.N. *fljót,* 'a stream,' fr. *fljót-r,* 'quick.' Three Fleet streams in England.

FLEURS Cas. (Kelso). Fr. *fleurs,* 'flowers.' *Cf.* CHAMPFLEURIE.

FLICHITY (Strathnairn). Loc. of G. *flichead,* 'moisture, oozy place,' W. It might be *fli(u)ch aite,* 'wet place.'

FLISK (Cupar). *Sic* 1250 and Fflisc. Perh. G. *fleasg,* 'a wreath, a ring.' *Pont* has a Flasckwood, N. Ayrsh.

FLODAVAGH (Harris). Either 'flood-bay,' fr. O.N., O.E. and Dan. *flód,* 'flood, flow of the tide,' or, more prob., fr. O.N. *floti,* 'a fleet.' The -vagh is O.N. *vag-r,* 'bay, cove.'

FLOTTA (S. Orkney). *Sagas* Flotey, O.N. for 'fleet-isle,' O.N. *floti,* 'a fleet'; but *flota-holm-r* simply means 'an islet.'

FLOWERDALE (W. Ross), aptly so called, is quite modern. *Cf.* Flowerburn, Rosemarkie, *sic* 1794.

FOCHABERS (Elgin). 1124 -oper, 1238 -obyr, 1325 Fouchabre, 1514 Fochabris. Prob. Pict. G. *fothach abair* or *obair,* 'lake marsh, lakelike marsh.' The *s* is not used in local pron.

FODDERTY (Dingwall). 1238 de Fortherdino, 1257 Fortherdy, 1275 Fotherdyn, 1548 Fothartye, 1572 Foddertie. Fodder- is hardened form of G. *fothir*; see FEDDERAT and FETTERANGUS. The -ty is termin. as in CROMARTY. But FODDERSLEE, Roxburgh, will be fr. a man, ? *Forthhere* or *Frodhere.*

FOGO (Duns). *c.* 1150 Fogghou, *a.* 1300 Foggov, 1352 -owe. Prob. *fog how,* 'hollow,' O.E. *holg, holh,* Sc. *howe,* 'in which fog, aftermath or second growth is found'; W. *ffwg,* 'dry grass.'

FOINAVEN Ben (Durness). G. *foinne bheinn,* 'wart mountain.' It has three protuberances.

FOLDA (Alyth). Doubtful. ? G. *faoghail daimh,* 'ford of the ox.'

FOLLA RULE (Fyvie). 1245 Folayth, 1364 Fouleroule, *a.* 1400 Folethrule, Foleroule. Prob. G. *foladh,* 'a covering, a hiding-place,' and see RULE and ABBOTRULE.

FONAB (Pitlochry). G. *fonn aba,* 'land of the abbot.'

FOOTTIE, FUTTIE (Aberdeen). 1337 Foty, 1583 Futismire; also Fotyn. Some think fr. St. *Fotinus* of Lyons, martyred 177; see *Aberd. Brevy.* But more prob. a loc. of G. *fòid,* 'peat, turf,' 'at the peaty place.'

FORBÉS (Alford). *Sic a.* 1300 but 1433 -bas. O.Ir. and O.G. *forba,* 'field, district,' with common Pict. ending of place, *-ais.*

FORD (Dalkeith, L. Awe). Da. F. *c.* 1130 Forda. O.E. *ford,* 'a ford.' Five in England.

FÓRDOUN (Kincardine). *a.* 1100 *St. Berchan*, Fothardun, *Colgan* Forddun, *c.* 1130 Fordouin. May be 'field with the fort,' G. *dùn, duin*, or 'Wood on the hill.' See FEDDERAT and FETTERANGUS.

FORDÝCE (Portsoy). *a.* 1300 -dyse. See above. G. *deas* is 'south,' also 'trim, fit.'

FÓRFAR. *Sic* 1137, but *c.* 1200 -fare. Doubtful. Accent may have changed. Perh. O.G. *fothir fàire*, 'land or wood on the ridge.' See above. Perh. fr. G. *faire*, 'a watch, a guard.'

FORGAN (Newport). *c.* 1144 Foregrund. W. takes it as 'terraced slope above the bog,' O.G. *gronn*. But *fothir grund*, 'field with the good bottom,' seems likely too. *Cf.* FETTERANGUS, and LONGFORGAN. For FORGANDENNY, Perth, 1505 Forgundynye, see also DENNY.

FORGLEN (Turriff). *Sic* 1314, but *c.* 1210 Forglint. O.G. *fothir glind*, 'field or wood in the glen.' *Cf.* above.

FORGUE (Huntly). *a.* 1300 Forge. O.G. *fothir gaoith*, 'field, wood of the wind, windy place.' *Cf.* above. The surname is spelt Forgie.

FORMARTIN (Central Aberdeen). 1433 Fermartyn. G. *ferann Martain*, 'Martin's land' (W.). What Martin we know not.

FORRES (Moray). 1187 Fores, *c.* 1190 -ays, 1283 -ais, *Chron. Melrose* ann. 897 Villa Forensis. G. Farais. G. *foir*, 'brink, edge, border,' with common Pict. suff. of place -ais.

FORSE (Lybster), FORSS (Thurso). *Orkn. Sag.* Fors, N. for 'waterfall.' *Cf.* all the North. Eng. Forces.

FORSINAÍN and FORSINARD (Sutherld.). Hybrids, N. *fors*, 'waterfall' and G. *an fhàin* (nom. *fàn*), 'in the low-lying place,' and *an àird*, 'on the height.'

FORT, ST. (Newport). Silly mod. corrup. 1312 Sannforde, 1449 Sandfurde, yet also 1684 Santford, and Sanctfuird too is on record. With this 'sandy ford,' *cf.* Sandyford, Glasgow, 1517, curiously, Saintfoorde.

FORTEVIOT (Perth). *c.* 970 *Pict. Chron.* Fothuirtabaicht, *c.* 1165 Fortheuiet, *c.* 1175 Forteuiet, 1187 Fertheviot, 1280 -teuyoth, but 1251 Forteviot and *Bk. Scon.* p. 20, Fetherteviet. For For- or *fothir* see FEDDERAT and FETTERANGUS. W. thinks *Tabaicht* a place in Ireland ; but it suggests G. *t'abachd*, 'abbey.' R. TEVIOT is not the same.

FORTH R. and Frith. *c.* 90 *Tacitus* Bodotria, *c.* 150 *Ptolemy* Boderia (not same name as Forth. W. thinks, fr. O.Ir. *bodar*, W. *byddar*, 'deaf' or 'silent' one ; *cf.* TAY). *c.* 720 *Bède* Sinus Orientalis ('Eastern Gulf'), *a.* 800 *Nennius* Mare Freisicum (*i.e.*, sea haunted by Frisian pirates), *c.* 970 *Pict. Chron.* Ripae vado-rum Forthin, 1072 *O.E. Chron.* Gewæde, Scodwade (*Ann. Waverley* ibid.) *i.e.*, 'Scots' ford'; so *wade* may be meant for a tr. of a name like Forth, *c.* 1140 *Orderic* Scotte Watra, *c.* 1155 *Brut* Escoce Watre, *a.* 1150 *chart.* Forth, *Ir. Nennius* Foircu, *Bk. Lecan* Muir n-Gíudan ('sea of the Jutes,' *cf.* INCHKEITH), *a.* 1200 *Descrip. Alban.* Scottice (*i.e.* Gaelic) Froch, Brittanice (Welsh) Werid, Romana (O.E.) vero Scottewatre, *c.* 1210 *Jocelyn* Litus Fresicum (see above) but flumen Fordense, *c.* 1225 *Orkn. Sag.* Myrkvifiord ('dark, murky frith'). A bay of many names. W. holds that Forth is W. *gwerid* fr. O. Celt. Voredia or Voritia, 'slow-running one.' The river is slow. But forms like Foircu and Froch suggest G. *foir* or *fraigh*, 'rim, edge, border, boundary of a country,' *i.e.* between Saxon Lothian and Celtic Fife. The present form Forth was prob. influenced by O.N. *fjorð-r*, 'fjord.'

FORTH (Lanark). Old var. of *ford*, as often in North. England.

FORTINGALL (Kenmore). G. Fartairchill. *c.* 1240 Forterkil, *a.* 1300 Fothergill, 1544 Fortyrgill. By common transposing of *r*, fr. O.G. *fothir* 'field, wood,' see FEDDERAT, and possibly *choill*, 'wood' or *cill*, 'church.' In this region we would not have O.N. *gil*, 'ravine.' W. connects with the tribe *Fortrenn* or *Verturiones*, and seems to think the name may mean 'fortress (W. *gwerthyr*), church.'

FÓRTROSE (Cromarty). 1455 Forterose. Prob. G. *foter*, compar. of *fo*, *rois*, 'under, beneath, the promontory.' *Cf.* MONTROSE.

FORTS AUGUSTUS, GEORGE and WILLIAM (Inverness). Ft. A. named, 1716, fr. Wm. Augustus, Duke of Cumberland; Ft. G. named, 1748, fr. George II; Ft. W. named, *c.* 1690, fr. William III, though a fort was built here in 1655.

FORTON, FORTUNE E. and W. (Drom). *a.* 1150 Fortona. Porh. *ford- ton* or village. *Fort* is a late word.

FOSS (Pitlochry). *c.* 1370 Fossache. G. *fasadh*, 'a station, a dwelling.' We get the fuller gen. in Bràigh Fasaidh, 'brae of Foss.' *Cf.* Fasag, Torridon.

FOSSOWAY (Kinross). *c.* 1210 Fossedmege, 1476 Fossochquhy. W. derives fr. O.Ir. *fossad mag*, 'firm plain.' As likely is O.G. *fasach*, G. *fasadh mhagha*, 'dwelling in the plain'; *cf.* above. Old forms prohibit equating with Fosavei vik, Norway, 'way to the waterfall' (at Rumbling Bridge).

FOTHRINGHAM Hill (Forfar). *Sic* 1492, but 1424 Fodryng-, Fodiheryngham. Same as Fotheringay, N'hants, *c.* 1060 Fodringeya, 'isle of *Fordhere's* descendants.' See -ing, p. 52, and -ham.

FOULA (Shetland). Pron. Foola. O.N. and Dan. *fugl-ay*, 'fowl isle'; sea fowl abound; *cf.* Fugloe, Faroes. Dr. Wilcock, Lerwick, held this was Thule, as its far-out, lone site suggests; and *th* and *f* do interchange, as in N.E. dial. Firsday for Thursday and as in Fenglesham, Deal, in 831 Thenglesham, and FRESWICK.

FOULDEN (Ayton). *c.* 1098 Fugeldene, 1250 Fulden. O.E. *fugel denu*, 'wooded vale of birds.' *Cf.* DEAN and Foulden, Norfk.

FOULFORD (Crieff). Here perh. tautology. G. *faoghail*, 'a ford.' But also name of an old, low-lying street in Berwick.

FOUNTAINBRIDGE (Edinburgh). On map of 1730, among gardens.

FOURMAN, The (Strathbogie). G. *fuar monadh*, 'cold hill,' which it is. *Cf.* Formond, St. Andrew's.

FOVERAN (Ellon). Prob. *Bk. Deer* Furene, *a.* 1300 Fouerne. Prob. G. *fuaran*, O.G. *fobhar*, 'a well.'

FOWLIS (E. Ross, Crieff). Ro. F. 1381 Estir foulis. Cr. F. 1147 Foulis, *c.* 1198 Fougles, *c.* 1208 Foglais. G. *fòlais*, *i.e. fo-ghlais*, 'sub-stream, burn.' (W.)

FOYERS (L. Ness). 1769 Fyers. G. *fo thir*, lit., 'under ground,' the water seems to dash away so. But W. holds it is O.G. *foithir*, 'terraced slope'; see FETTERANGUS. The Falls in G. are *Eas na smuid*, 'fall of the spray.' *Cf.* Foyness, Beauly, G. Phoineas, 1221 Fotheness (*fodha*, 'under').

FRASERBURGH. 1592 *grant.* Infra dictum burgum de Fraser, 1597 *Acts Jas. VI.* The toun and burghe of Faythlie, now callit Fraserburghe. Land here bought by Sir Wm. Fraser of Philorth, 1504. Frasers in Scotland fr. *c.* 1150; orig. *Fresel* or *Frasel.* Rich. Fresle is in *Dom.*

FRENDRAUGHT (Forgue). 1282 Fferinderahe, -ach. Prob. G. *fearrainn doireach*, 'woody land.'

FRESWICK (Wick). *Orkn. Sag.*, Thresvik (for *th cf.* FOULA). Prob. '*Frisians*' bay,' N. *vík.* *Cf.* Freston, Ipswich, *Dom.* Frisetuna.

FREUCHIE (Falkland). 1508 Fruchy; *cf.* 1479 Freuche, Banff, and 1548 Freuchy, L. Broom. G. *fraochach*, here in loc., 'heathery place,' *fraoch*, 'heather.' *Cf.* Fraoch, L. Awe, 1315 Frechelan ('isle'), and Freuch, Stoneykirk.

FRIOCKHEIM (Arbroath). Pron. Fréakem. 1608 terrae de Freok, 1663 Friock; and Philip Frek or Freke was bailie of Forfar, 1395–8. O.E. *frec*, *fric*, Sc. *freck*, *frack*, 'quick, ready'; *cf.* Freckenham, Suffk., *Dom.* Frakenaham. The Ger. *-heim*, 'home,' was added, *a.* 1830, by its owner, Jo. Andson, who had lived long in Germany.

FROBOST (S. Uist). 'Seed-place,' N. *frjo.* See p. 42.

FRUID Water (Hart Fell). W. *frwyd*, 'impulsive, hasty' burn. *Cf.* RENFREW.

FRUIN Glen (Helensburgh). *Sic* 1351, but *c.* 1225 Glean freone, Glanfrone. Prob. G. *fraon*, *-in*, 'place of shelter among hills.' W. prefers *freoine*, 'rage.'

FUINAFORT (Bunessan). G. *fionna phort,* 'white, fair port or bay.'

FULLARTON (Irvine, Maryton). Ir. F. 1327 Geoffrey de Foullertoune, king's falconer, 1391 Foulertoune. 'Hamlet of the fowler,' O.E. *fugelere* ; *fugel,* 'a fowl.'

FURNACE (Inverary), FURNESS (Gairloch, Ross). G. *fuirneis,* 'a furnace.' Sites of old iron works.

FUSHIEBRIDGE (Gorebridge). On analogy of W.'s derivation of Feshie, Fushie may be G. *fuathasisidh* (dat. of *innis*), 'at the spectre haugh.'

FYNE L. *Sic* 1555 ; but 1580 Lacus Finis a Fino fluvio. G. *loch fionna,* so given to me by old fishermen, 1903, 'bright, clear loch.' Some Gaels say, *loch Briagh,* 'fine, bonnie loch.' But W. says it is G. Fìne, fr. *fine,* 'a vine,' *fìon,* 'wine,' which it is hard to accept. For the pron. Fyne *cf.* ABOYNE.

FYVIE (Turriff). *a.* 1300 Fyvyn. Perh. G. *fiamh,* 'a track,' here in loc.

GADGIRTH (Coylton). *Sic* 1558 but 1508 Gait-. Prob. fr. *gad* sb. 4 in *N.E.D.*, a land measure of varying length, and *girth* or GARTH, 'enclosure.'

GÁDIE R. (Oyne). W. says, fr. G. *gad,* 'a withe,' but the *a* there is short, so perh. pre-Celtic.

GAILES (Troon). *a.* 1371 Gaylis. Doubtful. Perh., as in Gayles, N. Yorks., 1258 Austgail, fr. N. *gil, geil,* 'ravine' ; in later Eng. *gill* comes to mean 'narrow stream.' Jam. gives *gail, gell* as Ayrsh. for 'chink, creek' ; *cf.* Galefield, Cumberld.

GAIRLOCH (W. Ross) and GARELOCH (Helensburgh). Ro. C. 1275 Gerloth (*t* for *c*), 1366 Gerloch, 1574 Gar-. He. G. 1272 Gerloch, *a.* 1350 Keangerloch, *i.e.*, Garelochhead. Also *Pont* Gherloch, *i.e.*, Gairloch, Kells. G. *gearr,* 'short.'

GAIRN (or Gairden) R. (Crathie), GAIRNEY Br. (Kinross), GAIRNEY Water (Glenmuick). Root perh. G. *gearain,* 'to sigh, groan.'

GAIRSAY (Orkney). '*Garek's* isle,' N. *ay, ey.* *Cf.* Gair- or Garson, 3 in Orkney, 1565 Garsoind, -sent, prob. fr. N. *sund,* 'a strait, a sound.'

GALA R. (Galashiels). *c.* 1143 Galche, Galue, 1268 Galu, *a.* 1500 Gallow. W. is sure, fr. O.E. *galga,* 'the gallows,' *cf.* GALLATOWN. There seems no analogy for such a river-name, and it is no back-formation. The river is named long before the town, and 'gallows' is most unlikely. In a Melrose charter, *c.* 1143, we read 'Galche et Leder' (the R. Leader), but in another, of same date, we have 'inter Galue et Leder.' Thus Galche will be an error, and Galue will be for W. *gal gwy,* 'clear, fair stream,' G. *geal.* *Cf.* Gala Lane, Carsphairn, *Pont* Gallua Lane (*lane,* Sc.

for 'slow brook'). *Cf.* too W. *gwala*, 'the full stream.' According to Border usage Galawater means, the valley through which Gala flows.

GALASHIELS. 1237 Galuschel, 1416 Gallow-, 1442 Galowayscheelis, 1503 Galloschelis. See above. *Shiel* or shieling is 'hut,' O.N. *skali*, still used in N. for a temporary or shepherd's hut. *Cf.* O.N. *skjól*, 'a shelter,' *skyli*, 'a shed.'

GALBRAITH, Inch (L. Lomond). 1342–62 Galbrath, 1464 Gaw-[1296 Galbrathe, Wigtown]. A family of Galbraith, 1492 -breytht, used to live here. G. *gall-Breatnach*, 'stranger Briton or Welshman, Lowlander.'

GÁLCANTRY (Ft. George). G. *geal ceann-tire*, 'clear promontory.'

GAL(L)ATOWN (Kirkcaldy). Orig. 'gallows town.' *Cf.* GALA.

GALLON Head (Lewis). G. *gallan*, 'a pillar, standing stone.' *Cf.* Achagallon, W. Arran, and GALLANACH, Oban, 'place full of (basaltic) pillars.' G. *gallan* also means 'coltsfoot.'

GALLOWAY. *c.* 970 *Pict. Chron.*, Galweya, *c.* 1125 *Wm. Malmesb.* Wal(l)wetha, *c.* 1150 *Bk. Leinster* Gall Gedelu, *c.* 1175 *Fantosme* Gavelens = Galwegians. *Orkn. Sag.* Gadd-Gedlar, *c.* 1250 Galeweia; also 1158 Galovidienses. W. *Gallgwyddel*, G. *Gall-Gaidhel*, 'stranger Gael,' prob. fr. Galloway being long a province of Anglian Northumbria.

GALLOWFLAT (Rutherglen). 'Plain, flat of the gallows.' *Cf.* SKINFLATS.

GALSTON (Kilmarnock). 1260 Gauston, *c.* 1375 *Barbour* Gawlistoun. *Galls' i.e.*, strangers' (G. *gall*) town. *Cf.* GATTONSIDE.

GALTY, common rock name in Orkney. O.N. *galti*, 'a boar.'

GALVELBEG and -MORE (Crieff). 1529 Galvelmoir, 1535 Galdwelbege; also Galtwalmor, Galmor, Galven. Gald-, Galtwal must be corrup., but Galven is G. *gailbheinn*, 'great, rocky hill.' Galvel- must be transposition of G. *gabhal*, 'fork.' Galvelbeg is certainly at 'a little fork'; the 'big fork' is now obscured by houses. *Cf.* GAVELL and 1372 'Galvilgil,' Wamphray.

GAMESCLEUCH (Ettrick). *Old* Gamelscleuch. 'Gemmell's cleuch,' fr. O.N. *gamel*, 'old'; *cf.* Gamelshiels Cas., S. Haddington, 1539 Gamylshelis. For *cleuch* see BUCCLEUCH.

GAMRIE (Banff). Pron. Gǽmry, *c.* 1190 Gameryn, *c.* 1200 -ery. M. suggests G. *gamhainn-airidh*, 'stirk shieling.' *Cf.* AUCHENGANE and AUCHTERGAVEN.

GÁNNAVAN (Oban). 1502 Gannewane. G. *gainmhein*, 'a sandy beach,' which it is. Perh. Garavan, Mentone, may be the same. It has a sandy bottom, though not beach.

GANTOCKS (rocks off Dunoon). G. na Gamhneachan, 'the stirks,' *gamhainn*, 'a yearling beast.' Also name of rocks, L. Broom.

GAR-, GAIRBRAID (Glasgow). 1515 Garbred. G. *gearr bràghaid*, 'short gulley or neck.'

GARDERHOUSE (Lerwick). O.N. *garð-r*, 'enclosure, garden.'

GARGUNNOCK (Stirling). *c.* 1470 -now. Perh. G. *gart guineach*, 'sharp-pointed enclosure.' *Cf.* Girgunnochy, Stoneykirk.

GARIOCH (Old Meldrum). *c.* 1170 Garuiauche, *c.* 1180 Garvyach, 1297 Garviagha, *a.* 1500 *Bk. Clanranald* Gairfech. Either G. *garbh achadh*, 'rough field,' or better, *garbhach*, 'rough place.' *Cf.* Garwachy, Penninghame, 1506 -vake, 1507 -wachy.

GARLETON (Haddington). *c.* 1150 Garmeltun. 'Village of *Garmel*,' perh. var. of *Germær*, in *Onom.*

GARLIES (Minigaff), GARLIESTOWN (Sorbie). *c.* 1370 -leyis, 1457 -lois, 1497 Gerrolis, 1548 Garles, 1551 Garrules. G. *ceathramh lios*, 'quarter land of the castle' (Sir H. Maxwell). But G. *gearr lios*, 'short enclosure,' must also have been thought of.

GARMOUTH (Fochabers). *c.* 1650 -mogh, -moch, Germoch. Local pron. uncertain. Prob. G. *gearr magh*, 'short plain.' The -mouth is a mod. corrup. by persons who did not know Gaelic.

GARNGABER (Lenzie). G. *gart an ghabair*, 'goats' enclosure'; *cf.* Glengaber, Yarrow, and Ringaber, Buchanan (*roinn*, 'a point'). But *cabar*, 'antler' and 'stake,' seems also possible.

GARNGAD (Glasgow). 1446 Gartyngad. G. *gartan gad*, 'little enclosure with the withies.'

GARNKIRK (Glasgow). 1515–66 Gartynkirk. Looks like above, 'little enclosure for hens.' G. *cearc, circe*. But it seems 1116 *Inquisitio* Lengartheyn, where Len- will be O.Celt. for 'church,' G. *Lann*, W. *llan*, and so -kirk simply replace Len-.

GARRABOST (Lewis). Perh. *Geirra's, Garri's* farm or 'place,' N. *bolstað-r*, see p. 42. *Cf.* Garrisdale, Canna, L. Garrasdill, Kintyre. But perh. fr. N. *geiri*, 'gore, triangular strip of land.

GARRIONHAUGH (Cambusnethan). 1126 Garin. G. *gearran*, 'a work-horse,' in Eng. fr. 1540, see *N.E.D.* s.v. *garron* sb.[1]; and HAUGH, 'meadow.'

GARROCH Head (Bute). 1449 Garrach, *old M.S.* Ceann garbh, 'rough head,' = GARIOCH.

GARRY R. (Inverness and Perth). G. Garadh. In. G. 1307 Glengarech, -ach, 1325 -gareth, *a.* 1500 *Bk. Clanranald* Gleann Garadh; but often Garrif, which is G. *garbh*, 'rough.' W. thinks of *garidh*, 'a copse, a rough place'; and R. Garry, Kinlochewe, is a' Ghairbhe, 'the rough river.' But locally Inv. G. is held to be fr. *Garry*, a follower of Fingal; *cf.* Uamh Garridh, Glenquoich, 'Garry's cave.'

GARRYNAHINE (Lewis). Norse G. *gearidh na h'aibhne*, 'copse, rough land, by the river,' N. *gerði*, 'strip of enclosed land.' *Cf.* PORTNAHAVEN.

GARSCADDEN (Irvine). 1373 Gartscadane. G. *gart sgadan*, 'enclosure for herrings,' ? for curing. *Cf.* Culscadden, Sorbie, *Pont* Coulskadden. G. *cùil*, 'a nook.'

GARSCUBE (Glasgow). 1457–8 Gartskube. G. *gart sguaib*, 'enclosure for corn-sheaves.'

GARTCLOSH (Stirling), -CLUSH (Lanarksh.). As above and G. *clois*, 'a ditch.'

GARTCOSH (Glasgow). 1520 -gois. 'Enclosure with the hole or cave,' G. *còis*. *Cf.* Cash Bag. (*beag*, 'little'), Kirkmaiden.

GARTH (Aberfeldy). O.E. *geard*, O.N. *garð-r*, M.E. *garth*, 'enclosure, garden'; *cf.* APPLEGARTH. Common in old Shetland as *-gaard*, 1360 Basse- and Vallegaard, Sandwick, etc.

GARTHDEE (Aberdeen). Aberdeen Sc. *garth*, 'dam, weir for catching fish,' also 'gravel, river shingle.' See DEE.

GARTIE, Mid and West (Helmsdale), GARTY (Kilmuir Easter). 1368 Gorty. G. *gart*, *gort*, 'corn enclosure,' here in loc.

GARTLY (Insch). *a.* 1237 Garentuly, *a.* 1500 Grantuly, 1600 Gartullie. G. *garan tulaich*, 'thicket on the hill.' *Cf.* GRANDTULLY and MURTHLY.

GARTMORE (Aberfoyle). G. for 'big enclosure.'

GARTNATRA (Bowmore). G. *gart an tràga*, 'field on the strand.' Names in Gart- are very common in Islay, Gartchossan (*cossan*, 'foot-path'), -loist (*loisgte*, 'burnt'), -main (*meadhan*, 'middle'), etc.

GARTNAVEL (Glasgow). G. *gart n' abhal*, 'enclosure with the apples' = ORCHARD or APPLEGARTH.

GARTNESS (Drymen, Islay). Prob. G. *gart an eas*, 'enclosure by the waterfall.'

GARTNEY (Callander). G. *srath Ghartàin*, fr. some man. There is a *Gartnait* in *Bk. Deer* and *Gartnach* in *c.* 1120 charter. *Cf.* Lairig Ghartain, Glen Etive and 1452 *chart.* Balgartynnay.

GARTOCHÁRN (Balloch). 1485 Gartcarne, 1494 Garncarn, 1605 Gartoquharne. Prob. 'enclosure with the cairn,' G. *a' chàirn*.

GARTSHERRIE (Coatbridge). 1593 -sharie. 'Enclosure of the foals,' G. *searrach*, here in loc. *Cf.* Barsherry, Balmaclellan.

GARTURK (Coatbridge). 'Enclosure of the boars or hogs,' G. *torc*, *tuirc*. *Cf.* TURK.

GARVALD (E. Lothian, Peebles), GARVALT Burn (Braemar). E. Lo. G. *sic* 1250. G. *garbh alld*, *allt*, 'rough stream.' *Cf.* GARREL or Garvald, Lochmaben and Kilsyth. The -el is -ald shortened.

GARVE L. (Strathpeffer). G. *garbh*, 'rough.'

GARVEILEACH Isles (Jura). *a.* 558 *Vit. Brendan* Ailech, prob. Elachnave in this group. 1390 Garbealeach, 1589 Garowhellach, -whileach. G. *garbh eileach*, 'rough island-rock.'

GARVELLAN (Durness). 1580 *Buchanan*, Garvellan id est aspera insula. G. *an garbh eilean*, 'the rough isle.'

GARVOCK (Laurencekirk) = GARIOCH.

GARWOLING (Kintyre). *Old* -foling. G. *gart feòirlinn*, 'farthing land.' See p. 36.

GASK (Dunning, Turriff, Strathnairn). Du. G. *c.* 1208 Gaisk, Gask. O.G. *gasc*, 'nook, gusset, hollow.' *Cf.* FINGASK and Gergask, Laggan. GASCAN, Shieldaig, is 'little tail or extremity.'

GASSTOWN (Dumfries). Founded by Jos. *Gass*, *c.* 1812.

GAS Water (E. Ayrsh.). G. *gas*, 'a branch,' or ? N. *gás*, 'a goose.'

GASSIESLACK (Aberdeensh.). G. *gasach*, 'full of branches,' here in loc., and *slack*, 'hollow'; see BEESLACK.

GAT-, GAITEND (Beith). 'End of the gate,' Sc. for 'road.'

GATEGILL (Girthon), GATEHOPE (Peebles). 'Ravine,' and 'sheltered valley of the goats,' N. *geit*. See HOBKIRK.

GATESHAW (Morebattle). As above and see SHAW. But perh. *a.* 800 *Hist. St. Cuthbt.*, Gistatun. Only a *Gistheard* in *Onom.*

GATTONSIDE (Melrose). *c.* 1143 Galtuneside, 1539 Gawtonesid. 'Hamlet of the stranger,' G. *gall* + *side*, in names meaning 'slope' or perh. 'seat.' *Cf.* MUIRAVONSIDE, also GALSTON and WALLACETOWN.

GAÚLDRY (Cupar). Prob. G. *gall doire*, 'strangers' wood.'

GAUZE (Bo'ness). *Old* Gawes. Prob. fr. *gall* sb.[2], in Sc. 6–9 *gaw*, 'a bare spot in a field.'

GAVELL (Kilsyth). *Sic* Pont, 1694 Gaball. G. *gabhal*, 'a fork, a junction.' *Cf.* Tighnagavil, Bute.

GAVINTON (Duns). Called so, *c.* 1760, by David *Gavin*, its proprietor, who built it then.

GEANIES (Fearn). Pron. Gáynes. *c.* 1500 Genes, 1529 Gathne, -enn, 1561–66 Éstir, Westir and Midil Gany. Difficult. W. thinks of a pl. of N. *gjá*, 'goe, chasm.' But surely it is loc. of G. *gaothanach*, 'windy place,' as indeed it is, with an Eng. pl., or, as the natives thought at least 50 years ago, + *ness*.

GEAR (Orphir). 1503 Gyre, 1595 Gera. Perh. N. *geir-á*, 'auk isle,' as in Geirum or *geir-holm* (see HOLM), Barra.

GEDDES Ho. (Nairn). 1238 -deys, 1442 Meikle Geddes. G. *gead*, 'a patch, spot of ground, ridge,' with ending *-ais*, suff. of place.

GELDER Burn (Balmoral). G. *geal dobhar*, 'clear, fair stream.'

GELSTON (Cas. Douglas). 1296 *Ragman R.* Gevelestone, 1329 Geuylstoun, 1426 Gevyls-, Gilliston, 1466 Gelstoun. The man's name here is corrup., perh. *Gebhild* or *Gebweald*, in *Onom.*

GEORGEMAS (Thurso). Market held here on Apr. 23, *St. George's mass* or feast. *Cf.* Hallowmass.

GERMAIN'S, St. (Seton, E. Lothn.). 1296 La maison de seint Germeyn. *Germanus*, bp. of Auxerre, came to Britain, 429.

GHENAGHAN, Is. (L. Lomond). G. *geangach*, 'crooked, thick and short place,' with *-an* termin.

GIFFEN (2, N. Ayr). *a.* 1233 Giffin, 1278 Gyffin. As the sites show, W. *cefn*, 'a ridge.' *Cf.* Cefn, St. Asaph's, and Kevan Howe, Whithorn.

GIFFNOCK (Glasgow). Dimin. of above.

GIFFORD (Haddington). 1580 Giffordiensis. Said to be fr. a Hugo Gyffard, *c.* 1180; and Walterius Gifardus came over in 1066. But such a pl.-name is contrary to analogy, and Gif- is prob. fr. O.E. *gifla*, 'fork, forked opening.'

GIGHA Is. (Kintyre, N. of Barra). Kin. G. *Hakon's Saga* Guðey, 1263 Gudey, 1309 Gug, 1335 Gythe, 1343 Geday, *c.* 1400 Gya, 1510 Giga. A curious assortment! Col. Lumsden suggested, O.N. *God-*, *Guth-ey*, 'God's isle'; and there is a N. name *Gyða*. N. *gjá-ey*, 'goe, rift isle,' seems to suit some forms.

GIGHT, Braes of (Fyvie). *c.* 1374 le Geth. G. *gaoth*, 'a marsh,' but *cf.* EDINGIGHT.

GILABOLL (Helmsdale). 'Place of gills or ravines.' See *bol* p. 42.

GILCOMSTON (Aberdeen). 1361 Gilcolmystona. 'Hamlet of the *gillie* or servant of St. *Colm* or Columba'; *cf.* p. 65, GILMERTON and Glanderston, Kinnethmont, *a.* 1238 Gillandreston.

GILLESPIE (Old Luce). *Pont* Killespiek. G. *cill easbuig*, 'cell, church of the bishop,' L. *episcopus*. *Cf.* GILCHRIST, Urray, 1569 Kylchristan.

GILMERTON (Edinburgh). *c.* 1200 Gyllemoreton, -muriston. 'Village of the servant,' G. *gille*, 'of Mary,' the Virgin, G. *Moire*. *Cf.* Gilmorton, Lutterworth, and GILCOMSTON.

GILNOCKIE (Canonbie). G. *geal cnoc*, in loc., 'at the clear hill.'

GIRDLE Ness (Aberdeen). 1654 Gridle Ness. Sc. *griddle* or *girdle* is 'a gridiron'; in Eng. as *gredil a.* 1225.

GIRNIGO (Wick). *Sic* 1547. Perh. 'gaping inlet or goe,' O.N. *gjá*; *cf.* O.N. *girna*, 'to yearn, desire.'

GIRTHON (Gatehouse). 1300 *Close R.* Gerton. Perh. fr. a man *Gert*, in *Onom.* As likely fr. *garth*, M.E. also *girth*, 'yard, garden,' see APPLEGARTH.

GIRVAN R. and town (S. Ayr). 1275 -ven, 1328 Gervan. G. *gearr abhainn*, 'short river,' as contrasted with the Stinchar. But Garvan, L. Broom, is G. for 'rough place.'

GIZZEN BRIGS (shoal, Dornoch Firth). W. derives fr. N. *gisnar*, 'leaky,' the Sc. *gizzened*, and *bryggja*, 'bridge.' There seems nothing more likely for the first part. The second is as likely *brig*, 'a jutting-out reef,' as in BRIDGENESS and Filey Brigs.

GLACK (Newtyle). G. *glac*, 'hollow, valley.'

GLADHOUSE (S. Midlothn.), GLADSMOOR (Kirkcolm), GLADSMUIR (Tranent). *c.* 1142 Gledehus, 1183 -wis. 1328 Glademor, 1542 Gladismure. O.E. *glida*, Sc. *gled*, 'the kite, the *gliding* bird.' *Cf.* GLEDSTANES.

GLÁMAIG (mtn., Skye). Prob. O.N. *glám-r*, poetic name for the moon, with *-aig* termin. O.N. *glam(m)* is 'noise, din.'

GLAM(M)IS (Forfar). Pron. Glamms. 1187 -mes, 1251 Glemmis. G. *glamhus*, 'a wide gap,' hence 'open country.'

GLASGOW. 1116 Glasgu, 1122 *Papal mandate* Glasguensis episcopus, 1158 Glasgow, 1165–78 Glascu, 1185 *Jocelyn* Cleschu.[1] Rhys said, W. *glas chu* (G. *glas cu*), 'greyhound,' Kentigern or St. Mungo of Glasgow being called, *Vitae Sanct.*, In glas chu, 'the grey hound.' Has any place-name such a meaning ? W. *glas cu*, 'dear stream,' the Molendinar, is possible. As likely is W. *glas cau* (pron. kay), 'green hollows,' which agrees with the vulgar pron. Gles-cay. There are 2 Glasgows in Aberdeensh. and Gleschu Beag, Islay. *Cf.* LINLITHGOW and PLASCOW.

GLÁSMONT (Kirkcaldy). 1178 -month. G. *glas monadh*, 'grey hill.'

GLASS R. (Beauly). 1309 Straglass. G. *glas*, 'grey, dark-looking.'

GLASS (Huntly). O.G. *glas*, 'a river.' *Cf.* DOUGLAS.

GLASSARY (Lochgilp.). 1251 -ered, 1284 Glasrod, *c.* 1315 Glassereth, 1355 -sre, 1394 Glaster. G. *glas airidh*, 'grey or green shieling or hill-pasture'; *cf.* ASSARY. But 1394 is fr. *tìr*, 'land.'

GLASSAUGH (Portsoy). Pron. Glássaw. 1531 Glashauch, 1539 -sauche. Hybrid. O.G. *glas*, 'stream,' and HAUGH, 'river meadow.'

GLASSERTON (Whithorn). Pron. Glaiston. 1451 Glasar-, 1473 Glassertoune. In early chrons. seemingly confused with Glastonbury, the famous Somerset monastery. Prob. fr. a man *Glaser*, as in Gleaston, N. Lancs., *Dom.* Glasserton.

[1] Oldest MS. Deschu (D error for CL). Joc. says: 'Cathedralem sedem suam in villa dicta Cleschu quod interpretatur Cara Familia, quae nunc vocatur Glasgu.' This derives the name fr. W. *clas*, 'enclosed place or area, sanctuary, cloister, family'; and 'dear cloister,' though not 'dear family,' is quite possible.

GLAS(S)FORD (Hamilton). *c.* 1210 Glasfruth, -furth, 1296 Glasford. Orig. W. *glas ffridd* or G. *glas fríth,* 'green forest.' The change to *ford* was easy through its old form FORTH.

GLASTERLAW (Forfar). Hybrid. G. *glas tìr,* 'green land,' and *law,* O.E. *hlǽw,* 'hill.' *Cf.* Glastry, Dunblane.

GLEDSTANES (Biggar). 1296 *Ragman R.* Gledestane, 'kite's rock' or 'stone'; see GLADHOUSE. Hence the surname Gladstone.

GLEN or THE GLEN (Innerleithen). Already so called, 1296. For many Glens see under their rivers, ALMOND, ARAY, etc.

GLENAPP (Ballantrae), GLENNAPP (Berwicksh.). Ba. G. *c.* 1370 Glennop, is said to be Glen Alpinn, where K. Alpinn was slain, 750. Prob. both are 'glen of the abbot,' O.G. *ab.* *Cf.* APPIN.

GLENBOIG (Coatbridge). Local pron. Glenbōg. 'Soft, moist glen,' G. and Ir. *bog, buige,* 'soft.'

GLENBUCK (Muirkirk). G. *boc, buic,* 'a buck, a he-goat.'

GLENCAIRN (Thornhill). 1179 -karn. G. *càrn, càirn,* 'cairn, heap of stones.'

GLEN CALADH (Kyles of Bute). G. *caladh,* 'a harbour, a ferry.'

GLENCAPLE (Dumfries). *Sic c.* 1240. G. *capull, -uill,* 'a mare.' *Cf.* KINCAPLE.

GLENCHALMADALE (N. Arran). O.N. *Hjalmund-r dal,* 'glen of *Hjalmund,*' in G. *Calman.*

GLENCOE (N. Argyll). 1343 Glenchomure (G. *comar, chomair,* confluence,[1] 1494 Glencole (*caol,* 'narrow'), 1500 -cowyn, -coyne, 1623 -coan. Now in G. *gleann comhann, cumhann,* 'narrow glen,' *cf.* Glencune, Haltwhistle. See how names can alter! The river's name is Coe or Cona, hence the title of Ld. Strathcona.

GLENCORSE (Penicuik). 1298 *Close R.* -crosk. G. *crosg,* 'pass, crossing.' *Cf.* ARNGASK.

GLENCROE (L. Long). G. *cro,* 'circle, hut, sheep-fold.'

GLENCRUITTEN (Oban). 1502 -crutten. G. *cruitein,* 'little humpback.' *Cf.* 1378 *Ulst. Ann.* Cellach MacCruitin.

GLENDALE (Skye). Tautology, G. and N. Also in Northumberland.

GLENDARUEL (Cowal). 1238 Glen da rua, 'of the two points,' G. *ruadha,* 1314 -arewyle, 1445 -rowale, 1478 -derouane, 1508 -rouell, 1723 darowal. *Glen Masan MS.* Gleann na ruadh, Glend daruadh. Natives make the R. Ruel, *ruadh allt,* 'red stream,' fr. a bloody fight here. W. says it is, 'glen of the two red spots,' and compares the Ir. Deargail. Mack. helpfully compares W. *rhuddell,* 'red' and *rhuawl,* 'roaring.'

[1] The Glen starts just where the two parts of L. Leven meet.

Glendinning (Westerkirk). 1384 -donwyne. 1471 -dinwyne. W. *glyn din gwyn*, 'glen of the fair hill.'

Glendoick (Errol), taken by some fr. St. *Duthac* of Tain, *cf.* Duich and our surname Doak.

Glenduckie (N. Fife). 1392 -duky, *a.* 1500 *Aberd. Brev.* -deochquhy; also -duachy, 'glen of sorrow,' G. *dubhaiche. Cf.* Glendowachy, Gamrie, *c.* 1320 -douachy.

Gleneagles (Blackford). *c.* 1165 Gleninglese, 1508 -negas. G. *gleann n' eaglaise*, 'glen of the church.'

Glenelg (W. Inverness). *Sic* 1292, but 1282 -helk. Prob. fr. a man *Eilg*, 'the noble,' root akin to Elgin.

Glenfinnan (W. Inverness). W. says, 'glen of *Fingon*,' same name as in McKinnon. M. held it was *gleann an oin*, 'glen of the one,' a very curious name!

Glengarnock (Kilbirnie). [*Cf. c.* 1240 Dalegernoc.] Prob. G. *gearanach*, 'sighing, groaning' river. But *cf.* next.

Glengirnaig, -ock (Ballater, Atholl). 'Glen of the little crier.' G. *goirneag*. The -aig is a dimin.

Glengonar (Crawford). *Sic* 1239, but *c.* 1240 -goneur, -gonever. G. *goin-fheur*, 'couch grass.'

Glengyre (Kirkcolm). G. *gadhar* or *gaothar*, 'a greyhound.'

Glenhinnisdale (N. of Skye). W. conjectures, fr. a man nicknamed 'tinder,' O.N. *tund-r. Cf.* Talisker.

Glenhowl, -houl (Carsphairn, Glenluce). 1563 -hovyll, *Pont* -howill. G. *gobhal, -ail*, 'a fork, a branching.'

Gleniffer (Paisley). Perh. W. *glyn dyfr*, 'glen with the stream,' *d* lost by aspiration. But 1372 *R.M.S.* Glenifern, Argyll, is fr. G. *aifrenn*, 'the mass.' See Inchaffray.

Glenkens, The (Dalry, Gall.). 1181 -kan, 1368–9 -ken, see R. Ken. The pl. *s* refers to the four parishes along the river.

Glenkindie (Strathdon). 'Glen of the dark head.' G. *cinn duibhe*.

Glenlívat (Craigellachie). G. gleann Liòmhaid. M. and W. think fr. same root as Glenlyon.

Glenlochar (Cas. Douglas). G. *luachair*, 'rushes.'

Glenlyon (Cent. Perthsh.). *Sic* 1522, but 1328 -lyoun, *c.* 1380 *Fordoun*, -leoyne, 1508 -leehane. Doubtful. Perh. G. *lì omhuinn*, 'coloured river'; perh. fr. *lighe*, 'a flood.'

Glenmidge (Dumfries). Perh. like Midgeley, W. Riding, 1234 Miggeley, fr. O.E. *mycge*, M.E. *migge*, 'a midge.'

Glenmorison (L. Ness). *Ulst. Ann.* 638 Glinnemureson, 1479 Glenmorison. G. *mòr easan*, 'big waterfalls,' seen well fr. the road.

GLENMUICK (Ballater). Pron. -mík. 1451 Mukvale, 1571 Glenmuk. G. *muc*, *muic*, 'a sow.'

GLENORCHY, -URCHY (Dalmally). *c.* 1240 -erochy, 1292 -urwy, 1510 -vrquha. G. gleann Urchaidh. Doubtful. W.'s O.Celt. *ar cet*, 'on the wood,' seems far-fetched. Mack. thinks of W. *erch*, 'gloomy,' while form *c.* 1240 suggests G. *earrach*, *-aiche*, 'the bottom of a dish.'

GLENPROSEN (Kirriemuir). 1463 -prostyn, 1524 -prossin, -osswym. Doubtful. *Cf.* O.G. *brosnach*, 'a river.' G. root *brosn-*, *brosd* is 'stir, excite,' W. *prwst*, 'bustle.' *Cf.* too W. *prwyst*, 'an obstacle.'

GLENQUAICH or -CUAICH or -QUOICH (several). G. *cuach*, *-aich*, 'a quaich, a drinking cup.'

GLENRISDELL (Tarbert, L. Fyne). 1495 -restill, 1511 -rysadill. O.N. *hris-dal*, 'copsewood glen'; *cf.* Risabus, Islay. For the tautology *cf.* Strathhalladale.

GLENSHEE (Blairgowrie). 1495 -schee. G. *sìth*, *-he* means 'a fairy, a hill, and peace.'

GLENSHIEL (L. Duich). O.N. *skjól*, 'shelter, shieling.' *Cf.* GALASHIELS.

GLENSHIORA (Badenoch). G. *sioro*, root *sìr*, *siòr*, 'long.' *Cf.* SHIRA.

GLENTROOL (Minigaff). *c.* 1375 *Barbour* -trewall, *Pont* Truiyill. G. *t-sruthail*, 'stream.'

GLENTROMIE or -TRUIM (Badenoch). G. *troman*, here in loc., 'the dwarf elder,' Ir. *trom*, *truimm*, 'elder tree,' as in Trim, Meath.

GLENWHILLIE (New Luce). G. *gleann choille*, 'glen with the wood.'

GLOMACH, Falls of (Kirtail). Root prob. O.N. *gláma*, 'whiteness.'

GLOON Burn and RIG of GLOON (Minigaff). G. *glùn*, 'the knee, projecting hill.'

GLOUPHOLM (Shetland). O.N. *glóp-r*, 'soft,' and see HOLM. But note too, O.N. *glup*, 'throat,' and *gloppa*, 'a hole.' *Gloup* is a name for a sea-cave, with a funnel at its inner end, through which the sea spouts up.

GLOWER-O'ER-EM (Linlithgow). Name of a hill with a wide view; Sc. *glower*, 'to stare, gaze.' Also near Bamburgh.

GOATFELL (Arran). *Pont* Keadefell Hil. G. Gaod, older Gaot, Bheinn, which M. derived fr. N. *geit*, 'goat.' We find the same name in Keitval, S. Uist. Fell is N. *fell*, 'hill,' or *fjall*, 'mountain.'

GODSCROFT (Abbey St. Bathan's). 'God's field' or 'acre'; see CROFTHEAD. So named by Hume, *c.* 1630. Orig. it was Gowk's, *i.e.*, Cuckoo's, Croft.

GOGAR (Edinburgh, Menstrie). Ed. G. 1233 fluvius de Goger, 1250 Gogger, 1335 Coger, 1650 Gawger. W.'s idea, W. *go cor* or *gor*, 'under the coping or battlement,' then 'a small spur,' seems dubious. The name is difficult.

GOGO Burn (Largs). *Sic* Pont. Perh. N. *gauk-á*, 'cuckoo's' or 'gowk's stream'; *cf*. Gowk Craigs near by. *Cf*. too W. *gogof*, 'a cave.'

GOIL, L. (Firth of Clyde). G. Goil. 1430 -goyle, while Glengyle, L. Katrine, is also pron. in G. Goil. Prob. fr. G. *gall*, *goill*, 'a stranger.' Phonetics, though not the site, are against *gobhal*, *-ail*, 'a fork.'

GOIN, L. (Fenwick). G. and Ir. *geadh*, gen. pl. *geadhan* (pron. goin), 'a goose, a barnacle duck.' *Cf*. Loughnagoyne, Mayo.

GOLSPIE (Sutherld.). 1330 Goldespy, 1448 Golspi, 1550 Golspiekirk-toun (Kirkton farm still there). Perh. 'dwelling of a man *Gold*,' a known name. See -by, p. 41; *p* for *b*, as often *pol* for *bol*. The old name was Kilmaly.

GOMETRA Is. (Mull). 1390 Godmadray, 1496 Gowmedra. '*Godmadr's* or *Godmundr's* isle,' N. *ay*, *ey*.

GORBALS (Glasgow). 1521 baldis. Difficult. Perh. W. *gor buw-allt*, 'spacious, cattle-hillside'; *cf*. Builth in *Pl. N. Eng. and W*. Med. L. *garbale*, 'a tithe,' fr. *garba*, 'a sheaf,' does not suit well either phonet. or in meaning.

GORDON (Earlston). 1250 -din, 1289 -dun. W. *gor din*, 'spacious hill'; *cf*. GOURDON.

GORDONSTOWN (Elgin, Aberdeensh., Kirkcudbt.). The Elgin estate was purchased, 1638, by Sir Robt. Gordon, vice-chamberlain of Scotland. Kirk. G. is *R.M.S.* 1507 'Terra de Gordonstoun nuncupata Bennayed' or Bennaheid.

GOREBRIDGE (Dalkeith). 'Bridge at the *gore*,' O.E. *garu*, 'a triangular or wedge-shaped piece of land,' same as a *gore* in a dress. *Cf*. Kensington Gore, etc.

GORGIE (Edinburgh). *c*. 1200 -gin, *c*. 1250 -gyn, *c*. 1320 -gy. Perh. W. *gor cyn* (G. *geinn*), 'spacious wedge' or 'wedge-like field.'

GORTLECH (Ft. Augustus). G. *goirt leac*, 'stone in field or standing corn.' *Cf*. cromlech, 'crooked stone.'

GOURDIE (Murthly). *c*. 1120 Grudin. Difficult. *Cf*. next; also G. *grùid*, 'dregs.'

GOURDON (Fordoun). 1315 Gurdon. Prob. = GORDON. Perh. G. *gaoirdean*, var. of *gairdean*, 'an arm.'

GOUROCK (Greenock). W. thinks G. *guireoc*, 'a pimple,' so 'a hillock'; as this lacks confirmation, perh. *cùrrog*, 'the little corner.'

GOVAN (Glasgow). *Sic* 1275, but *c.* 1134 Guven, *c.* 1150 Gvuan, 1518 Gwuan. GOVANHILL (Glasgow and Carstairs). H. M'Lean said, G. *gudhbhan*, dimin. of *gudhbh*, 'schoolhouse, study.' It may be 'dear rock,' W. *cu faen* ($f = v$); *cf.* GLASGOW.

GOWANBANK (Arbroath, Falkirk). Sc. *gowan*, 'a daisy,' G. and Ir. *gugan*, 'a flower, a bud.'

GOWRIE (Angus). *c.* 1120 Gowrin, *a.* 1200 Gouerin, *c.* 1200 Gowrie, 1298 Gouary. 'Goat-place,' G. *gabhar*, *gobhar*, 'a goat,' with -ie loc. *Cf.* Gabhran, old name of Ossory, Leinster, and INVERGOWRIE.

GRAHAM'S DYKE (Falkirk). Name for the Roman Wall. *c.* 1370 *Fordun* says, called Grymisdyke because destroyed by Gryme, grandfather of K. Eugenius. 1649 *Acts Sc. Parlmt* Grahames Dyk. *Cf.* 1045 *chart. Eadweard* Grimes dic, in England.

GRAHAMSTON (Falkirk). Modern. It stands on 'Graham's Muir,' *sic* 1774, named fr. Sir John de Graham, slain here, 1298. Grahamstoun, Blairhoyle, Perthsh., was built, *c.* 1600, by Gilbt. Graham. The first Graham on record is *c.* 1128 *Holyrood Chart.* Wm. de *Graeme* or G[a]ham, 1139 Graham, *i.e.*, 'gray house.' It may have been orig. in Northumbld.

GRAIN. O.N. *grein*, Sw. *gren*, 'prong, branch of a tree.' In Tweeddale and Liddesdale applied to branches of a valley up where it splits into 2 or 3 small glens, and to the burns or waters there, *e.g.*, Grain Burn near Coulterwaterhead and Rashiegrain, Teviothead; also 'the Granes o' the Gauch,' Cabrach. *Cf.* 1303 *Gest. Dunelm.* Lithegrains.

GRAMPIANS. 1526 *H. Boece* identified this range with Mons Grampius (read Graupius), Tacitus *Agric.* 29. Wh. Stokes thought the root Celt. *gruq*, 'curved, rounded,' O.W. *crup*, 'a hump.' Dyack prefers *gra-uq*, 'hill-like place,' as in the Graian Alps.

GRANDTULLY (Aberfeldy). *a.* 1400 Garintully, 1492 Grantuly. G. *garan tulaich*, 'thicket on the hill'; *cf.* GARTLY. Sometimes called Baile na Grandaich, 'the Grants' village.'

GRANGE (many). 'Farm,' see ABBOTSGRANGE. The Edinburgh G. was a farm belonging to St. Giles' Church, 1506 Sanctgely-Grange.

GRANGEMOUTH (Falkirk). Owes origin to the Forth of Clyde Canal, begun 1768, at whose mouth and at the mouth of the Grange Burn it stands. The latter is named fr. ABBOTSGRANGE.

GRANTON (Edinburgh). *c.* 1200 Grendun. O.E. for 'green hill,' but 1544 Grantaine Crag. Two Grendons in England.

GRANTOWN-ON-SPEY. The oldest-known Sc. *Grant* is Gregory le Grant, *a.* 1250, prob. a Gael, no Norman. Ir. *grant* is a grizzly, hairy man. But in Eng. we have Grantham, Lincs., *sic* in *Dom.*, where Grantley, Ripon, is Grenteleia ; *cf.* too Bede's Granta-cæstir, now Cambridge.

GRANTSHOUSE (Berwicksh.). Named by the N.B. Rly. Co. fr. 'Tammy Grant's Inn.' He was a Highlander, *c.* 1800.

GRAVIR (Lewis). N. for 'pits, graves,' O.N. *gröf*, Dan. *graf*, Sc. *graft*, 'a grave.'

GRAY MORE (Deeside). O.Celt. *gra mòr*, 'big hill.' *Cf.* GRAMPIANS.

GREENGAIR Hill (Dalry, Gall.). *c.* 1280 *Bagmund's* R. Greenquer ; see QUAIR. GREENGAIRS (Airdrie). A *gair* is a strip of green grass in a bare or upland spot. *Cf.* Barty's Gair, Coquetdale and Ferniegair, Hamilton.

GREENLAW (several). Berwick G. 1250 Grenlawe. On *law* see p. 52.

GREENLOANING (Auchterarder). Sc. *loan* or *loaning* is 'a green lane,' O.E. *láne*, Fris. *lona*, *lana*, 'a lane.' For the -ing *cf.* shieling.

GREENOCK. *a.* 1400 Grenok, 1635 Greinok. Also, N.W. of Stirling and S. of Callander. Dimin. of G. *grian*, *grèine*, 'the sun.' Several Greenogs (Ir. *grianóg*) or 'sunny little hills,' in Ireland. But some Gaels call the seaport Ghónait, ? meaning. L. GRENNOCH (Minigaff) and GRENNICH (N. Perthsh.) are fr. G. *greannach*, 'rough, gravelly.'

GRENAN (Bute), GRENNAN (Penpont, several in Galloway). Bute G. *sic* 1400. G. *grianan*, 'a sunny spot, a summer house, a mountain peak.' *Cf.* above.

GRÉSKINE (Beattock). Prob. O.G. *creas cinn*, 'on the straight or narrow head or height.'

GRETNA (Carlisle, Old Luce). Ca. G. 1223 Gretenho, *a.* 1245 -hou, 1376 -howe, 1576 Gretnay. Seems, 'at the great height,' O.E. *hó*, or rather, 'hollow,' O.E. *holh*, Sc. *howe*.

GRIMSAY (L. Eport), GREMSA (Orkney). The man '*Grim's* isle,' N. *ay*, *ey*.

GRIMSHADER L. (Lewis). '*Grim's sæter*' or summer farm. See FLASHADER.

GRISAPOLL (Coll). O.N. *gris*, Sc. *grise*, 'a young pig,' and *poll* for N. *ból*, 'place, village.' *Cf.* ULLAPOOL.

GRODOK (Keith). 1187 Gradokk. Prob. G. *grodach*, 'putrid, rotten spot.'

GROUNDWATER L. (Orphir). 1595 -wattir. 'Shallow loch,' Dan. *grund*, 'a shoal, a shallow,' O.N. *grunn-r*, 'shallow.' *Cf.* Ullswater, Wastwater, etc.

GRUDNESS (Shetland). Fr. O.N. *grjót*, 'stones, rubble,' O.E. *gréot*, 'sand, grit,' or Sw. *groda*, 'a frog,' and *ness*.

Gruinard, -art (Islay, Gairloch, Shetland). Is. G. 1595 Girnard, Ga. G. 1580 Gruinorta. Either fr. O.N. *grœnn*, Dan. and Sw. *grön*, 'green,' or fr. N. *grunn*, 'shallow.' Gair. G. is pron. Groon- or Grinard, and is very green and very shallow. The -ard, -art is for *fjord*, 'bay'; see p. 34.

Gryfe Water (Renfrew). *c.* 1140 Stratgruia, *c.* 1160 Strath Grief, 1173 Stragrif, -gryff. Perh. W. *grif*, 'frog-spawn'; but *cf.* O.N. *gryfja*, 'a narrow valley.' W. compares Glen Grivie, Glen Affric, and suggests Ir. *grìobh*, 'claw, talon.'

Guardbridge (St. Andrew's). Built by Bp. Wardlaw, *a.* 1440.

Guay (Dunkeld). Pron. Guy. *Sic* 1457. G. *gaoth*, 'a marsh.'

Guildtown (Perth). Founded, 1818, on the lands of the *Guildry* of Perth.

Guisachan (Beauly). Pron. Ghéesăchan. 1221 Gulsackyn (*l* error for *i*), 1578 Guisachane. G. *guithsachan*, 'pine forests,' *giuthas*, 'a pine, a Scots fir.' *Cf.* Inverghuisachan, L. Etive.

Gulberwick (Lerwick). *Orkn. Sag.* Gullberu-vik. O.N. fr. 'yellow town (N. *bœr*) bay.'

Gullane (N. Berwick). *c.* 1200 Golin, 1250 -lyn, 1458 Goulyne, Guling. Perh. orig. W. *golyn*, 'guard of a sword,' referring to the shape of the site; but now G. *guallan*, 'a shoulder,' as in the Guallan, Applecross.

Gunnershaw (Dunipace). 1622 -schaw. 'Shaw, wood of *Gunner*,' as in Gunnerskeld, Shap.

Gunsgreen (Eyemouth). 1542 Gunisgrene. '*Gunn's* meadow.'

Gushetfaulds (Glasgow). Sc. *gushet*, 'a triangular corner,' Fr. *gousset*, 'a gusset in dress or boot.' *Fauld* is *fold*, O.E. *fald*, lit. 'enclosure by felled trees.'

Guthrie (Arbroath, Airth). Ar. G. 1359 Gutherie, 1361 Gothry. G. *gaothair*, 'windy place,' here in loc.

Gyle, Glen (L. Katrine). 1463 *R.M.S.* Glengell. See Goil.

Gylen (Kerrera). Pron. güälen. G. *gabhalan*, 'the little fork.' *Cf.* the common Ir. Golan, Goleen, Gowlan.

Haamer (several, Shetland). O.N. *hamar-r*, 'a hammer, a crag.'

Habbie's How (Carlops). See 1725 A. Ramsay *Gentle Shepd.* '*Halbert's* hollow,' O.E. *holg*, *holh*, fr. *hol*, 'a hole.'

Habchester (hill, Ayton). *c.* 1390 in *Diplom. Corresp. Rich. II*, p. 85. Abchestoclaw (*oc* error for *er*). 'Camp of *Abbe*,' *cf. Dom.* Yorks, Abbetune, now Habton. See *chester*, p. 56.

Hadden Rigg (Kelso). 1540 haulden rigg. Prob. 'Haldane's Rigg.'

HADDINGTON. 1098 Hadynton, *c.* 1139 Hadintunschira, *a.* 1150 Hadingtoun. 'Hading's village.' *Hadding-r*, in sagas, is patronymic, fr. common O.E. *Hadda*, and one of the traditional founders of the Danish kingdom. *Cf.* Haddington, Lincs.

HADDO Ho. (Methlick, Forgue). Me. H. *sic* 1654, but 1382 Haldawach. Like HADDOCH, Cairnie, corrup. of *half-davoch*; see DAVA. *Cf.* Lettoch, Urray, G. *leith dabhach*; *leth*, 'a half.'

HAGGS, The (Castlecary). O.E. *haga*, 'a hedge,' O.Sc. *hag*, 'copsewood.' *Cf.* The Hag, Parton and Foulden, Berwicksh., and Haggisha', Strathbogie.

HAILES, NEW (Musselburgh). *c.* 1150 Hala, 1250 Halis, 1467 Newhal. O.E. *heal(l)*, O.N. *höll, hall*, 'a public room, a hall.'

HAIRMYRES (E. Kilbride). First syll. see HARBURN; the second is O.N. *mýrr, mýri*, N. *myre*, 'swamp, fen.' *Cf.* Halmyre, Kelton, 1640 -mure, and HARLAW.

HALBEATH (Dumfermline). G. *choil beath*, 'wood of birches,' G. *coille*, Ir. *caill*, 'a wood,' *c* lost by aspiration.

HALIVAL (mtn, Rum, and 2, Skye). O.N. *hjalli-fjall*, 'fell, hill with the ledge or terrace.' *Cf* p. 38.

HALKERSTON (Midlothn., Moray). Mi. H. 1354 Haukerstoun, Mo. H. *c.* 1200 Halkertoun. 'Hawker's, *i.e.*, fowler's village.' O.N. *hauk-r*, 'a hawk.' *Cf.* FULLERTON, and for *l cf.* next.

HALKIRK (Thurso). *Sic* 1500, *Sagas* Há Kirkiu, 'high church,' 1222 Hakirk, 1274 Haukyre, 1601 Halkrig, still the local pron. through confusion with O.N. *hrygg-r*, 'a ridge.' The *l* shows the influence of O.N. *hall-r*, 'slope,' so common in Scandinavian place-names. On *kirk* see KIRKABY. *Cf.* HALCRO Hd., S. Ronaldshay, 1492 Haucro, fr. *kró*, 'a pen.'

HALLADALE, even Strath Halladale (Reay). *c.* 1230 Helgedall, 1274 Haludal. 'Holy dale, vale of saints,' O.N. *heilag-r*, Dan. *hellig*, O.E. *hálig*, 'holy,' *hálga*, 'a saint, a hallow.' *Cf.* Halliford and -keld in *Pl. N. Eng.*

HALLIN-IN-VATERNISH (Skye). O.N. *höll, hall*, 'a hall,' with suffixed art. 'the.' See VATERNISH.

HALLRULE (Hobkirk). *c.* 1560 Harroull. Modern 'refining' for the older Harrule, *i.e.*, Haraway Rule, *Rula Herevei*. See ABBOTRULE.

HALTERBURN (Yetholm). *a.* 800 *Hist. St. Cuthbt.* Eltherburne. *Elther* cannot be *halter*, in O.E. *hælftre*. But *Eltor*, *Altor* are names in *Onom.*

HALY- HALLYBURTON Ho. (Kettins). *c.* 1200 Haliburhtoun, O.E. or M.E. for 'village by the holy enclosure,' *c.* 1244 Halibortone. On *burh* see p. 50.

HAMILDEAN (Lyne). '*Hamil's* woody glen.' See next and DEAN.

HAMILTON. 1291 Hamel- ; surname also occurs as Hambleton. Walter FitzGilbert, called Hamilton, is known as the landlord, 1296 ; while, 1266 *Sc. Excheq. R.* we have Will. de Hamyll, king's falconer. The old name was CADZOW.

HAMMA VOE (Yell). *Sagas* Hafnarvag. O.N. for 'bay of the haven,' O.N. *hömn, höfn*, gen. sing. *hafnar*, gen. pl. *hamna* ; and *vag-r*, 'bay, inlet,' Icel. *vog-r*. *Cf.* Hammerclet, *sic* 1503, Sandwick, Orkney; see CLETT.

HANDA (Eddrachilis). Aspirated form of SANDAY.

HANGINGSHAW (many). Selkirk H. 1456 Hangandschaw, *i.e.*, 'hanging wood,' one on the side of a hill. See SHAW and *cf.* *a.* 1200 *Newminst. Chart.* Hangandescawe.

HARBURN (Carnwath). O.E. *ða hára stan*, so often found in boundaries in *Cod. Diplom.*, is 'the hoary (O.E. *hár*), ancient stone.' *Cf.* Hare Stane, Edinburgh, and Hare Stanes, Kirkurd. *Har, her*, in S. are for *higher*, compar. of *high*, O.E. *héah, hiera, héra*. This may be the meaning here and in next.

HARDEN (Hawick). *Chron. Melros* Harehouden. 'Higher HOWDEN.' *Cf.* above.

HARDINGTON (Lamington). 'Dwelling of *Harding*.' *Cf.* H., Yeovil, *Dom.* Hardintone and Harding(e)stone, N'hants, *sic* Dom.

HARLAW (Aberdeen). 1549 Hayr-. 'Boundary hill,' O.E. *hlǽw* ; see HARBURN. *Cf.* Harelaw, 1490 Harlaw, Lochore, Herlaw, E. Kilbride, Haerfaulds, Legerwood, HARSTANE and HARTREE.

HARLOSH (Dunvegan). G. *chàrr lois*, 'rock of the fire.' *Cf.* Ironlosh, 1456 Arnglosh, Balmaclellan.

HAROLDSWICK (Unst). 'Bay,' N. *vík*, 'of (prob.) K. *Harold*' Hardrada, d. 1066.

HARPORT L. (W. Skye). Either fr. O.N. *hár-r*, 'old, hoary,' or *há-r*, 'high.'

HARRAY (Orkney). *Saga* Herad, O.N. for 'territory.' See BIRSAY.

HARRIS (Out. Hebrides, Rum). Heb. H. *c.* 1500 *Bk. Clanranald* Heradh, 1542 Harrige, 1549 the Harry, 1588 Harreis [1585 Herres, Glenelg]. G. Na h'earradh. Prob. fr. N. *har*, 'high,' *hœri*, 'higher' ; but *cf.* HARRAY. Gillies says, Glen Harris, Rum, is 'glen across,' G. *thairis*.

HARSTANE (Kirkurd). See HARBURN, and *cf.* Haer Cairns, 2 in Perthsh.

HARTFELL (Roxburgh), HARTHILL, etc., fr. O.E. *heor(o)t*, O.N. *hjört-r*, 'hart, male deer.' *Cf.* 1225 Hertesheued ('head'), Lanarksh., and 1250 Hertleburne, E. Lothian.

HARTREE (Biggar). See HARBURN.

HARVIESTON (Gorebridge). 1250 Heruistun. 'Harvey's dwelling.' *Cf.* HALLRULE.

HASKEVAL (mtn, Rum). O.N. *haska fjall*, 'dangerous hill,' an appropriate name. On -val see p. 38, and *cf.* Hestaval, Lewis. N. *hesta*, 'horse, stallion.'

HASSENDEAN (Hawick). 1155 Halestonesden, 1158 Hastenden, *c.* 1320 Hass-. O.E. *hálig stán denu*, 'DEAN of the holy stone.'

HATLOCK (Tweeddale). The root idea of *hat* both in O.E. and O.N. is 'covering,' and -lock is O.E. *loca*, 'enclosure.' *Cf.* Porlock, Somerset.

HATTON (many). Old forms needed. Hattonknowe, Eddleston is *a.* 1400. Haltoun, 'village by the hall,' while the 4 Hattons in Eng. are said to be all *heath -town*. Proof lacks.

HAUGH (common). *E.g.*, *a.* 1150 Galtuneshalech, now GATTONSHAUGH, Melrose. O.E. *halech, healh*, 'a flat meadow by a riverside'; *cf.* SAUCHIE. The Haugh, Inverness, is G. An t'alchan, interesting keeping of the old *l*, seen also in the Eng. surname Greenhalgh. But Haugh in some names is O.N. *hauga*, 'a mound.'

HAWES Inn (S. Queensferry). O.E. and O.N. *háls*, North. E. and Sc. *halse, hause*, 'neck, throat,' hence 'narrow opening, defile, col.'

HAWICK. *a.* 1183 Hawic, -wich. O.E. *héah wíc*, M.E. *wick, wich*, 'high dwelling or village.' *Cf.* BERWICK.

HAWTHORNDEN (Roslin). 1296 Hauthorndene. *Cf.* DEAN, DENBURN.

HEATHERWICK (E. of R. Don). *a.* 1315 Hathirwych. = HEDDERWICK.

HEBRIDES. 77 *Pliny*, (H)æbudes, *c.* 150 *Ptolemy* Aibouda (perh., too, same as his Epidii, placed in Argyll), *a.* 300 *Solinus* Hebudes, *Ulst. Ann.* 853 Innsegall, 'isles of strangers,' *i.e.*, Norsemen. By Norse always called Sudreys, 'South isles,' as opposed to Nordreys, the Northern Orkneys. The *u* is supposed to have become *ri* through some printer's error. Hebrides is the regular spelling in 1526, H. Boece *Hist. Scotland.* Origin unknown. Suggestions are Bret. *heb eid*, 'without corn,' or *heb boued*, 'without food.' Prob. pre-Celt.

HECKLEGIRTH (Annan). 'Church field or yard.' See ECCLES and APPLEGARTH, and *cf.* Hecklebirnie ('of St. Brandan'), Cairnie.

HECLA Mt. (2 in Out. Hebrides). As in Iceland, 'hooded shroud,' O.N. *hekla*, 'a cowled or hooded frock,' O.E. *hacele*, 'a cloak, a hackle.'

HEDDERWICK (E. Lothian, Montrose). E.L.He. 1094 Hatheruuich [*c.* 1200 Hatherwic, Northumbd.], O.N. *hather, hader wíc* or O.N. *heið-r vík*, 'dwelling among heather,' or 'heath bay.' See Hatherleigh, *Pl. N. Eng.* *Cf.* HEATHERWICK.

HEE Ben (Reay). Prob. 'hill of peace,' G. *shìthe, i.e.*, quiet, peaceful hill. *Cf.* TEE.

HEITON (Kelso). 1152 Hetona. 'High village,' O.E. *héah*, 'high.' Seven Heatons in England.

HELENSBURGH. Founded, 1776, by Sir Jas. Colquhoun, and called after his wife.

HELL (Sanday), HELLMUIR L. (Hawick). N. *hella*, 'flat.'

HELL'S GLEN (Lochgoilhd). G. gleann Ifrinn ('Hell'). M'Kinnon thought this mistaken for 'glen of the masses or offerings,' *aifrionn*.

HELMSDALE (Sutherland). *Orkn. Sag.* Hjalmunddal, other saga, Hialmasdal, 1290 Holmesdale, 1513 Helimsdaill. '*Hjalmund's* dale,' or 'valley of the helmet,' O.N. *hjalm-r*, Dan. *hjelm*. *Cf.* Dalhalmay close by, and Helmsley, Yorks, fr. a man *Helm*.

HEMPRIGGS (Wick). O.N. *hamp-r*, Dan. *hamp*, 'hemp.' See RIGG.

HERBERTSHIRE Cas. (Denny). *Sic c.* 1365, but 1426 baronia de Herbertschire. 'Shire, share of *Herbert*,' prob. he landlord of Dunipace, *c.* 1200 *Cambusken. Chart.* The tradition about a 'halbert's share' is unfounded, for *halbert* is unrecorded till 1495. So Halbert's Bog, Bannockburn, will also be fr. a man. *Herbert* in the Saintonge dialect becomes *Albert*.

HERIOT (Stow), HERIOTFIELD (Methven). *c.* 1200 Heryt, 1250 -ieth, *c.* 1264 -ewyt. O.E. *here-geatu*, 'army equipment,' a 'heriot,' payment to the lord of a fee on death of vassal or tenant.

HERISHADER (Skye). '*Sæter*, summer farm, of the lord,' N. *herre*, O.E. *hearra*. See FLASHADER.

HERMISTON (Currie, Salton). Cu. H. 1233 Hirdmannistoun, Sa. H. 1186 Hirdmanestun. 'Village of the herdman.' *Cf.* HALKERSTON.

HERMITAGE Cas. (Riccarton Junc.). 1300 Eremitage Soules. Fr. *ermite*, Gk. *erēmītēs*, 'a hermit,' *erēmos*, 'solitary.' *Cf.* vicarage. Hermitage, not in *N.E.D.* till 1290, is in *c.* 1212 *Pontefract Chart.* Heremitagie.

HERRIES (Dumfries). *c.* 1139 Herziz, 1175 Heriz, 1578 -eis. A Norman *Heriz* came over in 1066.

HESTAM (Lewis), HESTAN Is. (Auchencairn). O.N. *hest-r holm-r*, 'horse islet'; *ham* and *holm* often interchange. But -an may be for the suffixed art. 'the.' *Cf.* Hestwall, Sandwick, Ork.

HESTERHEUGH (Yetholm). *a.* 800 *Hist. St. Cuthbt.* Hesterhoh. Prob. hybrid, W. *ystre*, 'dwelling,' *cf.* YESTER, and on prefixed *h cf.* p. 54 + O.E. *hóh*, 'height,' the Sc. *heugh*, prob. influenced by O.N. *hauga*, 'mound.' *Cf. c.* 1200 *Coldstr. Chart.* Huyisheuigh.

HIGH BLANTYRE. See BLANTYRE. High, Higher are common prefixes in England; very rare in Sc.

HIGHLANDMAN (Crieff). The Highlandman's Loan, once the direct road S. fr. the Highlands, passes here. The earliest use of *Highland* seems *c.* 1425 *Wyntoun*, 'the Scottis Hielandmen.'

HIGHTAE (Lochmaben). Prob. fr. O.E. and O.N. *tá*, 'toe'; *cf.* O.N. *tjá*, 'to mark.' But *N.E.D.* gives little help here.

HILLSWICK (W. Shetland). *Saga* Hildiswik, N. for 'battle bay,' *vík*.

HILTON (Urray, Whitsome). Ur. H. 1456 Hiltoun, Wh. H. *c.* 1098 Hyltun. 'Hill town.' Ur. H. shows early Eng. influence in Ross.

HINTON (Anwoth). O.E. *hina-tun*, 'hind's, servant's place.' *Cf.* CARLETON.

HIRSEL, The (Coldstream). *Sic* 1572, but *a.* 1166 Herishill, *a.* 1232 Hirsill. 'Hill of the lord,' O.E. *hearra*, N. *herre*. But now *hirsle* in Sc. means 'a flock, a fold.'

HOBKIRK (Hawick). 1220 Hopechirke, 1586 Hopeskirk, *Pont* Hoppkirk, and still sometimes Hope-. Sc. *hope* (O.E. *hop*, 'bit of enclosed land,' O.N. *hop*, 'little, land-locked bay') is 'a valley among hills, a place of refuge,' found *c.* 1200; see KAILZIE. *Cf.* HOPE, KIRKABY and KIRKHOPE.

HODDAM (Ecclefechan), HODDOM (Parton). Ec. H. 1116 Hodelm, 1179–80 Hodelma, 1185 *Jocelyn* Holdelm, 1292 Hodalmia, *c.* 1320 -holme. *Hold*, 'a fortress,' in North pron. hod; but -am, -elm is doubtful. It can hardly be orig. *holm*, 'meadow near river or sea,' for there is no trace of that in North. Eng. till long after 1116; *cf.* DURHAM. It may be O.E. *ealm*, 'elm.' *Ham* and *holm* often interchange; *cf.* YETHOLM.

HOE Pt. (Duirinish). O.N. *há*, 'high,' O.E. *hóh*, 'a hoe,' a spur, a hill.

HOGSTON (Ruthven). 1306 Hoggistoun. Prob. fr. a man *Hoge*, *Hoga*, names in *Onom.*, as in Hoggeston, Bucks, and Hoxton, London, both *Dom.* Hocheston, and former, 1200 Hoggeston. But Sc. *hog* is 'a young sheep.'

HOLBURN Hd. (Thurso). 1526 Howbrown. Cannot be = Holburn, London. Perh. it is fr. N. *hóll*, 'a hill,' and *brúni*, 'burning,' so perh. 'beacon hill.'

HOLLAND (N. Ronaldsay, Papa Westray). *Sic c.* 1500. Dan. *höi land*, 'high land.'

HOLLANDBUSH (Denny). 1707 Hollin-, 1769 Hollybush. Sc. *hollin*, O.E. *hollen*, adj. fr. *holen*, *-egn*, 'a holly.' *Cf. c.* 1250 *Cart. Kelso* Hollanmedu.

HOLM (Orkney). 1482 Hom. O.N. *hólm-r*, 'an island, a meadow near river or sea,' easily flooded, Dan. and O.E. *holm*, 'a small river-island'; often interchanged with *ham*, 'home.' But Glenholm, Peebles, *c.* 1200 Glenwhym, *c.* 1300 -whim, 1530 -quhome, is prob. fr. O.W. *gwym*, 'sleek, glossy.'

HOLY ISLE (Lamlash). *Sagas* Melansay. 'Melan's' or 'St. Molios' isle.' His well here was famed for its cures. *Cf.* LAMLASH.

HOLY LOCH (Dunoon). *O. Stat. Acct.* L. Shiant, G. *seunta*, 'blessed.' It is associated with St. Mund; see KILMUN and *Life Fintan Munnu*, c. 28, where the region is 'the Holy Land of Promise.'

HOLYROOD (Edinburgh). *c.* 1128 *foundation charter* Ecclesia Sancte Crucis, 1392 Holyrud, 1504 Abbey of the Holy Croce. *Rood* is O.E. *ród*, 'rod, pole, cross.' For the legend *re* David I and the 'holy rood,' see Grant, *O. and N. Edinburgh*, I, 21.

HOLYTOWN (Coatbridge). 1792 Hollytown, still its usual pron., just as in Holyhead.

HOLYWOOD (Dumfries). 1252 de Sacro Nemore ('grove'), 1289 de Sacro Bosco ('wood'), 1296 de Saint Boyse (*i.e.*, *bois*). An abbey once here. Its old name was Darcongall, 'wood,' G. *daire*, 'of St. Congal.'

HOMELIKNOW (Coldingham). 1198 -lenolle. '*Homil's* hill'; *cf.* Homildon Hill, Wooler, and see KNOWE.

HOOL, HOOLIN (common in Shetland). O.N. *hóll*, 'hill, knoll.' The -in is the suffixed art. 'the.' *Cf.* Tolin, Eigg.

HOPE Ben and L. (Eriboll). See HOBKIRK. The Hoobs in Shetland are the same.

HOPEMAN (Burghead). Village founded in 1805. Said to be Fr. *haut mont*, 'high hill,' as old people still call it—the Haudmont, old name also of an estate here.

HOPRINGLE. See PRINGLE.

HORNDEAN (Norham). *c.* 1100 Horverdene, Horeuordane, 'DEAN of *Heoroweard*,' a name in *Beowulf*.

HOROGH (Barra). O.N. *horg-r*, 'a heathen place of worship,' = Harrow, Middlesex.

HORRISDALE Eilean or Isl. (Gairloch) = TORRISDALE.

HORSE Is. (Ardrossan). *Chart.* Horrsey. N. for 'isle like a horse.'

HOSH (Crieff). As its site shows, aspirated fr. G. *cois*, 'the foot.' *Cf.* Choish, Stirlingshire.

HOUNAM (Kelso). *c.* 1150 Hunedun, *c.* 1200 Hunum, 1237 Honum, 1544 Hownome. 'Hound's home,' O.E. and Dan. *hund*, 5 *hown*. *Cf.* EDNAM, EDROM, and 1385 Hond (Hound) watre, R. Tweed.

HOUNDWOOD (Grantshouse). *c.* 1200 Hundewde. Near by is Harewood, named in same charter of William the Lion.

HOURN, L. (W. Inverness). 1542 *Dean* of *Lismore* Sowrnne, 1772 Jurn. In G. Shuirn. W. says, G. *sorn*, *suirn*, L. *furnus*, 'a kiln,' so, 'furnace-shaped gully.'

HOURSTON (Orkney). 1492 Thurstath. 'Thor's stead,' N. *stað-r*, 1503 -stacht, 1595 Hurstane. *Cf.* Hurteso for Thurstainshow.

HOUSTON (Johnstone). *c.* 1200 Villa Hugonis, *c.* 1230 Huston, *c.* 1300 Houstoun, 'Village of *Hugo*' de Paduinan, *c.* 1160 in *Paisley Chart.* *Cf.* SYMINGTON.

HOUTON (Orphir). Pron. Hoo-ton. 1627 Howton, 1662 Houth-. Prob. O.N. *há tún*, 'high district.'

HOWDEN (Midcalder, Ancrum). *a.* 1236 Hauden, 1296 Haudene (Midc.), Houedene (Anc.). Prob. 'DEAN in the how or hollow,' O.E. *holh, holg*. Several in England. *Cf.* HOWGATE ('road'), Penicuik.

HOWFF (farm, Orkney). Sc. *howff* is 'a rendezvous, house of call.' But N. *hof* is properly 'God's House.' The Howff, 1565 Houf, is name of the chief burial-place in Dundee.

HOWMORE (Eriska). 1703 Hoghmore. Hybrid. O.N. *haug-r*, 'burial mound,' and G. *mòr*, 'big.'

HOWPASLEY (Roberton, Roxb.). 1494 Howpaslot. See HABBIES HOW and PAISLEY.

HOXAY (S. Ronaldsay). *c.* 1390 Haugaheith, O.N. for 'mound in the heath or waste,' 1562 Hoxa. The -ay is 'island.'

HOY (Orkney). *Orkn. Sag.* Haey. 1492 Hoye, *c.* 1580 Hy. *Há -ey* is O.N. for 'high isle.' *Cf.* HYSKER.

HUGHSTOWN (Beauly). Named fr. *Hugh* Baillie, son of a former proprietor.

HUMBIE (Haddington, Aberdour, Fife). [1545 Humby, ? Balerno.] Prob. 'Hound's dwelling,' O.E. *hund*, here prob. a man's nick-name, and O.E. *bý*, Dan. *bi, by*, 'dwelling.' We find Sir Alex. Hundby in Edinburgh, 1450. '*Hume's* dwelling' is less likely.

HUME (Greenlaw). *c.* 1127 *Lib. Dunelm.* Houm, 1250 Home. See HOLM, pron. in Sc. howm, and *cf.* Cheadle Hulme, Chesh. Home and Hume regularly interchange.

HUNA (Canisbay). *Sagas* Hofn, O.N. *höfn, hömn*, 'haven,' with *a, ay, ey*, 'island,' prob. referring to Stroma opposite. *Cf.* 1550 'Hunday,' Orkney.

HUNGRY HILL (Carron, Stirl'g). HUNGRY KERSE (Br. of Allan). *N.E.D. hungry* 6 gives several quots referring to poor, starved land, earliest 1577. *Cf.* 1361 'Hungyrflat,' Liddesdale. The Eng. names like Hungerford all come fr. O.E. *hangra, hongra*, 'a hanging wood, a hillside.'

HUNTER'S QUAY (Dunoon). Called after the Hunters who once held Hafton estate here.

HUNTINGTOWER (Perth). Hunting seat of Ld. Ruthven. *Cf.* Castle Stalker.

HUNTLAW (Roxburgh). *Sic* 1170. 'Hill of the hunter,' O.E. *hunta.*

HUNTLY (N. Aberdeen). 1482 -lie. Orig. name of a Berwicksh. hamlet, *a.* 1180 Huntleie, now extinct. Transferred N. by the then Earl of Huntly. 'Hunting lea or meadow.' *Cf.* Huntley, Glouc.

HURLET (Barrhead). Prob. Celt. *chur let(h)*, 'turn, bend of the hillside,' G. *car, cuir*, 'bend'; *cf.* STRACHUR, and W. *llethr*, G. *leathad*, 'slope'; *cf.* CROMLET and Passelet, old form of PAISLEY.

HURLFORD (Kilmarnock). Seems to be 'whirl-ford' on R. Irvine. *Cf. hurlpool* and *-wind*, old var. of whirlpool and -wind, Whirlow, Sheffield, 1501 Hurlowe, and Hurlditch, N. Devon, 1351 Whuruel, dych. Root O.N. *hvirfla*, 'to turn about,' O.Dan. *hvirrell-* O.E. *hwyrfel*, 'an eddy.'

HUSEDALEBEG and -MORE (Skye). Hybrids. O.N. *hús-dal*, 'house valley,' and G. *beag*, 'little,' *mòr*, 'big.'

HUTTON (Berwick, Lockerbie). Be. H. *c.* 1098 Hotun, *c.* 1300 Hutona, 1548 Hooton. Lo. H. 1306 Hotone. Not *hut-town*, for *hut* is not O.E., but 'village on the HOE or projecting heel of land.' Seven in England.

HYLIPOL (Tiree). *Sagas* Heylipol. 'Shelter place,' N. *hæli bol.* *Cf.* p. 42.

HYNDLAND (Glasgow). 1538 *Rental Bk.* 'Fermeland callit the Hynde land,' *i.e.*, lying back fr. the Clyde. *Cf.* 1543 Hyndlandis, Udston, 1171 Hindhop, Berwicksh., and Hinshelwood, Carnwath, *i.e.*, hind-shiel ('hut')-wood.

HY- HANISH (Tiree). O.N. *há*, Dan. *höi næs*, 'high ness' or 'cape.' *Cf.* VATERNISH.

HYSKER (off Rum, Harris, etc.). 1703 Haisker. *Cf.* above. 'High rock or skerry,' N. *skjær.*

IBERT (Balfron, Killearn). G. *iobairt*, 'offering, sacrifice.' *Cf.* INCHAFFRAY.

IBROX (Glasgow). Prob. G. *ath bruic*, nom. *broc*, 'ford of the badger.' *Cf.* Ebroch, Kilsyth, *Pont* Abbroch, 1508 'Ebrukis,' near Dundee and *c.* 1200 Monabroc, 'badger's hill,' Strathgryfe. *Broc* is 'badger' in both G. and O.E. *Cf.* BROXBURN. The *x* is = *cs*, a pl.

IDRIGILL Pt. (Skye). Prob. as in Udrigill, Gairloch, O.N. *ytri gil*, 'utter, outer cleft or gulley.'

IDVIES (Montrose). 1219 Edevy, 1254 -evyn. Prob. G. *fhada, fhaide abh* or *abhuinn*, 'long stream,' *cf.* ADVIE; with *s* Eng. pl.

INCH, INSH (many), INSCH (Aberdeensh.). Kincraig I. 1226 Inche. Ab. I. *a.* 1300 Insula. G. and Ir. *innis*, 'island,' also 'pasture ground, links.' Wigtown I. is so called fr. the island in the White Loch there. *Cf.* MARKINCH.

INCHADDON (Taymouth). 'Isle of St. *Aidan*,' d. 651.

INCHAFFRAY (Muthil). *c.* 1190 'Incheaffren . . . Latine Insula Missarum,' 1290 Incheafraue. 'Isle of the offering,' *i.e.*, the mass, G. *aifrenn*, *aoibhrionn*, late L. *offerens*, 'the offering.' *Cf.* the name Jaffrey.

INCHARD, L. (W. Sutherland). G. Uinnisard, for which M. suggested O.N. *engis-fjörthr*, 'meadow's frith.' *Cf.* p. 34.

INCHBARE (Brechin). G. *innis bàire*, 'meadow of the battle' or 'game.'

INCHBERRY (Fochabers). G. *innis a' bhàraidh*, 'hurling mead' (W.).

INCHBRAYOCK (Montrose). *c.* 1250 Inchebryoc. 'Mead of St. or Bp. *Brioc*,' a W. and Breton 6th cny. saint. *Cf.* St. Briac, Brittany.

INCHCAILLOCH (L. Lomond). 1411 Innischallach. 'Isle of nuns,' lit. 'old women,' G. *cailleach*. Ruins of a nunnery here.

INCHCAPE ROCK (Arbroath). *Old* Inchscape. Hybrid. 'Isle like a basket or hamper,' O.N. *skeppa*, Dan. *skæppe*, Sc. *skep*. An old name for it was Skelly Ettle, 'rock to aim at or take as a mark.'

INCHCOLM (Frith of Forth). *c.* 1123 *Alexr. I's chart.* Insula Sancti Columbæ, 'St. Columba's isle,' G. *innis Choluim*; *cf.* p. 65. In 1605 *Macbeth* St. Colmes Ynch.

INCHES (Douglas). G. *innis*, 'meadow, links,' with Eng. pl. *Cf.* Perth Inches.

INCH GALL (Ballingry). 'Isle of,' G. *gall*, 'a stranger.' Lochore, which once surrounded it, is now drained.

INCHGARVIE (Queensferry). 1491 *R.M.S.* -garde, *Pont* Garwy. 'Rough, rocky isle,' G. *garbh*, 'rough.'

INCHINNAN (Paisley). 1158 -enan, -ienun, *a.* 1173 -inan. Prob. G. *innis Fhinnan*, 'isle of St. *Finnan*'; see KILWINNING. The old parish name was Kilinan. The 'inch' is the angle made by the junction of Gryfe and Cart.

INCHKEITH (Firth of Forth, hill, Lauder). *a.* 1200 Insula Keð, 1461 Ynchkeyth. *c.* 720 *Bede* has Urbs Giudi in the Firth of Forth, which *Bk.* of *Lecan* calls 'Sea of Giudan' or 'Giuds,' perh. *Jutes* fr. Jutland. Skene thought it fr. a son of the Pict. prince *Che*, *Gaeth* or Giudid Gaeth brechach. Prob. no connexion with KEITH.

INCHMAHÓME (L. of Menteith). *Sic c.* 1550, but 1238 -maquhomok, 1296 l'Isle de St. Colmoc, 1301 Enchimaholmok. 'Isle of St.

Macholmoc,' Ir. pet name of St. Colman, *c*. 520. *Cf*. PORTMAHOMACK, KILMACOLM and p. 67.

INCHMARLO (Banchory). 1494 -merlach. 'Meadow of the thief,' G. *mear-*, *meirlach*.

INCHMARNOCK (Bute, Ballater). From St. *Marnock*, pet form of St. Ernan; see KILMARNOCK.

INCHMARTINE (Errol). 1324 Inchemartyn. See KILMARTIN.

INCHMICKERY (Queensferry). G. *innis an bhicaire*, 'isle of the vicar,' fr. Inchcolm monastery.

INCHMOAN, -MOIN (L. Lomond). *a*. 1350 Ynismoin, 1545 Inchemone. 'Isle of the moss,' G. *moine*.

INCHMURRIN (L. Lomond). 1395 -muryne, 1405 -moryne. Perh. fr. G. *muireann*, *-inn*, 'a fish spear.' But ruins of a chapel here, said to have been dedicated to St. *Mirrin*, patron st. of Paisley.

INCHNADAMPF (L. Inver). 'Pasture of the ox,' G. *damh*. *Cf*. Toldamh, Blair Atholl.

INCHTAVANACH (L. Lomond). 1395 Elanvanow. 'Isle of the monks,' *m(h)anach*. Also called DEVANNOC.

INCHTURE (Errol). 1183 -ethore. Prob. 'mead of the pursuit or search,' G. *'a thòire*.

INCHYRA Ho. (Perth) and GRANGE (Polmont). Pe. I. 1324 -esyreth, 1365 Inchyreth. G. *iar*, *siar*, 'the west,' with -eth termin. The Pol. name is modern; formerly Kersiebank.

INGAN (hill, Kinross). G. *ionga*, *ingne*, 'a nail, talon, claw,' fr. its shape.

INGLESTON (Twynholm). 'Village of the *Inglis*,' or 'English'; or 'of a man *Inglis*.' *Cf*. *a*. 1246 *Paisley Chart*. Ingliston.

INGSETTER (Orphir). *Sic* 1503. O.N. *eng-sœter*, 'meadow pasture'; now the surname Inkster. *Cf*. ENZIE.

IN(N)ISHAIL (L. Awe). 1379 Insalte, 1542 Inchalt. G. *innis àilt*, 'stately, charming isle.'

IN(N)ISTRYNICH (peninsula, L. Awe). 1662 Inchstrenick. Prob. 'isle of badgers,' G. *strianaich*. McKinnon thought of 'isle of artists or sculptors,' *Druineach*.

INKERMAN (Paisley). From the Crimea battle, 1854.

INKHORN (New Deer). Perh. O.N. *enge örn*, 'meadow of the eagle.' *Cf*. ENZIE and INGSETTER.

INNELLAN (Dunoon). Native pron. Eénlan. 1571 Inellane. Prob. G. *en eilean*, 'bird isle,' *i.e.*, the Perch, a favourite lighting place for birds.

INNERHADDEN (Kinloch Rannoch). *Old* Inverchadden. Perh. O.G. or Ir. *inbhir chadain*, 'confluence at the little rock or summit.' G. *inbhir*, 'mouth of a river, or confluence,' is purely Gaelic, the Brit. or Pict. is *aber*; see p. 10. In names there is constant fluctuation between inner- and inver-, the *bh* getting lost by aspiration.

INNERLEITHEN (Peebles). *c.* 1160 Innerlethan, 1275 -lethain. See above. 'Confluence of R. Leithen,' which may be G. *liath*, *lèithe*, 'grey,' or, as in LEITH, fr. W. *lleithio*, 'to moisten.' The -an, -en is suff., perh. as in CARRON. *Cf.* 1227 *Reg. Dunferm.* Aqua de Letheni, prob. LYNE BURN.

INNERPEFFRAY (Crieff). 1200 Pefferin, 1296 Inrepeffre, 1391 Inverpefir, *a.* 1470 Pollpefery. There is no R. Peffray here, but there is a Pow. See above and PEFFER.

INNERWICK (Dunbar). *a.* 1173 Ennyrwic, 1250 Inuerwike. Prob. O.N. *eng-r vík*, 'close, narrow bay.' A rare case of Norse settlement in this region. But I. in Inverness is 1679 Innervuick, 'confluence of the buck,' G. *buc*, *bhuic*.

INSCH, see INCH.

INSHAIG (Argyll), INSHOG, -OCH (Nairn). G. *uinnseog*, 'little ash tree.'

INSHEWAN (Tannadice, Glen Quiech). Prob. G. *innis Eoghain*. 'Ewan's meadow' (W.).

INVER (many). See INNERHADDEN and *cf.* Aber, L. Lomond. Tain Inver was orig. Inverlochslin.

INVERALLOCHY (Fraserburgh). 'Beautiful confluence,' G. *àilleach*, here in loc.

INVERAMSAY (Inverurie). 1260 -almeslei, 1355 Inuiralmusy, 1485 Inveralumsy, -ramsay. 'Confluence at the damp or dirty rock,' G. *àil musaich*. *Cf.* An giuthais mosach, E. Ross, 'the nasty firwood.'

INVERAN (Bonar Br.). G. *inbhiran*, 'little confluence.'

INVER-, INNERARITY (Forfar). 1250 Inuerarethin. Prob. same as in Aradie, Urray, fr. root meaning 'slow' (W.). *Cf.* INVERQUHARITY.

INVERARNAN (L. Lomond). *Sic* in G. 1394 Hernane. ? G. *airne*, pl. *airnean*, 'sloes.'

INVERARAY. 'Mouth of the ARAY.' Dates fr. 1742.

INVERCANNICH (Beauly). Perh. O.G. *canach*, 'standing water.'

INVERCAULD (Braemar). *Sic* 1547. Perh. G. *càllda*, 'quiet.'

INVERCHAGGERNIE (Crianlarich). Said to mean 'confluence of the shinty scrimmage,' G. *gagernaich*, *i.e.*, the whirlpool here when the river is in spate.

INVERCHARRACH (Cabrach). 1296 -kerack, 1474 Ennercheroche. G. *carrach*, 'rough, stony ground.'

INVERCHAOLAIN (Rothesay). May be fr. G. *c(h)aolan,* 'little strait,' at Colintraive.

INVERDOVET (N. Fife). 1251 -dofacta, 1296 Inredovet, 1391 Inverdubet; also -dufatha, -doveth. Prob. G. *dubhach,* 'dark place'; but *atha* is 'a kiln.'

INVERESK (Musselburgh). *a.* 1093 Inneresc, *c.* 1150 Inverex, Infresc. See ESK.

INVERESKANDY (Fern). G. *inbhir uisgain duibh,* 'confluence of the dark little stream.'

INVERFARIGAIG (L. Ness). M. said, Farigag is 'lower ravine,' fr. G. *far,* 'below,' and *gàg,* 'cleft.' W.'s connecting with *fairge,* 'the ocean,' seems dubious.

INVERGORDON (E. Ross). *Sic* 1760. Named fr. Sir Alex. Gordon, its then proprietor. Formerly Inver- or Inchbreckie, G. *breac,* 'speckled.'

INVERGOWRIE (Dundee). 1124 -gourin, *c.* 1160 -goueren. This must mean, 'GOWRIE at the mouth of the Tay.'

INVERIE (Ft. Augustus, Oronsay), INVEREY (Braemar). Ft. A. I. 1508 Inverry. The -ie, -ey is perh. always for 'river,' as in EYE or EY. Inverry was also old name of Abercrombie; now there is the Inweary Burn.

INVERÍNATE (Lochalsh). G. In'irionait. 1571 Innerenede. W. thinks G. *inbhir Dhuinnid,* 'confluence of the brown river'; *cf.* Coire Dhuinnid close by. But, as in 1571, the centre *i* has a strong *ee* sound; so perh. *dhìon-aite,* 'refuge place.'

INVERKEILOR (Arbroath). *c.* 1200 Innerkeledur, -kileder, *c.* 1270 Inverkiletyr. Prob. O.G. *cìl dobhar,* 'ruddle or clayey river.' *Cf.* CALDER and Kielder, Cheviots.

INVERKEITHING (Dunfermline). *a.* 1057 Hinhirkethy, 1114 Innerkethyin, *c.* 1200 Inverchethin, 1229 Innerkeithing. Keithing Burn is prob. as in KEITH, with *-in* termin. *Cf.* next.

INVERKEITHNY (Turriff). As above, in loc. The stream is now Burn of Forgue.

INVERKINDY (Rhynie). Kindie Burn is G. *cinn duibh,* 'black head.'

INVER-, INNERKIP (Greenock). *c.* 1170 Innyrkyp, 1303 Inverkippe. Kip is G. and Ir. *ceap, cip,* 'block, tree trunk,' in G. 'a shoe-last.' *Cf.* Edinkyp, L. Earn and Barkip, Beith.

INVERLEITH (Edinburgh). *c.* 1130 Inverlet. 'Mouth of the Water of Leith.' I. is a fair distance fr. the sea, one of many proofs that the Firth of Forth was once much larger.

INVERMEATH (Perthsh.). 1183 Inuirmed, 1542 Innermeith. G. *mèath,* 'soft, rich in soil.'

INVERMORISON (L. Ness). G. *mòr easan,* 'the big waterfall.'

INVERNAHYLE (Appin). 'Confluence *na h'aoidhle*,' prob. 'of the adze' (W.). *Cf.* LOCH GILP.

INVERNESS. *a.* 1300 -nis, *c.* 1310 Invirnisse, 1509 Innernis. See NESS.

INVERNOOK Bay (Jura). 'Confluence at the nook,' G. *an uige*. *Cf.* CRAIGNEUK.

INVERQUHARITY (Kirriemuir). 1444 Innerquharady, Inercarity, 1508 Glenquharade. 'Confluence of the pair of streams,' G. *c(h)araid*, here in loc. *Cf.* CART.

INVERSNAID (L. Lomond). 'Confluence of Arklet and Snaid,' G. and Ir. *snàthad*, 'a needle.' *Cf.* Snaid, Glencairn.

INVER-, INNERTIEL (Kirkcaldy). 1358 Inuertele. R. Tiel is ? G. *t'sìol*, 'spawn, fish-fry, seed.' *Cf.* CAMUSTEEL.

INVERUGIE (Peterhead). *a.* 1300 Innerugy. R. Ugie is G. *ùigeach*, 'full of nooks or corners,' Norse G. *ùig*, 'a nook.'

INVERUGLAS (L. Lomond, Badenoch). G. *inbhir Dhuibh glais*, 'confluence of the DOUGLAS' burn.

INVERURIE (Aberdeensh.). *Sic* 1199 but *c.* 1175 Enneroury, *a.* 1182 Inuerurin, *a.* 1300 Innervwry. See URIE.

IOCHDAR (S. Uist). G. 'the bottom, nether lands.' *Cf.* YOKER.

IONA (Mull). 634 *Cummian* Huensis (not *Hiiensis*, W.) abbas, *c.* 657 *Cummine Ailbe* and *a.* 700 *Adamn.* Ioua insula (2 late MSS. Iona [1]), *c.* 730 *Bede* Hy, Hii, *c.* 831 *Walafrid Strabo* Eo, *a.* 900 *O.E. Chron.* Ii, *a.* 1100 *ibid.* Hiona-Columcille, *c.* 1080 *Tighernac* Ia, gen. Iae, Ie, *Four Masters* Ia, Hi, *Ulst. Ann.* Hi Coluim-Cille. *Aoi*, 'isthmus,' and *i*, 'island,' are Norse G., so inadmissible before 700. The N. for 'isthmus' is *eid* and Iona is Eidi in a Saga (Johnstone 232). Wh. Stokes thought Iona cognate with Ir. *eo-rna*, 'barley,' and that Hy, Hii is a different word. W. derives fr. O.Ir. *eo*, 'yew.' Iona is also called Icolmkill, in G. to-day Ee Choluim-cille, 'isle of C.,' pet name of St. Columba. *Cf.* Kilcolmkill, once on L. Aline, Kilcalmkill, Sutherld., and Aoi Columcille, Lewis (*cf.* EYE), while this last is also the name of Iona, *Annals Innisfailen* ann. 807.

IRONGRAY (Dumfries). 1298 Drungray (scribe's error), 1468–9 Yrnegray. Corrup. of G. *àird an greagh*, 'height of the horse stud.' *Cf.* ARBUCKLE, ERNGATH and HARLOSH.

IRVINE, R. and town (Ayrsh.). *c.* 1130 Strathyrewen in Galwegia, *a.* 1190 *Bened. Peterb.* Hirun, *a.* 1200 *Hoveden* Irewin, 1205 Irving, 1295 Orewin. Celt. for 'green river,' as in R. Irfon, Cardigan, W. *ir*, *yr*, 'fresh, green,' and *afon*, 'river.'

ISBISTER (Whalsay). 1595 -buster. As ice is rare in Shetland perh. not O.N. *íss-bolstað-r*, 'ice place,' *cf.* p. 42, but fr. a man,

[1] Iona was orig. a mistake for Ioua.

'*Ine's* place,' as in Isehaugh, Northumbd., 1370 Ineshaulgh. Yet Henderson says, Isay, Harris, is 'ice isle.'

ISLA, R. (Banff, Angus). An. I. 1187 Strathylaf, 1195 Glennilef, 1233 -ylif, and prob. Hilef mentioned in Angus by Bp. Andrew, 1165. Wh. Stokes thought, perh. cognate with O.H.G. *ílen*, mod. Ger. *eilen*, 'to hurry'; *cf.* ULLIE, R. Ill, Alsace, and R. Ille, central France. M. thought both this and next prob. O.Celt. *pi-la*, 'fat, drink, water, flow.' W. connects with next.

ISLAY. *c.* 690 *Adamn.* Ilea, *a.* 800 *Nennius* Ile, *Sagas Il*, *c.* 1375 *Barbour* Yla (this is very near the mod. pron.), *c.* 1450 Yle. Doubtful. W. thinks it O.Celt. for 'swollen place.' Perh. fr. a man *Ile* in *Four Masters.* Adamn.'s Ilea, like Egea, etc., must be an adj. The *s* is a recent innovation. *Cf.* Ila or ULLIE, old name of Helmsdale R.

ISLE Toll (Auldgirth). G. *isle*, compar. of *iosal*, is 'lower.' But this may not be G. *Cf.* Isle Rig, a hill, Dalry, Galloway.

ITLAW (Banff). Doubtful. The *-law* is 'hill,' and with It- we may compare ETIVE, G. Eite.

JANET'S BRAE (Peeblessh.). Said to be 'Danes' BRAE.' But there is a Janetstown, Wick.

JAW, Easter and Wester, JAWCRAIG (Slamannan). 1451 Estir Jal, 1745 Jall-, 1761 Jawcraig. 'Bare crag or rock,' O.N. *gall*, 'barren'; *cf.* YELL, and Sc. *ba'* for *ball*, etc.

JED. R. and JEDBURGH (Roxburgh). *a.* 800 Gedwearde, *a.* 1016 *O.E. Chron.* 952 Iudanbyrig, *a.* 1100 Geddewrde, *c.* 1130 Gedword, *c.* 1145 Jaddeuurd, *c.* 1160 Jeddeburgh, 1251 Jedwarth, *c.* 1500 -ward, 1586 Geddart; *cf.* 'Jeddart justice' and its old pron. Jethart. Here too is Bonjedward, *a.* 1300 Bondjeddeworth, *a.* 1328 Bonjedworth, 'foot of Jedburgh.' G. *bonn*, 'base, bottom.' R. Jed, *a.* 1140 *Order. Vital.* Zeda (*i.e.*, Yeda), is prob. fr. W. *gwd*, 'a turn, twist.' The 2nd syll. was orig. and even still, O.E. or M.E. *worth*, *word*, 'open space, then farm'; *cf.* POLWARTH, *Pl. N. Eng.*, p. 60, and Donauwerth on Danube; also re *fjord*, p. 34, for similar phonetic changes.

JEDBURGH KNEES (hill, Carsphairn). *Knees* is prob. O.E. and Dan. *næs*, 'ness, cape, nose'; *cf.* Calf Knees near by. But why Jedburgh here?

JEMIMAVILLE (Cromarty). A mod. type of name happily confined chiefly to across the Atlantic.

JOCK'S LODGE (Edinburgh). 1650 Jokis Lodge. *Jock*, Sc. for John, is said to be fr. an eccentric beggar who had a hut here.

JOHN O' GROAT'S HOUSE (Wick). Tradition says, an octagonal house with 8 windows and doors and a table with 8 sides.

'John o' Grot of Duncansbay, baillie to the Earl in those pairts,' 1496–1525, is on record. Grot may be O.N. *griót*, 'pebbles.'

JOHNSTONE (Lockerbie, Paisley, W. of Haddington), while Perth, *a.* 1220, was Sanct Johns toun. 1194–1214 Gillebert de Jonistune in Annandale, 1275 Johnnestoun, 'town of John,' his father, *c.* 1170–94. Pais. J. only dates fr. 1781.

JOPPA (Portobello). Called, *c.* 1780, after Joppa in Palestine.

JORDANBURN (Edinburgh) and other names in Jordan- seem mod. But we have 1595 'Jordenhill,' Glasgow.

JUNIPER GREEN (Edinburgh) is little over a century old.

JURA (Hebrides). *Ulst. Ann.* 678 Doirad Eilinn, 1335 Dure, *c.* 1598 Dewra *alias* Jura, G. Diura. As 678 shows, 'island,' G. *eilean*, 'of Doirad,' not N. *dýr-ay*, 'deer isle.' Very few N. names in Jura. Jurby, Man, is *old* Ivorby.

KAIL Water (Jedburgh). 1165–1214 Aqua de Calne. W. thinks O.Celt. *calona*, 'calling one.' Sc. *kail* is impossible. On *water*, *cf.* GALA.

KAILZIE (Innerleithen). *c.* 1200 Hopekeliov, *c.* 1265 -kelioch, 1358 Hopkeiloc, *c.* 1430 -Calye. Prob. G. *ceileadh*, 'a hiding-place,' so the name is tautologic. On *hope* see HOBKIRK.

KAMES (Kyles of Bute, Mainland, Shetld.). Bu. K. *a.* 1204 Cameys, 1475 -ys. G. *camas*, 'creek, bay,' *cf.* CAMBUS. But Sh. K. is O.N. *kamb-r*, 'comb, crest of a hill.' *Cf.* Camb Hill, Mid Yell.

KATEWELL (Kiltearn). G. Cìadail. N. *kví dal*, 'fold dale'; *cf.* Ardchiavaig, Islay, and QUINISH, also Cheadle, Kiddal in *Pl. N. Eng.*

KATRINE, L. (Callander). 1463 Loch Ketyerne (*R.M.S.*), 1682 Kittern, 1791 Catherine [*cf.* *c.* 1210 Gyllebert de Kathern, ? near Kingussie]. Prob. O.G. *cat*, 'battle,' or O.Celt. *cet*, *chet*, 'wood,' of EARN, G. *Eireinn*, not, 'of hell,' *ifrinn*. *Cf.* CATHCART and the Kittern, rock, St. Agnes, Scilly.

KEDSLIE (Dryburgh). *c.* 1150 Caddyslea. '*Cade's lea*' or 'meadow.'

KEIG (Alford). Pron. Kaig. *a.* 1200 Kege. Perh. O.G. *caidhe*, 'a quagmire'; *cf.* too *ceig*, 'clotted mess, clumsy appendage.' *Cf.* Monkeigie, Aberdeensh., *a.* 1182 Monkegyn.

KEIL(L)OR, R. (Angus), Easter and Wester K. (Newtyle, Kettins). 1296 Keloure, 1365 Kellor. See INVERKEILOR.

KEIL, KIEL (Kintyre), KEILLS (Lochgilphead). G. *cille*, 'a church, a graveyard.' *Cf.* KELLS.

KEIR (Thornhill, Br. of Allan). Pict., W. *caer*, 'a fort.' *Cf.* Keer or the Keir, Belhelvie.

KEISS (Wick). Prob. fr. O.N. *keisa*, 'to jut out.'

KEITH (Banffsh.). 1187 Geth, *c.* 1220 Ket and Kethmalruf ('of St. Maolrubha'); also *c.* 1250 Ketmariscalli ('of the marshal'). The upper part of the E. Lothian R. Tyne is Keith Water and near by is Keith-Humbie, *c.* 1160 Keth. Celt. for 'wood,' O.W. *cet, chet*, W. *coed*. Keith Hall, Inverurie, was called after the Kintore family. *Cf.* next.

KEITHAN (Keith), KEITHOCK (Brechin). *c.* 1130 Chethec, *c.* 1200 Kethet (*t* error for *c*). Both dimin. 'Little KEITH.'

KELBURN Cas. (Fairlie). 1417 Caleburne, later Kilburne. Hybrid. Prob. G. *call*, 'a hazel,' and Sc. *burn*, O.E. *burna*, 'stream.' *Cf.* too Kilburn, *Pl. N. Eng.* and O.N. *kill*, 'a narrow bay.'

KELLAS (Elgin, Dundee). Pict. G. *ceallais*, 'church place.' *Cf.* ALVES, etc.

KELLIE, -Y (Buchan, Carnbee, Arbirlot). Bu. K. 1183 Kellin, 1280 Kelly. Ca. K. *c.* 1140 Chellin. Prob. Pict., W. *celyn*, 'holly'; *cf.* LESLIE. But Collyland, Alloa, will be fr. G. *coille*, 'a wood.'

KELLS (Glenkens). G. *ceall, cill*, 'cell, church,' with Eng. pl. But Dan. *kell* is a spring, as in Kellhead, Dumfries. Kells, Co. Meath, is Ir. *ceann lios*, 'head enclosure' or 'fort.'

KELSO. 1126 Calkou, *c.* 1145 Chelchehov, *a.* 1153 Calchoh, 1158 Kelcou, *c.* 1203 'Ordo Kelchoensis,' *c.* 1420 *Wyntoun* Kelsowe, 1447 Calcouia, 1554 Kalyhow. In the old Welsh bards Calch-vynyd, O.W. for 'chalk, limestone height,' W. *mynyd*. The 1st syll. is O.E. *cealc*, L. *calx, -cis*, 'chalk, lime'; the 2nd is Sc. *heugh* or *howe* or HOE, 'height.' *Cf.* HESTERHEUGH.

KELTNEY Burn (Fortingall). G. *allt challtnigh*, prob. 'burn of hazels,' *calltuinn, -ne.*

KELTON (Cas. Douglas). *c.* 1200 Cheleton. Prob. as in KEILLS and KELLS. *Cf.* POLTON.

KELTY (Kinross), KELTY Water (Gartmore). Ki. K. 1250 Quilte. G. *coillte*, pl. of *coill*, 'a wood.' *Cf.* Keelty and Quilty, Clare.

KELVIN, R. (Glasgow). *Sic c.* 1200, 1208 -vyn. Prob. G. *caol abhuinn*, 'narrow water.'

KEMBACK (Cupar). *Sic* 1517 but 1250 Kenbak. G. *ceann bac*, 'head of the hollow' or 'of the stopping, restraining ground.'

KEMNAY (Kintore). 1348 Camnay, 1492 Kennay. Prob. G. *ceann a' maigh*, 'head of the plain.'

KEN, R. and L. (Kirkcudbt.). 1181 Glenkan, 1580 *Buchanan* Kennum. O.G. *can*, G. *cain*, 'white, dear.'

KÉNMORE (Aberfeldy, Applecross). Ab. K. *sic* 1258. G. *ceann mòr*, 'big head or height.' *Cf.* Malcolm Canmore and Kenmure, Kells. But, curiously, on L. Tay, some natives still say, *a' ceann a'mhùil*, bad Gaelic for 'the head of the loch.'

KENNAGEALL or WHITTEN Hd. (L. Eriboll). G. *an ceann geal*, 'white head or cape.' White is O.N. *hvít-r*, O.E. *hwít*. Whitten has become in G. Pūitig, *i.e.*, N. *hvít vík*, 'white bay.'

KENNET (Clackmannan). 1344 Canet. G. *ceann ath*, 'head, chief ford' or ferry over R. Forth. But in 1256 Kenneythes, 1561 Kennetis, old name of Fodderty. W. doubtfully connects the mid-part with W. *yd*, O.Ir. *ith*, 'corn.'

KÉNNOWAY (Leven). 1250 -achyn, -achi, *Aberd. Brev.* -oquy. Prob. G. *ceann achadh*, 'head, chief field.'

KENTALLEN (Ballachulish). G. *ceann t'saileinn*, 'head of the little inlet.' *Cf.* KINTAIL and SALEN.

KENVAR (Tiree). G. *ceann a' mhara*, 'the end of the sea.'

KEPPOCHHILL (Glasgow). 1521 -pok [1358 Keppach, Lennox.] G. *ceapach*, 'place full of stumps or tree trunks,' *ceap*, 'a block, a shoe-last.' *Cf.* Keppach, Applecross (*sic* 1662), Fodderty and Lochaber.

KERRERA (Oban). *Sagas* Kjarbarey, 1461 Carbery. Doubtful. Henderson suggested N. *kiarr-àr-ey*, 'copse-water-island.'

KERRIEMORE (Glenlyon). G. *ceithramh mòr*, 'big quarter' or 'fourth part.' *Cf.* KIRRIEMUIR.

KERRYCROY (S. Bute). 1449 Kervycroy. G. *ceithramh cruaidh*, 'hard, firm quarter.' *Cf.* CROY.

KERRYSDALE (W. Ross) is mod., but Kerry R. is N. *kjárr-á*, 'copse river.'

KERSE (Grangemouth, Lesmahagow) = CARSE. *Cf.* Kersland Barony, Dalry, Ayrsh.

KERSHOPEFOOT (Canonbie). 1595 *Mercator* Kirsopfoote. Usually thought, 'refuge place (see HOBKIRK) of the Kerrs.' But they dwelt at the other end of Roxburgh, so Kers- will be KERSE. *Cf.* Priesthope, Walkerburn, and the surname Kirsop.

KESSOCK Ferry (Inverness). 1437 Estir Kessok, 1564 Kescheok. From St. *Kessog*, 'Little Kess,' b. of royal blood at Cashel, d. at Luss. *Cf.* St. Makessog church, Auchterarder, and Tommachessaig, Callander.

KETTINS (Coupar Angus). 1264 thanage of Kathenes, 1292–3 Ketenes; also Kethynnes. Prob. G. *cathan-ach*, 'place belonging to soldiers,' G. *cathach*, 'a warrior,' here with the common Pict. *-ais*, suff. of place.

KETTLE or KINGSKETTLE (Cupar). 1183 Cathel, *a.* 1200 Cattel, 1558 Kettil, Chapel-Kettle. Prob. not 'hollow like a kettle,' O.E. *cetel*, O.N. *ketill*. Prob. Pict., W. *cuddial*, 'a retreat, private place'; *cf.* CUTHILL, Balmacathill, Balnakettle, Fettercairn and CAERKETTON. The 'Kings' comes fr. its nearness to Falkland Palace.

KETTLESTER (Yell). 'Place of *Ketill*,' Norse settler there. Ketill Flatnose invaded Scotland, A.D. 890, and *cf. c.* 1150 Kettilstoun, Stirling, Kettleburgh, Suffk., and Kettlesing, Leeds.

KIL(L)ARROW (Islay). Pron. -arúa, -arú. 1500 -molrow, 1511 -morow, 1548 -marrow, 1661 Killerew. 'Church of St. Maolrubha,' see p. 68, so not = KILMALLOW. G. *cill* is a survival of the old dat. or loc. of *ceall* (L. *cella*), 'hermit's cell,' then 'church,' esp. a parish church, then 'a graveyard, a grave'; *cf. cinn* in KINALDIE, etc. The regular G. form is seen in Loch nan ceall, 'loch of the churches,' W. of Mull. Names in Kil- may also come fr. G. *caol*, 'narrow,' *cùil*, 'nook, corner,' and *coill*, 'a wood.' *Cf.* KILMAROW.

KILBAG Hd. (Lewis), KILBAGIE (Clackmannan). Prob. fr. St. *Begha*. See KILBUCHO.

KILBARCHAN (Johnstone). *Sic a.* 1246. 'Church of St. *Berchan*,' Ir. saint, prob. 7th cny. *Cf.* the Market or Feill Barachan, Aberfoyle, and next.

KILBERRY (Kintyre). G. *cill Bhearaigh. Sic* 1492, but 1531 -berheth. Prob. fr. the Ir. abbot St. *Berach*, friend of Columba. But an old charter has Ecclesia Sti Berchani, see above.

KILBIRNIE (Beith). 1413 -byrny, *Pont* Killburney. Prob. fr. St. *Brendan*, friend of Columba, who made the famous 7 years' voyage. Birnie's well is here, and its fair is on 'Brinnan's Day.'

KILBOWIE (Clydebank). 1233 Cullbuthe, 1273 Cultbovy, 1330 Cultboy. G. *cùl buidhe*, 'yellow back' (of the hill). *Cf.* CULDUTHIL and Drumbowie, Linlithgow. Cult- stands for G. *coillte*, 'woods.'

KILBRANDON (Oban) and K. or KILBRENNAN Sound (Kintyre). Former is 'church of St. Brendan,' see KILBIRNIE; latter is 1549 Culibrenyn, 1796 Kyle Brannan, 'Strait, Kyle,' G. *caol*, 'of St. Brendan.'

KILBRIDE, E. and W. (also many). East K. 1181 Killebride, 1218 Kilbrigde near Crieff, 1249 Ecclesia Beati Brigide Virginis in Lorn, 1298 Kirkebride, *c.* 1300 Kylebride, Dumfries, *c.* 1400 St. Briged Kirk, Arran. 'Church of St. *Brigit*' or Bridget of Kildare, 452–523.

KILBUCHO (Biggar). *c.* 1200 Kelbechoc, Kylbeuhoc, *c.* 1240 Kylbevhhoc, 1475 Kilbouchow, 1567 -bocho. 'Church of St. *Begha*,' female disciple of St. Aidan and abbess Hilda, 6th cny. Same as St. Bees, Cumbld. St. Bees' well is near the old Kilbucho church. The -oc is a dimin. *Cf.* KILBAG.

KILCÁLMONELL (Kintyre). 1247 Ecclesia Sti Colmaneli, 1327 Kylcolmanel. 'Church of *Colmanela*,' see COLMONELL. Gaels call the place where the church was Clachan, *i.e.*, 'church.'

KILCHÁTTAN (Bute, Colonsay). Bu. K. 1449 Killecatan (the *c* or *ch* is still pron. hard). 'Church of St. *Catan*' or 'little cat,' an Ir. abbot, friend of Columba. *Cf.* ARDCHATTAN.

KILCHOAN (Ardnamurchan, Kiltearn). From St. *Congan* or *Comhghain,* uncle of St. Fillan, *c.* 750. The mod. form of the name is seen in KIRKCOWAN.

KILCHOMAN (Islay). 1427 Killecomman, 1508 -comane. From St. *Commanus* of Tyrconnell, 7th cny., brother of Cumin, abbot of Iona, where latterly he lived.

KILCHOUSLAND (Kintyre). *Old* Kil-, Quhitlawisland. G. *cill Chuisilein.* Curious name; perh. 'church of St. *Constantin,*' King and martyr, 590. *Cf.* St. Cousland's fair, Angus and Kildus(k)-lan, L. Gilp.

KILCHRENAN (Dalmally). (? in 1240 *chart. Alex. II re* Argyll, Kerchennan), 1361 Kildachmanan, Ecclesia Sti Petri Diaconi, 1600 Kilchranan. The old form is 'church of the dean,' G. *dachman, deadhan*; dean and deacon were often confounded. The present name is perh. fr. *Creathanmhnan,* son of Cathair the Great of the Ui Cormaic.

KILCHRIST (old name of parishes, Muir of Ord and Strath, Skye). Latter 1505 Kilcrist, Cristiskirk, 1574 Kirkchrist = Christchurch. *Cf.* Kirkchrist, Glenluce and KILTRINIDAD.

KILCHURN Cas. (Dalmally). Pron. Kilhúrn. 1432 Kylquhurne, 1723 Caolchuirn, 1751 Cheulchern. G. *caol a' chuirn,* 'straits, narrows at the cairn,' G. *càrn.* L. Awe narrows here. *Cf.* Kilhern, New Luce.

KILCÓNQUHAR (Elie). *Sic* 1461 and 1480 Kylconchare, but 1228 Kilconcath, 1250 -kunekath, *c.* 1300 Kalconewauth. The local pron. Kinyúchar and 1699 Kinneuchar give a later form, G. *cinn uachdair,* 'at the head of the high land.' W. ignores old forms and points to an Ir. St. *Conchobar*; *cf.* Inchconaquhar, L. Lomond. Mack., p. 177, is very wild. An obscure St. *Concad* comes nearest the early forms.

KILCOY (Killearnan). 1557 Culcowy; also Culcolly. G. *cùl coille,* 'back of the wood.' *Cf.* COWIE.

KILCREGGAN (Firth of Clyde). 'Church on the little crag,' G. *creagan.* An old church said to have been here.

KILDA, St. (island, Atlantic). There is no such st., see p. 71, and *cf.* Keldebreck, Stennes.

KILDALLOIG (Campbeltown). 1481 -lok. G. *cill Dallòic,* 'church of the Ir. St. *Dalloc,*' dimin. of *dall,* 'blind.'

KILDALTON (Islay). 1548 -tane. 'Church of the little foster- or godchild,' G. *daltain, i.e.,* branch, affiliated church.

KÍLDARY (Invergordon). G. *caol daire*, 'narrow oakwood.' *Cf.* KILCHURN.

KILDONAN (many). Suthld. K. *c.* 1230 Kelduninach, 1332 Kyldonane. 'Church of St. *Donan*,' martyred at Eigg, 617.

KILDROSTAN. 'Church of St. *Drostan*,' whom *Bk. Deer* calls pupil of St. Columba; prob. dwelt *c.* 700, in Glenesk, Angus, where Drostie's Well is. The name is now found only in Walter Smith's poem, but *cf.* CRAIGROSTAN, Ardtrostan, L. Earn, and Kilruskan, W. Kilbride, *Pont* Kilrouskan.

KILDRUMMY (Rhynie). *Sic c.* 1280 but 1238 Keldrumin, 1295 Kildromy. G. *coil droma*, 'wood on the hill-ridge,' *druim*, 'the back, a ridge.'

KILDUFF (Drem). *a.* 1150 Kipduf, *c.* 1165 Kepduf, so orig. G. *ceap dubh* (O.G. *duf*), 'dark stump.' *Cf.* KIPPEN.

KILDUICH (L. Duich), KILDUTHIE (Loch of Leys and Kincardine). 'Church of St. *Duthac*,' famed for his miracles, d. *c.* 1062. *Cf.* DUICH.

KILELLAN (Lochalsh, Campbelton). Lo. K. 1659 Killeallane. 'Church of St. *Fillan*,' see St. FILLAN'S. *Cf.* Cill Fhaelain, Leinster, and Kilallan, Houston.

KILFEATHER (New Luce). 'Church of St. Peter,' G. *Phetir*, *Pheadair*. *Cf.* Kilphedre, S. Uist.

KILFINICHEN (Mull). 1561 Keilfeinchen, *c.* 1640 Kilinnachan (*f* lost by aspiration). Prob. 'church of St. *Findchan*,' one of Columba's monks.

KILFINNAN (E. Loch Fyne). *c.* 1240 Kylfinnan, Killinan (*cf.* above). 'Church of St. *Finnan*' or '*Finnian*,' founder of great Ir. mission college at Clonard, who also lived at St. David's and at Whithorn, d. 579. Another *Finan* was sent fr. Iona to succeed bp. Aidan at Lindisfarne. *Cf.* INCHINNAN and KILWINNING.

KILGRASTON (Br. of Earn). 1608 Kilgirstoun, 1661 -gristoun. No trace of church here, and the old spellings connect with *grass*, in Sc. 4–9 *gers*, *girs*, in Eng. 4–6 *gris*. It must be a corrup. perh. of G. *cùil creas duin*, 'nook in the narrow hill'; *cf.* EDDERTON.

KILKENZIE, -CHENZIE (Campbeltn., Maybole). (1561 Sgeirkenze, G. *sgeir*, 'a rock.') 'Church of Kenneth,' G. *Coinneach*. *Cf.* Kilkenneth, Tiree and Colonsay, and the name Mackenzie.

KILKERRAN (Maybole and old name of Campbeltown). *a.* 1250 -chiaran. 'Church of St. *Kiaran*,' founder of Clonmacnoise monastery, d. 545. *Cf.* Aultkieran, Ft. William, Kilcheran, Lismore, G. *cille Chiarain*, and Kilkeran, Islay.

KILLAIL (W. L. Fyne). Pron. -awl. Perh. fr. St. *Agil*, *c.* 650; or can it be fr. St. *Olaf*?

KILLASSAR, -ESER (Stoneykirk). 1562 Kyllasser. Prob. fr. one of the many Ir. St. *Laissars* or *Laisres*. It may be G. *coill aisre*, 'wood in the pass or defile,' *aisir*.

KILLEAN (Muasdale, Lismore and Torosay). 1243 Killiean, *a.* 1251 Ecclesia Sti Johannis, 1545 Killane. 'Church of St. John,' G. *Iain, Eoin*. But Barnean, Penninghame, is fr. G. *en*, 'a bird.'

KILLEARN (Stirlingsh., old parish name, Jura), KILLERN (Anwoth). St. K. *c.* 1250 Kynerine, -hern, 1275 Kyllarn, 1320 Kynherin, *c.* 1430 Killern. An. K. 1575 Killerne. Stir. K. was orig. G. *cinn*, 'at the head,' but now *cill*, 'church,' *earrain*, 'of the division or district.'

KILLEARNAN (Muir of Ord, Kildonan, Suthld.). G. *cill Iarnain*. Mu. K. 1569 Kyllarnane. 'Church of St. *Ernan*,' here in root-inflected form. He was uncle of Columba.

KILLEN (Avoch). *c.* 1338 -ayn, 1456 -an. G. *cill Annaidh*, which W. thinks not fr. St. *Anne*.

KIL(L)ENNAN (Kintyre and Islay). G. *cill Fhìonain*. Both 1588–89 Killenane. Prob. = KILFINNAN.

KILLÉRMONT (Glasgow). Prob., like the W. Llanarmons, 'church of St. *Armon* or *Garmon*,' *i.e.*, St. *Germanus*, bp. of Auxerre, sent to Britain by Pope Celestinus, *c.* 430. The *G* is lost by aspiration.

KILLGALLIOCH (Inch. Wigton). 1600 Cullingalloch, *Pont* Kilgaillach. Prob. G. *coill gealaich*, 'wood of the moon,' over which it is seen rising.

KILLICHRONAN (Mull). M'Kinnon said, G. *coille chronain*, 'wood of the low, crooning murmur' as of bees or a brook. But Gillies thinks fr. St. *Cronan*, founder of Ir. abbey of Roscrea and visitor of St. Columba.

KILLICRANKIE (Blair Atholl). G. *coille chreitheannich*, 'wood of the aspens,' still found there. But Gaels call it *cath raon Ruaraidh*, 'battle of Rory's meadow.'

KILLIEHUNTLY (Badenoch). G. *coille chunndainn*, 'wood of the confluence.' *Cf.* BOHUNTIN.

KILLIN (L. Tay, R. and L., Foyers, Garve). Tay K. 1318 Kyllyn. Prob. G. *cill fhiom*, 'white church'; *cf.* Finlarig, L. Tay. But the L. Tay K. is the Macnabs' burying-place, so may be like Killean, common name for 'grave-yard' in S.W. Ireland.

KILLINTAG or -UNDINE (Morvern). 1542 -indykt. G. *cill Fhionntain* or *-taig*, 'church of little Finnan'; see KILFINNAN.

KILLIN-, KILLENTRINGAN (Portpatrick). *Pont* Kilantrinzean. 'Church of St. *Ringan*' or '*Ninian*'; see p. 65. This must be late Gaelic.

KILLISPORT, L. (Knapsdale). G. *caoilas port*, 'port, harbour, in the strait.' *Cf.* KYLE(S).

KILLÓCHAN (Girvan). Prob. G. *coil lochain*, 'wood by the little loch.' W. thinks it 1505 *R.M.S.* Killunquhane, fr. *Onchon* of Connaught.

KILLORAN (Colonsay). 'Church of St. *Odhran*' or '*Oran*,' d. 548. Colonsay, not ORANSAY, was sacred to him.

KILLYWHAN (Kirkgunzeon). G. *coille bhan*, 'white, fair wood.' But Barwhanny, Kirkinner, 1426 -quhony, seems to be a loc. fr. G. *cóinneach*, 'moss, fog.'

KILMACÓLM (Greenock). *c.* 1205 -macolme, 'church of my Colm' or Columba; see p. 65. The former pron. Kilmálcolm was due to supposed derivation fr. Malcolm, *Bk. Deer* Malcoluim.

KILMADÓCK (Doune). 'Church of St. *Modoc*,' a Welsh saint. It may be fr. St. *Cadoc* of Llancarven, once in central Scotland, 6th cny.; *cf.* Landoc, Cornwall, and see p. 69.

KILMAHÓG (Callender). 'Church of St. *Hog*' or '*Chug*,' whose festival is on 26 Nov. But perh. fr. St. *Cocca* of Kildare.

KILMAICHLIE (Inveraven). 1544 Kynimachlo, 1649 Kinmachlone. Said to be 'church of bp. *Machal*' (*d.* 498). *Cf.* Kirkmaughold, I. of Man.

KILMALLIE (Ft. William). 1296 -malyn, 1372 -malde, 1532 -male. G. *cill màille*, where *maille* seems a stream name, as in DALMALLY and Culmaly, 1275 -malyn, old name of Golspie. *Cf.* Knockmallie, Glencairn. W. thinks of an unknown St. Màillidh.

KILMALLÉW (Morvern). Pron. -mălū(e). 1508 -malew; also -maluog. 'Church of St. *Maluog*' or '*Moluoc*,' prob. friend of Columba, and = 'my dear little Leu' or St. Lupus, found also in Killaloe, Clare (*cf.* p. 67). One must contest W.'s derivation fr. Ir. *Liba* or *Liuba*. Kilmalew, *sic* 1529, old name of Inverary, was 1304 Kylmalduff, 'church' or 'wood,' *maoil duibh*, 'of the bare, black rock.' *Cf.* Kirk Malew, I. of Man, also Kilmaluog, old name of parishes in Raasay and Kilmuir, Skye, and Davoch maluag, Urray.

KILMARDINNY (New Kilpatrick). *Sic* 1680 but 1545 -merdunny. Doubtful. Perh. G. *coil meardhan* (here in loc.), 'foolhardy wood.'

KILMAREE Lodge (Broadford). 'Church of St. *Maobrubha*,' see MAREE.

KILMARNOCK. *Sic c.* 1400 but 1299 Kelmernoke. 'Church of St. *Marnoc*,' *i.e.*, ma Ernanoc, 'my dear little Ernan,' priest, uncle of St. Columba; see p. 67, and *cf.* 1255 *Reg. Dunferm.* Dummernech.

KILMARÓN (Cupar). 1245 -merone, 'Church of my own *Ron*' or St. Ronan; see next.

KILMARÓNOCK (Balloch). *c.* 1325 -merannok, -moronock, *c.* 1330 -maronnok, and KILMARONOG (L. Etive). 'Church of *Maronoc*,' *i.e.*, 'my dear little St. Ronan,' abbot of Kingarth, d. 737. *Cf.* p. 67.

KILMARÓW (Kintyre). *a.* 1251 Ecclesia Sancte Marie, 1631 Kilmaro. Orig. 'Church of Mary' the Virgin, G. *Maire*, *Moire*; but now 'church of *Mallrubha*' and so = KILLARROW.

KILMARTIN (Lochgilphd). 'Church of St. *Martin*' of Tours, teacher of St. Ninian, *c.* 380.

KILMAURS (Kilmarnock). 1413 Sancte Maure, 1498 Kilmaweris, 1515 -mauris, 'Church of St. *Maurus*,' a French saint, *c.* 550.

KILMAVEONAIG (Blair Atholl). 1275 -meuenoc, -mevenet (*t* for *c*). 'Church of my dear little *Beoghna*,' abbot of Bangor, d. 606 (W.). *Cf.* p. 67.

KILMELFORT (Ford, L. Awe). 'Church of MELFORD.'

KILMENY (N. Fife, Islay). Fi. K. 1250 Kylmanyn, 1518 Kilmainy. Prob. same as Isl. K., G. *cille mhanaich*, 'cell, church of the monk' (Rev. J. G. Macneill). W. derives Innermany, Contin, fr. G. *mèinnidh*, fr. *mèinn*, 'ore.'[1]

KILMICHAEL (Lochgilphd). 1240 Kelmikkel. 'Church of St. *Michael*' the archangel. Also in Cromarty in 1535.

KILMINSTER, L. (Wick). Pron. Kilmster. Prob. not fr. Kil- 'church,' but, dwelling of some Norseman with a name like *Ceolmund*. See -ster, p. 42.

KILMODAN (L. Riddon). *Sic* 1250. 'Church of St. *Modan*,' colleague of St. Ronan, 8th cny. Ardchattan's name was once Balimhaodan.

KILMONIVAIG (Spean Br.). Pron. -néevaig. 1449 -manawik, *c.* 1600 -manevak, 1602 -navag. 'Church of my own *Naomhan*' or 'little saint,' the Neamhan Mac ua Duibh of *Martyrol, Donegal*. *Cf.* Dunivaig, Islay, and see p. 67.

KILMORACK (Beauly). 1437 -rok. 'Church of St. *Moroc*,' said to be abbot of Dunkeld, *c.* 600. M. said, = *Mobharroc*, 'my dear little St. Barr'; *cf.* DUNBAR. This pet name, as Maworrock, is found connected with Lecropt.

KILMORE (Loth, Lorn). Lor. K. 1304 Kylmoor. 'Big,' G. *mòr*, 'church.' But it might be = KILMORIE.

KILMORICH (Lochgoilhead, Dunkeld). Lo. K. *sic* 1511, but *c.* 1246 Kellemurthe, Kelmurkhe. 'Church of *Muireadach*' or '*Murdoch*,' of uncertain date; perh. abbot of Iona.

KILMORIE, -RY (several). Arran K. 1357 Ecclesia Sancte Marie de

[1] W.'s connecting Kilmeny and Forgandenny with a St. Eithne seems contrary to evidence.

Arane, 1483 Kilmory, 1595 Kyrkmorich. L. Gilp. K. 1469 Kylmor. 'Church of Mary' the Virgin, G. *Moire*. Common in Ireland, where the name is sometimes *coill mhòr*, 'big wood,' but commonly *cill mòr* (Joyce).

KILMUIR (Skye, E. Ross). Skye K. is = KILMORE. Rs. K. 1296 Kilmor, 1394 Culmor, 1475 Kilmur, 1569 Estir Kilmure, Kylmuir Westir, may be G. *cùl mòr*, 'big back' of the hill. But to-day in G. it is *cill Mhoire*, 'Mary's Church.'

KILMUN (Holy Loch, Glenaray and L. Awe). Hol. K. *sic c.* 1240, but 1294 Kylmon, *c.* 1410 Kilmond, 1643 -mund. 'Church of St. *Mund*.' Fintan Mundu or Munnu was an Ir. friend of St. Columba. *Cf.* St. Mund's church, Lochleven.

KILNINIAN (Mull). 1561 -noening. Perh. fr. St. *Nennidius*, friend of St. Bridget, 5th cny., and prob. the *Ninnidh* of Lough Earn. Name remodelled after St. *Ninian* of Whithorn.

KILNINVER (Oban). 1250 Kyllivinor, 1558 Kylnynvir. G. *cill an inbhir*, 'church at the confluence.'

KILPATRICK, OLD and NEW (Dumbarton). 1233 Kylpatrick, 1298 Kirkpatricke super Cludam. 'Church of St. *Patrick*,' perh. b. near here, *c.* 380.

KILQUHANITY (Kirkpatrick Durham). 1488 Culconnady, *Pont* Kilwhonnaty, 1684 -quonadie. Perh. G. *cùil*, 'nook' of Suibhne Mac *Cinaeda*, K. of Galloway, *c.* 1000. W. derives Killiehonnet, Lochaber, G. *cill Chonaid*, fr. a *Conat*, *i.e.*, 'little hound'; it may be the same name.

KILRAVOCK (Nairn). 1225 -revoc, 1282 -rethuoc, 1295 -ravoc. In G. *Cill rathag*, so perh. fr. *rathach*, 'lucky, prosperous,' rather than *riabhach*, 'brownish, brindled.' M. thought the root *ràth*, 'a fort,' but admitted the name had changed. *Cf.* RAIGMORE.

KILRENNY (Anstruther). *c.* 1160 -rinny, 1583 Kylmarynnie (pet form of st.'s name). Prob. fr. St. *Irenaeus* of Lyons, *c.* 180. St. Ir(e)nie's well is here. Bp. Forbes took it fr. *Ethernan* or *Ernan*, uncle of St. Columba. But 1250 Kilretheni might be fr. G. *rathain*, 'ferns.'

KIL- CHILRYMONT, old name of St. Andrew's. *Tighern*. Cind righ monaigh, O.G. for 'head of the king's mount,' *c.* 1130 *Eadmer* Chenrimunt, *Flor. Worc.* Cenrimunt. *Cf.* Balrymonth near by.

KÍLRY (Kinghorn, Alyth). Ki. K. 1178 Kyllori, G. *cill' Mhoire*, 'church of Mary' the Virgin. But the accent has changed.

KILSPINDIE (Errol). *c.* 1250 Kynspinedy, Kinspinithin, *c.* 1470 Kilspynde. Doubtful. Orig. perh. G. *cinn spùinneadaire*, 'at the height of the plunderer.' Now perh. 'church of *Pensandus*,' disciple of St. Boniface, *c.* 700. The name once recurred at Aberlady.

KILSYTH (W. Stirlingsh.). Pron. -séith. *Sic* 1239, but 1210 Kelvesyth, 1217 Kelnasydhe, 1511 Kilsith. 'Church,' G. *ceall* or 'wood' G. *coill*, 'of the arrows,' *saighead*, gen. *saighde* (*cf.* 1217); *cf.* Coolsythe, Antrim. W.'s connexion with a St. *Syth* is impossible. The only known Sytha or Zita is an Ital. st. of uncertain date, never mentioned in Scotland till the 16th cny. There is no proof that *na* or *ve* (in 1210) ever did or could = *ma*, 'my dear'; *cf.* p. 67.

KILTÁRLITY (Beauly). *c.* 1225 Kyltalargy, 1279 Keltalargyn, 1384 Kyntallirty. 'Church of St. *Talorgain*' or '*Talarican*,' 'the bright-browed,' an Ir. saint, d. 616.

KILTEARN (Dingwall). 1226 Keltierny, 1296 -tyern. 'Church of the Lord,' G. *Tighearna*; so = KILCHRIST. The Chiltern Hills are prob. W. *cil tiern*, 'nook, refuge of the chief.'

KILTRINIDAD (N. Uist). *Sic* in *Pont*. Now Teampul na Trianaide, 'church of the Trinity.'

KILVARIE (Muckairn). 'Church of Mary' the Virgin, G. *Mhaire*.

KILVAXTER (Kilmuir, Skye). Hybrid. 'Church of the *baxter*,' *i.e.*, baker.

KILWHISS (Ladybank). 1593 -quhus. Perh. G. *coill chuais*, 'wood in the hollow.'

KILWINNING (Ayrsh.). *a.* 1160 Killvinin, 1184 *Bened. Peterb.* Ecelesia Sti Vinini, *a.* 1300 Kynwenyn, 1357 Kylvynnyne. 'Church of St. *Vinin*' or '*Wynnin*,' W. form of *Finnan*; see KILFINNAN. *Cf.* Caerwinning, Dalry, Ayrsh., *Pont* Kaervinnen.

KIMMERGHAME (Duns). *c.* 1337 *Reg. Dunferm.* Kymbirchame (*c* for *t*). Prob. to be identified with *c.* 1098 *Durham chart.* Cynebritham, '*Cynebrith's* home or village,' O.E. *hám*. Sim. Durham, ann. 854 has Tigbrethingham next Mailros, where again T is prob. error for C.

KINALDIE (Aberdeensh., St. Andrew's). *Kin*, *cinn*, older *cind* is the old dat. or loc. of G. *ceann*, W. *penn*, 'head, promontory'; *cf.* *Kil*, s.v. KILARROW. Except in Canmore and the occasional Cantire, *ceann* in names always becomes Ken- or Kin-. Kinaldie is *cinn alldain*, 'at the head of the little brook,' here in loc.

KINBLETHMONT (Arbroath). 1189 Kynblathmund, 1322 Kynblankmounthe. 'At the head of the flowery mount,' G. *blàtha monaidh*. Form 1322 is a Sassenach's attempt!

KINBRACE (Sutherld.). G. *cinn a' bhràiste*, 'seat of the wearer of the brooch,' *bràistich*, *i.e.*, the chief of the Gunns.

KINBUCK (Dunblane). *c.* 1208 Kenbuc, 1266 Kinbucche. 'Buck's head,' G. *boc*, *buic*. *Cf.* DRUMVUICH.

KINCAID (Lennoxtown). 1238 -caith, 1250 -cathe. 'At the head of the quagmire,' G. *càidhe*, or 'of the pass,' *cadha*.

KINCAPLE (St. Andrew's). 1212 -pel. 'Mare's head,' G. *capuill*. *Cf.* PORTINCAPLE.

KINCARDINE (county, K. on Forth, K. O'Neil, also Auchterarder, Bonar Br. and Boat of Garten). County 1295 Kynge Carden. Forth K. 1195 Kincardin. O'Neil *c.* 1200 Onele, 1277 Kincardyn, 1337 Kyncardyn de Nelee, K. O Nelee. Au. K. 1172 Kincarden, 1239 Kyncardin. Bon. K. 1226 Kyncardyn, 1536 Kincarn. Pict. G. *cinn chàrdain*, 'at the head of the wood,' W. *cerddyn*, 'a wood, a brake.' The O'Neils were a royal Ir. family.

KINCLAVEN (Stanley). 1195 -clething, 1264 Kynclevin. 'At the head of the slope or breast of the hill,' G. *cliathain*; *cf.* 1116 *Inquis.* Carcleuien. But later, 'of the kite,' *clamhain*.

KINCRAIG (Kingussie, Elie). 'At the head of the rock,' G. *creag*, *craige*.

KINDROCHIT (Braemar). 1245 -ocht. 'At the head of the bridge,' G. *drochaid*. *Cf.* DRUMNADROCHIT and Kintrockat, Brechin, 1574 Kindrokat.

KINFAUNS (Perth). Pron. -fánns. *c.* 1200 -fathenes, *c.* 1230 -faunes, *a.* 1578 -phans. 'Head, height with the coltsfoot,' G. *fathan*, with Pict. suff. of place *-ais*; *cf.* ALVES, etc.

KINGARTH (Bute). *Tighern.* ann. 737 Cindgaradh, *i.e.*, 'head of the enclosure or yard,' *a.* 1204 Kengarf, 1497 Kingarth. G. and Ir. *gàradh* is the M.E. *garth*.

KINGENNIE (Broughty Fy.). 1290 -galtenyn, 1391 -tny, 1473 Kyngenny. 'Height of the maker of promises,' G. *gealltanach*, here in loc.

KING EDWARD (Banff). *a.* 1300 Kynedward, *c.* 1320 Kinerward; also Kinedar. Local pron. Kinédart. Perh. 'at the head of the division,' G. *eadaradh*, fr. *eadar*, 'between.' This is a very old corrup. *Cf.* Cairn Edward, L. Ken.

KINGHORN (Fife), KINGHORNIE Cas. (Kinneff). Fi. K. *c.* 1136 Chingor, *c.* 1140 Kingornum, -gorn, *c.* 1150 Kyngor, -goren, 1280 -korn. Ki. K. 1654 Kingorny. W. is sure these are fr. an unrecorded *gronn* or *gorn*, 'a marsh'; *cf.* Pitgorno, Strathmiglo. 'Height of the beacon,' fr. *gorn*, 'firebrand, ember,' seems as likely. Any idea of King horn is quite recent.

KINGLASSIE (Leslie). *c.* 1153 Kinglassin, 'at the head of the stream,' O.G. *glàs*, here in loc. Near by is Finglassie, G. *fionn*, 'white, clear.' *Cf.* Edinglassie, Strathdon and 1296 *a.* 'Petglassi.'

KINGLEDORES Burn (Tweedsmuir). *Sic c.* 1200, 1359 Kylgildorys. Prob. G. *cinn gheal* (or *gile*) *doruis*, 'at the head of the clear opening.'

KINGOLDRUM (Kirriemuir). 1454 Kyncaldrum. 'At the head of the narrow ridge,' G. *caoil druim*; or fr. *coll*, *call*, 'a hazel.' (W.)

KINGSBARNS, etc. Of most of these many names in Kings- there is little to say. *E.g.*, KINGSWELLS, Aberdeen, dates *a.* 1600, but its origin is unknown.

KINGSCAVIL (Linlithgow). 1451–98 Kincavil, which is prob. G. *cinn caibeil*, 'head chapel.' But now usually taken as 'King's *cavel*,' Du. *kavel*, 'lot, parcel'—king's allotment or share of land. *Cavel* is found in Eng. *a.* 1300; see too Jam., s.v.

KING'S CROSS (Lamlash). *Sic* 1757, but *c.* 1450 Pennycrosche, see p. 36.

KINGSEAT (Dunfermline) was near Dunfermline palace.

KINGÚSSIE (Inverness-sh.). *c.* 1210 -guscy, *c.* 1237 -gussy, 1380 Kyngucy, and so still pron. or else Kineúzie. 'Head of the firwood,' G. *giùthseach*, 'a pine,' here in loc.

KINÍNMONTH (Mintlaw). 1165 -munth. G. *cinn fhionn monaidh*, 'at the head of the white or clear hill.' *Cf.* 1382 Kynmunthe, now Kinmont, Methven, and Kinmount, 1529 Kynmund, Cummertrees.

KINKÉLL (several). St. Andrew's K. 1199 Kinnakelle, Auchterarder K. 1200 Kinkelle. Garioch K. 1298 Kynkelle, *c.* 1320 Kingkell. Cromarty K. *a.* 1300 Kynkell, *c.* 1350 -kellee, in G. *cinn na coille*, 'at the head of the wood.' This known G. form and the accent make G. *cinn ceall*, 'head church,' impossible.

KINLAS (strath, L. Lomond). G. *cinn ghlais*, 'at the head of the stream.'

KINLOCH (many). Rossie K. 1220 Kindelouch, *c.* 1270 Kyndelouch, O.G. *cind a' loch*, 'at the head of the loch.'

KINLOCHRANNOCH. *c.* 1532 Kenloch-, etc., see RANNOCH, etc.

KINLOSS (Forres). 1187 Kynloss, *a.* 1200 Kinlos. Prob. 'height of herbs,' G. *lus*, *lois*, O.G. gen. *lossa*. (W.)

KINMUCK (Inverurie). G. *muc*, *muic*, 'a pig.'

KINMUNDY (Aberdeen). 1137 Kynmondy. Prob. = Kinmont, see KININMONTH, here in loc., 'at the head of the hill.'

KINNÁBER (Montrose, Islay). Mo. K. *c.* 1200 Kinabyre, 1325 Kynnaber. 'At the head of the estuary,' Pict. G. *aber*.

KINNAIRD (Brechin, Lindores, Larbert). Br. K. 1183 and Li. K. 1281 Kinard, La. K. 1334 Kynhard, G. *cinn àird*, 'at the head of the height,' or 'high point.' Kinnaird Head is thus a tautology. *Cf.* Kinnairdie, Dingwall, 1381 Kynardy, a loc., and L. Kinord, Ballater, G. *òrd*, 'a hill.'

KINNEFF (Stonehaven). *Sic* 1361. Doubtful. Seems O.G. loc. *cinnaibh*, 'at the headlands,' G. *ceann*, 'a head,' referring to the bold cliffs here. *Cf.* MORAY.

KINNEIL (Bo'ness). 1250 Kinel, 1336–7 Kynnevel. *c.* 720 *Bede* speaks of Penneltun, at the end of the Roman Wall, which Picts called *Peanfahel, i.e.*, Wallsend, W. *penn*, 'head,' and O.W. *guaul*, W. *gwal*, G. *fàl, fàil*, 'a wall.' So *Ir. Nennius*: Penguaul quae villa Scottice Cenail, Anglice vero Peneltun dicitur. *Cf.* Camden *re* Tynemouth: 'called Pen-bal-crag, that is, the head of the rampire in the rocks.' 'Kynnevel' will be O.G. *cinn fhàbhail*, 'at the end of the wall.'

KINNEIR (Fife). *c.* 1200 Kyner. G. *iar*, 'the west.' *Cf.* KINNOIR.

KINNELL (Killin, Arbroath). Ki. K. G. *cinn alla*, 'at the head of the crag.' (W.)

KINNELLAR (Kintore). 'At the head or end of the deers' walk,' G. *eilear*.

KINNESSWOOD (L. Leven). 'At the head of the waterfall,' G. *eas*.

KINNÉTHMONT (Huntly). 1198–9 Kelalcmund, *a.* 1300 Kynalchmond, -akemond. 'Church,' G. *ceall* or 'height,' *cinn*, of St. *Alcmund*, bp. of Hexham, *c.* 780. The mod. spelling Kennethmont is due to association with St. *Kenneth*.

KINNETTLES (Forfar). *c.* 1226 Kynetles, 1296 Kynathes. Prob. 'head, height of the glimpse, passing view, or breeze,' G. *aiteal*, *-eil* with Pict. suff. of place *-ais*; *cf.* ALVES, etc. 'Kynecles' (see ECCLES) also occurs, because a church once stood at the head of the valley.

KINNING PARK (Glasgow). Dates fr. 1871, built on site of Kinning Ho., also recent.

KINNOIR (Huntly). 1222 Kynor. 'At the east head,' G. *oir*, 'east,' also 'border, edge.' *Cf.* KINNEIR.

KINNOULL (Perth). 1250 Kynul. W. must be wrong in saying it is G. *Cinn alla* and so = KINNELL. It must be 'height like an apple,' G. *ubhal*, or perh. fr. *mhaol*, 'bald, bare,' *mh* lost by aspiration.

KINPURNIE (Newtyle). Pict., 'at the head of the pasture land,' *pourain*, here in loc. See POWRAN and PURIN.

KINRÁRA (Aviemore). *c.* 1338 Kynroreach, 1440 -rorayth, 1603 Kynrara. Prob. G. *cinn ruaidh ràtha*, 'height of the red fort'; *cf.* Craiganra, Kildonan. M. thinks *ro, ra* may mean 'great, noble.'

KINROSS. *Sic c.* 1214 but *c.* 1144 Kynros, *c.* 1150 Chinross. 'At the head or end of the word,' Celt. *ros*. *Cf.* Culross and Kinrossie, Scone, a loc.

KINSLEITH (? Fife). 1315 Kyndesleue. O.G. *cind a' sleìbhe*, 'at the head of the hill.'

KINTAIL (L. Duich). 1509 Keantalle, 1535 Kyntaill, 1574 -tale. G. *ceann t'sàil(e)*, 'at the head or end of the salt water.' *Cf.* p. 20.

KINTESSACK (Forres). 1237 -essoc. Prob. G. *cinn t'easaige*, 'squirrel's head.' *Cf.* KINBUCK, -MUCK, etc.

KINTORE (Inveruire). *c.* 1190 Kynthor, 1273 -tor. 'At the head of the mound or hill,' G. *tòrr*.

KINTRADWELL (Brora). *a.* 1500 Clyntraddel, 1509 Clentredaill, 1563 Clyntredwane. Fine example of corrup. or popular etymology. G. *claon Tradail*, 'slope of St. Triduana,' locally pron. Trullen, in sagas Tröllhæna, a reputed miracle-worker, *c.* 600. *Cf.* Cairntrodlie, Peterhead, St. Tredwell's L., Papa Westray, St. Trodline's Fair, Forfar, and CLYNE near by.

KINTRAE (Elgin). 'At the head of the bank or shore,' G. *traigh*.

KINTYRE (Argyll). *Sic* 1266, but *c.* 150 *Ptolemy* *'Επίδιον ἄκρον*, whose equivalent is found in *O.Ir. M.S.* ard Echdi i Cinn Tire, 'height of Echde in Kintyre.' The Epidii were a Brit. tribe. *a.* 700 *Adamn.* Caput regionius, *Ulst. Ann.* 807 Ciunntire, 1128 Kentir, *c.* 1200 Chentyr, Mael Chinn Tire, 1307 le Moel de Kentyr, *Gododin* Pentir. G. *ceann tìre*, 'at the head or end of the land.' *Cf.* KINNEIL.

KIPPEN (Stirlingsh.). *Sic* 1238, G. *ceapan*, 'little stump,' *cf. a.* 1272 Kyppen, Cromarty, and Kippenross, Dunblane.

KIPPENDAVIE (Dunblane). 1475 Kepan Davy. 'Hillock, lit. little stump, at the pit or hollow,' G. *dabhach*, here in loc.

KIPPFORD (Dalbeattie). G. *ceap, cip*, 'tree-stock, stump.' Kipp is or was common hill name in Peeblessh., *N.E.D. Kip* sb[2]. *Cf.* Makeness Kipps, Eddleston.

KIRKABY (Unst), KIRKAPOL (old name of Tiree parish). Ti. K. (? 1375 Kerrepol, G. *coire*, 'a hollow'), 1561 Kirkapost (see *bolstaðr*, 'place,' p. 42), 1599 Kirkcapoll. 'Church place,' see -by and -pol, pp. 41–2, and *cf.* Kirkebo, Sogne Fjord. *Church*, north. *kirk* is Gk. *κυριακόν*, lit. 'of the Lord,' in O.E. in 696 *cirice*, 870 *circe*, 960 *kirke*; in O.N. *kirkiu, -ia*. *Cf.* HOBKIRK, SELKIRK, *a.* 1124 Selechirche, etc. Kirkaby is the common Eng. Kirby.

KIRKANDRERS (Kirkcudbrt). 1295 -andres, 1426 -dris. See ST. ANDREWS.

KIRKBEAN (Kirkcudbrt.) *Pont* Kirbyinn. Doubtful. May be fr. *Beòan*, an Ulster priest, *c.* 750.

KIRKBUDDO (Guthrie), now CARBUDDO. 1463 Kirkboutho, 1473 Kerbutho. Skene says, fr. St. *Buite* or *Boethius*, friend of K. Nechtan, who came fr. Ulster, d. 521. *Cf.* Monboddo, Fordoun.

KIRKCALDY. Pron. -káddy. *a.* 1093 Kirkaladunt, *c.* 1128 Schira de Kircalethyn, *c.* 1130 -caladin, *c.* 1150 -calathin, -caladinit, -kaldin, 1451 Kircaldy. The 1st syll., as in KIRKINTILLOCH, is G. *cathair*, 'fort.' The rest W. J. Liddall derived—and it is prob.—fr. *Calatin*, father of famous magicians in *Bk. Leinster*. But *c.* 1180 -caladin suggests G. *cala dìon*, and *c.* 1150, -cala--dinit, *cala -dìon-aìt*, 'harbour of refuge.'

KIRKCOLM (Stranraer). Pron. -kúm. 1186 Kerkecolemm, 1296 Kyrkum. 'Church of St. *Colm*' or '*Columba.*' *Cf.* p. 65.

KIRKCONNEL (Sanquhar). 1347 Kyrkconwelle, 1354 -conevel. 'Church of St. *Convall.*' Seven Ir. saints so called.

KIRKCOWAN (Wigtonsh.). Pron. -kuan. 'Church of St. *Comhghan*,' uncle of St. Fillan. *Cf.* Lincuan near by.

KIRKCUDBRIGHT. Pron. -koóbry. 1278 Kirkudbrid, 1291 -cut-brithe, *c.* 1450 Kirkubrigh. 'Church of St. *Cudberct*,' the great Cuthbert of Melrose, *c.* 700. *Cf.* the Ir. Mac Oubery.

KIRKDOMINE (head of R. Stinchar). *Old* Kildomine. 'Church of the Lord,' L. *Dominus*. *Cf. Bk. Deer* Bal Domin.

KIRKENNAN (Buittle, Miningaff). Perh. *c.* 1280 *Bagmund's R.* Kirkelene, 1454 -ynnane, 1464 -ennane. Prob. 'church of St. *Eunan*' or '*Adamnan*,' as in Killeonan, Kintyre, 1481 -ewnane, and ROWARDENNAN. *Cf.* p. 68.

KIRKGUNZEON (Dalbeattie). Pron. -gúnnion, *c.* 1200 -wynnin, 1275 -gunyen, 1469 -gunzean. 'Church of St. *Wynnin*,' see KILWINNING. The *gu*, W. *gw*, sounds *w*.

KIRKHILL (Inverness). In G. *cnoc* or rather *crochd Mhoire*, 'Mary's hill.'

KIRKHOPE (Ettrick), K. CLEUCH (Durrisdeer). *c.* 1340 Kyrchop, -khop. 'Church valley,' see HOBKIRK. *Cleuch* is 'ravine,' see BUCCLEUCH.

KIRKINNER (Wigtown). 1326 Ecclesia Ste Kenere de Carnesmall (1319 -moel, old name of this parish), 1584 Kirkinver. Prob. fr. St. *Kennera*, virgin and martyr, who went with St. Ursula to Rome.

KIRKINTILLOCH (Glasgow). Gloss on *Nennius* Cair Pentaloch, *c.* 1200 Kirkentulach, 1288 -intolauche. G. *cathair*, W. *caer*, 'fort,' then the older Brit. *pen* has been changed to G. *ceann*, *cinn tulaich*, 'at the head of the hill.' *Cf.* KIRKCALDY. Perh. the battle of Circind, 596, was here.

KIRKLEBRIDE (Kirkpatrick Durham). *Pont* Kirkilbryde. Tautology = Kirk KILBRIDE.

KIRKLISTON (S. Queensferry). 1230 Lyston, 1250 Listun, 1298 Templum de Lystone, *c.* 1300 Templehiston. 'Church of Liston,' *i.e.*, village, O.E. *tún*, *tón*, 'of *Lisa*,' a man in *Onom.* It was a Templars' church. New Liston is near by.

KIRKMABRÉCK (Creetown). 1534–7 *R.M.S.* -makbrek. 'Church of *Mabrec*,' 'my dear Brec or Brieuc.' Doubtful if of 4th or 6th cny.

KIRKMADRÍNE (Stoneykirk). *Old* -madroyn. 'Church of my own St. *Draigne*,' perh. Welsh, *c.* 500. Prob. seen also in Kirkdrain, -dryne, Kirkmaiden.

KIRKMAHOE (Dumfries). 1275 -maho, *c.* 1280 Kirmaho, 1319 Kirkmahook. 'Church of St. *Mohoc*,' Eight Ir. saints so called.

KIRKMAIDEN, MAIDENKIRK (S. Wigton). 1469 -medun, 1473 -midyne. *Aberd. Brev.* says fr. Ir. St. *Medana*, contemporary of Ninian, *c.* 390. St. Medan's cave is here. W. prefers *Mo-Etain*, virgin, of Tuam.

KIRKMICHAEL (several). Grantown K. G. *cill Mhìcheil*, 'church of St. Michael the Archangel.' *Cf.* KILMICHAEL.

KIRKNESS (Orkney, Kinross). Or. K. 'ness, cape with the church.' Ki. K. W. J. Liddall thought, G. *cathair cinn eas*, 'fort at the head of the waterfall.' *Cf.* KIRKINTILLOCH. But it is already *a.* 1100 Kyrkenes. KIRLAUCHLIN, Stoneykirk, site of a fort, is wrongly spelt by the Ordn. Survey, Kirklauchlin.

KIRK O' MUIR (Fintry). *Sic* 1576, but 1459 Capella Beate Marie in mora de Dundaff, so, 'church of Mary.'

KIRKOSWALD (Maybole). 'Church of *Oswald*,' k. of Northumbria, d. 642, regarded as saint and martyr. Also in Cumberld.

KIRKPATRICK DURHAM (Dalbeattie), -FLEMING, -IRONGRAY and -JUXTA (Dumfries). 1248 Kirkepatrike, *c.* 1280 *Bagamund*, K. Dureant. 'Church of St. *Patrick*,' great Ir. saint, 5th cny. K. Juxta, L. for 'next,' older Kilpatrick, was so called *a.* 1500, to mark it off fr. K. Fleming. This last and K. Durham were prob. called after early proprietors.

KIRKSHEAF (Tain). 1560 Ker-, 1607 Kirkskeith. Some say, *kirk scat*, 'land given as tribute to the church' of St. Duthus close by, O.N. *skatt-r*, 'tribute,' O.E. *sceat*, 'money.' W. says, prob. G. *cathair sgèith*, 'fort of the hawthorn,' or *sgàtha*, 'of dread,' and says, *cf.* the now defunct Dunskaith, Nigg. This, as he does not note, is 1461 Dunschath, -scacht, while Dunscaith, Sleet, is 1505 Dunskahay, all pointing to G. *sgàtha*. But the *th* must have been mute by 1560. So phonet. most prob. is, 'CARSE, Kerse of loss or damage,' making it all N., fr. *skaðe*, 'hurt, damage.' *Cf.* 1567 Kirkskeith, near Avoch.

KIRKTON, very common, like Eng. Kirton. 1136 *Reg. Aberd.* Kyrkton, etc.

KIRKURD (Biggar). *c.* 1180 Ecclesia de Orda, 1186 E. de Horda, *c.* 1320 Urde, 1382 Kyrkhurde. G. *òrd*, *ùrd*, 'a rounded or hammerlike height.' *Cf.* ORD. Ladyurd, 1296 Ledyorde, and Netherurd, *sic* 1398, are near by.

KIRKWALL. *Sic* 1488 but *c.* 1225 *Orkn. Sag.* Kirkiuvagr, 1329 -waghe, 1364 Kyrkvaw, *a.* 1400 -cwav, 1438–1554 -waw, 1529 -wallia. O.N. *kirkiu-vagr*, 'church on the bay.' An interesting study in the 'liquids.' *Cf.* SCALLOWAY, etc.

KIRN (Dunoon). Modern. Sc. *kirn*, O.E. *cyrn*, O.N. *kirna*, 'a churn,' fr. the churn-shaped quarry out of which it was built.

KIRRIEMUIR (Angus). 1229 Kerimure, Kermuir. G. *ceathramh* (pron. cerrou) *mòr*, 'big quarter' or 'division.' Kerimor, *sic* 1250, was one of the quarters of Angus. Prob. *a.* 1130 *Sim. Durh.* Wertermor, where Werter– will be O.E. *feorde*, 'a fourth.' Also called Kilmarie, 'Mary's church,' with which the mod. pron. Kirriemare has nothing to do; *cf.* Stanissmare, pron. of STENHOUSEMUIR. Diack says, in G. *Cearrainn muir*, fr. Mary. If so, a late form.

KIRRIEROACH, -ROCK (hill, Barr). *Pont* Kererioch. G. *coire riabhach*, 'greyish, grizzled ravine.'

KIRTLE, R., KIRTLEBRIDGE (Annan). *Kirtle*, 'a short gown,' is very unlikely. Prob. W. *cyrddell*, 'the meeting' of Winterhope Burn and Kirtle.

KISCADALE (Whiting Bay). *Pont* Kiskidel. O.N. *kistu-dal-r*, 'glen of the chest or coffin,' Sc. *kist*.

KISHORN, L. (W. Ross). 1464 Kischernis, 1472 Kysryner, 1499 Kischrin, 1554 Kessarne, 1575 Kisyrne. W. says, G. Cis-orn, N. *Keis horn*, 'bulky cape,' influenced by G. *roinn*, 'point, cape.'

KITTLEGAIRY HILL (Soonhope, Peebles). *Kittle* is Sc. for 'tickle,' so this may be something G. like that, ? *tigh coill giorra* (gen. of *geàrr*), 'house in the short wood.' *Cf.* the Den of Kittlemannoch, Garioch.

KITTYBREWSTER (Aberdeen). The reputed female innkeeper is a myth. 1615 'the den callit Kittiebrouster,' while we have here 1376 Browster Lands. Kitty- will be as in next, and the rest is for 'brewer.' *Cf.* Kitty Frist Well, *sic* 1796, Kilsyth.

KITTYSHALLOCH (Minigaff). G. *cèide sealgaich*, 'green or hillock for hunting,' *sealg*, 'the chase.'

KNAICK, R. (Ardoch). G. *cnac*, *cnaic*, 'a crack, a fissure.'

KNAPDALE (Argyll). 1292 Knapedal, 1335 Knappedol. O.N. *knapp-r* (G. *cnap.*) *-dal*, 'knob dale,' glen with hillocks. On the coast is Knap Pt. *Cf.* the Knappis, Tingwall, NABDEN, and Knapp Hill, Woking.

KNIPE, The (hill, New Cumnock), G. and W. *cnap*, 'knob, button, little hill,' O.E. *cnæp*, 'hill-top.'

KNOCK (many). G. and Ir. *cnoc*, 'a hill,' in W. Highlands often *crochd.* Sir H. Maxwell gives 220 Knocks in Galloway.

KNOCKÁNDO (Rothes). 1685 -andoch. G. *cnoc cheannachd*, 'hill of commerce,' market-hill.

KNOCKANKELLY (Whiting Bay). 1783 Nockenkelly. G. *cnoc an choilich*, 'hill of the moor cock.'

KNOCKBAIN (Cromarty). G. *bàn, bàine*, 'white, fair.'

KNOCKDOLIAN (Colmonell). 1296 Knoudolyan, *a.* 1328 Knokdolian, *Pont* -dolean, 1684 -dallien. Brit. or Pict., W. *cnwc deillion*, 'hillock of the blinded one'; W. *dallu*, G. *dall*, 'to blind, mislead.' In Eng. 'The Mock Crag,' because, when seen out at sea, often mistaken for Ailsa Craig. *Cf.* Pen Rhiw Ddollion, Bettws y Coed.

KNOCKFARREL (Strathpeffer). G. *cnoc farralaidh*, 'hill of the high, projecting stone house.' (W.).

KNOCKLEGOIL (Baldernock). 'Hill of the stranger's grave,' G. *cill goill*; *gall*, 'a stranger.' It was a cairn full of cinerary urns.

KNOCKOLLOCHIE (Aberdeensh.). G. *cnoc mholach*, 'rough, bushy knoll,' here in loc.

KNOCKQUHAM (Aberdeensh.). 'Hill with the breast or pap,' G. *a 'mhaim*, nom. *mam*.

KNOCKRIOCH (Argyll, several). G. *riabhach*, 'brown, brindled.'

KNOCKSTING, L. (N. Kircudbt.). 'Hill with the pool,' G. *staing*.

KNOWE (Kirkcowan, etc.). Sc. *knowe*, O.E. *cnoll*, Dan. *knold*, W. *cnol*, 'a (rounded) hillock, a knoll.' *Cf.* Pow fr. *poll*, and *a.* 1094 *chart.* Knolle, in Lothian.

KNOYDART (Slect Sound). 1309 Knodworath, *a.* 1328 -worth, 1343 Cnudeworth, 1517 Knodart. In G. Crojarst, K. Canute or '*Cnut's fjord*,' here seen in several corrup. Cnut invaded Scotland, 1031. *Cf.* MOYDART.

KYLE (district, Ayrsh.). 750 Contin. *Bede* Cyil, *c.* 1150 Chul, *a.* 1173 Kyle, 1179 Kiil, *Taliesin* (O.W. bard) Coelin. Prob. fr. Coel Hen ('the aged'), the famous 'old King Cole,' *c.* 400; *cf.* Coilsfield and Coylton in Kyle. But some old forms suggest G. *caol*, 'a strait.'

KYLE-ÁKIN (Lochalsh). *Kyle, kil, col, hil* are all approximations to the sound in different parts of G. *caol, caoil, caolas*, 'a strait, a frith,' fr. *caol*, 'slender, narrow.' See COLINTRAIVE, EDDRACHILIS, KILCHURN, etc., also AKIN. *Cf.* 1549 Dunnakyne.

KYLE RHEA (Sleat). G. *caol Reathainn*. This R., in legend, is said to be one of the Feinn.

KYLE SCON, SKU (Assynt). G. *caol(as cumhann*, 'narrow strait or frith.' The *s*, through ignorance, has been transferred fr. noun to adj.

KYLES of BUTE. G. na Caoil Bhodach. See above.

KYLLACHY (Tomatin). 1162 Kylachie. G. *coileachaigh*, 'place of moor cocks.'

LACHSAY (Skye). N. *lachs-á*, 'salmon river.' *Cf.* LAXA.

LADHOPE (Galashiels). Prob. 'shut-in valley with the *lade*,' Sc. for 'a mill race,' O.E. *lad*, 'way, course, canal.' See HOBKIRK.

LADYBURN (Greenock), LADYSMILL (Falkirk), etc. *Pont* Ladiesmill, all prob. fr. 'Our Lady,' the Virgin Mary.

LADYBANK (Cupar). Lindores monks dug peats here fr. 13th cny., hence called 'Our Lady's Bog,' but also Lathy bog, prob. G. *leathad bog*, 'moist slope'; last cny. 'improved' to Ladybank. *Cf.* 1592 Lady-Bank near Arbroath.

LAGAVOULIN Bay (Islay). G. *lag a 'mhuilinn*, 'bay of the mill.' *Cf.* MOULIN.

LAGG (Arran, Ayr, Jura). G. and Ir. *lag*, 'a hollow, a cave,' same root as O.N. *lag-r*, 'low.' *Cf.* LOGIE.

LAGGAN (Badenoch, Bonar Br.). G. *lagan*, dimin., 'little hollow.' LAGGANKENNEY, L. Laggan, *c.* 1230 Logykenny, 1239 Logyn-, 1380 Logachnacheny, is fr. St. *Cainneach*, Kenneth or Kennie, of Achaboe, Ir. friend of St. Columba.

LAID (Durness). G. *lad*, *laid*, 'water course, foul pool,' same as Sc. *lade*; see LADHOPE.

LAIGH CARTSIDE (Johnstone). 'Low place beside R. CART,' O.N. *lag-r* M.E. *lagh*, Sc. *laigh*, 'low.' *Cf.* Laighdoors, Muthil.

LAIKER (Crieff). Jam. has *lagger*, *laiger*, 'mire, a muddy place.' Not in N.E.D.

LAIRG (Sutherland). *c.* 1230 Larg. G. *learg*, 'a plain, little eminence, beaten path.' *Cf.* LARGS.

LAMANCHA (Peebles). The Grange of Romanno was so called, *c.* 1736, by Adml. Sir A. Cochrane, who had lived in this province of Spain.

LAMBERTON (Ayton). *c.* 1098 -tun (two hereabouts at this date), 1235 -tona. May be 'village of *Lambert*.' But Lamerton, Tavistock, is of quite uncertain origin; the root may be *lamb*, *cf.* LAMMERMUIR.

LAMINGTON (S. Lanark). 1206 Lambinistun, 1296 -byngestone, 1539 Lammyntoun. Fr. a man *Lambin* found here *a.* 1150. *Cf.* p. 52.

LAMLASH (Arran). 1329 *Exch. R.* Almelasche, *c.* 1377 *Fordun* Almeslache, *Hacon's Saga* Malasey, ? *c.* 1500 Helantinlaysche (= H-elan-Molaysche), 1549 Molass, *Pont* Lamlach. From St. *Las*, commonly in his pet form *Molas*, *-lios*, *-laise*, 'my flame.' Of the 3 so-called this is Molas of Leighlin, grandson of K. Aidan, *c.* 610. Dr. Cameron of Brodick held Lamlash a corrup. of G. *eilean Molais,* 'isle of M.' Holy Island used to bear this name, but it seems phonet. unlikely as origin of Lamlash. The G. name to-day is *loch Mo-, Malais,* which would easily become Lamlash.

LAMMERLAWS (Burntisland). These grass-topped cliffs must be same as LAMMERMUIRS, of which one is Lammerlaw. *Sc.* law is O.E. *hlǽw,* 'mound, hill,' now *low.*

LAMMERMUIRS (E. Lothian). *a.* 800 Lombormore, 1114 Lambremor. Prob. not G. *Lombair mòr,* 'big, bare surface with a little grass,' but O.E. *lombor mór,* 'lambs' moor.' *Lombor* and *lambre* are early plurs. of O.E. *lamb.*

LANARK. 1116 Pathelanerhc, 1172 Barlanark, 1159 Lannarch, 1289 Lanark, 1375 Lanrik, *c.* 1430 Lamarke. L., like LANRICK and DRUMLANRIG, is W. *llanerch,* 'a forest glade,' as in Lanerchbrook, Hereford, and Lanercost, Cumbld., *sic* 1169.

LANDALE, -DELLS (Berwicksh.). *a.* 1188 Laundelis, 1296 -les; also Landel. Brit. *lann dail,* 'church in the field.' O.W., Bret. and G. *lann,* W. *llan,* O. Ir. *land* (same as O.E. *land*) is rare in Sc. names, but *cf.* LHANBRYDE, LONGFORGAN, etc. It means a fertile, level spot; then, an enclosure; then, a church; *cf.* the similar gradation in L. *templum.*

LAN-, LINDIFFERONE (Monimail). 1315 Lediferine. Prob. Brit. for 'enclosure by the little stream,' W. *dyffryn.* *Cf.* above.

LANGAVAT L. (Lewis). N. *langa vatn,* 'ling (the fish) loch' or 'water'; or perh. fr. O.N. *lang-r,* Dan. *lang,* 'long.' *Cf.* LANGAVILL, Mull, fr. O.N. *völl-r,* 'a field.'

LANGHAUGHWALLS (Hawick). *Cf.* 1273 Langeshahe, ? E. Lothian, and see HAUGH. LANGSIDE (Glasgow). *c.* 1600 'the Langsydfield.' LANGTON (Duns), *sic c.* 1150, also old name of Laurieston, Falkirk, 1393 Langtoune. *Cf.* 'the lang toun o' Kirkcaldy.'

LANGHOLM (S.E. Dumfries). Pron. Lángŏm. *Sic* 1376, but 1776 Langham; once Arkinholm. *Ham,* 'home' and *holm,* 'meadow' often interchange, *cf.* HODDOM, etc. *c.* 1550 a Schort Holm and a Langholme are found near Glasgow.

LANGLOAN (Coatbridge). 'Long country lane,' Sc. *loan,* O.E. *lane,* as in Lover's Loan.

LANGWELL (W. Ross and Caithness). N. *lang völl-r,* 'long field.' *Cf.* LANGAVILL.

LANRICK (Callander). 1669 Lennerick, but *sic* 1791 *O. Stat. Acct.,* and there said to be G. *làrig, làirich,* 'moor or hill.' This is wrong; it is = LANARK. But LANRIG, Whitburn, is prob. Sc. = Long ridge.

LANTON (Jedburgh). Prob. = LANGTON.

LARACHBEG (Morvern). G. for 'little house, farm, or ruin,' *larach* may mean all these.

LARBERT (Falkirk). *Sic* 1251, but 1195 Lethberth, *c.* 1320 -berd, 1481 Lethberdschiells, 1680 Larber (so often pron. still). G. *leth*, W. *lled*, is 'a half, a share'; but the present form seems fr. *làrach*. See above. The -berth is W. *perth*, 'brake, wood.' *Cf.* Narberth, Pembroke, *c.* 1248 -berd.

LARG Hill (Inch). LARGO (Ayrsh.). *c.* 1140 Larghes, 1179 -gas, 1318 -gys. G. *learg*, *lairig*, 'side or slope of a hill, beaten path,' with Pict. suff. of place *-ais*; *cf.* ALVES, etc., also LAIRG and Largue, Cabrach.

LARGIEBEG and -MORE (Whiting Bay). G. for 'little and big slope,' here in loc. See above.

LARGO, LARGOWARD (Fife). 1250 Largauch, 1279 -aw, 1595 -go. G. *leargach*, 'steep, sloping field.' The -ward expresses direction, as in homeward, toward, etc.

LARIG (hill, Dava). G. *larig*, 'path, way.' LARIG GHRUANACH, Aviemore, is G. for 'forbidding, dreadful pass.'

LASSODIE (Dunfermline). Prob. G. *leas aodann*, 'garden slope' or 'face' = Lessuden, old name of St. Boswells, *c.* 1200 Lassedwyn, O.W. *eiddyn*, 'a slope'; *cf.* EDINBURGH.

LASSWÁDE (Dalkeith). *a.* 1150 Las, -Leswade. O.E. *læs wæd*, 'ford on the meadow-land,' see *lease* sb[1] in *N.E.D.* *Cf.* Landwade, 1210 Landwath, Cambs.

LATHERON, LATHERONWHEEL (S. Caithness). Pron. Lahran. 1274 Lagheryn, 1275 Laterne, 1515 Latheroun, 1565 Lethrin. Prob. G. *laghran*, *ladhran*, 'prongs, forks,' referring to the two valleys here. Forms 1274–75 show it cannot be, as Dr. M'Lauchlan thought, = LORN. Latheronwheel, *old* -fuil, is prob. fr. G. *poll*, *phuill*, 'pool, stagnant water.'

LATHÓNES (St. Andrew's). Doubtful. Perh. O.G. *lath chonais*, 'mire, marsh, of the quarrel.'

LATHRISK (Falkland). 1183 Loschiresk, 1243 Losceresch, 1250 Lorresk, 1296 Laskreske. It seems G. *loisgear Esc*, 'swift ESK' or 'stream'; only the Eden is sluggish. The church here was dedicated St. Itharnaisc, son of Oengus; but Itharn- could not be = Loschir-.

LAUDALE (Strontian). 'Low dale,' O.N. *lag-r*, Dan. *lav*, 'low.'

LAUDER (Berwicksh.), LAUDERDALE. 1250 Lawedir, 1298 Loweder, 1334 Lawadyr. 1165–1214 Lauuedder-, 1298 Lauder-, 1560 Lawtherdale is the valley of R. Leader, *a.* 800-1150 Leder, *c.* 1160 Ledre. Lauder is prob. = LOWTHER, but R. Leader may be W. *lledwr*, 'the spreader.'

LAURENCEKIRK (Kincardine). Prob. fr. St. *Laurentius*, martyr, *c.* 260 ; *cf.* next. Formerly Conveth, prob. same name as Conway, see *Pl. N. Eng. and W.* The Mill of Conway, pron. Kunwah, is still here.

LAURIESTON (many). *Laurie* is dimin. of *Lawrence*. Kinneff L. 1243 Laurenston, 1461 -restoun. Davidson's Mains L. 1290 *Excheq. R.* Laurencystun, 1456 Laures-, 1492 Laurans-, 1512 Lowristoun. L. Falkirk, formerly LANGTON, was Merchistown in 1774, and renamed after Sir Lawrence Dundas of Kerse. Edinburgh L. is fr. Lawrence, son of Edmund of Edinburgh, to whom the abbot of Kelso granted a toft between West Port and Castle, 1160. Larriston Fell, Roxburgh, is the same name. *Cf.* the Eng. *Larrie* and Sc. *Lowrie*.

LAW (Carluke). Sc. *law*, O.E. *hlæw*, 'mound, hill,' in Eng. names -low, Marlow, Taplow, etc. *Cf.* FERRIELOW.

LAWERS Ben (L. Tay), LAWERS (Comrie). Some say G. *lathar*, 'a hoof,' so 'cloven ben,' but in G. it is Làthur. I did not find natives say Labhar (W.). *Cf. c.* 1150 *Reg. Dunferm.* Lauer.

LAXA (Shetland). O.N. *lax-ay*, 'salmon isle.' But LAXAY (Islay, Lewis), 'salmon river,' *á*. *Cf.* LACHSAY and Laxay, I. of Man.

LAXFORD L. (Shetland, Sutherld.), and LAXVOE (O.N. *vág-r*, 'bay'). Laxford is 'salmon *fjord* or bay,' Shet. L. 1488 -furde, Suth. L. 1559 -fuird. *Cf.* MELFORD

LEADBURN (Penicuik). *c.* 1200 Lecbernard. '*Bernard's* stone' or 'grave,' G. *leac*. The corrup. is remarkable.

LEADER R. See LAUDER.

LEADHILLS (S. Lanark). Lead, O.E. *léad*, has been mined here since 1239.

LECKMELM (L. Broom). 1548 Lachmaline, 1574 Lochmalyne. G. *leac Mailm*, 'stone of Malan,' which he is said to have flung over fr. across the loch. *Cf. Ulst. Ann.* 677, 'the battle of Liace Maelain,' and DUNFERMLINE.

LECKNARY (L. Fyne). G. *leac nathrach* or *nathaire*, 'flat stone of the serpent.'

LECROPT (Br. of Allan). 1260 Lecroith, 1390 -cro, 1512 -crop, 1550 Lekraw. Prob. 'flagstone' or 'grave on the little knoll,' G. *leac*, and *croit*, 'hump, knoll,' or O.W. *crup*, 'hump, haunch.' *Cf.* Carrickcroppan, Armagh, fr. the dimin. G. and Ir. *cnapan* or *crapan*, 'hillock.'

LEDAIG (Connel Ferry). G. Ledac. Perh. 'hindrance bay,' fr. O.N. *letja*, 'to hinder,' referring to Falls of Lora at mouth of L. Etive, and Norse G. *aig*, N. *vík*, 'a bay.'

LEDI Ben (Callander). 1794 Ben Le Di, 'mount of God,' *Dia*, gen. *dè*. Perh. a trace of Druid worship.

LEDINGHAM (Culsalmond). 1195 Lethgavel, ? *a.* 1600 -gauin, 1600 Leth-, Lettingham(e), 1640 Leding-. Instructive change. G. *leth gabhail*, 'half, landshare at the fork,' then *gamhainn*, 'of the stirks.' But early taken for a Saxon name in -ham.

LEE PEN (Innerleithen). *Sic* 1715, LEEFELL (Yell). O.N. *hlie*, *hle*, Dan. *hlæ*, O.E. *hléo*, 'shade, shelter,' the 'leeside,' Pen is Brit. form of G. *ceann*, 'head, headland.' M. says, Ben Lee, Skye, is fr. N. *hlíð*, 'a slope.'

LEEDS, NEW (New Deer). Leeds, Yorks, *Bede* Loidis, is of doubtful origin.

LEET R. (Coldstream). *a.* 1200 Let = LEITH. LEETHOLM, see HOLM.

LEFFENBEG (Kintyre). G. *leth-pheghinn beag*, 'little halfpenny,' a land-measure. *Cf.* Levencorrach, S. Arran, *corrach*, 'steep,' and Lephinmor, Strachur, also p. 36.

LEGERWOOD (Earlston). *Sic* 1158 but 1127 Ledgardesude, 1160 Legerswood. 'Wood,' O.E. *wudu*, 'of *Leodgeard*,' in *Onom*.

LEGLAN Wood (Auchincruive). *c.* 1470 Laklyne. Prob. G. *leac lann*, 'tombstone enclosure, graveyard.'

LEGSMALEE (Kinghorn). *a.* 1169 Ecclesmaline, later, Eglis- Egsmalye. 'Church of St. *Maline*,' said to be an Ir. 7th cny. saint. *Cf.* ECCLES.

LEITH and WATER of L., LEITHEN R. (Innerleithen). *c.* 1145 Let (in INVERLEITH), 1439 Leicht, 1570 Leth, W. *lleithio*, 'to moisten, overflow.' The -en in Leithen is adjectival. *Cf.* Lethen Burn, trib. of Findhorn, and *Nennius* Liethan, S. Wales, also Carleith, Duntocher, 1699 Caer Lieth, and LEET.

LENDAL Water (Girvan). G. *lèan dail*, 'marsh meadow.'

LENI-, LYNIEMORE (Catacol). G. *lèana mòr*, 'big, marshy flat.'

LENNEL (Coldstream). *c.* 1098 Leni-, 1127 Lienhale, *a.* 1166 Laynal. 'Poor-soiled nook,' O.E. *hlæne*, M.E. *lene*, 'lean,' found in this sense *c.* 1375, and *healh*, dat. *hale*, 'nook, corner,' usual origin of the common Eng. ending -hall.

LENNOX (Dumbarton). 1174 Leuenaichs, 1175 Levenax, *c.* 1210 -ach, 1234 Lenox, 1296 Levenaux, Lumenach (*cf.* LOMOND). O.G. MS. Lemnaigh. G. *leamhanach*, 'place abounding in elms.' *Cf.* LEVEN.

LÉNTRAN (Inverness). Perh. G. *lean traona*, 'marsh of the corn-crakes.'

LENY (Callander). 1237 Lani, 1238 -nyn. G. Lànaigh. G. *lèana*, 'a boggy meadow, a marsh,' here in loc.

LENZIE (Glasgow). *c.* 1230 Lenneth, *c.* 1300 Lengze, 1373 Leyneghe, 1451 Lenye. Prob. as above ; the -eth will be for *-ach*, here in loc.

LEOCHEL CUSHNIE (Alford). *c.* 1200 Loychel, *a.* 1300 *Regist. Aberd.* Lochel and Cuscheny. These parishes were united in 1795. L. is prob. G. *lòchail,* 'dark clearing.' See CUSHNIE.

LERNOCK (Balfron). G. *leatharnaich,* 'place at the one side or edge.' *Cf.* Learnie, Cromarty, which is a loc.

LERWICK (Shetland). *Sic* 1625. N. *leir vík,* 'mud bay.' *Cf.* Lervik, Norway.

LESLIE (Fife, Garioch). Ga. L., *c.* 1180 Lesslyn, 1232 and often Lescelin, *a.* 1300 Lessly. Fife L. is named fr. this one. Pict., W. *llys,* G. (*leas*) *celyn,* 'court, garden of hollies.' *Cf.* ROSLIN.

LESMAHAGOW (Lanark). 1148 Ecclesia Machuti, but *c.* 1130 Lesmahagu, 1158 -magu, 1298 Lismago, 1316 Lesmachute. The 1st syll. is prob. not ECCLES but G. *leas,* 'enclosure, garden,' 'of St. *Machute,*' whom Loth identifies with the Breton St. Maclovius or Malo. Sigebert, *re* ann. 561, speaks of 'Macutes also called Maclovus.' W. thinks Mahagu = Mofhegu, *i.e.,* 'my own St. Fechin,' see ECCLEFECHAN.

LESSUDEN or St. Boswell's, see LASSODIE.

LESWALT (Stranraer). *Sic* 1426 but 1607 Lesswoll. Brit., W. *llys,* G. *lios,* and W. *gwelt,* 'enclosure for grass.' (W.) *Cf.* Drumwalt, Mochrum.

LETHAM (many). Birgham L. *sic* 1166. Arbroath L. 1284 Latham. Same as Lathom, Ormskirk, *Dom.* Latune, and Laytham, Yorks, *Dom.* Ladon, corrup. loc., 'at the barns,' O.N. *hlaða,* early loaned in O.E. This loc. type is very common in *Dom.* Yorks, and the ending now is always -am, -om, or -ham.

LÉTHENDY (Blairgowrie), LETHENTY (Inverurie). Bl. L. 1285 Lenth-, 1296 Laughendy, 1451 Lethindy. G. *leathan tigh,* 'broad house'; or the ending may be suff. of place; *cf.* CROMARTY.

LETHNOT (Brechin). 1275 Lethnoth, 1359 -notty, but 1328 Petnocy ('bit of land on the hillock'). G. *leth,* lit. 'half,' becomes 'piece of land,' like *pit, pet,* see PETTY. The 2nd part may be G. *nochd,* 'of watching, observation,' or *nocht,* 'naked, bare.' Lightnot, Gamrie, 1225 Lethenoth, will be the same. *Cf.* TAP O' NOTH.

LETTERFEARN (L. Duich). *Sic* 1509. G. *leitir* (*leth-tir*), Ir. *leitar,* 'land on a slope,' *fearna,* 'with the alders.' *Cf.* O.Ir. M.S. Letherpen, Argyll, and Letter on a 1745 map N.W. of Campsie; common in Ireland, Letterfrack, -kenny, etc. *Cf.* too DULLATUR.

LETTERFINLAY (L. Lochy). 1553 Lettir-. '*Finlay's* land on the slope.' See above.

LETTERPIN (Girvan). 'Slope of the pennyland,' See above and PINMORE.

LEUCHARS (St. Andrew's). *a.* 1300 Locres, 1639 Leucheries. G. *luachair*, 'rushes,' with *-ais* suff. of place; *cf.* ALVES, *etc.* *Cf.* Leuchar, Skene, Luichar L., Lewis, and Auchleuchries, N. Aberdeen, perh. *Bk. Deer* Lurchari, also Tamleuchar, Selkirk, *c.* 1185 Tumloher, G. *tom, tuim*, 'a knoll.'

LEUCHAT (Aberdour, Fife). *c.* 1214 Lowchald. ? G. *laogh allt, alld*, 'calf stream.'

LEVEN (lochs Kinross and N. Argyll, R. Dumbarton, town Fife), LEVENHALL (Musselburgh). Ki. L., *a.* 955 Lochleuine, 1145 -lewyn, 1156 Lohuleuene. Ar. L., *a.* 1100 *Tighern*, 704 Glen lemnæ. Du. L. *Nennius* Lemn, -man, 1238 Levyne, 1370 Lewyne. G. *leamhan*, 'an elm,' *cf.* LENNOX. *c.* 150 *Ptolemy* calls L. Long Lemannonius,[1] obviously the same root. W. *llevn*, G. *sleamhuinn*, 'smooth,' would suit in some cases. Colin Livingstone said, neither *llevn* nor *leamhan* would suit the Arg. L., which is pron. llé-un, and so may be G. *lèan*, 'swampy place.' *Cf.* LYON, and Leven in *Pl. N. Eng.*

LEVENWICK (Lerwick). O.N. *hlæ-vang-vík*, 'bay of the warm, sheltered garden or haven.' *Cf.* MAVEN.

LEVERN (Paisley). Prob. = LEVEN. *Cf.* Morven and Morvern.

LEWIS. *a.* 1100 *Gael. M.S.* Leodus, *Sagas* Lyoðhus, *c.* 1225 *Orkn. Sag.* Liódhus, 1292 Lodoux, 1449 Leoghuis, 1580 -gus. Perh. O.N. *hljóð-r hús*, 'silent, melancholy house,' or, as in sagas, *ljoð-hús*, 'house of song.' Many think corrup. of G. *leoig*, 'a marsh,' *leogus, -ghuis*, 'marshiness'; appropriate enough, but not agreeing with earliest forms.

THE LEYS (Inverness). G. *an leàs*, 'sunny spot.' But LEYSMILL (Arbroath) is prob. fr. a man *Leys* or *Lees*.

LHANBRYDE (Elgin). *c.* 1210 Lamna-, Lamanbride, G. *lann na Brid*, 'church of St. Bride.' See LANDALE and KILBRIDE.

LIBERTON (Edinburgh, Carnwath). Ed. L. 1128 and Ca. L. *c.* 1186 Libertun; 1369 Nethirlibertona. Cannot be, as often said, *leper-town*. All analogy makes it, 'village of' some one, *e.g.*, *Leodbeorht* or *-burh* or *Liutbirga* (a woman), names in *Onom.* *Cf.* Lebberston, Filey 1206 Ledbrigton.

LIDDESDALE (Roxburgh). 1179 Lidelesdale, 'dale of the Liddel Water,' *c.* 1160 Lidel, *c.* 1470 Ledaill. Prob. reduplication, O.N. *hlý dal*, 'shelter dale.' But Li- may be G. *lì*, 'coloured.'

LIFF (Dundee). *Sic* *c.* 1120, but 1250 Lif. Perh., like Clonliff, Ireland, Ir. and G. *cluain luibh*, 'meadow of herbs.'

LILLIARD'S EDGE (Ancrum). *Sic* 1743 but *c.* 1200 Lilisyhates, *a.* 1300 Lillesiet, *c.* 1380 Lylyet Cros, 1548 Lylgearts Croce. 'Gate, road,' O.E. *geat*, Sc. *yet*, 'of *Lille*.' *Lil* and *Lilla* are

[1] Of course Lac Leman, the Lake of Geneva, *Cæsar* Lemanus, Gaul, *lemo, limo*, 'an elm,' is also the same.

names in *Onom.* Edge is common hereabouts for a sheer, steep hill. *Cf.* next.

LILLIESLEAF (St. Boswell's). *Sic* 1696 but 1116 Lilleseliva (? -cliva), 1147–51 Lyllescleue, 1186 -sclif, 1296 -slyve, 1721 Lilsly, still the local pron. Not 'lily's leaf' but 'Cliff,' O.E. *clif*, 'of *Lille*,' perh. a Northumb. thane whose death led to introducing Christianity hereabouts.

LIMEKILNS (Dunfermline, Avoch). Du. L. 1561 The lymekill, 1584 The Lyme-kilnes. LIMERIGG (Slamannan), see RIGG.

LINCLUDEN (Dumfries). 1452 Lyncludene. 'Pool,' W. *llyn*, 'on R. CLUDEN.'

LINCUMDODDIE (extinct hamlet, Peebles). W. *llyn cam*, 'crooked linn or pool' and Sc. *doddie*, 'rounded hill,' see DODD.

LINDEAN (Selkirk, also old parish now in Galashiels). 1275 Lyndon, 1353 Lindene. W. *llyn din*, 'linn, pool by the hill,' but influenced by DEAN.

LINDERTIS (Kirriemuir). *Old* Lan-. G. *lann dàirte*, 'enclosure of the heifer,' with *-ais* suff. of place.

LINDORES (Newburgh). *a.* 1182 Lundors, 1199 -doris, 1203 Londors. G. *linne*, W. *llyn*, 'pool, loch,' G. *doruis*, 'at the opening.' *Cf.* Puldores Burn, Carsphairn.

LINDSAYLANDS (Biggar). Lindsays in Clydesdale *a.* 1200; the first known, Randolph de Limesay or Lindesey ('lime-tree, linden isle'), was nephew of William the Conqueror and came over with him.

LINGA (Shetland). *Sagas* Lyngey, O.N. for 'ling, heather isle.' *Cf.* Lingholm (see HOLM) Stronsay and Lingrow, Scapa.

LINLATHAN (Dundee). 1359 Lumletheyn. G. *lòm leathan*, 'broad, bare surface.' *Cf.* LUMLAIR.

LINLITHGOW. *c.* 1138 Linlidcu, 1147 -litcu, 1156 Lillidchu, 1264 Lenlithgow; and, contracted, as often still, *a.* 1300 Lithcowe, 1489 Lythgow. Brit., W. *llyn lled cu*, 'dear broad lake,' *cf.* GLASGOW, PLASCOW. But early associated with G. *liath cu*, the 'grey dog' on the burgh seal. Much in W., p. 384, is quite fantastic.

LINNHE, L. (Argyll). G. *linne*, 'pool, enclosed sea-loch.'

LINSIDE (Sutherland). G. Lianasaid, N. *lín setr*, 'flax shieling' = LINSHADER, Lewis. (W.)

LINTALEE (Jedburgh). *Sic a.* 1369 *Scalacron.* Doubtful. Perh. G. *lionta lia*, 'flat, big stone.'

LINTON E. and W., and near Kelso. E. L. 1127 Lintun. W. L. 1567 Lyntoun. O.E. *lín tún*, 'flax enclosure,' *cf.* linseed, and Linmill, Alloa; but Linwood, Paisley, is prob. hybrid, W. *llyn*, 'a pool.'

LINTRATHEN (Kirriemuir). *c.* 1250 Lum-, Luntrethyn. G. *lòm*, *luim*, 'bare spot' or *lann*, 'enclosure' and ? W. *traethen*, 'sand-bank' (Mack.). If so, Pict.

LISMORE (Oban). *Tighern*, 611 Lesmoir, 1251 Lesmor, 1549 Lismoir. G. *leas*, *lios mòr*, 'big enclosure or garden,' L. is so fertile.

LISSA (Mull). Corrupt form of LAXA.

LITTLE FERRY (Dornoch). G. Port Beag. 'Littles,' so common in Eng., are very rare in Sc. But *cf.* LITTLE DUNKELD, *sic* 1505.

LIVILANDS (Stirling). 1457 Levilandis, 'level lands,' O.Fr. *livel*, in Eng, 1362 *livel*. *Cf. Dom.* Kent, Levelant and *a.* 1400 *Rent. St. Andr.*, Lufelandis.

LIVINGSTONE (Midcalder). *c.* 1128 Villa Leuing, *a.* 1150 Leuinestun, *a.* 1224 Levingstoun. 'Abode of *Leving*,' the common O.E. *Leofwine*, an early Saxon settler.

LOADBERRIE (Kirkwall). Perh. O.N. *hlað-berg*, 'projecting pier, rock where a ship is loaded,' *hlað*, 'a pile, a stack.'

LOANHEAD (Edinburgh), LOANS (Troon) see LANGLOAN.

LOCHABER (Ft. William), L. LOCHABER (Troqueer). *a.* 700 *Adamn.* Stagnum ('standing water, swamp') Aporum, 1297 Lochabor, 1309 -abre. G. *abar*, 'a marsh.' The earliest *loch* so named is perh. *c.* 1123 Lochtei or Tay.

LOCHALSH (W. Inverness). 1449 -alche, 1464 -alsche, 1510 -elch. G. Lochaillse, *i.e.*, 'fairy.' But perh. *c.* 150 *Ptolemy* Ouolsas which M. derived fr. root *vol-*, 'to roll as a wave.'

LOCHANBENNET (Glencairn). Perh. 'Little loch,' G. *lochan*, 'of St. *Benedict*,' follower of St. Boniface, *a.* 700. *Cf.* Lochans, Stranraer.

LOCHANDORB (Dava). G., 'loch of tadpoles,' *doirb*. But 1386 *Cal. Docts. Scotld. II*, 223 Louchondoun, G. *an duin*, 'of the castle.'

LOCH-AN-EILEIN (Rothiemurcus). G., 'loch of the island.'

LOCHAR-BRIGGS, -WATER, -WOOD (Dumfries). 1347 Lougherwode, 1487 Lochirwood. G. *luachair*, 'rushes.' *Cf.* Locher Moss, Longformacus, and LEUCHARS. Briggs is O.E. *bricg*, Sc. *brig*, 'a bridge.'

LOCHBUIE (Mull). 1478 -bowe, 1549 -buy. G. *buidhe*, 'yellow.' *Cf.* KILBOWIE.

LOCHBURNIE (Glasgow). G. *bùrn*, *bùirn*, 'fresh water,' here in loc.

LOCHEE (Dundee). Prob. fr. G. *iodh*, 'corn.' *Cf.* TIREE.

LOCHEIL (Ft. William). 1528 -iell. G. Lochioll. G. *ial*, 'gleam of sunshine.' Gillies prefers *iall*, 'a thong.'

LOCHGAIR (Inverary) = GAIRLOCH.

LOCHGELLY (Dunfermline). G. *geal*, *gile*, 'clear, white.'

LOCHGILP (L. Fyne). *a.* 1246 Louchgilp ; also Polgilib. G. *loch a' gilb*, also *gilab*, *gelb*. G. *gileab*, *gealb*, *gilb*, 'a chisel,' fr. its shape.

LOCHGOIL, -INVER, etc. See GOIL, INVER, etc.

LOCHHEAD (several) = The G. KINLOCH. *Cf.* 1296 Gilbert de Lakenheued ('lake-head') del counte de Lanark.

LOCHINVÁR (Dalry, Kirkcud.). *Sic* 1540 but 1578 -war. G. *loch an bharra*, 'loch on the height.'

LOCHLEE (Brechin). G. *liath*, 'grey, pale,' or *lì*, 'coloured.'

LOCHLUICHART (Garve). G. *lùichart*, 'a castle.' But W. prefers to call it, loc. of *longphort*, 'encampment, shieling.' *Cf.* LUNCARTY.

LOCHMABEN (Lockerbie). 1166-1296 Locmaban, *c.* 1320 Lochmalban (*l* prob. error), 1502 -mabane. *Mabon* (W. *mabon*, 'youth, hero') or *Maponos* was the Brit. sun-god, and *Mabon* is still a Border name. *Cf.* Carmaben, Dolphinton and the Lochmabenstone, Gretna, 1309 Clochmabenestane, a tautology. G. *cloch*, 'a stone.'

LOCHMADDY (N. Uist.). G. *madadh*, 'wolf, wild dog'; *cf.* Pulmaddy, Carsphairn. But 1703 *Martin* says, fr. the quantities of big mussels or 'maddies' on the rocks there, and M. agrees.

LOCH NA CUITHE (not Caoidh, as in O.S. map, N. Inverness). G. *cuith*, 'pit, gully or snow-wreath.' (W.)

LOCH NAN DUBRACHAN (Skye). Prob. G. for 'loch of the wells.' (W.)

LOCHNAGÁR (mountain, Braemar). 1640 Loch Garr, 1807 *Byron* Lachan y Gair or Loch na Garr. G. *gàire*, 'laughter.' The O.G. name seems Ben Chiochan ('little pap'), R. Gordon's map, 1640.

LOCHORE (Lochgelly). *Sic* 1245, but 1231 -or. G. *odhar*, 'grey.'

LOCHRUTTON (Kirkcudbt.). 1296 -ryertoun, -rynton, 1300 Loghroieton, 1466 -rewtoune. Doubtful. Perh. G. *ruaidh dùin*, 'of the red hill.'

LOCHS (Lewis). 1549 *Monro*, 'the Loches'; called, he says, fr. the number of small lochs there ; *c.* 1620 Loghur, *cf.* LEUCHARS.

LOCHWINNOCH (Beith). 1158 Lochynoc (very near the local pron. still), *a.* 1207 -winnoc, 1710 -whinyeoch. *Winnoc* is dimin. of St. Wynnin. d. 579 ; see KILWINNING.

LOCHY, R. and L. (Inverness-sh.), LOCHAY R. (L. Tay). *a.* 700 *Adamn.* Lacus Lochdiae, 1472 Locha, 1496 Loquhy. Prob. too *Adamn.* Nigra Dea. If so it is O.Ir. *lòch*, 'dark, black,' and *dea*, 'river goddess'; *cf.* DEE. In G. it is Lochaidh.

LOCKERBIE (Dumfriess-sh.). 1306 Lokardebi. '*Locard's* or *Lockhart's* dwelling' (on *by* see p. 41). Locard came N. with the early Bruces. *Cf.* Lockerley, Romsey.

LOGAN Pt. (S. Wigtown), LOGAN Water (Lesmahagow). *a.* 1204 rivulus de Logan. G. *lagan*, 'a little hollow,' *cf.* next and LAGGAN.

LOGIE, many. Br. of Allan L. 1184 Logyne, several *c.* 1210 -gyn, *c.* 1250 'Logie Mehed in Athollia' (*cf.* LOGIERAIT), 1257 Logibride, ? Logiebride, Auchtergaven (see KILBRIDE), 1270 Logy, Logie Easter, Ross-sh., *cf.* 1299 Logyiastre, Perthsh., *a.* 1300 Logy, Logie Buchan. The final *n* in old forms prob. always scribe's flourish. If so, O.G. *logaidh*, loc. of G. *lag*, *luig*, 'a hollow, a pit.' Logiepert, Montrose, see PERTH. As to Logie-Coldstone, Tarland, these were two parishes united in 1618, Logie and 'Codilstan,' possibly, as in Coldstone, Devon, *Dom.* Coltrestan, 1346 Codelstan, 'coulter (O.E. and L. *culter*), ploughshare stone.'

LOGIERAIT (Ballinluig). *a.* 1200 Rate, Rath. See above, and G. *ràth*, 'a circle, a fort.'

LOGIERIEVE (Ellon). 'At the greyish, brindled (G. *riabhach*) hollow.'

LOMOND, L. and Ben, LOMOND Hills (Fife). A shifty name. Ptolemy's Kolpos Lemannonios (O.G. *leman*, 'elm') is L. Long. *a.* 900 *Nennius* Stagnum Lumonoy, *v.r.* Lumonui, Limmonium, Lommon; while, according to M., 919 *Index to Nennius* says, L. Lummonou is in the land of the Picts and in Eng. is called Loch Leven. With this agrees the Inverness G. pron., Beinn Laomuinn, but at Inversnaid it is pron. Lŏwman; in Eng. always Lōmon (d.) Root here is Pict., W. *llumon*, 'a beacon,' as in Plynlimmon; *cf.* G. *laom*, 'a blaze of fire.' 'Beacon' suits well for the Ben and Lomond Hills, Fife, *sic* Pont., 1594 lie Lowmondis. But the 'elm' root, O.G. *leman*, G. *leamhan*, is seen in 1225 *Chart. Paisley* lacus de Leven, name now only of the river, here amnis de Leven, flowing out of L. Lomond; also perh. *a.* 1200 Ir. *Nennius* L. Lomnan, *c.* 1225 L. Lomne. But *a.* 1350 lochlomond, 1498–1633 Lowmond, 1580 *Buchanan* Lominius lacus, 1791 L. Lomin; these two last, spellings of Gaelic residents; and all these rather suggest G. *loman*, *-ain*, 'banner, shield'; for the *d cf.* DRUMMOND. It is curious there is a L. LEVEN at the foot of Lomond Hills. *Cf.* LENNOX.

LONG, L. (Firth of Clyde). In G. *Long*, but by some *loch fada*, 'long.' *c.* 1225 Long, but it is prob. *c.* 150 *Ptolemy* Lemannonios Kolpos ('gulf'), see above and LEVEN. 1776 Loung, ? G. *long*, *luing*, 'of the ship'; in N. it was Skipa fjord.

LONGFORGAN (Dundee). 1178-82 Forgrund, 1250 Forgrund in Gouirryn, 1315 Lon forgaund, Longforgrund, 1461 Langforgend, 1661 -gund; but *Acta Sanct.* Lanfortin. The 1st syll. is prob. G. *lann*, 'enclosure, church'; perh. *lòn*, 'a marsh.' See FORGAN. Monorgan near by, *c.* 1250 Monorgrund, has lost *f* by aspiration; G. *monadh*, 'a moor.'

LONGFORMACUS (Duns). *c.* 1340 Langeford Makhous, 1430 Lochyrmacus. G. *lann fothir Maccus,* 'church on the field or slope of Maccus,' found in the district, *c.* 1150. See MAXTON and above.

LONGHOPE (Stromness). For *hope,* 'refuge,' see HOBKIRK.

LONGMANHILL (Gamrie) may be a corrup., but *cf.* Standingmanhill, Fordyce and Stonemanhill, Fyvie.

LONGMORN (Elgin). Pron. Lang-. *Old* Longmorgan. Prob. 'church,' G. *lann,* 'of *Morgan,*' see MUIRAVON. There was a church here.

LONGNIDDRIE (E. Lothian). 1424 Langnudre, 1595 -nedre. Prob. as above and see NIDDRIE. Old chapel here.

LONMAY (Buchan). *a.* 1300 Lunme, *c.* 1445 Lymaij, *a.* 1500 Lummey. G. *lòn maigh,* 'marsh, meadow, in the plain.' *Cf.* CAMBUS O' MAY.

LORA, FALLS of (L. Etive). Taken fr. *Ossian,* supposed to refer to them. Perh. fr. G. *labhra*; *labhar,* 'loud-sounding, noisy,' though these sea-falls are hardly that.

LOREBURN (Dumfries). *Old* Lordeburn, but early Lore-. Root perh. as in O.Ir. *lòthur,* 'canal,' Bret. *laouer,* 'trench.'

LORN (Oban). *a.* 1166 *Ailred* Insulanis et Lavernanis ('men of Lorn'), 1304 Lorne, *a.* 1500 *Bk. Clanranald* Lagarne, Ladharna. (*Cf.* LATHERON.) From *Loarn, -ern,* reputed first K. of Scots in Dalriada, *c.* 500; root Celt. *lovern-,* 'a fox.'

LOSKIN, L. (Dunoon). G. *losgann,* 'a frog.'

LOSSIE, R. and -MOUTH (Elgin). If Ptolemy's Loxa, cannot be O.N. *laxa-á,* 'salmon river.' Root perh. W. *lloesi,* 'to pour' (Mack.). But LOSSIT, Kilsyth, is G. *loisit,* 'kneading-trough,' hence 'rich, productive field.' *Cf.* 1233 Losset, Old Kilpatrick, now Lusset.

LOTH (Brora). G. *làth(ach),* 'clay, mud, or, fine alluvial soil,' as here.

LOTHIAN. *c.* 970 *Pict. Chron.* Loonia, 1091 *O.E. Chron.* Loðene, 1095 Lodoneium, *c.* 1145 -onesia, 1158 in Loeneis, *a.* 1166 *Ailred* Laudonia, *c.* 1200 Louthion, *c.* 1600 Lawdien. Prob. fr. an unknown man. *Onom.* has *Leodwine, Lodowin.* *Cf.* Londesborough, Yorks, *Dom.* Lodenesburg.

LOTHRIE Burn (Leslie). 1250 Lochris (? *s* for *e*), 1294 -ry. Prob., like LOCHRIE, Strathbogie, fr. G. *luachrach,* 'place full of rushes,' here in loc.

LÓUDOUN (Kilmarnock). *Sic c.* 1140, but *c.* 1200 -dun, 1296 Loghdune, *Barbour* Lou-, *v.r.* Lochdon. Prob. 'flame hill,' O.E. *dún,* or 'beacon'; O.N. *loge,* in Eng. *c.* 1200 *loghe, c.* 1330 *lowe,* Sc. *low,* 'a flame, a blaze.' W.'s origin fr. Celt. *Lugdunon,* 'fort of the god Lugus,' as in Lyons, is not so likely.

LOVAT (Beauly). Pron. Lŭvat, *c.* 1235 Loveth, 1294 -et. Pict. for 'muddy place, swamp' (M.). W. says, root *lobh*, 'to rot.'

LOWES, L. of (St. Mary's Loch and Dunkeld). Pron. as in cows. 1506 *Rent. Dunkeld* Cardeny betwix the lowis. Perh. reduplication; in Speed's map, 1620, *lough* is general for loch, lake in N. England; *cf.* Forest of Lowes, *sic* 1329, once in Tynedale. Loweswater, 1189 Lawes-, Cumbld. may be fr. a man *Hlæwa*, in *Onom.*

LOWLANDS. The adj. Lowland as applied to Sc. is first in 1508 *Dunbar* lawland. 'Lowlands' is first in *N.E.D.* in 1631. In G. *Galldachd*, 'strangerdom,' as opposed to Gaeltachd, 'Gaeldom,' the Highlands; also *Machair*, 'the plain.'

LOWTHER Hills (Dumfriessh.). Perh. = LAUDER. O.Ir. *lòthur*, 'canal,' Bret. *laouer*, 'a trench.' *Cf.* Leuther, trib. of N. Esk, LOREBURN and Lowther, Cumbld.

LOY GLEN (Spean Br.). *Sic* 1568. 'Glen of the calf,' G. *laoigh* (W.). In Glengarry this makes Glenluie. Natives told the writer, 1891, it was Gloy. ? G. *gloath*, 'noise.' 1196 *Hoveden* has Locloy, ? near Nairn.

LOYAL Ben (Tongue). 1601 Lyoll. G. Laghail. Doubtful. M. thought O.N. *leið-fjall*, 'levy or slogan hill'; *cf.* Layaval, S. Uist and Laiaval, N. Uist. W. thinks O.N. *laga-völl-r*, 'law field,' where official meetings met. Henderson prefers *fjall* to *völl*.

LOYNE, R. and L. (L. Garry). G. *loinne*, 'beauty,' or 'of the glade,' var. gen. of *lann*.

LUBNAIG, L. (Callander). Named fr. its shape, fr. G. *lùb*, 'a bend, curve,' with double dimin. *-an* and *-aig*.

LUCE, OLD, NEW, GLEN (Wigtown). 1220 *Pat. R.* Glenlus, 1347 Luse. G. *lus*, 'herb, plant.' But Dunluce, Portrush, is Ir. *dùn lios*, 'strong fort.'

LUCHIE (Pitlochry). Prob. loc. of G. *laoghach*, 'place of calves or fawns.'

LUFFNESS (Aberlady). 1180 -fenac, *c.* 1250 -nauch, 1451 Lufnois, 1585 -nes. G. *luibheanach*, 'place full of little herbs or plants.' There is no ness.

LUGAR, R. (Auchinleck). *Sic. c.* 1200, but 1202 Lughor, *Pont* Ludgar little and meikle. May be = LEUCHARS. W. prefers W. *llug*, 'bright.' Pont's form looks like G. *lod, luid gearr*, 'short pool.'

LUGGIE Water (Cumbernauld). *c.* 1300 -gy. Might be loc. of G. *lag, luig*, 'a hollow.' Perh. case of river-worship, as in R. Lugg, *Pl. N. Eng.*, fr. a Celt. god *Lug*, W. *llug*, 'bright.'

LUGTON (Neilston, Dalkeith). Very likely corrup. of W. *llug din*, 'bright hill'; *cf.* DUBTON.

LUIB (Killin). G. *lùb, lùib,* 'a bend, a curve.'

LUING I. (Oban). Pron. Ling. G. *long, luing,* 'a ship.' *Cf.* Portnaluing, opposite Iona, *Adamn.* Lunge.

LUMGAIR (Kinneff). *c.* 1220 Lunkyrr, 1651 Lumger; also Lonkyir. This last is G. *lòn ciar,* 'dark brown or grey marsh.' But Lumger will be as in LUMLAIR, old name of Kiltearn, 1227 Lemnelar, 1548 Lymnolar, G. *luim* (loc. of *lòm*) *na làr,* 'bare surface of the mare' (W.). So, G. *luim gearr,* 'short bare surface.'

LUMPHANAN (Mar), -PHINNANS (Dunfermline). Ma. L. *a.* 1100 *Tighern.* Lumfanan, 1299 -fannan. G. *lann Finain,* 'church of St. Finnan'; see KILWINNING and *cf.* Llanfinan, Anglesea.

LUMSDEN (Alford). Name taken N. *c.* 1825, fr. lands near Coldingham, 1098 *chart.* mansio Lummesdene. *Lumme* is unknown. See DEAN.

LUMWHAT (Auchtermuchty). G. *lòm, lùim chat,* 'bare surface of the wild cat.' *Cf.* ALWHAT, LUMGAIR and Lynchat, Badenoch.

LUNAN Bay (Montrose). 1189 Innirlunan, 1296 Inverlounan. G. *lunn,* pl. *lunnan,* 'waves.'

LUNCARTY (Perth). 1250 Lumphortyn, 1358 Lonfordi, 1461 -gardi. K. Meyer said, Ir. and G. *longphort,* lit. 'ship's harbour,' then 'encampment,' often in Ireland as Longford; *cf.* Athlunkard, Limerick, Auchluncart, Banffsh., LOCHLUICHART and 1564 'Luncartis in Glentilth.' The -y is the loc.

LUNDIE (Dundee). 1510 -deif. G. *lòn dubh, duibh,* 'dark marsh'; *cf.* Duff. But L. Lundie, Glengarry, is loc. of next.

LUNDIN LINKS (Leven). *Sic c.* 1200. G. *lunndan,* 'a green, wet place.' London may be the same.

LUNNA and -STING (Shetland). *Old* Lundseidsting. O.N. *lund-r,* 'a grove,' common in pl.-names, *eid* is 'isthmus,' and *þing* is 'meeting, assembly,' while *a* is 'island.' *Cf.* TINGWALL.

LURG Hill (Cullen). G. *lurg,* 'a gradually declining ridge.' *Cf.* PITLURG.

LUSS (L. Lomond). 1225 Lus, 1250 Luss. Must be, like LUCE, G. *lus,* 'herb, plant.' *Cf.* CRUACH LUSSA.

LUSSA (Mull). O.N. *ljoss-á,* 'bright, clear river.'

LUTHERMUIR (Laurencekirk). O.E. *lýðre,* 3–4 *lithere, luther,* now *lither,* 'bad, sorry, hurtful' moor.

LUTHRIE (Cupar). Prob. = LOTHRIE.

LYBSTER (Caithness). The *y* pron. as in lyre. 1538 Libister. N. *hliebolstað-r,* 'shelter place,' see p. 42. *Cf.* BILBSTER and LEE.

LYNE Water (Peebles). *c.* 1190 Lyn, *c.* 1210 Line, 1399 Leigne. Corn. *lin*, W. *llyn*, G. *linne*, 'pool, stream, linn.' But Lyne Burn, Dunfermline, is 1227 aqua de Letheni; see LEITHEN.

LYNTURK (Alford). G. *linne*, (W. *llyn*) *tuirc*, nom. *torc*, 'pool of the wild boar.'

LYNWILG (Aviemore). 1603 Lambulge, *Pont* Lynbuilg. G. *lann*, 'enclosure,' or *linne*, 'pool' 'of the bulge or bag,' *bolg*, *builg*. *Cf.* BOGIE.

LYON, R., see GLENLYON. But LYONSHIELDS (Beith), pron. Lansheils, is perh. fr. G. *lann*, 'enclosure,' and see GALASHIELS.

MACBIE HILL (Dolphinton). 'Coldcoat,' bought by Wm. Montgomery, 1712, renamed by him after Macbeth or Macbie Hill, Ayrsh., 1508 Makbehill.

MACDUFF (Banff). So named by Jas. Duff, Earl of Fife, in 1783.

MACHAR, OLD and NEW (Aberdeen). *a.* 1300 Ecclesia beati Sti Machorii. *Machor* was a disciple of St. Columba. *Cf. Bk. Deer* Acchad (G. *achadh*, 'field') Madchor, N.W. of Deer.

MACHÓULSTON (Coylton). 'Village of Finn *MacCool*' or 'Fingal,' the Ossianic hero. But Mahoúl, Glasserton, is G. *maothail*, 'soft, spongy land.'

MACHRA-, MACHRIHANISH (Campbeltown). W. says, G. *machair Shanais*, 'plain, links of Sanas.' Who was he? Locally it is taken fr. *annais*, 'stormy, noisy.'

MACHRIE Bay (W. Arran). G. *machair*, 'field, plain,' here in loc. Also MACHRIEMORE ('big') and -BEG ('little'), Kintyre.

MACLEOD'S MAIDENS (rocks off Duirinish, Skye). Macleods first appear in Skye, 1343. But one is found at Forfar, 1227.

MACMERRY (Tranent). Perh. G. *màg(h) mire*, 'plain of the merry or wanton'; Merry is a Sc. surname. The root of *màg* is prob. *màg*, 'palm of the hand.'

MADDERTY (Crieff). *a.* 1100 *Tighern.* ann. 669 Madderdyn, 1185 Maddyrnin, *c.* 1199 Maderdin, -nin, 1219 Madirdi. Old folks used to speak of 'the plain o' Mathertie.' Prob. G. *meadair Ethernain*, 'little pail, round wooden dish, of Ethernan, Ydarnan or Itharnan.' This saint, to whom the church was dedicated, d. among the Picts, 669.

MADDISTON (Polmont). 1366 *R.M.S.* Mandredestona, later Mandrestoun, 1424 Mandirstoun, '*Mandred's* village.' Good study in disappearance of liquids (*n* and *r*). *Cf.* Manderston, Duns.

MAESHOW (Stennis). Famous chambered cairn; *sagas* Orkahaug, 'mighty cairn'; *how* is fr. *haug*. The Maes- is perh. O.N. *mœrst-r*, 'greatest,' *i.e.*, most famous. Possibly a hybrid fr. G. *màs*, 'a buttock.' *Cf.* CYDERHALL.

MAGBY (Ayr). 'Dwelling of *Mæg*,' a name in *Onom.* On *-by*, see p. 41.

MAGDALEN GREEN (Dundee). Site of a chapel to St. Mary Magdalen.

MAGGIEKNOCKATER (Dufftown). G. *màg an fhucadair*, 'field of the fuller.' *Cf.* 1653 Don. Roy M'Nuguttar, Comrie.

MAGUS MOOR (St. Andrew's). Same as MAGASK (Kingskettle), 1517 Over-Magask, 1585 Magas. G. *magh gasc*, 'plain with the point of land' (W.). See GASK.

MAHAICK, L. (Doune). G. *màg fhaitche*, 'plain of the green fields.'

MAIDENHEAD Bay (S. Wigtown). Prob. corrup., in this wanton county, of O.E. *meddan hyð*, 'middle port' or 'Hythe.'

MAIDEN PAP (hill, Caithness, Colvend, and 2 Riccarton, Roxb.). Ca. M. 1595 *Mercator* Mayden papes. Named fr. their shape. The Maidens is name of rocks near Kirkoswald; *cf.* the Middens off Leith and p. 171.

MAINLAND (Orkney and Shetland). Both in *Sagas* Meginland, 'the main or chief land, continent.' O.N. *megin* is lit. 'might.'

MAINS. Common in Sc. for 'farm-house, group of small houses, mansion.' *N.E.D.* says, short form of *domain*; but full proof is lacking. MAINSRIDDELL (Dumfries) gives the owner's name. Gervase de Ridale, *i.e.*, Ryedale, Yorks, Norman favourite of David I, came N. with him.

MAKÉRSTON (Kelso). 1159 Malcaruistun, 1241 -rvestun, 1298 -ristona. '*Malcarf's* village.'

MALSAY (Shetland). Prob. O.N. *a, ay*, 'island,' 'of the stipulation or agreement,' *mál*. But MALLAIG (N.W. Argyll) is prob. 'bay,' Norse G. *aig*, N. *vík*, 'of sea-gulls, maws or mews,' O.N. *má-r*, found as *mall*, *e.g.*, in 1698 Martin, *Voy. St. Kilda.*

MAMBEG (Gareloch). 1248 Mambege and Mammore, 1545 Mawbeg. G. *màm beag* and *mòr*, 'little and big hillock like a breast,' L. *mamma*. *Cf.* Cioch Mhor, 'big breast,' Ben Wyvis.

MAMORE Forest (Lochaber). *a.* 1310 Maymer, 1502 Mawmor, 1504 Mammore. G. *magh mòr*, 'big plain.'

MANISH (Harris). O.N. *má-r*, 'mew, sea-gull,' and *næs*, 'ness, promontory.'

MANNOFIELD (Aberdeen). Robt. Balmanno so named his family estate, *c.* 1790.

MANOR (Peebles). Pron. Mǽner. 1186 Maineure, 1323 Mener. W. *mænor*, 'stone-built mansion.' G. *mainnir* is 'a cattle-pen.' *Cf.* Manorbier and Manordilo, Wales.

MANOR SWARE, SWIRE (Peebles). O.E. *swéora, swíra*, 'neck or pass on a mountain top, a col.' *Cf.* Reidswire, 1515 Redis swyr, and Swyre or Sware, Dumfries; also 1525 Howtell Swyre, Cheviots, Northbld.

MANUEL (Polmont). *c.* 1190 Manuell, 1301 -ewell. A priory founded here in 1156; called, 1707 The Nunnery of Emanuel. But there is no proof that this place is contraction of Immanuel, even though Manuel is a common name. Quite likely it is W. *maen gwel,* 'rock of the sight or view.' There is Ardmanuel, 1681 Arnm-, Kippen, ? 'Height of Manuel'; but if so, why the art. *n* or *an,* 'the'?

MAR (Aberdeensh.). *a.* 1150 *Bk. Deer* Marr. Wh. Stokes thought, a tribe-name cognate with Marsi and Marsigni.

MARCHMONT (Duns). Only so named *c.* 1670, by the first Earl of Marchemont, who orig. wished to be called Earl of March, but Chas. II forbade. *Cf.* 1461 la Marchemond, 'boundary hill.'

MARÉE, L. (Ross). 1633 Maroy, 1656 Mourie. W. says, G. Maruibhe, but old natives say as in Eng. Not fr. the Virgin Mary, but fr. St. *Maelrubha,* who arrived hereabouts fr. Bangor, Ireland, 671. *Cf.* Ardmaree, Berneray.

MARGARET'S, ST. (Edinburgh), ST. MARGARET'S HOPE (Queensferry, Orkney). *c.* 1425 *Wyntoun,* Saynt Margretys Hope, 'haven, refuge (see HOBKIRK) of princess M.,' 'maid of Norway,' d. in Orkney, 1290. The Edinb. places are called fr. Q. Margaret, wife of Malcolm Canmore, d. 1093.

MARK, MARKIE, R. (several). G. *marc,* 'a horse,' with -ie loc.

MARKINCH (Fife). *a.* 1055 Marchinke, 1183 -inge, *a.* 1200 Marcinche, *c.* 1290 Markynchs. G. *marc-innis,* 'horse-meadow'; *cf.* INCH. But the ending was prob. influenced by N. *eng,* 'meadow.'

MARNOCH (Huntly). From St. *Marnoch,* pet form of Ernan, who d. here, 625. *Cf.* KILLEARNAN.

MARSCOW (Skye). O.N. *má-r skóg-r,* 'sea-mew's wood.'

MARTIN'S, St. (Scone). St. *Martin,* of Tours, was teacher of St. Ninian of Whithorn, *c.* 380.

MARYBURGH (Dingswall, also old name of Ft. William). From *Mary,* wife of William III, d. 1694.

MARYCULTER (Deeside). The Templars erected a chapel here to St. Mary, patron of their order, 1487. *Cf.* COULTER and PETERCULTER.

MARYHILL (Glasgow). Named, 1760, fr. *Mary Hill* of Gairbraid, the proprietrix. With MARYWELL, Aboyne, *cf.* LADY- and MOTHERWELL.

MARYTON (Montrose). *a.* 1220 Marington, *c.* 1600 -iton. Not fr. *Mary,* but prob. fr. a man, ? *Marinus* or *Marcwin,* in *Onom.*

Masson, Glen (Kilmun). G. *gleann measain*, 'glen of the puppy or lapdog.' But *a.* 1500 *old MS.* gleann masain, and 1323 Invermesane, *c.* 1370 -measan, Wigton. Perh. fr. a man, *Masson.*

Masterton (Dunfermline). *c.* 1140 Maistertone, *c.* 1248 Villa magistri, 1296 Meystertone. 'Village of the master,' O. Fr. *maistre*, L. *magister.*

Mauchline (Kilmarnock). Ir. *Nennius* Machlind i Cuil, *c.* 1130 Machline, *a.* 1177 Mauhhelin, *c.* 1200 Mauchlyn. G. *magh linne* (W. *llyn*, O. Ir. *lind*), 'plain with the pool.'

Maud (New Deer). Root prob. G. *maodh*, 'soft, moistened.' *Maud*, 'a plaid,' is a late Sc. word.

Mauldslie (Carluke). 1304 Maddisley; also Maldisley. 'Lee, meadow (O.E. *léah*), of ?' The Norm. family De Monte Alto has now as one of its names Maude; see Mold, *Pl. N. Eng. and W.*

Maven, -vine (N. Shetland). Jakobsen says, 1403 Nordhan Mæfeid, *i.e.*, 'North of the narrow isthmus,' 1481 Normaueth. But the present ending is prob. fr. O.N. *vang-r*, 'garden, home.'[1]

Mavisbank (Polton). Sc. *mavis* is 'a thrush,' Fr. *mauvis*, med. L. *malvitius*, root unknown.

Mawcarse (Kinross). Tautology. G. *magh*, 'a plain,' and Carse.

Mawkinhill (Greenock). Sc. *mawkin* is 'a hare.' Orig. *Malkin*, dimin. of Maud or Matilda.

Maxpoffle (St. Boswell's). 1317 -poffil. On Max- see next. *N.E.D.* says *poffle* is 'a small parcel of land, a pendicle,' origin unknown, *cf.* pightle. *Cf.* too the Paphle, Kinross; but its old form seems Popilhall; fr. *popple*, dial. for 'poplar tree,' O.E. *popul*, as in the Eng. Poppleton and -well-.

Maxton (St. Boswell's). 1165–1214 Mackus-, -istun, Maxtoun, *c.* 1240 Makestun. From a man *Maccus*, *c.* 1144 in *Chart. Melrose.* A Maccus was King of the Isles, 973. See -ton, p. 47.

Maxwellheugh (Kelso; see Hesterheugh), Maxwelltown (Dumfries), -ton Braes (Sanquhar). Maxwell is 'wiel' or 'pool of Maccus'; *cf.* The Weal, Maryculter. It was once the name of a parish near Melrose. In 1144 we find Joh. de Mackeswel, 1190 Maxwell. *Cf.* Bothwell, Ordwiel, Bunkle, and the Max Wheel, Kelso.

May, I. of (Frith of Forth). *c.* 1143 *chart.* and *c.* 1200 *Gervase* Mai, *c.* 1165 *Vit. Kentigern* Insula May, *Orkn. Sag.* Maeyar. O.N. *má-ey*, 'sea-mew's isle.'

[1] Schütte, *Gothon. Nations*, II (1933), 442, thinks the ending *-vin*, a very early form, suggests Norse settlement here by the 6th cny.

MAYBOLE (Ayrsh.). 1275 -boill, 1371 -boyl; also Minibole (G. *moine*, 'a moss, a bog'). G. *magh baoghail*, 'plain, moor of danger.'

MAYISH (Brodick). G. *maothais*, 'soft place,' *-ais* suff. of place.

MEALFOURVOUNIE (L. Ness). G. *meall fuar mhonaidh*, 'hill of the cold moor.' Of hills called Meall, lit. 'lump, boss,' Sutherland is full—Meall Garve, Horn, etc. There is even a sunk rock, the Mell, Costa, Orkney.

MEALLANT'SUIDHE, part of Ben Nevis, pron. antée. G. 'hill of the seat.' *Cf.* BEALLACHANTUIE.

MEARNS (Kincardine). *a.* 1200 Moerne, 1337 Miernys. Seems G. *magh Eireann*, 'plain of Eire'; see EARN, and *cf.* MOY and next. In G. a'Mhaoirne, 'the Stewartry,' fr. Ir. and G. *maor*, 'steward.'

MEARNS (Glasgow). *Sic c.* 1160, but 1178 Meorns, 1188 Mernis. 'Plain of EARN,' see above. Water of Earn flows through. The -is or -s is prob. the common *-ais*, suff. of place.

MEDWIN, R. (Carnwath). Brit. *med abhuinn*, 'river extended and full.' *Cf.* R. Medway, Kent, W. *med gwy* ('stream').

MEGGAT Water (St. Mary's L.). *c.* 1206 -gete. G. *meigead* is 'the cry of a kid.' But W. says 'bogginess,' fr. W. *mig-n*, 'bog.' *Cf.* MÉGGERNIE, Glen Lyon, 1502 Megarie.

MEGGINCH (Errol). *c.* 1200 Melginch, *c.* 1240 -ginge, later Melkinche. Perh., as in Cnoc Malagan, Sleat, fr. O. Celt. *mal(a)g*, 'noble,' and *innis*, 'meadow by a river' (W.).

MEIGLE (Newtyle, and hill, Galashiels), MEIGLE Bay (N. Ayrsh.). Ne. M. 1183 Miggil, 1296 Miggyl. The Bay is N. *mjó gil*, 'narrow gill' or 'opening.' W. derives the others fr. W. *mig-dol*, 'bog meadow.' But *cf.* *Cockersand* (Lancs.) *Chart.* Migedale, and Mýdale, Iceland, fr. O.E. *mycge*, M.E. *migge*, O.N. *mý*, 'a midge, gnat'; so this may be 'midge gill.' *Cf.* GLENMIDGE and MIGDALE.

MEIKLE EARNOCK (Hamilton). Sc. *meikle, muckle*, O.E. *mycel, micel*, 'great, large.' See EARNOCK.

MEIKLEOUR (Coupar Angus). 1214 Ure, *a.* 1244 Hure, 1296 de Magna Hure, 1376–7 Muchyluere, 1507 Mekleour. 'The big yew tree,' G. *iubhar*; see above.

MELBY (Shetland). *Old* Medalboer, O.N. for 'middle dwelling,' see -by, p. 41, and *cf.* Norby, Shetland.

MELDRUM, OLD and NEW (Garioch). 1291 Melgedrom, 1296 Melkidrum. Seems like MEGGINCH, fr. O. Celt. *mal(a)g druim*, 'noble hill-ridge.'

MELFORD, -FORT, L. (Lorn). 1403 Milferth. O.N. *mel-r fjorð-r*, 'sand-dune, sand-bank firth or bay.' *Cf.* EISHORT and MELVICH. Milford Haven is of same origin.

MELNESS (Tongue). 1546 Melleness. As above, with *ness*, 'nose, cape.'

MELROSE (Roxbh., Gamrie). Ro. M. *c.* 700 and *Bede* Mailros, *a.* 1124 Malros, *Sim. Durh.* Melros. Brit. *maol, mail ros,* 'bare moor.' *Cf.* Marloes, Pembk., *Tax. Eccl.* Malros.

MELVICH (Reay). O.N. *mel-r vík,* 'sand-dune, sandbank bay.' *Cf.* Achmelvich, Assynt, and MELFORD.

MELVILLE (Lasswade, Ladybank), MT. MELVILLE (St. Andrew's). Galfrida de Malevile, a Norman, is found in Lothian, 1153 and Philippus de Malavilla, *c.* 1230–50. Four Mallevilles or 'bad townships' in Normandy. In *Antiq. Taxat.* the old parish of Melville, Newbattle, is spelt Maleuile, Malauill, also Mailvyn, Maleuyn, hence the surname Melvin, with which Melville often interchanges. The Fife M.'s are recent; Mt. Melville was formerly Craigton.

MEMSIE (Fraserburgh). Perh. G. *màm sìth,* 'breast-like, rounded hill.' *Cf.* CAMPSIE and MAMBEG.

MEMUS (Kirriemuir). Perh. G. *magh meas,* 'plain of fruit.' *Cf.* MEY.

MENDICK (W. Linton). *a.* 1190 Menedicte (Lat. gen.), *c.* 1215. Mynedicht. British. W. *mynyddig,* 'hilly,' would be abnormal. Prob. Corn. *menedh ithic* (*th* muted), 'large hill,' which it is.

MENMUIR (Brechin). *c.* 1280 Menmoreth. Prob. like Ir. Meenmore or *meen mòr,* 'big mountain-meadow,' influenced by O.E. and O.N. *mór,* 'a moor,' in Sc. *muir.* The -eth will be termin.

MENSTRIE (Alloa). 1261 Mestryn, 1263 -treth, 1315 -try, 1505 Menstray. W. *maes-dref, -tref,* 'hamlet in the plain' (W.). *Cf.* NIDDRIE.

MENTEITH (S. Perth). 1175–8 Menetethe, -thet, *a.* 1185 -ted, 1234 Mynyn-, Mynteth, 1724 Monteath. 'Moss, moor,' G. *moine,* 'of R. TEITH.' With 1234 Mynyn- *cf.* W. *mynyndat,* Corn. *menit, -eth,* 'a moor.'

MERCHISTON (Edinburgh, Falkirk). Ed. M. 1266 -chinston, *c.* 1277 *Newbat. Chart.* Merhammeston, 1357 Merchamystona, 1494 -anistoun. 'Village of a man *Markham*' (*Onom.* has only *Mearc.*), confused with *merchant.*

MERKLAND (Glasgow). 1518. 'Ane markland off Gwuan (Govan),' *i.e.*, rented at a mark.

MERRICK (Minigaff). *Pont* Maerach Hill. G. *meurach,* 'pronged or branching place.'

MERSE (Berwicksh., Twynholm). Be. M. 1560 The Merse. O.E. *mersc,* 'marsh'; *merse* in Sc. is 'low, flat land,' not in *N.E.D.* till 1810.

MERTOUN (St. Boswell's). 1250 Meritun (*a.* 1182 Mertona, now Mortonhall, Edinburgh). O.E. *mere-tún,* 'hamlet by the mere' or 'lake.' *Cf.* Merton, N. Devon, *sic* in *Dom.*

MERVYNSLAW (Jedburgh). *c.* 1200 Xernwingeslawe. In this charter, *Nation. MSS. Scotld.* I, 37, *x* stands for *h*, so prob. 'heron's wing hill,' O.E. *hlǽw*. 'Heron' is not in *N.E.D.* till 1302, but this Fr. word was already known here; *cf.* 1144 *Lib. Calchou* (Kelso) Jordanus Hayrun. Changed later to Mervyn- or Marvin-, still a surname.

METHIL (Leven). 1250 -kil. G. *maoth coill*, 'soft, boggy wood.'

METHLICK (Ellon). *a.* 1300 -elak. G. *maoth tulach*, 'soft, boggy hill.' *Cf.* MORTLACH.

METHVEN (Perth). Pron. Meffan. *a.* 1150 Matefen, 1172–8 Mafen, *c.* 1211 Methfen, 1304 Mehtven, 1500 Mechwynn. Prob. W. *medd faen*, 'mead stone' (W.). There was a St. Methvanna's Market, in Fowlis Wester, near by—a dubious saint.

MEY (Dunnet). Loc. of G. *magh*, 'a plain.' *Cf.* MOY, MYE.

MIÁVAIG (Lewis). Capt. Thomas said, O.N. *mjó-r vag-r*, 'narrow bay.' *Cf.* ARISAIG.

MIDCALDER, etc. See CALDER, etc.

MIDDLEBIE (Ecclefechan). *c.* 1280 -elby. 'Middle village,' O.E. and Dan. *middel*, and see -by p. 41. *Cf.* next.

MIDDLEM or MIDHOLM (Selkirk). 'Middle home' or 'meadow.' *Ham* and *holm*, q.v., constantly interchange. MIDDLETON (Midlothian), 1313 Medilton, is similar. Common in England.

MIDLAND (Orphir). 1263 Meðal-land, O.N. for 'middle land.'

MIDMAR (Echt). *a.* 1300 Migmarre. Prob. 'bog,' W. *mig-n*, 'of MAR.' *Cf.* MEGGAT.

MIGDALE (Bonar Br.). Prob. 'midge dale,' see MEIGLE.

MIGVIE (Stratherrick, Tarland, Kirriemuir). Ta. M. *c.* 1160 -aveth, 1183 -uuith. Str. M. is G. Migeaghmaidh, which W. connects with Celt. *mig*, 'bog'; while -veth will be Brit. equivalent of this G. ending, so 'hill-face'; *cf.* ANWOTH and AVIEMORE.

MILK, R. (Annandale). 1116 Abermelc. 'Milky' river, O. Ir. *melg*, 'milk.' *Cf.* 1272 *Cart. Levenax* rivulus de Melych and *c.* 1150 *Reg. Dunferm.* Schira de Gatemilc, near Perth.

MILLBREX (Fyvie). 1577 Mylbrex. Prob. *mill-breaks* or pieces of land broken up by the plough; *cf.* 1794 *O. Stat. Acc.* XI, 152. It might be G. *meall breac*, 'speckled, round hill,' with Eng. pl. *s*.

MILLEUR PT. (L. Ryan). *Pont* Mullawyr. G. *meall odhar*, 'grey hill.'

MILLIFIACH (Beauly). G. *meall a' fitheach* or *fhithiche*, 'hill of the raven.'

MILLIG (Helensburgh). 1294 Muleig, 1644 Milligs. Dimin. of G. *maol*, 'little, round hill.'

MILLIKEN PARK (Johnstone). Founded 1856, and called after Major Milliken, who bought the estate 1733. Milliken is var. of Milligan, Mulligan, G. *maolagan*, 'little shaveling.'

MILLISLE (Whithorn). *Pont* Milnisle. O.E. *mylen*, *miln*, 'a mill.'

MILLTIMBER (Aberdeen). *Timber* is here 'a wood'; see *N.E.D.* *s.v.* sb[4]. *Cf.* Newtimber, Sussex, 1283 -bre.

MILNATHORT (Kinross). Local pron. Millsyforth. 1359 Moloworth, -forth cum molendino, 1372 Milnethort, 1491 The Myllis of Fortht, 1645 Gordon's map, 'Thuart Mills' on 'Fochy Burne.' Curious. 'Mill,' O.E. *miln*, 'on Forth or Fochy' burn. Meaning of this last doubtful, *cf.* FORTH; -thort will be transposition of Forth. But Thorter Fell, New Abbey, is O.N. *þwert*, 'athwart,' Sc. *thortour*, 'transverse, cross.' The 1359 Molo- prob. represents 'mill.'

MILNGAVIE (Glasgow). *Pont* Milgúy, and so pron. still. G. *muileann-gaoithe*, 'a wind mill.'

MILNGRADEN (Coldstream). 1095–8 Greiden(e), 1515 Gradon, *a.* 1850 the Graden. O.E. *græg* (O.N. *grá-r*) *dene*, 'grey-looking DEAN.' Miln- was prefixed by David Milne-Holme, *c.* 1845.

MILTON, many. 1479 Myltoun of Methat, Kilmuir Easter. Twenty Miltons, mostly 'mill-villages,' in England.

MÍNARD (L. Fyne). 'Small bay,' O.N. *minni*, O.E. *min*, *fjord*. See p. 34.

MINCH (channel, Lewis). In W. Ross it has no name; but, by some, at N. end, called Cuan Laodhasach, 'Lewis Sea,' and at S. end, Cuan Sgiathanach, 'Skye Sea.' Prob. Minch is a sailors' name, *cf.* ST. KILDA, mistakenly picked up fr. Norsemen, who would speak of C. Wrath or Butt of Lewis as *megin nös*, 'great ness'; *cf.* Mygennæs, Færoes, and *megin-land*, 'mainland.' *Megin* regularly becomes Min-, as in MINGINISH, MINGARRY, MINGULAY, and *min-nish* would soon become Minch.

MINGARRY (Ardnamurchan). G. Mioghairidh, 1493 Mewar, 1499 Mengarie, 1505 Meary. O.N. *mikinn* (acc. masc. of *mikil*) *garð-r*, 'great enclosure' (M.). *Cf.* next.

MINGINISH (Skye), MINGULAY, -LA (Out. Hebrides). Sk. M. is in G. *rudha mòr*, 'great ness'; see MINCH. Heb. M. is G. Miodhulaidh, 1580 Megala. Prob. 'great isle,' N. *mikill-a*, though it may be 'middle isle,' O.N. *meðal*, Dan. *middel*.

MINISHANT (Maybole). G. *muine seant* (L. *sanctus*), 'sacred thicket.' *Cf.* CLAYSHANT.

MINNI-, MONIGAFF (Newton Stewart). 1504 Monygof, 1573 Mynnie Gof. W. *mynyd y gof*, 'hill of the smith,' or G. *moine gobha*, 'moor of the smith.'

MINTLAW (Peterhead). 'Hill,' Sc. *law*, O.E. *hlǽw*, 'on which grows mint,' O.E. *mint*. *Cf.* Minstead, Hants, *Dom.* Mintestede.

MINTO (Denholm). *Sic* 1275, but 1166 Munethov, 1296 Mynetowe, *c.* 1320 Minthov. May be as above; but prob. O.W. *minit*, W. *mynydd*, 'a hill,' and Sc. *how*, O.E. *holh*, *holg*, 'a hollow, a hole.' *Cf.* STOBO, also Minton, *Pl. N. Eng.*

MOCHRUM (Pt. William). 1329 Mouchrome, 1341 Machrome. Old loc. G. *mo chruim*, fr. *magh crom*, 'crooked plain.' *Cf.* MOY and MEARNS.

MOFFAT (Dumfriessh.). 1179 Moffet, 1296 -fete. Prob. as above, O.G. loc. *mo feta*, G. *magh fada*, 'long plain,' exactly the site.

MOI-, MOYDART (Arisaig). *a.* 1292 Muddeward, 1309 Modworth, 1372 Mudewort, 1532 Moydort. *Mud* is not a N. root, so prob. '*fjord*, bay of *Mundi*' (M.). *Cf.* the name Tormoid fr. Thormund, and KNOYDART.

MOLENDINAR Burn (Glasgow). 1185 *Jocelyn* Mellindonor. Said to be rivus molendinarius, 'miller's stream.' But 1185 looks like G. *meall an dhonair*, 'hill of the stranger,' where now is the Necropolis.

MOLLAND (Drymen). G. *mòilean*, 'a little lump.' *Cf.* DRUMMOND.

MONADHLIATH Mtns. (Inverness-sh.). Pron. Monachlée. G. 'grey, or light blue mountain or moor.'

MONAN'S, St. (Elie). 1565 Sanct Monanis. Perh. bp. of Clonfert, d. 572. Said to be *c.* 1143 *I. of May chart.* Inverrin.

MONCRIEFF Hill (Perth). *a.* 1100 *Tighern.* ann. 726 Monid Croib, 728 Monagh Craebi, *a.* 1400 *Ann. Clonmacn.* Moynid Crewe. G. *monadh craoibh*, 'hill with the trees.'

MONCUR, -QUHUR (Carmylie). *c.* 1240 Muncur, 1245 -chur. G. *moine chuir*, 'moss, moor with the bend,' G. *car*, *cuir*. *Cf.* STRACHUR.

MONDYNE(S) (Fordoun). 1251 Monachedin. G. *monadh eadain*, 'moor with the slope or hill face.'

MONESS (Aberfeldy). Looks like G. *moine eas*, 'moor of the waterfalls.' But W. says, *i mbun eas*, 'near waterfalls.'

MONÉYDIE (Luncarty). 1285 -edy. Prob. = MONDYNE, here in loc.

MONIACK Easter, Wester (Beauly). 1221 Monychoc, *c.* 1235 Monchitech. Prob. G. *moine chiteach*, 'showery moor.'

MONIAIVE (Thornhill). The -aive pron. as in ivy. *Sic a.* 1684, but 1560 Monyyfe, 1636 -eve, 1779 Minnyhive. Prob. G. *moine èibhe*, 'moss, moor of the cry or howl.'

MONIFIETH (Carnoustie). 1178 Muni-, *c.* 1205 Monifod, *c.* 1220 -fodh, -foth, Munifeth, 1242 -feit. G. *moine fòide*, 'moss, moor with the peats.' *Cf.* Monfod, Ardrossan, 1150 Monfoit, 1321 -fode.

Monikie (Carnoustie). Pron. -éeky. *c.* 970 *Pict. Chron.* Eglis ('church') Monichti, 1178–98 Monickyn, Munickkin, 1189–99 Munickky; Monechata and Monichi also occur. May be fr. a saint, see Eglismonichty. But it may be G. *moine èchta,* 'moor of slaughter.'

Monimail (Ladybank). 1250 -mel, 1275 -ymaile, 1495 -meal (so still pron.). G. *moine mil,* nom. *meall,* 'moss, moor with the hill.'

Monimusk (Alford). *Sic* 1315 but *c.* 1170 Monimusc. Perh. G. *moine muiseig,* 'bog of the scolding woman'; but *Musk* is an old Ir. personal name. *Musk* sb. is not in Eng. till *c.* 1400.

Monkcroft (Crieff). 1271 Mukracht, *c.* 1609 Muckcroft. Modern corrup. of G. *mucaireachd,* 'a herding of swine.'

Monkland, Old and New (Glasgow). 1323 Munkland—belonging to the see of Glasgow. Monkton (Prestwick). Pron. Múnton. 1163 Munctune, 1275 Monktoun. It belonged to Paisley Abbey.

Monquhítter (Turriff). Perh. G. *monadh mhiodair,* 'moor or hill with the pasture-ground.'

Monreith (Mochrum). 1481 Mureith, 1491 -rith, later Menrethe. Perh. G. *muin riabhach,* 'grey back.'

Monteith, see Menteith. Monteviot, see Teviot.

Montgreenan (Kilmarnock). 1480 -grenane, *Pont* Mongrynen. G. *monadh grianain,* 'hill of the sunny spot' or 'summer-house.'

Montrose. *c.* 1178 Munros, *a.* 1200 Vetus Monros, 1296 Montrose, 1322 Monros, 1488 Montross. G. *moine rois,* 'moss on the promontory,' which applies to the site of Old Montrose.

Monynut Water (Lammermuirs). *c.* 1200 Monimet, Maninet, *Pont* Monynett. G. *moine,* 'moss, moor,' and perh. *neid,* 'with the circular hollow,' lit. 'nest.' W. cannot say.

Monzie (Crieff). Pron. Mŏnée. 1226–34 Mugedha, Muyhe, 1282 Moythethe. W. thinks, G. *mag iodh,* O. Ir. *ith,* 'plain of corn,' influenced by G. *moine,* 'moor.' *Cf.* Moy and next.

Monzievaird (Crieff). *c.* 1200 Muithauard, 1203 Monewarde, 1251 Moeghavard, 1279 Morgoauerd (corrupt). G. *magh,* in its form Moy, 'plain,' or *moine,* 'moor,' *a' bhàird,* 'of the bard or rhymer.' *Cf.* above.

Moonzie (Cupar). *c.* 1230 Mooney, and so still pron. May be = Monzie.

Moorfoot Hills (S. Midlothian). *c.* 1142 Morthwait, -thuweit. O.N. *mór þveit,* 'moor place,' lit. 'bit cut off.' *Cf.* Murraythwaite.

Morangie (Tain). Pron. Mórinjy. 1457 Morinchy, 1520 -inch. G. *mòr innis, innse,* 'big inch' or 'links, meadows.' *Cf.* 1550 Morinche, Killin.

Morar (Arisaig). *a.* 1292 Morderer, 1343 -hover, Morware, *a.* 1371 Moruar, 1372 Moreobyr. G. *mòr dhobar,* 'big water.' But *a.* 1500 Moiroin, 1517 Moroyn. G. *mòr sròn,* 'big nose or cape.'

Moray. *c.* 970 *Pict. Chron.* in Moreb (a loc.), *a.* 1100 *Tighern.* Moreb, 1124 *Bk. Scon* Morauia, *c.* 1136 Muref, *a.* 1199 -ewe, *c.* 1205 *Layamon* Muræf, -æiue, *Ulst. Ann.* ann. 1085 Muireb, *c.* 1225 *Orkn. Sag.* Mærhaefi, *c.* 1295 Morref, *Ann. Innisfail* Muriamh ('men of Moray'). The first part is G. *muir, mor,* 'the sea.' The second is prob. the old loc. *-aibh,* so, 'beside the sea'; *cf.* Morrab, Penzance, the same word, and Gallaibh, 'among the strangers,' old name of Caithness, also Kinneff. But, though there is no *t* in the oldest forms, W. is sure it is Celt. *Mori-treb,* 'sea settlement,' W. *tref, tre,* 'a house,' *cf.* Niddrie. It is useless, as some do, to compare Morfe Forest, Salop. 736 *chart.* Moerheb. It is far fr. the sea, and is prob. W. *morfa,* Corn. *morva,* 'moor, marsh.'

Moray Firth. *Orkn. Sag.* Breidafjord, 'broad firth.'

Mordington (Berwick). *c.* 1098 Morthintun, 1240 -dingtona. Prob. 'village of the sons of *Morta,*' 1 in *Onom.*, see p. 52. But Ardnimord, Kirkcowan, 1527 -namoird, 1627 -enmort, is 'height of the murder,' G. *an moirt.*

More, Ben (many). G. *mòr,* 'big.'

Morebattle (Kelso). *a.* 800 *Hist. St. Cuthbt.* Scerbedle (*Sc* error for *M.*), 1116 Mereboda, 1170 -botle, 1575 Morbottle. O.E. *mere-botl,* 'lake-dwelling.' *Botl* is cognate with the common O.N. *ból*; *cf.* Newbattle and Harbottle, Rothbury. The 1116 -boda is early form of *booth* (O.N. *búð,* Dan. and Sw. *bod,* 'abode'), earlier than any in *N.E.D.*

Morel (Tomatin). G. Mòirl. Doubtful; not = Balmoral.

Morham (Haddington). *Sic* 1250 and Morton (several) *sic* 1220, both are 'village on the moor,' O.E. and O.N. *mór.*

Mormond (Fraserburgh). G. *mòr monadh,* 'big hill.'

Morningside (Edinburgh, Bathgate). 'Morning seat,' see Muiravonside.

Morphie (St. Cyrus). *a.* 1370 -phy, -fy. Prob. Pict., W. *morfa,* Corn. *morva,* 'a moor, marsh.' W. says it also means 'a sea plain.'

Morrone (hill, Braemar). G. *mòr sròn,* 'big snout or headland.'

Mortlach (Dufftown). 1157 Murthilloch, *a.* 1300 Morthilache, 1639 Murthlack. G. *mòr t(h)ulach,* 'big hillock.' *Cf.* Murthly.

MORVEN (ben, Ballater). G. *mòr bheinn,* 'big ben.' The Argyll M. is a bad spelling of next.

MORVERN (N. Argyll). *Sic* 1390, but 1343 Garwmorwarne (G. *garbh,* 'rough'), 1475 -varne, *a.* 1500 *Bk. Clanranald* Na Morbhairne; so in G. still, sometimes Mhorarnia. M. says, G. *mòr bhearna,* 'big passes,' or, as Gillies renders, 'big cleft,' which runs right through Morvern.

MOSSAT (Kildrummy). *Old* Massach. Either G. *mosach,* 'nasty, stinking place,' or *measach,* 'place full of fruits.' For ending *cf.* ELLIOT.

MOSSFENNAN (Broughton). *a.* 1249 Mospennoc, 1296 Mesfennon. Prob. orig. W. *maes pennog,* 'plain with the little hill.' Influenced by Eng. *moss* and G. *bheinnan,* 'little ben.'

MOSSGIEL (Mauchline). O.N. *gíl,* 'a narrow glen.'

MOSSPAUL (Ewes Water). The -paul is prob. W. *pwll,* 'pool, stream'; *pawl* is 'a pole, stake.' MOSSPEEBLE close by is fr. W. *pebyll,* 'tents'; *cf.* PEEBLES.

MOTHERWELL (Lanarksh.). *a.* 1250 *M. Paris* Matervelle, 1265 Moydirwal, 1362 Modyrwaile, 1373 -vale. Either 'well,' O.E. *wella,* or 'pool, eddy,' O.E. *wæl* (*cf.* BOTHWELL) 'of the mother,' L. *mater,* O.E. *módor,* O.N. *móthir,* prob. the Virgin Mother, *cf.* LADY- and MARYWELL.

MOULIN (Pitlochry). 1207 Molin, 1323 -lyn. G. *maolinn,* 'bare hillock' (W.). MOULINEARN may be M. FEARN, *f* lost by aspiration, as alders were plentiful there.

MOUND, The (Dornoch). This mound or breakwater, built at the head of L. Fleet, 1816, must not be confounded with the oft-mentioned 'The Mounth,' *i.e.,* the Grampians, 1198–9 Muneth, G. *monadh,* 'a hill.'

MOUNT BENGER (Yarrow). 1423 Mountbergeris, Montbargere, 1563 -bern(e)ger. G. *bearna geàrr,* 'the short pass.'

MOUNT FLORIDA and MT. VERNON (Glasgow). Recent. The latter is in Glasgow directory, 1787.

MOUNTHOOLY (Aberdeensh. and Roxbh.). Perh. G. *monadh chùile,* 'hill with the corner or nook,' *cùil.* But Tomnahulla, Galway, is Ir. and G. *tuam na h'ulaidh,* 'mound with the altar tomb'; in G. rather, 'grave with the treasure.'

MOUSA (Lerwick). Pron. Moosa. *Orkn. Sag.* Mósey. Doubtful. Perh. O.N. *mose,* Dan. and Sw. *mos-a,* 'moss isle'; *cf. c.* 1500 Nethirmousland, Stromness. Jakobsen says, fr. O.N. *mó-r,* 'a moor,' where *r* may not belong to the root.

MOUSWALD (Ruthwell). Pron. Mŭsald. 1303 Mousewald, *a.* 1321 Musfald, *c.* 1340 -fold. O.E. *meós-fald* or Dan. *mos-fold,* 'moss-grown enclosure.' *Cf.* FAULDHOUSE.

MOWHAUGH (Morebattle). *c.* 1150 Moille. Prob. G. *moil, -le*, 'a heap'; *cf.* W. *moel*, 'a hill,' and see HAUGH.

MOY (2 in Inverness). *c.* 1235 Muy, 1497 Moye. In G. a' Mhoigh, loc. of *magh*, 'at the plain'; *cf.* MOCHRUM, Muuie, Sutherland, 1379 Muuge, and MYE.

MOYNESS (Forres). 1238 Moythus, *c.* 1285 Motheys. G. *maothais*, 'soft place'; *cf.* ALVES, FORRES, etc.

MUASDALE (Kintyre), MUSDALE (Rum). Either fr. O.N. *mús*, Dan. *muus*, 'a field mouse,' or O.N. *mose*, 'moss.'

MÚCHALLS (Aberdeen). 1302 Marisio quod vocatur anglice Muchelli. *Cf.* 'Muchals or Muchil in Mar,' 1268 Mukual, and *a.* 1321 Mukulis, -cullis, Perthsh. Prob. G. *mucail*, 'place full of swine.' The district E. of St. Andrews, now 'Boarhills,' was 1183 Mucrosin or Muckross, 'pig's, boar's wood.'

MUCK (Hebrides). *c.* 1370 *Fordun* Helantmok, G. *eilean muc*, 'isle of swine.'

MUCKAIRN (Taynuilt). G. Mùcharn. 1527 Mocarne, 1723 Mucarn. Prob. G. *muc-chàrn*, 'sows' cairn or heap.'

MUCKERSIE, see CARSE.

MUCKHART (Dollar). 1250 Mukard. G. *muc-àrd*, 'boar's height.'

MUCKLE FLUGGA (Unst). 'Big precipices,' Sc. *muckle*, O.N. *mi-, mykill*, 'big,' and *flug*, pl. *fluga*, 'precipices.'

MUGDOCK (Strathblane). *Sic* 1680 but *Ann. Cambr.* 750 Magedauc, Mocetauc, 1392 Mukdoc. Prob. G. *mag a' dhaboich*, 'plain of ploughed land.' *Cf.* DOCHART.

MUGDRUM I. (Newburgh). *c.* 1190 Mukedrum. G. *muc druim*, island like 'a sow's back.'

MUGSTOT, -STAD (Skye). 1773 -stot. 'Monk's place,' O.N. *muk-r*, 'monk,' and *stað-r*, see p. 42. *Cf.* Baile Mhanaich ('of the monk'), Uist, and Mangaster, 2 in Shetland, also Mockley Wood, Henley in Arden, *c.* 1250 Monkelee.

MUICHDHUI Ben (Braemar). G. *beinn muic duibhe*, 'mountain of the black boar.'

MUIRAVONSIDE (Polmont). Quite a recent 'improvement.' *c.* 1190 *chart.* Sedem Sancti Morgani, *Eng. vsn.* Morganes sete, 'Seat, residence of Morgan,' who would be fr. Wales; *cf.* LONGMORN. But 1508–9 Morowyngsidis, 1693 Mor(e)vinside, 1707 Moran-, 1722 Muiring-, 1725 Muiraving-, 1733 Muiravenside. *Morrowing* (Chaucer) and *Morrin* or *morwyn* (1503 *Sc. Acts*) are old forms of *morning*. Thus the name is = MORNINGSIDE or 'seat,' as *side* often means.

MUIRDRUM (Carnoustie). Hybrid. See DRUM. MUIRHOUSE (Edinburgh), see MURROES. MUIR of ORD (Beauly), see ORD.

MUIRNEAG (Lewis). G. dimin. of *muirn*, 'cheerfulness, joy,' name of fine hill, the only one fishers here can see far out at sea. *Cf.* Muirne Meall, Islay, 'joy hill,' an unusual order in G.

MULBEN (Elgin). *a.* 1328 Molben, 1367–8 Mulbynne. G. *maol beinn*, 'bare, round hill.'

MULL I. *c.* 150 *Ptolemy* Maleos, *a.* 700 *Adamn.* Malea insula, *Sagas* Myl, *Act. Sanct.* Mula, 1542 Mowill. G. Muile. Wh. Stokes thought this Pict. for 'mountainous.' W.'s suggestions are doubtful.

MULL of DEERNESS or MOULHEAD (Orkney). *Sagas* Múli, 1795 Mule of D. MULL of GALLOWAY, *c.* 1375 *Barbour* Mullyr Snwk. 1536 *Bellenden* Ane gret snout of craggis . . . callit be the peple the Mulis Nuk, 1564 the Mule of G. Mull in Wigtown is now pron. Moyle. G. *maol*, 'brow of a rock, cape,' fr. *maol* 'bald, bare,' cognate with O.N. *múli*. Then see *N.E.D. nook* sb[4], and *snook* sb[1], which means 'promontory,' so Mullyr (Norse gen.) Snwk, etc., are tautologies. *Barbour* already calls the MULL of KINTYRE 'the Mole.'

MUL-, MALLOCH (Falkirk). G. *mullach*, 'a small hill.' *Cf.* Balmalloch, Kilsyth, and Balmullo, Leuchars, *sic* 1517.

MUMRILLS (Falkirk). 1552 Mum-, Munmerallis. Perh. G. *moine*, 'moss,' or *màm*, 'round hill,' 'with the oaks,' Ir. *ral*, *rail*, 'an oak'; perh. 'of the mistake,' G. *mearail*.

MUNCHES (Buittle). *Sic* 1457, but 1486 -cheis. O.G. *moine cheis*, 'moor of the furrow' or 'the swine.'

MUNGAL (Falkirk). 1508 Monguellis, 1552 Ovir et Nethir Mongwell, *Pont* Mungill. G. *moine*, 'moss'—the site was once a bog—and perh. O.W. *gwawl*, 'a wall,' *i.e.*, the Roman Wall near it.

MUNLOCHY (Fortrose). *Sic* 1328 but 1605 Mullochie. Diack says, in G. *magh n' lòchaidh*, 'plain of the black place.' But W. holds it is *mun* for *bun locha*, 'at the foot of the loch.'

MURKLE (Thurso). *Old* Myrhol. O.N. for 'dark, murky hole.' *Cf.* Markle, E. Linton—*mirk* in Sc. 6–9 is *mark*—and Mircol, Lewis.

MÚRLAGAN (Inverroy, L. Ness, etc.). In. M. 1466 Murvalgane, 1476 Murlagane, 1568 Moir-valagane. L. Arklet M. 1505 Murvalgan. Strathtummel M. *old* -vullagan. G. *murbhlagan*, pron. murrulagan, dimin. of **murbhlag*, Adamn. *murbulc*, 'sea-inlet like a sack,' *muir*, 'the sea.' (W.) *Cf.* VORLICH.

MURRAYFIELD (Edinburgh) seems called after Arch. *Murray*, an early 18th cny. advocate.

MURRAYTHWAITE (Ecclefechan). *a.* 1300 Moryquhat, 1303 Mourythwayt, 1550 Murfatt. 'Moory clearing,' O.N. and O.E. *mór*, 'a moor'; the adj. not in *N.E.D.* till 1387; and O.N. *þveit*, 'place, bit cut off.' Thwaites are common S. of Carlisle. *Cf.* MOORFOOTS and Nether Murthat, Kirkpatrick juxta. The surname Murray comes fr. MORAY. The Murray family became landlords here in 15th cny., hence change of spelling.

MURROES (Dundee). *c.* 1205 Muraus, 1250 Moreus, 1372 Morhuse, while 1376 Morhuse is Muirhouse, Edinb. Prob., as locally interpreted, 'moor-houses,' O.E. *mór-hús*.

MURTHILL (Tannadice). 1360 Murethlyn, *c.* 1390 Morthyll. Prob. G. *mòr tulach*, 'big hill,' and so = MURTHLY (Dunkeld). But the ending has been conformed to Eng. *hill*.

MÚRTLE (Cults). Prob. G. *mòr tuil*, 'big stream' or 'flood,' the Dee. *Cf.* DUTHIL.

MUSAL (Durness). 1560 Moswell. Prob. N. *mose-fjal*, 'moss fell' or 'highland.' Fell in Hebrides is usually -val; see p. 39.

MUSSELBURGH (Midlothian). 1189 Muxelburg, 1200 Muschel-, 1250 Muskilburk, O.E. *muscle, musele*, 'a mussel.' On -burgh see p. 51.

MUTHILL (Crieff). Pron. Mewthil. *c.* 1198 Mothel, *c.* 1200 Muothle. Not O.E. *mót hil*, 'hill of the meeting,' *cf.* the Mute Hill Scone, but G. or Ir. *maothail*, 'soft, spongy ground'; and Muthillock, Drumblade, and the 2 Moathills, Aberdeensh., have prob. similar origin.

MUTTONHOLE (said to be 16 in Sc.). 1601 'The Mutton hoill, Cowper, Perth.' Often thought *moot-town-hill*, see above, but the *u* or *oo* here is long and in Mutton-, short. So *cf.* Mitton, common Eng. name; *Dom.* has 6 Mitunes, 2 Mutones, which *a.* 1300 become Mutton; prob. fr. O.E. *gemythan* or *mythe*, 'waters' meet, junction of two streams or roads.'

MYE (Buchlyvie). *Sic* 1510. G. *maigh*, loc. of *magh*, 'a plain.' *Cf.* MOY.

MYLNEFIELD (Dundee). O.E. *miln*, 'a mill.'

MYRESIDE (Edinburgh). O.N. *mýri, mýrr*, 'bog, swamp.' *Cf.* WHITEMIRE.

NAB, The (Lerwick). N. *nabbi*, 'a knoll, a point.' NABDEN (Paxton). *c.* 1100 Cnapadene, *c.* 1120 Cnapedane. 'DEAN, valley by the hill-top,' O.E. *cnœp*, N. *nabbi*, W. and G. *cnap*, 'knob, little hill.' *Cf.* KNAPDALE.

NACKERTY (Bothwell). G. *cnac àirde*, 'crack, fissure height.'

NAIRN, R. and town. G. Narrun. *c.* 1200 *Hoveden* Ilvernarran (*l* for *n*), 1236 Inuer-, 1283 Inernarn (still heard). Wh. Stokes thought it = next. Inchnairn, Lochalsh, 1548 Inchenarne, G. *innis an fhearna*, 'alder-haugh,' cannot be the same.

NAVER, R. (Sutherland). G. Na'r, Stranar. Prob. *Ptolemy's* Nabaros, 1268 Strathnauir, 1427 -nawarne. Perh. pre-Celt. cognate with Navarre. Perh. fr. Celt. *nabho*, 'divided.' It is so, at its mouth, by a high bank. M. preferred *nav*, *snav*, G. *snàmh*, 'to swim, flow,' and W. root *nabh*, 'cloud, fog.' *Cf.* R. Nevern, Pembroke, *Hen. Hunt.* Navarri, 1603 Ysh nyver. NAVAR, Brechin, W. thinks 'sanctuary,' Celt. *nemed*, 'of St. Barr,' 1232 Neuethbarr; see DUNBAR.

NAVIDALE (Helmsdale). G. *Neimhe' dail.* Hybrid. O. Celt. *nemed*, see above, and DALE.

NAVITY (Kinross, Cromarty). Ki. N. *old* Nevathy, -ody. Cr. N. 1578 Navite. G. Neamhaididh for *neimhidh*, 'church land, hallowed meeting-place'; *cf.* the common Celt. *nemed- et*, see above.

N(E)ANT, R. (L. Etive). G. *nenaid* pl. *neannta*, 'nettles.' (W.)

NEDD (Assynt). G. 'sheltered place like a nest'; *cf.* Corn. *neid*, 'a nest,' and Neath, Wales.

NEIDPATH Cas. (Peebles). Prob. fr. Dan. *nöd*, 'neat-cattle.'

NEILSTON (Barrhead). *c.* 1160 -toun, *a.* 1214 Neleston. The O'Neils were a royal race in Ireland. Neil is for Nigel.

NELDRICKEN, L. (Minigaff). Dimin. of ELRICK, with *an*, 'the,' prefixed. (W.)

NELL, L. (S. of Oban). G. *loch nan eala*, 'loch of the swans.' L. Nell, Ledaig, *sic* 1772, is a sea-loch with a transferred name. Its true name is ARDMUCKNISH.

NEMPHLAR (Lanark). *Sic* 1404. Prob. G. *naomh làr*, 'sacred ground'; *cf.* Celt. *nemed*, 'sanctuary.' For the intruded *p cf.* INCH na DAMPH.

NENTHORN (Kelso). *c.* 1150 Naythinthern, 1159 Neithanesthyrn, *c.* 1204 Naythansthorn, 1296 Nethenthyrn. Prob. boundary mark like Nicor's and Tiw's thorn (O.E. *þorn*), Green *Mak. England* 183. As to this *Nethan* or *Nechtan cf.* CAMBUSNETHAN.

NESS, L. and R. (Inverness, Lewis). *a.* 700 *Adamn.* R. and L., Nesa, Nisa, *a.* 1300 Nis. Origin unknown. Lewis N. is O.N. and O.E. *næs*, 'nose, cape.'

NESTING (Lerwick). O.N. *næs þing*, 'cape of the thing or meeting.' *Cf.* TINGWALL.

NETHERCLEUGH (Lockerbie), see BUCCLEUCH. NETHERURD, see KIRKURD.

NETHY, R. and Br. (Grantown). See ABERNETHY. Henderson thought fr. root of *nixie* (*niks-a*), water-spirit. When Nethy is in spate they say, Tha na neithichean a tighinn, 'the nixies are coming.'

NEVIS, Ben and R. (Ft. William). G. Nibheis, pron. Néevush. *Sic* 1532, but 1552 Nevess, 1769 -ish. Colin Livingstone suggested G. *ni-mhaise*, 'no beauty,' appropriate to this ungainly ben. But M. connected with the nymph *Nebestis*, fr. *neb*, 'cloud.' W. prefers O.Ir. *nem*, 'the venemous'!

NEW ABBEY (E. Kirkcudbt.). 1310 La Novelle Abbey. The Abbey of Sweetheart or Douce Cœur founded here by Lady Devorgilla, 1275.

NEWARK (Pt. Glasgow, Yarrow, Sanday). Ya. N. 1508 Newwerk; *cf.* 1492 'Newark one Spey.' 'New work' or 'castle'; *cf.* bulwark, outwork, etc., Wark on Tweed, 1138 Werch, and Newark, Notts, 1066 Newarcha.

NEWARTHILL (Motherwell). *Pont* Neuwhil. Tautology. G. *nuadh àrd*, 'new height.'

NEWBATTLE (Dalkeith), NEWBOTTLE (Beith). Da. N. 1141 Niwebothla, *c.* 1145 Newbotill, 1295 Neubattaill, *a.* 1500 Nowbatile, 1825 Newbottle. O.E. *neowe botl*, 'new dwelling,' as opposed to Elbottle, Dirleton, 'old dwelling,' site of convent fr. Berwick on Tweed. *Cf.* MOREBATTLE and Newbottle, Durham.

NEWBIGGING (several). Oxnam N. 1153 -bigginghe, Edinb. N. 1331 -byggyn. *Bigging*, Dan. *bygning*, is Sc. for 'building,' in Orkney (S. Ronaldshay) 'a group of buildings.' The earliest quot. in *N.E.D.* is *c.* 1250. Five Newbiggins in England.

NEWBURGH (N. Fife, Ellon). Fi. N. *a.* 1130 *Sim. Durh.* ann. 756 Ad Niwanbyrig, id est, ad Novam Civitatem, 1266 *chart.* Novus burgus juxta monasterium de Lindores. 1309 Noviburgum. So it is not very new! On *burgh* see p. 50.

NEWBURN (Largo). *c.* 1135–1250 Nithbren. Prob. Celt. *newydd bryn*, 'new hill,' or fr. W. *pren*, 'tree.' (W.) But Newburn, Northumbd., is *a.* 1130 Nyweburne. *Cf.* NITH.

NEWCASTLETON (S. Roxbh.). 1275 Cassiltoun. NEWMILNS or 'mills' (Kilmarnock), 1503 Newmylns. NEWPORT (Dundee). There is a *c.* 1200 Newporth, *Melrose Chart.* I, 33. Nine in England.

NEW GALLOWAY (Kirkcudbt.). 1682 The New Town of GALLOWAY.

NEWHAVEN (Leith). 1510 *Edinb. Chart.* 'The new haven lately made by the said king,' James IV., 1536 The New Havin.

NEWINGTON (Edinburgh). Here quite recent, but often in *Dom.* as Newentune, Neweton, 'new town,' On *ing* see p. 52.

NEWLANDS (Peebles, Falkirk). Pe. N. 1275 Newlandis. But N., Lanarksh. is *old* Nevylands, G. *neimhidh*, 'church land.' *Cf* NAVITY.

NEWSTEAD (Melrose). *Stead* is O.E. *stede*, Dan. *sted*, 'a place'; *cf.* farm-steading, and N., Notts, 1189 de Novo Loco. Near by is Red Abbey Stead.

NEWTON (many, over 30 in England), NEWTON DON (Kelso), *c.* 1152 Newtoun. The Dons were lairds. NEWTON GRANGE (Dalkeith), see ABBOTSGRANGE, NEWTON or KIRK- (Midcalder), 1250 Neutun. NEWTON of AYR, *c.* 1280 Newtoun de Are. NEWTON STEWART (Kirkcudbt.). Wm. *Stewart,* 3rd son of Earl of Galloway, obtained charter here, 1677.

NEWTONMORE, better -MUIR (Kingussie). G. *Baile ùr an t'slèibh,* 'new village on the moor.'

NEWTON WOOLMET (Dalkeith). *c.* 1150 Wymet; also -med, -meth, Womett, *c.* 1630 Umat. Pron. Oomet. G. *uamhach,* 'place full of caves.' For the ending *cf.* ELLIOT. Omit is an Edinb. surname.

NEWTYLE (Coupar Angus). *a.* 1182 Neutyle, 1199 -tile. G. *nuadh tulach,* 'new hill.' *Cf.* NEWART.

NIDDRIE (Musselburgh, Winchburgh). *a.* 1249 Nodref, 1266 Noderyf, 1296 Nudreff, 1506 Nudry, 1572 Nidderie. W. *nuadh tref,* 'new house or settlement' = Newton. (W.) N. MARISCHALL (Liberton). 1363 Nudre Marescalli, lit. 'of the horse tender, farrier.' But the Sc. *Marshal* was a high officer of state; *c.* 1144 *Reg. St. Andr.* Malothen le Mareschald. The earliest in *N.E.D.* is 1258.

NIGG (Aberdeen, Invergordon). Ab. N. *c.* 1250 Nig, Nyge. In. N. 1257 Nig. This seems a case of survival of the art., G. *an uig,* 'the bay'; or *n'eig,* 'the notch,' loc. of *eag.* (W.)

NINIAN'S, St. (Stirling). [1147 Egglis, G. *eaglais,* 'church,' 1207 Kirketoune], 1242 Ecclesia Scti Niniani de Kirketoun, 1301 Seint Rineyan. 1457 Sanct Rynnans chapel. Many chapels in Sc. dedicated to St. Ninian, see p. 65.

NIS-, NESBIT (Edrom, Jedburgh, Biggar). Ed. N. *a.* 1138 Nesebite. Je. N. *c.* 1130 Nesebita, 1147–50 Nesbet, *c.* 1260 -byth. Prob. *Ness-bit,* 'prominent projecting site,' which always seems to suit, O.E. and O.N. *nœs,* 'nose, ness, cape,' mid. Eng. and Sc. *nese,* and O.E. *bita,* O.N. *biti,* 'a bit, a mouthful.' *Bit* is Sc. for 'piece of ground.'

NITH, R. and NITHSDALE (Dumfries). Perh. *c.* 150 *Ptolemy* Noouios, *Bede* Nidd and Nid-uari,[1] tribe of Galloway Picts, 1181 Nud, *c.* 1240 Nyth. *c.* 1124 Stranit, 1124–40 Strad-nitt, 1181 -nud, all strath-, but 1256 Niddesdale. Prob. root as in W. *newydd,* G. *nuadh,* L. *novus,* 'new.' *Cf.* NEWBURN and NUDE.

NITSHILL (Paisley). ? 'nuts hill,' O.E. *hnut,* Sc. *nit,* 'a nut.'

NODDSDALE (Largs). Pron. Noddle. *Pont* Nodsdale, Noddisdale, through which is 'Nodle fluvius.' O.N. *nauta, nauts dal,* 'neat or cattle dale.' *Cf.* NOLTLAND.

[1] That is Nidwara, 'dwellers by the Nith.'

NOE Glen (Ben Cruachan). The G. pron. varies between *gleann nodha* and *otha*. Perh. G. *nodha*, 'new,' *i.e.*, fresh, green.

NOLTLAND (Westray, Ork.). O.N. *nauta-land*, 'cattle,' Sc. *nowt*, 'land.' *Cf.* NODDSDALE.

NONAKILN (Rosskeen). 1563 Newnakle. G. *Neo' na Cille*, 'glebe of the church.' (W.)

NORMAN'S LAW (Cupar). Hill called after Aymer de Valence, earl of Pembroke, reputed defeated here, 1298.

NORRISTON (Stirling). *Norrie* is a common Sc. surname. *Cf.* Norrie's Law, Largo.

NORTON (Ratho). *c.* 1380 Nortoun, 'north town.' About 60 in England.

NOSS of BRESSAY (Lerwick). *Sagas* and 1539 Nos. O.N. *nös*, 'a nose,' akin to *ness*. *Cf.* the Scaur Nose, Portknockie, 1728 Scarr noss. See SCAR.

NOUP, NOOP (Westray, Ork.). O.N. *gnup*, 'a peak.'

NOVÁR (Dingwall). *Pont* Tenuer. In G. *tigh n' fhuamhair*, 'house of the giant.' (W.)

NUDE (Badenoch). *Sic* 1375. G. Noid. Root perh. as in NITH.

NUIS Ben (Arran). Pron. Noosh. Prob. = Noss; if so, a similar hybrid to GOAT FELL, G. Gaod Bheinn.

NUNTON (Lochmaddy). *Cf.* MONKTON and MUGSTOT.

NYADD (Stirling). NYDIE (St. Andrew's). 1144–1220 Nidin (*n* scribe's flourish), 1471 Westir Nydy. Perh. G. *nead*, *nid*, 'a nest,' with -ie loc.

OA, Mull of (Islay). G. *maol na Ho*. 'MULL of the howe or cairn,' N. *haug-r*.

OATHLAW (Forfar). 1635 Ouathlaw. Prob. O.G. *abh-ach*, 'river place' on S. Esk. *Cf.* AWE, *old* Ow, and Outh Muir, Saline; and see LAW.

OBAN. G. 'little bay,' land-locked. *Cf.* Openan, Gairloch, G. *obainean*, 'little bays.' *Cf.* next.

OBBE (Portree). G. *òb*, *òba*, 'a bay,' prob. fr. O.N. *hóp*, 'a sheltered bay.'

OCCUMSTER (Lybster). Perh. 'place of' some man; see -ster, p. 42. Perh. O.N. *álka-heim-r*, 'auk home's' place.

OCHIL Hills (Clackmannan). *a.* 700 *Geogr. Ravenna* Cindocellun (or *cind Ochil*, *cf.* KINALDIE), *c.* 850 *Bk. Lecan* Sliab ('hill') Nochel, 1461 Oychellis, 1580 Ocelli montes. Near Besançon, France, and twice in W. Spain were hill-ranges called by Romans Ocellum, which must be Celt., cognate with O.Ir. *achil*, W. *uchel*, 'high,' ACHILTY, Aldochley, Luss, AUCHELCHANZIE, OGLE and next.

OCHILTREE (Linlithgow, Auchinleck, Penninghame). Au. O. *a*. 1200 Okeltre, *c*. 1317 Houchiltre, 1537–72 Vchiltre, Pe. O. 1506 Uchiltre. W. *uchel tre*, 'high house.' *Cf.* Ptolemy's Uxellon near the Solway.

OCHTER-, AUCHTERTYRE (Crieff, Lochalsh.). Lo. O. 1495 Wochterory, 1527 Ochtertere. G. *uachdar tìre*, 'upper part of the land.' *Cf.* AUCHTERARDER. OCHTERLONY (Rescobie), 1296 Oghterloveny, 1391 Ochterlowny, is fr. G. *lob(h)anach*, here in loc., 'marshy, what one wallows in.'

OCTAVULLIN (Islay). G. *ochdamh a' mhuilinn*, 'eighth (L. *octavus*) part of the mill.' On these land measurements see p. 36.

ODAIRN, L. (Lewis). O.N. *oddi örn* or *arn*, 'point of the eagle.'

OFFERANCE (Buchlyvie). 1451 lie Offeris (another, 1510, near Denny), *Pont* Offron, O. Ir. *oifrend*, W. *offeren*, G. *aifrionn*, 'offering, the mass.' *Cf.* ORRIN.

OGILFACE (Torphichen). *Sic* 1386, but *c*. 1200 Ogel-, Okelfas. Brit. *ocel fas*, 'high station,' W. *faes*, aspirated fr. *maes*, 'field.' *Cf.* OCHIL and FASLANE.

OGILVIE Glen (Glamis). *c*. 1205 Ogilvin, 1296 Eggilvyne, also *c*. 1200 Purin Ogguluin, later Pury Ogilvy (see PURIN); and 1172–8 Oggoueli, 1239 Ogeluin, Auchterarder. Brit. *ocel*, O.W. *ugl*, 'high'; *cf.* OCHIL, and perh. *ma*, *fa*, 'plain' (W.), but as likely, G. *bheinn*, 'hill.'

OGLE GLEN (Killin). See above and OCHIL. *Cf.* Ogle, Northumbd., *sic* 1180.

OICH, L. (Ft. Augustus). *Sic* 1769. G. O'aich. Perh. G. loc. for 'water, stream,' *cf.* BANNOCK. M. says, 'awesome,' fr. Celt. *ut*, 'dread.'

OLDCAMBUS = ALDCAMBUS.

OLDHAMSTOCKS (Cockburnspath). 1127 Aldehamstoc, Haldehastok, 1567 Auldhamesokkes. O.E. *ald hám stoc(c)*, 'old home stock,' lit. 'stake.' The common Eng. Stoke just means 'place.' *Cf.* AULDHAME, STOCKBRIDGE and Knockstocks, Penninghame, where the ending has become G. *stoc*, *stuic*.

OLD MAN of HOY (Orkney). A striking high rock there.

OLD SHORE (Durness). *Chart.* Ashlair, Aslar. Corrup. of Ashir, G. *fhas thìr*, 'productive, cultivatable land.'

OLLABERRY (Lerwick). *Saga* Olafsberg, 'King *Olaf's burgh*,' see BORGUE and *cf.* TURNBERRY. St. or K. Olaf the Holy, was King of Norway, 1015–30.

OLNAFIRTH (Delting). 'FIRTH, bay like the forearm,' O.N. *öln*, *alin*, Sw. *aln*, the Eng. *ell*.

OLRIG (Thurso). *c*. 1230 -rich, 1587 -rik. Prob. 'Alder ridge,' O.N. *ölr*. See RIGG.

OMOA (Holytown). Iron works here, 1787, called after *Omoa*, Honduras, by Capt. Dalrymple of Cleland, a commander at its capture, 1779.

ONICH (Ballachulish). Some say G. *ochanaich*, 'wailing for the dead,' because they started here for the burial-place on Mungo's Isle. More prob. G. *omhanaich*, a loc., 'place full of foam,' referring to the stormy waves; *cf.* Nonach, Lochalsh. (W.)

ONWEATHER Hill (Tweeddale). Perh. W. *onn gwerthyr*, 'ash-tree fortification.'

ORAN-, ORONSAY (Colonsay and several). 1549 Col. O. Ornansay, Skye O., Oransay. 'St. Oran's isle,' O.N. *ay*, *ey*, *a*, or 'isthmus' G. *aoi* (see COLONSAY). *Oran* or *Odhran* was an Ir. friend of St. Columba, *d.* 548.

ORBLISTON (Elgin). No old forms and difficult. ? G. *iorbull*, *earball fhoistine* (*fh* mute), 'remote, calm spot.' *Earball* is a point or extremity of land, common in Ireland as Urball, and *foistine* is 'calm, rest.'

ORCHARD (Hamilton). 1296 Jordan del Orchard, 1368 Terrae de Pomario, 'lands of Orchard,' O.E. *ort-*, *wyrtgeard*, 'wort or root yard, garden.'

ORD (Helmsdale). MUIR of ORD (Beauly). G. *òrd*, 'a steep, rounded height.' Thus Ordhead, Tillyfourie, is a tautology. Ord, 1208 Orde, also occurs near Tweedmouth.

ORDIQUHILL (Fordyce). Pron. Ordifŭll. G. *òrd a' choill*, 'rounded height with the wood,' or *a' phuill*, 'by the pool.' *Cf.* Camoquhill, Balfron, *c.* 1350 Camkell, 1513 Canquhole, and LATHERONWHEEL.

OREVAL (Harris, Uist). N. *orri-fjall*, 'moorfowl fell.' (Henderson.)

ORKNEY. *Strabo* fr. *Pytheas* *c.* B.C. 330 Orkas, *Ptolemy* Orkades *nēsoi*, 45 A.D. *Pompon. Mela* Orchades. *c.* 970 *Pict. Chron.* Orkaneya, *Nennius* Orc, 1066 *O.E. Chron.* Orcanege, 1115 'jarl i Orkneyium,' *c.* 1175 Orkenie. 'Whale isles,' O.N. *ay*, *ey*; Gk. *ὄρυξ*, *-υγος*, L. *orca*, N. *orc*, 'a great fish, a whale,' same root as L. *porcus*, 'a pig'; *cf.* p. 10. The Romans perh. took their name fr. *Orkas akra*, prob. Dunnet Head.

ORLOGE KNOWE (Kirkcolm). O.Fr. *horloge*, L. *horologium*, 'sundial, water-clock.' See KNOWE.

ORMIDALE (L. Riddon), GLENORMIDALE (N. Arran). '*Orme's* dale' or 'valley'; or fr. O.N. *orm-r*, 'a snake, a worm.' With the tautology Glenormidale *cf.* Strathhalladale.

ORMISTON (Tranent, Abernethy, Perth), GLENORMISTON (Innerleithen). Tr. O. *sic* 1293, but *c.* 1160 Ormystone. '*Orme's* village'; *cf.* the Eng. Ormesby and Ormskirk.

ORMSARY (Ardrishaig). 'Orme's shieling or hut,' N. *erg*, in G. *airigh*.

ORPHIR (Kirkwall). *c.* 1225 *Orkn. Sag.*, Örfura, Jorfiara, *Flatey Bk.* Orfiara, *c.* 1500 -phair. *Örfiris-ey* or *a* is O.N. for an island showing above the waterline at ebbtide, fr. *ör*, 'out of,' and *fjara*, 'low water, foreshore.'

ORR, ORE Water (Leven). Might be G. *odhar*, 'grey.' Perh. pre-Celt. name for 'water,' as in URR.

ORRIN, R. (Urray). G. Oirrinn. 1257 Inueraferan, 1440 Inverafferayn, *Pont* Glenavaryn. G. *aifreann*, *oifreann*, 'offering, the mass.' *Cf.* OFFERANCE. (W.)

ORTON (Fochabers). 1542 Urtene; also Ortane. Prob. G. *oir dùin*, 'at the border or edge of the hill,' *cf.* DUBTON, EDDERTON.

ORWELL (Kinross). 1330 Urwell. Prob. G. *ùr bhail*, 'new village,' *cf.* FARNELL.

OSPISDALE (Dornoch). 1384 Hospostyl. 'Dale,' it is said, 'of *Ospi*,' brave N. leader who fell here, 1031. But perh. 'of the hospice,' Fr. *hospice*, L. *hospitium*; *cf.* DALNASPIDAL. Obsdale, Rosskeen, 1548 Obstuill, is N. *hóps-dal*, 'bay dale.' (W.)

OSTAIG (Sleat). Norse G. for 'east bay,' O.N. *aust-r vík*. *Cf.* ARISAIG.

OTTER FERRY (L. Fyne). 1490 ly Ottyr, 1627 Ottir. As the site shows, G. *oitir*, 'a reef.' *Cf.* DUNOTTAR.

OTTERSTON (Aberdour, Fife). *Old* Otherston. *Ohthere* or *Other* was a Saxon settler; *cf.* Outerston, Midlothn. But OTTERBURN (Longformacus), *c.* 1210 Otyrburn, is fr. O.E. *oter*, 'an otter.'

OUAN, UAINE, L. (Crieff). Prob. *Sim. Durh.* ann. 756 Ouania. G. *uaine*, 'green, pale,' or *uan*, *uain*, 'a lamb.'

OUSE, stream near Jedburgh, OUSSIE, USSIE, L. (Fodderty). Celt. for 'water,' Ir. *os*, same as Eng. R. Ouse; see *Pl. N. Eng.* and OXNAM.

OUTON (Whithorn). 1451 Otoun in Farnis, 1473 Otanys, *old MSS.*, Litill Owtoun, etc. 'Out town,' outside the town.

OVERSCAIG (Lairg). 'Upper strip of land,' N. *skiki*. *Cf.* ABERSCROSS.

OXGANG (Grangemouth, Kirkintilloch, Mouswald). 1472 Crauford de Oxingangis. Grant of land of as much as an ox could plough or *gang* (Sc. for 'go') over in a day. See *N.E.D. s.v.*

OXNAM (Jedburgh). *c.* 1150 Oxene-, Oxanaham, 1177 Oxeham, *c.* 1360 Oxinghame. O.E. *oxena hám*, 'oxen's home'; *cf.* Oxenholme, Kendal, and Oxendean, Duns. It stands on a little stream, the Ousenan or Oxnam, so possibly, as some think it is in Oxford, Ox is var. of Celt. *oc*, 'water.' The district can never have been very good for oxen. But *ousen* may be the regular North pl. of *ox*; see *N.E.D.* s.v.

OXTON (Lauder). *c.* 1200 Ulfkilston—a caution in contraction. *Ulfcytel* is a common O.E. name.

OYKELL, R. (Sutherland). [*Ptolemy* Ripa Alta.] 1365 Okel, 1490 Ochell, 1515 Akkell. Brit. for 'high,' W. *uchel*, Gaul. *uxellos*; *cf.* OCHIL. This is *c.* 1390 *Flatey Bk.* Ekkjalsbakki, 'coast, border of R. Oykell.'

OYNE (Insch). *a.* 1182 Uuen, *a.* 1300 Ovyn. Perh. G. *omhan*, 'froth, foam.' *Cf.* ONICH.

PABAY (Barra), PABBAY (S. Uist, Skye). Ba. P. 1580 Paba. O.N. *pap-ay*, 'priest isle' = PAPA.

PADANARAM (Kirriemuir). Fancy name, meaning Padan in Syria. See Gen. xlviii. 7.

PADDY'S MILESTONE is Ailsa Craig, *Paddy*, 'the Irishman.' PADDY'S SLACKS, Border name, *old* Paddock slack, where *paddock* is Sc. dimin. for 'toad,' often *puddock*, and *slack* is O.N. *slakki*, 'a hollow, a dip in the ground'; in Sc. also 'a morass,' *cf.* Chamar Slack, Cullen.

PAINSTON (Haddington). 1430 Payinstoun. 'Pagan's town'; *pagan*, 4 *paygane*, L. *paganus*, 'a rustic,' early became a surname. It recurs in Kilmafaddon or -makfadzean, New Luce, (see the author's *Scottish Macs* s.v.) 'church of the son of the pagan.' The early forms make it unlikely to be 'son of Paddy' or Patrick. (M.) It is *Pont* Kilmacphadzen.

PAISLEY. 1157 Passeleth, 1158 Paisleth, *a.* 1163 Passelet, -lay, *c.* 1170 Pasletum, 1508 Paislay, *c.* 1550 Passele. Prob. W. *pasgell llethr* (Mack.), 'pasture slope'; *cf.* CROMLET, G. *crom̃ leathad*, and How Pasley, Roxbh., 1494 Howpaslot (*o* for *e*). Kuno Meyer conjectured it was corrup. of L. *basilica*, 'court of justice, then, Christian church,' O.Ir. *baisleac*, while the mod. G. is Paslig. But the evidence proved so unsatisfactory he abandoned this in a letter to author, 7.6.1913.[1]

PALDY'S WELL (Fordoun). Called after St. *Paldoc*, see ABERFELDY.

PALINKUM (Kirkmaiden). *Pont* Poolinkum. G. *poll linne cam*, 'stream with the crooked pool.'

PALNACKIE (Buittle). Prob. G. *poll na cnaic*, here in loc., 'stream at the fissure.'

[1] W. does not state the evidence adequately. There is no proof *baisleac* was ever used in Sc. or that -leac ever becomes -ley. To-day's Argyle Gaels who say Paslig are not the same Brit. race who named Paisley. Conceivably it may represent a form not otherwise found—W. *pas*(*gell*) *llyg*, 'meadow of the mouse or shrew.'

Palnure (Minigaff). 1527 Glenewir, *Pont* Polnewyir. G. *poll n' iubhar*, 'stream with the yews.' *Cf.* Dunure.

Panbride (Carnoustie). *c.* 1200 Pannebrid, 1485 Panbrid. Seems 'headland of St. Bridget'; see Kilbride, with *pann* Brit. or Pict. for G. *ceann*, 'head.' W. prefers W. *pant*, 'hollow, valley' in face of early Panne-. *Cf.* Panlathy Mill, Panmure, *chart.* -lathyn, G. *leathan*, 'broad,' and next.

Panmure (Carnoustie). 1286 Pannemore. See above. G. *mòr*, 'big,' is often confused with Sc. *muir*, Eng. *moor*.

Pannanich (Ballater). Accent uncertain, and W. hesitates. Perh. Pict. *pann eanaich*, 'height of hunting.' *Cf.* above.

Papa, Little and Stour (Shetland). Papa Stronsay and Westray (Orkney). *Sagas* Papey and P. litla, 1229 Papey stora. O.N. *pap ey*, 'isle of the priest or "father" of a monastery.' *Papa* is same root as our papa and pope. O.N. *stor*, *stora* is 'great.'

Papill (Yell, Unst), Papley (Mainland and S. Ronaldshay, Orkn.). Papl. is *c.* 1225 *Orkn. Sag.*, Papuley, -li, 1369 Pappley, 1506 Pappale. 'Isle,' O.N. *ay*, *ey*, 'of the *papulus* or little pope or priest.' *Cf.* above, Papadil ('dale'), Rum, and the Papyli, Iceland.

Paps of Jura. So called fr. their shape. 1703 *Martin*, 'the two highest (hills) are well known to seafaring men by the Name of the Paps of Jurah.'

Parbroath (Cupar). 1315 Partebrothoc, 1593 Parbroith, now pron. Pitbrod. Pict. G. *perta* (W. *perth*) *brothach*, 'muddy, filthy wood.' *Cf.* Arbroath and Perth.

Pardovan (Linlithgow). Pron. -dúvan. *a.* 1150 Pardufin, 1296 Purdevyn, 1372 -dovine. Parduvine (Carrington). *c.* 1142 Pardauearneburn. Perh. seen too in *a.* 1093 *Reg. Dunferm.* Pardusin (*s* for *v*), said to be also Pardew. W. *parr ddwfn*, 'deep-lying parcel of ground.' (W.)

Parenwell (Kinross). Well of the saint, in W. *Piran*, Corn. *Peran*, Ir. *Kieran*, of Clonmacnoise, 6th cny. *Cf.* Kilkerran and Peranwell, Cornwall.

Park (often). 1264 *Sc. Exch. R.* Joannes de Parco. O.E. *pearruc*, G. *pairc*, 'enclosed field, park.' Parroch or Paurich, Freuchie, may be the same; perh. G. *peurach*, 'place full of pears.'

Partick (Glasgow). *c.* 1136 Perdeyc, 1158 Pertheck, 1483 -hic. Dimin. of O.W. *pert*, *perth*, 'a thicket,' or *perthog*, 'full of bushes.' *Cf.* Perth.

Parton (Cas.-Douglas). 1426 Portoun, *Pont* Parton. G. *portan*, 'little harbour.' *Cf.* the Ir. Parteens.

PATHSTRUIE (Forgandenny). O.E. *pæth*, *path*, 'a path,' in O.Sc. 'a steep ascent,' *cf.* PATHHEAD, Kirkcaldy and Dalkeith; and G. *sruthan*, 'little stream,' here in loc., *cf.* STRUAN and 1116 *Inquis.* Pathelanerhc. But *path* may be Pict. G. *peth* or *pit*, 'piece of land,' see p. 28.

PATNA (S. Ayr). Named *c.* 1810, after Patna on the Ganges, where a former laird is said to have made his money.

PAXTON (Berwick). *c.* 1098 Paxtun. Not 'village of peace,' L. *pax*, but 'of *Pace*,' same name as in *Dom.* Surrey, Pachesham.

PEASE Br. (Cockburnspath). 1502 'the Path of Pease,' 1548 the Peathes. This may be simply the O.E. pl. *pæðes*, *peðes*, 'paths.'

PEAT Inn (Ceres), PEAT HASS (Carsphairn). *Peat* is first *c.* 1200 in *Melros Chart.* peta, origin unknown. Hass is O.N. *háls*, Sc. *halse*, 'the neck or throat,' then 'gap, opening.' *Cf.* the hawse of a ship, Deerhass, Durrisdeer and HAWES.

PEATON (L. Long). 1680 Alterpittoune, 1792 Piton. Quite doubtful; perh. fr. *peat*, see above.

PEEBLES. 1116 Pobles, 1126 Pebles, *a.* 1136 Peples, *c.* 1141 Pebbles. W. *pabell*, pl. *pebyll*, 'a tent.' Pibble, Kirkmabreck, may be the same. Sir H. Maxwell thinks, G. *pobull*, 'meeting, place of assembly.'

PEFFER, R. (E. Ross) and Burn (Duddingston, Aberlady). Ro. P. 1350 Strathpefir. Ab. P. *c.* 1160 Pofre, later Pefer. *a.* 1130 *Sim. Durh.* Pefferham, E. Lothian. W. *pefr*, 'fair, beautiful.' W. says, in G. Pheofhair, others say Feothar. *Cf.* INNERPEFFRAY and Inverpeffer, S. of Arbroath.

PENCAITLAND (E. Lothian). *a.* 1150 -catlet, *c.* 1210 -cathlan, 1250 -katland. O.W. *pen chet*, 'head of the wood,' and *llan*, 'enclosure' (*a.* 1150 -let will be 'slope,' see PAISLEY). *Cf.* BATHGATE. Fountainhall, close by, before 1688 was Woodhead, plainly a translation.

PENCHRISE PEN (Stobs). 1380 -criz, later -christ. O.W. *pen crys* (G. *chriosa*), 'height with the band or girdle round it.'

PENDR(E)ICH (Tweeddale, Br. of Allan). Br. P. 1288 Petendreich, 1503 Pettyn-. Brit. or Pict. *pet an drych*, 'farm, croft of the view,' W. *drych*, but W. says 'of the hill-face' = PITTENDREICH. But Tw. P. may be fr. W. *penn*, 'height.'

PENICK (Nairn). *Sic* 1672, but 1571 Mekill Pennik. Pron. Painick. Perh. G. *peighinneach*, 'spotted, dappled place.' It may be 'pennyland,' see below.

PENICUIK (Midlothian). 1250 -icok, 1296 -ycoke. W. *penn y cog*, 'hill of the cuckoo.'

PENIFILLER (Skye). 'Fiddler's,' G. *fidhleir*, 'pennyland.' See p. 36.

PENINERIN (S. Uist). G. *peighinn an aorainn*, 'pennyland for the mass'; *cf.* OFFERANCE and see p. 36.

PENNAN (Fraserburgh). *Sic* 1654. Brit. for G. *ceannan*, 'little head or headland.' Pen- is very rare N. of Perth.

PENNILEE (Paisley). Prob. 'lea, meadow let at a penny,' see p. 36. But perh. Celt. *penn na lighe*, 'headland of the spate.'

PENNINGHAME (Newton Stewart). Pron. Pennicum. 1576 Pennegem. *Pont* Pennygham. 'Penny holding,' O.E. *peneg*, *pening*. A frequent land-measure in W. of Scotland. *Cf.* Pennington, Ulverston, *Dom.* Pennegetun, and below.

PENNYGANT (Liddesdale). Prob. W. *penn y gwant*, 'height of the butt or mark.' Also in Yorks.

PENNYGHAEL and PENNYGOWN (Mull). 'Pennyland of the Gael' and 'smith,' G. *gobhann*, see p. 36. *Cf.* Pennycastel, Arran, Pennycross, Mull, *a.* 1600 Peanagross, Pennyfuar, Lorn, 1596 -furt, Pennymuir, Borgue, and Pennytown, Kells. For -fuar, see BALFOUR.

PENNYTERSAN (Kilmalcolm). Brit. *penn tarsuinn*, 'oblique hill.' *Cf.* Ben TARSUINN.

PENPONT (Dumfriessh.). Pron. -púnt. W. *penn pont*, 'hill of the bridge,' L. *pons*, *-tis*. *Cf.* 1316 Kinpunt, Roxbh.

PENRIOCH (Arran). *Old* Pennerivach. G. *peighinn riabhach*, 'speckled pennyland.' See p. 36.

PENTLAND FIRTH. *a.* 1100 *Arnor* Pettlands fjordr. Sagas tell, the Norsemen learnt this name fr. the natives. 1403 Mare Petlandicum, 1595 Pinthlande Firth, 1701 Pightland F. 'Pentland' is a recent 'improvement.' 'Land of the Picts,' O.E. *Pihtas*, *Peohtas*. *Cf.* 1226–34 *Inchaff. Chart.* Villa mea Petlandi, *c.* 1272 Pechlandy.

PENTLAND HILLS (Midlothian). *Sic* 1250 but *a.* 1150 Pentlant. Rhys thought, W. *penn llann*, 'height over the enclosed land,' *llann* being cognate with O.E. and O.N. *land*, and the *t* coming fr. *ll* now pron. *thl*. It might mean 'the pent land,' only *pen*, 'to shut in,' is not found till *c.* 1200.

PENTOOT (Glencairn). W. *penn twt*, 'height of the look-out hill.' *Cf.* Toothill, *Pl. N. Eng.*

PENVENNA, -NY (Stobo). W. *penn faen*, 'head stone.' (W.)

PERCEBIE, PIERCEBY Hall (Dumfries), PERCETON (Irvine). 1520 Peristoun. 'Dwelling of *Piers* or *Percy*.' See -by, p. 41.

PERCLEWAN (Dalrymple). Prob. G. *pairc leamhan*, 'park with the elms.' *Cf.* BLALOWAN.

PERSIE (Blairgowrie). *a.* 1214 Parthesin, 1529 Perse. Prob. Pict. *perthais*, here in loc., 'wood place.' See next and *-ais*. But

PERSEBUS, Mull and Islay is 'farm of the parson or priest,' G. *pearsa*. See *bus*, p. 42.

PERTH. *Sic a.* 1150, but *c.* 1128 Pert, 1220 St. Johnstoun or Perth, 1527 *Boece* Bertha, prob. meant for G. *barr Tha*, 'height over Tay,' Kinnoull Hill. W. *perth*, 'a thicket,' Gaul. *perta*, 'a wood.' *Cf.* LOGIEPERT and Aberpert, Wales.

PETERCULTER (Deeside). The Church of COULTER was dedicated to St. *Peter*. *Cf.* MARYCULTER opposite.

PETERHEAD. *Chart.* Petri promontorium, 1595 Peterpolle (*poll*, 'a head'), 1654 oppidulum Peter-head. It was founded, 1593.

PETTICUR (Kinghorn). *c.* 1150 Petioker, 1277–1610 -ocher, though 1268 Petecor (? *car*, *cuir*, 'at the bend'). As the *o* persists, prob. O.G. *pette ocar*, 'croft of extortion,' i.e. high-rented. See PETTY.

PETTINAIN (Carstairs). *c.* 1150 Pedynnane, -uenane, *c.* 1130 Padinnan, *c.* 1580 Pettynane. O.G. *pette nan en*, 'croft with the birds,' or, like Balmain, Aviemore, *an athain*, 'at the little ford.' *Cf.* next.

PETTY (Ft. George). *a.* 1250 *M. Paris* Petin, *a.* 1400 Petyn. *Cf. a.* 1150, *Bk. Deer* Pette meic Garnait; there is still Petmegartney, Mearns. *Pit*, spelt also *pedy*, *peth*, *pet*, *pette*, *pith*, *put*, is Brit. or Pict. for 'piece of land' then 'hamlet'; in S. often rendered by *baile*, *cf.* PITLOCHRY. In W. *peth*; its true G. equivalent is *cuit*, 'a portion.' In root perh. same as med. L. *petia*, *pecia*, our *piece*.

PETTYVAICH (Kiltarlity). 'Croft with the byre,' G. *bhàthaich*.

PHILIPHAUGH (Selkirk). 1265 Fulhope, 1502 Philiphalch, 1510 Phillophaugh. 'Foul hope' or shut-in valley; *cf.* the surname Filshill, fr. Foulshields, Yarrow, 1375 Fouleschelis, and Philip, Northumbd, 1331 Fulhope, O.E. or O.N. *fúl hóp*. Also see HAUGH.

PHILIPSTOUN (Linlithgow). *Sic* 1546, but 1615 Grange Philpenstone (? 'filliping stone'), a name still found near Bo'ness.

PHILORTH (Fraserburgh). *Sic* 1361 but *a.* 1300 Fylorthe. (Perh. *Bk. Deer* Orte). Perh. G. *feill ghort*, 'market field.' *Feill* is 'a feast, fair, market.'

PHYSGILL (Glasserton). 1469 Fischgill, 'Fish gill' or 'narrow opening.' N. *gil*. *Cf.* AUCHINGILL.

PIEROWAAL, -WALL (Westray). Prob. not fr. *pier*, but 'little bay,' O.N. *vág-r* as in KIRKWALL, and Sc. *peerie*, 'little,' common in Orkney, N. *piril*, 'a small person'; *cf.* the Peerie Sea, Kirkwall.

PIKE, The (Selkirk and Roxbh.). Common on both sides the Border, for 'a pointed hill,' and recorded fr. c. 1250, see *N.E.D.*, *pike* sb.[2]

PILRIG (Leith), PILTON (Granton). 'Peel ridge.' *Cf.* PILMUIR, St. Andrew's, 1296 Pylemore, Pillmuir, Coldingham, 1296 Pylmor, and see RIGG. *Peel* is found, 1298, as L. *pelum* (O. Fr. *pel, piel,* Fr. *pieu,* L. *palus, -um,* 'a stake') *re* a palisade or stockade at Lochmaben. *Pile, pyle* is often used for 'tower, stronghold' in the 14th cny. *Peel,* in mod. sense of 'border tower,' is not found till 1726; but *cf.* 1422 Mote sive Pele in *Pl. Names Sussex* II, 431.

PINDERICHY (Glen Ogil, Angus). Brit. or Pict. *penn doireach,* here in loc., 'woody height,' G. *doire,* 'a forest.'

PÍNKIE,- KEY (Musselburgh, Duns). Mu. P. *c.* 1260 Penke, 1548 Pynky. Brit. *penn Ce,* 'height of Ce,' see INCHKEITH. But PINKHILL (Corstorphine) is prob. 'little hill,' same root as *pinkie.*

PINMORE (S. Ayr). G. *peighinn* (fr. N. *penning-r*) *mòr,* 'big penny-land,' see p. 36.

PINWHERRIE, -IRRIE (S. Ayr). 'Pennyland' (see above), perh. 'of the copse,' G. *an fhoithre,* or *a 'choire,* 'of the corrie' (Henderson), *cf.* Kinwhirrie, Forfar. *Cf.* too W. *gwyr,* 'pure, fresh.'

PINWINNIE (Airdrie). May be W. *penn gwynn,* 'white, fair height,' here in loc. As likely, G. *peighinn mhoine,* 'penny-land on the moor.'

PIRN MILL (W. Arran). Sc. *pirn* is 'a reel, bobbin.' But PIRN (Gala Water) *c.* 1400 Pren, Pyrn, and PIRNHILL (Innerleithen), are fr. W. *prenn,* 'a tree.' So is PIRNTATON, Stow, 1565 Princado, 1598 Pryntatoun, 1608 Pirntaiton, and, perh., W. *tiddyn,* 'a small farm' (W.). But PIRNIE Lodge, Slamannan, may be as in KINPURNIE.

PITALPIN (Dundee). Perh. 'Land of K. Kenneth MacAlpin,' *c.* 850. See PETTY.

PITCAIRN, and -GREEN (Perth). 1247 Peticarne. 'Croft with the cairn or barrow,' G. *càirn.*

PITCAPLE (Inverurie). 'Croft of the mare,' G. *capuill.* *Cf.* KINCAPLE.

PITCHIRN (Alvie). 'Croft with the rowans,' G. *chaorunn.* *Cf.* Loch a 'chaoruinn, Islay.

PITCORTHY (Carnbee). *a.* 1093 Pittecorthin, *a.* 1150 Petcorthyn, *c.* 1195 Pethcorthing, Pitcortyne. Prob. 'croft of the pillar stone,' O.G. *coirthe.*

PITCOX (E. and Midlothian), G. *coig,* 'a fifth part,' with $x = gs$, so an Eng. pl.

PITCULLO (Leuchars). *Sic* 1517. Prob. 'field of *Cullo.*' *Cf.* Edenticullo, Ireland, 'slope of the house of Collo,' Ir. *tigh Colla.*

PITFIRRANE (Dunfermline). *Sic* 1561 but *c.* 1200 Pethfuran. 'Croft with the well,' G. *fuarain.*

PITFODDLES (Aberdeen). 1525 Petfothellis, Badfodullis (G. *bad*, ' a thicket '). Perh. ' croft of the foundling or waif,' G. *faodail*. But W. says, fr. *fodàl*, ' a subdivision,' a supposed word nct found in any Dict.

PITFOUR (Avoch, Old Deer), PITFURE (Golspie). Av. *c*. 1340 Pethfouyr. Pict. = BALFOUR. *Cf*. 1539 Inchfure alias Petfure, Kilmuir Easter.

PITGAVENY (Elgin). Perh. *a*. 1100 Bothnguanan, 1187 -gouane, 1251 -gauenan. G. *both an ghobhainn*, ' house of the smith ' ; *cf*. Botarie, Cairnie, G. *both airidh*, 1662 Pittarie. Dr. McLauchlan said, Bothnguanan is Boath near Forres. W. derives Pitgav. fr. *gamhain*, ' a stirk,' which is prob. right.

PITILIE (Aberfeldy). Pron. -éelie. G. *pit a' dhile*, ' croft of the heavy rain.' *Cf*. Cnocadile, Duncansbay.

PITKEATHLY, -CAITHLY (Br. of Earn), *c*. 1225 Pethkathilin, 1461 Petcathle. May be fr. G. *càithlich*, ' seeds, chaff,' or *ceathachail*, in loc., ' misty, foggy.' W. thinks fr. a man *Cathalan*. *Cf*. BALCAITHLY.

PITKELLONY (Muthill). ' Field of the multitude,' G. *coilinne*, fr. *comh-lion*, or ' of the truant or poltroon,' G. *coilleannich*, here in loc.

PITKERRALD (Glen Urquhart). From *Cyril* or *Gerald*.

PITLESSIE (Ladybank). ' Croft with the garden,' G. *lios*, *-ise*.

PITLOCHRY (Perthsh.). G. Bailechlochrie, first *ch* silent. Either ' hamlet of the assembly ' or ' convent,' G. *chlochar*, *-air*, or ' of the stepping stones,' Ir. *clochran*, here in loc.

PITLOUR (Kinross). ' Hamlet of the lepers,' G. *lobhar*. *Cf*. *c*. 1190 Petenlouer, Aberdeensh.

PITLURG (Banffsh.). 1226 Petynlurg, 1230 Petnalurge. ' Croft on the ridge,' G. *lurg*, *-uirg*, sb. femin.

PITMEDDEN (Dyce). Prob. called after St. *Medan*, friend of Drostan. *Cf*. St. Meddan's, Troon. It may be fr. G. *meadhon*, ' middle.'

PITMILLY (Crail). 1211 Putmullin, G. *muileann*, *-inn*, ' croft with the mill.' *Cf*. Pitmillan, Foveran, *c*. 1315 -mulen, and perh. *Bk. Deer* Pett in Mulenn.

PITRODIE (Errol). ' Croft by the road,' G. *ròd*, here in loc.

PITSCOTTIE (Cupar). 1358 Petscoty. ' Croft with the little flock,' G. *sgotan*, here in loc.

PITSLIGO (Fraserburgh). *Sic* 1467 but 1426 Petsligach. ' Shelly croft,' G. and Ir. *sligeach*. *Cf*. Sligo.

PITTEDIE (Kirkcaldy). *c*. 1360 Pethidy, -edy, Pittedye. ' Croft on the hill face,' G. *eadainn*, here in loc.

PITTENDREICH (several). Lasswade P. 1140 Petyndreih, -endreia. Elgin P. 1238 Petendrech, Brechin P. 1545 Pettyndreiche. Prob. as in PENDREICH, though some think 'croft of the Druid or magician,' G. *draoidh*.

PITTENWEEM (Anstruther). *a.* 1150 Petnaweem, -neweme, 1528 Pittenwemyss. 'Land by the cave,' O.G. *uam*, G. *uamh*. *Cf.* WEMYSS.

PITTÓDRIE (Aberdeen). O.G. *pit fhodraidh*, 'croft by the wood' or 'on the slope,' loc. of *foder*; see FEDDERAT.

PITY ME (S. of Jedburgh). Pron. Peety Mei. W. *peth y midd*, 'piece of the enclosed, cultivated ground.' W. *peth* is cognate with *pit*, see PETTY; and final *dd* in W. easily falls away. Also on Redewater.

PITYOULISH (Abernethy, Inv.). *Old* Putgaldish. The *gald* is Norse G., N. *kelda*, Ger. *quelle*, 'a spring, a well,' and -ish is the common *-ais*, suff. of place, *cf.* WYVIS. In G. now Bail gheallais, fr. G. *geal*, 'white, clear'; *cf.* ABERGELDIE.

PLADDA (S. Arran). 1549 Flada, 1609 Pladow, Dan. *flad-a*, 'flat isle'; O.N. *flat-r*, 'flat.' *Cf.* Bladda, Jura, Fladay, Barra, and Fladda, Treshnish Isles.

PLAINS (Airdrie, Ladybank). PLAN (Beith). *Cf.* PLEAN.

PLANTATION (Govan). In 1783 'Craigiehall' was bought by Jo. Robertson, who had made his money in W. Indian plantations.

PLASCOW (Kirkgunzeon). W. *plas cu*, 'dear place or homestead.' *Cf.* GLASGOW and LINLITHGOW.

PLEAN (Bannockburn). 1215 Plane, 1449 le Plane, 1745 Plen, usually called 'the Plean.' Pron. Plain, Plen. Prob. Brit. *plane*, *plen*, L. *plan-um*, 'a plain,' not in *N.E.D.* till 1297 and fr. O. Fr. *Cf.* 1116 *Inquis.* Planmichel, and Plenmeller, Haltwhistle, 1255 Plenmeneure, 1279 Playnmelor.

PLENDERLEITH (Roxburgh). 1296 Prendrelathe, *c.* 1320 -derleith, Plenderlathe, 1587 Premderleith. Prob. O.W. *premter lleth*, 'presbyter's, priest's slope.' *Cf.* PRENDERGAST.

PLENPLOTH (Stow). 1593 -ploif, 1598 -ploff. Prob. as PLEAN, 'plain with the hamlet,' W. *plwf*, which is L. *plebs* 'community,' and same root as Plou- so common in Breton names.

PLEWLANDS (Edinburgh, Peeblessh.). Ed. P. *sic.* 1528. [1450 Pleulande, Berwksh.] 'Ploughed lands,' Sc. *pleu* or *pleugh*, 'a plough.' *Cf.* 1589 Plewlandis, Bolton.

PLOCKTON (Strome Ferry). G. am Ploc. Hybrid. G. *ploc*, 'a large clod or turf, a block' + Eng. -ton.

PLORA Burn (Traquair). *Sic* 1468. Seems Brit. for G. *blorach*, 'noisy,' *blor*, 'a loud noise.'

PLUCKERSTON (Kirriemuir). *Old* Locarstoun, fr. a man *Lockhart*.

PLÚSCARDEN (Elgin). 1124 Ploschardin, 1226 Pluscardyn, 1461 -carty. Pict. *plus cardin*, W. *plas cerddyn*, 'place with the wood or brake.' *Cf.* KINCARDINE.

POGBIE (Upp. Keith, E. Lothian). Prob. fr. a man *Polga* in *Onom.*, or the like. See -by 'hamlet' and *cf.* BEGBIE.

POLKEBUCK Burn (Muirkirk). G. *poll cabaig*, 'pool like a cheese.' Sc. *kebbuck*. 'Pool' is G., Ir., and Corn. *poll*, W. *pwll*, Bret. *poull*, and may mean either running or standing water, stream or pool.

POLKEMMET (Bathgate). 1375–6 -camet. Prob. G. *poll camaidh*, 'pool at the bend' of the meandering Almond.

POLLOKSHAWS and -SHIELDS (Glasgow). 1158 Pull-, Pollock, Brit. for 'little pool,' see POLKEBUCK. Peter, son of Fulbert, took the local name Polloc, after 1153, and gave to Paisley Abbey the church of Polloc. See SHAW, and for -shields or 'shielings,' GALASHIELS. *Cf.* Pulloxhill, Beds, *c.* 1200 Polochessele.

POLMADIÉ (Glasgow). *a.* 1189 -macde, 1318 -made, 1654 Pomadi. Perh. this was a sacred spot, and so G. *poll màig De*, 'burn, pool in the field of God,' *Dia*. The latter part may be fr. a man *mac Dith* or the like. (W.) But POLMADDIE Hill, Barr, like Pulmaddy Burn, Carsphairn, is fr. G. *madadh*, 'dog, wolf.' At the latter hunting dogs used to be kennelled. POLMOOD, Tweedsmuir, is fr. Brit. or G. *mòd*, 'gathering, fold.'

POLMAISE (Stirling). 1147 Polle-, 1164 Polmase, 1372 Polmas mareschelle (now P. Marshal, *cf.* NIDDRIE MARESCHAL). 'Pool of beauty,' G. *maise*, though W. says fr. W. *maes*, 'a plain.'

PÓLMONT (Falkirk). Pron. Pómon. 1319 Polmunth, 1552 -mond, *Pont* Poumon. 'Stream or pool on the moorland hill,' G. *monadh*. The accent has changed. *Cf.* ESSLEMONT.

POLNAR (Inverurie). Seems fr. G. *nàr*, 'shameful.'

POLNASKY Burn (Mochrum). Perh. 'stream of the love-token,' G. *n'aisge*.

POLSHAG Burn (Carsphairn). *Pont* Poushaig. G. *poll seabhaig*, 'stream of the hawk.'

POLTALLOCH (Kilmartin). 'Stream of the smithy,' G. *teallach*.

POLTON (Lasswade). 'Hamlet on the river' Esk. *Cf.* LINTON and 1365–6 *R.M.S.* Poltona, Wigtown.

POLWARTH (Duns). *a.* 1200 Polwrth, *c.* 1200 Powiourd, 1250 Poulwrd, 1299 Powelsworthe. 'Place, homestead,' O.E. *worþ*, 'on the pool.' *Worth* is a very common Eng. pl. name ending. *Cf.* JEDBURGH.

POMATHORN (Penicuik) seems recent.

POMONA or Mainland (Orkney). *c.* 1380 *Fordun* Insulæ Pomoniæ, 1529 Pomonia, *c.* 1670 -na. Said to be fr. L. *pomum*, 'apple,' because Mainland is, as it were, in the middle of the apple. This is dubious, L. *Pomona* was goddess of fruit trees, and so very inappropriate for Orkney. Prob. there has been erroneous connexion with the *pomōna* or 'harvests,' which Solinus connected with Thule.

PONFEIGH (Lanark). 1370–71 Pollynfeyche. G. *poll an f(h)eidh* or *feigh*, 'pool of the deer.'

POOLEWE (L. Ewe). G. Puileu. See POLKEBUCK and EWE.

POOLTIEL, L. (Duirinish). Seems 'pool, loch of the fish-spawn,' G. *t'siol*, *sil*.

POPELSHEAL (Haddington). 1430 Popil, late O.E. *popul*, 'poplar,' and see GALESHIELS. A *sheal* was usually a summer pasture. *Cf.* too PEEBLES.

PORT BANNATYNE (Rothesay). Ninian Bannachtyne of Kames granted lands here to his son Robert, 1475. There was a Bannachtyn, 1455 *Sc. Excheq. R.*, prob. near Largo, which seems now Bannaty, said by W. J. Liddall to be *old* Balnechtan, 'farm of Nechtan.' But the orig. one for the surname was prob. in Roxbh, 1294 *Lib. de Calcou* Nicol de Benauthyn, prob. old dat. of G. *beannacht*, 'a blessing,' then 'place where a saint lived,' as in Beannachd Aonghuis, Balquhidder. (W.)

PORTS CHARLOTTE and ELLEN (Islay). Named, 1828, fr. Lady *Charlotte*, mother, and in 1821, fr. Lady *Ellenor*, first wife, of W. F. Campbell of Islay.

PORTENCALZIE (Kirkcolm). 1525 -incalze, *Pont* -cailly. G. *portan cailliche*, 'little harbour of the nun.'

PORTERFIELD (Renfrew). 1361 -felde. Prob. fr. a man *Porter*. The Eng. sb. is first in *N.E.D.* in 1382.

PORTESSIE (Buckie). G., 'harbour at the waterfall,' *eas*, in loc.

PORT GLASGOW. Site feued by Glasgow Town Council, 1668.

PORTINCAPLE (L. Long). *a.* 1350 -kebillis, -chapil, 1395 -cable. 'Harbour of the chapel,' G. *caibeal* ; not = PITCAPLE.

PORTINCRAIG (Tayport). *a.* 1237 -encrag. 'Harbour at the crag,' G. *creag*, *craige*, orig. the rock on which Broughty Cas. stands.

PORTINCROSS (W. Kilbride). 'Harbour at the cross,' G. *crois*. *Cf.* Portnacroish, Appin.

PORTKNOCKIE (Cullen). 'Harbour by the little hill,' G. *cnocan*, here in loc.

PORTLETHEN (Aberdeen). G. *leathan*, 'broad.'

PORTMAHOMACK (Tain). 1678 -machalmok, *a.* 1700 Portus Columbi (an error). 'Harbour of *machalmac* or *mocholmoy*,' *i.e.*, my own little Colman, name of many saints. See p. 67, and *cf.* Kilmachalmag, Kincardine and INCHMAHOME.

PORTMOAK (Kinross). *a.* 1150 -moack, *c.* 1152 -emuoch, 1187 -moog, 1250 -mochoc, Porthmook; also *a.* 1107 *Reg. St. Andr.* Petnemokane. 'Harbour of St. *Moach* or *Mouc*,' companion of Brendan, who perh. built the first church here.

PORTNAHAVEN (Islay). G. *port na h'aibhne*, 'harbour on the water.' *Cf.* AVON.

PORTOBELLO (Edinburgh). 1753 Porto-Bello. Portobello Hut was built, *a.* 1750, by a Sc. sailor, who served under Adml. Vernon, to commemorate his victory at Portobello ('fine harbour'), Darien, 1739.

PORTPATRICK (Wigtown). So named, 1630, fr. the famous St. *Patrick*, L. *Patricius*. There was a chapel Patrick here long before. *Cf.* next.

PORTREE (Skye). 1549 -ri. 'Harbour of the king,' G. *port righe*, 'Port Royal'; so called fr. James V.'s visit here, 1540. *Cf.* Port-an-righ, Saddel, and Inchree, Onich. Port-rig is the name of Portpatrick in *Bk. Leinster*.

PORT SONACHAN (L. Awe). Dimin. of G. *sonnach*, 'palisade, wall, castle.'

PORTSOY (Banff). 'Harbour of the warrior,' G. *saoi*, *saoidh*.

PORTYERROCK (Whithorn). 1647 -erack; also -carryk. 'Harbour at the crags,' G. *carraig*. The *y* is for aspirated *c*. *Cf.* CARRICK.

POSSIL (Glasgow). 1241 -ele, 1512 -ell, -il. Prob. *post-wiel*, 'fish-pool with the *post*,' O.E. *post*, 1340 *pos.*, *cf.* Postwick, Norfk, *Dom.* Possuic. On *wiel*, *cf.* BOTHWELL; also *cf.* next.

POSSO (Manor). *c.* 1400 -ow, -aw. May be Brit. for 'calm water,' O.W. *poues*, 'rest, repose.' (W.)

POWBURN (Edinburgh). *Sic* 1663. *Pow* is Sc. for 'a sluggish stream,' softened form of *pool*; see POLKEBUCK. *Cf.* Pow, New Abbey and Powmill, Plean.

POWGREE (Beith). G. *poll greighe*, 'stream of the herd' of deer.

POWRAN (Glencairn). 1580 -ane. POWRIE (Dundee, Glamis). Gl. P. *c.* 1200 Pourin. Brit. *pourain*, G. *pòr*, *pùir*, 'pasture land'; The -ie is a loc. *Cf.* BALFOUR, Porin, Strathconon, and PURIN.

PREASANDYE (Stirling). G. *preasan dubh*, 'dark, little thicket.'

PREMNAY (Insch). 1198–9 Prameth. Prob. Pict. *pren a' mhaigh*, 'tree in the plain,' W. *pren*, Ir. *cran*, 'a tree.' *Cf.* KEMNAY.

PRENDERGAST (Ayton). 1100 -negest, *c.* 1150 -dergest. O.W. *premter gest*, *cest*, 'presbyter's, priest's deep glen'; but *cf.* Fris. *gaast*, 'a morass.' Also in Pembroke. *Cf.* PLENDERLEITH. But W. *pren* is 'a tree.'

PRESCALTON (Moray). G. *preas calltuinn*, 'copse of hazels.'

PRESHOME (Buckie). Might be 'priest's home,' and Pressen, S. of Coldstream, is pron. Préssom. But here prob. corrup. of G. *preasan*, 'little thicket.' *Cf.* next.

PRESS (Coldingham), PREAS (Sutherland). G. *preas*, 'a copse, thicket.'

PRESTON (several). 'Priest's village.' Many in England; *cf.* Prescot. PRESTONGRANGE at PRESTONPANS is *c.* 1240 Grangia de Preston; see ABBOTSGRANGE. The latter is 1587 Saltprestoun, 1611 Prestounepannis. Salt pans made here by Newbattle monks, *a.* 1200.

PRESTWICK (Ayr). *Sic* 1158 and 1160 Prestwick usque Pulprestwick (*pul* for *pool*). 'Priest's dwelling,' O.E. *wíc*, rather than 'bay,' O.N. *vik.* Also in Northumbld.

PRINGLE or HOPRINGLE (Stow). *c.* 1275 Hoppringyl and so till 1585. 1463 Pringil (surname). O.N. *prjónn gil*, 'narrow valley of Prjonn,' lit. 'knitting pin, peg,' found in 13th cny. as sur- or nickname; Sc. *preen*, 'a pin.' See HOPE and *cf.* DUNRINGIL.

PRINLAWS (Leslie). Hybrid, Pict. *pren*, 'tree,' and Sc. *law*, 'hill.' *Cf.* next.

PRINSIDE (Yetholm). *a.* 1140 Praunwesete; also Prenwensete, 1502 Prymsid. Also hybrid. W. *pren gwyn*, *gwen*, 'fair, white tree,' and *seat*, see MUIRAVONSIDE. *Cf.* PRIMROSE, Midlothn.; also W. of Inverkeithing, *c.* 1150 *Reg. Dunferm.* Primros, 1450 Prumrosse. Prob. W. or Pict. *pren ros*, 'tree on the moor'; *cf.* RESTINNET.

PROAIG (Pt. Ellen). Corrup. of O.N. *breið-r vík*, 'broad bay' = BRODICK.

PROSEN, see GLENPROSEN.

PROVANSIDE (Glasgow, now away). 1522–3 'The prebend of Barlanark, otherwise called Provand,' 1613 Provanside. Med. L. *prebenda*; but Sc. *provand* means 'provender.' *Cf.* Praunston, Balfron, 1817 Provenstoun.

PULCAIGRIE Burn (Kells). G. *poll cathagrach*, 'stream abounding in jackdaws,' *cathag*, here in loc. *Cf.* Drumcagerie, Kirkcowan.

PULHAY Burn (Carsphairn). 'Burn of the swamp,' G. *chaedhe.*

PULTENEYTOWN (Wick). Founded, 1808, by the British Fisheries Socy.

PUMPHERSTON (Midcalder). 1684 Phumpherstoun. The name *Pumpher* is prob. Dan. dial. *pamper*, 'a short, thickset man.'

PURIN (Freuchie) *sic* 1517; also Pourane. See POWRAN.

PYATKNOWE (Biggar). *Pyat* is Sc. dimin. for *pie*, 'magpie,' L. *pica.* See KNOWE.

Quair Water (Traquair). 1116 Quyrd, 1174 Cuer, 1184 Queyr. Corn. *quirt*, later *gwer*, 'green.' *Cf.* 'the green, green grass o' Traquair kirkyard.'

Quanterness (Kirkwall). O.N. *Kantari*, lit. 'Canterbury,' 'a bishop,' an element in a good many Norse names. See Ness.

Quarff (Shetland). 1569 Quharf. O.N. *hvarf*, O.Sw. *hwarf*, 'a turning, hidden corner, shelter.' *Cf.* C. Wrath and R. Wharfe, Yorks.

Quarrell (Carron, Falkirk). 1298 Querle, 1510 le Quarrell. Old Sc. and M.E. for 'a quarry,' O.Fr. *quarriere*, Fr. *carrière*, med. L. *quarriaria*, *quadriaria*, 'place for squaring stones.'

Quarter (several). West Quarter (Falkirk). *Sic Pont.* Dunipace Q. 1510 ly Quartir. *N.E.D.* calls it an Ir. land-measure.

Queensberry Hill (Drumlanrig). 'Queen's hill or fort.' It is a queenly hill. See Turnberry. The Earl of Q. was created, 1633.

Queensferry N. and S. (Firth of Forth). 1183 Passagium S. Marg. Regine, *c.* 1295 Queneferie, 1461 Quenis Fery. So called because Margaret of England, wife of K. Malcolm Canmore, 1057–93, crossed here. *Ferry* is not in *N.E.D.* till 1440 ; but already 1087 *Dom.* Yorks, we have Ferie, *i.e.*, Ferrybridge.

Queenzieburn (Kilsyth). *Pont* Goyny. Perh. G. *caoin*, *-ne*, 'gentle.'

Queich, R. (Braemar). G. *cuach*, 'a cup, a quaich.' The stream bed is full of circular holes ; *cf.* Glenquaich. But Inverqueich, Alyth, 1296 *Ragman R.* Entrekoyt (entre- for eutre, Norm. spelling of *auchter*, see Auchterarder), 1374 Inu'euyth, is prob. fr. Brit. *coit*, 'a wood' ; see Quothquhan.

Quendale (Sumburgh). *Sic* 1503. O.N. *kvan*, 'a wife,' Dan. *qvinde*, O.E. *cwen*, Sc. *quean*, 'a woman.' See Dale.

Quien, L. (Bute). Prob. G. *cuithean*, 'little trench or pit.'

Quils (Perthsh.). G. *coill*, 'a wood,' with Eng. pl. ; *cf.* Cults and Kelty. But Quilt, Edmonstone, Stirling, is the G. pl. *coillte*, or else *cuilt*, 'a nook' ; *cf.* 1377–8 *R.M.S.* Qwylt(s), Peebles.

Quinag (mtn., Assynt). Pron. Köneag. Either G. *cuinneag*, 'churn, milk-pail,' fr. its supposed shape, or *caoinag*, dimin. fr. *caoin*, 'beautiful' ; *cf.* Coshquin, Derry.

Quinish (Mull). 1561 Quyneise. N. *kví næs*, 'fold cape.'

Quiraing (mtn., Skye). O.N. *kví rong*, 'crooked enclosure.' *Cf.* Quoyloo.

Quivox St. (Ayr). This is the Ir. St *Caemhan*, in his pet form Mochaemhoc (see p. 67), Latinized Pulcherius, d. *c.* 750.

QUOTHQUHAN (Thankerton). *c.* 1210 Cuthquen, 1275 Knokquhan (G. *cnoc*, 'hill'), 1403 Quodquen, 1662 Cothquhan. O.W. *chet*, *coit*, W. *coed*, 'a wood,' and *gwen*, 'clear, white.' It is a wooded hill now. *Cf.* Cefn Coed, Hereford, 1227 Kevenesquoyt, and *a.* 1600 Coitquoit, 1610 Quotquoit, W. Linton.

QUOYLOO (Stromness). [1329 Leika kvi, later Lykquoy, S. Ronaldshay, and 1482 Quhitquiy, Ork.] O.N. *kví hlœ*, 'warm fold.' A *quoy* is an enclosure or fence of turf or stones. Quoyland is common in early Orkn. rentals, also names like 1546 Queybewmont, Kirkwall, 1502 Gloupquoy, Deerness, etc. *Cf.* Dan. *kovi*, O.Du. *coye*, 'a hollow, an enclosure' found in Shetland as Whee. *Loo* is Dan. *hlœ* O.N. *hlie*, O.E. *hléo*(*w*), 'shelter,' or, as adj., 'warm.' *Cf.* LEE.

RAASAY (Skye). 1263 Raasa, 1501 Rasay, 1526 Rairsay. Puzzling; but M. and Henderson agree it is N. *rár-áss-ey*, 'roe-ridge-isle.' *Cf.* RARNISH and see -ay.

RACHAN Mill (Biggar). 1458 The Rawchan. G. *racan*, 'arable land.'

RACKWICK (Westray, Hoy). We. R. *Orkn. Sag.* Rekavik. Ho. R. 1503 Rakwik. O.N. *reka-vík*, 'bay full of wrack, cast-up seaweed,' *reki*, *-ka*, Sw. *wrak*, same root as *wreck*.

RAFFORD (Forres). *a.* 1700 Raffart; also Rathard. G. *rath àrd*, 'high fort'; there are ruins of such here. *Cf.* ALFORD for *th* become *f*.

RAHÁNE (Gareloch). *Old* Rochean, Raheavin, 1723 Rachein. Perh. G. *rath chàin*, 'fort of the tax or tribute'; but -eavin looks like *èibhinn*, 'happy, glad.'

RAIGMORE (Strathdearn). *Old* Ravochmore. M. thought G. *rathag* (dimin. of *rath*) *mòr*, 'big fort.' *Cf.* CROSSRAGUEL and KILRAVOCK.

RAIT (Errol, Nairn). Er. R. 1284 Rath, G. for 'fort.' *Cf.* LOGIERAIT.

RAITH (Kirkcaldy). *c.* 1320 Rathe. Prob. as above; but *cf.* O.Ir. *raith*, 'fern, bracken.'

RAMÓRNIE (Cupar). 1439 Ramorgney, 1512 -gany. Perh. G. *rath Morganaigh*, 'fort of the clan Morgan.' (W.)

RAMSEY (Whithorn). O.E. *rammes-ige*, 'ram's isle.' *Cf.* Portramsay, Lismore, and Ramsey, Hunts, 1050 Rammesege.

RAMSHORN (once estate, now parish church, Glasgow). 1241 Ramnishorene, 1494 Ramyshorne. O.E. for 'horn, spur of land belonging to *Ramni*,' a Saxon settler. *Cf.* Ramnigeo, Orkney, and Ramsbury, Wilts, *c.* 1100 Reamnesbyrig. Form 1241 bars derivation fr. O.E. *erne*, 'house,' as in WHITHORN. *Horn* is *sic* in O.E.

RANFURLIE (Br. of Weir). G. *rann feòirlinn*, here in loc., 'part, division let at a farthing rent.' See p. 36.

RANKEILLOR (Cupar) [Ade de Rankeloch here, 1293]. 'Part division on the KEILOR,' name now lost here. See INVERKEILOR.

RANNOCH (N. Perth). 1505 -ach. G. *raineach*, 'place of fern, bracken.'

RANZA, L. (Arran). 1433 Lockransay, 1549 -renasay. N. *reynis á*, 'rowan tree river.' (M.) *Cf.* Reynisnes, Iceland.

RAPERLAW (Lilliesleaf). *Sic c.* 1150. Perh. 'land, hill of *Ræfmær*,' in *Onom.*

RAPLOCH, The (Stirling). *Sic* 1329 but 1359 Roppelache, 1361 Raplach. G. *rapalach*, 'noisy, bustling place,' *rapal*, 'noise.' *Cf.* Moss Raploch, Kells.

RARÍCHIE (Fearn). 1333 -echys, 1368 -icheis, 1476 Wester Rarethe. Prob. G. *rath riachaidh shios* (where *h* silences *s*), 'fort of scratching,' as by brambles. There was a fort here. (W.) *Cf.* Corrichie, Echt. But Dunriachie, Dores, will be fr. *riabhach*, 'dappled,' here in loc.

RAR-, RANISH (Lewis). O.N. *rár-næs*, 'roe-deer cape.' *Cf.* RAASAY.

RASHIEDRUM (Denny). Hybrid. Sc. *rashie*, 'rushy,' and G. *druim*, 'hill-ridge.'

RATHELPIE (St. Andrew's). 1183 -pin. 'Fort,' G. *rath*, 'of King *Alpin*.' *Cf.* PITALPIN.

RATHEN (Lonmay). *a.* 1300 -yn. G. *rathain*, 'ferny place,' O.Ir. *raith*, 'fern.' *Cf.* 1238 Inuerathin near Fochabers.

RATHÍLLET (Cupar). *a.* 1200 Radhulit, 1455 Rothulyt. 'Fort,' G. *rath*, 'of the Ulsterman,' *Ulad.* (W.). *Cf.* the name MacInulty.

RATHMURIEL (Garioch). *Sic* 1198–9. W. says, 'fort of *Muirgheal*,' 'sea-white,' a lady's name. As likely, like Dun Muirgil, Taynuilt, fr. *Muriel.*

RATHO (Midlothian). 1250 -eu, 1292 Radchou, 1293 Rathou. Prob., W., *rathau*, 'mounds, hills.' *Cf.* Dalratho, *c.* 1160 Daratho, Grangemouth, and for the ending *cf.* STOBO.

RATHVEN (Buckie). *Sic* 1366. Pron. Raffen. Prob. O.N. *rauð-r fen*, 'reddish fen or marsh.' For *th* become *f*, *cf.* ALFORD.

RATTRA (Borgue), RATTRAY (Blairgowrie, Peterhead). Bl. R. 1291 Rotrefe, 1294 Retref, 1305 Rothtref. W. or Pict. *rath tref*, 'fort or mound dwelling,' W. *tra, tre, tref*, 'house.' Dr. J. Anderson thought RATTAR BROUGH, Dunnet, the sagas' Rauda Biorg, 'red headland,' as it is. *Cf.* ROTHIEMAY.

RAVELRIG (Midcalder). 1683 -ridge. *Ravel*, *N.E.D.* *sb*,[2] is 'a railing.' But RAVELSTON, to the N., is fr. a man, whose name in O.E. would be *Ræfcytel* or *Ræfwulf*.

RAVENSTRUTHER (Carstairs). 'Raven's marsh,' see ANSTRUTHER. *Raven* may be a man, O.E. *Ræfen*, *-fwine*.

RAWYARDS (Airdrie). Prob. corrup. of G. *rath àrd*, 'high fort.' *Cf*. BARNYARD and Benraw, Ireland, Ir. *beinn rath*.

RAYNE (Insch). 1137 Rane, 1261 Ran. G. *rann*, *rainn*, 'part, division.'

REAWICK (Scalloway). O.N. *rifa vík*, 'rift, cleft bay.'

REAY (N. Sutherland). *c*. 1230 Ra, *c*. 1565 Ray. G. *rèidh*, pron. ray, 'smooth, level; a plain.'

REDCASTLE (Dingwall, Arbroath). Di. R. 1455 Redcastell.

REDDEN (Spronston). *c*. 1145 Rauendena, 'raven dell.' See DEAN.

REDDING and -MUIRHEAD (Polmont). *Pont* Redding. Not as in 1195 Redinche, E. of Polmaise, 'red-looking links,' but, as in 1609 Roundredding, Dumbarton, 1530 Ridinghill, and *Pont* Paddock ridding, Ayrsh., also 1459 Rydynland, 1546 Raddindyke, Lanarksh., all prob., like the several Reddings or Riddings, Glouc., fr. O.E. *hryding*, dial. *rudding*, 'a clearing.'

REDGORTON (Perth). *c*. 1250 Rothgortanan, Rogortenen; but *a*. 1215 *Lindores Chart*. Ràthangothen. Prob. G. *rath gortain*, 'fort in the little enclosure.' For Ro- *cf*. ROTHIEMAY.

REDHEUGH (Cockburnspath). *c*. 1220 Redehouh. On *heugh*, 'height,' see HESTERHEUGH. *Cf*. 1552 Reidhcuche, ? near Falkirk.

REDNOCK (Pt. of Monteith). *a*. 1500 -nauch. Perh. G. *reudanach*, 'place abounding in moths.'

REELICK (the Aird, Inverness), RUILLICK (Beauly). Be. R. 1584 The Relict. O.G. *rèilig*, 'churchyard,' fr. L. *reliquiæ*.

REISS (Wick). O.N. *hreysi*, 'a cairn.'

RELUGAS (Dunphail). *Old* Relucos. Perh. G. *ruith luaith gais*, 'stream of the swift foot,' *gais* for *cais*, gen. of *cas*, *cos*, 'a foot.'

RENDALL (Pomona). *Sic* 1612, *saga* Rennadal. 'Rivulet dale,' *fr*. O.N. *renna*, 'to run,' or else fr. *rend-r*, 'striped.'

RENFREW. *Sic* 1160, but *c*. 1128 Reinfry, 1147–52 Renfriu, 1158 Reinfrew. W. *rhen friu*, 'flowing brook'; *friu*, *frwd* is fr. *frw*, *frou*, 'impulse.' *Cf*. The Fords of Frew, Kincardine-on-Forth. Old forms make W. *rhyn*, 'a point,' less likely.

RENTON (Coldingham, Dumbarton). Co. R. 1098 Reguintun, *c*. 1200 Regnintun, Reningtona. 'Village of' a man with one of the many O.E. names in *Regen-*, as *Regenbald*, *-hild*, etc.

Du. R. was so named in 18th cny. after a Berwicksh. Cecilia Renton, who married Alex. Smollett, M.P., of Bonhill.

RERRICK, -WICK (Kirkcudbt.). 1487 Reryk. Perh. O.E. *reáfere-wic*, 'dwelling of the robber or reaver,' O.Sc. *revar*. Sir H. Maxwell takes it fr. O.N. *rauð-r*, 'red,' as in Rarick, I. of Man.

RES-, ROSCOBIE (Forfar), ROSCOBIE Hill (Dunfermline). Fo. R. 1226 Roscolpin, 1251 -solpin; also Roscollyn and *Aberd. Brev.* Roscoby. O.G. *ros colpa*, 'moor of the horse or cow,' with *n* scribal flourish. W. prefers G. *sgolbach*, 'thorny place,' in loc.

RESÓLIS (Cromarty). 1662 Reisolace. G. *ruigh soluis*, 'slope of light,' ? fr. a beacon. *Cf.* Barsolis, -us, 3 in Galloway, 1623 -sollis.

RESTALRIG (Edinburgh). *Sic* 1526. Now, very rarely, pron. Lestarick. *c.* 1210 Lestalrig, *c.* 1230 Lastalrich. W. *llys tal rhych*, 'hall, mansion on the lofty ridge.' The liquids *l* and *r* easily interchange. *Cf.* L. Restal, Glencroe.

RESTINNET (Forfar). *c.* 1150 Rostinoth, *c.* 1200 *Gervase*, -not, 1268 Restenet, 1289 Rustinoth. Prob. Pict. or O.G. *ros tened*, 'moor of the fire.' *Cf.* Afon Tanat, Denbigh. (W.) W. *rhos*, 'moor,' is pron. roose. *Cf.* Roose, Glam.

RESTON (Berwick). 1098 Ristun. 'Village of *Ris*' now *Rhys*. *Cf.* the W. prince, in 1053 *O.E. Chron.* called *Ris*, *Res*, and *Dom.* Restone, Devon, and Riseton, Chesh.

RHICONICH (Eddrachilis). G. *rudha coinnich*, 'point, cape covered with moss or fog.' Near by is RHIVOULT, fr. G. *m(h)uilt*, 'a wether,' same root as *mulct*. Sheep were a common fine. RHIDORROCH, Ullapool, is *ruigh dhorcha*, 'dark slope.'

RHU COIGACH, etc. G. *rudha*, 'point, cape,' is specially common in Sutherland. See COIGACH, etc. RHU DUNAN, Skye, is 'cape at the little hill.'

RHYND (Br. of Earn), RHYNIE (Gartly, Fearn), RHYNNS Pt. (Islay), RHYNNS of GALLOWAY. Br. R. *a.* 1147 Rindalgros (*cf.* DALCROSS). Ga. R. *c.* 1230 Rhynyn, Ryny. Fe. R. 1529 Rathne, *c.* 1564 Rany. Gall. R. *old* Ryndis, 1460 le Rynnys; *cf.* Ir. *Life St. Cuthbt.*, Regio quæ Rennii vocatur in portu qui Rintsnoc (MULL of Galloway) dicitur. Rhynie, Fearn, will be G. *rathan*, 'little fort,' in loc. All the rest fr. O.Ir. *rinn*, *rind*, G. *roinn*, W. *rhyn*, 'a point of land.'

RÍBIGILL (Tongue). 1530 Regeboll. Curious transposing, N. *hryggar-bol*, 'farm on the ridge'; see -bol, p. 42. But -gill is N. *gil*, 'narrow inlet.'

RICCARTON (many). Kilmarnock R. 1208 Ricardten, 1230 -deston. Currie R. *c.* 1320 Richard-, 1391 Ricardistone. Hawick R. 1376 Ricarden. '*Richard's* village.' On the Kilm. R., see WALLACETOWN.

RICHORN (Urr). 1486 Raehern, 1507 Reicharne, 1623 Richorne. O.E. *ræce* (4–7 *rach(e) erne*), 'hunting-dog house.' *Cf.* WHITHORN.

RIDDON, L. (Kyles of Bute). G. *rùdan* is 'a knuckle'; but this is either corrupt or G. *ruadh dùn*, 'reddish hill.' The true name is said to be Ruel, see GLENDARUEL.

RIDDRIE (Glasgow). Perh. G. *ruadh airigh*, 'reddish hill-pasture,' *cf.* AIRDRIE. But Raddery, Rosemarkie, is G. *radharaidh*, 'arable field not in tillage.' (W.)

RIGG (Gretna). Sc. *rig*, 'ridge, furrow, hill-ridge,' O.E. *hrycg*, O.N. *hrygg-r*, Dan. *ryg*, 'ridge,' lit. 'back.' *Cf.* DRUM.

RINGFERSON (L. Ken). 1462 Farsynne. G. *roinn farsuinn*, 'wide point.'

RINNES, Ben (Aberlour). = RHYNNS, with common ending *-ais*, see p. 9.

RIRAS, RERES (Largo). Pron. Reéres. *c.* 1290 *Reg. Dunferm.* Shire of Rerays. Prob. G. *riarachas*, 'a distribution, sharing.'

RISELAW (Berwicksh.). Perh. fr. a man *Rhys*, see RESTON.

RISK (Minigaff). G. *riasg*, *reisg*, 'a moor, morass.'

RIVALDSGREEN (Linlithgow). Prob. corrup. of '*rye-field*,' *cf.* 1263 Riefield, Sussex, now Rivall farm.

ROAG (loch, W. Lewis, Knapdale). Kn. R. 1511 Roage. N. for 'roe -deer bay,' see RODIL and ASCOG.

ROBERTON (Lamington, Hawick). La. R. *c.* 1155 Villa Roberti fratris Lambini (*cf.* LAMINGTON), 1229 Robertstun, 'Village of *Robert*' or *Rodbeard*, *-beart*, 'red beard.'

ROBROYSTON (Glasgow). 1587 Robres- Roberstoun. Mod. corrup. of '*robbers*,' or perh. '*Robert's town*.'

ROCKVILLA (Glasgow). Named fr. the house of Robert Græme, sheriff substitute, 1783.

RODIL (Harris). 1580 Roadilla, 1682 Rovadil. Either 'dale of the roe,' O.N. *rá*, Dan. *raa* (pron. ro), or fr. O.N. *rauð*, 'red.' (M.) *Cf.* Attadale, 1584 -dill.

RÓGART (Golspie). *Sic* 1546, but *c.* 1230 Rothegorth. O.N. *rauð-r garð-r*, 'reddish enclosure'; *cf.* G. *gort*, 'a field.'

ROGIE, Falls of (Strathpeffer). 1472 Rewgy. ? G. *raog*, *raoig*, 'rushing.' W. hesitates; perh. G. *mòr agaidh*, 'great cleft.'

ROLLOX St. (Glasgow). Also called St. Roque, Rowk, Rolloc. A chapel to St. *Roche* (d. Montpellier, 1327) built here, 1502.

ROMANNO Br. (W. Linton). *c.* 1160 Rothmaneic, *c.* 1200 Rumanach, *a.* 1300 Roumanoch, 1530 Romannose. G. *rath manaich*, 'fort, circle of the monk.' *Cf.* ROTHES.

RONA (Skye, N. Uist), N. RONA (N. of Lewis). *Saga* Hrauneyjar. 'St *Ronan*,' abbot of Kingarth, d. 737, in wild N. Rona. Here is Teampull Rona or 'St. Ronay's chapell'; *cf.* Port Ronan, Iona, and St. Ronan's Wall, Innerleithen. But the place-name is prob. N. *hraun á*, 'rough, rock-surfaced isle.'

RŎNACHAN (Kintyre). G. *roinneachan*, 'place full of little points or promontories,' *roinn*.

RONALDS(H)AY, N. and S. (Orkney). Two distinct names. No. R. *Orkn. Sag.* Rinarsey, *Fordun* Reualdisay (*u* for *n*), *a.* 1600 Rinarsöe. Native pron. Rinnalsay. 'Island,' N. *a. ay*, 'of *Ringan*,' *i.e.*, St. Ninian, see p. 65. So. R. *Sagas* Rögnvalsey, 1329 Roghnalsœy, Rognaldzœ. 'Island of *Ronald* or *Rognvald*,' 'gods' wielder,' jarl of the Romsdal, whose brother Sigurd was first jarl of Orkney, *c.* 880.

ROOE, ROOENESS VOE (Shetland). *Sagas* Raudey mikla (O.N. *mikill*, 'great') and Raudaness vagr (O.N. for 'bay'). Raudey is 'red isle,' O.N. *rauð-r, raud-r*, Dan. and Sw. *röd*, 'red.'

ROSA GLEN (Arran). 1450 -rossy. O.N. *hross-á*, 'horse river.'

ROSCOBIE, see RESCOBIE.

ROSEHEARTY (Fraserburgh). 1508 Rossawarty. Prob. G. *ros Abhartaich*, 'cape of Abartach,' an Ir. sept. (W.).

ROSEMARKIE (Fortrose). *c.* 1128 Rosmarkensis, *c.* 1190 *Bened. Peterb.* Rosmarkin, 1257 Rosmar(a)kyn, 1510 -rky. G. *ros maircnidh, marcanaidh.* Prob. 'cape of the horse-burn,' G. *marc*, 'a horse.' *Cf.* Rosemarket, Pembroke, *Pl. N. Eng. and W.*

ROSHVEN (Arisaig). O.N. *hross fen*, 'horse fen.' *Cf.* RATHVEN.

ROSLIN, ROSSLYN-LEE (Midlothian). *c.* 1240 Roskelyn. W. *ros celyn*, 'moor of hollies.' *Lee* is O.E. *léah*, 'meadow.'

ROSEHALL (Invershir.). In G. *innis na lion*, 'meadow of the fishing nets.' (W.) ROSEHAUGH (Fortrose). *Sic c.* 1680; really Rosauch, 'promontory,' G. *ros*, 'above AVOCH.'

ROSNEATH (Gareloch). *a.* 1199 Neveth, 1225 Rosneth, 1447 -neveth. G. *ros reimhidh*, 'cape of the sacred meeting-place,' O.Ir. *nemed*. Two Neimhidhs in Ross-sh., 1 in Banff, 1 in Fife, etc. Connexion with a W. bp. Nevydd seems ill-founded.

ROSQUE, L. (Achnasheen). G. *loch chroisg*, 'loch of the crossing or pass,' *crasg*.

ROSS, shire. *a.* 1100 *Life of St. Cadroe* Rossia. W. and Corn. *ros*, 'a moor.' *Cf.* MELROSE. But The Ross (Borgue) and Ross of Mull, arc G. *ros*, 'cape, peninsula.'

ROSSALL (Mid Atlantic). O.Ir. *rossàl*, loaned fr. O.N. *hross-hval-r*, 'a walrus.' But Rossal, Suthld., is *hross-völl-r*, 'horse-field.'

ROSSDHU (L. Lomond). *c.* 1225 Rosduue, 1315 -dufe, *a.* 1350 Elanrosdui (a gen.), 1595 -doy. G. *ros dubh*, 'dark, black cape.'

ROSSIE (Fife, Strathearn, Montrose). Fi. R. 1187 Rossyn, 1488 -sy. St. R. *c.* 1272 Rossy. Perh. all G. *ros-ach*, here in loc., ' promontory place.' W. prefers *ròsach*, ' rose-place, shrubbery.'

ROSSKEEN (Invergordon). 1257 Roskwin, 1270 -ken, 1575 -kin. The Ir. Rosskeens are Ir. *ros caein*, G. *caoin*, ' pleasant, dry wood ' ; but W. prefers Ir. *ros cuinche*, ' arbutus head.'

ROSYTH (Dunfermline). Pron. -syth as in scythe. *c.* 1170 Rossyth, 1363 Westir Rossith, 1473 -itht. Hybrid. G. *ros*, ' headland ' and O.E. *hiðe*, ' landing-place, hythe ' ; *cf.* Lambeth, 1041 Lambhythe.

ROTHES (Elgin). *Sic* 1238. O.G. *roth*, G. *rath*, ' fort,' with *-ais* suff. of place, as in ALVES, etc. *Cf.* ROTHIEMAY.

ROTHESAY. *Sic* 1401 but 1321 Rothersay, *c.* 1400 Rosay (still at times so-called), *a.* 1500 Rothissaye, *c.* 1590 Rosa. G. *baile Bhòid*, ' town of Bute.' Name orig. applied to the castle, an islet in a moat. It prob. was ' Rother's isle,' N. *a*, *ay*, all other forms being contractions. The *Rother* may have been the Capt. *Ruðri* in *Hakon Saga*.

ROTHIEMAY (Huntly). 1430 Rothmay. G. *ràth a' mhaigh*, ' fort in the plain ' ; *cf.* CAMBUS O' MAY. ROTHIE-NORMAN (Fyvie) 1362 Rothynormain, is named fr. the family of *Norman* of Leslie, Garioch.

ROTHIEMURCUS (Aviemore). 1226 Rathmorchus, 1472 -amurcus, 1499 Ratamorkas. G. *rath a' m(h)òrchuise*, ' fort of pride or pomp.' But M. says, either ' fort of *Muirgus*,' or, as explained locally, ' of the big firs,' *mhòir ghuithais*.

ROTTEN Row (street, Glasgow, farm, Carnoustie). Gl. R. 1283 In vico qui dicitur Ratonraw (O.E. *raw*, ' a row '), 1434 Ratown rawe, 1452 Vicus Ratonum (' village of rats '). Several like names occur, 1400–1600, all over the Lowlands and even in Menteith. M.E. and Sc. *rottin*, ' a rat,' can hardly be the origin ; for there are or were many Rotten Rows all over England, esp. Yorks ; and, as the early forms always have *a*, it is prob. *rotten*, dial. *ratten*, Dan. *raaden*, in the sense, ' extremely soft, friable of soil,' so in *N.E.D.* fr. *c.* 1440. *Cf.* Redford, Co. Durham, 1369 Rutynford. Thus Rotten Row would be the opposite of the almost as common Eng. Hardgate.

ROUKEN Glen (Glasgow). *Old* Rooken. Prob. G. *ruicean*, ' pimple, pustule,' and so, ' a hillock.' *Cf.* 1364 Ruchane, 1369 Rowcan, Dumfs.

ROUSAY (Orkney). *c.* 1260 Hrolf-, Rolfsey, 1369 Rollisey, 1529 *Jo. Ben*, ' Rowsay, Raulandi Insula.' ' *Rolf's* isle,' N. *ay*, *ey*. *The* Rolf founded the Norse settlements in Gaul, 911–27—in O.Fr. *Rous*, L. *Rollo*.

ROW (Helensburgh). Pron. Roo. 1638–48 Rue, Row. G. *rudha*, ' a cape, a point.' *Cf.* Rowallan, Ayr, 1498 -allane.

ROWANTREE (Barr). Dan. *rön, rönne-træ*, Sw. *rönn*, 'the mountain ash,' in Sc. 'the rowan.'

ROWARDÉNNAN (L. Lomond). Pron. Ru-. G. *rudha àirde Eonain*, 'Cape of Eunan's hill.' See St. Adamnan, p. 68.

ROWBER (Sanday, Ork.). O.N. *ranða berg*, 'red hill.'

ROXBURGH. *Sic* 1158, but 1127 Rokisburc, *a.* 1130 *Sim. Durh.* Rochesburh, 1147 -burg. 'Burgh, castle of *Hroc*,' O.E. for 'the Rook'; *cf.* Rook Barugh, N. Yorks, 1140–80 Rochesberc, -berg, *Dom.* Beds, Rochesdone, and Lincs. Rochesha.' Also *cf.* CRAWICK and BORGUE.

ROY Br. (Spean Br.). 1568 Glenroy. G. *ruadh*, 'red, reddish.' *Cf.* Rob Roy.

RUBISLAW (Aberdeen). 1348 Rubbys-, 1473 Rubbislaw. Prob. '*Rubie's* or *Reuben's* hill.' *Cf.* Ruberslaw, Jedburgh, fr. O.E. *Rudbeort*, Rupert.

RÚCHIL, R. (Comrie). G. *ruadh thuil*, 'red flood,' but RUCHILL (Glasgow), pron. *ch* guttural, is G. *ruadh choil*, 'red wood.' *Cf.* 1140 *Newbatt. Chart.* Ruchale.

RUDHA. G. for 'cape, point,' see ROW. Thus Rudha Suisnish (= ness), S. Skye, is a tautology.

RÚISGACH (Glen Lyon). 1502 Ruskich. 'Place where swords were bared before a fight,' G. *ruisg*, 'to strip, make bare,' with *-ach* suff. of place.

RULE, ROULL, R. (trib. of Teviot). Forms see BEDRULE. Doubtful. Perh. W. *rhull*, 'hasty, rash,' fr. *rhu*, 'a roar.'

RULLION Green (Penicuik). Looks like G. *ruithlean*, dimin. of *roth*, 'little wheel.' But it is said to have been also called Yorling's Green.

RUM (Hebrides). *a.* 1100 *Tighern.* 677 Ruim, 1292 Rume, *c.* 1370 Rune. G. *rum, ruim* is 'a place, space, room.' But Capt. Thomas made this aspirated form of G. *druim*, 'hill-ridge,' and the name orig. *i-dhruim*, 'isle of the ridge.' Wh. Stokes said, this lozenge-shaped isle is prob. cognate with Gk. ῥύμβος or ῥόμβος.

RUMBLETON Law (Greenlaw). 'Hamlet of *Rumbeald*,' in *Onom.*

RUMBLING BR. (Dollar and R. Bran). *Cf.* Routing Br. Kirkpatrick Irongray, fr. Sc. *rout*, 'to roar, bellow.'

RUSKIE (Menteith). 1472 -ky. G. *riascach*, 'boggy place,' *riasg*, 'a bog.' *Cf.* Rusco, Girthon and *c.* 1397 *chart.* Glenrustok, -rusco, Peeblessh.

RUTHERFORD (Kelso). *Sic c.* 1215, but 1296 Rother-. 'Ford for cattle,' O.E. *hrypera*. *Cf.* many Eng. Rothers-, *e.g.*, Rotherfield, Tunbridge Wells, 880–5 Hrytheranfelda; and *cf.* Oxford.

RUTHERGLEN (Glasgow). *Sic a.* 1150, but 1276 Ruthglen, *a.* 1300 Ruglyn (so still often pron.). Ruther- will be as above; but the orig. name was G. *ruadh gleann*, 'reddish glen.'

RUTHRIESTON (Aberdeen). *a.* 1370 -ristoun, 1531 Radruston. Prob. fr. *Ruadri* or *Rothri*, mormaer or earl of Mar, *c.* 1130.

RUTHVEN (many). Perth R. *c.* 1198 Ruadeuien, Rotauin. Huntly R. *c.* 1200 Ruthaven, *a.* 1300 Rothuan, Rothven; also Ruven. Meigle R. 1200 Ruotheven, 1291 Rotheivan. Often pron. Rívven. Old forms strongly point to G. *ruadh abhuinn*, 'reddish river,' or else Pict. or W. *rhudd faen*, 'red rock.' But there is nothing like these near Huntly, so sometimes it is = RATHVEN. *Cf.* METHVEN.

RUTHWELL (Annan). Pron. Rívvel. O.E. *róde well*, 'rood or cross well.' A very ancient 'rood' here. *Cf.* Rothwell, Leeds and Kettering, *Dom.* Rodewelle.

RYAN L. (Stranraer). *c.* 150 *Ptolemy* Rerigonios Kolpos ('gulf'), *Taliessin* Loch Reon, *c.* 1301 louch ryan, 1461 Lochrian. Prob. fr. Celt. *Rigon*; Ptol's Reri- is prob. just a scribe's reduplication. *Rigon* becomes in W. *rhion*, 'lord, chief,' just as Chiltern, Bucks, 1009 Ciltern, is W. *cil tiern*, 'nook of the chief,' fr. O. Celt. *tigern*, G. *tighearn*. *Cf.* Seskinryan, Ireland.

SADDELL (Kintyre). 1203–1503 Sagadul(l); also Saghadul. In G. Sà'adal. Henderson thinks, 'dale where wood was sawn,' N. *sag*, 'a saw.' *Cf.* 1662 Sacadaill, Applecross.

SALACHAN (Morvern, Lorn, etc.). Mo. S. *Adamn.* Coire Salcain, 'willow,' G. *sailech*, 'copse.' (W.) 1436 Salachin.

SALEN (Mull, Sunart). S. *sàilean*, 'little inlet or arm of the sea.' *Cf.* KENTALLEN.

SALINE (Dunfermline). 1613 Sawling. Med. L. *salina*, M.E. *c.* 1450 *salyne*, 'salt pit,' fr. L. *sal*, 'salt.' *Cf.* 1143 *chart.* Una salina in Carsach (Carse of Forth), and Saling, Braintree.

SALISBURY CRAGS (Edinburgh). *Old* Sarezbury Crags. 1554 *Council Min. Edinb.* Arthur Sett, Salisberie and Duddingstoun Craggis. Late tradition says, fr. the Earl of Salisbury who came to Scotland with Edward III, 1355. By common change of liquids O.E. *Chron.* ann. 552 Searobyrig or Sarumburg, becomes by *c.* 1110 Salesburia.

SALLACHY (common). Kincardine, Ross 1529 Salki. O.G. *saileach*, G. *seileach*, 'place of willows.' *Cf. c.* 1320 *Excheq. R.* Salakhill, Stirlingsh.

SALSBURGH (Holytown). 1839 Sallysburgh. O.E. *salh*, 'willow,' is impossible. A 19th cny. freak, named fr. some forgotten *Sally*.

SALTCOATS (Ardrossan). 1548 -tes, *Pont* -cottes. 'Salt-workers' cots or huts.' *Cf.* 1471 Saltcotis, St. Andrew's and CAULDCOTS.

SALTON (E. Lothian). *a.* 1140 Saulestoun, 1250 Sawilton. Doubtful. Perh. 'hamlet of *Savile*'; *cf.* 1216 Ralph de Sayvile, Yorks, which may mean 'of Sévilly,' Orne, France. Less likely is 'hamlet of *Sules*,' fr. Ranulph de Soulis or Sules, who came with David I fr. Northants, where the family were named fr. the bailiewicks called Sule, Fr. *souille*, 'miry place.' Salton York, *Dom.* Saleton, is fr. O.E. *salh*, 'willow, saugh.'

SANDAIG Bay (Knoydart). 'Sandy bay,' O.N. and Dan. *sand* and Norse G. *ag*, *aig*, N. *vík*, 'a bay.' SANDAY (Orkney, N. Uist, Canna) Or. S. *sic* 1369, N.U.S. 1561 Sand. 'Sandy isle,' N. *a*, *ay*, 'island'; *cf.* Glensanda, Lorn, Sanna, Mull and Ardnamurchan.

SANDSTING (Shetland). *c.* 1524 -isting. '*Thing* on the sands,' O.N. *þing*, Dan. and Sw. *ting*, which in O.N. means 'assembly, parish,' and also 'district or shire.'

SANDWICK (Shetland, Stromness, Stornoway). Sh. S. 1360 -vik. Str. S. *c.* 1225 Sandvik, fr. O.N. *vík*, 'bay.' *Cf.* Senwick, Kirkcudbt., 1456 Sannak, *Pont* -nick, see SANDAIG.

SANNOX (N. Arran). Prob. = SANDAIG, 'sandy bay,' with Eng. pl. $x = cs$. There are N., S. and Mid Sannoc, all in *Pont*, and spelt Sennoc(h); also 1489 Nethirsannak. But SANNOCH, Kells, may be G. *samhnach*, 'place of sorrel.' *Cf.* SAVOCH.

SANQUHAR (N. Dumfries). Pron. Sánkar. *a.* 1150 Sanchar, *c.* 1280 Senechar, 1298 -whare. G. *sean cathair*, 'old fort'; seen aspirated in Shanquhar, Gartly.

SARCLET. See SCARCLET.

SAUCHEN (Aberdeen), SAUCHIE (Stirling, Alloa). Al. S. 1208 Salechoc, 1240 -whoch, 1263 -whop, *a.* 1328 Salacheth, 'Field, HAUGH, of willows,' Sc. *sauch*, O.E. *salig*, *salh*, L. *salix*. *Cf.* Saughall, Chester.

SAUGHTON (Edinburgh). Pron. *gh* guttural. *c.* 1130 Saletunia, 1150 Salectuna, *c.* 1320 Salchton. 'Hamlet by the willows.' See above.

SAUL-, SOULSEAT Abbey (Stranraer). 1457 Saulsede, L. Sedes Animarum, 'seat of souls'; *cf.* SYDSERF. Sir H. Maxwell prefers O.E. *sáwl scéat*, *scéot*, 'the due for a dead soul.'

SAVAL BEAG and MORE (mountains, Reay). G. *sabhal beag* and *mòr*, 'big and little barn,' fr. their shape. As the *av* in Saval is long, W. suggests N. *há fjall*, 'high fell,' which accords with analogy.

SAVOCH (Deer). G. *samh-ach*, 'place of sorrel'; Sanachan, Lochcarron, 1583 Safnachan, is the dimin.

SCALLOWAY (Shetland). O.N. *skaalr-vàgr*, 'bay with shielings or booths around.' *Cf.* GALASHIELS and STORNOWAY.

SCALPA (Skye), SCALPAY (Harris). Ha. S. *sic* 1549. 'Island,' N. *a*, *ay*, 'shaped like a boat,' O.N. *skálp-r*. *Cf.* SCAPA.

SCAMADALE (Kilninver, Jura). O.N. *skamm-r*, 'short.'

SCANIPORT (Inverness-sh.). G. *sgainidh-port*, 'harbour, ferry at the rent or cleft.'

SCAPA (Kirkwall). *Sic* 1579, also Scalpay, *Orkn. Sag.* Skalpeið, 'boat isthmus.' *Cf.* SCALPA.

SCAR Hill (Anwoth, Rerwick). N. and Dan. *skjær*, 'cliff, rock, scaur'; *cf.* O.N. *skor*, 'a cleft in a precipice.'

SCARBA (Jura). 1536 Skarba. N. *skarf-a*, 'cormorant isle.'

SCAR-, SARCLET (Wick). It is hard to pron. both *c*s. Prob. O.N. *skari klett-r*, 'sea-gull's rock or cliff.' But Vigfússon gives *klettascora*, 'a scaur.'

SCARFSKERRY (Dunnet). 'Cormorant rock.' See SCARBA and SKEIR.

SCÁRINISH (Tyree). 'Cormorant ness,' N. *næs*, 'cape.' See above.

SCARRISTRA (Harris). As above. The *-stra* is the latter part of *bolstaðr*, 'place,' see p. 42. *Cf.* 1562 Scarrabolsy, Islay.

SCATWELL (Contin). N. *skatt-völl-r*, 'field for which scat or due was paid,' common grazing ground. *Cf.* BRAWL.

SCAVAIG, L. (Skye). Perh. 'bay,' Norse G. *aig*, N. *vík*, 'which scrapes boats,' O.N. *skav*, 'scraping, peeling.'

SCHALLASAIG (Colonsay). Perh. 'shell bay,' N. *skjæl*, *skel*, 'a shell,' and Norse G. *aig*, 'bay.' Perh., like SCHALLANISH (Jura, Mull), fr. N. *skali*, 'bald pate, headland,' with *nish* for *ness*.

SCHIEHALLION (Rannoch). 1642 Schachalzean alias Uchel Hills (see OCHILS). Often thought, fr. its shape, G. *sich* or *sine chailinn*, 'maiden's breast,' just like Sichnanighean, mountain, N. Arran, *nighean*, 'maiden,' and Maiden Pap, Caithness. M. and W. say, *sìth Chailleann*, 'fairy hill of the Caledonians'; *cf.* DUNKELD and Rohallion near it. In G. palatalized *s* before a slender vowel aspirates to *sh*.

SCHILLEY. See SELLAY.

SCHIVAS (Tarves). Perh. fr. G. root *siabh*, 'to drift, like snow,' with *-ais* suff. of place.

SCIENNES (Edinburgh). *Sic* 1667 but 1575 the Senis. Pron. Sheens. The Monastery of St. Catherine of *Siena*, Italy, was here.

SCONE (Perth). *Sic a.* 1300, but *Pict. Chron.* Scoan, *c.* 1020 Sgoinde, *a.* 1100 Scoine, *c.* 1170 Scoone, and still pron. Skoon. In G. Sgàin. Wh. Stokes says, Pict. Perh. G. *sgonn*, *-uinn*, 'lump, mass.'

SCOONIE (Leven). 1156 Sconin, 1250 -yn. G. *sgonn*, *-uinn*, here in loc., 'lump, block of wood.'

SCOTCH DYKE, SCOTS GAP, on Borders. The true adj. is Scots or Scottish, *e.g.*, 1549 *Compleynt Scotl.* prol. 'Oure Scottis tong.' But Scotch was in reputable use by 1591, when Spenser speaks of 'an old Scotch cap.'

SCOTLAND, also SCOTLANDWELL (Leslie). *c.* 940 *Geirason* Scotland, *c.* 1000 *Ælfric* -lande, *Orkn. Sag.* Skotland. *c.* 360 *Ammian. Marcell.* xxi gives our first mention of *Scoti*, fr. Ulster, and *Jerome* a little later speaks of 'Scotica gens.' The O.W. was *Yscotteit*, which Rhys thought fr. W. *ysgthru*,' to cut, sculpture'; and *c.* 630 Isidore says the Scotti were so called fr. tattooing themselves with iron points. Scotland did not include Lothian till after Layamon, *c.* 1205. Scot. Well is 1329 *Sc. Exch. R.* ballivus Fontis Scocie.

SCOTSCALDER (Caithness). The part of CALDER dale possessed by the Scots or Celts as contrasted with Norn Calder near by, possessed by the Norse; 1538 Scottis- and Norne-caldar.

SCOTSTOUN (Aberdeen, Glasgow). *Cf.* Scotton, Yorks, *sic* in *Dom.* and Scotby, Carlisle, *c.* 1139 Scotebi.

SCOUGAL (N. Berwick). Pron. Skole. 1094 Scuchale, 1311 Sco-, 1495 Scowgale. Prob. 'wood neuk,' O.N. *skog-r*, Dan. *skov*, 'a wood,' and *hale*, see LENNEL, and *cf.* Scugdale, N. Riding.

SCOUR, SGUR, common Norse G., in N. *skjær*, *sker*, a mountain, a 'scaur,' *e.g.*, SCOUR OURAN, L. Duich, prob. fr. St. Oran, G. *Odhran*, SCOUR-nan-GILLEAN, Skye, Rum, 'servants' hill,' Sgur Ruadh ('red'), W. of Beauly and Lochcarron.

SCOURIE (W. Sutherland). G. Sgoghairigh, which is Norse G. for 'wood shieling,' O.N. *skog-r* and G. *airigh.*

SCRABSTER (Thurso). 1201 Skarabolstad, *Orkn. Sag.* -bolstr, 1328 Scrabester, 1557 -bustar. N. *skjære bolstað-r*, 'rocky place.' See p. 42.

SCRAPE (Manor). A rounded hill, 'scraped' bare. The sb is not in *N.E.D.* till 1781.

SCREEL, Ben (Glenelg, Kelton). Ke. S. *Pont* Hill of Skyll. In G. Sgridheal. Prob. O.N. *skriða fjall*, 'landslip fell.' *Screel* is well known in the Lake District for a steep slope of loose stones.

SCRIDAIN, L. (Mull), SCRIDEN (N. Arran). G. *sgrìdan*, 'stone-covered slope,' root as above. *Cf.* Sgreadan, Kintyre.

SEAFIELD (Cullen, S. of Edinburgh, Leith, Kirkcaldy). Ki. S. 1440 Seefelde. As in Seacroft and Seathwaite, N. of England, prob. fr. O.E. *sæcg*, *secg*, 5 *sege*, 'sedge.'

SEAFORTH, L. (Lewis). 'Sea frith or *fjord*.' Sea is O.N. *sæ-r*, Dan. *sö*.

SEATON (Longniddry) and PT. SETON. *c.* 1210 Seaton, 1296 Seytone. Called after the *De Sey* family, fr. Say, Indre.

SELKIRK. *Sic* 1306, but 1113 Selechyrca, *a.* 1124 -chirche, 1147–52 Selkyrke, *c.* 1190 Seleschirche; also 1560 and later Selcraig. Prob. not 'church among the shiels,' as in GALASHIELS, but 'church in the hall or house,' O.E. *sele, sæl.* O.E. *sealh, salh,* 'willow' does not suit phonet. See KIRKABY.

SELLAY, SHELLAY or SCHILLEY (Out. Hebrides). 1580 Seila. O.N. *sél-r,* Dan. *sæl,* 'a seal,' and *ay, ey,* 'island.'

SELMA (Ledaig). *Ossian* says, his father reigned at Selma, supposed to be BEREGONIUM. The meaning is doubtful.

SERF'S ST. (isle, L. Leven). *Serf* or *Servanus* was prob. tutor of St. Kentigern at Culross, *c.* 520.

SGUABACH (Badenoch, Ross-sh.). G. 'the sweep of the wind.'

SGUR NA LAPAICH (R. Farrar). G. 'rock of the muddy' river. *Cf.* SCOUR.

SHAMBELLY (New Abbey). 1601 Schambellie. G. *sean baile,* 'old house or village'; *s* aspirated by rule. *Cf.* shanty or *sean tigh,* 'old house,' also Shenvalie, Appin, and *c.* 1380 Shenvale, Dunfermline. Seanbhaile occurs 83 times in S.W. Ireland.

SHANDON (Helensburgh). G. *sean dùn,* 'old fort.'

SHANDWICK (Fearn). N. *sand-vík,* 'sandy bay,' the only such hereabouts. Gaelic tongues put in the *h.*

SHANISH (Inverness). G. *loch na seann innse,* 'of the old haugh.'

SHANKEND (Hawick). O.E. *scanca,* Dan. *skank,* 'leg, shin-bone.'

SHANNO (Montrose). 1576 Skannack. G. *sgean-ach,* 'clean, neat place,' or fr. *sgann,* 'herd, drove place'; *-ach* suff. of place.

SHANT Glen (Arran). G. *seunta, sianta,* 'a charm.'

SHANTER (Ayr). G. *sean tìr,* 'old land.'

SHAPINSAY (Orkney). *Orkn. Sag.* Hjalpandisay, 1492 Schalpandsay 1529 *Jo. Ben.* 'Schapinschaw dicta the Shipping Isle' (fr. O.N. *skip,* 'ship'). Ben is wrong. It must be '*Hjalpand's* isle.'

SHAW (many). O.E. *scaga,* O.N. *skóg-r,* Dan. *skov,* in Eng. *a.* 1300 *shawe,* 'a wood.' *Cf.* O.E. *haga,* 'hedge,' now haw.

SHAW-, SHEABOST (Barra). 'Sea place,' O.N. *sjá-r,* 'the sea.' On *bost* for *bolstað-r,* see p. 42. *Cf.* SKEABOST. SHEBSTER, Reay, is prob. the same.

SHEDOG (Arran). G. Shaidhac. Perh. G. *sèidheach,* 'blowy, windy place.'

SHERRAIG Glen (Brodick). 1450 Glenservaig, 1590 Sherwik. O.N. *skir, skærr vík,* 'bright, clear bay'; it leads down to such.

SHET-, ZETLAND. *Sagas* Hjalt-, Hetland, 1289 Rymer *Fœdera* Shetland, 1369 Hjatland, 1403 Zetlandie. The name is thought inexplicable ; perh. fr. N. personal name *Hjalti*, which is prob. the Sc. *Sholto*. The Z is Sc. Y, to give sound of Hj. In *Tacitus* it is Thule.

SHETTLESTON (Glasgow). 1170 *Papal Bull* villa filii Sadin, *a*. 1186 Inienchedin (O.G. *inghean*, 'daughter'), villa filie Scadin. Schedinestun, 1515 Schedilstoune. 'Village of *Sca-*, *Scedin*,' *Onom.* has only Sedwine. The liquids *n* and *l* easily interchange.

SHEUCHAN (Stranraer). 1667 Sewehane. G. *suidheachan*, dimin. of *suidhe*, 'a seat.' The *sh* comes late. *Cf.* Seeghane and Seehanes, Ireld.

SHIANT Isles (Minch), Ben SHIANTA (Ardnamurchan). G. *seunta*, 'enchanted, sacred,' fr. *seun*, 'a charm.' *Cf.* MINISHANT and Penzance, 'holy headland.'

SHIB-, SKIBBERSCROSS (Sutherland). Pron. Shéever-. 1360 Sibyrs-(k)oc, 1535 Heberriscors, 1562 Syborskeg, Schiberskek. In G. Siobarscaig. W. says, N. *siðu-bur-skiki*, 'side-bower-strip'; *cf.* ABERSCROSS. But the first part may be fr. a man *Sæbeorht*; *cf.* similar forms of Sepscott, *Pl. N. Devon* 68.

SHIEL, L. (Moydart). *Adamn.* Sale. G. Seile ; or Saoil (W.). Uncertain.

SHIELDAIG (L. Torridon). Perh. 'sheltering bay,' Norse G. *aig*, N. *vík*, and O.N. *skjöld-r*, 'a shield.' W. says, fr. N. *sild*, 'herring.'

SHIEL HILL (4, Galloway), SHIELDHILL (Falkirk, Lochmaben), SHIELHILL (Stanley, Oathlaw). 1629 prob. Stan., Shilhill, 1745 Falk. Shielhill, and so still pron. Prob. all as above, 'shielding, sheltering hill,' and not as in GALASHIELS.

SHILLINGLAW (Traquair). 1512 Schelyn-. Not fr. *shilling*, but *shieling*, 'pasture for cattle' and *law*, 'hill.' *Shieling*, which also means 'a hut,' was early in Sc. fr. N.; *cf.* 1150–53 *Reg. Dunferm.* 33 Rectas divisas et scalingas de Fathenechten. *N.E.D.*'s earliest is 1225.

SHIN, L. (Lairg). 1595 Shyn. 'Loch of the charm,' G. *seun*, *sian*, *cf.* SHIANT. But SHINNOCK, Kirkcowan, 1633 Shanknock, is G. *sean cnoc*, 'old hill.'

SHIRA, R. and L. (Inverary), SHIRRAMORE and -BEG (Badenoch). In. S. 1572 Shyro. Ba. S. 1603 Schyroche. Perh. fr. G. *siar*, 'western'; but W. prefers *siòrabh*, 'lasting river.' *Mòr* is 'big,' *beag*, 'little.'

SHISKINE (Arran). *a*. 1250 Cesken, 1550 -kane. G. and Ir. *sescenn*, *seasgan*, 'a marsh.' *Cf.* Cessintully, Menteith, 1305 Seskentully, and Sheskin, Seskin, Ireland.

SHOTTS (N. Lanark). 1399 Bartramshotts. O.E. *scéat*, 'corner, nook, then, division of land'; *cf.* Aldershot, Shotover, etc. Also Coxithill, St. Ninian's, 1328 Terra de Kokschote, 1584 Cockshothill. This *shot* is not in *N.E.D.* till 1490.

SHUNA (Luing, Appin). *Sic* 1511, but *Adamn.* Sainea, *c.* 1380 *Fordun* Sunay, 1580 Senna Eilean. G. *seun, -na,* 'a protecting charm'; *cf.* SHIN. SHONA, Moydart, is 'look-out isle,' O.N. *sjóna,* 'sight'; but Adamn. could not have a N. name.

SHURRERY (Halkirk). 'Pig-shieling,' O.N. *sý-r,* accus. *sú,* and G. *airigh.* (M.) *Cf.* BLINGERY.

SIBBALDBIE (Applegarth). 'Dwelling of Sibbald,' O.E. *Sigebeald;* and see -by. *Cf.* 1328 Sybbalbe, near Burntisland.

SIDLAW Hills (Angus). 1799 Seedlaws. Perh. fr. *side,* 'seat'; *cf.* MORNINGSIDE and G. *suidhe,* O.G. *suide,* 'a seat.'

SILLIEBABIE (? St. Andrew's). *Sic* 1517 *Inquis.* Perh. O.G. *seileach beabh,* here in loc., 'willow by the grave.' Said to be the origin of *bawbee.*

SILLYCHARDOCH (Aberdeensh.). G. *seileach a' cheardaich,* 'willow by the smithy.' *Cf.* DALNACARDOCH.

SIMPRIN (Duns). 1159 Simprig, *c.* 1160 Sympering, 1250 Simp'nge, *c.* 1300 Sympring. Like Sempringarth, Lincs., prob. patronymic fr. an unrecorded *Sindbeorn.* We have *Sindbeorht, -perht* and *Sigebeorn.* See -ing, p. 52.

SINCLAIRTON (Kirkcaldy). From the *St. Clairs,* earls of Rosslyn, whose former seat, Dysart House, is near by.

SINK (Plean). 1819 Sike. O.E. *síc,* Sc. *sike, syke,* 'watercourse, rill, then, marshy hollow with streams, a ditch.' North. E. and Sc. *sink* mean much the same. See N.E.D. *sink* sb. 7.

SINNAHARD (Lumsden). Prob. G. *sine na h'àrde,* 'height with the boss,' *sine,* 'a pap.'

SKAIL, L. (Sandwick, Ork.). Common Ork. farm name, O.N. *skali,* 'a shieling.' *Cf.* GALASHIELS and Seascale, Cumbld.

SKEABOST (Portree). Perh. 'place set askew,' O.N. *skeif-r,* 'skew, oblique.' W. derives fr. a man *Skith.* See *bost,* p. 42.

SKEDDIN (Freuchie). 'Shedding, shed,' O.E. *sced.*

SKEIR, SKERRIES, common name for rocky islets, esp. in Minch—Skeirinoe, etc. N. and Dan. *skjær,* 'cliff, rock,' with pl. as in Pentland Skerries; 1329 Petland-Sker, and the SKARES off Cruden. *Cf.* Auskerry, E. of Orkney, *saga* Austr-sker, 'eastern rock,' SCARCLET and SCOUR.

SKELBO (Dornoch). *c.* 1210 Scel-, *a.* 1300 Scellebol, 1455 Skelbole. 'Shelly place,' O.N. *skel,* O.E. *scel,* 'a shell'; and see -bol, p. 42. An Eng. scribe, 1290, writes it Schelbotel, see MOREBATTLE; and *cf.* SKIBO.

SKELDA Ness (Shetland). Prob. 'shield or shelter isle,' as in SHIELDAIG, with N. *a, ay,* 'island.'

SKÉLMORLIE (Wemyss Bay). *c.* 1400 -morley. Prob. like Skelmersdale, Ormskirk, *Dom.* Schelmeresdale, 'lea, meadow of *Scealdamer*,' a known O.E. name. See LEE.

SKELPIE (Kingskettle). G. *sgealbach*, here in loc., 'place full of splinters or shells.'

SKELSTON (Dumfries). 'Farm town made up of shielings or huts,' O.N. *skali*. See GALASHIELS.

SKENE (Peterculter). *Sic* 1318. *Cf.* 1290 Johannes Skene. Ir. or G. *sceathin*, 'a bush.' *Cf.* SKEENGALLIE, Kirkinner, fr. G. *gallach*, 'standing stones,' here in loc.

SKERRINGTON (Ayr). 1507 Skyrrenetoun. 'Village of *Scira*, *-an*,' 2 in *Onom*. See -ing, p. 52.

SKERRY, often SKERRY-VORE (Tyree). G. *mòr*, 'big.' See SKEIR.

SKIACH, R. (Kiltearn), SKEOCH (Bannockburn). Ba. S. 1317 Skewok, 1329 -eokis, *Pont* Skyoch. G. *sgitheach*, 'blackthorn.' But St. Skeoch's or St. Skay's burying-ground, Craig, Montrose, and a vanished St. Skeoch's chapel, Bannockburn, are fr. *Skiath* or *Skeoch*, a royal Munster saint.

SKIBA (Islay). Dan. *skib-aa*, 'ship-water' or 'stream.'

SKIBO (Dornoch). 1275 Schytheboll, 1557 Skebo. In G. Sgiòbul. Perh. fr. O.N. *skeið*, 'a warship,' and see -bol, p. 42. W. prefers '*Skithi's* place' here and in SKIARY, L. Hourn, G. *airigh*, 'shieling.' Glen SKIBLE, Skipness, 1511 Skippail, is prob. the same.

SKILLYMARNO (Auchnachar, Aberdn.). *a.* 1150 *Bk. Deer* Scali merlech or -lie. N. *scali*, 'hut,' and G. *merlach*, 'thief' (M.). *Cf.* GALASHIELS.

SKINFLATS (Grangemouth). No trace of a tannery here. But connexion with O.E. *scén*, Ger. *schön*, 'beautiful,' is very doubtful. *Flats*, 'meadows,' is common hereabouts—Millflats, etc. It is found in names as early as 1296.

SKIPNESS (Tarbert). *c.* 1250 Schepehinch, 1260 Skipnish, 1262 Schypinche. 'Ship ness,' O.N. *skíp*, Dan. *skib*, O.E. *scip*, 'a ship,' and O.N. *næs*, 'cape,' or G. *innis*, 'island, peninsula.' *Cf.* INCH and ARDALANISH.

SKIRLING (Biggar). *a.* 1400 Scrawlin, *c.* 1535 Scraling. Prob. 'Scaur, scar,' O.N. *sker*, in Eng. *c.* 1350, 'rock, crag,' and O.E. *hlynn*, 'torrent, pool,' W. *llyn*. *Cf.* Dunskirloch (G. *sgeirleach*, 'rocky'), Kirkcolm.

SKYE. *c. Ptolemy* Ski- Skētis, *a.* 700 *Adamn.* Scia, *Tighern.* Scith, *c.* 1100 *St. Berchan* Do bhile sgiath, 'from the shield's edge,' prob. meaning Skye, *Sagas* Skið, Skid, 1266 Scy, 1292 Skey. Prob. Ir. *sciath*, G. *sgiath*, 'a wing,' fr. its shape. *Cf.* Dunskey, Portpatrick.

SKYREBURN (Anwoth). Prob. fr. SKEIR, 'a rock.'

SLAINS (Cruden). 1165–9 Slanes, *c.* 1280 -nys. G. *sleamhuinn*, 'smooth,' with *-ais* suff. of place. *Cf.* 1549 'Loch of Slene,' [1] and Slane, Tara.

SLAMANNAN (S. Stirling). *Sic* 1365, but 1250 Slethmanin, *Chron. Iona* ann. 711 Campus Manonn; pron. *a.* 1800 Slaym-. 'Moor, hill-face,' G. and Ir. *sliabh*, 'of *Manau*,' see CLACKMANNAN. *Cf.* Cremannan, Balfron, and Slamonia, Inch.

SLANGER and SLANGHILL Burns (Largs). N. *slangi*, 'a snake.' The -hill is perh. for N. *gil*, 'gill, ravine.'

SLAPIN, L. (S. Skye). Perh. fr. N. *slappi*, 'a lump fish.' There is a G. *slabhgan*, 'a reddish seaweed.'

SLATEFORD (Edinburgh). Hardly as in next. Must be as it stands, but ? why. *a.* 1700 Edzell was Sclaitford.

SLEAT (Skye). *a.* 1400 Slate (so pron. still), 1475 Slet, 1588 Slait. O.N. *slett-r*, 'smooth,' *slétta*, 'a flat piece of land.' The Sound is sheltered, and the island remarkably level for Hebrides. But Ardenslate, 1401 -inslatt, Dunoon, is 'slatey height,' G. *sgleàt*, 'a slate.'

SLEWCREEN (Kirkmaiden), SLEWNARK (Portpatrick). G. *sliabh crion*, 'withered moor or heath,' and 'moor of the pig,' O.G. *an arc*.

SLIACH (Drumblade, Glengairn). Dr. S. *c.* 1375 *Barbour* The Slevach. G. *sliabh -ach*, 'moory, hilly place.'

SLIDDERY (S. Arran). *Pont* Sleadroi. In G. Slàidridh or Slaiteridh, but G. origin seems impossible. 'Slippery'; *sliddery* is in Eng. *a.* 1225, O.E. *slidor*, 'slippery.' *Cf.* Slidderick, Kirkmaiden, and SLIPPERFIELD.

SLIGACHAN, -ICHAN (Skye). G. 'abounding in shells,' G. *slige*, 'a shell,' with *-ach* suff. of place and *-an* termin. *Cf.* Geodha ('goe') Sligach, Durness.

SLIN, L. (Tain). *c.* 1560 Lochislyne. W. says, not G. *sleamhuinn*, 'smooth,' but *slinn*, 'a weaver's sleye.' *Cf.* SLAINS.

SLIOCH (mtn., L. Maree). G. *sleagh*, 'a spear.'

SLIPPERFIELD (W. Linton). *Sic* 1682. *Slipper*, obs. or dial. for 'slippery.'

SLOCKGARROCH (Portpatrick). G. *sloc carrach*, 'rough, rocky pit or hollow.'

SMAILHOLM (Kelso). Pron. Smailom. *a.* 1246 Smalham. O.E. *smæl hám*, 'small house'; or perh. 'village,' called fr. a man *Smail* or *Small*. On interchange of -ham and -holm *cf.* HOLM.

[1] This is a ballad title in *Complaynt Scotld.*, prob. not L. Slin.

SMEATON (Ormiston, Carsphairn). Or. S. *c.* 1150 *Dunferm. Chart.* Smithetune; also *ibid. c.* 1160 Smithebi. 'Smooth, level village,' O.E. *smethe, smoethe. Cf.* Smeaton, Pontefract, *Dom.* Smethe-, Smedetun.

SMERBY, High and Low (Kintyre). O.N. *smjórr bi,* 'butter house' or 'hamlet'; same root as *smear*; seen also in Smerrin, Shetland, N. *smör-vang-r,* 'butter field.' See -by, p. 41.

SMOO, Cave of (Durness). Icel. *smuga,* 'a hole, hiding-place,' fr. *smúgja,* 'to creep,' same root as *smuggle. Cf.* Pettasmog, 'Picts' hole,' Unst.

SNÁEGOW (Dunkeld). 1506 Snago. 'Snowy gully or ravine,' O.N. *snœ-r,* Dan. *snee,* 'snow,' and O.N. *gjá,* 'goe, cleft.'

SNAPE (Coulter). O.N. *snáp-r,* 'apex, pointed end,' Dan. *sneb,* 'beak,' Sc. *neb. Cf.* Snab Hill, Kells, Snape, Sussex, *sic* 1279, and 4 in Northumbld. and Durham. Snabothalgh, *sic* 1325, Northumbd., may be a dimin.

SNIZORT (Skye). 1501 Snesfurd, 1526 Sneisport, 1662 Snisort. 'Fjord, frith of snow,' O.N. *snæ-r, snæs.* Henderson suspected here a Norseman *Sní,* as *æ* would not yield *i. Cf.* KNOYDART.

SOAY (Braeadale). 1549 Soa. 'Pig isle.' Dan. and Sw. *so,* 'a *sow.*' But, as the *o* is long, perh. fr. O.N. *sauða,* 'a sheep.'

SOLLAS (Lochmaddy). G. *solus,* 'a (beacon) light.' *Cf.* RESOLIS.

SOLSGIRTH (Dollar). 1573 Solissgarth. 'Garth, enclosure of *Soli,*' 1 in *Onom. Cf.* APPLEGARTH.

SOLWAY FRITH. 1218 *Patent R.* Sulewad, *c.* 1300 Sulway; also Sulliva. Also called Tracht-Romra (*Adamn.*), 'Strand of the mighty sea,' and Scottiswathe, N. and Dan. *wath,* 'ford.' Cannot be fr. the tribe *Selgovae.* It is 'muddy ford,' O.N. *söl,* O.E. *sol,* 'mud,' prob. same root as *soil* sb[3]. Henderson suggests N. *soll,* 'swill,' *sull-r,* 'a boil.' Silloth on Solway, 1537, Silleth, may be the same name.

SOONHOPE (Peeblessh.). *c.* 1200 Swhynhope, 'shut in valley for swine,' O.E. *swín,* Dan. *svün*; but *soon* is Sc. pl. of *soo,* 'a sow'; *cf.* shoe and shoon. On *hope,* see HOBKIRK.

SORBIE (Whithorn), SOROBY (Tyree). Wh. S. *Pont* Soirbuy. Ty. S. 1461 Sourbi, 1561 Soiribi, 1615 Sorbi. 'Dwelling amid the mud or swamp,' N. *saur.* On -bie, see p. 41. *Cf.* Sourby, Ewesdale, and Sowerby, Yorks, *Dom.* Sour-, Sorebi.

SORN (Mauchline). G. *sorn,* 'a snout, a kiln.'

SOURIN (Raasay). Perh. root as in SORBIE, with *-in,* N. art.

SOUTHWICK (Colvend). Prob. *c.* 1280 *Bagamund* Suchayt, 'south thwaite,' 1482 Suthek. O.E. *súth wíc,* 'south house' or 'hamlet.'

SOUTRA (Fala), SOUTRIES (Beith). Fa. S. *c.* 1160 Soltre, 1455 Sowtra, 1461 Soltra. Perh. Brit. *sul tra, tre,* 'watch-tower,' lit. 'outlook house.' *Cf.* W. *sulw,* 'a sight, a view.'

SPEAN, Br. (Ft. William). 1516 Spayng, 1552 Spane. Thought a dimin. of SPEY. W. compares Speen, Newbury; but see *Pl. N. Eng.* s.v.

SPELVE, L. (Mull). Prob. Pict. for 'stony.' *Cf.* G. *sgealb,* W. *ysgolp,* 'a fragment, a splinter.'

SPEY, R. *Sic* 1451, *c.* 150 *Ptolemy* Tvesis (prob. a shot at a Brit. name; W. *chw* is an awkward sound), 1124 Spe. Wh. Stokes thought its root, Ir. *sceim,* G. *sgeith,* W. *chwyd,* 'to vomit, spue.' It is the swiftest river in Sc. W. is strangely dogmatic that it is Ir. *scé,* W. *yspyddad,* 'hawthorn.'

SPIGIE, L. (S. Shetland). Prob. fr. Sw. *spigg,* 'a stickleback.'

SPINNINGDALE (Ardgay). 1464 Spanigidill, 1545 Spanzidaill. Prob. fr. Icel. *spanning,* 'temptation,' but it may be fr. *spinning,* Icel. and Sw. *spinna,* 'to spin.'

SPITTAL (many). *c.* 1160 De Ospitali. *Spital* is the old form of *hospital* or hospice, in G. *spideal.*

SPOTT (Dunbar). 1298 Spot (1327 de Spotis, ? Peeblessh.). O.N. *spotti,* 'bit, piece,' in Eng. *a.* 1200. *Cf. c.* 1200 *Coldstream Chart.* Pratum qui vocatur Bradspotes. The earliest in *N.E.D.* in this sense is *c.* 1440. *Cf.* Spotland, Lancs.

SPROUSTON (Kelso). *a.* 1124 Sprostona, *a.* 1147–52 Sprouis-, *a.* 1250 Sproueston. 'Village of *Sprow,*' 3 in *Onom.* *Cf.* Sprouston, Norwich, and *Dom.* Chesh. Sprostune.

SPYNIE (Elgin). *c.* 1220 Spyny. W. connects with SPEY and L. *spina,* 'a thorn.'

STACK, often in Caithness. O.N. *stak,* G. *stac,* 'cliff, isolated rock,' cognate with Eng. *stack.* *Cf.* Car Stackie, Durness, where we have the adj. *stacach,* 'abounding in precipices,' in loc.

STAFFA (Mull). N. *staf-ay,* 'isle with the staves,' *i.e.,* its basaltic columnar rocks. In STAFFIN, Portree, the N. art. *inn,* 'the,' is suffixed. The rocks are very similar.

STAIR (Ayr). G. *stair,* 'stepping stones, path over a bog.'

STANDALANE (Falkirk, Peeblessh., Dumfries). Humorous name, given to a solitary house.

STANHOPE (Drummelzier). O.E. *stan,* 'stone, rock.' On *hope,* 'an enclosed valley,' see HOBKIRK.

STANLEY (Perth). Named *c.* 1700 fr. Lady Amelia Stanley, daughter of Earl Derby, and afterwards M'chess of Athole. Five in England, *c.* 938 *chart.* Stanleage, 'stony lea.'

STAPLEGORTON. Old name of Langholm. *c.* 1180 Stapel- 1493 Stabilgortoun. O.E. *stapole, -ple,* 'a post, then, a market'; *cf.* Barnstaple; and G. *gortan,* 'a little field or garden.'

STAR (Markinch). O.N. *storr, starar,* M.E. *star,* 'sedge.' *Cf.* Starry shaw ('sedgy wood'), Benhar, and Starbeck, Harrogate.

STARTA of Sanday, The. O.N. *stert-r,* O.E. *steort,* 'the tail.' *Cf.* Start Point (as this is also called), Devon, and the bird red-start.

STAY-THE-VOYAGE (Kirkcowan). *Cf.* the Rest and be Thankfuls.

STEELE ROAD (Hawick). Jam. says Sc. *steel* is 'a wooded cleugh or precipice'; but O.E. *steall* is 'place, stall.' *Cf.* 1136 *Reg. Dunferm.,* Aldestelle, ASHIESTEEL, and Steel, Hexham, 1268 Stele.

STEMSTER (Wick, Orkney). Wi. S. 1557 Stambustar. Or. S. 1559 Stembister. 'Place like the stem or prow of a ship,' O.N. *stafn, stamn,* O.E. *stemn.* See *bolstað-r,* p. 42.

STENHOUSEMUIR (Larbert). Local pron. Stánismare. *c.* 1200 Johannes de Stan hous, M.E. for 'stone house,' 1264 Stanus. Oldest Eng. name in the shire. *Cf.* STONEHOUSE.

STENNIS, -NESS (Stromness). *c.* 970 Steinsness, *c.* 1500 Stanehous (an ignorant Anglicising), 1700 Stennis. '(? standing) stone ness' or 'cape.' O.N. *steinn,* Sw. and Dan. *sten,* 'stone.'

STE(I)NSCHEL (Skye). Prob. N. for 'stone shieling or booth.' *Cf.* above and GALASHIELS.

STENTON (Haddington). *a.* 1150 Steinton, 'Stone village.' The forms show N. influence; see above.

STEPPS ROAD (Glasgow). Road made with staves, O.Sc. *steppe, stap,* O.E. *stæpe,* lit. 'a step.'

STEVENSTON (Saltcoats). 1246 -toun, 1437 Stewynstoun. 'Stephen's or Steven's village.'

STEWARTON (Kilmarnock). 1201 -toun. Village of Walter, High Steward (O.E. *stiweard,* lit. 'sty-keeper') or Seneschal of David I, *c.* 1140.

STEY GAIL (steep hill, Leadhills). Sc. for 'steep gable,' O.N. *gafl,* also Sc. *gavel.*

STICHILL (Kelso). *Sic c.* 1200, but *c.* 1270 Stichehill. 'Pathway hill,' O.E. *stig,* 3 *stighe,* 'a footpath.' *Cf.* The Sty Pass.

STINCHAR, R. (Ballantrae). 1538–9 -chear, 1682 -siar. Perh. river with 'the awry turn,' G. *staon char.*

STIRKOKE (Wick). Perh. O.N. *sterk-r ak-r,* 'strong, vigorous field,' lit. 'acre.'

STIRLING. *a.* 1124 and *Bened. Peterb.* Strevelin, *c.* 1125 Struelin, *a.* 1182 Striuellin, *c.* 1250 Estriuelin, 1295 -evelyn, 1455 Striviling, *c.* 1470 Sterling, 1682 Strivelinge, *c.* 1130 Striuelinshire.

Brit. or W. *ystre Felyn* (G. *Mhelain*), 'dwelling of Velyn,' aspirated form of Melyn, Meling, often confused with MELVILLE, and perh. found also in DUNFERMLINE. W. *felyn* is 'yellow,' aspirated in Melyn llyn, Llanrwst; a man Velyn is in 1312 *Patent R.* *a.* 1100 St *Berchan* has a Sruthlinn near Perth, lit. 'river-pool,' perh. a 'shot' at this Brit. name by a Gael. The mod. G. is Sruithla; *cf. Dean of Lismore's Bk.* 161, 'Duncan a Sruthlee.' To derive Stirling fr. this mod. G. is to ignore the early and persistent *v* and *n*. Gaels themselves are very uncertain. *E.g.*, the Dean of Lismore, *c.* 1542, writes under 1124 Strieveleich, but under 1213 Streulyne.

STOBCROSS (Glasgow). 1573 Stobcors. See STOBO and BEAN-CROSS.

STOBINEAN (mtn., S. Perth). 1783 -inian. This seems a mod. invention. In G. it is *am beinnean*, 'the peak.'

STOBO (Peebles). 1116 Stoboc, 1170 Stubho, 1186 Stobhou, 1206 -bbo, 1223 Stobohowe, 1296 Stubbehok. O.E. *stubb*, O.N. *stubb-r, stobbe* Sc. *stob*, 'a stump' and, either HAUGH, 'pasture,' *cf.* forms of SAUCHIE, or *how*, O.E. *holh*, *holg*, 'a hollow.' *Cf.* *c.* 1200 Poltenstobbeh, in this parish.

STOBS (Hawick). *c.* 1360 -bis. 'Place of stumps.' See above.

STOCKBRIDGE (Edinburgh, Cockburnspath). Wooden bridge there, made of stocks or stakes, O.E. *stocc*, lit. 'tree-stump,' prob. same root as *stick*. *Cf.* Stockbridge, Sussex, *Dom.* Estocbrigge.

STOCKING Hill (Old Luce). Sc. *stoken*, 'enclosed,' *steek*, 'to fasten, enclose,' *N.E.D.* *steek* vb.^{1}.

STODFAULD Burn (Cullen). *Sic* 1542. Same as Stotfold, Herts. 1007 Stodfald, O.E. for 'fold, enclosure for the breeding stud.'

STOER (Lochinver). *Orkn. Sag.* Staur, O.N. *staur-r*, 'stake, pole.'

STONEHAVEN (Kincardine). 1629 Steanhyve; also Stonehive. O.N. *steinn höfn*, 'stony haven'; *hive* seems a local Sc. form.

STONEHOUSE (Larkhall, Sorbie, Twynholm). La. S. 1275 Stanehouse, 1298 Stanhus, and this is usually the pron. still. *Cf.* STENHOUSE.

STONEYBRIDGE (S. Uist). G. *staoni-brig*, N. *stein brekka*, 'stone slope.'

STONEYBYRES Falls (Lanark). To take this as it stands, fr. Sc. *byre*, 'cow-house,' would hardly make sense. Prob. corrup. W. *son y byddariad*, 'noise of deafening,' would be a bold guess. The *dd* easily becomes mute, and *-iad* would easily drop. Then some Scot would think the ending *-byre* and add an *s*.

STONEYHAUGH (Liddesdale). 1376 Stanyhalch. See HAUGH.

STONEYKIRK (Portpatrick). 1535 Steneker, 1546 -akere, 1735 Stevenskirk. Sir H. Maxwell says, dedicated to St *Stephen*, in Sc. *Steenie*. But 1546 looks like 'stony acre' or 'field.'

STORMONTH (district, E. Perth). *c.* 1250 Starmun, 1292 -monthe. Prob. G. *starr monadh*, 'crooked, distorted hill,' rather than fr. G. *stair*, 'stepping stones.' (W.)

STORNOWAY (Lewis). G. sronbaidh ('point bay'). 1511 Stornochway, 1549 Steornaway, 1716 Stornbay. 1549, close to present pron., suggests 'steering, steerage bay,' O.N. *stjórn vág-r*. *Cf.* SCALLOWAY.

STOW (Galashiels). 1560 Stow of Tweeddail. O.E. *stow*, 'place, town.'

STRACATHRO (Brechin). *c.* 1212 Stracatherach, *Fordun* -cathrow. G. *srath*, O.G. *srad*, usually spelt in Eng. *strath*; but, as final *th* becomes mute, we often find only *stra*. Already used separately 1540 *R.M.S.* Cum lie strath. The *t* is an Eng. device to aid pron. In G. *sr* is always *sr*. Occasionally we find *c* or *k*, see STRATHMIGLO. In W. *ystrad*, *cf.* ANNANDALE and YESTER, also 1298 *Welsh writ* Strat Tewy. Stracathro is 'valley of the seat,' G. *cathair*, *-rach*.

STRACHAN (Banchory). Pron. Strawn. *a.* 1153 Stratheyhan, 1333 -echin, 1599 -auchtyne; also -auchin. Perh. 'valley of the little horse,' G. *eachain*; *cf.* too *achain*, 'prayer.'

STRACHÚR (L. Fyne). 1368 -ore, 1490 -quhour. 'Valley with the twist or turn,' G. *cor*, *chur*.

STRAITON (Edinburgh, Maybole). Ed. S. 1296 Stratone. Not '*straight* village,' that is a late adj., but, like Stratford and the Eng. Strettons, *Dom.* Stratone, 'village on the Roman road,' L. *stratum*, O.E. *strœt*, our *street*.

STRALACHLAN (Strachur). 'Valley of *Lachlan*' or '*Lochlin*.' A Gileskel M'Lachlan found in Argyll, 1292. See STRACATHRO.

STRAMALLOCHY (Dalmally). Often Glen Strae. This is far more expressive, 'glen with the humped, rounded hills,' G. *meallach*, here in loc.

STRANRÁER. *c.* 1320 -rever, 1556 Stronerawar, 1600 Stranraver. G. *sròn reamhar*, 'thick point,' lit. 'nose,' *i.e.*, the Loch Ryan peninsula. *Cf.* Canrawer, Galway.

STRATHALLAN (S. Perth). 1187 Strathalun, -alin. See ALLAN.

STRATHARDLE (Skye, Perthsh.). Sk. S. *c.* 1160 -erdel, 1542 -ardol. Pe. S. *c.* 1200 -ardolf, 1561 -dell. Prob. tautology. 'Glen, dale with the river,' N. *áar dál*.

STRATHAVON (Banffsh.). *c.* 1190 -ouen, STRATHAVEN (Lanark). Pron. Stráven. 1552 Straithawane, 'Valley of the AVEN or AVON.'

STRATHBLANE (Milngavie). *c.* 1200 Strachblachan, -blahane, 1238 -blachyne, *c.* 1240 Stratblathane, *c.* 1300 Strablane. 'Glen with the little flowers,' G. *blàthan.*

STRATHBUNGO (Glasgow). Local pron. Strabungy. G. *srath Mhunga,* 'valley of St. Mungo or Kentigern,' *c.* 550.

STRATHCLYDE. *a.* 910 *Asser* Stratduttenses (*d.* for *cl*), 875 *O.E. Chron.* (Worc.), 'Stræcled Weala cyning,' 977 *Hist. Briton.* Strat Clut, *a.* 1150 *Gaimar* Streclued, *c.* 1097 *Flor. Worc.* Rex Streatcledwalorum. See CLYDE.

STRATHEARN (Perthsh.). *Pict. Chron.* Sraithh'erni, *c.* 1185 Stradearn, *c.* 1190 -herin, Stratherne, *a.* 1200 Sradeern. See EARN.

STRATHENDRY (Leslie). *a.* 1169 -enry, 1319 -anery. = ENDRICK.

STRATHERRICK (L. Ness). 1282 -arkik; later, -keg. G. *srath fharagaig,* 'lower ravine river,' fr. *far,* 'below,' and *gag,* 'a cleft.'

STRATHKINNESS (St. Andrew's). 1144 Stradkines, 1156 Kinninis, 'Valley at the head of the waterfall,' G. *cinn an eas.*

STRATHMARTINE (Dundee). 1250 Stratheymartin (-ey, sign of loc.). 'Glen of St. *Martin*' of Tours. *Cf.* KILMARTIN.

STRATHMIGLO (Auchtermuchty). *Sic* 1517, but *a.* 1200 Scradimigglock, 1294 Stramygloke, *c.* 1385 -miglaw, 'Valley of the swine-pen,' G. *muclach. Cf.* DRUMMUCKLOCH.

STRATHPEFFER, see PEFFER.

STRATHWILLAN (Brodick). *Old* Terrquhilane. Dr. Cameron said, G. *tìr Chuilein,* 'land of Cuilean,' K. of Alban, 10th cny. Natives say: 'land of the whelp,' G. *cuilein.* No strath here.

STRATHY (Thurso). Loc. of G. *srath,* 'at the strath.'

STRATHYRE (Callander). 1457 -yire. 'Valley of the land,' G. *thìre*; so Rev. J. M'Lean. But natives call it Strahür, which is = STRACHUR.

STRAVITHIE (St. Andrew's). 1144 Struuithin, 1471 Strawithly, -wethy. Prob. 'rich, fertile,' G. *mheith,* 'strath,' in loc.

STRAWFRANK (Carstairs). 1528 Strafrank. G. *srath Frangach,* 'French valley,' referring to the many Norman settlers in Clydesdale.

STRICHEN (Maud). Perh. G. *striochan,* 'little streak or line.'

STRING, The. Popular name of the Monimore road, Arran. *Cf.* The String of Lorn, *sic a.* 1678; it is a mountain ridge.

STRIVEN, L. (Rothesay). 1400 Lochstryne, 1525 *R.M.S.* -strewin, 1595 Skruien (*cf.* STRACATHRO). W. says, G. Sroigheann, of obscure meaning. But natives say, stra-ínn, G. *srath Fhionn,* fr. the Ossianic hero Finn, of whom the district is full of supposed reminiscences.

STROMA (Pentland Firth). *Sic* 1455, *sagas* Straumsey, 1539 Strome. 'Island,' N. *ay*, *ey*, 'in the stream or current,' O.N. *straum-r*, Dan. *ström*. The firth here runs like a river. *Cf.* Stromoe, Faroes.

STROME (W. Ross, Reay). W. Ro. S. *sic* 1472, 1492 Stromecarranach ('of L. Carron'). See above.

STROMNESS (Orkney). *Sic* 1492, *sagas* Straumsness. See above.

STRONACHLÁCHAR (L. Katrine). G. *sròn a' chlachair*, 'cape,' lit. nose, 'of the mason.' STRONECLACHAN, Killin, is fr. *clachan*, 'village.'

STRONE (Dunoon). 1240 Strohon, *c.* 1400 Stron. G. *sròn*, 'nose, cape.' *Cf.* Stroan, Kells and Minigaff, and Stronehill, Luss.

STRONGARVALTRY (Callendar). *Sic* in *O. Stat. Acc.* 1791, where it is said to be 'nose, point, at the rough brook,' G. *garbh allt*, in loc.

STRONSAY (Orkney). *c.* 1225 *Orkn. Sag.* Stiornsey, 1529 *Jo. Ben* Stronsay vel Sdronsay. *c.* 1225 must be 'star-like island,' O.N. *stjarna*, 'a stir'; but 1529 suggests Gaelic influence.

STRONTÍAN (L. Sunart). 1789 -tean. G. *sròn tiahhain*, 'cape with the little hill.'

STROQUHAN (Girthon). Prob. G. *srath bhan*, 'white, bright valley.'

STROWAN (Crieff). STRUAN (N. Perth, Skye). Cr. S. *c.* 1200 Struuin. G. *sruthan*, 'little stream.' STRUEY, S. Arran, gives the loc.

STRUMINOCH (New Luce). G. *sròn meadhonach*, 'middle height or promontory.'

STUC a CHROIN (Ben Vorlich). G. *stuc a' chroinn*, 'horn, projecting hillock with the tree or like a plough,' *crann*. *Cron*, 'round hollow,' common in Ir. names, seems also possible.

STUDY, The (Glencoe). G. *an t'innean*, 'the anvil,' fr. the rock's shape. Study is the Sc. *stithy*, O.N. *steði*, 'an anvil.'

SUAINABOST (Butt of Lewis). 'Swain's, boy's place,' O.N. *sveinn*, Sw. *sven*, O.E. *swán*; or fr. K. *Sweyn* of Denmark and England, d. 1014. See for *bost*, p. 42.

SUILVEN (mtn., Lochinver). Perh. G. *sùil-bheinn*, 'eye-like ben,' fr. its shape, or 'prospect hill'; *cf.* SOUTRA. W. says, hybrid, fr. N. *súl-r*, 'a pillar.'

SUISGILL Burn (Kildonan, Suthld.). Said to be N. *seyðis-gil*, 'gill, ravine of the saithe or coal-fish.' But how comes it here? In G. it is *saigh*, *saoidh*.

SULLAM (Lerwick). O.N. *sule- heim-r*, 'home of the gannets or solan geese'; *cf.* HODDAM, also Sule-skerry, W. of Stromness, 1424 Soolsker, and Salishader, Skye; though here M. preferred N. *súl-r*, 'pillar'; -shader is fr. *setr*, see p. 42.

SUMBURGH HEAD (S. Shetland). *Sagas* Sunnboejar höfði, Svinborg, 1506 Swynbrocht. Prob. 'the swain's castle or hold'; see SUAINABOST, BORGUE and BROUGH, and *cf.* SWANNAY. Höfði is fr. O.N. *höfuð*, 'head'; and S. Roost is N. *röst*, 'a whirlpool,' lit. 'strife.' *Cf.* Rouste, an eddy, Guernsey.

SUMMERFORD (Falkirk). Borrowed fr. one of the Eng. Summerfords, *Dom.* Chesh. Sumreford, 'place on a river fordable only in summer.' *Cf.* the common Winterbourne, and Summerton, New Luce. The Summer Isles, L. Broom, have no G. name as a group. Sheep are 'summered' there.

SUNART, L. (Morven). 1372 Swynwort, 1392 -awort, '*Fjord*, bay of K. *Sweyn*,' in L. chrons. *Suanus*, *Sueno*, d. 1014. See KNOYDART.

SUTHERLAND. *c.* 1250 Suthernelande, 1300 -erlandia, in N., Sudrland, 'southern land,' compared with the Nordreys or Orkneys. *Cf.* Sudreys, N. for the Hebrides.

SUTORS of CROMARTY. 1593 *Act Parlmt.* Craiges callit the Sowteris. G. na Sùdraichean or 'the Tanneries' (W.). Two cliffs on either side the firth's mouth. Form influenced by Sc. *sutor*, 'shoemaker.'

SWANNAY (Kirkwall). 1696 *Torfæus* Sviney, N. for 'isle of swine,' *cf.* SWONA; but now 'isle of swans,' O.N. *svan-r*, 'a swan.' *Cf.* Swanbustar, *sic c.* 1500, still a district in Orphir.

SWARTABACK (Orphir). 1502 Swarthbak, 1595 Swartabreck. O.N. *svart-r brekka*, 'dark,' lit. 'swarthy, hill-slope.' *Cf.* CLIBRECK.

SWEERIE (burn, Freuchie). Prob., as a place for courting, fr. G. *suire*, 'a nymph,' or *suiriche*, 'a wooer.'

SWERDALE (Creich). 1275 Swerdisdale, 1508 Suerdule, 'dale of the green sward or turf,' O.N. *svörd-r*, Dan. *svaer*. *Cf.* Swordale, Kiltearn, 1479 Sweredull.

SWINEY (Lybster). *Sic* in *Orkn. Sag.* Jos. Anderson thought it so called fr. being the property of Grim of SWONA. *Cf.* Sviney, Faroes.

SWINTON (Duns). *c.* 1098 Suineston, *c.* 1120 Suin-, Swintun. 'Village of *Suen* or *Swegen*,' a common O.E. name, not, 'of the *swine*.' But *cf.* Swinewood, Ayton, 1098 Swinewde and SOONHOPE; also Dalswinton. Four in England.

SWONA (Scapa Flow). *Orkn. Sag.* Sviney, see SWANNAY; other *sagas*, Swefney, 1564 Swonay. *Cf.* O.E. *swán*, M.E. *swon*, 'a swineherd.'

SYDSERF (N. Berwick). 1290 Sideserfe. 'Seat of ST. SERF.' *Cf.* MORNINGSIDE. He lived at Culross and was reputed friend of St. Mungo.

X

SYMINGTON (Troon, Biggar, Fountainhall). Tr. S. 1160 'Inter terram Simonis Loccardi and Prestwick,' 1293 Symondstona in Kyl. Bi. S. *c.* 1189 Villa Symonis Lockard, *a.* 1300 Symondstone. 'Village of *Simon* Lockhart,' a local knight. *Cf.* CRAIGLOCKHART.

TAIN (E. Ross). 1226 Tene, 1257 Thayn, *c.* 1375 Tayne. [1369 *Recds. Earld. Orkn.*, 2nd ser. 16, Sira Christian of Teyn seems in Orkney.] Much disputed. *Cf.* R. Tene, Staffs., *Dom.* Tene, *a.* 1400 Teyne. Phonet. most prob. is O.N. *teinn*, 'twig, osier,' cognate with O.E. *tænil*, dial. *tenel*, 'a basket,' so Tain Water may be like R. Tone, Somerset, O.E. *Tan*, *i.e.* 'twig.' But *cf.* O.Ir. *tàin*, 'water.' (Mack.) In G. it is Baile Dhubhaich, from St Duthac.

TAING of TORNESS, The (Shetland). O.N. *þang*, 'a low, projecting cape.' Tor- is prob. the god *Thor*.

TALISKER (Raasay). Capt. Thomas's rule is, where a N. name in H has been thought a G. gen. the *h* is dropped and *t* prefixed. Thus the orig. name here will be N. *hjalli-sker*, 'shelf-like rock or SKEIR.' *Cf.* Talladale, L. Maree, N. Hjalladal. No G. word can be written in nom. beginning with *h*.

TALLA (Tweedsmuir, castle, L. of Menteith). W. *tal*, 'that tops or fronts, a brow,' name appropriate to the precipitous burn. *Cf.* the bard Taliessin, W. for 'bright-browed.' W. says, An Talla, L. Broom, is G., 'the hall.'

TALMINE (Tongue). G. *talamh mìn*, 'smooth, level land.' *Cf.* Talnotry, Minigaff, 'dung (*otraigh*) land,' but 1572 Tonnotrie.

TAMFOUR Hill (Falkirk). 1617 Thomfour, 1632 Tomefurhill. G. *tom fuar*, 'cold knoll,' influenced by *Thomas*, Sc. *Tam*.

TANDLEMUIR (Lochwinnoch). 1460 Tandil-. Prob. fr. O.N. *tand-r*, *-dri*, 'fire,' hence Sc. *tandle*, *-nle*, 'a large bonfire,' esp. at May Day or Hallowe'en.

TANDOO (Portpatrick). *Pont* Tondow. G. *tòn dubh*, 'dark height like a rump or buttock.' *Cf.* THUNDERGAY.

TANKERNESS (Kirkwall). 1502 -arnes. 'Ness, cape of *Tancrad* or *Thancred*.' *Cf.* THANKERTON.

TANNADICE (Forfar). 1250 Tanethais, 1266 -nethes, 1322 Thanachayis. Prob. G. *tanach-ais*, 'thin place,' *-ais* suff. of place.

TANNAHILL (Kilmaurs). 1599 Tannochill (surname). G. *teannach*, 'narrow place.' *Cf.* Tannach, Wick, Tannack, Kilbirnie.

TANNER, TANAR Water (Aboyne). 1511 Glentannyr. G. *teannair*, 'the noise of the sea in a cave.' (But it is now pron. Tana, G. *tana*, 'thin, slender.') Thought connected with Tanaros, trib. of R. Po, 'the thunderer,' L. *tonitru*, 'thunder.'

TANNIEROACH (Old Luce). Prob. G. *tamhnach ruadh*, 'red meadow.' The -ie is loc.

TANTALLON Cas. (N. Berwick). *a.* 1300 Dentaloune, 1389 Teintalon, 1481 Temptallon, 1572 Tomtallon. First, W. *din talgwn*, 'high-fronted fort,' then G. *tom talain*, 'knoll of the feats of arms.' *Cf.* 1254 *Patent R.* Tantalon, Tontolon, Gironde.

TAP O' NOTH (hill, Strathbogie). The *o* in Noth is short. G. *taip a' nochd*, 'hill of observation,' lit. 'showing, revealing.' *Cf.* Toothill, *Pl. N. Eng.*

TARBAT (E. Ross), TARBET (L. Lomond, Kirkmaiden), TARBERT (L. Fyne, 5 in Mull, etc.). Ross T., 1226 Arterbert, 'high Tarbert,' 1257 Tharberth. Lom. T., 1392 Tarbart. Fy. T. *Sagas* Torfnes, *Ulst. Ann.* 711 Tairpirt Boetter (opposite Bute), 1326 Tarbart. G. *tairbeart*, 'isthmus,' place over which a boat can be drawn, fr. *tar*, 'across,' and *ber*, 'bring, bear.' (M.) Both Magnus Barefoot and Robert the Bruce dragged their galleys across at L. Fyne.

TARBOLTON (Ayr). *a.* 1177 Torboultoun. Hybrid. G. *tòrr*, 'hill, mound, castle' and BOLTON.

TARBRAX (Carmdath.). G. *torr breac*, 'speckled hill,' with Eng. pl., $x = cs$. *Cf.* 1591 Torbrax, Torphichen.

TARF(F), R. Name of several violent streams. G. *tarbh*, 'a bull.'

TARLAND (Aboyne). 1183 Tarualund, *a.* 1300 Taruelayn, Tarhlund, 1492 Terlane. G. *tarbh-lann*, O.G. *land*, 'bull-enclosure.' Celt. *lann* is cognate with Eng. *land*. For Tarland, S. Ronaldsay, *sic* 1492, see next.

TARRADALE (Conon Br.). 1240 Taruedal, 1309 -delle, 1320 Tarrodall. N. *tarf-r dal*, 'bull dale.'

TARREL (Tarbat). 1368 -ell, 1579 Mekill T. G. *tar àl*, 'over the cliff,' its very site. *Cf.* the Undercliff, Ventnor.

TARSKAVAIG (S. Skye). 'Across,' G. *tar*, 'fr. SCAVAIG.' But perh. N. *thorska vík*, Norse G. *aig*, 'cod bay.'

TARSUINN, Ben (Arran). G. 'oblique, diagonal ben.'

TARTRAVON (Torphichen). 1508–9 Tortrevin. W. *tor tra Afon*, 'hill or castle over the Avon.' *Cf.* TARBRAX.

TARVES (Udny). *Sic* 1165–9, but 1287 -uays, *a* 1300 -vas. G. *tarbh-ais*, 'bull place.' On *-ais*, see p. 9.

TARWILKIE (Balmaclellan). 1604 Tragilhey. Brit. *tra*, *tre*, 'house,' or G. *tìr*, 'land,' *giolcaidh*, 'of rushes,' G. *giolc*, 'reed, rush.'

TASSIESHOLM (Wamphray). Prob. 'river-meadow, HOLM,' of an unknown man, ? *Tosti*. But Drumtassie, Slamannan, is fr. G. *tais*, *-se*, 'moist, damp.'

TAY, R. *c.* 80 *Tacitus* Taus, Tanaus (*n* for *v*), *c.* 150 *Ptolemy* Taoua, *c.* 600 *Amra Columcille* Toi, Tai, *a.* 1100 *St. Berchan* Toe, *c.* 1123 Lochtei, 1199 Thay, *a.* 1300 Tay. G. *tamh*, 'rest, quiet, sluggishness.' *Cf.* R. Taw, Devon.

TAYANTRUAN (Pitlochry, Carradale). G. *tigh an t'sruthain*, 'house on the little stream.' *Cf.* next.

TAYCHREGGAN (L. Awe). G. *tigh a' chreagain*, 'house at the little crag.' *Cf.* G. *teach* and W. *ty*, 'a house.' TAYINLOAN, Argyll, is fr. G. *lòn*, 'marsh, meadow.'

TAYNUILT (L. Etive). G. *tigh an uillt*, 'house on the burn,' *allt*.

TAYVALLICH (Crinan). 'House in the pass,' G. *bhealaich*.

TEALING (Angus). 1206 Thelin, 1497 Teling. Prob. Pict. *Cf.* W. *teiling*, 'enveloping,' or *telain*, 'beautiful.'

TEANINICH (Alness). G. *tigh an aonaich*, 'house on the market-place.'

TECHMUIRY (Fraserburgh). G. *teach muire*, 'house of leprosy, leper hospital.' *Cf.* 1233 Dumtechglunan, Kilbowie.

TEE, Ben (L. Ness). Local pron. Hee. 'Ben, hill of peace,' G. *sìth*, *i.e.*, tame-looking hill. But M. says fr. *sìdh*, 'conical hill, fairy knoll'; *cf.* Bailintian, fr. *sidhean*, 'fairy knoll.'

TEITH, R. (S. Perth). Forms see MENTEITH. Obscure (W.).

TEMA, R. (trib. of Ettrick). *a.* 1185 Thimei. Same as R. Thames, *Cæsar* Tameses; root W. *tam*, 'spreading, quiet, still.'

TEMPLE (Gorebridge), TEMPLAND (Lockerbie, Rhynie), TEMPLELANDS (Strathmartine, Denny). 1329 Tempilland. Lands belonging to the Knights Templars. But G. *teampull*, L. *templum*, 'church,' occurs often as a Hebrides name; also Teampull Columchille, Benbecula.

TÉNANDRY (Blair Atholl). *Tenandry* is an O.Sc. charter-term, found 1391 = *tenantry*, or the holding of a tenant, a piece of land or a house. *Cf.* 1498 Fennek in tenand, *i.e.*, Finnich Malise, Killearn. M. was a faithful vassal of the earl of Lennox, *a.* 1400.

TERERRAN (Moniaive). G. *tìr iaran*, 'western land'; but older Trorarane, ? G. *treamhar earrainn*, 'farm at the division or boundary.' *Cf.* TROQUEER.

TERREGLES (Dumfries). c. 1280 *Bagamund* Tranagles, 1350 Travereglys. G. *treamhar eaglais*, W. *eglwys*, 'farm of the church.' Also 1461 Torriculis, -ekillis. *Cf.* TRANENT.

TEVIOT, R. (Hawick). ? *a.* 600 *Avellenau* Teiwi, *a.* 800 Tefe, *a.* 1130 *Sim. Durh.* Tefegedmuthe, *c.* 1160 Teuiot. TEVIOTDALE, *c.* 1117 Teuegetedale, *c.* 1128 Teuiethes-, *c.* 1150 Tesweta-, Teuiedesdale, *c.* 1200 Teuidale, *a.* 1300 Tyvidale. TEVIOT (pron. Teeit) WATER is Teviotdale above Hawick, not applied to R. Teviot itself. Root prob. W. *tyw*, 'spreading around'; *cf.* R. Teifi, Cardigan and Tavy, Devon. The names *Tywi*, *Teifi* often occur in the earliest W. or Brit. writings. The early *-ged*, *-get* is for O.W. *gueid*, *guith*, 'a division.'

TEXA (Islay). *c.* 1380 *Fordun* Helan (G. *eilean*, 'island') Texa, 1549 *Munro*, 'In Erische (Gaelic) Tisgay.' Prob. N. *t-heggs-ay*, 'bird cherry isle.' On *t-h* see TALISKER.

THANKERTON (Carstairs). *c.* 1180 Villa (1232 Ville) Thancardi, Tancardestun, *c.* 1320 Thankaristone, 1359 -garton. 'Village of *Thancard*,' a Fleming. *Cf.* TANKERNESS and Thankard, old name of Kilbirnie loch. Also once called Woodkirk. It is phonet. possible Fankerton, Denny, may be the same; *cf.* Fuirsday for Thursday, etc.

THIEVESHOLM (Orkney). The public gibbet once stood here. See HOLM.

THIRLSTANE (Ettrich). *c.* 1150 -estan, *a.* 1196 Tirlestan. Prob. 'pierced stone,' fr. *thirl*, 'to drill.' *Cf.* Thirlstone, Devon, 1240 Therlestone.

THOM, L. (Greenock). Called after Robt. *Thom*, the engineer who constructed it, 1827.

THOMANEEN (Milnathort). *Old* Tomenayne. G. *toman eun*, 'little knoll with the birds.'

THORNILEE (Renfrew). *c.* 1340 -yle. THORNTON (Dysart, Keith, Mearns). Me. T. *a.* 1153 Thornetowne. Prob. fr. a man *Thorn* rather than fr. *thorn*; 12 in England, 34 times in *Dom.* Yorks.

THORNKIP (Colvend). G. *ceap*, 'stump, block,' Sc. *kip*, 'sharp-pointed hill.' *Cf.* KIPFORD and Makeness Kipps, Eddleston.

THREEPNEUK (K'patrick-Irongray), THREEPWOOD (Lauder, Br. of Weir, Beith, Lanarksh.). La. T., *c.* 1230 Trepewode, Be. T. *c.* 1140 Trepwood, 1369 Trepwode. M.E. *threap*, 'a scolding contest,' fr. O.E. *þreapian*, 'to reprove, afflict.' *Neuk* is Sc. for 'nook.' *Cf.* Threepwood, Northbld.

THREPLAND (Biggar, Banff). [*c.* 1250 *Reg. Dunferm.* Threpland, Burntisland.] Bi. T. 1296 Threpe-. 'Debateable land,' see above. *Cf.* 1449 *Treaty*: 'The landez callid Batable landez or Threpe landez'; also Threapland, Cumbld. and Yorks.

THRIEVE (on R. Dee, Kirkcudbt.). Ir. or G. *treabh*, 'a farm,' cognate with W. *tref*, *tre*, 'house'; *cf.* the Gaul. A-treb-ates, 'the near dwellers.' Trebb and Trave, farm names in N. Ronaldsay and Sanday, are akin.

THROSK (S. Alloa). *Sic* Pont, but 1246 Threske, 1252 Trost, 1311 Tresk. Brit. *tre esc* or *usc*, 'house on the river' Forth. *Cf.* Thirsk, Yorks, *Dom.* Treske.

THRUMSTER (Wick). A man, '*Thrum's* place.' See *stað-r*, p. 42.

THUNDERGAY (W. Arran). *Old* Tonregethy. Now G. *torr na gaoith*, 'hill of the wind,' windy hill. Orig. *ton re gaoithe*, 'backside to the wind.' *Cf.* Tonderghie, Whithorn, 1589–90 Tondirgeich, *Pont* Tonreghe, and 1571 Tonergeche, Dunure. Craignathunder, Benachie, must have a different origin.

THURSO, R. and town. 1152 Thorsa (river). *c.* 1200 *Hoveden* Turseha (town), *Orkn. Sag.* Thorsey, 1547 –so. Not 'Thor's river,' but O.N. *þjórsa-á*, 'bull river.'

THURSTON (Dunbar). 1292 Thureston, 'Village of a man *Thor* or *Thur*.' *Cf.* the Eng. Thurleigh and -low.

TIANAVAIG Ben (Portree). Norse G. *t-hjóna-vaig*, 'servants,' 'domestics' bay,' N. *hjón* and *vík*. *Cf.* TEXAY.

TIBBERMORE, -MURE (Perth). *c.* 1200 Tubermore. G. *tiobar mòr*, 'big well.' *Cf.* MUIRDRUM.

TIENDLAND (farm, Elgin). *Tiend* is Sc. for 'tithe,' O.N. *tíund*, Sw. *tiende*, 'a tenth.' *Cf.* MERKLAND.

TIGHARRY (L. Eport). Prob. G. *tigh charraigh*, 'house on the rock.'

TIGHNABRÚAICH (Kyles of Bute). G. 'house on the bank or slope.' *Cf.* Balnabruaich, Tarbat, Ross.

TILLICOULTRY (Dollar). 1195 Tulycultri, *c.* 1199 Tullicultre, -try, 1270 -cultrane ; also Tuligcultrin. Either G. *tulach cùl tire*, 'hill at the back of the land,' the Carse, *cf.* COULTER ; or, fr. G. *cuilteir*, pl. *cuiltearan*, 'a skulking fellow.' The -y in both sylls. is a loc. *Cf.* TILLYSKOOKIE.

TILLIECHÉWAN (Bonhill). Pron. Tillyhéwan. 1548 Tullychquhewin, 1608 Tillichewin. G. *tulach chumhainn*, 'narrow hill.'

TILLIETUDLEM (Craignethan). Fancy name in Scott's *Old Mortality*.

TILLYEVE (Aberdeensh.). 'Hill of the cry or howl.' G. *èibhe*. *Cf.* MONIAIVE.

TILLYFOUR, and -RIE (Chapel of Garioch, Tough). G. *fuar*, 'cold' ; –ie is loc.

TILLYMORGAN (Culsalmond). A hill ; but here perh. G. *teaglach Morgain*, 'family,' hence 'ground of the family, of Morgan.' The clan is found in *Bk. of Deer* ; Pict. *Morcunn*, O. Bret. *Morcant*, 'sea-bright.' The hill is 1510 Knockmorgan. *Cf.* 1511 *R.M.S.* Dawargemorgane (*cf.* DAVA).

TILLYSKOOKIE (Aberdeensh.). 'Hill of the soft, boorish fellow.' G. *sgugach*, with *-ie*, loc.

TILT, R. (Atholl). 1564 Glentilth. Rev. J. M'Lean, Pitilie, did not recognize this as G. Obscure.

TINGWALL (Scalloway). *Sagas* Thingavöll, O.N. for 'meeting of the *Thing*' ; *cf.* DINGWALL and *c.* 1500 Tyngwale, Rendall, Ork., and a lost Tingwal, 1145–8 in a N. Yorks chart. Perh. Tingall Top, hill near Abernyte, is the same. *Cf.* too TINVALD.

TINNIS (Yarrow). 1455 Tynnes, 1541 Dynnesdale ; TINNIS Hill (Liddesdale), *c.* 1570 Dennys ; and TINNIES, once a castle, Drummelzier. W. *dinas*, 'fort, castle.' *Cf.* Pendennis, Falmouth.

TINTO (hill, S. Lanark). *c.* 1315 -tou ; in Sc. Tintock. G. *teinteach*, 'place of fire' (W.). Knocktentol, Balmaclellan, is G. *cnoc tendail*, 'hill of the bonfire.'

TINWALD (Dumfries). *Sic c.* 1320 but *c.* 1280 Tynwalde. O.N. *þingvold*, 'meeting place,' lit. 'fold, of the Thing' or local assembly. Also in I. of Man. ; *cf.* DINGWALL, TINGWALL and Thingvellir, Iceland.

TIPPERLINN (once a village, now a road, S.W. Edinburgh). O.Ir. *tipra*, G. *tiobar linne*, W. *llyn*, 'well by the pool.'

TIPPERTREOCH (Crieff). 'Well of the ploughman,' G. *treabhach*.

TIPPERTY (several). 1501 -tay ; 1591 Tibbertey, Logie-Buchan. Prob. loc. of O.G. *tiobartach*, 'well-place.' (W.) *Cf.* Cloch in Tiprat, *Bk. Deer*, prob. the Logie T.

TIPPETCRAIG (Bonnybridge). 'Craig, rock *tipped* with a house.' *Cf.* Tappitknowe, Denny.

TIREE (Hebrides). *O.Ir. poem* Tir Iath, *a.* 700 *Adamn.* Terra Ethica, *c.* 1225 *Orkn. Sag.* Tyrvist, 1343 Tiryad, 1354 Tereyd, *c.* 1360 Tirade, 1467 -oda ; also Terra Hith, and prob. 1231 *papal bull* Chorhye (*cf.* the mod. G. pron. Chíŕee). Wh. Stokes said, Ir. *tìr etha*, 'land of corn,' it is so fertile. W. is doubtful. *Hith*, *Ith* may be a man. Several Ir. places are called Mag-Ithe, 'plain of Ith.' G. *tìr* and L. *terra* are cognate.

TIRRY, R. (L. Shin). ? G. *tuireadh*, 'a lament, dirge.'

TITABOUTIE (3, Aberdeensh.) = Lookabootye, also a place-name, fr. *toot* v., 'to peer or gaze about,' so found *a.* 1225 ; in Buchan pron. teet, see Jam. s.v. *tete*.

TITWOOD (Glasgow). 1513 Tytwoyd. Tit- will be as above, see *toot* sb^1. *Cf.* Toothill, *Pl. N. Eng.* found as early as *Dom.* Lincs, Totele, now Tothill ; also *cf.* 1550 Tidwood, Dunlop.

TOB (Lewis). G. *t'ob*, 'the (little) bay.'

TOBERMORY (Mull, Alness). (*c.* 1200 *Bk. Scone* Tubermore.) Mu. T. 1540 Tibbirmore, 1730 Topur Morry. G. and Ir. *tobar* (O.Ir. *tipra*, O.G. *tiobar*) *Moire*, 'well of Mary,' the Virgin = LADYWELL. *Cf.* Toberonochy (fr. *Donnachaidh*), Luing ; also Moray charters, *c.* 1240 Tubernacrumkel and -nafein, and 1591 Inverness chart. Toberdonich, G. *domhnaich*, 'of Sunday.'

TOCHIENEAL (Cullen). 1567 -ynell. G. *teach an aoil*, 'house of the lime,' *i.e.*, lime-kiln.

TOD RIG (Kirkinner). (*c.* 1200 *chart. re* Coldstream, Thothrig might = Todrig.) 1470 Todryk (surname). RIGG, 'ridge of the fox,' Sc. *tod*, so called fr. his bushy tail, fr. O.N. *toddi*, 'a mass of wool.' *Cf. c.* 1170 Todholys, Liddesdale.

TOFTCOMBS (Biggar). Dan. and late O.E. *toft*, 'a field, house, site,' O.N. *topt*, *toft*, 'land,' and O.E. *comb*, *cumb*, 'a vessel, a valley'; *cf.* W. *cwm*, 'a hollow.' *Cf.* Colbinstoft, Fetlar, and COOMLEES.

TOFTINGALL (Halkirk). Hybrid. 'Croft of the stranger,' G. *an-gaill*.

TOKAVAIG (Skye). Norse G. for N. *t'hauka vík*, 'hawk bay.'

TOLAIN (Eigg). Norse G. *t-hólinn*, 'the hill,' suffixed art.

TOLSTA Head (Lewis). 'Place of the toll or custom-house,' O.N. *toll-r*; as likely fr. a man *Tolli*. On *sta* for *stað-r*, place, see p. 42.

TOM-A-MHÒID (Dunoon). G. 'hill, knoll of the court of justice,' G. *mòd*, 'a court, an assembly.'

TOMÁTIN (Carr Br.). 'Knoll of the juniper,' G. *aitein*.

TOMBEA (Pass of Leni). Pron. -bay. 'Hill of birches,' G. *beath*. *Cf.* AULTBEA.

TOMICH (Rosskeen, Beauly). G. *tomach*, 'place of knolls,' *tom*.

TOMINTOÚL (Banffsh.). Pron. -tówl. G. *toman t'sabhail*, 'little hill like a barn.' *Cf.* CAIRN TOUL and 1570 Tullichintaul, Dumbtn.

TOMNAHURICH (Inverness). 1690 Toim-in-hurich. M'Kinnon said, prob. G. *tom na h'iubhraich*, 'hillock with the junipers,' G. *iubhar*, 'a yew.' The name (Wardlaw M.S. Tom ni Fyrich) till recently is said to have been *tom na fhiodraich*, 'of the timber,' *i.e.*, for gathering sticks. Here M. was sceptical. *Iubhrach* also means 'a boat,' and may do so here, fr. the knoll's shape. Portnachuraich, Iona, is fr. G. *curach*, 'a hide-boat, a coracle,' another word.

TOMNAVOULIN (Craigellachie). 'Knoll of the mill,' G. *an mhuilinn*. TOMNAVOWIN, Cabrach, is prob. the same.

TONGLAND (Kirkcudbright). *c.* 1150 Tuncgeland, 1457 Tungland. O.N. *tunga*, O.E. *tunge*, 'a tongue'; not in *N.E.D.* for 'spit of land' till 1566, but Tong, Bradford, is *Dom.* Tuinc, 1202 Tanga. Tongabrey, Orkney, is O.N. *tanga-breiði*, 'broad spit of land.' *Cf.* next.

TONGUE (N. Sutherland, Inch). Su. T. 1542 Toung. O.N. *tange*, *tunga*, 'tongue, spit of land.' *Cf.* above.

TORBANEHILL (Bathgate). Tautology. G. *tòrr bàn*, 'white, clear hill.' The TORRS are sandhills, Bay of Luce. Tor is a common hill name in Devon and Cornwall.

TORBOLL (Sutherland). *c.* 1230 Thoreball, 1575 Thuriboll. 'The god *Thor's* place'; see *bol*, p. 42, and *cf.* THURSTON.

TORDUFF (Currie). *a.* 1200 Turdaphe. G. *torr dubh*, 'dark hill'; *cf.* Tarduff, Polmont. But -daphe will be *damh*, 'ox.'

TORE (Inverness). G. *torr*, 'heap, mound, tower,' Ir. *tor*, W. *tur*, 'tower.' *Cf.* Tur, W. Calder. TORLANE (Dalry, Gall.) is fr. G. *leathann*, 'broad.'

TORMASDALE (Islay). N. *Ormas-dal* (see ORMISTON), to which Gaels, by rule, have prefixed T.

TOROSAY (Mull). *Sic* 1390, but 1561 Toirrasa. '*Thor's* isle,' N. *ay*, *a*, 'island.'

TORPHICHEN (Bathgate). *Sic* 1540, but 1296 Thorfighyn, Torphychin. G. *torr phigheainn*, 'magpie's hill.'

TORPHIN (Colinton), -PHINS (Aboyne). 'Clear, white hill,' G. *fionn*.

TORRANCE of CAMPSIE. 1554 Torrens, WATER of TORRANCE (Drumblade). Prob. G. *torran*, 'little hill,' with common Eng. pl. (*ce* = *s*). L. *torrens*, 'a torrent,' would be abnormal. But TORRAN Rocks, Ross of Mull, are said to be fr. G. *torrunn*, 'thunder.'

TORRIDON (W. Ross). G. Torr(bh)eartan. 1464 Torvirlane, 1584 Torrerdone, 1663 Torriden. W. says, it means, 'place of transference or portage.'

TORRISDALE (Kintyre). G. Tòrasdal. *a.* 1251 Glentoresdale. 'Dale, glen of *Thori*.'

TORRY (Aberdeen), TORRYBURN (Dunfermline). 1350 Torry. G. *torr*, 'a hill,' here in loc.

TORSONCE (Stow). Perh. 'hill of good luck,' G. *sonais*.

TORTHORWALD (Dumfries). 1287 -thorald (so still pron.), 1297 Thortharalde. Hybrid, 'Hill of *Thorald*.'

TORVEAN (Inverness). G. *torr Beathain* is 'tower of some St. Bean or Beyn,' but

TORWEAVING (Pentlands) is W. *tor gwefyn*, 'hill of moths or insects.'

TORWOOD (Larbert, New Luce), TORWOODLEE (Stow). La. T. *c.* 1140 Keltor, G. *coill torra*, 'wood of the hill or fort,' so Torwood is a half translation. See LEE.

TOUGH (Alford). Pron. Toogh. *c.* 1550 Tulluch or Tough, 1605 Towch. G. *tulach*, 'hill, mound.' TOUCH or TOUGH Hills, Stirling, are the same, 1329 Tulch. Also TOUCHADAM, Stirling. 1359 Tulk-, 1455 Tuchadam, 'hill of Adam,' but accent may have shifted, and so orig. 'hill of the ox,' O.G. *dam*, G. *damh*. *Cf.* Toughgorum, and -mollar, farms near by, 1368 Tulchgorme (G. *gorm*, 'green') and 1359 Tulkmaler, fr. G. *màlair*, 'a merchant, a renter.'

TOWARD (Rothesay). *Sic* 1498. Said to have been G. *rudha tonn àrd*, 'cape of high waves.' G. *toll àrd* (fr. 'a hole' or cave near) and *taobh àrd*, 'direction cape,' are both phonet. possible, but seem abnormal. Perh. an O.N. name, fr. *tá*, N. *taa* (pron. to), 'tip of a ness,' lit. 'toe,' or fr. *tó*, 'grassy spot,' and *ward* for *fjord*, 'bay,' as in Muddeward or MOIDART.

TOWIE (Alford). *Old* Tolly. G. *toll, tuill*, 'hole, cavity,' here in loc. *Cf.* LOGIE.

TOXSIDE (Gorebridge). *c.* 1142 Thocchesheued, 1587 Toksyde. 'Head, height,' O.E. *héafod*, 2–5 *heved*, 'of *Tochi* or *Toki*,' in *Onom.* *Cf.* SYDSERF.

TRABROUN (Tranent). 1296 Trebrun. 'House on the hill or slope,' W. *tra, tre*, 'house,' and *bryn*, O.G. *brun*, 'slope.'

TRADESTON (Glasgow). The ground here was bought and laid out by Glasgow Trades House, 1790.

TRAILTROW (Cummertrees). 1116 *Inquis.* Kevertrole (K for Tr), later Travertrold. Hybrid. G. *treabhar*, 'farm, house' (*cf.* TRANENT), and Dan. and Sw. *trold*, O.N. *troll*, 'a fairy,' a Robin Goodfellow (*cf.* Pow for *poll*). *Cf.* Trailflat, Tinwald, *c.* 1200 Traverflat (*cf.* BAMFLAT). This last shows W.'s W. *tref yr* or *ar*, 'house of the' or 'on the,' will not do.

TRANABY (Westray). 'Abode of cranes,' O.N. *trani*, Dan. *trane*. On -by see p. 41, and *cf.* CANISBAY.

TRANENT (Prestonpans). *Sic c.* 1210, but *c.* 1144 Treuernent. Brit. or G. *treabhar*, 'ploughed land, farm,' 'by the dell or stream,' W. *nant*. *Cf.* Trierman, Gilsland, 1169 Treverman.

TRANTLEBEG (Forsinard). Hybrid. O.N. *trani-dal*, 'crane dale,' and G. *beag*, 'little.' *Cf.* OSPISDALE.

TRAPRAIN LAW (Haddington). *Sic a.* 1700, but *c.* 1370 Trap-, Trepprene, 1451 Trapren. W. *tra, tre pren*, 'house by the tree.' Also called Dumpender Law [1174 Dumpeleter in Cludesdale] *c.* 1180 Dunpelder, *Vit. St. Monen.* -peleder, 1547 -prender. W. *dyn peledyr*, 'fort of the spear shafts,' *paladyr*. *Cf.* DRUMPELLIER; also Trahenna, Tweeddale.

TRAQUAIR (Innerlaithen). *Sic* 1265, but 1116 Treverquyrd, *c.* 1135 Trauercoir, *c.* 1140 Trauequair, 1174 Trauercuer, 1225 Trefquer, 1275 Trakwair, 1506 Trawere. 'Farm,' Brit. or G. *treabhar*, 'on QUAIR Water.' But W. *tref, tra, tre*, is 'house.'

TREARNE (Beith). *Sic* 1413, but *a.* 1233 Triern, *Pont* Triorn. Perh. Brit. *tre àirne*, 'house among the sloes.' But *cf.* TRYORNE, with which it has been confused.

TREIG, L. (Lochaber). G. *treig*, 'abandonment, desolation.' Fit name.

TRELONG Bay, TRELUNG Ness (St. Cyrus). Pict. or Brit. *tre luing*, 'house of the ship, boat-house.' There are two instances of Tre- in Stratherrick.

TREMUDA Bay (St. Cyrus). Prob. Pict. or Brit. for 'house on the cove,' W. *mwdd*, 'an arch, a spring, a cove.'

TRESHNISH Isles (Mull). Prob. O.N. *tres næs*, 'ness, cape of trees.' But *cf.* CRAIGNISH, fr. G. *innis*, 'meadow.' TRESTA (Shetland) is 'tree-place'; trees are very rare here. See *stað-r* or *sta*, p. 42.

TRILLEACHAN (L. Etive). G. 'the pied oyster-catcher.'

TRINAFOUR (Struan). Pict. or Brit. for 'house on the pasture land,' W. *tre*, *tra*, 'house.' See BALFOUR and *cf.* Tirafour, Lismore.

TRINITY (Edinburgh), TRINITY GASK (Crieff). A Trinity Lodge was built, 1783, on lands of the Trinity House, Leith, a house for seamen, orig. partly of a religious nature. The first Trinity Ho., Deptford, 1514, certainly was. See GASK.

TRIOCHATAN, L. (Glencoe). G. Triachtan. Prob. Brit. *tre*, 'house' and ?. Natives make it G. *loch na tri caochan*, 'loch of the 3 streams,' which is very doubtful. Achatriochatan, 1723 -trichitan, is close by.

TROCHRY (Dunkeld). *c.* 1650 -rig. Hybrid. G. *droch*, *troch*, 'bad, dangerous,' and RIGG.

TROON (Ayr). 1371 le Trone, 1464 le Trune, *Pont* the Truyn. W. *trwyn*, in G. *sròn*, 'nose, point, cape.' Also near Camborne, Cornwall. *Cf.* Duntroon, L. Crinan.

TROQUEER (Dumfries). *c.* 1380 Treqvere; also Traquire = TRAQAIR, 'green house.' *Cf.* Trowier, Girvan, 1430 -were.

TROS(S)ACHS (Callander). *Sic* 1791. Not a G. word. W. says, 'the cross places,' fr. W. *traws*, O.W. *tros*, 'across.' So, Brit. or Pict.

TROSTRIE (Twynholm). 1456 -taree, *Pont* -tari. Brit. *tros tire*, 'across the land,' W. *tir*. G. *tìr*. W.'s *tref*, 'house,' will not suit the old forms.

TROSWICK (Dunrossness). O.N. *tros vík*, 'bay full of rubbish or old leaves.' *Cf.* Trossevigen, Egersund.

TROTTERNISH (Skye), TRUDDERNISH (Islay). Sk. T. 1309 Trouter-1573 -tyrnes, ? 1588 Trottwayshe, *a.* 1700 *M'Vurich* Trontarnis. In G. Trò(n)dairnis. N. *Throndar-næs*, 'bear's cape,' or fr. a man *Thrond*; *-nish* is common for *ness*.

TROUP Head (Gamrie). 1296 Trup, 1382 Trowpe. Prob. *true hope* or harbour of refuge. *True* is O.E. *tréowe*, but O.N. *trygg-r*; *cf.* *c.* 1205 'treow castle,' also Phaup, Ettrick, for *faw hope*, Bacup, Lancs. *c.* 1200 Fulebachope, and St. MARGARET'S HOPE.

TRUFF Hill (Kirkmaiden). By common transposing of *r*, fr. O.E. *turf*, O.N. *torf*, 'turf.' See *N.E.D.* s.v.

TRYORNE (once in Roxburgh). 1116 Keveronum (K for Tr. as in TRAILTROW), *a.* 1124 Treueronum. Perh. Brit. or G. *treabharan*, 'little farm.' But *cf.* TREARNE.

TUACK (hill, Kintore). G. *tuagh*, 'an axe,' fr. its shape.

TUBEG-, MORE (Assynt). G. 'Little and big side of land,' G. *taobh*, W. *tu*.

TULLIALLAN (Alloa). G. *tulach àluinn*, 'lovely hill,' or fr. *àilean*, 'hill on the green meadow.' The Ir. Tullyallan is fr. *àlainn*.

TULLIBARDINE (Crieff, Moray). Cr. T. 1234 Tulibarden, 1461 Tulybardyn, -dy. 'Hill, mound of the warning,' G. *bàrdainn*; the *li* or *ly* is loc. *Cf.* DUNAVERTY.

TULLIBELTANE, -TON (Auchtergaven). 'Hill of the beltane,' G. *bealltainn*, an old Celt. celebration on May Day, when great bonfires were lit on the hills. M. says fr. O.Ir. *beltene*, fr. *belo te(p)nia*, 'bright fire,' same root as *bale* fire and Cym*beline*. Nothing to do with the god Bel or Baal.

TULLIBODY. Old charters imply there was such a place S. as well as N. of Forth, near Alloa. Nor. T. 1147 Dunbodeuin (*dùn*, hill), *c.* 1150 Dumbodenum, 1195 Tullibotheny. So. T. *c.* 1147 Tulibodevin, *c.* 1150 -body, 1195 Tulybotheuyn, *c.* 1200 Tulliboyene. 'Hill with the house on the river,' G. *both*, O.G. *bod*, 'house,' and *abhuinn*, *aibhne*, 'river.' *Cf.* RUTHVEN.

TULLOCH (Dingwall). 1542 Tulche. G. *tulach*, 'hill, hillock.' *Cf.* TOUGH.

TULLYBOLE (Kinross). 1685 -boal. Prob. 'hill of danger,' G. *baoghail*. *Cf.* MAYBOLE.

TULLYMET (Ballinluig). *c.* 1200 Tulichmet, Tulimath. 'Soft,' G. *maoth*, or 'rich, fertile,' *meith*, 'hill.'

TULLYNESSLE (Alford). *a.* 1300 Tulynestyn, *a.* 1500 -nestil. Prob. 'hill of the charm or spell,' *an eoisle*. *Cf.* ESSLEMONT.

TULLYPOWRIE (Perthsh.). 'Hill of pasture,' Brit. *paur*, here in loc. See BALFOUR.

TUMMEL, R. (Perthsh.). Perh. *Ptolemy's* town Tamia. G. Teamhal, Taimhail. Perh. Celt. *tam*, 'dark' (the Eng. *dim.*), 'the shadowy, obscure' river; *cf.* Dun Teamhalach, E. end of L. Tummel, spelt in O.S. map Duntanlich. W. thinks it cognate with Thames, etc.; see TEMA.

TUNDERGARTH (Lockerbie). 1215–45 Thonergayth. Doubtful. Perh. fr. W. *tyndir*, 'lea land, fallow.' O.N. and Dan. *tundr*, O.E. *tynder*, 3–7 *tunder*, is 'tinder.' *Garth* is 'enclosure'; see APPLEGARTH.

TURC, Ben (Glen Shee, Kintyre), Glen TURK (Wigtown, *sic* 1462), BRIG O' TURK (L. Katrine), TURKEY Burn (Glen Queich). G. *torc*, *tuirc*, 'a wild boar.'

TURNBERRY (Girvan). *c.* 1200 Turnebiri, 1286 -byry, 1301 Tornebiri. Prob. hybrid, Norm. Fr. *tournei*, *tornei*, 'tourney, tournament,' and O.E. *byrig*, *burg*, 'fort, castle'; *cf.* QUEENSBERRY. Eng. *turn*, 'a corner,' comes in rather late. *Cf.* too *Dom.* Salop and Devon, Torneberie.

TURRET (Crieff, Glenroy). Might be G. *turaid*, 'a turret,' fr. the shape of the rocks. W. says fr. *tur*, 'dry,' with a dimin.

TURRIFF (N. Aberdeen). Perh. *c.* 1150 *Bk. Deer* Turbruad, 1273 Turrech, *a.* 1300 -reth, *a.* 1500 -reff. Perh. a name which has changed. Orig. G. *torr bruid*, 'hill of anguish' or 'of the stab'; or perh. 'fort of *Brude*.' Now it might be for G. *tùrach*, 'tower-place.'

TUSHIELAW (Ettrick). *Sic* 1602. Prob. fr. *tissue* sb. 2, 'a band or girdle,' in Sc. *c.* 1450 *tusche*. Possibly fr. *tushy*, *c.* 1430 *Lydgate*, for 'tusky.' Law is Sc. for 'hill.'

TUSKERBUSTER (Orphir). 1627 Tuske-. Now pron. Tusherbist. O.N. *torf-skeri*, 'turf-shearer, peat-cutter,' in Ork. and Shet. *tuskar*, and *bolstað-r*, 'place,' see p. 42.

TWATT (Stromness). 1563 Tuait, 1595 Twat (surname). O.N. *þveit*, 'a thwaite, a place'; see MURRAYTHWAITE.

TWECHAR (Kilsyth). 1369 Tweoures. Perh. G. *tuath a' chuir*, 'north of the turn,' G. *cor*, *cf.* STRACHUR. This suits the site of the original farm.

TWEED, R., TWEEDSMUIR (Peeblessh.). ? *a.* 600 *Avellanau* Tywi, *Bede*, Tu-Twidus, *a.* 800 Tweoda, *c.* 970 *Pict. Chron.* Tede, *c.* 1120 Tweda, -oda, *c.* 1180 Tved. Prob. fr. W. *twyad*, 'hemming in,' *twy*, 'to check, to bound.'

TWEEDLE (Lochcarron). G. Ta'oudal. N. *t-haga-dal*, 'pasture dale.' (W.)

TWISLEHOPE Burn (Newcastleton). 1376 Cwys-, 1541 Twylishop. O.E. *twisla*, 'a fork, branching of two streams,' as here. *Cf.* Twizel, Coldstream, *c.* 800 Twisle. Form 1376 and the present pron. Coozelop, show influence fr. O.N. *kvísl*, same meaning. For -hope see HOBKIRK.

TWYNHOLM (Kirkcudbtsh.). *c.* 1200 Twenham, *c.* 1360 Twynem. 'House,' O.E. *hám*, 'in between,' O.E. *twéon*; *holm*,'meadow,' and *ham* constantly interchange. *Cf.* the Rom. Interamna and Twynham, Christchurch, *Dom.* Tuinam.

TYDEAVERYS (Balmaclellan). *Pont* Tydauarries. G. *tùd a' bharra*, 'heap on the top or height,' *barr*, with common Eng. pl. *s*. *Cf.* Tudhope, Jedburgh. It may be from the common O.E. *Tuda*.

TYNDRUM (N.W. Perth). G. *tigh an druim*, 'house on the ridge.'

TYNE, R. (E. Lothian). Perh. *Ptolemy's* Tina; it may be the Eng. Tyne, *Bede* Tinus, Tyne. Either W. *tyno*, 'green plot, dale,' or *tynu*, 'draw, pull,' G. *teann*, 'to move, stir, proceed.'

TYNECASTLE (Edinburgh). History seems lost.

TYNINGHAME (Haddington). *a.* 800 *Hist. St. Cuthbt.* Tinninga, 1094 Tiningeham, 1265 Tynynham. (Perh. *Bede* Incunening-hum, *c* for *t.*) 'Home of the Tyne dwellers.' See on *ing*, p. 52. There is also TYNEHOLM.

TYNRIBBIE (Appin). G. *tigh an ribe*, 'house of the snare or trap,' perh. referring to a tavern once here.

TYNRON (Moniaive). G. *tigh an sròin*, 'house on the point.'

TÝRIE (Fraserburgh, Kirkcaldy). Fr. T. *a.* 1300 Tyry, 1595 Tyer, Ki. T. *a.* 1328 Tyri,- 1440 -ry ; also 1296 Tiry, Perthsh. G. *tìr*, *tìre*, 'land.' *Cf.* ALTYRE and STRATHYRE.

UAMVAR (Kilmadock). O.G. *uaim*, G. *uamh bharra*, 'cave on the height,' *barr*. *Cf.* WEEM and LOCHINVAR.

UDDINGSTON and UDSTON (Glasgow). 1475 Odingstoune. 1529 Uds-, 1543 Eddestoun. Former perh. 'village of the god *Odin's* or *Woden's* descendants'; see -ing, p. 52, and *cf.* THURSTON. But Ittingston, Huntly, 1534 Utins-, 1677 Uttingstoun, may be fr. *Witting*, descendant of *Witta*, common O.E. name ; not = WHITTINGHAM. Latter will be fr. a man *Udd*, in *Onom.*

UDNY (Ellon). *c.* 1400 Uldeny, 1417 -nay. G. *alldan*, 'little stream,' here in loc., fr. *allt*, *uillt*, 'stream.' *Cf.* AULDEARN.

UGADALE (Kintyre). *a.* 1251 Ugladull, 1542 Vughedall. N. *ugladal*, 'owls' valley.'

UIG (Skye, Lewis). Sk. U. 1512 Wig, 1552 Vig. Le. U. 1549 Vye, *c.* 1620 Vyg, Oig. G. *ùig*, 'nook, cove,' fr. O.N. *vík*, 'bay.' *Cf.* WICK.

UISKENTUIE (Islay). G. *uisg' an t'suidhe*, 'drink,' lit. 'water, at the seat'—place where funerals halted for a drink—of *whisky* ! *Cf.* BEALLACHANTUIE and BAD na CARBAD. Wisheach, Gartly, is G. *uisgeach*, 'watery place.'

UIST, N. and S. (Out. Hebrides). 1282 Iuist, 1292 Guist, 1344 Ywest, 1373 Ouiste, Huwyste ; also Ewyst, the pron. now. O.N. *í-vist*, 'an abode,' lit. 'in-dwelling'; same root as Eng. *was*, Goth. *wisan*, 'to stay.'

ULBSTER (Wick). 1538 -bister. O.N. *Ulf-bustar*, 'Ulf's,' *i.e.*, 'the wolf's abode.' See p. 42, and *cf.* ULSTA.

ULLADALE (Strathpeffer). G. Ulladal. 1476 Elodil, 1479 Ulladall. Prob. O.N. *öla -dal-r*, 'valley of alders,' *öl-r*. W. prefers '*Ulli's* dale.' *Cf.* next.

ULLAPOOL (W. Ross). *Pont* -bill. The ending is *pol*, *bol*, 'place,' see p. 42. *Ulla* may be for K. *Olaf*, *cf.* OLLABERRY. There seems no local tradition. *Cf.* 1415 Ulyshaven, Angus.

ULLIE Strath, through which R. Helmsdale flows. G. Uille or Iligh. Prob. *Ptolemy* Ila. Obscure. *Cf.* ISLA, ISLAY.

ULLOCH (Balmaghie). *Pont* Vlioch. G. *uallach*, 'proud, high' place.

ULSTA (Shetland), ULSTON (Jedburgh). *c.* 1150 Ulvestoun. 'Place,' N. *sta*, see p. 42, or 'village of *Ulf*,' *i.e.*, the wolf.

ULVA (Aros). 1473 -way. 'Wolf's' or 'Ulf's isle.' O.N. *úlf-r*, Dan. and Sw. *ulv*, 'wolf,' and *a*, *ay*, 'island.'

UNGANAB (N. Uist). G., 'ounce-land of the abbot,' O.G. *unga*, L. *uncia*, 'an ounce,' *i.e.*, the rent was an ounce of silver. See p. 35, and *cf.* BALNAB.

UNICH, R. (Edzell). G. *uinich*, 'bustle, hurry.' It is a rapid stream.

UNST (Shetland). *Sagas* Ornyst, Örmst, Aumstr, *c.* 1524 Ounst. Perh. O.N. *örn-vist*, 'eagle's dwelling.'

UNTHANK, common farm name. Mosspaul U. 1228 Vnthanc, 1290 Wnthanke. O.E. *un-þanc*, 'ingratitude,' referring to the barren soil. *Cf.* Winthanke, St. Andrew's. Two in Northumbld., *c.* 1200 Unthanc. This use is not in *N.E.D.*

UPHALL (Bathgate). Its old name was Strathbroke, *i.e.*, BROXBURN. *Cf.* 1297 'Adam de Uphal de Vileby,' prob. Wilby, N'hants.

UPLAWMOOR (Neilston), also called Ouplaymoor. More light needed.

UPSETLINGTON (Ladykirk). *c.* 1098 Upsetinton, *a.* 1200 Upsedilingtoune, 1183 Upsetling-, *c.* 1210 Hupsetlintun. A patronymic, see -ing, p. 52; it is hard to say fr. what man. *Ulfcytel* seems nearest, and it is far away.

URIE, -Y (Stonehaven, Huntly). Hu. U. 1260 Ouri, *a.* 1328 Ure and see INVERURIE. Prob. G. *iubharach*, here in loc., 'abounding in yews,' *iubhar*.

URQUHART (several). Kilmorack U. *Adamn.* Airchardan, *a.* 1150 Urchard. Elgin U., 1165 Urecard, *c.* 1200 *Gervase* Hurcard, *c.* 1340 Urquhart; also Owrchard. Conon Br. U. 1340 Urchard. Airchardan will be Pict., *air*, 'on, upon,' and W. *cardden*, 'a wood,' so, Woodside. *Cf.* Urchany, Nairn, G. *air canach*, 'on the standing water.' (M.)

URR (Dalbeattie). *c.* 1280 *Bagamund* Urrer, 1607 Or. Prob. pre-Celt. for 'water, river,' Basq. *ur*. *Cf.* ORR, and O.N. *örr*, 'swift.'

URRAY (Muir of Ord). G. Urrath. 1546 Vrray, *c.* 1565 Vurray. G. *air rath*, 'on-fort,' *i.e.*, 'repaired fort.' (M.)

USAN (Montrose). Prob. a Pict. dimin., *cf.* next.

USSIE, L. (Fodderty). G. Ŭsaidh. 1463 Usuy, 1476 Ouse, 1527 Housy, 1594 Ussay. Pict., of unknown meaning. (W.) See OUSE.

UTHROGLE (Cupar). G. *uachdar*, 'upper part,' see AUCHTERARDER, and OGLE.

UYEA Sound (Unst). O.N. *öyja*, 'island.'

VAT-, WATERNISH (N. Skye). 1501 Watternes. Prob. 'ness, promontory, like a glove,' O.N. *vött-r*. *Cf.* Waterford and next.

VATERSAY (S. of Barra). 1580 -sa. Looks like 'glove isle,' N. *ay, a*, see above, or fr. a man *Vöttr*; *Onom.* has *Wetta*. M. prefers N. *vatrs* (gen. of *vatn*) *-ay*, 'water isle,' which seems curious. O.N. *veth-r*, Sw. *väder*, 'weather, violent wind,' also seems a possible root.

VELLORE (Polmont). Named *a.* 1800 fr. an Indian town near Madras.

VEMENTRY (Shetland). N., '*Vémundr's* isle,' *-ey*, *-ay*.

VENLAW (Peebles). *Sic* 1469 but 1451 -lau. Tautology, G. *bheinn* and O.E. *hlǽw*, 'hill.' *Cf.* Penlaw, Dumfries.

VENNACHAR, L. (Callander). *c.* 1375 *Fordun* Banquhar, *M'Farlane* Bennachar, and so = BANCHORY. But 1794 *O. Stat. Acct.* says, Vennachoir, G. *bhana choir*, 'fair corrie' or 'valley.'

VENUE, Ben (Trosachs). 1794 Benivenow. G. *beinn mheanbh*, 'little ben' compared with Ben Ledi. *Cf.* YARROW.

VICE, LOCHAN of (Tungland). *Pont* Voyis. G. *lochan* is 'little loch.' *Voyis* is possibly O.Fr. *voyes, voies*, 'ways, roads,' found in Sc. *a.* 1578.

VIDLIN (Shetland). O.N. *víd-r*, Dan. and Sw. *vid*, 'wide'; -lin may be N. *lund*, 'a grove.'

VIGEAN'S, St. (Arbroath). *Vigeanus* is L. for St. *Fechan*, abbot of Fother, W. Meath, d. 664. *Cf.* ECCLEFECHAN.

VINEGAR Hill (Kingussie). Said to be G. *fionna gabhar*, 'white goat.' But M. says, fancy name.

VIRKIE (Dunrossness). O.N. *virki*, 'a work, a bulwark, a castle.' *Cf.* outwork and WORK Hd.

VOE (Shetland, common name). O.N. *vág-r*, Icel. *vog-r*, 'little bay.'

VOGRIE (Borthwick). *c.* 1160 Vogeryn, 1336 Wogrym, 1377 Vogry. G. *a' mhogur*, *-uire*, 'bulky, clumsy' place.

VOIL, L. (Balquhidder). Aspirated form of G. *moil*, 'a heap,' or *boil*, 'fury, rage.' But Auchenvole, Kirkintilloch, is prob. 'field on the bare hill,' G. *mhaoil*, 1658 Auchinvale.

VORLICH, Ben (L. Earn and Lomond). (L. Earn, 1543 Ardiuurlik, *c.* 1800 -vurlig.) Lom. V. *Pont* Binvouirlyg, 1794 Benvurlich. W. says, G. *beinn Mhurbhlaig* or *Mhur'laig*, 'ben of the sea-inlet shaped like a sack,' *cf.* MURLAGAN. W. says, only younger people say Mhurlaich or Vurlich, the older all said Mhur'laig. This is not so. Vurlich has been common since the Gael who wrote the *O. Stat. Acct.* 1794; and in 1917 the writer, after careful enquiry, found no Gael (and he found several) on L. Earn who said Mhur'laig. It is hard to believe that so commanding a landmark as the L. Earn Ben could be named fr. a tiny inlet, fr. which it is barely visible. There must have been early confusion with L. Lomond Voirlich, where the inlet is clear. 'Ben of the kingfisher,' G. *mhùirlaich*, seems possible. The bird was here.

VOXTER (Delting). N. *vog-setr*, 'bay place.' See VOE and DALSETTER.

VRACKIE, BHRAGGIE, Ben (Golspie, Blair Atholl). G. *beinn bhreac, bhrice*, 'spotted, speckled ben.' *Cf.* BREAKACHY.

VUILLIN, SCUIR (Achnasheen). G. *sgùrr a' mhuilinn*, 'rock of the mill.'

WADDENSHOPE (Yarrow). 1262 Waltamshope. Wadden- might be fr. common O.E. *Wada, -an* ; but Skeat says, Wealtham is O.E. for 'unsteady, ill-built home' or 'house.' For *hope* see HOBKIRK.

WALKERBURN (Innerleithen). Stream where *wauking*, fulling or dressing of cloth was done, O.E. *wealcere*, 'a fuller.' *Cf.* WAUK Mill, Walkern, Stevenage, and *Dom.* Chesh. Walcretune.

WALLACESTONE (Polmont). The stone commemorating Wallace's battle of Falkirk, 1298, was erected in 1810 in place of an older slab. WALLACETOWN (Ayr), *old* Walenseton. 'Village of the strangers,' the Welsh, Britons fr. Strathclyde, O.E. *wæl-*, *welisc*, 'a foreigner.' In 1160 *Paisley chart.* we find 'Ricardo Walas,' perh. the earliest mention of the name Wallace. He came fr. Salop to Riccarton, Ayrsh. Le Waleys, later Wallis, was a common Eng. name in 13th cny. *Cf.* Walesby, Newark, *Dom.* Walesbi, GALSTON and WALSTON.

WALLS (Hoy, N. Shetland). Ho. W. *Orkn. Sag.* Vagaland, *saga* Valey, 1492 Wawis. Prob. corrup. of Waa, O.N. *vágar*, 'voes, bays.' But Valey may be N. *val-ey*, 'wall, rampart island.'

WALLYFORD (Musselburgh). Sc. *wa(l)ly*, 'ample, large,' of obscure origin.

WALSTON (Biggar). 1275 Wail-, 1293 Waly-, Walliston, *a.* 1375 Welchetoun = WALLACETOWN. *Cf.* Walsall (O.E. *hale*, 'nook').

WAMPHRAY (Beattock). 1275 Vam-, 1590 Womphray. O.G. *uaim phraimh*, 'cave of slumber' or 'sorrow.' *Cf.* UAMVAR.

WANDELL (Lamington). *c.* 1116 Quendal. O.E. *cwen*, 'a woman, a queen,' O.N. *kván*, 'a wife,' and *dal*, 'dale, valley.'

WANLOCKHEAD and -WATER (Leadhills). 1563 Wenlec. Prob. W. *gwen llech* (G. *leac*), 'white, clear flagstone.' To the E. is Midlock Water, which may be W. *med llwch* or *llwg*, 'extended, spread-out pool or marsh.'

WARDIE (Leith). Prob. O.E. *worði*, common charter name for a 'farm.' *Cf.* Word, Kent and Sussex.

WARDLAW (Beauly), WARDLAWHILL (Glasgow, Ettrick). Be. W. 1210 Wardelaue. *Law*, hill, where *ward* or *guard* was kept for the Norm. lord, Jo. Byset ; oldest Eng. name in Ross-sh.

WARRISTON (Edinburgh). [*c.* 1320 Wairistoun, Dundee ; 1391–2 Warynstone, Currie], 1581 Waristown. 'Hamlet of *Warin*' ; *cf.* 1215 *Patent R.* Comes Warren.

WARTHILL (Rayne), WARTLE (Inveramsay). 'Ward, guard hill' ; *cf.* Warthill, Yorks, *Dom.* Wardille, and O.N. *varði*, 'watch-tower,' origin of several Shetld. names—Vordeld and the Vord, Unst, Vardhill, Fetlar, etc.

WATERBECK (Ecclefechan). Tautology. Both *water* and *beck* mean 'brook' ; *cf.* Wansbeckwater, and see GALAWATER. WATERFOOT (Mearns) is 1593 Watterfut.

WATERNISH, see VATERNISH.

WATERSTON (Fern). 1329 Walteristoun. 'Village of *Walter*.'

WATTEN (Wick). *c.* 1230 Watne. O.N. *vatn*, 'water, a loch.'

WAUCHOPDALE (Langholm). *a.* 1214 Walc-, 1220 Walleuhope, 1247 Waluchop, *c.* 1330 Wachopdale, 1340 Walghopp. O.N. *valg-r*, *volg-r*, O.E. *wealg*, 'warm, lukewarm' *hope* or shut-in valley, see HOBKIRK.

WAUK MILL (several). 1561 Walkmiln. Sc. *wauk*, 'to full, dress cloth,' O.E. *wealcan*, 'to turn about,' O.N. *válka*, 'to full' ; same as Eng. *walk*.

WEDALE (Stow). *Sic c.* 1160, but 1370 -dalle, 1560 Weddaill, and *Chron. Melros* re 1184 Wedhale (loc. of O.E. *healh*, 'nook, corner'). Legend says, 'vale of woe,' O.E. *wá*, *wǽ*, Dan. *vee*, fr. a great defeat of the Angles by K. Arthur. But prob. fr. Sc. and M.E. *wad*, *wed*, 'a mortgage or pledge.'

WEDDERBURN (Duns). 1296 Wederburne. Sc. *wedder*, O.E. *wether*, 'a ram.'

WEEM (Aberfeldy). O.G. *uaim*, 'a cave' ; *cf.* UAMVAR and WEMYSS, also *O. Ir. MSS.* Doilweme, near Dull.

WEIR, WYRE (Rousay). *Sic* 1529 Jo. Ben, but *Orkn. Sag.* Vigr, *c.* 1500 Wyir. O.N. *vigr*, 'a spear,' an island name in Iceland.

WEMYSS, E. and W. (Fife), WEMYSS BAY (Largs). Fi. W. 1239 Wemys, *a.* 1300 Whense, 1638 Weyms, 1639 Easter Weimes = WEEM, with common Eng. pl. *s*. *Cf.* Port Wemyss, Islay.

WEST CALDER (1183 West Caledoure), WEST LINTON (formerly Linton Roderick), etc. See CALDER, etc.

WESTERDALE (Halkirk), -KIRK (Langholm). O.N. *vest-r*, 'West.' But Westerkirk is 1296 to 1641 Westerker, 1329 Wastyrkyr, prob. W. *caer*, 'fort.' WESTERHALL (Pettinain) 1455 -raw or 'row.' Changed to –hall by Jas. Johnston, 1605 ; but now often again WESTRAW. *Cf.* Nunraw, Haddington.

WESTRAY and PAPA WESTRAY (Orkney). Sic *Orkn. Sag.*, *c.* 1260 Vesturey. O.N. *vestr-ay*, 'western isle.' See PAPA. WESTRUTHER (Greenlaw). *Sic a.* 1300. 'West marsh.' See ANSTRUTHER.

WEYDALE (Thurso). Prob. 'way, road dale,' O.N. *veg-r*, Dan. *vei*.

WHALSAY (Shetland). *Saga* Hvalsey, O.N. for 'whale's isle.'

WHAM Glen (Kilsyth). 1298 Glenwhym. O.G. *uaim*, G. *uamh*, 'a cave.'

WHAUPHILL (Kirkinner). Sc. *whaup*, 'a curlew,' named fr. the sound of the bird's cry.

WHEE, see QUOY.

WHIFFLET (Airdrie). 1683 Hifflet. Very doubtful. Rhys suggested 'whin, furze, flat.' Perh. W. *chwif llethr*, 'the turn of the slope.' *Cf.* CROMLET and SKINFLATS.

WHINNEYLEGGATE, -LIGGATE (Kirkcudbright). From *whinny*, 'full of whins,' and *liggate*, O.E. *leag-geat*, 'field gate post.' *Cf.* Liggatcheek, Dalry, Gall., and Whinny-fold, Cruden.

WHITBURN (Bathgate). 1296 Whiteburne, 'white stream.'

WHITCHESTER (Longformacus). *c.* 1210 Witchestyr, *c.* 1380 Whitchestre, Qwytchestrys. 'White camp,' see p. 56. Also called Whitster, *cf.* Glo'ster. There may have been 2 in S.E. Scotland.

WHITEFARLAND (Arran). 1356 Quhitforland. O.N. *hvitt for-landi*, 'white-looking land 'twixt sea and hill.'

WHITEFIELD (Elgin). 1226 Whytefeld. Early case of an Eng. name here.

WHITEINCH (Glasgow). *Inch* is 'meadow, links.' See INCH.

WHITEMIRE (Forres). 'White-looking swamp,' O.N. *mýrr*, *mýri*, N. *myre*, 'swamp, fen.' *Cf.* BRABSTERMYRE, Drakemire, Berwicksh., and *c.* 1200 *Newbot. Chart.* Wytteriggemyre.

WHI(T)TEN Head. See its Gaelic form KENNAGEALL.

WHITERASHES (Udry). *Rashes* is Sc. for 'rushes.' *Cf.* Rashiehill, 2 in Stirlingsh. WHITERIGG (Airdrie). 1572 Quhitrig. See RIGG.

WHITHORN (Wigtown). *Bede* H.E. III, iv. Vulgo vocatur Ad Candidam Casam eo quod ibi ecclesiam de lapide, insolito Brettonibus more, fecerit. *O.E. Chron.* ann. 565 Hwiterne, *c.* 1140 Candidae Casae id est Hwiternensi ecclesiae, 1159 Whitherne; *old MS.* Futerne (*cf.* Aberdon. *f* for *wh*). O.E. *hwít erne*, 'white house,' in L. *candida casa*, the clay house built by St. Ninian, *c.* 380. Name prob. taken by him fr. St. Martin's community near Poitiers—Locotegiacum, Gaul. *leuc-teg-ac*, 'white house place.'

WHITING BAY (Arran). Named fr. the fish *whiting*, lit. 'little white thing.' In G. also called Eadar da Rudha, 'between the two points.'

WHITLETTS (Ayr). Perh. *white flats*. *Cf.* WHIFFLET.

WHITSOME (Chirnside). 1296 Whyte-, 1300 Quitesum. 'Home,' O.E. *hám*, 'of a man *White*.' *Cf.* EDROM.

WHITSTER, see WHITCHESTER.

WHITTERHOPE (Liddesdale). 1340 Wytwrahop, 1500 Quhitterhop. O.N. *hvitr hóp*, 'white narrow vale,' see HOBKIRK. The *wra* in 1340 is O.N. *wrá*, 'corner, landmark.' *Cf.* WRAE.

WHITTINGEHAME (Haddington). With its inj pron. *cf.* dial. Notinjam for Nottingham. *a.* 1232 Witingham, 1250 Whitingham. 'Home of the *Whitings* or sons of White'; *cf.* p. 52. Also near Alnwick, *c.* 800 Hwitincham, 1104–8 Hwittingaham.

WHITTON (Morebattle). Perh. *a.* 800 *Hist. St. Cuthbt.* Waquirtun (this scribe's spelling is reckless), 1285 Wytton. 'White hamlet.'

WHUP (Sanday). O.N. *hóp*, 'haven, hope.'

WIAY (L. Bracadale). O.N. *vé-ay*, 'house isle.'

WICK (Caithness). *Sic c.* 1375 *Barbour*, 1140 Vik, 1455 Weke. O.N. *vík*, Sw. *wik*, 'a (little) bay.'

WIDEWALL (S. Ronaldsay). *Orkn. Sag.* Vidivag(r), O.N. for 'beacon voe or bay.' *Cf.* KIRKWALL.

WIES-, WEISDALE (Voe, Shetld.). O.N. *vés-dal*, 'dale of the mansion.'

WIGTOWN. 1266 Wige-, 1283 Wyggeton. 'Village of *Wig* or *Wiga*,' several in *Onom.* But WIGG, Whithorn, is prob. O.N. *vig-r*, 'a spear.'

WILSONTOWN (Carnwath). Founded, 1779, by two brothers *Wilson*.

WILTON (Hawick). *a.* 800 Wiltuna, *c.* 1170 Wilth-, Wiltona. 'Village of *Willa*,' a common O.E. name. Three in England.

WINCHBURGH (Linlithgow). 1375 Wynchburch. Prob. 'castle,' O.E. *burh* (*cf.* BORGUE), 'of *Winca, -co*,' in *Onom.* *Cf.* the Eng. Winchcombe and -field.

WINDHOUSE (Shetland). Corrup. of O.N. *vind-áss*, 'windy ridge.'

WINDLESTRAE LAW (Tweeddale). O.E. *windelstréaw*, 'a dry, thin stalk of grass, left to wither.' Law is O.E. *hlǽw*, 'hill.'

WINDYGATES (Markinch), WINDYGATE Mill (Cheviots). *Old* Windeyetts, Windgate. O.E. *geat*, 'a gate,' but in Sc. 'a road.' *Cf.* Wingate, Durham, *c.* 1150 Windegat. WINDY GOUL (Edinburgh, Tranent). G. *gabhal*, 'a fork, a pass.' *Cf.* Goul, New Machar, *sic* 1137, and Windy Gyle, Northumbld.

WINTON (Ormiston). *c.* 1160 Wyn-, 1210 Winton. 'Hamlet of *Wine* or *Wini*,' common in *Onom.* Three in England.

WIRRAN (hill, Lethnot, Angus). G. *fhuaran*, 'a water spring.'

WISHAW (S. Lanark). Prob. 'SHAW, wood of *Wice*,' as in next. But Wishaw, Tamworth, *Dom.* Witscaga, is fr. a man *Wita*.

WISTON (Lamington). *c.* 1155 Wicestun, 1159 Ville Withce, *c.* 1190 Ecclesia de Wische, 1406 Wyston. This 12th cny. knight, *Withce* or *Wice*, is well known in his charters.

WOLFLEE (Hawick). *Pont* Oulie, 1700 Woole. Same as Woolley, Hunts, *O.E. chart.* To wulfa leage ('lea, meadow'), 1180 Wulfelea.

WOLFSTAR (E. Lothian). First so spelt 1855 Ord. S. map. Local pron. Foulster. 1276 Fuylstrother, 1505 Foulstruther. 'Foul,' or perh., 'fowls' (O.E. *fugol*), marsh.' See ANSTRUTHER.

WOODWICK (Orkney). Pron. Withik. O.N. *viði vík*, 'wide bay.'

WORK Head (Kirkwall) = VIRKIE, 'work, bulwark, castle.'

WORMIT (N. Fife), WORMIT Hill (once, Falkirk). Fi. W. 1440 -et. O.E. *wyrm*, 'serpent, worm.' The -et may be termin., or for 'wood' as in Coquet, O.E. *cocwudu* (*wormit* is Sc. for 'wormwood')—or for 'height, head,' as in AIKET.

WRAE (Tweeddale). O.N. *vrá*, *rá*, M. Sw. *vraa*, 'a nook, a cabin.' *Cf.* Woodrae, Finhaven, 1549 -wra.

WRAITH (Rerwick). G. *rath*, 'rampart, circular fort.' *Cf.* RAITH.

WRANGHAM (Garioch). *Sic* 1261. Rare type of name so early here. 'Home,' O.E. *hám*, 'of the Varangians,' O.N. *Væringi*, 'men of plighted faith,' name of the Normans in Russia.

WRATH, C. (Sutherland). *Sic* 1638, but 1583 Wraith, 1595 *Mercator* C. Wrayght or Faro Head. O.N. *hvarf*, 'a turning out of sight, a shelter,' *hverfa*, 'to turn round.' *Cf.* Hvarfs-gnipa ('peak'), O.N. for C. Farewell, Greenland. Lewis Gaels say An Carbh, others, An Parph or Barpa (hence form 1595), both corrups. of *hvarf*.

WYSEBY (Kirtlebridge). 'Dwelling of *Wyse*,' O.E. *wis*, 'the wise man.' See -by, p. 41.

WYVIS, Ben (Strathpeffer). Pron. Ooash. 1608 Weyes (W for U), 1776 *Pennant* Wewish. G. *beinn fhuathais*, 'ben of the bogle, spectral ben.' The *f* is retained in Cabar Fuais. *Cf.* AUCHTERHOUSE, AULDHOUSE and Waas, Glencairn.

YAR-, YERROCK Pt. (Whithorn). Prob. G. *garbh-ach*, 'rough place.' *Cf.* next.

YARROW (Selkirk). Also called St. Mary's Kirk of Lowis. *c.* 1120 Gierua, *c.* 1150 -wa, *Chron. Melr.* Gyrwa, 1508 Yarou. Jarrow-on-Tyne is 793 *Alcuin* Ecclesia Gyrvensis, *Sim. Durh.* Gyruum, Girwe, -vum. May be fr. the tribe *Gyruii* (Bede). But more prob. G. *geàrr*, *giorra*, 'short,' or *garbh*, 'rough,' and *abh*, 'stream.' *Cf.* VENUE, L. AWE, Yar on Tweed, and R. Yare, *Pl. N. Eng.*

YELL (Shetland). *Sagas* Jala, Ala, *c.* 1524 Yell. O.N. *gelld*, *gall*, 'barren.' *Cf.* JAWCRAIG.

YESTER (Haddington). 1295 -tre, 1407–10 Yhestir. W. *ystre*, 'dwelling.' *Cf.* STIRLING.

YETHOLM (Kelso). *a.* 800 *Hist. St. Cuthbt.* Gatha'n, 1233 Jetham, *c.* 1244 Yetham, *c.* 1420 Kirkyethame, 1608 Toun-Yettam. 'Hamlet,' O.E. *hám*, 'at the gate.' O.E. *geat*, Sc. *yett*, between Scotland and England. *Cf.* Yetts o' Muckhart, mouth of a pass in the Ochils. *Cf.* too the Eng. Gatton and Yatton; and with *c.* 1420 and 1608 *cf.* GOLSPIE. See HOLM.

YOKER (Glasgow). *Sic* 1505, but *Pont* Yochyrr, 1632 Yocker. G. *iochdar*, *iocar*, 'the bottom, low-lying ground'; *cf.* 1466 *Dunferm. Chart.* Yochry Den.

YORKHILL (Glasgow). Perh. fr. the visit of the Duke of York, 1681. He passed this way to Dumbarton.

YOUCHTRIE HEUGH (Kirkmaiden). G. *uachdarach*, here in loc., 'upper place'; *cf.* AUCHTERARDER. Heugh is 'height,' see HESTERHEUGH.

YTHAN, R. (Ellon). 1373 aqua de Ethoyn, 1477 Ithane. W. says = R. Ieithon, Radnor, Welsh for 'the talking one,' W. *iaith*, 'language.'

ZETLAND, see SHETLAND.

BIBLIOGRAPHY

DICTIONARIES :

The Oxford English Dictionary, 1884–1929.

Gaelic, Highland Society's Dictionary, 2 vols., 1828.

M'Leod and Dewar, 1853.

Welsh, Pughe & Pryse, 2 vols., 1866–73.

Icelandic or Old Norse, Cleasby & Vigfusson, 1874.

JO. VEITCH : *History of the Scottish Border*, 1878.

W. F. SKENE : *Celtic Scotland*, 3 vols., 1876–80.

P. W. Joyce: *Irish Names and Places*, 3rd edit., 2 vols., 1871.

ALEX. M'BAIN : *Place Names, Highlands and Islands, of Scotland*, 1922.

W. J. LIDDALL : *Place Names of Fife and Kinross*, 1896.

JAS. M'DONALD : *Place Names of Strathbogie*, 1892.

Place Names of West Aberdeenshire, 1899.

DON. MACKINNON : 'Place Names of Argyle,' in *Scotsman*, 1887–88.

SIR HERB. MAXWELL : *Scottish Land Names*, 1894.

Place Names of Galloway, 1930.

H. C. GILLIES : *Place Names of Argyll*, 1906.

GEO. HENDERSON : *Norse Influence on Celtic Scotland*, 1910.

W. J. WATSON : *Place Names of Ross and Cromarty*, 1904.

'Some Sutherland Names of Places,' in *Celtic Rev.*, II, 361–8.

History of the Celtic Place Names of Scotland, 1926.

FRANCIS DIACK : *Révue Celtique*, 1922, two articles.

BRÖGGER : *Ancient Emigrants*, 1929.

W. C. MACKENZIE : *Scottish Place-Names*, 1931.

EDW. ELLICE : *Place-Names of Glengarry and Glenquoich*, 1931.

GUDMUND SCHÜTTE : *Our Forefathers, the Gothonic Nations*, 2 vols., 1929–33.

J. B. JOHNSTON : *Place Names of Stirlingshire*, 2nd edit.

Place Names of England and Wales, 1915.

The Scottish Macs, 1922.

W. G. SEARLE : *Onomasticon Anglo-Saxonicum*, 1897.

F. GROOME : *Ordnance Survey Gazetteer of Scotland*, 6 vols., 1882.

J. BARTHOLOMEW : *Survey Gazetteer of the British Isles*, 1927.

Also J. Stevenson, *Calendar of Documents relating to Scotland*, 3 vols., 1881 *sq.*, *Register of the Great Seal* (*R.M.S.*), 1306 on, *Scott. Exchequer Rolls*, 1266 on, and the many Abbey and other Charters published by the Bannatyne, Maitland and other clubs. Likewise the *Origines Parochiales*, 1851–5, Vol. I, Dumbarton, Renfrew, Lanark, Peebles, Selkirk, Roxburgh ; Vol. II, Argyle, Western Isles, Lochaber, Bute, Arran, Ross and Cromarty, Sutherland, Caithness.

INDEX

SPECIALLY OF NAMES NOT UNDER THEIR ALPHABETICAL ORDER IN THE LIST